TRADITIONAL WISDOM AND SUSTAINABLE LIVING

TRADITIONAL WISDOM AND SUSTAINABLE LIVING

(A Study on the Indian Tribal Societies)

Editors
Hrishikesh Mandal
Amitabha Sarkar

Anthropological Survey of India

GYAN

Traditional Wisdom and Sustainable Living
(A Study on the Indian Tribal Societies)

ISBN : 978-81-212-1164-2

Published in 2013 in India by
Gyan Publishing House
23, Main Ansari Road, Daryaganj,
New Delhi - 110002
Phones : 23282060, 23261060
Fax : (011) 23285914

E-mail: books@gyanbooks.com
website: gyanbooks.com

Laser Type Setting : Rajender Vashist, Delhi
Printed at : Chawla Offset Printers, Delhi

Contents

Preface

The idea of ecology and traditional wisdom was first conceived as a national project of Anthropological Survey of India in 1998 under Ninth plan. It was a multidisciplinary project but focused on anthropological perspective.

The project was framed and executed through subsequent discussion with Dr R.K. Bhattacharya and Dr J.K. Sarkar, the then Director and Deputy Director of the Survey, respectively. They suggested that the study of the project should be specific and restricted to a particular domain.

India is a large country with varied geographical phenomena inhabited by different communities distributed across the country. Thus the varied geo-cultural landscape embedded in rich traditional wisdom developed in different ecological zones under respective domains of their own cultural heritage, which is a very difficult task for its projection within a limited plan period.

After thorough discussion, it was suggested that the project would be restricted in the study of traditional knowledge in tribal society only. Initially Dr B.R. Rizvi and Dr Hrishikesh Mandal were the co-ordinators of the project. Since Dr Rizvi was entrusted for some others important official work as a regional head of North-Eastern Region of the Survey, the entire responsibility of the project was given to Dr Mandal as co-ordinator.

Since it was a multi disciplinary project, the researchers to be involved, were taken from different disciplines of the survey. The project co-ordinator is indebted to Dr R.K. Bhattacharya and Dr J.K. Sarkar, for their suggestions in framing their national project in which 15 researchers of different disciplines from different regional offices of the Survey were involved and untiring effort of their contribution to this project and its successful completion in time was invaluable.

The plan project was titled– "Management of Environment and Natural Resources: A Study on Traditional Wisdom among the Indian Tribal Societies". It is the outcome of the concept of 'Ecology and Traditional wisdom'. Traditional Wisdom is the acquired knowledge of experience developed through a process of cognitive sense of invention over generations. The son of a fisherman who usually catches fish in deep see, can acquire the technique of his father's profession by virtue of his inherent traditional wisdom. So, the study of wisdom is a logical and justified belief which is in agreement with some facts based on ecological conditions. So, the definition of the concept involves logistic, cognitive processes, perception, communication, association and reasoning but to be accepted and acknowledged by the traditional societies.

The field work for the study was undertaken in two phases. Before the beginning of project, a workshop was conducted in the field at Pakur of Jharkhand to test the methodology, questionnaires, selection and identification of study area, process of interaction for collecting data relating to the specific problem of our objectives. Our main thrust was to identify the threads of indigenous knowledge of tribal communities from their traditional occupations. It was decided in the field of workshop that two types of studies were to be chosen – one approach unit and another away from easily accessible places to identity the factors of traditional wisdom in the management of natural resources, specially uses of folk medicine, craftsmanship, application of cognitive experience for their sustainable development still practised in their societies.

Diversification in physical characteristics as well as cultural landscape of India which has been reflected in the management of natural resources has a distinctive character of ecological niches among the tribal communities inhabiting in different ecological zones. About 427 tribal communities (census 1981) are distributed throughout the country. The distributions of their traditional societies are closely associated with the regional variation reflecting in the management of biodiversity based on traditional wisdom. Utilisation and production of resources are very much linked to the terrain character along with the climatic conditions. In the hilly terrain terrace and shifting cultivation have been practiced, but on the plateau and deltaic region cropping patterns are of different types. This operational planning of farming is linked to ecological processes within the respective landscape with the social processes adopted through generations which is called traditional wisdom. Sustainable development has to be considered in the context of the ecological frame work within which the system operates. Traditionally different tribal communities have different mode of operation in utilizing their natural resources for sustenance. Modern process of development with the change of ecosystem from the traditional character affects the biodiversity instead of sustainable development.

In the Himalayan region rough terrain and unfertile soil with limited water resources have forced the tribal people to acquire knowledge of transhumance system for sustenance. The practice of shifting cultivation with cattle herding is still prevailent in the Himalayan region from western Himalayan region to North-Eastern region of India. But increased human population pressure and decline in land area are the resultant effect of cropping pattern in shifting cultivation. Preservation of forests in the name of sacred landscape adds a new dimension to our understandings in the management of natural resources and environment in the backdrop of cultural ecology inherently developed through the respective traditional wisdom of societies that leads to their sustainable development. A number of development programmes have been taken up by the government, but the development programmes launched by the government have not been accelerated up to the expectation to the indigenous people of the area.

It is observed during my visit to many places of Eastern Himalayan region since 1973, where the Mompas, Sherdukpen, Daflas, Khasis are closely associated with the nature for their sustainable development. In the district of Bastar in the then Madhya Pradesh, I visited Abujhmarh area a number of times during 1980-90. It is felt that the tribals mostly depend upon forest products and agriculture (specially shifting cultivation) for their livelihood. They were least bothered about the modernisation of the civilised world. They are rather satisfied with the nature's gift available within and around their habitats.

In fact, deprivation or problems started, when the government planning do not take cognisance of the mental altitude of the tribals and as a result their traditional knowledge for their livelihood has become inactive and ultimately damaged their social system as acquired through generations making a balance with the eco-system of their own habitats through a long process of traditional wisdom for sustainable development.

It is also observed that deprivation started, when Abujhmarh was opened up with certain administrative restrictions. As a result they are neither fully exposed to the outside world, nor can they sustain their traditional way of living. In fact, they have been kept isolated as living specimens of an open zoo in the name of preservation of primitive tribal culture. It seems that they are living in 'in an island within mainland' Dr Samira Dasgupta and others associated with the project have depicted a very clear picture of livelihood of the tribals which is controlled by gifts of nature, but their sustainable development has been interfered by the wrong planning of the government.

In Andaman Islands, the same picture has been depicted by Dr Umesh Kumar and Samir Biswas who studied intensively on Jarawas, Onges and Shompens primitive tribes of the islands. They have projected in their study that the march of civilisation, for some reasons has a paralysing effect on tribal people. As a result the development programmes instead of being beneficial to the tribals have in a way proved a curse to them because of our philosophy of development.

The Baiga of Baiga Chak who are staying in the hilly region are much more dependent on natural resources available in their habitats. They were originally shifting cultivators, locally called 'Bewar' cultivation. But this shifting cultivation in the Baiga Chak was permitted in a controlled manner so as to regulate, control and finally to establish a system of permanent cultivation. But the tribals were not ready to accept the modern method of cultivation instead of practising shifting method which was acquired through generation for their sustainable development and also intermingled in their socio-economic condition. Dr Sumit Ghosal has illustrated a picture of traditional wisdom still prevailent in their society for livelihood and also their response to the development programme of the government planning adjusting with the ecological conditions inherited by their societies.

It concludes that the government machinery can articulate the welfare planning and programmes in a mutually integrative and participative performances. The planning as a collaborative undertaking has to take the tribals into confidence. In this connection the traditional village Panchayats should have full jurisdiction on overall development programmes relating to the interest of the tribals and their societies as a whole.

Lastly, the remarks of Verrier Elwin, an eminent anthropologist are significant. "We do not want to preserve the tribesmen as museum specimens but equally we do not want to turn them into clowns in a circus. We do not want to stop the clock of progress but we do want to see that it keeps the right time." So, traditional wisdom should be preserved and can articulate the welfare planning and programmes.

Since it is a national project of the Survey, we are to consider the study of morphological and climatic character of the sub-continent and its natural resources which depict a picture of regional variations in respect of cultural landscape of tribal societies inhabiting as indigenous population group. They have their own cultural heritage specially based on traditional knowledge or wisdom. So, we have considered to undertake our study according to the regional variation of the country so as to enable us to project a complete picture of "unity in diversity" among the tribal societies.

For the convenience of the study, the village as a unit inhabited by major tribal population (more than 60 per cent) was taken into consideration with a special observation of its location in order to compare the physical and cultural landscape for understanding dissemination of knowledge. Operation of farming system under different attitudes and terrain character have depicted a different pictures among the different tribal groups. India as a sub-continent can be divided into the following ecological zones : 1. Northern Hilly Region, 2. North-Eastern Region, 3. Eastern Region, 4. Western Desert and Semi-Desert Region, 5. Central Highland and Plateau Region; and 6. Bay Islands. So, the scholars involved in the project have given identical picture of the respective physical and cultural landscape.

The hilly tracts of sub-Himalayan region in the north are mainly inhabited by the Dogras, Gujjars and the Gaddis. Terrace cultivation and rearing of livestock are the main occupation. In the high Himalayas, the tribals live with their flock, which also help them in transporting belongings during the period of transhumance. They shift along with their flock, Thus the villages remain unoccupied for some months in a year.

The North-eastern Region has accommodated a number of tribes which constitutes about 50 per cent of the total population of the region. In the higher altitude the scope of agricultural activities is very restricted either in '*jhum*' or shifting cultivation or in cattle rearing as primary occupation of the tribal communities following transhumance system. Terrace cultivation on the slope of the hills is also practised by them. Among the tribes Khasi, Naga, Purum, Mompa, Sherdukpen, Dafla are important.

The topography of eastern region is varied in nature comprising deltaic plain, plateau sub-region of Jharkhand and highlands of Orissa. In deltaic sub-region Santals, Orans, Mundas as dominating tribal groups have changed their traditional occupation to settled cultivation. The same picture was also depicted by Dr Archana Dutta and Mrs Sanchita Ghatak on the study of Sauria Paharia of Rajmahal Hills. Dr S. Gangopadhyay and Mr Sunit Mandal depicted a changing pattern of traditional occupation among the Malpaharia of Rajmahal Hills in Jharkhand maintaining their traditional heritage.

The western region mainly comprises Rajasthan and Gujarat under the study. In Rajasthan, Bhils, Garasias, Minas, Patelias, Sahariyas are important. Mr Santanu Mitra has studied on the Bhils of Rajasthan. The domain of the tribal groups are mainly characterised by the hilly terrain with low productivity (banjar land) spotted with thorny bushes, Sabai grass, bamboo bushes and plants of cactic nature, like *babul*, *siris* and date-palm. The main agricultural products are *bajra* and *jowar* (millet group). Agriculture is their primary occupation.

Central region under the study comprises mainly Bastar district of Madhya Pradesh. In Bastar the Abujh Marias of the Abughmarh Hills (i.e., the sub-group of the Gond community) and the Baigas of the Baiga Chak, practise shifting cultivation as their traditional occupation.

The tribes of the Bay Islands have been known as aborigines from ancient times. Among them Onges, Jarawas, Nicobarese, Sentinalese, Shompens are the tribal groups. The Andamanese are of mixed group. The thick evergreen tropical rain forests and mangroves fringed long indented coast line provide varieties of terrestrial and aquatic resources for their livelihood. Hunting, gathering and finishing are their traditional livelihood.

The project co-ordinator is deeply indebted to all the contributors of the book who took pains during their intensive field work and valuable contributions for the same.

As a project Co-ordinator, I am also extremely grateful to Dr R.K. Bhattacharya, Former Director and Dr J.K. Sarkar, of the Survey, not only for giving me the scope of the project, but also for giving us continuous support and co-operation.

During preparation of methodology and questionnaire I was continuously supported by Dr Archana Dutta, Mrs Sanchita Ghatak,

Dr S. Gangopadhyay, Dr Sumit Mukherjee and Dr Umesh Kumar. I express my gratitude and thanks to Prof. K.K. Misra, Director of Anthropological Survey of India for his kind permission for publication of this volume. I am very much thankful to Dr Amitabha Sarkar who has taken a great pain for initiating the idea of bringing out this volume in a publishable form. I also thank to the publisher of this book.

I hope that this book will give an immense scope to think of the concept of Traditional Wisdom to be applicable in a wider scale of national planning to preserve the cultural heritage of our ancient India.

Hrishikesh Mandal

Project Co-ordinator

List of Contributors

1. **Dr. Hrishikesh Mondal :** Human Ecologist (Superannuated), Anthropological Survey of India, Kolkata – 16. Presently Director, Netaji Subhash Engineering College, Techno City, Garia, Kolkata – 152
2. **Dr. Amitabha Sarkar :** Superintending Anthropologist (Cultural), Anthropological Survey of India, Kolkata – 700016.
3. **Dr. (Mrs) Samira Dasgupta :** Assistant Anthropologist (Cultural), Anthropological Survey of India, Kolkata – 700016.
4. **Shri Sunit Mondal :** Research Associate (Cultural) (Superannuated), Anthropological Survey of India, Eastern Regional Centre, Salt Lake, Sector-V, Kolkata – 700091.
5. **Dr. Sudhansu Gangopadhyay :** Research Associate (Ecology), Anthropological Survey of India, Eastern Regional Centre, Salt Lake, Kolkata – 700091.
6. **Dr. (Mrs) Archana Dutta :** Research Associate (Ecology) (Superannuated), Anthropological Survey of India, Eastern Regional Centre, Salt Lake, Kolkata – 700091.
7. **Ms. Sanchita Ghatak :** Research Associate (Ecology) (Superannuated), Anthropological Survey of India, Kolkata – 16.
8. **Dr. Samit Ghosal :** Anthropologist (Cultural), Anthropological Survey of India, Nagpur.
9. **Shri R.B. Thakre :** Research Associate (Ecology), Anthropological Survey of India, Nagpur.
10. **Shri Santanu Mitra :** Assistant Anthropologist (Cultural), Anthropological Survey of India, Kolkata – 16.
11. **Dr. Umesh Kumar :** Human Ecologist, Anthropological Survey of India, Kolkata – 16.

12. **Shri Samir Biswas :** Research Associate (Ecology), Anthropological Survey of India, Port Blair, A & N Islands.
13. **Dr. R. R. Gowloog :** Anthropologist (Cultural), Anthropological Survey of India, Shillong, Meghalalya.
14. **Dr. Sumit Mukherjee :** Research Associate (Ecology), Anthropological Survey of India, Kolkata – 16.
15. **Shri Pijush Chowdhury :** Research Associate (Cultural) (Superannuated) Anthropological Survey of India, Eastern Regional Centre, Kolkata.

1

Introduction

Hrishikesh Mandal and *Amitabha Sarkar*

Environment is the surrounding space in which organisms find themselves during their span of life and survive by interacting with the existing elements on the earth. Each of these elements affects the other and in turn all jointly affects the environment. So, the habitation or space where the man lives is his environment. Over the years the processes of development, may be of social, economical, industrial, or technological, has led to a massive degradation of environment. Hence it is found necessary for proper management of environment and natural resources. Some questions that may be raised in this connection are : what are the environmental factors that should be taken into consideration in our study and how the natural resources are being managed by the tribal communities of our country; what kind of procedures should be adopted for analysing the environmental situation and how can the traditional environmental planning and management of the tribal, who are actually with and kin with the physical environment around them; be integrated with the present day modern development planning and management. Considering of all these questions will lead us to know the traditional knowledge of the tribal groups of our country in this aspect and also help to implement a programme for environmentally sustainable development. Natural resources basically include atmosphere, water and land including flora and fauna, which determines the quality of physical environment of mankind, while these are utilised for our benefit.

The present treatise is limited to the study only of Traditional Knowledge of the tribal people of our country in the process of management of environment and natural resources through which they eke out their subsistence for survival. Traditional knowledge usually covers traditional and tradition based cultural expressions in forms such as stories, music, dance, artworks and crafts including signs and symbols and other recurring expressions of traditional concepts. It is knowledge handed down from one generation to another through oral tradition and that suggests a sense of common or communal ownership. It is the systematic body of knowledge acquired by local people of a particular geographical niche which they acquired over experience, informal experiment and intimate understanding of local conditions and provides a productive context for activities designed to help the communities. **This knowledge is the product of centuries of trial and error, natural selection and keen observation that can form a knowledge base on which researchers and planning executors can plan their research strategy and experimental procedures.**

Our conception of knowledge is bounded by the philosophy and methods of western world of science It is the anthropologist especially cultural anthropologist and ecologist among a few have recognised that there are myriad sciences embedded in the cultures of other ethnic groups who are mostly either marginalised or live in secluded hilly-forest terrain of the civilised world. To-day we have realised and recognising the importance of various local or community based knowledge systems for conserving and preserving the environment in sustainable developmental way.

The tribal communities traditionally live in the hilly and forest regions, which are usually not easily accessible because of terrain character. Their economy is largely self-sufficient, unstructured, non specialised and non-commercialised. Their social system is simple. But with the advent of time this situation is becoming changed. Vargin natural resources of some tribal regions have been destroyed or damaged due to establishment of industry, mining activities or dam or reservoirs etc.

The level of tribal economy in our country is uneven. On one extreme there are tribal communities who are at the food gathering and hunting stage and the other extreme many among them are at par with the modern agricultural and industrial societies. Similarly differences are also observed in their educational level. In some places of our country like Bastar region of Chhattishgarh, Koraput and Malkangiri of Odisha, Malwa region of Madhya Pradesh, western part of Rajasthan, some pockets of Santal Pargana, Sundarban region- the delta of South Bengal etc. literacy rate among the tribal are sufficiently low, while in some other areas the rate of literacy is sufficiently high. Thus, the tribal areas present a complex socio-economic situation which has been reflected through utilization of their natural resources. Their cultural heritage in fact lies in the management of their physical environment, where they live in, and the study in this regard will try to reveal their traditional knowledge about the process of utilization and preservation of natural resources existing in and around their habitats.

The researchers involved in various eco-cultural zones for digging out the empirical situation and finally presented in the following pages which certainly indicate the process of adaptation with the local condition in various degree and accordingly their socio-cultural situation are also tuned. This being a kind of survival strategy in particular eco-cultural zone.

II

The panorama of Indian tribal situation is full of cultural diversity. In one locale these tribal are not only pre-literate but possess lack of technological support for their sustenance, while in other area the tribal are sophisticated, highly technologically skilled, literacy rate is quite high and fully exposed to world competitive market economy with all sorts of modern gadgets of communication. Under this backdrop the present treatise is prepared where our researchers are confined their study on selected locales among marginalised as well as least known tribal groups of India.

Defining the Study Area

Natural resources mainly comprise land and water resource. Land resources include flora and fauna of forests and hill areas, cultivable lands, mining and quarries. Water resources involve management of inland water, tidal water, saline and brackish water, management of lagoons water, management of desert areas and also management of water for irrigation, drinking purposes etc.

As the management process is proposed to be understood from the tribal societies living in various ecological settings and pursuing various economic activities as traditional occupation such as hunting, food gathering, shifting cultivation, terrace cultivation, wet and settled cultivation, horticulture, trapping of fish and birds, pastoral, transhumance system etc. India can be divided into following ecological zones or regions mainly based on terrain character, distribution of forests and vegetation, mining and water resources.

1. Himalayan region
   - (a) Western Himalayas
   - (b) Central Himalayas
   - (c) Eastern Himlayas

2. Foot hills or Terai region
3. Plains
4. Upland/ Plateau region
5. Coastal region
6. Desert region
7. Island

Unit of Study

Tribal village of the respective ecological zone is the unit of study. Village will be selected according to major tribal concentration depending on natural resources as their subsistence. Besides indigenous people have the power to make decisions concerning the sustainable use and management of natural resources and often this is also governed by village committee or institution.

Methodology

Tribes of different traditional occupations chiefly depending on natural resources of their respective locale of habitation are to be studied from one or two villages of each selected ecological zone. All information pertaining to village level technique and technology i.e. indigenous knowledge for sustainable use to be documented, occupation depending on the management of natural resources, farming system including cropping patterns, use of traditional folk medicines and craftsmanship are to be extracted through interviewing, discussion, case histories, observation and some structured schedules.

Distribution of tribes in the following pages on the basis of their occupations and resource management under the following occupational pattern is shown:

Major Traditional Occupational Pattern	Ecological Zone Under Study	Tribal Group
(A) Shifting Hill Cultivation	Plateau	1. Abujh Maria, 2. Bison-Horn Maria, 3. Sauria Paharia, 4. Mal Paharia
(B) Settled Cultivation	(a) Gangetic delta-Sundarban.	5. Munda and Oraon
	(b) Desert	6. Bhil
	(c) Plateau	7. Baiga
(C) Fishing/ Plantation	Island	8. Nicobarese
(D) Terrace Cultivation	Himalayan region	9. Khasi of Meghalaya

Scope of Study

(i) To access indigenous knowledge of tribal communities from their traditional occupations.

(ii) To understand local resource use practices

(iii) To know the impact of utility of traditional know- how on modern methods of preservation and conservation of natural resources.

(iv) To understand the gravity of practice and deviation from their traditional norms in environmental management for sustainable living.

III

In order to focus the different dimensions of the trends and patterns of management of environmental perspectives flourished differently according to the varied geo-physical nature and extent which have got multifarious criterion. These are needed to be checked and evaluated. Various indigenous communities living in these specific ecological zones from time immemorial could have been able to make these favourable and by means of which they sustain themselves. It is to be noted that living in the lap of diversified environment the indigenous groups of humanities have found different means to bring the adverse as well as hostile geo-physical milieu in their favour by the direct and indirect application of their indigenous expertise. It is to be noted with great concern that these proficiencies are not the result of some person for a limited duration, rather these are outcome of the innumerable persons through generation. Naturally it is a very long time affair and is based on the close and friendly relation with the ecological settings. The methodologies of observations and related comprehensions very naturally differ from community to community; the specific thinking pattern and working procedure execute characteristic mode of life which deserve close-set study and analysis to help solve the different dimensions of the present day problems arising out of environmental hazards. The indigenous knowledge span many a time may enlight some sudden points.

In the different papers presented here an earnest as well as deep quest has been made in bring out the basic test of the patterns and perspectives of the management of environment and natural resources of the different tribal groups living in the nine selected region of India. The first paper has been presented by Dr. (Mrs.) Samira Dasgupta. It highlights the traditional tribal wisdom in the Bastar region. In the beginning of her study she focuses the significance of the Abujh Maria in the background of its geo-physical, historical and socio-cultural nature and extent. Ader village, studied here, is surrounded by forested mountains. The interactions of the villagers with ecological perspectives have been put forwards thought the analysis of their living style and modes of adaptation with the help of their tradition oriented understandings. With the help of a large mass of concrete examples the author has been able to bring out the very mechanism of the traditional wisdom of these people in managing the environment and natural resources.

The next paper is presented by Sri Sunit Mondal and Dr. Sudhansu Gangopadhyay. They have centred round their study on the environment management of the Malpharia of Rajmahal Hills. The study area is situated in *Damin-i-Koh* region which is characterised by the hilly region. After putting forward the long and significant historical perspective of the region the authors have put forward the geological standpoints. In this region of hilly landscape this authors has selected Amirjola village exclusively inhabited by the Malpaharia. The economy of the people and their settlement patterns are evaluated along with the cultural background after community concerned. Then their traditional ideas on the land and nature have been evaluated in the background after native thinking pattern. These people cultivate by the adoption of slash and burn cultivation locally known as *khallu*. In addition to this crops are raised on the land slopes of the foot hills. The patterns of cultivation as well as the methodology differ according to the nature of land and in this sphere various technological details have been highlighted. These people are very much alert in the forest management and they have devised their indigenous way. Along with this the water management is also conducted with seriousness. Preservation of the water bodies, fishing management, protection of the contour *bandh* are their specific responsibilities. The lot of cultural practices in using and controlling the forest products have been pin-pointed carefully.

Dr. Archana Dutta and Mrs. Sanchita Ghatak have taken up their study on the Sauria Paharia tribe living in the hilly region and forest claded environment of the Rajmahal Hills. The study region has a close linkage with the *Damin-i-Koh* area of immense geo-political importance. The village Satia has been selected here which is situated on the Satia Pahar region of the Rajmahal Hills. The forest-oriented topography, hilly terrain, paucity of water have compelled the people to practice slash and burn cultivation. This *khallu*. Cultivation is of two types depending on the two factors – flat land type and slope of the hill. The Khallu land management is very tough and the Sauria Paharia have been able to a considerable extent to perform this practice. The crops are raised in these land applying their traditional wisdom which the people have developed through hazard and anxieties. The authors have put forward the different management procedural activities on land, crops, livestock and the forest. Rajmahal Hill forests resources are different types. They use these for food, drink and shelter, forests supply medicine, game animals, raw materials for cottage industries. The people are conscious on the conservation of forest resources, management of water through the adoption various norms and traditions.

Dr. Amitabha Sarkar and Sri Piyush Choudhury in their joint efforts has highlighted the picturesque Baster tribe – the Bison-Horn Maria. These people practise slash and burn cultivation, settled type of cultivation with plough. Wet cultivation is also seen among them. This tribal group of Bastar is provided with regional and historical background which the authors have drawn successfully. There the total territorial set up has been presented along with the in-depth study of the eco-zones of the villages taken up for the purpose of investigation. Among these tribal groups the management and utilization of vast natural resources are noteworthy. Especially the forest management and the utilization forest resources, indigenous health care practice have been explored in depth-oriented dimension putting concrete examples from various eventual activities. The role of these people in the sphere of conservation of forest is highly praiseworthy. Sacred grove or *tallin* among the Bison-Horn Maria is regarded as a dedicated site. Here the existence of the Mother Goddess is a dominating factor. The customary laws play the great role in the protection of the forest ecology. The authors have shown that the forest management device of these people are controlled and activated by the various belief and practices performed by socio-economic and ritualistic factors. All these have been shown and explained in the present work. Bison-Horn Marias expertise in the management of natural resources is governed by physical and social environment which the authors have carefully presented through the explanation of their day to day life and behaviour-patterns with the surroundings.

Dr. Samit Ghosal together with R.B. Thakre have gone to study the Baiga in specific socio-cultural surroundings of their traditional environment. The area under study is known as "Baiga chowk", situated in Madhya Pradesh. After referring the historical background and geographical set-up of the study area the authors have attempted to discuss the material and local life and activities of the Baiga tribe along with their economic understanding. Their specific dependence on forest has been highlighted. In the study the indigenous forest management of the Baiga has been discussed together with some observations on water resource management as well as the management of the wind and solar resources. In this connection the authors have put forward some suggestions.

Dr. (Mrs.) Samira Dasgupta and Dr. Amitabha Sarkar's paper examines categorically the nature and mode of applications of traditional wisdom among the Munda and Oraon tribes settled far away from their traditional home i.e., Chotanagpur in Jharkhand. It is interesting to note that in the completely changed ecological setting like Sundarban region dominated by salt water rivers and estuaries as well as the mangrove forest the original Chotanagpur tribes could have been able to adjust themselves with the alien geo-physical setting which all the time poses multitudinal problematic situations in their daily mode of life. After highlighting the specific geo-physical, environmental and ecological conditions of this landmass the authors have collected relevant data on the way of life and their adjustment from the different village settings inhabited by the Mundas and Oraons and then focus depth-oriented results of investigation in the management of forest. The management of land in three villages – Panchpukur, Konkandighi and Moghkhali – has been taken into consideration to highlight their indigenous comprehensions in the process of growing crops there. They have no doubt taken a great challenge to cope with the all rounded adverse situation. Thoroughly categorical analysis of the diversified data collected from total behaviour patterns of the Mundas and the Oraons the mechanism of their adoption of traditional knowledge of the alien ecological setting for fighting with the adverse situations with which they are completely ignorant. The paper is very interesting and noteworthy for the fact that it has tried to explore the basic dimensions of developing the indigenous knowledge pattern from the other human groups in a different eco-cultural setting for the purpose of managing the environment and natural resources of the where they have been compelled to take shelter due to unavoidable circumstances

Sri Santanu Mitra has taken up the Bhil tribes in Rajasthan and he has tried to present the patterns and perspectives of management of environment and natural resources of such a community which has been living in desert condition where the climate becomes severe hot in summer and cold in winter. The rainfall is trace. At the outset Sri Mitra has devoted himself to highlight the basic geo-physical setting of the region which very naturally indicate conspicuous unfavourable surrounding as it has been said here that the villages where the Bhils live suggest all characteristics of hot desert. The study has been conducted in Bharmasar and Roopsi villages where the vegetation is scanty and sparsely distributed. As a natural consequence the water resources are very limited. That studying the nature of people together with their material belongings the economic resources has been highlighted. Different land types utilised by the people for raising the houses, for grazing the animal etc. Because of their sterility these cannot be used in raising the crops. The soil types have been examined and reported. The villages are surrounded by hills and hillocks from where stones are collected to serve the different purposes including the making of images, bowls and other containers. But the forest resources are very scanty here. The Bhils are mostly engaged as labourers locally known as *Mantak Majduri*. Some lands are utilised for agricultural purposes but the work is heavily obstructed by the water scarcity. Very small amount of Bajra, Jowar, Pulses, Wheat and mustard are raised in the desert ecology. They put their specific stress on the conservation of water resources. Rain water is preserved in tank and well. In getting new sources of water the Bhils are seen to utilize their traditional wisdom in digging well in such places where they found rainwater accumulated during a heavy shower. Water preservation procedures of different types are the eminent features amongst these people. The Bhils are no doubt dependent on the natural resources for their day to day living. The study highlights the fact that the Bhils here are highly eco-friendly in nature. These are reflected in their every attempt to fight for survival.

Dr. Umesh Kumar and Samir Biswas study provides some significant information on the people of Katchal island in the Andaman & Nicobar archilepago. Katchal is the largest island in the central group of islands there. Katchal is provided with as many as 35 village amongst which Mildera is the largest and is inhabited by the Nicobarese along with some non-Nicobarese. The study was carried out here after the greatest havoc like tsunami. At the very outset the specific climate, flora and fauna and the type of people have been put forward which is followed by occupation pattern. Under the headline Resource Management and Socio-political system and Religion- the resource management is achieved in the Nicobarese society through the social structure, economic organisation, political system and religious beliefs and practices. The resources here are exclusively controlled and looked into by *kamunchiase.* The distribution of resources is not conducted by haphazard way rather the *kamunchiase* enters directly into the process. Each of the villages has one village council by the Captain having two assistants. It is a democratic organisation. At present these have been influence by tribal councils. Religion and shamanism are characteristically dominated in the line of thinking and behaviour-pattern of the people. The authors observe here that the religion is an adaptive mechanism to nature. Pigs are regarded as most important livestock as they have double-headed significance – biomass and social status. Pigs have considerable effect on eco-setting. The continuous digging and rooting activities of the pigs in the natural surroundings especially the forest soil increases various types of decomposition helping in adding various nutrients to the soil. In horticulture and water related activities these native people show tremendous expertise. Their oceanographic knowledge is based on basic scientific ideas fed by the native wisdom. It has been noted that in their resource management pattern there is a deep-based phenomenon of reciprocity. The impact of tsunami on these people, occurred in 2004, has been analysed in the background of their life, belief system and tremendous hazards. It is opined that tsunami has itched a permanent scar in the memory of the people concerned which is still to be looked into with sincerity and seriousness.

Dr. (Mrs.) R.R. Gowloog and Sri S. Mukherjee have presented their study on the Management of Environment and Natural Resources centering round the well-known Khasi tribe of N.E. India. The study has been conducted in Mawlam village, Meghalaya. The tribal wisdom of the tradition war Khasi people is the principal aim of the work. The village Mawlam has been selected for detailed study because of the fact that being located in a remote corner and exclusively dominated by the traditional religion known as *Niamtre.* The authors at the very beginning pointed out the significance of Khasi tribe and their continuous interactions with the natural resources. After putting some information on the history and geography of the region of study the authors have discussed the cultural set up.

The village people have been studied in the background of their material and economic life. Land tenure system has been illustrated. The land is utilised for Jhum cultivation or *Thang Shyrti*, It is highly influenced by the various customary rules, taboos and restrictions which reflect the traditional wisdom of the people towards management. Their practice of plantation, agriculture is also noteworthy. It is highly returnable. Besides various crops, oranges, lemon, bay leaf, areca nut, betel leaf as well as a kind of broom sticks are grown in abundance. Forest management work of the Khasis is centred round a long symbiotic relation between the people and the forest. Different ways of utilisation of forest resources have been summed up in five different types which are regulated by traditional ways. In bee-keeping and honey collection the War Khasis still proceed with the native knowledge system. Besides various collection from forest for daily uses the collection of medicinal plants from here deserve their native wisdom. Their joint activity with tradition orientation is highly seen in case of forest fire, water management and conservation of the surrounding landscape. It is their specific feature.

2

Management of Environment and Natural Resources : A Study of Traditional Tribal Wisdom among Abujh-Maria of Bastar

Samira Dasgupta

Introduction

India is a vast country with various cultural and religious groups and institutions. Among its population a considerable portion is occupied by the tribal people, distributed in various parts of the country. They have their own and unique cultural heritage which help them to maintain the traditional system of proper management (that is, control, utilisation, conservation and preservation) of environment and use of local resources for sustenance which deserves special attention to the present day social scientists.

It is deeply felt that the tribal communities in India witness the destruction of their habitat in which they are nourished and nurtured. Gradually they are being driven out of the jungle, the Valleys, and the mountains which are their original abode. Their life is intimately associated with their natural environment in which they live. When an ethnic group is forced to get out of its primaeval ground, its tradition is automatically destroyed and as a result "the nations aboriginal tribes with their rich cultural heritage and traditions that go beyond the Vedic times, even beyond the Aryan times seem doomed to extinction (Hindu, March, 1999).

Objective

Keeping all these in mind, the researcher tried to study the process of management of environment and natural resources by the Abujh Maria people, who still are less exposed to the outside world for their sustenance. In this situation it is expected that they are in advantageous position to keep their own traditional knowledge or wisdom less changed and less influenced by the outside agencies. The researcher is also interested to study how far their traditional wisdom is useful to maintain the eco-balance of the present situational contexts.

Selection of Village

The present work is done among the Abujh Maria of Ader village. Ader is an uniethnic, less exposed, forest village situated in the lap of at least 700 metres high mountain. In this situation how the people of the village adjust themselves to manage their natural environment and its natural resources utilizing their traditional knowledge is really an interesting phenomena for the present study.

Methodology

As per the convention in socio-cultural Anthropology, the study began in the village primarily with the establishment of rapport, so that the people of the village would never suspect the researcher as a stranger. On the contrary, she should be accommodated by them as one of the members of their society. Prelimthary census survey was done to collect the demographic data. The researcher recorded concrete case histories by open end questionnairre. Depth interview along with direct and indirect participation, genealogical method are also applied for the present study. Some of their songs and mythical stories are recorded which nicely reflect their ideas about nature, natural objects and the mode of use of the nature for their own sustenance.

Regional Background and local Environment

Abujh Marh is a place situated in the Bastar District of erstwhile Madhya Pradesh. Bastar district (undivided) lies at the extreme south-east corner of the state. Ecologically and Culturally Bastar is a part of Dandyakaranya forest. Bastar is 39,114 sq. km. in area and thus larger than Kerala state and Belgium country and nearly as large as Holland (Grigson, 1991). The district extends from 17°46′ to 20°34′ north latitude and 80°15′ to 82°01′ east, longitude. The district is bounded by Orissa on the east, Andhra

Pradesh on the south, Maharashtra on the West and Durg, Raipur of Madhya Pradesh on the north. "Bastar is still the most forested district with a forest cover officially estimated as 55.4%. The Bastar forests are tropical moist deciduous variety with sal shading into teak as the most import commercial species" (Sundar, 1977). "Both sal and teak have several associates (include Bija, Saja, Haldu, Dhaora, Mahua, Char, Tendu which together to nearly 85%. "Bamboo is another important forest product and it covers 20% of the total forest. It is told that the name Bastar comes from the word *bansta* or *banstari* or bamboo. As per Madhya Pradesh Environmental Status report (Bhopal, 1991) it is told that per capita forest area in Bastar is 9.5.

The greater part of Bastar district is a plateau. The plateau continues east ward to Jeypore of Orissa state. This plateau descends on the Chhattisgarh plain on the northern side. Godavari low lands are found towards south west side. The Indravati river bisects the district in two halves. The Sabri river flows along the south eastern boundary ends in the Godwari basin (ibid).

Physio-graphically the district is divided intothe following six divisions.

(i) Northern low land – Most of the parts of Kanker and Bhopalpatnam tehsils and northern part of Narayanpur tehsil come under northern low land where Kotri-Mahanadi Plains stretches.

Elevation in land surface extends upto 300 m. to 450 m. The land is underlain by granites and gneisses. It is diversified by a long narrow strip of Dharwar rock.

(ii) Keshkal Scarpment – South of northern low land, the land rises steeply for about 150 m. to 300 m. at Keshkal. It is marked by a Cuddapah and Vindhyan sand stone and quartzite capping of the granite and gneisses with the occurance of some Dharwar patches.

(iii) Abuli Marh Hills – Abujh Marh is about 95 Kms. long from north to south and about 55 kms. broad from east to west. 'Marh is situated at the Western part of the Bastar district in the Southern part of Narayanpur tehsil and the northern margin of Bijapur Tehsil. Narayanpur and Chote Dongar are situated at its eastern part. Abujh Marh is a hill range. Some of its crests and peaks in the Abujh Marh exceeds 900 metres height from the sea level. A large part of this area is rugged and dissected by numerous streams. The central part of the Abujh Marh hill range is formed of trap rocks and northern, southern and eastern edges have patches of Dharwar and cuddapah rocks, capping widespread granites and gneisses. The fisherland is formed due to the volcamic sway.

(iv) North-eastern Plateau - At the east of Abujh Marh hills the north-eastern plateau lies. It is the Bastar high land. Kondagaon and Jagdalpur tehsils come in this plateau. It slopes gently from about 750 metres high near Keshkal in the north and Tulsi Dongri in the south to slightly less than 600m, in the middle River Indrawali runs in the middle.

(v) Southern Plateau - It is slightly a lower plateau which includes Dantewada tehsil, northern parts of Bijapur and Konta tehsils. This plateau is formed of granitic and gneissic rocks. On the south-east portion, the plateau descends to the Godwari - Sabri low land. The Bailadila hills attains about 1100 m. elevation are formed of Dharwar formation.

(vi) Southern Low Land - The Sukma low land comes under the southern low land. It has a surface height of 150 to 300 m. continues south-west Konta, then to Golapalli hills and stretching northwards to Bhopalpatnam. The Godawari - Sabri low land extends from the southern boundary of the district to the base of the southern plateau. The Darbha Ghati of this southern low land is very steep. This low land is due to the denudation of the southern granites and gneisses by the numerous tributaries of Godavari and Sabri rivers which flow in Konta tehsil and Southern Bijapur.

Lithography

Lithographically Bastar is formed of various types of old rocks of Pre-cambrian and cambrian era. They are:

(a) The Dharwar,

(b) The Archaean Granites and Gneisses,

(c) The older trap.

(d) The Cuddapahs.

(e) The Vindhyans

(a) The Dharwar rocks are sedimentary and meta morphic in composition. The Dharwar rock occur in (i) the Bailadila hills on the Western boundary of the Dantewada tehsil (ii) The Raoghat hills on the northern margin of the Abujh Marh hills between Antagarh and Narayanpur tehsil and (iii) Chain of hills running from the midst of Pratappur and Koelibeda in Narayanpur tehsil upto north west to Bhanupratappur tehsil.

(b) The Archaean Granites and Gneisses : About three fourth of the dislrict is covered by Archaean granites and gneisses. Greater part of Bastar district consists of Granitoid gneiss.

(c) The Older Trap : The trap rocks of Bastar district are exclusive basic or basalt rocks, produced by Volcanic activity. They occur in Abujh Marh hills, West of Orcha and between Pratappur, Koelibeda, both located in Narayanpur tehsil.

(d) The Cuddapah Formation : Four areas of the district are covered by this formation. It extends from Mardapal, in Kondagaon tehsil to Tirathgarh, in Jagdalpur tehsil from Chitrakote to Jagdalpur and extends to the south - east border of the Kondagaon tehsil. In Bastar this cuddapah formation includes quartzite, sand stone, limestone, and phyllitic shales and possess nearby horizontal bedding.

(e) The Vindhyas Formation : The youngest formation of all the Bastar rocks, occur in small patches on the West and east of Keshkal, along the tehsil boundary between Kanker and Kondagaon. It is the composition of quartzitic sand stones.

Soil

In Bastar laterites and lateritic soils cover about three - fourth area of the district. It forms due to high humidity and tropical conditions. The soil is acidic. In the river base of Indrawati, Godavari and Mahmadi deposits of fresh alluvial soils are found. These are the most fertile soil for agriculture.

Climate

Bastar district can be divided into three climatic regions namely (1) humid, (ii) moist sub-humid (iii) dry sub humid. The climate is divided into four seasons namely:

(a) South-West monsoon season - June to September.

(b) Post monsoon - October- November.

(c) Winter - December - February.

(d) Summer - March - May / June.

Temperature : The mean temperature is about 20°C.

Rainfall : The monsoon starts in the month of June and continue is due to South-West monsoon wind.

Relative Humidity : It is higher during monsoon. Average rainfall is between 1000 mm to 1550 mm.

Ecoclimate : Ecoclimatically thi district is divided into Humid, Moist sub humid, Dry sub humid zones. Abujh Marh hills belong to the moist sub humid zone.

The present study deals with the Abujh Maria of the Abujh Marh hills. Due to this reason special emphasis is given to the Abujh Marh Hills.

Historical Background

Various prehistoric remains excavated and collected from Bastar at different times proves the remote antiquity of human culture in Bastar. Report of Bastar Development plan by the state planning board mentions, "about 350 A.D. Vyaghra Dev of Nal dynasty is said to have conquered northern parts of Dandakaranya and founded his dynasty" thus the Nal dynasty began. After Nalvans, Bastar passed through a dark era approximately for five hundred years. During this period the Chalukyas and the Ganga Kings of Orissa, some other kings of Trikuta, Vakatas ruled over Bastar. After that, Chhindak Nag Vansh kings became the ruler of Bastar. They are supposed to have started their reign from middle of 11th century. It is supported by the inscriptions and ruins in the temples at Dantewada, Bbairamgarh, Barsur and Kurushpal that in the eleventh century, a Telugu line of Nag Vanshi Kings reigned at Barsur in Dantewada tehsil and at Kurushpal near the Chitrakote falls of Indrawati river at Jagdalpur tehsil then known as Chakrakot (Grigson, 1991). About 200 years ago or less there were several Zamindaris at Bastar of whom Bhopalpatnam, Kutru, Kotapalli-Pamer the trends of which are continuing. In Kutru again there were three or four sub-zamindaris under the zamindars. It has been understood from records that before the kings migrated from Warangal, a nominal suzerainty of Warangal was there. Heads of local tribal Council and local chiefs used to rule the place. With the end of Nagvanshi dynasty Bastar passed through a traditional period. It was ruled by the Chalukyas. There were several raids between 844 and 1150 by the Chalukyas and Hoysala princes (ibid, 1991).

The first member of Kakatiya dynasty, entered in Bastar and established his Kingdom there and he was Raja Annam Deo. He was the younger brother of Raja Rudra Pratap. Actually he was a member of Chalukya Vansh but adopted by Rudmma of Kakatiya dynasty and as soon as he was adopted he became one of the member of the Kakatiya Vansh and then he became the king. Grigson has mentioned that Annam Deo established his Kingdom in Mudhota and Raipur in 1424. Raja Annam Deo ruled for 45 years and after his death the thorn was succeeded by Hamir Deo. After Hamir Deo, Raja Bhairaj Deo, Purushottam Deo became the King of Bastar. He visited Lord Jagannath at Puri of Orissa on foot. Seeing his devotion Lord Jagannath became very pleased with him and as per divine order, the King was offered a Chariot. He was the first man of Bastar started the festival of Goncha at Bastar. After him the fifth King was Jaisingh. Then Narayan Singh Dev ruled and succeeded by Raja Pratap Raj Deo who was succeeded by Jagdish Deo. Next it was ruled by the Kings Vir Naryan Deo, Bir ingh Deo, Digpal Deo, Rajpal Sing Deo, Raja Dalpat Deo. Raja Dalpat Deo shifted his capital to Jagdalpur. Then Dariya Deo succeeded the King who in turn was succeeded by his son Mahipal Deo. Then came Raja Bhupal Deo and next Raja Bhairam Deo became the king. During his reign in 1854 direct political relations with the British Government of India was started. He was succeeded by his son Rudra Pratap's daughter Prafulla Kumari Devi. During her reign hereditary title Raja was upgraded to Maharaja in 1932. After her death her son Maharaja Pravir Chandra Bhanj Deo became the ruler. He was the last king of Kakatiya dynasty at Bastar in the pre-independence period. During the Kakatiya dynasty the present day Bastar was divided into two states namely Bastar and Kanker. Bastar had five tehsils namely Narayanpur, Kondagaon, Jagdalpur, Bijapur and Konta. The four Zamindaris are Kutru, Bhopalpatnam, Pamed and Sukma. The Kanker state had only two tehsils.

The Kakatiya Kings mainly dealt with the administration of Bastar. They had an assistant called Dewan. In the tehsil level there were Tehisildars and Managers.

In 1948 these two feudatory states that is Bastar and Kanker are brought under the State of Madhya Pradesh.

The Original inhabitants of the district are tribal. 67.35% of the total population belong to the tribal group (1991) such as Abujh Maria, Bison-Horn Maria or Dandami Maria, Bhatra, Dhurwa or Parja, Dorla, Halba, and Muria. These tribal groups have their own separate territorial zones. The Abujh Maria are distributed in the North-Western part of the district. The Dandami Maria live in the south-central, Dorla in the southern part and western part of Bijapur, Dhurwa in south eastern part, Bhatra in the Indrawati plains, Halba in north and south Bastar and the Muria in the northern and north-eastern region of Bastar. Saora, Munda, Gadaba are also found but they are very small in number.

There are other local communities such as Koshta, Mahara, Painka etc. who are the weaving castes of Bastar. Kalal, Sundi are the distillers, Raut or Cow herders, Kumhar or potters, Teli or, oil pressure, Kewat or fisherman, Panera or Mali or gardener, Dhakar, Ghasi Ghadwa or brass / metal worker and musician etc. A sizeable population of immigrants are also found in Bastar, The businessmen from Orissa, Gujarat, Rajasthan, Uttar Pradesh, and persons from Andhra Pradesh, Kerala, Tamil Nadu, have migrated as merchants, money lenders, mining and forest officials and private employee. There are Bengalee refugee who have settled here. 60% of the Brahmin families are the migrants from Orissa and they are Aranyak Brahman. They were brought by Raja Purushottam Deo in the fifteenth Century A.D. Maithili Brahmans are also found who have migrated and settled there. A few Kayastha, and other caste people migrated to work as officials.

In Bastar Halbi serves as lingua-franca since the seventeenth century. Bhatri has a large admixture of Oriya. Telegu influence dominates in the South.

In Bastar there are 1003 females per 1000 males. Level of literacy is poor and 14.13% of the total population is literate of whom 20.99% are male and 7.29% are female.

The Area – Abujh Marh

Abujh Marh is situated in the north-east portion of Bastar. The name Abujh Marh means unknown hills (Abujh means unknown and Marh indicates hills). The original inhabitants of the area are a sub group of Gond tribe and named as Abujh Maria by the outsiders. They prefer to introduce themselves as Meta Koitor, The hilly tract of Abujh Marh which attains the height of at least 700 to 900 metres and is surrounded by dense forest. It highest position is 1200 metres near Todaur in Mangnar Pargana. The Abujh Marh region is 95 Kms. long from north to south and about 55 Kms. broad from east to west. It is populated by 17624 Abujh Maria people (1981 census) who are distributed in 236 villages.

"A large part of this area is rugged and dissected by numerous streams." "If any part of India is still terra incognita" to nearly all the travellers it is Abujh Marh which has infact always been an almost unknown backwater of the rivers of the Indian history - a land free from rules and regulations, inhabited by perhaps now the most primitive tribe - as popularised in anthropological literature between the Godawari and the garge.

Physiography of the studied village area

Abujh Marh is physically characterised by Dharwar rock structure. The Raoghat hills lies on the northern margin of Abujh Marh between Antagarh and Narayanpur in the Narayanpur Tehsil. Soil is mainly of lateritic type. "Rocks are usually covered with a layer of red lateritic soil having an acidic or neutral reaction (Roy, 1989). The texture of the soil varies from sandy to fine textured day soils. Abujh Marh hills comes under the moist sub-humid eco-climate. Indrawati river marks the southern limits, of the Abujh Marh hills and then turns south near the district boundary to meet Godavari.

VILLAGE AND DEMOGRAPHY

Village under study

It is not so necessary to utter that the people who live in Abujh Marh area live in isolated condition. Living in an expilicitly isolated set up in the Abujh Marh area. The people concerned completely depend upon their natural environment and resources in and around their habitat. Abujh Marh is consisted of 236 villages which are distributed in three tehsils namely Dantewada, Bijapur and Narayanpur. In Bijapur 39 villages and in Orcha block of Narayanpur tehsil there are 189 villages. Ader, the village under present study is situated in Orcha block. To substantiate data the researcher also visited and collacted data from Orcha, Gudari, Koduli and Becha villages. Except Becha all the other three villages come under Orcha block and Becha village comes under Dantewada Tehsil. The total area of Orcha block is 3880sq. km. and the total area under cultivation is approximately 2321 Hectors. Village Ader is situated at the western direction and 16 kms. far from Orcha block.

Village Ader attracted the researcher for the present study. It is situated in the lap of at least 700 metres high mountain which is crowded with forest growth. It is an uniethnic village. They have less interaction with the outsiders. There is a jeepable fair weather road from Orcha to Jatlur village - another 'village of the Abujh Maria people. On the way to Jatlur at the left hand side Ader village comes. The jeepable road is unmettalled, of red soil. The village is reached by traveling through the steep road. There are several big sal, sagun, mahua, sulphi and tendu trees at both the sides of the road. Plenty of fruit giving plants such as guava, mango, jackfruit, papaiya etc. are also found in the jungle of that valuable timbers. Trees like drum stick, date palm, harra, aonla and bamboo are not undommon here. A small variety of date palm tree grow in large scale in the area. These are locally known as Ind or Hind, These are used for thatching the houses. All the plants are necessary and important in the life of the people of the area. Plenty of grass grow by the sides of the road which look like the demarcating line between forest and road. Instead of using these grasses for thatching the roof, the people prefer Chhind leaves or Hind or Ind Kata (smaller variety of date palm leaves).

On the way to the village sometimes trees are found felled to clear a patch of land prepared for cultivation. It is interestingly found that these trees are cut not from the root but leaving atleast 2′ to 3′ height from the root. A *talao* (water tank) is located here and to proceed towards the village it is required the cross it.

Ader village is surrounded by forested mountains as mentioned above. There is a small *nulha* and four hand pumps which meet the daily need of water in the village. There is a small stream bed by some spring water looking like veins coming through the motches and holes in the hills. The water of stream is stored in a ditch which is used for cleaning, and washing purpose.

At the entrance of the village there is a middle school, a health centre and also an Anganbari, There is no market place in the village; the people of the village attend the Orcha market.

Due to this type of location where on one hand the village is situated in the lap of natural environment, the forested mountain and on the other hand the viilage is connected with the Headquarters by jeepable road and got some exposure of outside world; the researcher got interest in mind to see how far the people of this village are able to maintain and apply their indigenous methods or traditional knowledge for their sustenance.

Ader village is bounded by the village Chalcher, Gumagal in the north, Itulnar and Dhoudalbera/ Dondalbera in the south; Bade Tondabara in the east and Harbel, Kudmet, Jatlur in the west. The Ghotul (youth dormitory) of the village is situated at the southern periphery of the village. There are 52 Abujh Maria houses situated sporadically on the hill slopes. Entrance of most of the houses are facing the ghotul or constructed on the eastern direction.

Each village demarcates its boundary line by series of boulders and pebbles. There is atleast twenty five to thirty yards gap between the boundaries of the two villages. The gap is regarded as no man's land and is kept for protection of the village. The villagers observe *pir mansha ceremony*, through which they drive out the evils, diseases etc. from the village. They drive those in a particular place outside the village fanning those with old winnowing fans. Those winnowing fans are also left there along with the evils.

In the village, there is an *Udam gariya* or the seat of honour of the *Kaisekh gaita* (religious head). Tallur or seat of the village mother is situated at a corner of the village. Their *pen* deity place is located at another side of the village. It is told that their clan deity Karmaikola do not permanently stay in their village. She visits few other villages where people of the same *pen* live.

A big hut is found in the village which is known as *kurma-lon.* The women during their menstrual cycle come and stay there. There are houses where there is a separate room attached with the household. It is known as hala. Hala is the room built for the menstruating women far of the house. The village provides a resting place for the outsiders which is locally known as *thanagudi* in south Bastar.

House type

The houses are built generally at one corner of the homestead land. There is a Varandah infront of the rooms called as *angadi.* At the corner of the *angadi* there is a cooking place. During summer generally women sleep in the *angadi* with their children, and the husband sleep outside in the *algi.* A small chamber is there inside the inner room where their ancestors are believed to reside. It is also the store room. This room is known as *hanalkotla.* In one corner of the room a hanal or pot of the departed is kept. In the pot of offerings are made. People of other clans are not allowed to enter in the chamber. The hanalkotla is also known as *lonu,* women with their children are allowed to sleep in the *lonu* during rainy season and winter; generally the houses have got no *hala* or separate room for the menstruating women. In some houses *agha* or husband's separate room is there where women are tabooed to sleep. If there is no separate sleeping room for husband, the husband sleeps in the grannery. They construct a wooden platform named *alpanji* where the men sleep. Women are tabooed even to sit on it.

In general they have plenty of space in their homestead land. There is a boundary constructed by small wooden poles, grasses etc. They plant various types of trees, at the boundary of the homestead land. A portion of the homestead land called as *bari* land is also attached with their houses.

Their houses are built with the materials collected from forest. The structure of the house is made with logs of sal and sagun trees and bamboo. The height of the house is about 6' to 7' at the centre and slanted infront of the house. The sagun or sal logs vertically erected at the sides are with forked tops. These are forked to fit horizontal beams on those. In the partition walls also beams are used. On the houses in between the beams of salor sagun or saja logs, bamboo and other small branches are kept. The central beam must be the highest beam and made of saja log. The roof is also structured by wood. The gaps between the logs are covered by bamboo and other small trees. Roof is thatched by md *Kata* or *sawai* grass. The *sawai* grasses are supported by bamboo 'crised-crossed' outside the thatch. These are also tied with the beams. In this way they apply their traditional knowledge to protect their thatch. The grass is easily available in plenty in the jungle and in their *penda* land. Every year they change the straw or leaves of the thatch just before the onset of monsoon. They do it as the old grasses are dried up and become useless. It losses its character to protect them from rains, heat and cold. It gets destroyed by rains, winds, cold and hot throughout the year. Due to this reason, they change it every year. In some houses of Ader some tile roofed houses are also seen.

The slanting of the roof and its and entrance are not so high. It is to be entered in bending posture. In many houses there is no door. If there is any, it is a single or double doored house. It is constructed of wood and bamboo splits. Bamboo splits are fitted in a frame made of wood or bamboo. The entrance is not so high to protect the house from wind and dust. In the *algi* or Varandah infront of a house there are beams and a roof. The house is plastered by clay which is very hard and durable.

It is found from the above description that the Abujh Maria of Ader village live in a hilly, jungle village where they are very much dependent on the locally available jungle products to construct their hut. They apply their traditional wisdom to construct it suited to their local environment.

Demographic aspect of the studied village

In connection with the study of management of natural resources in Abujh Marh, the some other villages were also visited in Abujh Marh such as Gudari, Orcha, Jatlur, Becha and Koduli village and collected some qualitative data for the study. In Koduli village they live with the Bison-Horn Maria who have migrated from Dantewada and other areas and settled in village Koduli. In Orcha they have some interaction with the people of other communities also. All those will be described later in the chapter of social management. The quantitative data were collected from the village Ader. Here some of their demographic aspects are given below:

Table 1 : Family size

Number of Individuals	*Number of families*
One	-
Two	3
Three	13
Four	6
Five	6
Six	13
Seven	3
Eight	6
Nine	-
Ten	-

Average Family Size = 4.92 persons

Table I of family size depicts that the average family size is small and it is 4.2. It is mentioned earlier that the Abujh Maria live in such an ecological condition where they primarily depend on the local forest environment for their sustenance. In Such a situation they have uncertathity in their economic life and probably due to this rason it is found that they live in small families.

Table 2: Sex and age group-wise distribution

Age group	*Population*		*Total*
	Male	*Female*	
0-5	31(25%)	26(20.96%)	57(23.17%)
6-10	20(16.39%)	16(12.90%)	34(14.63%)
11-15	17(13.93%)	11(8.87%)	28(11.38%)
16-20	3(2.45%)	4(3.22%)	7(2.84%)
21-25	5(4.09%)	6(4.83%)	11(4.47%)
26-30	11(9.01%)	16(12.90%)	27(10.97%)
31-35	10(8.19%)	13(10.48%)	23(9.34%)
36-40	11(9.01%)	12(9.67%)	23(9.34%)
41-45	7(5.73%)	5(4.03%)	12(4.87%)
46-50	5(4.09%)	6(4.83%)	11(4.47%)
51-55	0(0.00%)	3(2.41%)	3(1.21%)
56-60	2(1.63%)	3(2.41%)	3(1.21%)
61+	0(0.00%)	3(2.41%)	3(1.21%)
Total	122(49.59%)	124(50.40%)	246

Here in this Table 2 of Sex ratio and age group wise distribution it is found that there are 246 Abujh Maria people live in the village Ader. Among these 246 Abujh Maria people 122 (49.59%) are male and 124 (50.40%) are female. Therefore sex ratio is 98.38 males per 100 female.

Again it is observed that the number of population is maximum, in the age group of 0-5. They are 57(23.17%). Among them 31(25%) are male and 26(20.96%) of the total 124 are female. Age group 6-10 comes next, holds 20(16.39%) of the total 122 males and 16(12.90%) females out of 124 females. In age group 11-15 there are 17(13.93%) males and 11(8,87%) females. Only 3 (2.45%) males and 4(3.32%) females belong to the age group 16 - 20.5(4.09%) males and 6(4.83%) females belong to the age group 21-25. Age group 26-30 holds 11 (9.01%) males and 16 (12.96%) females. Age group 31-35 holds 10(8.19%) males and 13 (10.48%) females. There are 11 (9.01%) males and 12 (9.67%) females in the age group 36-40. Age group 41-45 has 7 (5.73%) males and 5 (9.67%) females. There are 5 (4.09%) males and 6 (4.83%) females in age group 46-

50. Age group 51-55 has no male and it has 3 (2.42%) females, 56-60 age group holds 2 (1.63%) males and 3 (2.42%) females 61+ age group has no male and only 3 (2.41%) female. A rate of population increased is noticed among them.

The reasons behind the increase of population may be the practise of settled plough cultivation which is done among them along with their traditional shifting cultivation.

Table 3: Family Type

Sl No.	*Family Type*	*No. of Families*
1.	Nuclear with or without dependent	34
2.	Horizontally Extended	1
3.	Vertically Extended	-
4.	Polygynous nuclear family with dependent	2
5.	Broken family	6
6.	Composite family (Both vertically and laterally)	3
7.	Incomplete	4

Table 3 of family type depicts that among 50 families maximum number of families is; 34(66%) are of nuclear type. Nextly, comes the broken type of family and those are 6(12%) in number. 3(6%) are of composite type. Polygynous nuclear type of families are 2(4%) and laterally extended family is 1(2%). There are 4(8%) families which are incomplete type. Among the 34 nuclear families most of those are composed of husband, wife and their unmarried children. Except those there are another 2 nuclear families which are of polygynous type. It is found from the study that generally a son within a few years of his marriage constructs his new house which may be constructed in the same compound of his father's house or brothers, In aximum cases the hearth is only separated but the land is not divided and the sons collectively work together with the father. Here in such cases the production is divided among all of them.

Now the question arises why they form separate families?

Primarily it is told that due to maladjustment between women centering the job load is very common. Sometimes quarrel centers round food due to obvious reason. The Abujh Maria live in hills

Table 4 : Age group wise literacy among the Abujh Maria of Ader Village

Age group	Illiterate		Anganbari		Class I to IV		Class V to X		Higher Secondary		College level	
	M	F	M	F	M	F	M	F	M	F	M	F
0-5	23	21	8	4	-	1						
6-10	5	3	4	3	11	10						
11-15	5	10			3	1	9					
16-20	2	2					1	2				
21-25	4	4					1	2				
26-30	8	16					4					
31-35	6	13					2					
36-40	9	12					2					
41-45	4	5					3					
46-50	5	6										
51-55	-	3										
56-60	1	3			1							
60+	-	3										
Total	72	101	12	7	15	12	23	4	-	-	-	-
	(59.01%)	(81.45%)	(9.83%)	(12.29%)	(9.67%)	(18.85%)	(3.22%)	-	-	-	-	

and forests and very much dependent on forest resources to maintain their livelihood. They do hunting, gathering coupled with shifting cultivation. In hunting and gathering there are risks with regard to the resources under all conditions the quantum of food procured cannot be too high. So in a large family maladjustment and quarrel naturally arise centering around the sharing of food. So they feel it is better to form their separate families for the better management of family environment.

Table 4 of literacy shows that in the Village Ader: among total 246 people there are altogether 173 (70.32%) illiterate people. There is not a single person who has appeared the Madhyamic Examination and there is no person to got higher education. It is a fact that the maximum number of the Abujh Maria people of Ader have got no formal education. Among the literates women are very less in number. There are only 23(18.54%) females and 50(40.98%) males who have got some formal education.

Now the question arises, why the number of literates is so less. These people live in such an environmental surrounding where they primarily have to depend on the forest for their sustenance. For collection of forest products the children from their very childhood get engaged in the activities of collection and they think it is useless to send their children to schools. Formal education has no practical use in their life. On the contrary they feel it is necessary to engage their children in various economic pursuits. The Abujh Maria people live in an isolated condition. Most of their villages are inaccessible or less accessible for the outsiders. In such a situation the Government school teachers are reluctant to stay in those villages. They occasionally visit the village. It is also observed that in nearly all the villages (except two/three villages) the infra-structure to run a school is very poor. They have no separate room for the school. Government aids hardly reach to the students. The teachers are not given any incentives to run a school in such a remote area. So this situation does not permit the teachers to run the school in the proper way where the students and specially their guardians are very much reluctant to the formal education and thereby to educate their children.

Table 5 of marital status of the Abujh Maria people of Ader village shows that maximum number of population are unmarried. Among total 246 people 139 (56.50%) are unmarried, It is found from the table that upto the age of 20 there is not a single person who is married. The married persons are found from the age

Table 5 : Marital Status of the Abujh Maria of Ader Village

Age Group	*Unmarried*		*Married*		*Widow*		*Separated*		*Total*	
	M	*F*	*M*	*F*	*M*	*F*	*M*	*F*	*M*	*F*
0-5	31	26							31	26
6-10	20	16							20	16
11-15	17	11							17	11
16-20	3	4							3	4
21-25	4	4	1	2					5	6
26-30	1	-	9	15	1	1			11	16
31-35	-	1	10	11	-	1			10	13
36-40	-	-	11	12					11	12
41-45	-	-	6	3	1	2			7	5
46-50	-	-	5	5	-	1			5	6
51-55						3			-	3
56-60	1		1			2		1	2	3
61+						3			-	3
Total	77	62	43	48	2	13	-	1	122	124
	(63.11%)	(50.00)	(34.24%)	38.70%	1.63%	10.48%	0.00%	0.80%		

group 21-25. So it appears that they do not practise child marriage. Generally in their society though divorce is allowed, in practise it is not tolerated or encouraged and if it happens, the person is to go for remarriage. In this villag, only one women is seen still living separated. She is old and belongs to the age group 56-60 She has grown up children and she was deserted by her husband when shs had crossed her youth. Thus in such a situation she did not to like or rather it is unnatural to go for remarriage.

MANAGEMENT OF NATURAL RESOURCES

At the outset, it is necessary to clarify what is meant by Natural Resources. Natural resources are those which are gifted by nature and which are seen, or felt and utilised by the living beings - nature's specific creation. Natural resources include forest, land, water, sun, moon, stars, wind, animals - even the smallest creature of the earth - all the objects of our universe.

The present study indicates categorically how the sustainable use of the natural resources, is done by the Abujh Maria People for their sustenance without jeopardising the future of the next generation and how preservation and conservation or in a word management of natural resources is done by the people through their traditional knowledge or wisdom.

(a) Forest Management

It has already been mentioned that the Abujh Maria live in hills and forests in the midst of large timbers, crowd of small growing trees, clumsy and dusty shrubs and creepers. The hills look horripilant and occult and simultaneously very beautiful as those are decorated with the greenary, sometimes with thin silver threads of small streams running through the hills. Under this bounty of nature tnere are several footways even in the very difficultly accessible areas - which are created by the village people's movement in the forest to maintain their livelihood. In the forest there are chances to be lost even then as their life is very much oriented by forest. They say that jungle is their own place. From very childhood they used to go even to the dense areas of forest. Everyday they have to travel through forest. In a dense jungle they generally do not get confused or lost. They have got very good conception about the forest path. They opine that the Abujh Maria parents feed their children the half eaten food remants of dog or mouse/ rat. They believe that these animals are never lost in the jungle and when a person eats the said food, he or she gets that quality of these animals. They can even see the evil spirits and all the mischievous acts of the evil spirits as it is done by the dogs and bitches (if they drink even a drop of milk of a bitch).

There are various types of birds, leapard, hyana, beer, fox, jungle dog, wolf, tiger, jungle fowl, pigs etc. in the jungle. These are also the part and parcel of this particular ecological niche. The Abujh Maria live with these, adjust, accommodate and manage all these through their traditional knowledge which are also governed by various types of beliefs and practices, many of which have some scientific explanations also.

On forest management there are seven discussions, writings and researches. Srivastava A. and Pradeep Khanna (1995) wrote that forests are passed through atleast six phases starting from 2000 B.C. to 3000 B.C., of whom major activity was medication, hunting, and religious studies. At present in 1947 A.D. to 1980 A.D. Forests are used for agricultural activities, industry, township, transmission lines, roads etc.

They mentions "A forest eco-system has the capacity to meet the requliements of future generations comfortably and sustainably only when it is managed as an eco system". (ibid, 1995).

To the primitive tribal groups like Abujh Maria forest management is nothing but utilisation of forest for their sustenance. With this there are several necessities and social and cultural bindings through which conservation of forest is also done.

Abujh Marh hills is of deciduous nature. It is an unsurveyed zone. Here the land and the forest are completely owned by these people. Forest adjacent to a particular village is owned by the villagers as a whole. Regarding ownership some observations are made which will be discussed later. The ownership of forest vests on the villagers who own the forest collectively. Next, in case of some trees and plants specially the fruit bearing trees and the trees with economic value are owned by the families at individual level. Ownership of some plants such as mahua, mango, tamarind in the forest is very interesting. The ownership is seasonal. A person who firstly puts his dagger or axe on a particular tree at the beginning of the season, the tree would be regarded as owned by him only for that particular season. If there are several clan groups in the same village, forest is not demarcated clan wise for hunting and collection purposes.

(1) Hunting : Forest is the only source for hunting of birds and animals which are regarded as delicious food items for the tribal groups of the Abujh Marh area.

It is to be noted that inspite of having their habitation in forest itself, Abujh Maria are not so expert hunters like Dandami Maria and Muria. Their hunting techniques are very simple in general. They have some bows and arrows and some axes etc. only. They even have got no net.

Generally they hunt different types of birds such a.s Punari or Harial (a species of yellow dove), Gadra or Tota (Parrot), Irk or Chhota Tota (Small variety of parrot), Malk or Mur (Peacock) etc. Small animals such as Murali or hare, Gedka or jungle fowl, Bada Padin or boar, deers such as Kotri, Chital, Kodama, Sambar, etc. To them hunting is not considered as an occupation. It is an obligatory recreation specially during some rituals and festivals when it is performed collectively. But whenever they go to the forest for any type of slash and burn cultivation, and other reasons, they take their bow and arrow with them and keep the axe on shoulder during the time. These are taken not only as a protection from any ferocious animal but also with a hope to get a hunt.

Summer season is considered as suitable for hunting. During the months of schorching heat, animals comes out of forest towards the water sources to get some swampy muddy area and to quench their thirst. So chances are there to get a hunt near a water source. On the other hand, during rainy season and in winter the animals go and stay in the dense forest. During summer they get animals such as jungle fowl, peacock, wild boar etc. These are easily available. They take rest under green shadows specially during morning and after sunset. The Abujh Maria do not eat jackle, hyena, wild, dog, beer or Erju, Doyal or tiger, Nival or Chita, or leopard. Erju (bear) is a very mischivious animal who always tries to do harm. Those spit pointing the eyes of their opponent party, whom they regard as enemy. The victim gets some burning sensation with it and feels helpless. By this time the animal gets the opportunity to attack the person. The Erju runs very fast and can climb up a tree (in a upside down posture). So if a beer is met in a cross road, it is wise to throw something infront of it. The beer gets busy with it and within this time the person has to run away from the place. Tiger is an animal, whose position is at the top among the animals of the forest. They show reverence to this animal. They say if one happens to come across a tiger, it is a very bad omen for the person and also for the village. If a tiger comes near the village, they become sure that there is definitely some mistake done by any of the villagers such as eating of any new fruit or crop, cereal etc. before offering it to the deities in particular festival connected with eating of new seasonal products due to this the forest deity, Bhum deity and even the *pen* deities may become displeased and send the tiger to punish the villagers. In such a case they call the village Gaita to prescribe the remadies along with the identification of the culprit and the type of mistake. The Gaita through his chants and calculation detects the fault and prescribes remedies through certain ritual offerings. Due to this reason they are customarily not allowed to consume season's any new edible without offering it to the deities. This is one of the very vital point that their traditional beliefs and practises restrict them to destroy any edible before it is fully grown and ripened.

On seeing a hare in the jungle they are sure about their safe condition. There is no tiger in their path. On the contrary a restless manju or monkey gives signals and the birds cry when there is a tiger seen or smell very close to them. The Abujh Maria people also have got some instinct in this regard. They get smell of a beer, tiger and leopard etc. They can detect their movement through the foot marks or the excreta or by the examination of the half eaten fruit. They know in what situation they can get a hunt or may be attacked by some ferocious animal. When they go for hunting in the forest, they minutely try to keep their vigil on the way and try to identify the sounds in the jungle. There are various types of arrows for different animals. The arrow used to kill a bird is not suitable for a bigger hunt like wild bore. All these are suggested by their own traditional wisdom how to live along with their neighbouring animals and to utilise those for their own sustenance.

The Abujh Maria people take their domesticated dogs with them in the forest when even they go there. The dogs help them in searching a hunt, to drive it towards them and even to catch a hunt.

When a person is being isolated from the group or lost in the forest, he whistles in a particular sound signaling that he is lost. On hearing that specific indication the other persons make fruitful attempt to find out the lost one. If a hunt in seen he signals it to his other companions in the hunting party in a different type of whistle. It is very slow, very mild just like a whisper pointing the aim by fingers.

The field rats are caught from the field very easily. They identify the holes. Then dig a little portion of the hole, and put some *kosra* fixing a rat trap in the hole. The rats are fond of *Kosra*. When they come to eat it, immediately they are caught in the trap.

The hares are trapped by *moler funda or jail funda* - another variety of trap. It is fitted on the way of the hares. A hole is dug just very close to the trap. They urinate in it. When the hole is over saturated with the salt of urine, hares get attracted and come to eat it and they are trapped in the *funda*. Sometimes instead of trapped in the *funda* a hare falls in the hole and if there is any Abujh Maria close to the place, catches it immediately. They instruct their pet trained dogs to drive a hunt towards them. The dogs run behind the prey and either catch it or drive it to its master.

To catch a bird they collect oil extracted from green Velva seed. At first they keep the seeds in a pot and boil it. After that they take out the hot seed from the pot, keep those in a basket and by giving pressure and squizing the seeds they extract oil from it. Then they cut a portion of Eva marandu tree, extract resin from it, mix it with the Velva oil and prepare a paste which is annointed on a branch of *Dasing* tree. They place the branch on a mahua or tendu or a mango tree on a higher positiori.When a bird comes to eat the fruit, gets stuck with the branch of *Dasing* tree and can not fly away. The hunters take the advantage and hunt it.

They do fishing in the small nulhas of their area. In the Abujh Marh area fishing is not at all a regular practise. Fishing is done generally in certain rituals and festivals. Fishes are not got in plenty in that hilly area, but it is a very delicious item. So to get those in a good number, they are to restrict them from fishing daily and instead of this, fishing is associated with rituals and festivals. In this way they are to adjust with their local ecological niche. They do fishing by poisoning the water with the paste of bark of various types of plants such as Urthang, Pidin deli, Berma, Mardi, Manging, Kuang, Katoa, Pedra or Kutul fruit. They generally do not destroy these trees but try to conserve those for this purpose. These are mixed with the water of the nulha which immediately gets poisoned. The fishes are stupified by the action of it when they are easily caught. This poison is not harmful to them.

Women are not allowed to accompany any hunting expedition. They are strictly prohibited by social norms. Men are strictly tabooed to sleep with their wives at night if there is any hunting expedition on the next day. Hunting is an auspicious event. They have to offer with certain rituals and festivals. Sexual cohibition is not regarded as a very pure phenomenon. On the contrary, they mention this restriction is in practice prior to any auspicious event. So this taboo is also imposed prior to hunting expedition. They are not allowed to kill certain animals of their totems such as Kachvi, Kohami (a type of turtle), Usendi (monkey), Poyami (buffalo), Oyami (tortoise), Kuharami or Kadiri (Cuckoo), Sodi or Odi (tiger) etc. which help to maintain ecological balance.

(b) Collection

Forest plays a very important role in their material life; it gives them food, shelter, medicine etc. all the important and necessary items of their life. Forest contributes in their house making, in their food chart and also help them to earn cash. Collection of forest products is one of their essential factors of their daily routine. It is observed that collection is mainly done by women accompanied by their children. Men also collect jungle products especially wood, honey and resin etc. but the field of work of collection lies on women. The women are more efficient in this sphere . They have instinct to locate where an edible tuber is available or from where they can get some vegetables. They are very fast to pick up the mahua flowers fallen in the ground. Collection is not a heavy manual work. It needs less labour and minimum skill and for this no skill or training is requiried. From early morning till evening whenever women get anytime they go to the forest. Whenever they go to forest, they keep a basket and a digging stick with them. Generally early in the morning after leaving bed and getting fresh the male folk straight go to the forest to drink the juice of sulphi or sago palm tree. The women after taking their breakfast, they prepare the lunch and then set out to the *penda* field where their men became busy by this time. They go through the jungle and throughout the day they keep themselves busy in collection work along with the work in their land. When they just go to the jungle only for collection purpose, they come back home at mid-day when the sun reaches just at the top of their head. Then they take lunch and again go to the forest for collection and it is done till sun set. Interestingly it is found that utilisation and conservation of forest products are done nicely by them. Their traditional knowledge is not so poor in management of forest environment.

When one enters an Abujh Maria house, he or she has to enter the house opening or lifting the main- gate which is either made of wood or bamboo. The fencing of their houses are constructed, by wood specially of sagun, gambhar, bija, aden, sal and bamboo. All are collected from jungle. The central pole of the house is of aden log. Aden is one of the ritually most valuable tree. It is ragarded as very auspicious. The roof is thatched either by siyari or dabri grass or Chhind or hind or in katta leaves. Presently tiles are replacing the grass and leaves. Previously they had no conception of door. Now they construct it with wood. The houses are plastered with mud. Thus, it is seen that most of the items for construction of a house are collected from forest. Most of the times they construct sheds or rooms for their pet fowls on mahua and other trees. They construct it at a height. The shelter is known as *balla*. The pet birds climb up. to the shelter by a ladder and sleep during the night. They construct it to protect their pets from the attack of leopard or civet and even domesticated cat.

Their household materials of daily use and the materials associated with their economic life and various types of weapons are mostly made of wood, bamboo, grass, leaves, barks, seeds etc. collected from the forest. The handles of axe, adze spade are mode of the bija or sagun wood or wood of vara marum tree. Mushal is a club shapped wooden husker or pastle by which grains are husked in the *ahki* (hole) in the floor. Gudari or hoe is made of wood.

Among the hunting implements bow and arrow, axe, catapult are common. The bows and the arrows are made of bamboo splits. String of a bow which is known as *aund* is made of the thread of *siyari* or elephant creeper or with the thread of *chhind* leaves. Two sides of the string are tied strongly with the bow by silk thread extracted from cocoon of silk worm locally known as Kosa. Kosa threads are also found to tie on the shaft of arrow locally known as *meri*. It is made of bamboo. Kokri the digging stick is also known as *pushal* and made of a very hard wood. They use *dhaman* wood for that purpose. Plough is also made of the same wood. Plough share is of *dhaman* tree. Biasi is a leveller. It is also made of wood. They rarely have cots. If there is any, it is made of wood of bija or dhaman tree. The netting or threading is done by the ropes of Siyari creeper. They are more familier with alpanji

- a sleeping platform for the males only. Women are tabooed even to sit on it. It is made of the wood of *sagun* or *dhaman* tree. A *magh hai* or *Chatai* or mat is made of the bamboo splits. In their houses they keep coils of ropes of dried siyari bark twisted into twine ball are kept. These are used for various types of purposes such as tying of bundle, threading of cot etc. To extract rope, at first they cut the bark of siyari or vara marum tree keep it in water nearly for a month. By this time the gum of the bark of vara marum is washed out and the threads are easily separated.

Bamboo is a very important item to them. They weave various types of *duti* or basket with bamboo split. The baskets are of various shapes and sizes, The large sized *duti* known as *Kalduti* is the biggest or largest variety. The height of *Kalduti* is atleast 3 feet. These are used to store grain. The smaller type of basket is known as *murki,* is carried with them when they go to jungle for collection. Women generally pick up Mahua flower or tamarind in that basket and then those are stored in a basket of larger variety known as *gappaduti*.

Their rain hat or rehki or *reking* is structured by bamboo splits and veiled by *siyari* leaves. Rain coat or *taghali* or *tahali* is also made of bamboo splits and veiled by *siyari* leaves. Slyari leaves are also used to prepare a container for storing grains. Their tobacco pouch, known as *duingagota* is made of *timas* wood. Supa or winnowing fan is made of bamboo.

They use sal leaves as leaf plates, bowls and leaf cups. Paghas are nothing but gourd ladle used as a spoon to serve food and drink. There are small wooden sitting stools. They keep peacock or fowl feather in their houses to protect the house from all types of evils. They believe that these have some magical power to drive out evil spirits. They collect phulbehari grass or *epur* which are used as broom to sweep their houses.

Their musical instruments are prepared by wood and cow or deer skin. One of their very big drums is made of dried trunk of *sulphi* wood. When a sulphi tree losses its capacity to produce juice, they cut it and take its inner portion. It is then dried for preparing a drum. One end of it is covered by deer skin and the other side by cow hide. It is done to get two different varieties of sound effect from the two sides. A smaller variety of drum - *turburi* is prepared by some wood and covered with cow hide.

The Abujh Marh area is very rich with various types of edibles and non-edibles found in the jungle. People of the area have plenty of various types of food items which is thought by them as a blessing of the supreme authority. They collect vorious types of plants, roots, fruits, flowers, seeds, tubers, leaves etc. These are collected for their own consumption and other uses. If there is any excess quantity of collected material, they sell that in the market or exchange for some other necessary items available in the market. There are some items used as medicines.

Among the collected items *dargo* or *mahua* flower is very important. The flower is available during the months of February - March and April. Each and every Abujh Maria family has a number of mahua tree of their own. Except these trees there are several other *mahua* trees in the jungle which are owned seasonally as discussed earlier. If there is any *mahua* tree without even a seasonal owner, anybody can collect *mahua* of that tree. But in that case also they are to follow some rules. A person who reaches first to the tree, he or she is the owner of the tree for that day. They say that this flower starts felling from very early morning and continues to fall till mid day. So they start collection of *mahua* from very early morning.When flower falling stops they understand that it is noon and return home with their collection of *mahua*.

During this season they put controlled fire in the jungle to clear the dried leaves there. It helps them to locate *mahua* fallen in the ground. After collection, they spread those on a mat for drying there in the sun. After this these are gathered in a place and thrushed by a heavy flattened piece of wood, which looks like a cricket bat. In this process they separate stamen of the flower. After that again the *mahua* flowers are dried and stored. They say that they separate stamen from the flower to protect the flower from the attack of insects. The mand or liquor is prepared by this *mahua* flower is very tasteful. It has no bitter taste. They take the flower also by frying. It is also used to flavour *pej*. They store excess mahua flower for future use. In crisis period they sell or exchange the flower with the item needed.

They collect *aam* (mango), itta (tamarind), malli or aounla, *behera* (bayer), *garra* (sal seed), tendu, kusum bija, kosa (Cocoon of silk worm), *Char* (Diospyros melanoxylon), seona (Gmeliha arborea), jamun (Eugenia jambolana) etc. Sulphi or *gohgha* or sago palm juice is one of the main attraction of the forest products.

Mushroom, bora and various types of leafy vegetables are also collected.

They do not feel any need for collection of fodder. as there is a vast area full with jungle. Their cattles are free to move in the jungle as it is an unsurveyed zone. The cattles never face any crisis for food. They collect fuel wood from the forest for their own use. Generally they avoid to cut living trees to keep ecological balance but only cut the dried trees. Men generally cut a big tree into small pieces and these are tied into bunches by Siyari ropes. Women folk carry those on their heads. If the load is heavy, then it is carried by the men on their snoulder.

Forest provides them various types of roots, tubers, leafy vegetables, many of which are seasonal products. During summer they collect mati or tubers such as Kodo, Kaska, Gone, Kotosh, Kai, Kaiman, Keku, lekh, kasa, nangal, jule, pad, gunga, krish, nager, chhind, kaimul etc. Jabba or sag (leafy vegetables) such as Velvetun, Kodeli etc. Phool or flower like Velvetun, shund or tund, mahua or velva, nalli, mango, char, phanos, harra or kahkka, baira or jahka, tummer panding or tendu, itta or imli (tamarind) and seeds such as tora (mahua seed), juice such as Sulphi or gohgha (sago palm) etc. In monsoon they collect tubers such as Kash, Kaiman, tule, Kosa, pad, Kotosh etc. bota/ boda (a tuber grown under the foliage of sal leaves, jabba or leafy vegetables such as Kohak, mugur, erbor, Velvetun, Koliari etc., phool or flower such as shund or tund, basta or young bamboo shoot and various types of *Kuhku* or mushroom etc. In winter they collect tubers such as pido, gale, pad fruits such as karka or harra, janka or bayra, juice of suiphi or gohgha. Beside these they collect various types of non-edible items from forest such as Kohku or Velva, *arengi* or sal seed, sal twig, harra twig etc. Siyari and pubur leaves, sal leaves, tummer, akkakki (tendu leaves), chhind leaves are also collected. They collect kosa or silk cocoon and epur or fuljharia, wood, bamboo and serka grass. During monsoon the collection from jungle is not an easy matter . Generally they collect edibles and the most necessary and urgent items (such as medicinal herbs, shrubs, etc.) from jungle. In winter again they use the forest as one of their important economic source.

A list of collected materials from the forest is given below:

The third but another important part is that the forest plays an important role by providing various items with different items with medicinal value. In Ader village there is a Non-Governmental Organisation who runs a health centre. But the opportunity is very limited and the people of the village are not so interested to take medicines from that health centre. Instead they are very

A List of Collected Forest Items

Season	*Items*	
	Edibles	*Non-edibles*
Summer	Mati (Tubers)-Kodo, Kaska, Gone, Kotosh, Kai, Kaiman, Keku, Lekh, Rasa, nangal, Tule, Pad, Gunga, Langal, Rash, Krish, Nager, Chhind, Kaimul etc.	Seed-Kohka/Velva, Arengi/Sal Seed. Twig-Sal and Harra
	Jabba (Leafy vegetables)-Velvetun, Kodeli etc. Phool (Flower)-Velvetun, Shund/Tund, Irru or Mahua.	Leaves-Siyari or Pabur Sal, Tummer, Akkior Tendu leaves, Chind, Kosa (Silk Cocoon)
	Phal (Fruit)-Turguna, Ind, Kohka/Velva, nalli, Mango, Char, Phanos,. Harra or Kohkka, Baira or Jahka] Tummer Panding or Tendu, Imli.	Epur or Fuljharia Bamboo, Wood Serka Grass.
	Seed-Tora	
	Juice-Sulphi or Gorga/gohgha	
Monsoon	Mati (Tuber)-Kash, Pad, Kaiman, Tule, Kosa, Kotosh, Bota/ Boda (a tuber grown under the foliage of sal leaves). Jabba (Leafy Vegetables)-Kohak, Mugur, Erbor, Velvetun, Koliari	Bamboo and Wood and necessary items such as medicinal herbs, shrubs etc.
	Phool-Shund/Tund.	
	Basta-Young bamboo shoot Various types of Kuhku or Mushroom.	
Winter	Mati (Tuber)-Pido, Gale Pad. Phal (Fruit)-Kahka or Harra Jahka or Bayra,	Sal Leaves, Bamboo, Wood, Sarka Grass
	Juice-Sulphi or Gorga/gohgha	

much dependent on their indigenous health practices through various rituals, sorcery and also through medicines. The ingradients of those medicines are collected from jungle.

It is told that whenever a person becomes sick he or she immediately consults the *leske* or *sirha* of the village. The leske or sirha through his magical performances identifies the actual cause of the sickness. If the *leske* or the *sirha* gets some hints through their magical performances anybody has performed some mischivious magical performance or sorcery to do harm of a person who ultimately is ill, he (*leske*) or *sirha* prescribes remedies. If the *leske* or *sirha* is unable to identify the actual culprit, he takes the help of Log God or *pen* deity who by his divine power identifies the witch or the wicket person.

These leskes also act as medicine man. They believe that medicines are prescribed by the Heavenly Father and their ancestors are taught by Him. Generations after generation knowledge is maintained, applied and also transmitted to the persons of the next generation. Leske or *sirha* can detect the disease by beating of the pulse beat. Sometimes they consult the deities who prescribe remedies through dreams which may include some jungle products with some magical performances. But in all cases a ritual offering to the deities is compulsory.

Indigenous Health Practise

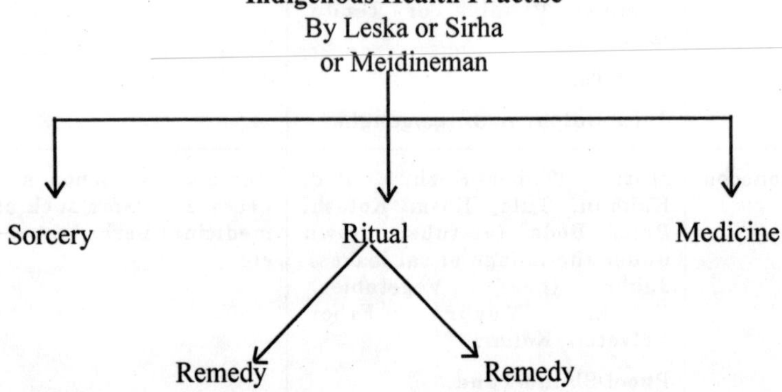

The common diseases are dysentry fever, malaria and skin diseases.

Now a list of some medicinal plants, herbs etc. which they often collect from forest is given below :-

Sl. No.	*Name of the disease*	*Herbs shrubs, plants etc., with English Equivalent*	*How to use / Method of use*
1.	Headache	Turguma fruit, Katta or Kota fruit	Boil the fruit is water. Then take the fruit Or fry the fruit and take it.
2.	Stomache	do	do
3.	Col, Caugh and Harra Fever (Muta Pasinta)	Harra	Grind it in water then keep it soaked in water for atleast 2 hours. Then drink the Water. It is taken for two to three times in Empty stomach.
4.	Cold, Caugh and Cracks In the Skin	Tora seed (Mahua seed)	At first the oil is heated then the Warm oil is massaged all over the body.
5.	Headache	Kohka / Velva seed	The seed is slightly broken and heated. The oil of the seed comes out and is applied on the forehead.
6.	Headache	Kaikat grass	Extract juice from the grass, then added with Fever Stomache water and boiled and drank or Grind the grass, boil it in water filter it by new cloth in a new pitcher and drink or sometimes they prepare tablets by those grass and taken with boiled water.
7.	Wound (Kahattom)	Bark of Mehenda sola tree	The bark is grinded. A sleeper juice comes out of that and is anointed at the place of wound, and the paste is not washed till the wound gets dried and automatically falls.
8.	Headache (one side)	A branch of Kata ban tree with its leaves	These are boiled in water. Then the water is massaged on the particular side of the forehead.

(contd...)

(contd...)

Sl. No.	*Name of the disease*	*Herbs shrubs, plants etc., with English Equivalent*	*How to use / Method of use*
9.	Sprain	Mud of ant hill	Collected mud and it is heated and then appointed at the place of sprain.
10.	Bone fracture	Bark of Mehenda sola tree	At first the bone is set and then they appoint of the sleepy juice at that place.
11.	Irregular menstruation	Bark of need (Azadirachta Indica) tree	Bark of neem tree is grinded and soaked in water for few hours and then the water is drank.
12.	Asthama (Dama)	Harra (Terminalia Chebula). Bayra (Terminalia bellirica) Aoula (Emblica officinalis)	All these are mixed and pasted together and then it is taken.
13.	Epilepsy (Mirgi)	Pharsa or palash twin and bark of mahua tree mixed and grinded together then soaked in water throughout the night and taken or neem twig.	These two are grinded together, soaked in water over night and next morning water is taken or the neem twig is grinded and soaked in water over night. Next morning that Water is taken.
14.	Wound	Kohka/Velva seed	The seed is slightly broken then heated. The oil comesout of the seed, applied in the wound. The wound will be heated.
15.	Wormicide	Baibairang (Babreng) Embelia Ribes	
16.	Blood pressure, Mental Derangement, Female disease, snake bite	Sarpagandha (Rauvolfia Serpentine benth)	

(contd...)

(contd...)

Sl. No.	*Name of the disease*	*Herbs shrubs, plants etc., with English Equivalent*	*How to use / Method of use*
17.	Skin disease	Karanj seed (Pongamia glabra, Alnus integrifolia)	
18.	To keep body cool	Tikhur-a tuber (Curcuma angustifolia)	Wash it in water for several times then grind it and soak in water. The Water is taken.
19.	Malaria	Chiraita (Swertia chirata)	Grind it and soak in water overnight and the water is taken.
20.	Barrennes	Sannhelup seed (crotolaria Juncea)	
21.	Constipation and snake bite	Erand seed (castor) Ricinus Communis.	
22.	Constipation	Amaltas fruit pulp (Cassia fistula)	
23.	Lencorhaea	Satyanasui seed and plant.	
24.	Tatti/Pet darna, (Dyarrhea)	To root of Duli tree.	It is grinded and soaked in water over night. Early in the morning it is drank.
25.	Sir Dukhna/Tala naunta (Headache)	Velva seed (Kohka seed)	Oil is extracted and heated and applied to the forehead where it is paining.
26.	Kahattom (cut/wound)	Kakar Indi tuber	Finely grinded and applied to the wound and bandaged. it sticks to the would till it is healed up. it takes nearly one month to get cured
27.	Netur pota (Blood dysentery)	Beng Podla Tuber	Grinded and soaked in water over night, taken in the morning.
28.	Mendur Nainta (Bodyache)	Pendra root	Grinded and taken.
29.	Kondang Putingta (Eye trouble)	Pittereka fruit (Green small	The fruit is taken as medicine.

Conservation of Forest

The next part of discussion on management of environment and natural resources deals with its conservation and preservation. The dictionary meaning of conservation and preservation do not vary but in the study of management these two terms are slightly different from each other. Both of these terms are used for protection of forest but where the people have their own concept and system of protection of forest, it is called as conservation and where forest is protected for commercialisation it is preservation. Conservation of forest is mainly done by the primitive people through their own cultural norms which are reflected through their own indigenous practises. (Sing A.K. Jabbi,1994).

The Abujh Maria, the indigenous people of the Abujh Marh hills are very intimate with their physical environment in and around which they live. They utilize the resources available in the forest of the region over generations for their sustenance. Side by side they have various cultural bindings which prohibit them to kill certain animals and to cut certain trees for different reasons and to burn these. They are tabooed to eat certain fruits such as mango, tamarind etc., certain flowers such as mahua, certain leafy vegetables such as Khatta bhaji prior to the performances of certain rituals. These implied restrictions help them to protect the forest from destruction and side by side it guides them on proper utilisation.

For conservation of forest sacred grove plays a vital role. Gadgil and Vartak opine that sacred grove is a patch of land with various types of trees. The land is definitely undisturbed. No tree of this area is cut as it has its association with some deities.

The Abujh Maria of Abujh Marh also have their sacred grove in each and every village. In the village Ader, there are sacred places known as *tallur* and - *pen rawar* situated in sacred grove. In the sacred grove there are several trees such as aden, saja, sal, sagun, harra, bans are found. They are tabooed to cut all the trees of the area. They are allowed only to collect dried up twigs, and leaves fallen in the ground. Sacred grove is regarded as the abode of a particular deity in whose name the place is established. The trees of the place have ritual value. It is believed that the deities sit on the leaves, branches of those trees. At the time of performance of any ritual the deities come on certain leaves. Their ritual bindings imposed restrictions which ultimately helped in conservation of their natural resources.

The tree aden or saja is very much important to them. It is very much liked by their deities. When a Sirha or a priest invites some deities through a prayer, he keeps an aden leaf in his palm. The deity responses very quickly. They can cut a dry Aden tree but not allowed to burn it. In house building there is a social norm that the central pole of a hut the deities will always be present in the house and protect them from all types of misfortunes. Aden trees are again important from economic point of view. Its leaves are a very delicious food item for the silk moth. This small creature lays egg on the leaf. The lurva of the worm is very much fond of this leaf and eat it and ultimately it forms cocoon. Silk Cocoon is a very costly item. The silk extracted from cocoon is of high quality. They collect the cocoons from jungle and sell those in the market. Similarly dhawra tree is also protected. It is also ritually very important and also the silk moths like the tree to complete their life cycle as in the aden tree. Sarai or Saja or aden tree is called as ammarum, bija tree is wengo, char as mormarum. They never urinate or spit in or close to the place. They never cut trees of *bij patar.* It is the place where they perform the *bijputni* and *ama khani* rituals.

They do not cut trees such as neem, harra, bayra, aonla etc. as these have got medicinal value. Naturally, these trees are very important in their life. They prepare indigenous medicines by barks, fruits, seeds, flowers, roots or tubers etc. of those trees. Trees like harra, bayra and aonla have economic value also. They sell the fruits of these trees in the Orcha market to the businessmen to earn cash or exchange it for getting other necessary items. Due to all these reasons they do not cut these trees and as a result conservation of these trees are being maintained.

The cutting of Kaliary tree is restricted . Its leaves are needed in several rituals. Bargat or banyan tree holds the top most position among all the trees in the forest for its ritualistic value; aden comes the next. Bat is more or less a spiral type of creeper with ritual value. This tree must be found in their sacred grove. Trecs like peepal, sal, dummar, jag dummar etc. also have ritualistic importance. The bark of the peepal tree is necessary for purification. When a person gets purified after the completion of some pollution period or becomes polluted because of touching a person passing through polluted person, water is sprinkled over him or her by peepal bark as they believe that peepal bark is very pure. They get incense from Sal tree which is very necessary in all of their rituals and festivals. They do not cut all these trees.

Velva tree has remarkable medicinal value. They believe that if any body cuts this tree, he or she will definitely suffer from wound in the stomach.

They are not encouraged to cut any fruit giving tree such as mango, tendu, imli, or atta (tamarind), Karia nerui or kala jamun also mahua tree. These are protected to havc food for their own consumption. Chiranji is a very costly type of seed. They sell Chiranji in the market to earn cash. Mahua flower is taken as breakfast. They prepare sweet dish with this flower. Mahua liquor locally known as *mand* is another important item in their all rituals, festivals and ceremonies. They are very much fond of it. Its seeds are collected and oil is extracted from the seed. The oil is massaged all over the body and head hair. It protects them from mosquiito bite. Their skin remain glazy even during the severe cold. Their hair remain black till very old age. Mahua flower and seed are also sold in the market or exchanged for getting other essential items. So here both the economic and ritualistic values are present. Keeping of a number of mahua tree is regarded as an asset for a family.

Similarly, Sulphi tree also has its importance due to its juice which is a very favourite drink to the Abujh Maria. The liquor has no intoxicating property when it is fresh but gradually it becomes intoxicated when it is not fresh. When a suiphi tree becomes old, it losses its juice giving character and becomes dry, its inner portion is taken out to prepare musical instrument, sometimes with the inner portion they prepare *roti*. Similarly tamarind and mango trees are also regarded as their assets.

Whenever they cut trees for *penda* cultivation, many times they cut alive and young trees (except those above mentioned trees). They say that they never cut any tree from its root but cut it leaving at least 2′ to 3′ height from the bases. It is done to protect the forest. They claim that after a few days new leaves will come out again from those trunks and it begins to grow but in true sense it is examined during the field investigation that most of such trees get burnt and destroyed during firing of *penda* field. According to them, Marai is a festival after harvest of all crops and cereals when their deities are entertained with the newly cultivated product. They havc a rule that prior to the performance of Marai if anybody sets fire in the jungle he has to pay *dand* (fine to the *jati panchayat*). They believe that the deities will be dissatisfied and feel insulted if they set fire for next season prior to the offering of all cultivated crops through this festival.

They never dig out a tuber wholly from the earth. They leave a small portion atleast for growing for the next year. They dig out only the big sized *tikhur*. The small sized one is left in the earth for further growth. In this way the conservation process of the tubers is being done.

They do not demolish an ant hill which is called *putlai*. They show reverence to it as they believe that *putlai* have some connection with their origin. It is observed that white ant of the ant hill is a delicious food item for the beers. So indirectly the protection of ant hill means the protection of white ant which indirectly helps the beer to get food and ultimately to its conservation.

Thus, it is seen that side by side with the utilisation of forest and its products, conservation is also being done by these people.

B. Land Management

The subsistance base among the Abujh Maria is cultivation along with collection of forest items. Both of these activities are solely dependent on their local ecological niche. To them cultivation is the family enterprise those who share the hearth - share the works of cultivation. Sometimes when an extended family is divided into smaller units, the land is not divided, there cultivation is a joint enterprise where the smaller units are tied together by an economic bondage which units them to work together and to share the harvest. They utilize their land for their sustenance, and at the sametime take several necessary measures for the conservation of their land for future utilisation.

To the Abujh Maria land is *bhum*, the abode of their deity Tallur Mutte; their own cultivated crops, cereals etc. such as Kohla or Kola Kosi or Kosra, Jhajmago or paddy, Pupul pusey or urad pulse, Armaribe or kang, Ikaliri and Gondo pokri other varieties of Kosra and Bismareh or lal bhaji are regarded as seven daughters of Bhum deity-Tallur. Traditionally the Abujh Maria are the shifting cultivators. Cultivation process is slash and burn cultivation. Presently they have acquired some knowledge of settled plough cultivation but this cultivation is not so popular like slash and burn cultivation, Traditionally the shifting hill cultivators used to identify their land in two varieties namely Kaghe or Kaghai and Paghe or Paghai. The land cleared to do shifting cultivation is Kaghe. or Kaghai jamin and the other land left fallow or the land where the vilisgi site is situated is called as Paghe or Paghai jamin.

Now-a-days usually they do not use these two terms, though these two terms have yet to get replaced by another two specialised terms.

The Abujh Maria classify their cultivable land as follows :

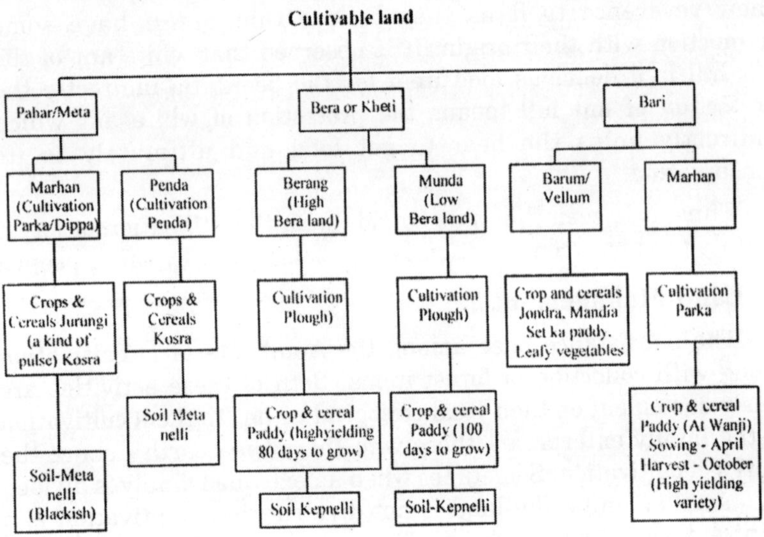

Land

The high land on the hills is known as Pahar. When such a cultivable land is situated at the flat table land on the hill top, it is known as *marhan* land in Abujh Marh. This type of land is smaller in size in comparison to the *penda* land and generally is cultivated for successive two years. Two types of cultivation in this type of land is done. These are *parka* and *dippa* cultivation. Another variety of land situated on the hill slopes is knoum as *penda* land and here the *penda* cultivation is done. *Parka, dippa* and *penda*–all these three types of cultivation in *pahar* are similar with a little difference which will be discussed later.

The next variety of cultivable land is known as or *bera* or *kheti*. The land is flat, low and suitable for paddy cultivation. The soil of this type of land is sticky having the capacity of water conservation. Soil of this type of land is suitable for paddy cultivation. This land is also divided into two types namely *barum* and *munda*. The *munda* land is very low lying land where the crop gets maximum water facility, very urgently needed for plough cultivation.

Third type of land is *bari* land or homestead land attached to or situated very close to their huts. This land is called as Barum or Vellum or Wellum where it is attached to the houses at low land. The another variety is marhan land which is very similar to the marhan land in *Pahar* or or *meta*. This type of land is attached to the huts, which are situated at comparatively high level. The *marhan* lands are higher than the *barum* lands. They cultivate a type of paddy called *atwanji* which requires less water and grows very quickly. The seeds are sown in April and these are ripened before Dushera.

Now a table on the possession of various types of land among the Abujh Maria families of Ader village is given.

Type of land	*Upto 2 acre*	*upto 5 acre*	*upto 8 acre*	*upto 12 acre*	*13 acre and above*
Bari	35	5			
Bera	20	21			
Pahar	7	32	9	1	1

In this table the lands are divided into three broad categories namely *Bari*, *Bera* and *Pahar*. It is found that maximum number of the people of Ader villag, possess Bari land upte 2 acres. When it is Bera land, maximum people have upto 5 acres. But in Pahar, maximum people possess 5 acres. In case of *Bari* land it is observsd that maximum number of families that is 35(67.30%) possess upto 2 acre of land, 5(9.6%) families have *bari* land upto 5 acres. There are 10 (19.30%) families who have no *Bari* land attached to their huts. In case of *Bera* land 20 (38.46%) families possess upto 2 acres, 21 families possess upto 5 acres. In case of land in Pahar there are 7 (13.4%) families who possess 2 acres 32(61.53%) families have land in *Pahar* upto 5 acres. 9(17.30%) families possess this type of land from 9 acre to 12 acre and 13+ acre is possessed by 1(1.92%) family.

The Abujh Maria people possess maximum amount of land in *Pahar*. They have informed that in Pahar they have a vast land. But they do not like unnecessary felling of wood or clearing of land for cultivation in *Pahar*. They only clear the land as per their necessity. In this way the manage to control the destruction of forest and do not generally destroy it more than their need. In this way the forest gets some protection.

There are 10(19.23%) families who have no *Bari* land. In al] those 10 cases it is found that the families have either migrated recently from some other village, or just have established their own separate family of procreation. Among the Abujh Maria of Ader 9(17.30%) families have no *Bera* land. They mostly earn the livelihood by cultivation in *pahar* and in their *Bari* land.

Now in the following Table Land – Man Ratio is given below:

Type of Land	*Total (in acre)*
Pahar (Marhan, Penda)	215
Bera	112
Bari	59½

Total land cultivated	386.5 acre
Total number of person	246
Therefore, Land-Man-Ratio	386.5 ÷ 246 = 1.5 acre

Occupational categories is given below:

Occupational Category	*Primary*		*Subsidiary*		*Total*	
	M	F	M	F	M	F
Cultivation (Parka, Penda and Plough)	53	28	2	45	55	73
Household work	-	75	-	4	-	79
Collection	-	79	54	-	79	54
Cattle herding	1	1	-	-	1	1
Service	2	-	-	-	2	-
Student	34	22	-	-	34	22
No work (either below 5 years of aged or old/physically handicapped)	32	22	-	-	32	22

Table on occupational categories shows that the Abujh Maria people engage in the work like cultivation (both *penda* and plough), collection, cattle herding etc. for their subsistence. Household work is one of the most important occupation for the women. Service is a new addition in their occupational categories. There are students also, who are also included in the table. cultivation and collection - these two are the main sources to earn their livelihood.

To the Abujh Maria men of Ader, cultivations (including *Parka*, *Penda* and *Kheti*) are regarded as their primary occupation. There are 53(43,44%) males out of 122 males whose primary occupatièn is cultivation. Only 2 (1.63%) males are there whose primary occupation is service and have taken cultivation as their secondary source of occupation. In case of females out of 124 females cultivation is the primary occupation for 28(22.58%) females and 45 (36.38%) females have taken it as their secondary occupation. Household work is solely done by the women. It is the responsibility and also primary occupation of 75 (60.48%) women, 4(3.22%) women do it as their secondary occupation. In case of those 4 women, they have other female members in their family who do the household work. These 4 women have taken cultivation as their primary occupation. Collection is mainly done by women, There are 79(63.70%) women, involved primarily in collection along with their household and other jobs. It is markedly observed that for men collection is regarded as their subsidiary occupation and out of 122 men 54(44.26%) do collection as their secondary occupation. It is found that women take more rssponsibility and burden of collection work as they ars regarded to have instinct to locate the forest products which is less in men. Again collection is tiring but one has to pay minimum labour in this work. So collection is the suitable work for the women. Men generally collect the forest products which need more strength and are to some extent regarded as hard work. They fell fire wood and cut those into small pieces and carry those on shoulder. Women also carry smaller bunches of firewood on head. Men mainly deal with the sago palm drink. They collect bamboo for basket making and Siari or elephant creeper leaves for use as plates and leaf cups, honey, gum etc. There are 34(27.86%) males and 22(17.74%) females who are students in Anganbari. Therefore, the Abujh Maria economy is primarily dependent on cultivation and collection. The Abujh Maria people of the village Ader both male and female claim that they also do wage earning in unskilled sectors but it is observed that very rarely any depelopmental work (such as road construction installation of tubewell etc.) is done here. If there is any such work, they are definitely recruited. Otherwise in cultivation they do not get any such job of wage earning. They extend their labour for one another on mutual understanding.

The Abujh Maria live in a vast area covering so many acres which is completely an unsurveyed zone. There is no government rule and restriction in felling trees or occupying land as per the need and wishes of the inhabitants. They are the only owner. Ownership of land here is firstly on village basis and then at clan basis. It is informed that sometimes the village site is abandoned for various superstitions reasons such as death, disease or any calamity. Previously, shifting of village was obvious. It was not only related with the superstitions but also for economic reasons for sustenance. They are traditionally the shifting hill cultivators and used to do slash-and-burn cultivation which is locally known as *penda* and *dippa*. In dippa cultivation, a plot can be cultivated for two years and *penda* is done is a field not more than four years. After four years of cultivation they shift to another land, leaving the previous land as fallow land for its regeneration and the nitrogenous balance is maintained in this process. They move from one to another land in a hill attached to their village. When all the lands of that particular hill are cultivated and exhausted, they leave the total hill and shift to another hill. Traditionally with the shifting to another hill for cultivation, they used to shift their village to a place very close or attached to the new cultivable area. In this way they used to shift from one hill to another for cultivation and again come back to the first site in rotation. The total period from leaving the first hill to resume the cultivation there takes atleast twenty years.

Regarding allotment of land it is seen that when they shift to a new site to prepare it for cultivation, the whole village people work together to clear the land. Generally the village *Gaita* in consultation with the village headman and other villagers allot the penda land for cultivation to the villagers. Plots once alloted for the work of cultivation becomes the property of the person or family till it is left after several times of cultivations. When it is left, it again becomes free of ownership. There is no guarantee that a man will have the same plot when he comes again to cultivate in the same hill after completion of cultivation in other hills under the same village.

In Abujh Marh any man can get a larger plot to work if he is able to cultivate it. But in practise one seldom, does it unless one has a large family. The land is divided among the clans. So the ownership of land vests to the clan and the pople of the same clan are alloted plots from-the portion of land. The plots are divided according to the needs. These are demarkated by tree stums. Generally, in the village members of same clan live together. So they do not face any difficulty in division of land. If there are two or more clans in a village, then they firstly divide the hill clan wise and after that smaller plots are alloted to the families of same clan.

Sometimes families of other clans migrate to another village leaving their own village due to some reasons. In such a case firstly the new comer goes and meets the village elders with an appeal to have some land. Generally after discussion with others, the headman and the *Gaita* allot some plots for cultivation. In lieu of the land the person or family concerned does not have to pay any cost or any. rent. Only a bottle of liquor is sufficient. It is offered to the village headman and the *Gaita*. It is told that generally after harvesting of the crop the new comer gives a grand feast to the villagers though it is not compulsory.

Now-a-days shifting of village along with shifting of *penda* site is not encouraged and recently stopped. Now they have some permanent rice field which are the private property of the families. Presently, they have got an idea to construct huts which are more durable and with various types of plants in the homestead land. Tube wells are installed by the Government to give them water facility. All these reasons restricted them to abandons village (only except the case of any calamity or disease).

The people of Ader village have their Pen deity Karmaikola They have five hills of their own where the people of Ader are allowed to cultivate. These hills are their own property. The property is owned by their ancestors from time immemorial as per the instruction of their *pen* deity. They cultivate these five hills one after another's completion, These are named as Ader, Thurthuli, Makori or Makowahi and Nernar and Keramtang. All of these mountains have their own Rani or Queen or Goddess. They do cultivation to all the hills staying at Ader village. Ultimately they have got interest to build a comparatively a permanent hut. They plant various types of fruit plants. In their *bari* land attached to their huts they cultivate various types of crops and cereals. So gradually they have got some attachment and attraction towards their huts and greenaries and specially to their rice field. Due to this they cultivate their *penda* slope even when it is at a distant place from their village, where their permanent rice fields are present. When the *penda* slope field is situated nearby, everyday early in the morning they go to the field, do cultitation work throughout the day and return to the village when it is dark. As a rule, after sowing when the seeds are germinated and the seedlings come out, the men are tabooed to sleep with their wives and to have any sexual relation as they are to stay in the field till harvest.

Their woman folk arive at the field everyday after sunrise with the day's meal. They stay in the field till sun set. The night meal is prepared in the field by them. Then taking their share with the men then they return to their homes.

When the load of work in the field is more during harvest, women have to go to the field very early morning and cook the day's meal also in the field. In this way they adjust with the situation. When the *penda* field is situated very far from their houses, the male members of the village stay in the field from the starting of work in the field.

Types of Cultivation

In case of *parka*, *dippa* and *penda* cultivations, cutting of the tree and bush wood and burning of those take place. The crop is raised on the ashes which act as fertilizer for production of those crops and cereals. But in the cultivation process differences are there. In case of *parka* cultivation the wood is felled in the jungle and then those are brought to a flat *marhan* land in the hills, then spread out to dry and when it is dried, it is burnt. It is burnt before the rain breaks. Then the seeds are broadcasted and eventually the crops and cereals are produced. Parka cultivation is done in flat *marhan* land. In this type of land various types of millets which are locally known as Kosra or Kohla are produced. A high yielding variety of rice which is known as *atwanji* is also cultivated. This variety of paddy needs a very short period to get matured. The seed is broadcasted in the month of April which ripens within September-October. In case of *marhan* type of *bari* land *parka* cultivation is also done.

Dippa cultivation is very similar to *parka* cultivation. It is also done in the flat land of hills. But in thts cultivation the land can be cultivated only for two years. In the first year they cut smaller trees and bushes and all other undergrowth in that particular land and burn it. The big trees are not felled during the first year. Those are protected by the girdles during first year, During first year of cultivation the land is fresh having its own capacity to produce good crop. Due to this they do not fell all the trees. They clear some portion of land to get space for cultivation. During next year or second year, they cut all the big trees and burn all those along with the stumps. Stumps are generally of bush wood. They say that during next year the land needs some added fertilizer as it has lost its original capacity due to cultivation in the previous year. After two successive years of cultivation, the cultivated *dippa* land becomes a deforested *marhan* land as its all the trees, bushes and even the brush wood are cleared and burnt. If anybody wants to cultivate again in that particular land he is to accumulate wood, cut and brought from other area, fired and cultivated. Then the cultivation is called as *parka* cultivation instead of *dippa* cultivation. In dippa cultivation various types of Kosra or millet are also cultivated.

Among all these three types of slash and burn cultivation, *penda*, the shifting hill cultivation is preferred most by the Abujh Maria because of the fact that a large quantity of crops and cereals can be produced through this type of cultivation.

Penda cultivation starts with the felling of trees in a particular hill slope selected for it. Cutting or felling of wood in a particular *penda* plot starts from the month *fagur/phagur* (Feb.-Mar). It continues upto Chait (March-April). Then those are spread in the field for drying. Firing of the wood is never done before the performance of Holi in the month of Phagur (February-March). According to them, one should not light fire in the field prior to the performance of Holi. Holi is believed as a festival when all the evils are burnt with the ritual firing of Holi. If one violets this social taboo he is punished as per their social rules and decision of their own jati panchayat. Some of them have informed that during that time they have just finished the harvest of kosra which are yet to be brought to the granary. If they light fire in the jungle, crops and cereals lying there may be destroyed. So this is avoided through their social bindings.

Before felling of the trees, they perform a ritual through which offerings are made to the Bhum deity-Tallur Mutte. This is done once in a land for the first time of its penda cultivation. In successive cultivations, they do not perform the ritual. The first time of cultivation is known as *pune-pendai* and successive *penda* cultivations are *parna penda.* Their lands are demarcated from one another by raising a row of some shrubs or keeping some stones in a row. Sometimes tree stumps are also kept along the boundary. During the month of *Vaisakh* or *mur* (April-May) after one or two showers they broadcast Kosra or Kohla seeds. Kosra or Kohla is a blanket term used for the crops cultivated in the penda plot. Kosra which are sown early during month of Landi or Jaith or (May-June) and Hai (June-July) they have less work in their penda land. During this period they become busy in their paddy cultivation in *bera* land. During sawan or Hagh (July-August) Chota Kosra starts to ripen. They start cutting Kosra. Along with Kosra they also cultivate *atwanji* rice - a variety of mountain rice which also ripens by this time. They complete harvest within the month Bhado or Eranj (August September).

Among the Chota Kosra *amu* (Panicum frumentaceum), Sika or Chikma or Turiya Kohla (Panicum miliare), Kodan (Paspalum scrobiculatum), mandia (Elunsive Coracana) and harua or light mountain rice are very important.

In the month of Hai (June - July) the cultivation of another type of Kosra named bara Kosra is done. During this period they also become busy in their *bera* land for plough cultivation. Even then they keep sometime to broadcast the seeds of Kulthi (Panicum miliaceum), Kodang, Kang (Setaria italica), bajra (Panicillaria spicata) with different varieties of pulses such as pupul or urad (Phaseolus radiates), arhar (Cajanus indicus) and jata/jatengi (Dolichos lab lab). These are harvested in Pandi or pand (November - December).

In Eranj (August-September) they cultivate Oskosra with the harvesting of Chhota Kosra; in this cultivation they cultivate various types of pulses such as (Phaseolus mungo), Kulthi (Glycine hispid) etc along with Kosra. This crop is harvested in Pusi (December-January).

During *penda* cultivation in the field, they keep some big trees without cutting those. They leave those as a support for growing creepers such as semi. In penda field they conducts mix cultivation. They cultivate barbati/ jurunga, semi/jatengi bangola (tomato), poyami or rahar, pupul or urad, gunei or kochei, rasa mati or Sakar Kanda simultanously along with Kohla. When they prepare land for or Kosra cultivation, they leave the leaves to get those spoilt and rotten. After that they dig some portions on the four sides of the land. Those rotten leaves are kept there which become fertilizer. They keep these in heaps of circle and sow seeds as already mentioned in these circles. The seeds which are sown in central position of the circle gets maximum fertilizer and gives the maximum product.

In penda land they broadcast kosra in a ratio *paili* (1 kg. 800 gms) of Kang or ark, a variety of paddy grain, 1 to 2 saili/Sali/soli

(1 soli is equal to ½ kg) of *gund* (a variety of kosra). Its colour is brown and it is very tasty especially the *pej* 1/2 to 1 *paili* of *jowar* (junam), semi, barbati, cucumber etc. along with 20 *paili* of Kosra seed.

In *dippa* and *parka* cultivation also the crops and the cereals are same as in *penda* cultivation. They specially cultivate mandia, jira along with Kosra. Even *setka* (high yielding variety) rice is also produced in those cultivation.

In *dippa* cultivation they cultivate Kosra, Kulthi Parbat (ram-tilla) (at a time in the same field during the time of Dushera. It takes two months to get ripened when it is reaped. Parbat or ramtila is an oil seed. They do not use it but sell it in the bazar.

Plough Cultivation

Plough cultivation is not their traditional calling. It is learnt later from the neighbouring tribal people such as Bison-Horn-Maria and Muria. Now-a-days they have acquired some permanent land for settled plough cultivation. This land is called as *bera jamin.* This type of land is again divided into two types namely *bergang* and *munda*. The first one is slightly a high *bera* land where the yield gets the lesser water facility. The next one is the *munda* land. It is situated at a low level where the yield gets comparativeluy more water facility. In *berang* or *bera* land which is also known as *batti* land several varieties of paddy such as barengi, kabri bat kabri etc. are grown. They get this harvest in eighty days. In *munda khet* they cultivate *luchai / luching, garakut, warangi, gurmati, guria* varieties of paddy. These take more time at least one hundred days to get ready for harvesting.

The land is ploughed four times for conducting plough cultivation. The first one is known as *patina*. It is done either after the first shower or after harvest of the crop during aghan or pand (Novembr - December) if the soil is wet. It is done to loosen the soil for which water can easily penetrate and soil gets wet.

Matana is the ploughing just done after the days of *patina*. It is done only when the soil is wet by which the soil of lower level is brought upward and the upper soil goes beneath it.

The third ploughing is known as *dora* or *mutgamana*. It is done to make the soil loose. When the soil becomes loose light and thin and perforated. All these are necessary for paddy cultivation. The water reaches upto its bottom. After third ploughing they do the broadcasting of seed.

The fourth ploughing or *biasi* is done when the plant is grown upto 1.5 to 2.5 feet height. They do this ploughing from atleast 1 feet distance from those growing plants. It is done to loosen the soil again is conducted just after weeding. If there is any weed left, it is also damaged by this *biasi*.

In plough cultivation during the month Chaita (March-April) in their *bera* land the work is started. Firstly, they dig the land. In Mur (April- May) and Na (May-Jun.) they do ploughing in the land. In Hai (June-July) they broadcast paddy seeds. Sometimes they sow the seedlings which are germinated separately in a *tokni* made of bamboo. They firstly keep some leaves in a *tokni*. Some paddy grains are kept on it and then they sprinkle some luke warm water and cover it loosely with another leaf. Within two to three days seedlings come out and these seedlings are sown in the field. In Hagh (July-August) and Eranj (August-September) weeding is done. In Eram (September-October) they start harvesting. During this month they harvest paddy of Vellum or barum land, These varieties of paddy grow earlier than the Vakosh and Koteng paddy of *munda khet*.

Their another type of land is *bari* land or kitchen garden. It is generally attached with their homestead land. They produce mustard in that land. The *bari* at high area is also known as *marhan* land. They do *parka* cultivation in that land and produce a variety of rice locally known as *atwanji*. A table on Land use and crop and cereal pattern is given below for ready reference:

Table : Land use and Crop, Cereal Pattern

Land Type	*Cereals, Crops and Pulses Cultivated*
Parbat/ Meta	Kohla or Kosra, Atwanji, Sawa or Ghatka (Chhota Kosra), Sika or Amu, Turiya Kohls, Hodon, Mandia, Harua (a variety of mountain rice), Kulthi, Kodong, Kand, Bangla (tomato), Bajra, various types of pulses such as Pupul or urad, poyami or Arhar, Jata, Jatengi, Sem, Mung, Chikma, Kochei or Rasamati, Sakar Kanda, Parbat (Ramtila).
Bera	Various types of paddy such as Barengi, Kabri, Bat Kabri, Luchai/ Luchang, Garakut, Warangi, Gurmati, Gurja.
Bari	Jondra, Rahar, Vegetables and Sarsa.

In case of *parka*, *dippa* and *penda* cultivation, ash functions as fertilizer. In such land no fertilizer is used. Once they used some chemical fertilizer supplied by the Government sources. That year they faced several death in the village, and ultimately they thought that the Bhum deity-Tallur Mutte got insulted for it and became very displeased. Due to this she caused sufferings for her people. After that incidence the use such fertilizer was stopped. It is said that the deity order the *gaita* through dream that such practice must be stopped once for all otherwise severe consequences would happen.

In *bari* land, they use only cowdung fertilizer. They use wood ash as insecticide.

They do not employ or engage any labourer on wage basis in any phase of cultivation. Whenever a cultivator needs any help or assistance, he requests his friends, relatives and other villagers to extend their hands of co-operation. In mutual understanding and co-operation they work for one another. Exchange of labour is a very common phenomanan in their society.A feast is generally given to the workers.

If anybody needs some cereals and grains (though it is a very rare occasion) he or she can ask for it to any of the villagers for which repayment is generally not done.

In case of all types of slash and burn cultivation, women have minimum work to do. Felling of tree and firing are done by the men, women can assist them. Digging of *penda* land is always done by men but in *dippa* land it is done by women. Sowing is done by broadcasting method by both the sexes. Similarly, harvesting is also a joint venture done by both the sexes. Women are not allowed to do threshing and winnowing. Winnowing is done by men during night when they take the help of wind. Threshing and winnowing are collectively done by the village males for one another.

The cultivated products are taken from field to granary by all the family members They do not like to mesure the products. They believe that their deity Tallur and their pen deity have blessing upon them. She has given plenty of food grains to them. It is not proper to measure these. Whenever they need it, they take out the needed quantity from the granary. Even then during the time of data collection a rough calculation is made of their product as per their version. But the researcher has got no chance to verify it.

Generally they produce crops and cereals for their own consumption. They sell some of their items such as Parbat, mustard etc. in the market.

It is worthy to mention that the Abujh Maria prefer to do *penda* cultivation and all the other typs of cultivation in Pahar or

Meta as according to them they have the ability to conduct mix cultivation and get varieties of crops and cereals. In *Bera jamin* they can cultivate paddy only and it depends on rain. Due to all these reasons they prefer *penda* most.

Conservation of Land

It has been understand from the mode of behaviour of these people that they utilise land tomaintain their livelihood but side by side with utilisation, conservation of land is also ione.

It is true that for slash and burn cultivation they are to cut several trees in jungle, not only to clear a patch of land but also to increase the fertility of land for better crop. As a result of this destruction of forest has been conspicuous which can not be ignored. To minimise this they do avoid to cut young growing trees and in case of grown up trees they do not cut a tree from its root but instead of it they cut it leaving at least 2′ to 2½ feet height from the field.

The do it for various purposes. Firstly these are left as a support for the creepers like seem, barbatti etc. Secondly, when a tree is cut in this way, it is alive and chances are there for its rejuvenation within three to four years. Thirdly, the trees restrict soil erosion to a great extent.

Socially and ritually implied tabooes for cutting several tress, restriction for cutting trees of economic importance and with medicinal value are not felled which is very much important for conservation of soil. It protects soil from erosion.

In their *bari* land they store all the garbages of their house and kitchen. They throw the roughage of vegetables, sweep all the garbages and accumulate those in that field. Cowdung are accumulated in their *bari* land. Sometimes their cattle also graze in that land and the excreta act as manure. The garbages get decomposed and spoilt which act as very good manure. Sometimes they burn those in the field itself to get quicker action.

In *penda* cultivation they do not cultivate a plot more than four years. After four years of cultivation they leave the land and shift to another plot for doing *penda*. The previous land is left fallow at least for twenty years. By this time gradually the land recovers from its less fertile condition. During this period the land is not used for cultivation. It is used as grazing land for cattle. It gets nitrogenous and other organic and inorganic substances from nature and its conditions of fertility graudally improve through time.

Management of other Natural Resources for their Sustenance

Apart from forest and land management for sustenance the other major thrusts are identified by Abujh Maria are water, solar and wind which are also part and parcel of their livelihood.

In regard to the water management among Abujh Maria, it is observed that they mainly depend on monsoon and their cultivable lands are rainfed. They have a knowledge that paddy is generally possible to produce in low land that is *bera* where they are able to store the rain water by erecting contour bunding. More so it is also reported that they also practise gravitational irrigation during monsoon which helps them to store required water in a specific paddy field and the excess water is allowed to pass in the next plot on the undulated land of the terrain. This technique they have learnt from the neighbouring Muria and the intruding Bison-Horn- Maria from whom they have got the knowledge of plough cultivation.

Apart from this at Orcha Block Head quarters, it is observed that some of them are aware of lift irrigation system through which Papaiya orchard is maintained by Horiticultural Department. At Gudari it is found that Panchayat has got a sanction to build a reservoir and it is under construction and as per plan it will store catchasnt water of monsoon and pisciculture would be introduced among the Abujh Maria for economic development.

It is found at the studied village and its neighbouring Abujh Maria villages that solar energy also plays a great role in their life. They fully depend on the solar energy for cultivation of their crop (which is also necessary along with water and soil), They fully depend on it for drying of their harvested crops and cereals. They keep maize in hanging position in their houses for drying, They use the heat of solar energy to dry mahua flower, tamarind, mango etc. They make the pith of suiphi tree dried which is eaten by them. They prepare *amchur* by dried mango. They even use sun ray to make flesh, fish etc. dried. All these dried things are preserved for future use. In this way importance of solar energy can not be ignored.

Lastly among the natural resources, the main function of wind in their abode is to accelerate threshing of their cereals in the open field. As per the direction of wind they thresh their harvested cereals and crops. They prefer night time for this threshing work as wind flows more in the evening than in the day time. Wind helps the dust and husk to flow away while cereals are kept aside.

Market

Market is a place where people gather to sell, purchase and exchange their essential, items. People of various communities, caste groups and economic categories gather together for the above mentioned business. In social-cultural anthropology the study of market is very essential. In the studies of centres and network of relationship - a social anthropologist can never ignore the study of market. Through the study of market a cross- sectional study of a given group can be done.

Bastar is a place where weekly market, locally known as *hat* or *bazar* is more common than the regular market. Even in the Jagdalpur city there is weekly market held on every sunday popularly called as *etowari bazar* which is a very important item in the life of the people of Jagdalpur and its surroundings.

In Abujh Marh previously there was no market. The people of Abujh Marh used to attend the weekly market at Dharwai which is located nineteen miles north of Orcha by road.

At present in Orcha - the Block Headquarters – there is a weekly market or bazar where the people of the whole Marh gather on wednesday in connection with sell, purchase and exchange of essential items of daily need.

Abujh Marh is a very remote, isolated place. Natural barrier limits them to travel far off villages to meet friends, kiths and kins, living at distant villages. The Abujh Maria are confined in their restricted zone. They hardly get any exposure to the places outside their own world-Abujh Marh. In such a situation the weekly market at Orcha is an important source to link up them with the people outside their world. Not only with the outside world but also with the people of their own world - the Abujh Marh because it is the only bazar situated in the Marh area. So people of the villages of the whole Marh gather in that place.

The Abujh Maria are very fond of *bazar*. Thus, Wednesday seems to be a festive day for all of them. They walk down long distances with whatever saleable merchandise they possess. Even they walk for more than a day to cover the path. In such cases they bring their ration along with this. They halt in the villages on their way during night and again start to walk to reach the with the rise of the sun.

In the Orcha bazar on each and every Wednesday from early morning, people come with their saleable items. Women come with head load of basket full several collected and cultivated items, Children accompany their parents - specially the mothers. Breast feed children are carried by their mothers, generally taken on their lap or backtied with a piece of cloth so that a mother can keep both of her hands free. Small girls carry smaller baskets on their head - and the boys carry the load on shoulder; they say that carrying something on head is very derogatary - a sign of weekness - a womanly character. They are the males of the forest very strong and steady. Their shoulders are very thick and strong to carry heavy load. Actually on shoulder they can carry more things which is not possible to carry on head.

In Orcha market businessmen from Narayanpur, Dantewada, Bijapur and Jagdalpur and other places of Bastar come to purchase the local items specially the forest products at a cheaper rate. Some of which are very important, having medicinal value. These are collected by the businessmen from Orcha market at cheaper rate and sold in bigger markets elsewhere at higher rate. Thus, the tribal market at Orcha is regarded as a very profitable market for these businessmen. A few years back Government has organised a co-operative society to check exploitation. The co-operative society purchase those items from the tribals at a higher and reasonable rate.

The Abujh Maria mainly purchase here salt, colourad beads, mirrors, colourad cloth pieces, silver ornaments etc. The people of Ghadwa community attend the to sell their items. The dokra items are specially the idols of several gods and goddesses worshipped by the Abujh Maria. These are very costly, people of the Marh can hardly afford to purchase it in cash. They exchange these items in exchange of their domesticated cattles. Shops of iron implements such as knife, plough share, sickles etc. are also brought by the Lohars of the villages outside Marh to sell those in the market.

It is observed that a number of women sit in one row or two rows facing each other by the side of the road at the outskirt of the bazar. They sit with their earthen pots full with *landa* or rice beer. The customers are mainly men. They take the drink in sal leaf cup and quench their thirst till they get fully drunk. According to the women folk, selling of *landa* and *mahua* liquor (which is also sold there in bottle) is not a job of men. Men are very much fond of liquor and their temptation can never restrict them to drink at the time of selling. So women take sole responsibility to sell the drink. Bazar is the place of enjoyment. Cockfight is another item of their enjoyment.

Small children are very much fond of *lai chana* (puffed rice and peanut). They collect separately silk cocoons from forest and sell those and by their earning they eat *lai chana*.

In bazar proposals of marriages are sometimes initiated. It is the centre from where they get news of girls of marriageable age. People get the important messages such as of meetings or of some festivals in the market. The young boys of some villages fix up date for communal hunting expedition. In this way Orcha bazar plays a very important role in the life of the people of Abujh Marh. Difficulties of their geographical isolation are met in this way.

The Abujh Maria of the studied Ader village also attend the bazar every Wednesday. They mainly come to purchase salt, cloth, iron implements, ornaments etc. from the market and sell their collected forest items and also some of their cultivated crops.

The following list will provide the nature of different items especially Minor Forest Produce (MFP) which are sold and exchange by them in the Orcha market or **bazar** or *hat*.

A. Non-Timber Minor Forest Produces

Sl. No.	*Forest Products*	*Cost*
1.	Itta (Temarind) with seed	Rs. 5/- per kg. (Private Businessman)
2.	Itta without seed	Rs. 6.75 per kg. (Government rate)
3.	Itta seed	Rs. 13/- per kg.
4.	Nalli (aonla)	Rs. 5/- per kg. (private Businessman)
5.	Harra	Rs. 5/- per kg. to Rs. 10/- per kg. (Rate varies depending upon quality)

(contd...)

Sl. No.	*Forest Products*	*Cost*
6.	Sal seed (Garra)	Rs.4/- per kg.
7.	Hahua flower	Rs. 5/- per kg. (Private Businessman)
8.	Epur of Fuljharia	Rs. 4/- to Rs.7/- per kg. (Rate varies depending on the quality).
9.	Kosa or Cocoon with Silk worm	0.80 paisa to Rs.1/-
10.	Kosa cracked and without worm	0.50 paisa.
11.	Kosa broken into pieces	0.25 paisa.
12.	Dhup	12/- per paili (1 Paili – 1700 gms.
13.	A bundle of 2500 tendu leaves	Rs.25/-
14.	Lasa or gum	Rs.4/- to Rs. 5/-- per kg.
15	A tunba full with honey	Rs. 4/- to Rs.5/-
16.	Dull(used to prepare some medicine)	Rs. 130/- per kg.
17.	Karkatia bija (used to prepare some medicine)	Rs. 10/- to Rs. 30/- per kg.
18.	Tikhur	Rs. 28/- per paili.

B. Cultivated Items in their Lands

Sl no.	*Cultivated Items*	*Cost*
1.	Sarso (Mustard)	Rs. 22/- per paili
2.	Zondra/Makai (Maize)	Rs. 20/- per paili or 0.50 paisa per piece
3.	Urad dal	Rs. 20/- per paili
4.	Hata sim	Rs. /- per done
	Vegetables	
1.	Papaya	Rs. 5/- for 6 to 8 piece
2	Gourd	Rs. 20/- for per piece
3.	Lady's finger	Rs. 2/- for 8 to 10 pieces.

In this way market plays a very important role in the management of economic and socio-cultural life of the Abujh Maria people adjusting with their local ecological niche.

Socio-Cultural Life in the Management of Environment and Natural Resources

To the Abujh Maria, the Abujh Marh hills and its forest are created by the heavenly father and created solely for them. Thus they automaticallay think that they are the sole incharge, proprietor of the hills and the adjoining forest. They utilize each and every opportunity of their habitat for sustenance. Side by side they are restricted to destroy forest as per their own wisdom. Rather their way of life centering round this hill-forest ecological setting is specifically governed by their self-imposition social and ritual norms and bindings, following of which, they consider, is their sacred and moral obligations.

Abujh Maria one of the particularly vulnerable primitive tribal group of India are distributed in the Abujh Marh hills of Bastar which is situated In the north-western part of the district. They are one of the sub-group of well known Gond tribe. The Gond designate themselves as Koitor which means man. The Abujh Maria are called as Meta Koitor as they live in the Meta Bhum that is, high land in the Abujh Marh hills.

The Abujh Maria tribe primarily is divided into two broad social divisions. These two subdivisions axe exogamous in nature. Each of these has several septs. The septs of a sub division are tied by Dadabhai or bhaiband relationship with each other that is; they are the consanguinal kins having relationship of brothers and marriage is prohibited among them. The septs of other sub division are related by mama bhai or akomama that is; affinal relationship with the septs of other subdivision. Marriage among the septs of two subdivisions are allowed Also it is noted that each sept has a number of *katta* or clan which are automatically exegamous in nature. Among them septs are known as *pen*. Each *pen* has its own deity and the pens are named after their deities. The deities are similarly related with each other by the same dadabhai and akomama relationship as mentioned earlier.

The studied village Ader is populated mainly by the people of Jodi Katta whose *pen* is Karmaikola and the associated deity is Karmaikola Devi. Their pen or sept is Karmaikola Devi. The *pen* or sept Karmaikola has several other *katta* or clan such as Mandor, Kohkonakha etc. They are all tied by *bhaiband* relationship with the Jodi Katta. Jodi Katta has some other bhaiband kattas such as Mukla, Wadde etc. who belong to some other *pens*. In the village Ader there are three families belong to Usendi Katta whose is Dewan Dokra. There are other four families of Parsak Katta whose *pen* is Sonkuar. One family is there of Korami Katta; Pen of Korami is Karmaikol Devi. Usendi and Parsak these two are related with Jodi Katta by *akomama* relationship. Pen Sonkuar of Parsak Katta is the eldest son of Dewan Dokra of Usendi Katta. Both of them are related with Karmaikola. Karmaikola is Dewan's sister and Sonkuar's aunt. She is married to Parkal Deo with whom Dewan Dokra has affinal or *akomama* relationship. In this way the deities are genealogically related with each other in their celestial world.

These Katta, pen bhaiband and akomma relationships are very important. To them among all the types of marriages cross-cousin marriage is preferred most. It is thought that in the myth of their origin there is a clear-cut picture of marriage by exchange and cross-cousin marriage. When there was no human being in the earth, Bhagwan - the heavenly father and his Dowki (wife) gave birth to two pairs of brothers and sisters. One pair was named as Neleria, and Nelire and the other pair is Bumeria and Bunire. They are the first Abujh Maria people holding two sub divisions. Now Neleria was married with Bumire and Bumeria is married to Nelire. Now these two couples gave birth to several children. Neleria and Bumirc's children are married with the children of Bumeria and Nelira, as the children of the same sept are not allowed to marry. Thus in this way the custom of cross-cousin marriage has appeared in their society and preferred most by them. Another explanation behind the preference of cross-cousin marriage, given by them, is that it minimises the expenditure of marriage. It is also found that they always try to arrange marriage in nearby villages. Geographical barrier limits them to negotiate marriages in far off villages. The villages surrounding their own village are inhabited by their cross-cousins. So automatically marriages are negotiated with the cross- cousins of nearby villages. Therefore natural environment plays a very important role in selection of mates.

It is already mentioned that their villages are either inhabited or dominated by the people of one clan or clans of the same pen. In the village Ader some other *pen* groups are also there but those are mostly having *akomama* relationship with the dominant Jodi clan. In Ader members of usendi and Parsek clans have come and settled through marital relationship.

The land is seen to be divided on clan basis amongst them. Each village has a jati panchayat which deals not only with the breach of social norms but also with the breach of any of their customary law in relation to the management of their natural environment. As for example, if anybody fells any wood which has some religious value and there is a polo (taboo) in cutting the tree- the panchayat calls a meeting in which the type and degree of punishment is accorded.

The division of land among the clan members is generally done by the village headman after consultation with the members of the village. He also allots land for the outsiders if any, who wants to settle in the village.

Each clan has its own totem such as Poyami (buffalo), Oyamai (tortoise), sodi (tiger) and Markami (tortoise) etc. They are tabooed to kill their totems. In this way the animals of the forest are protected. The *pen* deities have their own territory. A separate priest or *gaita* known as *Pen Wadde* is there who officiates all the rituals associated with *Pen* deity. Bhum Gatta officiates all the rituals of Bhum deity or *Tallur Mutte*. Pen Wadde's house is situated very close to the *pen-rawar* the seat of the clan deity. In the village Ader there is a *pen-rawar* and also a sacred place *tallur*. Tallur is the abode of Tallur Mutte that is Bhum deity or Dharti Mata or earth goddess. It is situated at the outskrit of the village. It is a very vast area full with forest growth. There are various types of plants and trees such as bamboo, sal, sagun, harra, barkat, aden or saja, mahua, dhaura, bija, siyari/sihari in the place. It is believed that the deity stays in that place. She stays just under a saja or an aden tree. They are strictly prohibited to disturb her by cutting any of the trees there.

The *pen* deity of Ader is Karmaikola. She is the deity of the Abujh Maria of some other villages namely Bade Tondabara, Durging, Orcha Metang, Markaveda etc. She visits all, the above mentioned villages and stays at each village for atleast three to six years. In all her villages she has her *pen-rawar*. Pen-rawar is also a similar place like *tallur* where the deity's seat is situated under an *aden* tree. All the trees of pen-rawar also are never be felled. These are rather protected from fire and other inauspicious events. They are not allowed to pollute the place. Restriction on felling trees in *tallur* and *pen-rawar* helps in conservation of forest through ritual bindings.

Tallur is regarded as the earth goddess and their most essential seven crops, cereals etc are regarded as her children as she produced those. So to get plenty of harvest thy worship her.

The religious activities of Abujh Maria are very much linked with their economic life. They believe that their *pen* deities, Tallur and their ancestors, always have blessings for them and through their supernatural power they give them plenty of crops and cereals for their sustenance. Due to this they never consume any of this harvested crops and cereals and season's new fruit and flower like mahua prior to the offering to their deities as well as to their ancestors. It is believed that breach of the taboo may bring catastrophe to the village. A person violating the taboo may be bitten by a snake or the village may be attacked by a tiger. In fact the period from Vaisakh to Ashad is a very busy period for collection of forest products including mahua. Mahua is stored for the whole year. Ritual offerings are essential for any edible items. It has an economic value also. So if anybody gets busy with consuming of those instead of collection, the collection process will hamper greatly. In case of mango, they are allowed to eat outside their houses but taboosd to carry those in their homes. The probable reason is that if they are allowed to take mango in their houses, all the mango will be picked up and collected prior to its full maturity. To protect the fruit from this situation, the ritual bindings have automatically restricted them. Matured fruit seeds may again germinate to a new mango tree and add some more plants in the forest. In this way conservation through ritual bindings are highly conspicuous here.

Land is regarded as the property of the clan deity. Starting from the selection of cultivable land till the consumption of the cultivated crops and cereals some ritualistic performances through which offerings are made to the deities invoking their blessings are obligatory. They perform a ritual in the *penda* field prior to the cutting of trees. In that field they worship *Tallur Mutte*, their clan god and Nelnarin Mata seeking permission to start *penda* cultivation. They also pray for their blessings.

They are tabooed to lit the forest before Holi. If it is done, the deities of jungle will be annoyed. So the firing of jungle is done after the performance of Holi. In fact this ritual binding is there to protect their harvested crop which are not brought to their houses till the performance of Koding ritual. Koding is performed during the month fagun. So if firing to the jungle is performed prior to that the harvested crop will be destroyed. To protect these this ritual binding is implied on them.

They perform a pre-sowing ritual known as Miching during the month saon or Hagh (July-August) in their field just before the broadcasting of Kohla nuka (a variety of Kosra). They perform this ritual to appease the earth goddess–Tallur Mutte seeking her blessings for good production. It is believed that if they sow Kohla without performing the ritual, the deities will be displeased and annoyed with them and their harvested crop may be eaten or destroyed by jungle animals.

After Kohla Tindana they are free to thrash their harvested crop but they are not allowed to bring these to their home prior to the performance of Kodding in the month fagun (February-March) when they offer the harvest to Tallur, Pen deity, and also to Nelnarin Mata who is recognised as Goddess Sitala in the Hindu ritual and pantheon.

They do thrashing when the harvested crop becomes dry. When the crops and cereals are harvested these are in wet condition and so immediately these are not threshed. These are kept in the open field for drying. After these become dry, threshing is easier. Due to this they keep the harvested crop and cereal in the field and due to this reason they are tabooed to lit fire in the jungle before Holi. By this time they bring all of their threshed crop in the granary. They perform Wanj Korta to offer harvested paddy along with various types of roots such gundeng, kayameta and vegetables to Tallur Mutte and *pen* deity. It is celebrated at tha end of bhado or eranj (August-September). Jona Kortam is a festival of jondra or maize associated with eating of newly produced maize. Another important new eating ceremony is Pupul Korta Tindana. It is performed in the month of Chait (March-April), when they offer pupul or urad to their deities. Along with urad they also offer various types of beans, kutki and other new items to the gods. Sometimes this festival is combined with another important festival known as Marai. Marai is a festival after harvest of several crops and cereals and before the starting of *penda* again. In Marai they invite formally the deities from neighbouring villages. They are entertained with newly harvested crop.

Tur Korta Tindana is a ritual through which they offer a variety of newly harvested Kohla and other vegetables to the deities.

Pune Nuka is performed after Wanj or Vanj Korta of paddy. Wanj Korta is a ritual associated with eating of newly harvested rice. When they do Wanj Korta, they thresh a little portion of paddy and offer to the deities. They do threshing by feet. It is probably due to the reason newly harvested crop is very soft and due to this probably they wait few more days for threshing those by cattle. They offer new crop to Nelnarin Mata known as Sitala Mata in the Hindu religions pantheon.

After performance of Pune Nuka ritual they are allowed to take the harvested paddy grain in their houses. Generally they are not allowed to consume the new rice prior to the performance of Pune Nuka. On the day of wanj korta they consume the new rice without washing it in water probably due to the softness of the crop.

In the month of Landi (May-Jun.) to Hai (June- July) they celebrate their most important and gorgeous festival kaksar. It is the ritual performed before the onset of rain. During rainy season they are to be engaged in their fields again and are to do hard, ardrous labour. Before that they have got sometime with lesser load of work. They utilize the time by performing several ritualistic functions. Among these Kaksar is the main. During Kaksar they worship all the *pen* deities. It is performed in Orcha proper. The villagers of Ader and other villages, even very far off villages like Lanka are invited and who come to attend Kaksar festival at Orcha with their *pen* deities. All the *pen* deties of bhaiband and akomama relationship are invited by Dewan Dokra - the *pen* deity of Usendi clan of Orcha. He invites them through his priest the Gaita. All the deities assemble there and are worshipped by all the Abujh Maria. Kaksar festival is performed to get blessings of all of their *pen* deities to have bumper crop. In this way they are governed by the ritual beliefs and practises in the management of their local resources through their traditional wisdom.

World View and Conclusion

A group of people's idea, thinking and understanding of all the world's animate and inanimate objects and happenings around them is the world view of the people. The world view of a population groups reflects the particular angle of vision in highlighing and comprehending the specific trends of the people processed in a particular fashion of understaqnding.

Adhikary (1984) mentions "World view of the people that is the way of the people see themselves in relation to the world (s) around them might give us a clue to the nature of their techno-economic adaptation as well as the perpetuation of their distinct socio-cultural identity, and would help us in comprehending the meaningful world they live in."

To the Abujh Maria, who live in association with hills and forest, Abujh Marh hills is their own world. They know that outside their own world there is a greater world about which they are least bothered. Each and every aspect, objects and happenings around them are thought, understood, and explained in their own way which are expressed through their traditional life ways and thought-ways which find place in their myths, folklore, feasts and festivals.

Myths and legends regarding the Universe of the people concerned

According to one of their myths, the earth, many years ago was very soft, very slippery as it was filled up with water. There was no human being in the world. Bhagwan send a wild boar to make the world suitable for human being. It came out from the heavenly forest Bantemeta and dug the soft mud of the earth and ultimately prepared the soft mud to stone which ultimately became rock. Gradually the villages were originated. Somewhere small drains also had arised. The path which it had taken became nullahs. Where it put his mouth, big rivers sprung up. The mountains formed by its excreta where it passed its urine, pits came. A frog was also sent by the heavenly father. By the jumping movement of the frog the land was levelled. After that heavenly father created human being. They call Sun as Pord and moon as *lenj*. Pord is male and *lenj* is female. Pord is male as it is very strong with its hot schroching heat and rays. Moon light is very mild it gives a very soothing atmosphere. They believs that moon is Sun's wife and stars which are known *Ukkam* are their children.

According to them Pogaiyo or east is the place from where the Pord (sun) rises and it sets in the irieburum or west. Sonkuar, one of their gods along with Marama and Bisharma constructed sun by the wood of Ilora Marang tree. Only one tree of that kind was sent by God from heaven. As per the order of the heavenly father the above mentioned deities constructed sun. After that they ditched it towards east and ordered it to give light to the earth. From that time till pate the pord is sincirely performing his duty. Everyday early in the morning it rises in the east and during evening it sets in the west and becomes a bull and runs throughout the whole night to cover the path from west to east to take prepara tion for the next morning.

Similarly *lenj* (moon) is constructed with the rest of the wood of that tree by the same persons. It rises from the west everyday in the evening and sets in the east everyday in the morning. They believe that every month on the day of Kumbh or *amavashya* the moon becomes old and it dies. On the next day a new moon borns and it becomes fully grown up moon on the fifteenth day when it looks totally round on the day of full moon or purnina locally called as nelta. After that, day by day it becomes old and it is seen through its decay and ultimately it is fully vanished or dies on the day of Kumbh. During the construction of both sun and moon, Sonkuar offered human sacrifice to the heavenly father to get his blessings for the success of the said work. After creation of Sun, Moon and their children the heavenly father sent two pairs of brothers and sisters and from whom the Abujh Maria people have originated.

Concept of time and Cognizence of their Season

The people of Abujh Marh count their months and days according to the position of the moon. Their month starts from the first day of the lighter half called as *ujera paksh* and ends on the last day of the darker half known as *lenjatu* or amavashya. The full moon day is regarded as the fifteenth day of the month.

They have informed that their ancestors taught them to count months with the moon instead of Sun. Moon changes its shape everyday which helps in counting the days. Sun has no such speciality. They have twelve months which are divided into three seasons namely summer monsoon and winter.

During the lighter half of fagun (February-March) they understand that the summer season is coming. Also they opine that when the mahua and palash flowers bloom, the mango trees start flowering, they get indication that the summer season is very near to them.

Another point to identify summer season is that the *sadka* grasses become dry. During summer season new *chhind* (date palm) leaves come out. When they see that new leaves began to appear in mahua tree, there is no flower in the tree, they understand that monsoon is approaching. Tha *fuljharia* in the jungle gradually stop blooming with the approach of rainy season. When sulphi or sago palm trees are ready to offer sweet juice, paddy is ready for harvest, the *fuljharia* trees are again ready to bloom, which indicate that winter is very close to them. During the lighter half of the month Katick (October-November) felt that the time to start harvesting of crop has reached and also winter is very close to them.

The people concerned thatch their huts during summer season by the new leaves of Chhind (date palm) leaves which is done during the summer. It is taken for granted that if they do not change with the thatch during summer, they will face difficulties in rainy season when the rain water may pour down profusely into the room through the old thatch which usually gets damaged within a year. So it is necessary to thatch the hut in every year during summer prior to the rainy season.

The people here are in a belief that plentiful production of mango in a year is indicative of heavy shower and a good harvest. When the new mahua leaves come, they notice it minutely. If the size of mahua leaves is large and the colour of the mahua leaf is very light, then there will be heavy rain.

If sarai (Sal) flowers grow in abundant there will be plenty of paddy in that year. If the mahua leaves are red, then the rain will be insufficient. If it rains during the month magh (January then it is a good sign for the cultivators. But if it is in fagun (Feburary-March) the cultivators will be in a pitiful condition as there will be want of rain.

They calculate the time and date seeing the position of sun and moon. When the sun is seen just at the top of the head in the mid sky, it is the time about 12'0 clock. Again they calculate time observing the falling of mahua flower from its tree. Generally *mahua* starts falling everyday from 4 am and continues to fall till 12 noon to 1 pm in the afternoon. When it stops falling, they come back to take their lunch. If it is a cold day, mahua starts to fall a little late at about 7 to 8 am but always stop failing at 12 noon to 1 p.m.

Way of counting days

To count dates they have a very traditional method. Suppose there will be a marriage ceremony after twenty days, they take a rope or string and gives twenty one knots. On each and every morning they untie one of the knots. The last knot is untied on the day of the performance of marriage. In this way they calculate the dates.

In this counting they keep bazaras a stigma. Suppose in twenty days there are two bazar days. They firstly tie two knots in a gap with each other in the string. Then counting the other days before and after the bazars they tie rest of the knots.

Beliefs in Natural objects in relation to their Celestrial World

According to them, Bhum or the Tallur Mutte is the mother

goddess who gives them the cultivated products. Her husband's name is Kanga. There are several stories on their love and conjugal life. Tallur has gave birth to seven children which are their crops and cereals. This is also discussed in the chapter of land Management. According to them there is no binding to fix up a date of marriage. But they generally avoid to settle it during the month of fagun (Feb.-Mar) as they believe that it is the time of firing the jungle. If the marriages are performed in this month, the bride will have a very violent or angry nature which may destroy the whole family. They prefer to arrange marriage during the month ashad or Hagh (June-July). Ashad is a month when they have plenty of mahua to quench their thirst. They believe that a bride of the month ashad will have a very peaceful and calm and quite nature which is necessary for progress of a family.

In fact the actual reason behind it is that they have heavy work in their *penda* land during the month of fagun so that hardly get time to attend any ritual and ceremony, if it is not so urgent and necessary. On the contrary though there are works in their cultivable land during ashad, even then it is not so hard and ardrous like cutting and burning of *penda* and get time to attend various types of rituals and ceremonies. There is another point which is probably more important. During this time they have plenty of mahua which is one of the very important item of their life and culture. Due to this reason ashad (June-July) is preferred most to celebrate a marriage ceremony.

When they start penda for the first day or if a person is going for any auspicious work such as negotiation of marriage etc. it is regarded as a very important and auspicious moment. At that time if a Dahoda/or Dahok bird shouts from the right hand side it is very unfortunate and they stop going. If the bird shouts from left side it is a very fortunate event. The Abujh Maria call eclipse as *garanj*. They fell very much afraid during this *garanj* period. According to their myth when the people of Ganda community of celestial world swallows sun or moon, the *garanj* happens.

Another myth tells that the Ghasias of celestial world hides from heavenly father and shadows sun and moon in demand of some loan from Bhagwan. Then the *garanj* occurs. Then Bhagwan pays the loan and immediately the Ghasia makes the sun and moon free and with it *garanj* comes to an end.

They call, whirlwind as *Wagawari*. Raobhut (a ghost) is responsible to create this. He roams in the air specially by the side of river. If one gets its touch, then inveriably he or she will be sick.

According to them stones grow everyday and gradually it takes the shape of a mountain finally.

Ulka or meteor is called as *ugu* by them. If one sees a falling *ugu*, it is a very unlucky event. They believe that in the village, any body will, die.

According to them river is created by the water flow coming from the lower level of earth.

Hail stone is called as *adraku*, but why it falls they have no idea about it.

They say that they can ses own image in a mirror and the image has also life. when one's soul enters in a mirror, his or her image is reflected. If one beats himself seeing the mirror, the image will also get the same beating.

There are *deos* in the radioset. They are not accustomed with television. Cave or *geda* or *Parum* is formed by the wild boar who was sent by God at the time of creation of earth.

Jogmirko or jonaki is not so important. They simply said if the *Jogmirko* or fire fly glows near surface, rain is soon to come. If in the rains the fire fly flies, the rain will stop.

Monday, Wednesday and Friday are lucky days for hunting.

They say that flower blooms to produce fruit from which seeds come ultimately giving birth to new tree.

When thunder is called as *gaj* which falls with the lightening. They say that in the heavenly abode the Lohar is busy to break stone. Some of small pieces of those stone chips slip and fall in the earth. Gaj always falls on a large tree. They also call it as *Kistaram*. Immediately after falling of a *Kistaram* they immediately sprinkle *harra pani* or water soaked in Kulthi to make the place cold and danger free.

They know that each and every plant has life and they can talk with each other. If they cut tree blood oozes out of it in the form of white liquid. Musar is rain when it starts they think Goddess Lakshmi has come to the earth and to give them plenty of wealth. They call rainbow as *bumtaras*. It comes just after a shower. It signifies that there will be no more rain that day when goddess Lakshmi comes with her assistant suchas *gurogunje* (thunder), *paksire* (water) and Barchire (wind), Jagmirse (lightening), Eranga mire (cold water). All of these have some supernatural power. Duo to this when anybody suffers from fever, the sorceror chants all these names to get their blessings for recovery.

Cloud is known as *mayal* Appearance of *mayal* signifies the chances of rains, When the *mayal* is black or brown, the rain will definitely come. But sometimes wind drives the cloud to some other places. If the cloud is very dark brown in colour and found in north-east direction, then heavy storm with shower will happen.

In this way their traditional myths, knowledge, beliefs and practises are very much oriented by nature through which their traditional wisdom is reflected. Even when they sing songs in the Ghotul, nearly all of those are related with nature such as

"Relo Relo Relo Dada
Japsi Karela"

means brother please come and give support to the creeper so that it can climb and grow in a proper way.

CONCLUSION

Human being just after their appearance in the world in the remote part period have got a very intimate relationship with the natural environment and its resources for their survival. The process continued through the ages. Their socio-cultural life was shaped and determined by the environment as it is told by Ratzel and Sempel in 1920 in the theory of environmental determinism. In this theory it is asserted that all the aspects of human culture and behaviour were caused directly by environmental influences. But in due course, gradually they could not be satisfied with the limited utilisation of nature. They became more ambitious, their demand and necessity began to increase day by day. Necessity and demand taught them how to utilise the natural objects more and more and automatically this brought them to invent improved and better technological devise and these supported them to rule over the nature as per their necessity, wishes and also whims.

Steward's (1955) model of cultural ecology gave emphasis on the relationship between the environment and exploitative techniques which ultimately becomes responsible for the economic, social life and population size of a group. These are coined by him as culture core.

Gradually in the name of utilisation, exploitation of nature began. Excessive tree felling is one of the ultimately has been identified as the resultant towards destruction. Due to the excessive tree felling at Kalahandi, a district of Orissa, neighbouring to Bastar, once was famous for its dense forest, cool and pleasant climate, and a good harvest, is at present a district where there is no rainfall, no greenary. There is only draught, scarcity of food and femine. It is because of excessive felling of trees in the forest, resulting deforestation and catastrophic change in climate. Similarly the very recent super-cyclone in Orissa, which according to the scientists, environmentalists and researchers has been resulted due to excessive cutting of mangrove forest. All these destructions are happened due to the exploitation of the natural environment. There are thousands of examples like these two. Invention of advanced technological devise is really helpful for progress and development but its implementation must always be positive, for the improvement of mankind and all other world objects around him, avoiding any type of destruction.

The Meta Koitor of Abujh Marh, who are known as Abujh Maria live in the lap of nature. They have a very limited technological knowledge and devise by which they utilise all of their natural tesources. The utilisation is generally limited. They have various types of socio-religions bindings which restrict them to exploit the forest according to their whims, and they do practise controlled utilisation of forest. Each and every step of their life and culture is seen have evolved in relation to their natural environment.

Their economic life is vary much dependent on hills and forest environment. As they are a group of slash and burn cultivators and gatherers, they have always been facing an insecurity and uncertainity of food which ultimately becomes the reason for the small family size. It is also supported by Greetz, Clifford's (1963) article on "Two types of eco-system" where he showed that the people who do slash and burn cultivation have small population size. On the contrary the settled cultivators' have large and extended family.

To control the family size, their customary laws have imposed various types of taboos to prohibit them from sexual co-hibition for most of the time in a year. A man is not allowed to stay in the village throughout the period of penda cultivation starting from seed sowing till the harvest of the crop. They are similarly prohibited to have any such relation on the night prior to hunting or any ritual performance. They believe that their deities will be displeased if one does the same. In this way they can have some control over the population.

Felling of trees for slash-sad-burn cultivation is a very hard and ardrous work, which restrict them to or limit them to cut excess tree or to destroy forest beyond the need. Their limited utilisation of forest along with their knowledge of regeneration of it and also various types of religious taboos for cutting various types of trees protect the forest from destruction. With it their efforts for conservation of forest also cannot be ignored.

Not only the trees, many animals and birds are also protected by their various types of social and ritual bindings. The following diagram shows how Management of environment and natural resources is done by the Abujh Maria.

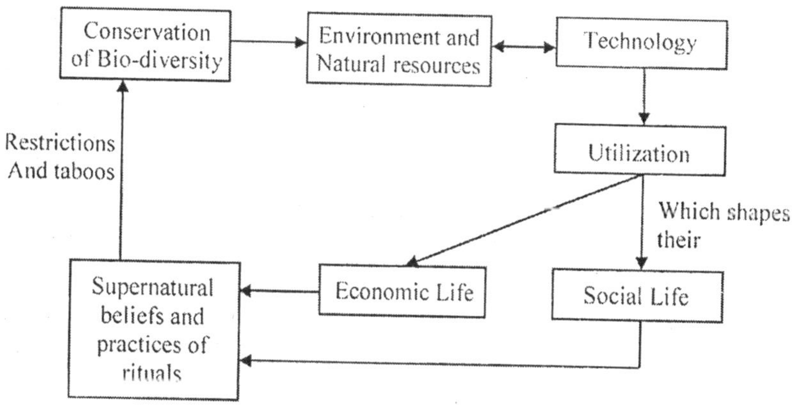

The Abujh Maria people in this way through their traditional wisdom is managing their environment and natural resources in such a situation when the whole world is suffering from natural disaster and destruction.

References

Adhikary. Ashim. K., 1984, *Society and world view of the Birhor*, Calcutta: Anthropologycal Survey of India. Memoir No. 60

Bates. M., 1953, "Human ecology", in *Anthropology To-day* (ed). A.L Kroeber, Chicago : University of Chicago Press.

Bennett, John. W, 1976, *The Ecological Transition, Cultural Anthropology and Human Adaptation*, New York :Pergamon Press Inc.

Conklin, H.C., 1954, "An Ethno-Ecological Approach to shifting Agriculture" New *York Academy of Science, Transacion*. Vol. 17, No. 2, pp. 133-42.

Crookshank, H, 1963, *Geology of Southern Baster and Jeypore from the Bailadila Range to Eastern Ghats*, Memoir of Geological Survey of India, Vol. 87.

Dasgupta, Samira, 1994, *Birjia : Society and Culture*, Calcutta: Firma KLM Pvt. Ltd.

Dasgupta. Samira Dasgupta, SamiraAmitabhaSarkar, 20032005, "A New Dimension of Social Organisation of Abujh Maria of Tribal Bastar : Communion between Celestial and Terrestial Life". *Journal of Indian Anthropological Society*, Vol. 38, pp. 41-54, Reflection of Ethno-Science: Study on the Abujh Maria, New Delhi:Mittal Publication.

Ellen. Roy, 1982, *Environment, Subsistence and System : The Ecology of Small Scale Social Formation*, Cambridge: Cambridge University Press.

Elwin, Verrier (reprinted), 1991, *The Muria and their Ghotul*, Delhi : Oxford University Press and Vanya Prakashan.

Evans – Pritchard, E.E, 1940, *The Nuer*, Oxford : The Clavendon Press.

Gadgil, M and V.D. Vartak, 1976, "The Sacred Groves of Western Ghats in India", *Economic Botany*, Vol. 70, pp. 152-160.

Geertz, Clifford, 1963, *Agricultural Involution : The Process of Ecological Change in Indonesia*, Berkeley : University of California Press.

Gell, Simeran Man Singh, 1992, *The Ghotul in Muria Society*, Switzerland : Hardwood Academic Publishers.

Gindi, Suresh Kumar, 1994, "Ethnomedicine among the Yanadi : A Hunter- Gatherer Tribe in South India", *GirijanSanskriti*, Vol. 2, No. 2.

Glasfurd, Capt. C.L.D, 1862, Reeport on the Dependency of Bastar.

Goodenough, Ward. H., 1956, "Componential Analysis and the Study of Meaning", *Language*, Vol. 32, pp. 195-216.

Grigson, Sir Wilfrid (reprinted), 1991, *The Maria Gonds of Baster*, Delhi: Vanya Prakashan, and Oxford University Press.

Hardesty, D.L., 1977, *Ecological Anthropology*, New York : John Wiley & Sons.

Harris, Marvin, 1968, "Emics", "Etics" and the "New Ethnography", in *Readings in Anthropology*, Vol. II, edited by Morton. H. Fried, New York : Thomas Y. Crowell Company.

Hugher, Charles, 1968, "Ethnomedicine", in *International Encyclopaedia of Social Science*, Vol. IV, New York : The Macmillan and Free Press.

Jay, Edward J., 1970, *A Tribal Village of Middle India*, Calcutta: Anthropological Survey of India, Memoir No. 21.

Knight, C.G., 1974, "Ethno Science as a Research Paradigm" in *Language in Anthropology*, (ed). W.C. Mccormack and S.A Wurm, Mouton : The Hague.

Kurup, A.M., 1963, "People of Unknown Hills", Vanyajati, Vol. X pp. 38-41.

Milton, Kay (ed), 1993, *Envirormentalism* : The View from *Anthropology*, London : Routledge

Negi, S. S., 1994, *India's Forests, Forestry and Wild Life*, New Delhi : Indus Publishing Co.

Pandey, Justice K.L, 1967, Report on the Disturbances which took place at Jagdalpur on the 25th March and 26th March, 1966, Madhya Pradesh, Home Department, Bhopal : Govt. of Madhya Pradesh.

Pranjpye, 1989, "Deorai", in *Deforestation and Drought*, (ed). N.D. Jayal, INTACH, New Delhi

Rappaport, Roy, A., 1967, *Pigs for the Ancestors : Ritual in the Ecology of a New Guinea People*, New Haven : Yale University Press.

Redfield, Robert, 1971, *The Little Community and Peasant Society and Culture*, Chicago : The University of Chicago Press.

Sahlins, Marshall. D., 1964, "Culture and Environment : The study of Cultural Ecology" in *Horizons of Anthropology* (ed). Sol Tax, London: Allen and Unwin Ltd.

Sarkar, Amitabha and Samira Dasgupta, 1995, *Spectrum of Tribal Baster,* Delhi: Agam Kala Prakashan.

Sarkar, Amitabha and Samira Dasgupta, 2000, *Ethno– ecology of Indian Tribes : Diversity in Cultural Adaptation*, Jaipur : Rawat Publications

Singh, K. S, 1994, *People of India, Vol. III, The Scheduled Tribe*, Delhi, Oxford University Press and Anthropological Survey of India.

Singh, Pramad, 1989, "ACollapsable Forest Ecology of India", in *Problem of Waste Land and Forest Ecology in India* (ed). Pramad Singh, New Delhi; Ashish Pub. House. pp. 227-245.

Sinha, Rajiv, K., 1995, "Contribution of Indian Tribals to Modern Civilisation; in *Tribals in India"*, ed. A.K. Singh and M.K. Jabbi, New Delhi : Har-Anand Publications.

Sinha, Rajiv, K., 1991, "Eco – System Preservation Through Faith and Tradition in India", *Jr. of Human Ecology*, Vol. 2, No. 1. pp. 21 – 24

Steward, J.H., 1955, *The Theory of Culture Change*, Urbana : University of Illinois Press.

Strong, F.M., 1992, "Only the Earth", *India International Centre,*Quartely, Vol. 19 No. 1 & 2, pp. 49-52

Sundar, Nandini, 1997, *Subalterns and Sovereigns : An Anthropological History of Baster*, 1854-1996, Delhi : Oxford University Press.

Vartak, V.D and M. Gadgil, 1991, "Studies on Sacred Groves along the Western Ghats from Maharastra and Goa : Role of Beliefs of Folklore", in *Glimpses of Indian Ethnobotany*, (ed). S.K. Jain, New Delhi : IBH.

3

Role and Status of Traditional Wisdom in the Management of Environment and Natural Resourcs in Tribal Societieis– A Case Study of the Malpahariya

Sunit Mondal and Sudhansu Gangopadhyay

Introduction

The study of environment and natural resources has become the basic aim of the project in order to know how or at what extent the traditional wisdom is operating in the tribal habitats of the respective eco-zones of the country where the process of interaction is discernable. In this connection it is desirable to understand, in brief, the components of environment, natural resources and traditional wisdom of which the inter actional process has become the main theme of the study. The natural environment means environment surrounding the tribal people and the basic components are terrain, climate, hills, slope etc. The natural things available in nature become natural resources when they are used for their maintenance. The ideal examples of these are land, forest, water resources etc. These are the immediate available natural resources in the reserve being area of the aborigines covered with hills and forests. The traditional wisdom i.e. indigenous idea and thoughts or peoples' perception about natural environment, way of cultivation, farming methods and techniques, idea on organizational network to prepare farming land, observances of rituals and customs in the hope of better output or preservation of natural resources, practicing different methods for forestry or indigenous way on controlling water in order to have uniform distribution of it which may be considered as the latent strength to utilize the natural resources in their own way. They way of management also conforms to the principles of preserving and conserving the natural resources also.

Selection of study unit

The selection of Amirjola village of Pakur district lying in Damin-i-Koh (meaning skirts of hills) as study area has been done to examine the concept of investigation pattern, as is indicated, traditional wisdom is operating for the purpose of interaction of natural resources in the area where land of hills and forest provide basic livelihood to the Malpahariyas. Damin-i-koh of Rajmahal hills as a preserve area of the aborigines has been considered as the best possible unit of the study where the imprints are still left out to know its traditionality in interaction process to possible extent in spite of changing scenario.

Nature of early and current works

The study of tribal communities in the area of Santhal Parganas of Damin-i-Koh of Rajmahal hills is not new. It can be traced in well documented form from early nineteenth century. The work is mainly restricted with the observation of the respective tribal groups in the form of various official documents. Among them, Dalton (1872), Risley (1892), Hunter (1863), O'Makey (1938), Mc. Phirson (1909), Gierson (1926) are mentionable. Missionaries like Skrefsrud (1887), Bampass (1909), Cuislaw (1949) were very much familiar specially with Santhal/Pahariya. The works of them do not provide only ethnographic detail, but also an attempt to reconstruct history of the area. In addition, there were various district gazetteers, census reports, and land-survey and settlement reports.

Again in the latter part of the 1st half or in the 2nd half of last century, monographs and articles based on extensive field work narrating various tribal aspects of life and society including changing scenario have come out. Among them, some are the examples on the works made by Sarkar, S.S. (1934), Vidyarthi L.P. (1964), Prasad. S.N (74,61), Verma (1977), Kumar, A (1986), and Sharma, B.K. (1992).

In continuation with the work, the survey has undertaken a project at the far end of the last century in order to note down the nature of traditional wisdom operating in the habitats of various tribal groups lying in the different eco-zones of India. Damin-i-koh of Rajmahal hills of erstwhile Santal Parganas of Bihar is such a eco-zone where the impression of traditional wisdom of tribal groups like Malpahariya or Sauria Pahariya is still left out amidist the forco of changing scenario.

Significance of study unit

Damin-i-Koh of Rajmahal hills as study unit has its significance which is guided by history, heterogeneous character in concentration of tribal groups and varied physical aspect and problems.

The situation of the studied village in Damin-i-koh has added another dimension which deserves mention. It was a Government estate covering an area pf 1,338 miles (3465 sq km) in the subdivision of Rajmahal, Pakur, Godda and Dumka. Damin-i-koh was a Persian name meaning skirts of hills named by Abdul Rasul Khan, the then in charge of Bhagalpur after Cleaveland's death in 1784 who was actually the founder of the estate. It was established with the idea of keeping the Pahariyas pacified and restricted them in the limits of the area at the initial stage. Later on, the idea was promoted to set the Pahariyas in the forest with the improvement of the country and civilization at the same time. But in course of demarcation of Damin-i-koh during the regime of Mr. J.P. Ward in 1824, it was found that the Pahariyas did not come down from hill slope and improvement of the area did not take place as expected but it was found during this time that a tribc of immigrant namely Santal likely to come from Singbhum was seen engaged in cleaning the forest and reclaiming the waste land. Thus it was proposed by him to introduce the Santals into the Damin-i-koh with a view to improve its land as there was no prospect of the hill men. Even in 1837 when Mr Pontet took the charge of Superintendent of the Damin-i-koh, the direction came to him to make the estate productive and to provide encouragement to Santals in the work of clearing jungle. Therefore, it becomes clear that the Pahariyas were not interested in doing cultivation in the area of plants and valleys. Instead, they were interested in cultivating the land in slope and top of hills where slope or dry cultivation and forestry become possible. Naturally, they have developed traditional wisdom as gained through day to day interaction with natural elements of low quality and relatively in isolated situation since long time. Again, the Pahariyas are branched into three groups i.e. the Sauria Pahariya and the Mal Pahariya, Kumerbhag Pahariya who are distributed dominantly in the North and Southern part of Damin-i-koh respectively. Out of these, the former two are declared as scheduled tribes.

Therefore, in order to understand the nature of traditional wisdom and its application on the utilization of natural resources specially of land and forest as a basic source of livelihood, it seems to be ideal to select the village of Amirjola of Amrapara block, Pakur district lying in the southern part of the erstwhile Damin-i-koh where the Malpahariyas form a sizeable section. In addition to this, it is also curious to know how the Malpahariyas a more Hinduised section of the tribe and a tribe in transition on the one hand and a tribe coming to the touch of more acculturation process operates their traditional wisdom which is gradually mitigating in the height of exposure to technical and scientific advancement and increasing education.

Regional Background

Introduction

The study area lies in the Amrapara block of Pakur district which has a total area of 1803 sq.km. Pakur is the only town of the district. It has six police stations in the district. Only Litipara and Amrapara fall within the Damin-i-koh area. Both these blocks are dominated by tribal people e.g. Sauria Pahariya, Malpahariya and Santals. The district Pakur was a part of Bhagalpur division and later on it came under the district of Santal Parganas in 1855 when it was founded. At present, it is a separate district which is bounded on the north by Dumka and Deoghar district and on the south and south-west by Dhanbad and Giridih district. On the east of it, lies Birbhum and Burdwan district. The then district had 277421 populations according to 1951 census. It covered about 1.77% of Malpahariya in relation to total population according to 1951 census. Again, the total Malpahariya population was 39,950 distributed over six divisions of the erstwhile Santal Parganas.

Terrain

Since it lies within Damin-i-koh meaning skirts of the hills, the area is made up of hilly-terrain and valleys. The main range of the district comes out of Rajmahal hills. It consists of a succession of hills, plateaus, valleys and ravines. The general elevation varies from 150 m to 250 m, though they might come down to height of

30m in the plain or river bed. Again, in some places height goes to more than 300m. However, it is surrounded by hills and covered with jungles and wild plants. The valleys have a picturesque landscape and slope is gentle with undulating terrain.

Drainage

There are also numerous small streams coming down to valleys and ravines. Bansloi is one of the broad streams intersecting the hills. It comes down to Amrapara valley where the river falls down from a rock about 3.50 m high. The water flows struck the river bed with force and create potholes in the bed. There are few hot springs in the region.

Geology

This region is a part of dissected upland of hard ancient which has a cover of thick lava flow in the east of erstwhile of Santal Pargana district. There is the evidence of Gondawana rock which occurs as inter-stratification of sale and sandstones.

Climate

In general, the region witness experience of hot summer, rainy season and cool winter. The summer season lasts from March to May in general, while the rainy season starts in the month of June and ends at October last week. Winter commences at November, and ends at February in general. The average annual rainfall at Amrapara is 1636 mm. Maximum temperature in May-June rises as high as 46.7°C.

Natural vegetation

The hill slope is dominated by Sal and bamboo though deciduous type of forest is found in the area of foothills, plains and valleys. Some of prominent trees are tamarind, mango, jackfruit, palm, date-palm, *Mendu, Mahua*, though there are different kinds of plants including trees used for fuel, fruit trees, bushy plants, creeper and sabai grass.

Soil

Soii formation is poor on slope and foothill while soil cover is good below the foothill where height falls down to about 75m. Below the foothill, the alluvial deposition is good and sometimes it is clayey and sticks when it is dry. However, it is fertile as a whole. Reddish type soil is found in the foothill and it is little bit inferior type. Minor millet type of crops are groiwn in this type of soil. In addition to this, heavy black clayey soil, clayey loam sand soil are also found.

Ethnic Composition

In respect of ethnic composition of the block, nearly 95% of population belongs to the Santals and Pahariyas. There are some Muslims in the area of Parerkala, Jamugrja, Chandpur and Amrapara. There are also some Kumhars, Bengalee people and Bhagats (business community) in and around Amrapara Bazar. According to 1991 census, the block Amrapara is inhabited by 14% tribal population in relation to the total population (2,76,188 pop).

Land-tumure system

In Damin-i-koh, under the official holding of Pradhan or Majhi (village headman) the entire land-holding system started to be governed by certain rules which got definite definition in respect of rent assessment and village boundary during Brown Wood's settlement in 1978-79. Subsequently, the principles became strict at the time of Mr. Quinn (1891), the then commissioner by way of noting the position of dismissal, prohibition of appointment of headman and transfer of the office of headman, rights and duties. However, pradhan would collect tax and settle all kinds of disputes. He would reform waste land and settle the case of vacant holding on account of the desertion of riot or death without heir. However, this kind of land tenure system is known as Pradhan-Jote. In general, land holders are known as ryots.

Communication and Accessibility

Amrapara block is chiefly infested with hills and jungle and therefore access to the hilly area is not easy due to undulating terrain. However, the main thorough fare is Dumika- Pakur Road passing through this block. Amrapara block lies at about mid point on Pakur- Dunuka road, while the block head quarter lies at a distance of about 55km from both the district headquarters. The block headquarter is connected by metalled road with neighbouring state West Bengal.

Geographical Background of the studied village

Amirjola village is lying at about 6km from Amrapara market place. The extension of the Amirjola village in terms of latitude and longitude is 24°31′30″N to 24°32′45″N and 87°33′50″E to 87°35′15″E respectively. The hills namely Gugurdi, Khando, Amirjola and low-lying area in south-east corner have marked relief pattern of the village. The height of the village varies between 60m and more than 180m while its highest spot is lying on about 200m. The relief pattern is easily understandable from two sectional profiles. Both the profiles indicate that the village has maximum height lying at Amirjola hill. Along east direction, the height gradually comes down on the eastern and western side of Amirjola hill. Again along the north point direction the height gradually descends towards south. Soil cover is well developed towards south and southeastern part due to decrease in height. But its formation is poor towards hill slope. It is little reddish and stony. Summer and winter both are severe partly due to rock type.

The village is fully inhabited by the Malpahariya community constituting 281 persons distributed in 58 households which are spread in Amirjola, Gugurdi, Khando and Mohulbona hamlets.

Cultural Set-up

Amirjola village is fully inhabited by the Malpahariyas. It has an area of about 2.50 sq.km with density of population as 114 persons per sq.km. But the density of population per sq.km. at block level is 174 persons per sq.km in 1991. The number of female is 965 per 1000 male. In respect of family type, it may be said that the nuclear type holds the major share of 64% of total households. The extended type family holds 22%. The broken type family has 14% in relation to total households.

Age break-up

In respect of age break-up, it may be said that 124 population i.e. 44% of total population lies below the age group of 15 which may be considered as non-working force due to minor age. Again, the age-group of above 55 years are seven in numbers i.e. 3% of total population which is also non working group due to old age. Therefore, about 47% of total population may be considered as non-working group due to minor age or old age. 53% of total population is lying in the age group to 55. The people of this age-group are actually working population. In the age-group of working force i.e. 15 to 55, the number of male and female is almost equal and the male population in the age-group of 15-55 is little higher than male and female members in other age groups. The age-break up of the village is as follows.

Table 1: Age break-up (Amirjola)

Age Groups	*M*	*F*	*Total*
0 – 14+	64	60	124
15 – 54+	76	74	150
55 – 60+	3	4	7
	143	138	281

Size

In respect of population size, it may be said that the village is basically a medium sized village i.e. 4 to 6 which would be 34 in numbers (59% to total households), while the size of 2-3 finds 14 in numbers i.e. 24% to total households. It is also to be added that the size of 7+ above is 10 in number equaling 17% to total households. The highest size of household is 12 member found at Amirjola hamlet. The average size of family is 5 in number. The medium sized family indicates the broad-base in resource management. Land and forest are major resource on which they are dependent. Now-a-days they do fishing as management of water resources. Besides, there is scope of doing farm labour even in the neighbouring district of West Bengal i.e. Burdwan, Birbhum. The family size has been placed here in a tabular form.

Table 2: Family size Amirjola

Size	nos.	%
2 – 3	14	24%
4 – 6	34	59
7 + above	10	17
Total	58	100%

Literacy

In literacy, it is observed that the village Amirjola has maximum literacy. Out of total population, 57% people are illiterate of which 36% is female and 21% is male. Only 43% of total people are literate amongst which 30% is male and 13% is female. Five male members have education above class XI standard, but none amongst the female. The lack of facility for getting education is conspicuous. In addition to this, the primary school is seen at the out skirt of the village which is not run properly due to lack of teachers and classrooms.

Economy

Amirjola village is basically dependent on agriculture, though there is scope for diversified occupation like selling of forest products and cattles, engagement as labour/farm labour in or around village or in the neighbouring districts of Burdwan, Birbhum of W.B., grazing of cattles and even selling of fish. It is revealed that 86% of total working force is primarily dependent on agriculture. Even labour either as farm labour or labour and cattle grazing engages 3% of total working force for each category. Even 5% of the total working force is engaged in service. The working and non-working force holds 52% and 48% respectively. The table shows dependency on occupation primarily.

Table 3: Primary Occupation (Amirjola – 281 Pop)

Agriculture	*Labour*	*Cattle grazing*	*Selling of Mahua flower in the form of liquor*	*House-hold work*	*Service*	*Total working*
127	4	4	1	3	8	147
86%	3%	3%	1% than	2%	5%	100%

It is also to be mentioned that 52% and 48% is meant for male working and female working force respectively. The Malpahariyas have taken farm labour, selling of different forest products including the sale of mahua flower as country liquor, cattle grazing, cattle selling, selling of fish as their secondary occupation in order to supplement their income. It is also observed that a few of them go to Burdwan/Birbhum in agricultural season as farm labour. Therefore, occupational pattern of the Malpahariyas indicates the broad-based resource management.

Settlement Pattern

The settlement pattern and house type of these people under study bears the evidence of influence of terrain and availability of natural resources. The village has an area of about 2.50 sq.km. and four tolas i.e. hamlets – Amirjola, Khando, Gugurdi, Mohulbona have sprung up in the area of foothills or low-lying area between the two hills. As for example, Khandotola has developed in the low-lying area in between Amirjola and Gugurdi hills. The rest are seen to have sprung up at foothills. The use of 'Khar' grass on roof and the use of 'Sal', 'bamboo' in the main structure of the house and the 'Damor' and 'Kend' as pillar clearly indicates the utilization of forest resource. Out of four hamlets, Amirjola is the biggest which is developed possibly due to availability of gentle slope.

Market

The role of market 'hatia' has a greater role in the life and society of the Malpahariyas as in all other tribal groups. The 'hatia' sits on Saturday and Tuesday at Amrapara bazaar. It is the place where they use to sell the forest, agricultural and water products. They purchase cloths, earthen pots, and the daily requirements from the bazaar. It is also the place where they meet different kiths and kins and get pleasure through such visit. Also, they attend Hiranpur market for selling cow/bullock, if necessary. Besides, they sell goat/pig at Amrapara 'hatia'. The seeds of *mahua nim, kusum* are sold in the market. The leaves of '*kendu*' and '*sal*' are also the saleable products. Along with these they sell tamarind mango, *kul* and other types of forest products. Country liquor extracted from mahua flower is also another saleable product. They even sell paddy, bean (*barbati*) in the market.

Cultural Background of the Community

The Malpahariyas may be said as a more Hindised section of the tribe due to the exposure and increasing transport network. The ethnic group is on transition. According to Risley, they used to live by hunting and shifting cultivation. However, at present they also take resort to settled cultivation, labour work, and other diversified occupation in selling forest products, fishing and trading of cattles etc. They speak a sort of corrupt form of Bengali. They have borrowed a good number of words from Hindi also. The Malpahariyas of Amirjola or nearby areas go often to Burdwan/ Birbhum districts of neighbouring West Bengal for subsidiary income. As a result, they are acculturated to a little extent in relation to other groups.

To them, marriage is an essential event. The matchmaker i.e. sithu or sithudar plays a vital role to find a bride among the Malpahariya society. The bride-price (pon-taka) is the usual practice among them. It is paid in cash and kind. The payment in term of cash usually varies between Rs. 9 and 13. Cloth, pulse, salt, tobacco, turmeric, mustard oil, pig are given in kind for bride-price.

The most usual practice of marriage like among them is marriage by bride-price or marriage by purchase. The role of matchmaker in selecting bride and payment of *pacho* or *mad* (country liquor) as gift to the matchmaker for finding a bride, payment of bride-price in cash and kind, feast to be held in both houses of bride and bridegroom, putting vermillion by the bridegroom are the important events in this marriage.

In addition, there are other forms of marriage by love or force, exchange, service, adoption which are few in practice. Marriage by adoption occurs, when there is no male member in the respective family. The adopted son-in-law is called 'Ghar-jawae or Ghar Damand' who looks after land and other natural resources in law's house.

Apart from marriage, there are other types of cultural practices among them. As for example, the Malpahariya woman wants to avoid to be alone in the forest or spring water during pregnancy in anticipation of getting harm by evil spirits. The period of pollution (chute) continues upto 5 days during child birth. After completion of pollution, the couple with new baby enters the house through ceremonial cleaning marked by purificatory bath and shaving of head hair of the child. The name is also given to the child after it. Ten days after death, a ceremony marked by shaving of beards and hair takes place. Cooked rice and chicken meat is made in the name of the deceased person. One year after death a great feast is held among people and relatives.

The landed property is normally divided equally among the sons. The females have no right to it. But in case of no male issue, daughter can get the property, if she stays with husband in the village.

The significance of the deceased person or ancestor has a great place in the mind of the Malpahariyas as they think the ancestors are with them even after death in order to help them. So, they recollect the ancestors in the form of ancestor worship. Again, the idea of spirits is very much embedded in their society, as they think the spirits are lying in the jungles and hills. So, it is necessary to appease them. Therefore, in the Malpahariya society, the nature of ancestor worship, worship of stones, hilly land along with certain trees, appeasement of spirits through offering sacrifices and worship have a great role in their mind.

Different kinds of social problems including divorce, adultory, elopement etc are discussed in the village council in addition to problems related to land, forest, water etc.

Social unit

Family is the basic social unit among the Malpahariyas. It is normally nuclear type in nature. Man, wife and unmarried sons, daughters become the members of nuclear family. In addition parents, unmarried brothers or sisters are seen in the family type which is called joint family. Married sons and daughters build up separate houses after their marriage. Sometimes married sons occupy the same courtyard and set up own house. Food is separately cooked by this family.

There are heriditory distinctions among the Malpahariyas. These are *Dehri, Singha, Grihi, Manjhi, Ahriti*. But these divisions are not exogamous clans because inter marriage among them is easily permitted. Clan is absent among them. During selection of married partner, they avoid *kins* upto third generation on bothsides.

Land management

Introduction

Land is a vital natural resource and it is also important as equal as forest, since it provides stable and other subsidiary foods to them. The traditional knowledge about land and nature plays a significant role for the effective use and management of land resource. The different practices of cultivation i.e. wet, dry and shifting cultivation have been developed as a way of management in accordance with indigenous basic idea of land and its quality. Again preference is attached with the practice of forest cultivation (shifting cultivation) and dry cultivation as it is related with the way of life and environmental situation. Particularly, hill and foothill slope favours the practice of two types of cultivation. Land management is also reflected in selecting suitable indigenous type of crops, farming methods and techniques, cropping area and pattern. It is also influenced by the organizational network. Naturally, traditional wisdom bears impression or using such techniques in the field of land management.

Traditional idea about nature and land

The idea about surrounding nature i.e. terrain, land type, soil and weather condition as perceived by them in their own way may be considered as latent strength to utilize land resources in a suitable way.

Terrain and slope – It is seen that the Malpahariyas of the Amirjola village have a fair idea of the surrounding hills and valleys. The three hills i.e. Amirjola, Gugurdi and Khando have surrounded the village. The hill Amirjola lies to the north of the village, while Gugurdi borders south-west corner of the village. The hill Khando marking the meaning a little bit low area between two hills of Amirjola and Gugurdi. The name 'Gugurdi' has been coined due to the presence of stones and pebbles here. In addition to this, they have the indigenous perception of the terrain and slope. They know the slope of hill by its own term 'dhasna' while rocky place is known as 'Chatan'. The hill top is marked by 'thal'. Large size stone is familiar as 'hatipahar' in their perception. Some times, this hathipahar indicates the boundary of the two villages of Amirjola and Harinduba. The foothills and relatively low area is known as 'Gadi'.

However, according to the geographical point of view, the village has three types of relief zones – (1) Upland (lying above 150m) found in the north and north-eastern part known as Amirjola hill and south-western part known as Gugurdi hill (2) Eroded land or foothill land (75 m – 150 m) lying in the central part of the village. Khando hill is found in this part (3) Plainland (<75 m) found in the south-western corner of the village.

Soil – Due to close proximity with nature, they have own experience about nature of soil condition. Perhaps, they understand the relation of slope and rain with the character of soil. Due to his fact, they have developed the idea of different types of soil in different slope with its specific nature. In the slope, reddish soil with pebbles and gravel is found. It does not allow standing water. But due to presence of roots in the soil, soil erosion does not take place. This soil is called 'Kankure lal mati'. But in the foothills, soil becomes red, but the soil does not have much pebbles and gravels as found in slope. But the land holds water due to causation of slope. Again, the black soil is found in the lower part of foothill i.e. almost plain land where soil is thick. Due to gentle slope and accumulation of organic matter and water, soil formation and fertility is good in nature. This kind of soil is locally known as 'Jetki'.

Weather

The local people have also a fair idea about seasonal wind and weather characteristics which act as instrument in conducting effective land management through the practice of different types of cultivation. As for example, they are very much aware of western wind which makes the advent of summer season. Similarly, dark cloud in the west raises the expectation of coming rainy season in their mind. They come to know the possibility of rain and storm with the help of natural phenomena when ants come out to the surface with eggs from the holes. They also expect storm when fish jumps out of water. The severity of winter is marked by the understanding when wind blows from north-west part and sky becomes clear. This kind of indigenous idea about sky and wind might have helped them to undertake agricultural operation in their own way.

Indigenous idea on farm and general land – The indigenous idea on different aspects of nature i.e. terrain, slope, soil, sky and wind etc leads to classification of land which ultimately helps to maintain nature and type of farming. This background acts as controlling factor for effective land management.

Farm land: Based on indigenous idea on surrounding nature, the farm land is basically divided into two types i.e. wet and dry land depending on the water holding capacity of land, though other divisions of land are influenced by terrain, slope, soil and type of cultivation, crops grown etc. It has an area of 258 acres which amounts to 42% of total land of the village.

Wet land

The wet land comprises of kheti / dhani jami (Paddy land). This land requires water to grow paddy in the terraced field. So its names is dhani/kheti jami. This type of land is found normally in the area lying below foothill or in the area where slope comes to be low. It is found in the south-east corner of the village which surrounds the Amrapara plain land. It is also found in the north-western part which descends in the Chotapaharpur plain land. The south-western corner of the village has also concentration of this land to a little extent due to close proximity of Amrapara plain land. Normally, this land lies in the height of 65 m – 75 m approximately, though its location is also influenced by gentle slope. It covers an area of 43 acre which has an equal area with 7% of total geographical land. This land has good soil formation with alluvial corner. The variation is also observed in soil characteristics. It grows paddy mainly, though it favours to grow potato, mustard, maize, and pulse like mosoor, khesary etc.

The dhani/kheti jami is divided into three types based on the qualities of alluvial coverage with its colour, stones and retention quality of water. The quality of land has been labelled in their own understanding developed through age-long interaction with nature.

As for example, the first class 'dhani jami' is known as dhani/kheti aoal. Its alluvial cover is fair in thickness. The presence of stones of any size is hardly found and it is black due to decomposition of leaves, paddy roots, and grasses. This type holds water due to having fair amount of clay and sand. The 'dhani/kheti aoal' has an area of 18 acres which is equal with3% of total land. This type of land is very good in terms of its output. It is suitable for heavy type paddy seed. Sometimes it allows two crops in a year. The second class 'dhani/kheti land' is termed as dhani/kheti doyem or bad locally. The label of land as doyem/bad depends upon presence of stones to a little extent and position of it in medium height in relation to kheti aoal. It requires light weight seed and it allows mosoor to grow after paddy. It covers an area of 10 acre and is equal with about 1% of total land. The third quality land is locally known as 'dhani/kheti/sem or dari'. This type of land does not have good soil, since it does not hold water to a maximum extent. Again its position is lying higher in relation to other types of land. It also favours light weight type paddy seed. It is growing one crop in a year. It has an area of 15 acres which is as equal as 3% of total land. The resource management quality is poor in terms of its output.

(1) Dry land

The dry land comprises of bari and bitho jami. The two types of lands do not hold water as they lie on slope or foothill. The degree of slope, soil condition and nature of dryness divides the land in two types I) bari and bitho jami. The total dry land of the village has 215 acres (35% of total land). II) Bari Jamin – This type of land is lying normally in the hill slope of medium range (10°) and in the height varying between 105m – 140m. In this village, this kind of land is found in the north-eastern corner of the village and west central of the village. It is locally known as bari/kuruwa bari. Since this land lies on hill slope i.e. bari, it is known as bari jamin. It is also reddish and is covered with pebbles gravel or large type of stones. But, erosion is less due to presence of roots of left out turnks cut out before the commencement of shifting cultivation. The presence of stones in the soil prevents erosion also. Based on year of holding, this land is divided into two(1) Jara bari (1st year land) (2) Kuruwa bari (2nd Year land). The land of jara bari grows *Kalai* (barbate-been type of crop) in the 1st year, while crops like gandi (Makai – maize), *Janta* (bajra), *Kokro* (sutri-pulse type), *Lahore* (Arhore-pulse type) are grown in the 2nd year. The first and second year of land occupies 21 and 19 acres respectively.

Therefore, land under '*kuruwa*' (shifting land) has equality with 6% of total land (40 acres).

(2) Bitho Jamin

This type of land is found in the foothill where slope comes to be less in relation to that of 'bari' land. The slope of this type of land lies between 4°-5°, while the range of height varies between 105m – 75m. It has little undulation. It is an eroded type of land. It is reddish in colour and it has the coverage of small pebbles and gravels, though degree of coverage varies from place to place. However, this type of land has become favorable for the growth of maize and other millet crops, when water stands less due to less rain. But, soil has become reddish when water stands in good amount due to heavy rain.It seems that organic and other nutrients are reached out to lower height and soil becomes reddish in colour with low nutrient capacity of the soil. Again, the type of land is divided mainly into two qualities on the basis of degree of stony coverage and undulation. However, the quality of land is reflected in their traditional wisdom through the naming of different names as obtained through experience and generation. As for example, the first class land of 'bitho' is named as 'dabor bitho' or 'bitho aoal', which means good land in terms of less stones, undulation and consequently development of soil profile. It grows maize and mustard. However, it has an area of 72 acre which is equal with about 12% of total land. Therefore, this kind of land bears good management quality in terms of resource utilization. The next quality of this land is called locally 'bitho doyem' when the stonny coverage and undulation is higher. Naturally, the soil formation is less and it becomes dry very soon. It allows to grow pulse type crops like 'kukro', 'Arhor' with having chance of mosoor. But maize is not grown in this land. The grade of this land covers an area of 101 acres (17% of total land). Practically, it is a type of land having one time crop in a year. Therefore, resource management quality is medium in nature.

(3) Ghar Ingna

This is actually homestead land and it is locally known as 'Ghar Ingna' meaning house and adjoining land. It is a part of 'bitho jamin' falling under dry land. It has an area of two acres of land occupying less than 1% of total land. Due to close proximity, they nurture the adjoining open space close to house with water in order to grow vegetables like brinjal, pamkin, gouard. Different kind of fruit trees like papya, banana, mango, jack fruit, ata (custard apple), *kul* (plum) grow on the bordering lines which act as fence. This land lies in the height varying between 105 m – 75 m.

Non-agricultural land

The non-agricultural land coprises of bon/ jongle, danga, rasta and jola and has an area of 349 acres which amounts to 58% of total geographical land of the village.

Bon/Jongle (Forest)

The village has a sizeable amount of forest equaling with 175 acres (29% of total land). It is locally known as bon or jungle which has three types known as bon (reserve forest-101 acres – 17% of total land), kurua jungle (jungle grown during regeneration period in shifting cultivated land – *Kuruwa* – 55 acres 9% of total land and bitho-doyem jungle (jungle allowed in the foothill slope – 19 acres – 3% of total land). The land of bon/jungle is mainly found on hill top, slope and foothill slope.

The *bon* is a reserve forest controlled by government, while other two forests – kuruwa jongle, bitho-doyem jongle are village forests which are owned by the respective family. The reserve forest lies above 10° slope and above 140m. It is found in the south eastern part and north western corner of the village. On the otherhand, Kuruwa Jungle and bitho-doyem jungle lies in the height of above 140m – 105m and 105m – 75m respectively. The *Kuruwa* and *bitho-doyem* jungle are restricted to the area lying at 8-10° and 4 °-5 ° slope respectively.

The forest species are basically deciduous in type with dominance of 'Sal', 'Mahua', Kendu, 'Bamboo' trees. There are also different kind of fruit trees like mango, 'Jamun', 'ata', 'bheloa' etc. It is also to be mentioned that 'jungle' grow in 'bari jamin' (shifting cultivated land) as regenerated forest, while some areas of 'bitho-doyem' jamin' (second class foot hill slope land) is allowed to grow species like 'sal', Mahua, Kendu and other fuel wood trees and fruit trees. This type of species allowed to grow in bitho-doyem jam in bears name such as 'am danga' (mango land), saldanga (sal land) tal danga (palm tree growing land), mohulbona (mahua growing land) depending on the dominant species grown in the area. The restriction is found to be imposed in reserved forest on curving trees, though it is allowed to use leaves, flowers, and roots for sustainable use. However, cultivation is followed as a way of management in 'bari jamin' after regeneration and use of forest produce is followed during regeneration with care.

Danga jamin including Chatan pathar (grazing land)

This type of land is meant mainly for grazing. In *danga,* there was patches of small jungle with some big trees. But presently such 'jungle' or trees are hardly found. Again, 'chatan' means large size of flat stone exposed on the earth's surface. 'Pathar' means stones or boulders of different sizes found on the land. But it is to be noted that grasses, bushes and small trees are found in between stones or exposed flat type stones. So, *chatan or pathar jami* is also used by grazing time to time as in case of *Danga jamin,* though both types of land is almost devoid of green cover. This type of land is found mainly in the central part of or southern most part of the village. It has an area of 166 acre which amounts to about 28% of total geographical land of the village.

Rasta and jola (Village road and water reservoir)

This kind of land has an area of 8 acres of land which amounts to 7% of total geographical land. The village road runs through four settlement units and ultimately it falls into two metalled roads lying to the east and west of the village. There are few water reservoirs lying in the south-eastern, north-western, south-western. Among them, Amirjola is the biggest of all water bodies. In addition to this, there are number of small streams radiating mainly from Amirjola and Gugurdi hill. Out of this land *'Rasta'* includes one acre (less than1 %) and *'Jola'* has an area of seven acres (1% of total land).

In this way, land has been divided mainly into six types according to people's perception, though broad-heads have been followed either on degree of dryness or on farm land/non-farm land. The total reflection has been made in the table as given in terms of its type, characteristics, area and quality in their traditional perception. Table – 4A, 4B.

Table 4A : Land Type and Characteristics (Peoples' Perception)
Farm Land

Sl. No.	*Land Major Div.*	*Land Minor Div.*	*Dry Wet*	*Height*	*Slope*	*Soil*	*Quality of land*
1.	Farm Land Dhani/Kheti Jamin (Paddy land)	(i) AAOL (1st class) (ii) DOYEM (2nd class) (iii) SEM (3rd class)	WET WET WET	Below 70m " "	1° - 2° " " "	Blacktype, fair aluvial coverage, less stone Thin alluvial coverage, clay less, Less sand and stone	Good Moderate/ Poor moderate.
2. (A)	Bari Jamin (Hill slope land)	(iv) (1st year shifting cult. Land) Jara Bari (v) Kuruwa Bari 2nd year shifting cult. Land.	DRY "	140m 105m " "	8°- 10° " "	Reddish covered with gravel pebbles, Large type stone found sometimes.	Moderate Moderate
(B)	BITHO JAMIN (Foot hill land)	(vi) (Homestead land) GHAR INGNA (vii) BITHO AAOL (1st class) (viii) BITHO DOYEM (2nd class)	DRY " "	105 – 75m " "	4° - 5° " "	Little undulation	Moderate Moderate Moderate

Table 4B : Land Type and Characteristics (Peoples' Perception)
Non-Agricultural Land

Sl.No.	*Land Major Div.*	*Land Minor Div.*	*Dry / Wet*	*Height*	*Slope*	*Soil*	*Quality of land*
3.	BON/JONGLE Forest Jungle	(i) BON	DRY	Above 140m	Above 10º	Rocky slope	-
		(ii) KURUWA JUNGLE	”		8º-10º	Stony slope	-
		(iii) BITHO DOYEM JUNGLE	”	140 m - 105 m ”	4º-5º	Stony slope	-
4.	DANGA JAMIN (Grazing land)	(iv) DANGA	DRY	105m – 75m	4º-5º	Stone, Large;	-
		CHATAN (Large stone)	”	”	“	Stone, Hill	-
		(v) PATHAR (stone)	”	”	“	Slope/ Hill top.	-
5.	RASTA and JOLA village (Road and water bodies)	(vi) RASTA	Dry	-	-	-	-
		(vii) JOLA	Water bodies	-	-	-	-

Farming method and techniques

The way of management of land has been made in tune with suitability of land according to theirspecific understanding in their own perception. Again, the way of management is reflected in the process of cultivation, selection of crop variety, crops grown, crop-season, techniques of sowing and harvesting, implements used, way of land preparation etc.

Pattern of Cultivation – The Land-types and characteristics as developed by own perception have a great bearing on the pattern of cultivation. The 'bari jamin' (shifting cultivated land) is characterized by the method of slash and burn cultivation in hill slope. The hill slope is meant for the growth of forest. But they have been able to raise certain types of crops preferable to them through shifting cultivation. The process of cultivation allows regeneration of forest and to cultivate for 3/4 years and two years respectively. The change of forest residues into fertilizer, prevention of soil erosion through cutting of trees at a height of 1.20m – 1.50m before the commencement of cultivation, placing crop-seeds into the holes are the unique features to raise certain types of crops even in the harsh environmental situation. Again, these kinds of features conserve the environment as well. Thus, the shifting cultivation may be said as the best possible way to extract resources to a certain extent out of such harsh lands.

Crops grown, crops variety and crops season –these concepts have got respective thinking and working pattern concerning the specific farm lands. It bears the evidence of management ability of the people through the selection of suitable crops in tune with land characteristics as gained from experience and continuous interaction with nature. The bari (shifting cultivated land) jamin grows *barbate* (bean) in the first year, while in the second year on the same land, crops like maize, bajra and sutri, arhor (pulse groups) grow. The selection of barbate (bean group) in the 1st year may be cited as an example of traditional wisdom because this kind of crops helps to enrich the soil by fixing nitrogen. The soil allows also good harvest of the crops in the 2nd year. The cultivation of maize and other crops of bazra, surti, arhor etc requires less amount of water and are grown in harsh situation. But the crop seed used in bari jamin is of large size and heavy weight in order to offer resistance to the stonny and sloppy soil. As for example, Asna type of heavy weight maize seed is grown here. The crop season is one time which continues before monsoon (June-July) and ends at Nov/Dec when harvesting is done though sowing and harvesting time of the crops varies little bit, but restricted within the time period as mentioned. As for example Kalai (Barbati – bean type) of 1st year crop has sowing time in Aug and harvesting time in Nov. in respect of gandi (makai – maize) of 2nd year, the sowing time is in June and the harvesting time is in early Nov. But in case of other crops of 2nd year, Jawla (Bajra), Konkro – (surti-pulse type), lahore (arhore-pulse type), the sowing time is almost same with that of maize, but harvesting time is little late than maize i.e. 1st Nov.-Dec. The sowing and harvesting time is guided mainly by the factor of seed characteristics.

The bitho jamin (dry land) is lying at foothill where slope ceases with undulating terrain. But it is basically rainfed. So, cultivation continues every year with some exception where land is not good. However, it is basically maize land, though konkro (sutri-pulse type), Lahore (arhar-pulse type) grow depending on the harshness and dryness of land. Sometimes, mustard is sown after harvest of maize in the land of bitho aaol where stone is less with good soil cover. Otherwise, the land is monocrop in nature. The seed used in bitho jamin is of lighter type in relation to that used in bari jamin since the land is less harsh in comparison to bari jamin. As for example, *Baria, Satpatia* is allowed to grow in good quality of bitho jamin. It is of a lighter type and it gets less resistance from such type of land. Due to lighter type, maize seed gets ripen only. It is sown in July, while harvesting is done in the last week of August to September mid week. The rabi crops of kurti, sarisa (mustard) are sown in the month of Sept. third week and are harvested in the month of Nov.-Dec.

The dhani jamin is lying far below hill slope where slope decreases. Naturally paddy is the main crop of such kind of land, though khesari (a kind of pulse) is grown on land in few cases. Thus it is called dhani/kheti jamin. Three varieties of paddy e.g. Chengul, bohal; askalma swarna and bhadoi are grown depending on the retention of quantity of water and alluvial cover of land. The chengul variety and bohal of heavy weight and darker type require a good amount of water with fair alluvial cover. The chengul and bohal varieties of paddy are finally suited to dhani/kheti aoal owing to their bifitting characteristics which are known to the Malpahariyas in their own perception. Again, swarna and askalma being lighter type require less water with medium cover of soil. Therefore, they are best suited to dhani/kheti doyem. Bhadoi kind of paddy requiring little water with stony soil is found to grow in dhani/kheti sem jamin. The more heavy is paddy seed, the more time is required to get matured. Therefore, chingul and bohal take more time to get matured when its transplantation s done by July 15 and its harvesting time is by Dec. while askalma, swarna and bhadoi being lighter variety are sown through transplantation by July 15 with its harvesting time by Oct. late or Nov. 15 at maximum. In such cases, mosoor, khesari (pulse type) are put on as rabi crops, if land permits.

Techniques of sowing and harvesting implements used and preparation of land

The usability of any natural thing such as land as resource depends not only selection of crop with its variety and proper season, but also mode of sowing and harvesting pattern with implements used and specific preparation of land if needed. These skills are considered as ways of management of a particular resource.

In case of bari jamin, sowing is following the method of putting seed into the hole. The holes are made at 60 m – 190 m interval. Two seeds of each crop are put in the hole. The method of putting seed into hole is followed mainly due to slope in stead of broadcasting as followed in foothill or gentle slope. Barbati (bean type crop) is sown in the first year, while maize, bazra (cereal group) and surti arhar (pulse group) grows in the 2nd year. The implements used is dao which is meant for cutting the trees during start of cultivation after regeneration of forest. Dangua (a stick made of dho tree) is used to make hole in bari jamin for putting seed into it. The preparation of bari jamin conforms to the management of land. As for example, in the month of March-April-May, thorny bushes, creeps, plants are cut and assembled in different places for the purpose of clearing the forest floor. The forest residues are allowed to get dried and they are burnt with fire. The residues get rotten with monsoon rain and are turned into organic fertilizers which becomes favourable for the growth of crops. Secondly, the trees are cut at the height of 1.20m – 1.50m. Due to this fact, soil erosion is prevented and creeper type plant barbate (bean type) takes the help for climbing up. Thirdly, fruit trees mango, bheloa, jamin, Ata etc and other useful trees like mahua, kusum, kendu, kurmu, muga are forbidden to cut. Fourthly, mix-cropping is followed in order to get two/three crops at one time. Therefore, these methods of farming as developed indigenously make the resource capability of land high in terms of prevention of soil erosion, enriching soil fertility and allowing other useful trees to grow at a time. In addition to this, availability of three to four crops from 2nd year bari jamin is an added advantage since this type of farming allows three to four crops in one season and harvesting is made for the crops within one and half month.

In bitho jamin, the farming method is little bit different. Here, ploughing is made for three times. Hal (plough), Kodal (spade) mai (ladder) are the instruments used in bitho jamin. The method of broadcasting is followed due to decrease in degree of slope. The use of organic fertilizer has been made either through the application of cow dung and decomposed leaves and grasses. Sometimes, they use chemical fertilizer in case of maize crops and in bitho aoal jamin.

In dhani/kheti jamin (paddy/wet land), the farming method is almost same except in few items. Plough and ladder are used for the purpose of ploughing and leveling of the land. But, transplantation method is followed instead of broadcasting as done in bitho jamin. This is mainly due to water requirement of the crop. Ploughing is required for three times in a year, while weeding has become necessary in the month of Sept. It is observed that dhani/kheti jamin is vary much prone to attacking of insects due to water accumulation and sticky soil. But it is interesting to note that insect attack is resisted by an attempt through placing the branches of sindua tree amidst paddy land. Another way of negotiating the problem of insect attack, if it happens in a greater context is that water is drained out at the time of water logging so that breeding of insect becomes less in lesser watery situation. Application of cow-dung or decomposed leaves or plant residues is the usual way to add fertility in the soil, though chemical fertilizer is observed to use in the paddy field. The lighter type of paddy seed variety such as askalm, bhadoi at dhani dyoem/semi jamin require less time to get matured allowing sufficient time in rabi season to grow the crops like sarso (mustard), khesari and kurti (Pulse type), alu (potato). The soil of such land type is not sticky as that of dhani/kheti aoal jamin. Therefore the selection of lighter variety may be said as technique to use the land of dhani/kheti doyem or semi for double crops in few cases.

Labour requirement for land preparation farming process

The cultivation for bari jamin require work specially at three stages i.e. land preparation made through cutting, felling, assemblage of forest residues; setting fire on the residues, sowing and harvesting. In one bigha of land, 4/5 labours are required to cut trees, bushes and to assemble the forest residues. Rs. 25/- and one time meal is to be provided to one labour. The system of exchange of labour is hardly found.

In bitho jamin, land preparation requires ploughing for three times. But leveling is not required. Ploughing is done at the interval of about one week. Weeding is also done twenty to thirty days after sowing. The rate of one labour for plough is Rs. 30/- plus one time meal per bigha of land. In case of weeding, Rs. 15/- plus one meal is required for one labour. In order to reap the crops, one labour is required for two days in one bigha of land. Rs. 20/- plus one meal is given for the purpose.

The rate of labour for ploughing one bigha of dhani/kheti jamin (wet land) is Rs. 30/- plus one meal. In this land, ploughing is required for three times. In transplantation, Rs. 25/- plus one time meal is needed for one labour. The weeding work needs 3-4 labours for two days for one bigha of land. Rs. 20/- plus one day meal is needed for one labour. Reaping needs one man for two days in one bigha of land to the work.

The total reflection of people's perception concerning the way of cultivation, selection of crop variety, crops grown, crop season, of sowing and harvesting, implements used, way of land preparation is presented in the following table.

Production rate

The rate of production and seed amount required may be cited as an indicator to assess the level of management in some

Table 5A: Land – Management (Peoples' Perception)

Sl. no.	*Land Major Div. Wet Land*	*Land Minor*	*Mode of way management*	*Crop-selection Major-type*	*Crop variety*	*Crop duration*	*Mode of cropping*	*Implements used*	*Techniques of sowing*	*Any other point*
1.	DHANI/ KHETI AMIN (PADDY LAND)	(i) AAOL (1st class) (ii) Doyem (2nd Class) Sem (3rd class)	DHAN CHAS (PADDY CULTIVATION)	DHANI (PADDY)	(i) Heavy weight and darker type chingul and Bhohal (ii) Lighter type swarna Ashaima Bhadoi	Paddy (i) July 15-Dec (Heavy weigh) (ii) July 15 to Nov 15 (Lighter type)	Once in a year	1. Plough 2. Leveller	Transp-lantation	1. Keeping away insect by way of placing branch of 'sindua' tree. 2. Regulating water by way of contour bundh. 3. Application of cow dung.
2.	Dry Land Bari Jamin Bitho Jamin	(i) Jara Bari (ii) Kuruwa Bari (i) Ghar Ingna (ii) Bitho Aaol (iii) Bitho Doyem	Bari Chas (Shifting cult.) Sukha chas (Dry cult) Housing, Growing of vegetables, fruits, flowers	Gangra (Bean) Gandi (Maize) Bajra; Pul-se etc) Brinjal, Pamkin, Patiya, Maize, Mustard, Pulse type	Heavy and Large size Asna type of maize)	Aug – Nov Maize – June – Nov July - Sept mid week	Once Once Mix cropping throughout the year (ii) norm-ally (iii) Once	Dao cutting Implements 1. Dangua (to nutral hole) Spade, plough, leveller	Putting hole Broad casting	4. Fruits and useful trees forbidden to cut. 1. Two years holding 2. 3-4 yr regeneration 3. Cutting of trees at 1.20 m-1.50 m height Application of cowdung

Table 5B: Land – Management (Peoples' Perception)

Sl. no.	*Land Major Div. Wet Land*	*Land Minor*	*Mode of way management*	*Crop-selection Major-type*	*Crop variety*	*Crop duration*	*Mode of cropping*	*Imple-ments used*	*Techniques of sowing*	*Any other point*
3.	Bon/ Jongle	(i) Bon (ii) Kuruwa Jongle (iii) Bitho Doyem Jongle	Forestry	-	-	-	-	-	-	1) Sustainable use 2) Practice of forest cultivation and raising of livestock 3) Fire control 4) Maintaining sanctity of the sacred grave
4.	Danga Jamin including Chatan Pathar	Chatan Pathar	Grazing	-	-	-	-	-	-	-
5.	Rasta and Jola	Rasta Jola	Movement in village Fishing Miscellaneous purpose	-	-	-	-	-	-	-

situations. As for example, bari and bitho jamin considered as hill slope and foot hill slope land respectively require more seed with increasing slope. The production rate is relatively fair specially in the first and second year of cultivation of kuruwa jamin in comparison to that of bitho jamin. The harvest of barbate (bean) in the 1st year of kuruwa jamin is believed as fixer of nitrogen enriching the soil fertility. Therefore, production rate is higher for the 1st year barbate (bean) is 6-9 quintal per hect., while 2nd year crop maize is 450-550 quintal per hec. But it is less in bitho jamin (foot hill slope) and the figure is 3.50 quintal per hec. The less production rate of maize in bitho jamin may be said due to continuous cultivation and lack of soil fertility. Again, in wet land where land management is good in terms of getting water and good alluvial coverage, the general yield per hec is 13.50 quintal for chengul variety of paddy land. But the production rate becomes less for lighter paddy seed requiring less water and poor coverage of soil. The production rate for swarna is 6.75 hec. The seed requirement per bigha is seen higher in higher slope due to requirement of heavier type which is able to offer resistance in harsh terrain. The table 6

Table 6: Production rate and seed amount
(Barbati – (bean), makai (maize) and dhani (paddy)

Land type and crop	*Seed amount in 1 kg per bigha*	*Production in quintal per hec*	*Production rate in quintal per bigha*
A. BARI (HILL SLOPE LAND) i) JARA BARI (1st year shifting cultivated land, Barbati (bean type)	5-10	6-9	.90-1.20
ii) KURUWA JAMIN – 2nd year shifting cultivated land Makai-maize	3-3½	4½-5½	.60-.75
B. BITHO JAMIN (foot hill slope land) – Makai maize	3	3½	.45
C. DHANI/KHETI JAMIN (WET LAND) – Dhani – paddy	5-8	3½	.80

Source: Field data.

stating seed amount per bigha and production rate in quintal per hec is given to know the situation.

Land holding and Land tenure

The degree of land holding shows the dependence or importance on type of land. It is observed from a general view that land hold by per capita is very meager in case of wet land, while it is maximum in case of dry land including bari and bitho jamin (hill slope and foot hill slope land). Again, per capita land hold is very less in case of bari jamin (shifting cultivated land). The maximum land hold in dry cultivation (.83 acre) per capita is due to maximum area under hill slope and foot hill slope for which the Malpahariyas have no other option but to take resort to shifting cultivation and other form of dry cultivation. The table shows per capita land hold for bari, bitho and dhani jamin.

Table 7: Per capita holding

* *Bari (shifting cultivated land)*	** *Bitho (foot hill slope land)*	*Dhani / Kheti (Wet/Paddy land)*
.14 acre (40 acre)	.69 acre (194 acre)	.15 acre (43 acre)

Source : Field data. Total land in bracket and per capita land outside bracket.

* Based on actual use of the land for the current year

** Total Bitho jamin including Bitho-doyem jungle.

The land holding by community shows that the Malpahariyas occupy total bari jamin but bitho and kheti jamin are hold by the Santals to a certain extent. The table shows community wise land hold.

Table 8 : Land holding (Community wise) area in acre

	*Bitho * (Foot hill slope land)*	*Dhani/Kheti (Wet land)*
Pahariyas	58 (81%)	36 (84%)
Santal and LOHAR	36 (19%)	7 (16%)
TOTAL	94 (100%)	43 (100%)

Total Bitho Jamin including Betho-doyem jungle

Source : Field data

The area is lying under pradhani system in which 'Pradhan' (village headman) not only collect the land rent, but also plays the main role to sort out all disputes or acts as arbitrator. He has a great role to perform all kinds of rituals and worship as a priest.

He is held in high esteem socially. Therefore, his role is significant in land management.

It has been observed that traditional wisdom developed through experience and interaction with nature since time immemorial has become very much useful in turning land as viable alternative resources next to forest. The usability of land as resource has been reflected in the mode of use by applying skill of farming methods and techniques including land preparation. The production rate and seed amount required has a some sort of reflection on quality of land and way of management. Again, the land-hold per capita indicates the importance of the perfect pattern of land in accordance with environmental situation. Similarly, control over land is full in case of bari jamin and almost dominant in bitho and dhani jamin to the Malpahariyas. The Santal has little control on land of bitho and dhani jamin, though they live in the surrounding region

Forest Management

Introduction

The basic aim of forest management is to ascertain the maximum benefits from the forest for the people in a continued fashion without jeopardizing the growth and regeneration of it. Therefore, in forest management people provides the way of management which is mainly influenced by the demand of the inhabitants. Thus people show the direction and forest shows the means of fulfilling peoples' needs. In order to achieve the economic and social need of the people the concept of modern forest management requires scientific technical and administrative assistance so that it would not jeopardize growth and regeneration. But forestry is grown normally in the land of low quality and relatively in isolated situation which the indigenous tribal people select as their habitat. Naturally, the forest management in this kind of isolated situation and tribal dominated zone has been made in a very natural way which is related with the way of tribal people and is developed through traditional wisdom. As a result of it, this kind of natural forest management is very easier, acceptable to them and less costly. Now, it is attempted to understand how the Malpahariyas have developed the indigenous techniques in preserving and conserving the forest with the help of combined practice of forestry, forest cultivation and livestock grazing in the backdrop of hilly terrain and isolated situation of Rajmahal hills. It is also interesting to note the mode of use of forest as well as sustainable need of life. Again, prevention of soil erosion, way of controlling fire have been developed in their own simplistic and indigenous way. Hunting is the age-old practice which acts as a source of food in the lean period and recreation, though its intensity is gradually decreasing with the reduction in forest area.

It is necessary to have an idea on the land meant for the use of forest cover, forest type, species composition, area under forest cover and wild life in the forest before going to the discussion on the ways of forest management by the Malpahariyas of Amirjola village of Pakur.

The land actually meant for forest is reserve forest which is locally known as 'bon' (17% of total village land). In addition to this, 'Kuruwa Jamin' (shifting cultivated land) allows jungle during generation period and bitho-doyem jamin (foot hill slope land – 2nd grade) allows jungle. The former is known as 'Kuruwa jongle' and the later is known as 'Bitho-doyem jungle' (9% of total land and 3% of total village land). The total forest cover in the village is 29% of total land (175 acres total forest area of the village).

The forest species grown in the area are basically deciduous in type with the dominance of Sal (Shorea robusta Gaerth), Mahua (Bassia latifolla Romb), Bamboo (Dendro alanus Strictus Wees), 'Kul', Palm, mango. The trees used mainly for fuel are 'simul', 'kusum', murga, dho, jibla, khair, gamar, dumur which are mainly taken out from 'kuruwa' land when the land is left out for regeneration of forest. The fruit trees 'bheloa', ata, bel, jam, bedana, papaya are found generally in this area. It is also seen that bitho-doyem jungle sometimes bears the name such as 'am danga' (mango growing land), sal danga (sal growing land) depending on the strength of the dominant species grown.

The wild life is an indication of degree of dense forest. It is believed that the area of Amirjola and the adjoining region was the habitat of leopard (chita bagh), tiger, bear etc. though bear is now found to a little extent. Monkey, jackal, lambri (Harpal), wild rat are found. Different kinds of birds such as titar, gundur, ghughu, dahuk, mayur/manjur (peacock), koyel are found in the forest. It is also fact that wild animals like tiger, bear, leopard, and jackal have either disappeared or the members of them have been decreased significantly due to depletion of forest. The continuation of hunting is still the source of inspiration and enjoyment and bears the testimony of prominent role of forest in the life and society in the past.

Ways and techniques

Forest is the major element in their life and society which has a reflection in the use of it in every sphere of life to them. The Malpaharyas have developed the ways and techniques for managing the forest resources in the form of sustainable use of the products in the different spheres of life such as making agricultural and hunting implements, use in house and building materials, use as fuel wood and organic manure, use as medicine, use in ritual, use as food and fodder. The mode and purpose of use of the product is important to them so that its regeneration, growth is not hampered. The control of fire is also a device known to them which is an indigenous way. Hunting though practiced in low intensity is a part of management. The continuation of forest cultivation and livestock grazing through forestry is a good way of management, since both the practices are complementary to each other without hampering its regeneration and the use of forest products continues to help the practices.

Mode of use in different spheres of life

Making agricultural implement

Hal (plough) - The plough is an important agricultural implement used in toiling agricultural land i.e. kheti (paddy) and bitho (dry land). The hal consists of two parts – the upper part forming wooden rod made of 'sal' tree. The lower part is made of kusum, babul and sal trees. The trees are found in bon, bitho-doyem jongle and kuruwa jongle. The woods are taken out from the trees grown mainly 'kuruwa jongle or bitho-doyem jongle' as because woods are forbidden to take out from bon (reserve forest).

Kodal (spade) – This agricultural implement is used for the purpose of digging the soil. The wooden handle is prepared from the wood of sal tree. The handle is attached with the iron plate of spade.

Dao and kachia (sickle) – The implements are used for cutting branches of trees, undergrowth twigs and paddy respectively. The wooden stick attached with dao and kachia is made from sal or dho tree.

Dangua (wooden stick) – The lengthy wooden stick made of sal, dho and kendu tree is used for making a hole in the 'kuruwa jamin (shifting cultivated land). A straight lengthy branch is cut out from the tree. The main tree would remain as it is and therefore no damage is caused to the tree.

Mai (Ladder) – This is used for levelling land at the time of other works such as house making. In order to make it, the wood of sal, gamar, babul tree is used. Only the branch and small part is used without causing any major damage to the tree.

Tanga (Axe) – It is also a useful instrument in order to cut trees/branches as and when necessary even in clearing jungles of 'kuruwa jamin'. The wooden part of the instrument is taken out from the branch of 'dho' tree, sal or bamboo. The small piece of branch in required and no damage is made to the tree as a whole.

Patta (Level or flat piece of wood) – It is used for threshing paddy. It is made from 'sal' and kathal wood.

Kula (winnowing fan) – It is used for sorting out the grains. It is made of bamboo which is a renewable resource.

Dheki (Husking item) – It is used for husking paddy. It is made of babul, kendu, kusum, or sal wood. The use of tree is done when it is absolutely necessary and sustainable purpose. This is taken out from the 'kuruwa or bitho jamin' of their own.

Tamni (bick axe) – It is used to dig the stonny and gravelly land. The wooden part is made of 'dho' tree grown in 'kuruwa or bitho jamin'.

Basal (to cut trees/to make piece of wood) – It is used to cut trees/ to make piece of wood. The attached rod with iron item is made of bamboo.

Housing implements

Aokhol (to husk paddy/dal) – It serves the purpose of husking paddy, dal etc. The main body of 'aokhol' is made of mango tree, dumur, gamhar, sal etc. The husking rod of it is made of khoyer. The trees of khoyer, dumur, gamhar grow in 'kuruwa jamin'. Therefore, its availability is not difficult.

Jhanta (broom) – It is used for cleaning room or homestead land. It is made of 'kher' grown in the 'kuruwa jamin' or in the jungle. Its growth is very normal.

Khotra (a type of container made of wood for giving feed to the pig) – This is the type of container made of simul wood. It is used for giving feeds to the pig.

Khochla (type of container made of bamboo for keeping different kind of grain) – This may be of different sizes, but made of bamboo.

Khat (cot) – The leg of it is made of bamboo or sal wood.

Use in house and building materials

The walls of rooms where the Malpahariyas live in, are made of earthen walls and kher (a kind of grass) used as roof material. Woods of different trees, bamboos are used in making structures of house. Sometimes, they have cattle shed of which structures are made of woods or bamboos. 'Kher' (a kind of grass) is used in roof. Straw is also used in roof. This is the use of building materials in traditional ways though 'khapra' (titles) or brick are used in case of 'Indira Abas Yoyona'. The main structure has the use of 'sal' wood or the use of bamboos in some cases. The wood of 'gamhar', 'kend' is used in making pillar in order to support the structure. The use of bamboo is found in making door, though the use of window is rarely found. The ropes made of 'chaklo' (bark) of kudrum tree are used in order to tie the structure.

Use as fuel wood and organic manure

The inhabitants of the villages use woods of different trees as fuel wood. Normally, the trees grow in regeneration period of 'kuruwa' land. The trees cut for this purpose do not have any significant use in other spheres. Again, the trees are cut in the height of 1.20 m – 1.50 m. So it does not affect soil erosion. They also use fuel wood of those trees grown in 'bitho doyem'. The trees cut before the growing of crop in 'kuruwa' jamin are known locally as 'kurum', 'murga' 'jibla', 'khoyer', 'Rang'. The thorny plants locally known as 'Kor', 'Kasari' and 'kande' which are also cut at the height of 1.20 m – 1.50 m.

The leaves, twigs and branches are used as organic manure when it gets dried in the sun, burnt and gets wet in the rains. This is an example of management of land through forestry.

Use as medicine

The use of roots, barks, stem, leaves as medicine is important to the tribal people of this area, as these are easy available, cheaper and only source to resist the different diseases in the isolated and hilly terrains. The plants used for this purpose may belong to creeper, bushy/thorny or large sized vegetation.

The roots of ghutri-alu are made to powder and paste. Then it is used on pain stricken area.

The paste made out of root of 'bichati' creeper is rubbed on the forehead to get relief from pain.

The root of goad plant is used for the purpose of recovery of pain in the belly. It is a creeper type plant.

The root of 'busha' a plant of bush type is applied as paste in order to check loose motion.

'Pujro', a small plant is useful to recover the wound happened due to cutting any part of the body.

Another creeper type of plant known as 'harjora' has an application as paste when any fracture of bones has happened.

The fruit of bheloa plant is applied through its juice on the injured area of body. It is of medium height plant.

The leaves of 'ajhar' plants are smashed and made to paste and its juice is applied on the nose when blood comes out of it due to injury or any other reason.

The juice prepared out of the roots of chirchira, a small plant, is applied orally two or three times daily in case of centipedes bite.

The oil made out of mahua seed is applied specially for chest pain. The application of oil is to be made in light warm condition.

The use of paste made out of leaves of ghiphor, a small plant, is applied on the snake bite area. The paste is also fed two to three times dailyto the affected person.

The use of bear hair is tied at the hand when any person is affected by malarial fever.

The juice made out of leaves of brahmi and tulsi is applied orally in order to lesson the effect of cough and cold.

Use as food and fodder

The uses of forest products like roots, tubers, fruits, are used as food to the Malpahariyas. Grass, leaves are found to be used as fodder.

The tender bamboo shoots and mushrooms are likeable food to them. They eat also different kind of fruits like bheloa, ata, khejur (date), kul, mango. Sometimes they also collect honey and consume it.

The leaves of gamhar, mango are used as feed to cow, goats etc. though straw is consumed by cow. The 'kher' grass locally grown in the forest is consumed by cow and goats.

Use as insecticides

The use of leaves and stems as insecticides either to protect crop-seed or crops in the field is known to them. The leaves of nim get dried and powdered. In this powder, crops are kept in order to make it free from insects. Sometimes, the leaves of *misinder* get dried and powdered. In the powder, the seeds of barbate (bean), bajra, arhar and surti (pluse type) are kept to make free from insects. The stem of 'sindua' tree is planted amidst paddy land to protect the plants from insecticides.

Use as commercial basis

The fruits of kusum, mahua, nim are used to extract oil and they are sold in the market. The leaves of kendu, sal are useful to prepare thali and these are marketable commodities. In addition to it, tamarind, mango, kul, bheloa, ata are marketable products. Even jharka (a kind of grass), daton (made of nim stem), simul (cotton) jackfruit fetch cash by sale.

Therefore, it is seen that the use of forest products like leaves, stems, barks, fruits, roots and tubers in different spheres has been made purely on sustainable uses. The extraction of parts of forest species do not cause damage or hamper forest regeneration and growth. In general, the mode of use conforms with the art of preservation and conservation of the forest in an indigenous way except some situation when species are required as a whole or in large amount specially in house making or some other items. But, they are very careful in such cutting which are normally followed in case of such tree grown in Kuruwa jamin (shifting cultivated land), or by 'bitho-doyem jamin' (hill slope land). Replanting is also done in such situation.

Hunting as a way of forest management

The hunting though practiced at low intensity may be cited as a way of management since they get hunting prey and recreation through the management of forestry. Hunting has been developed as a game or source of recreation or source of food in the off season through forestry. They do not eat the flesh of monkey, tiger or snake, even if, they are killed as hunting prey. They beat or drive away the animals which cause harm to the crops. They use bow, arrow and 'barsha' as hunting weapons. They hunt the birds as mentioned in wild life and animals specially wild rats, hare, wild pigs normally in the month of June, but it would stop in the rainy season. However, hunting gradually disappears with the disappearance of forest.

Way of fire control

The management of forest by way of controlling fire is known to the Malpahariyas in their indigenous conception. By this way, they control fire and restrict it to the area what they desire even in summer when there is possibility of catching fire. In addition to this, they clear the forest ground by way of burning twigs, undergrowth and the forest-cuts lying in the forest. After it, the mahua flower is collected from the clear forest ground at an easier way with minimum wastage.

In April-May, they put together all the undergrowth, twigs and forest cuts in Kuruwa jamin and in the areas surrounding the big trees. They arrange all the forest remnants at a safe distance from the main trunk of the big trees like mahua, kendu, tamarind, nim etc. and keep the heap of the forest-cuts at desired height so that fire would not be so much hight. As a result of it, it would not damage the big trees and its yield such as fruit, flower etc. Again, the heap of the forest-cut is lined in different rows with a desirable gap among them. So the fire would not spread horizontally and it would be restricted to the desired extent. Besides, they have a careful watch during the making of fire. In addition, cleaning of forest floor and cutting, pruning the trees annually allows the forest growth and regeneration well.

Indigenous way of administrative control on forest management

The Malpahariyas have their own committee consisting of seven or eight persons who look after how to use the forest products and follow the restrictions and rules in using it. The committee makes them aware about renewbility of the forest through the sustainable use. It is forbidden by the committee to cut the trees in the reserve forest. However, there is no restriction to collect leaves, roots, part of stem, flower only for the purpose of sustainable use so that it does not affect the growth and regeneration of the forest. They avoid cutting of fruits and other useful trees in 'Kuruwa jamin' (shifting cultivated land), when it is necessary to prepare the land for cultivation. They also cut the trees here at the height of 1.20 m – 1.50 m to avoid soil erosion. There is no participation of women in the traditional committee.

There is also existence of the committee formed by the Government. The committee consists of the members of the neighbouring villages. There is a forest guard provided by the forest department to look after the maintenance of the rules and restrictions.

Practice of forest cultivation and raising of livestock alone with forestry as a way of management

The continuation of forest cultivation though practiced at low intensity and raising of livestock in the forest land with the use of forest resources is their age-long habit which may be considered as a way of forest management.

The forest cultivation locally known as 'Kuruwa' allowed for two years in the 'bari jamin' (Hill slope land) and left for regeneration minimum for 3 years and its process of mechanism as already discussed do not cause any hamper to the growth and regeneration of forest, but also allows cultivation through addition of fertilizer made through decomposition of leaves, twigs, undergrowth and pieces of stems. More than 50% of total 'Kuruwa jamin' (55 acres) is under 'jungle'. Similarly, raising of livestock in 'bon' (reserve forest), Kuruwa jamin (hill slope land) and Bitho doyem (foot hill land) is the way of adjustment with the forest from which they collect feed of leaves grass etc. for the livestocks. Almost every household has cows, bullocks grazed in the forest lands. The ratio of cows and bullocks per household stands 1:.50 and 1 : 1 respectively in the village. They prefer selling of cows and bullocks to milching. Normally, cattle of such type are sold at Rs. 700/- 800/- at Hiranpur where fair of livestock is held every week. In addition, they sell pig and goat. Goat is sold at Rs. 250/- 400/- which depends on size of it. Pig of normal size is also sold at Rs. 250/- to 350/. Now-a-days they sell cow milk at Rs. 5/- per pai (one pai equals to ½ kilo). This kind of earning through raising of livestocks with the use of forest resources has helped to maintain livelihood as supplementary income specially in the year when there is shortage of crops.

It is revealed that the use and mode of use of various parts of forest species in various sphere of life are meant for sustainable purpose. This kind of mechanism helps to grow forest naturally. In addition, prevention, regulation and control of fire, exercising practice of forest cultivation and raising of livestock along with forestry, hunting as a way of management by way of getting food, recreation may be added as other aspects of management.

Water management

Introduction

The Malpahariyas specially of Amirjola village have limited use in water management which is simple in nature. Basically, they were dependent on forest even in the recent past when more than half of the total land of the village were under the cover of forest. In addition to this, the area is basically rainfed area and scope for surface irrigation is limited due to its hilly terrain. So, hilly terrain and dependence on forest resources and minor millet crops, barbate (bean type) grown on shifting cultivated land since time immemorial have made them limited in the use of water. The existence of water reservoir, two springs, wells have given them a scope to manage the water resources in different ways with the touch of the Santal community inspite of having backdrop for limited use of water management.

Water bodies

The use of water-reservoir has been started for the purpose of fishing in recent period. A small water-body is found in the southeast corner of the village where the surrounding hills come down and saucer type terrain is developed. Actually, it was a small natural reservoir fed mainly by rain water and it had no use to the people of the village upto 1965 when it was extended. Since then, water has been used for the purpose of fishing only. In addition to it, there are two small water reservoirs lying in the south west and north-west border line of the village. The area of the water reservoir amounts to an area of seven acres.

The reservoirs are owned by the Malpahariyas. The water of the reservoir is not used for irrigation, when it is in excess. It is channelised through the built up of canals to other neighbouring villages. However, it is seen now-a-days that water is used for irrigation in very few occasions during dry period. Now, it is also used for washing, cleaning and bathing.

Fishing as way of management

However, the major way of managing the water resources is fishing. During rainy season, fishlings of different varieties like 'rohu', 'mrigal', 'katla' brought from Murarai locality of Birbhum district are released in this reservoir of south-east corner. At one time, the fishes released in it weighted to an amount of 10 kilos. The price of fish per kilo is Rs. 200/-. In January, fishing harvest is done. It is striking to note that the Malpahariyas are mainly dependent on the Santal at the time of catching fishes as they do not have fishing nets. They are not expert in catching fishes. So, they take the help of the Santals of Chotapaharpur and Chilkajuri. In lieu of it, Rs. 5/- is to be given to the Santals per kilo of fish raised. It is reported, 39 kilos of fishes are caught during this season. In respect of marketing of fishes, normally they go straight to 'Hatia' (market place) at Amrapara either on Saturday or Tuesday (the day of hatia). They sell out the fishes by themselves there at the rate of Rs.40/- per kilo. Even a few years back, the 'Bhagat' (Marwari – a trading community) used to visit the village to take the sale. However, the practice is not in vogue in anticipation of having much more money by sale directly in the market.

Miscellaneous use

Apart from fishing in the natural reservoir, the people of the village use well water lying at Amirjola tola and spring water found at Gugurdi and Khando tola as drinking water. It is also striking to note that one well lying at the bed of natural reservoir of south east corner is used for the purpose of drinking water and other purpose like cleaning and bathing when the reservoirs get dried in the acute draught situation. In this way, use of water for cleaning utensils, clothes, bathing is restricted only to the use of spring water in acute drought situation, though its flow gets decreasing condition.

Contour bandh as a tool for distribution of water

In order to get water distributed specially on the dry and wet land, the method of making earthen bundh along the contour is followed. It is known as 'contour bandh'. In this way, water can not escape usually to the low ground, since the flow is regulated through this bandh. However, water is allowed to pass on the land lying in the lower height by narrow opening in the bandh in a convenient side of the land. This is their traditional method of regulating water-flow in the hilly terrain. Side by side, a trend is observed to chanelize water through built up channel constructed by the Govt. a few years back. The inception of pucca channel in recent years may lead to the development of irrigation of surface water through 'pucca' channel in the next future when the Govt. would take the control of the reservoir for irrigation. Ultimately it would result in the diversification of agriculture.

Management of environment and natural resources: A reflection at socio cultural level

Introduction

It is observed that indigenous idea and thoughts about the surrounding environment i.e. land type, terrain, slope, soil, wind, temperature, rainfall and the way of utilization of natural resources like land, forest, water have become latent strength to have a control over the resources in their favour. In the context of hilly terrain of Damin-i-kho in Rajmahal hills and practice of 'kuruwa' (hill slope cultivation) and 'bitho' (foot hill cultivation) primarily and traditionally, they have developed social norms, customs, ancestor and spirit worship, maintenance of rituals during agricultural operation which have a great reflection in the utilization and control of natural resources. As for example, prevalence of some sort of social practices like nucleated family, nearby marriage distance, joint venture of labour among the close blood relatives, role of pradhans specially as authority in solving land disputes and custodians of all lands, *gharjamai* (adopted son-in-law) through marriage be adoption bears some sort of evidence to control natural resources. Similarly, strong belief in ancestor worship with the idea of having beneficial role by them, idea of remaining in peace, good health and happiness have led them in the worship of spirits living in hills and forests where they reside and worship of gods, other deities in anticipation of good return or prevention of bad effect during agricultural operation. However, worship of stones, trees, agricultural lands for the appeasement of gods, deities, ancestor, and spirits has an indirect role to preserve wild life. Again, the uses of forest products signify the attachment of forest with life and society. This attachment acts as an instrument to control and preserve wild life also.

Social practice

It is seen that the village Amirjola has a greater percentage of nucleated family (64% of total households) with average size of family members less than 5. This may be due to much dependence on 'kuruwa' (shifting cultivation) and 'bitho chas' (foot hill cultivation) which is reflected at per capita land-holding for 'bitho' (.56 acre) and 'kuruwa' land (.13 acre- based on actual area used for 'kuruwa' of the year) and per capita 'kheti' land (.14 acre).

The nearby marriage distance (mostly within 20 kms) restricted within Amrapara block or nearby kathikund, Mahespur block indicates the distribution of Malpahariya people in the neighbouring blocks of Pakur district or Dumka district where similarities are found in terms of cultural practices including management of natural resources so that no difficulty would arise in social life.

In case of 'kuruwa' (shifting cultivation) and 'bitho chas' (foothill cultivation) specially they are much more dependent on brothers of close blood relatives particularly for engagement of labours. So exercising of joint venture is not uncommon, though it is found now in few cases with the introduction of cash money which is paid for labour.

As per social custom, the Malpahariyas give no right of property to female. As a result of it, any individual can adopt son-in-law (ghar-jawaee by way of paying bride-groom price), when there is no male heir in the respective family. In such a situation, ghar-jawaee has to reside in the village of bride and would look after land and resources.

In addition, they have committee members of own community consisting of 5 or six members at village level with 'Pradhan' as chief who actually looks after forest in the matter of sustainable use of forest and making the people aware about renewbility of forest. 'Pradhan', 'Ojha', Gorait may be considered, as the important posts in the level of village authority. These posts are hereditary in nature. The role of 'pradhan' is to play active role also in solving dispute of any kind including land. The collection of tax is also his duty. The role of 'pradhan' is also to perform 'puja' or rituals of social ceremony. In this connection, it is to be mentioned that 'pradhan' performs puja at deberthan or any kind of 'puja' in connection with forest land or water management. The function of 'Gorait' is to inform people about meeting or social function or 'puja' related to forest, land and water. It is also found in the village that 'Gorait' acts also as medicine man in addition to normal duty. The role of 'ojha' in general is to perform mainly as medicine man in order to make the people free from disease or evil spirits.

Cultural Practices

Maintaining sanctity as a way of preservation of forest resources

The customs and beliefs as maintained in the form of various worships, rituals centering round deities, spirits, or mother earth controlling the basic components like forest, hills, streams, spring as they believe, may be cited as traditional feeling on the management of forest at philosophical level. Some of the worships, rituals may be mentioned in order to illustrate the way of life making the mental make-up to use the forest resources in the form of maintaining sanctity.

Nahmat puja

It is a festival in relation to crop harvest. This 'puja' is held under the tree o 'kurum'/sal tree surrounded by stones. It is called 'Deberthan' in Malpahariya. It is known as 'Jaherthan' in Santalee language. The festival is centred round 'jag-singhi' diety of forest. It is made to appease her. It is performed by 'pradhan'. Different items like eggs of hen, batasa (made from sugar or gur), pan-leaves, vermillion, insense sticks, maize, minor millets, liquor (made from mahua flower) are offered to the dieity. The sal and kurum tree of this place are forbidden to cut and the sanctity of the place is maintained by them.

Baghasi Puja

It is held amidst jungle under any 'sal' tree. The worship has been made in the name of 'Baghase' in anticipation of no loss of domestic animals like cow, pigs by tiger, though it is now not found in the jungle. Items like egg, sugar, batasa (made of sugar/gur), kubutar (pigeon), flower are offered.The worship is made by *dehri* .The tree under which such worship is held, is not allowed to cut.

Bhui-deo Puja

This 'puja' is held in the foot hill of 'kunkur'. It is held under the tree of dho surrounding by big stones and 'bhelog' tree. The purpose of the worship is to satisfy the mother earth so that these would be no quake of earth and no erosion of land. They maintain the sanctity of the place. Trees grown here are not allowed to cut. It is held in Feb-April. It is conducted by the *'dehri'*. The basic requirement in the worship is the sacrifice of goat, pig, hen, pigeon with the offer of sugar, 'batasa' (a kind of sweetmeat), betelnut, betel-leave and country liquor made of mahua flower.

Respect to the Mother Earth: A mental boost up

The Malpahariyas are basically dependent on shifting and dry cultivation of hillslope and foothill respectively. So, they are much more careful in offering the 1st crop of the respective fields i.e. 'barbati' (bean) or makai (maize) to the mother earth. They believe that worship as a mark of respect to the mother earth at the time of sowing crop or harvest or certain time of year brings good crop and makes free from all bad effects. Some examples of such worship are cited here under.

Jara Puja

'Jara' means first year cultivation on shifting cultivated land where bean (gangra – barbate) is the only crop. It is known as 'barbati chaklo' (boiled bean) since time long. They are very much careful to have a good return of the crop in the first cultivation after fallow period of 5-6 years. The shifting cultivated land i.e. 'bari jamin' lying in the hill slope has the possibility of getting attack of wild animals specially by tiger, leopard and other animals like wild rats, bear etc. Therefore the 'puja' is conducted on the actual field in the hope of averting damages caused by these animals.

Makai Puja

Maize (Gandi-Makai) is an important crop grown in shifting cultivated land (bari-jamin) or foothill slope land (bithojami). The 'makai puja' is held in the event of maize harvest. It is worshipped with requisite reverence. Then the crop is offered symbolically to the ancestors. This special 'puja' is regarded as a mark of good output of the crops in addition to 'Maghi puja' held in the harvest of all crops.

Maghi Puja

This is held actually in the month of Magh (Jan-Feb) in order to mark the harvest of crops – maize, bajra (cereal crop), sutri, arhar (pulse type). The worship is held in the name of Jag-singh deity (deity of forest) who is believed to reside under the tree of 'kurum'. This place is called 'Deberthan'. This worship is done in the hope of good harvest.

Worship of Water Deity

The custom of maintaining worship to the respective deity/ spirit as seen in using forest and land, is also found in worshipping the water deity. It is scheduled to be performed in the month of Magh (Jan-Feb). The place of worship is done under the date palm tree in the north of the reservoir. The worship is held to appease the deity so that any harm to the users and creatures living in the reservoir can not take place. In this worship, a goat, two pigeons are sacrificed. In addition, sugar, 'batasa' (made of sugar/gur), flower known as dhutro, sila, available in the jungle are used in this worship. The materials are supplied by the owners of the reservoir and the worship is performed by the 'pradhan'.

Use of Forest Products in Ritual

The use of forest products in ritualistic performances is highly important rituals as equal in its use as is found in case of using these in medicines.

The liquor made out of fermentation of 'mahua flower' is highly used through its consumption in many festivals like 'Nahamad' (performed in connection with crop harvest), Bhuideo worship (performed in order to prevent soil erosion), 'Jara' worship (performed in anticipation of good crop) and 'Gaonali' worship (performed to keep peace in the village). The liquor extracted through the fermentation of 'Mahua' flower is either consumed by the villagers or offered to the respective deity. The worship is held under any tree like 'sal', 'kurum', 'mahua', 'bheloa' etc. It reflects the importance of trees to them. They do not cut the trees grown in the concerned places.

Even, the leaves of sal, am(mango) are used during rituals/ puja. As for example, 'sal' leave is necessary either to keep vermillion required for puja or to keep 'prasad' on sal. Again, 'character' (divorce) between man and woman is also marked by tearing 'sal' or 'am' leave. In addition to this, 'tulsi' leaf is required sometimes during puja. Flower of 'bashki', dhutro locally available is used during puja.

It is seen that forest, hills, streams, water reservoir are the integral part of their life. These are the basic components to their way of life. Naturally, the beliefs, customs, developed centring round deities, mother earth controlling those basic components are found reflected in the form of maintaining sanctity to the sacred place and the species grown in the place. The use of forest species in worships and rituals enhances strong bondage between forest and human life which ultimately make them careful about its preservation.

Conclusion

The present discourse helps to understand that traditional wisdom for the management of natural resources still becomes the major force in the areas of tribal concentration where modern management has not attained to the extent of desired expectation due to relative isolation or historical/cultural background of the area and population group. The course of discussion has helped to develop the idea that hilly slope of undulating land of poor quality type lying in relatively isolated situation and the forest cover on it have become the major source of livelihood to the Malpahariyas who are considered as one of the indigenous group of Rajmahal hills. It reveals from an intensive survey at the village of Amirjola that 35% hilly slope and foothills land and 29% of forest land i.e. 64% of total geographical land have left them no other alternative to the Malpahariyas but to conduct shifting cultivation (kuruwa) on hill slope and slope cultivation locally known as 'Bitho chas' on foothill slope and forestry on land covered by Reserve Forest, jungle allowed for regeneration on shifting cultivated land (Bari jamin) or jungle allowed on 'Bitho doyem' land (second class foothill slope land). It is also observed that 28% of total land of the village can not be used now by the Malpahariyas for any other purpose excepting its use in grazing due to stone coverage of the land or the rocky nature leading to barreness of it. The attachment of the Malpahariyas towards land specially of hill slope and foothills and forest as major natural resource for their livelihood is conspicuously evident from the historical perspective of the region. Therefore, the Pahariyas of the area did not show much interest towards cultivation in the plains in spite of demarcation of the Rajmahal hills as 'Damin-i-koh' (meaning skirts of hills) between 1824 and 1833 with a view to keep them pacified initially and to improve themselves by switching over towards cultivation in the plains and valleys and reformation of the area. The age-long attachment of them to 'kuruwa' (shifting cultivation) on hill slope, Bitho chas (slope cultivation) on foothill slope and practice of forestry in the land of poor quality rests on some basic qualities of traditional wisdom which has active and eco-friendly role for the management of natural resources without jeopardizing the growth and preservation of regeneration of forest species and natural resources.

It is also necessary to mention a few aspects of their society which has some roles or influence in management of natural resources. As for example, the larger percentage in illiteracy (57% illiterate of total people of the village) is due to engagement in farm activities or forest collection, cattle rearing as well as movements towards neighbouring districts of West Bengal as farm labour. Again, the greater percentage of nucleated family (above 64% of total households) with average family size less than 5 may be due to 'kuruwa' (shifting cultivation) and 'bitho chas' (foothill cultivation). The nearby marriage distance is necessitated to find out the similarities in cultural norms especially in terms of land and forest management inevitable for their life and culture which are available in the nearby similar ecological set-up. Again, the system of joint venture in cultivation though found in few cases specially of 'kuruwa' (shifting cultivation) and 'Bitho chas' (foothill slope cultivation) indicates the necessity of close-ties among the blood relatives of nearby generations, since the cultivation requires hard and hazardous job starting right from preparation of land to harvesting of crops. 'Ghar-jawee' (adopted son-in-law) is such a social custom by which they want to keep control of land within village. Similarly, 'Pradhan' (village head man) has a significant role in performing 'puja' relating to land, forest and water management. Again, forest, hills, streams, springs, water-reservoir are their integral part of life. These are the places where deities and spirits reside. The strong attachment with them makes the people believe that worship to them is obvious in order to have a good return and to avert impairment. They are also highly obliged to the mother earth whom they worship at the time of sowing or harvesting time. This mental make-up has given a feeling of sanctity to the sacred place which indirectly helps for preservation.

The study reveals the basic principles of traditional wisdom of the Malpahariyas operating for the management of principal natural resources i.e. land and forest and the utilization of water-resources pointing out various empirical contexts.

The forest growth becomes natural in the hilly land of the area. The use of diversified materials from the vast natural resources in serving the multivarious essential purposes in the daily mode of life and activities of the people as exemplified in the overall earlier discussions indicates the integrated attachment of these to the people concerned i.e. the Malphariyas. The mode of use and sustainable purpose of it which carry out the sense of wisdom in management purpose, does not affect the growth and regeneration of species. Again, clearance of forest floor in order to collect 'Mahua' flower from clean floor with minimum wastage and to turn the forest residues into organic manure in shifting cultivated land have necessitated them to know the art of fire control by way of keeping gap of the residues and careful watch so that fire would be restricted at their control. The hunting practiced at low intensity at present bears evidence of close attachment with it. The people get hunting prey and recreation through the management of forestry. The exercise of different practices i.e. shifting/forest cultivation and raising of livestock in combination with forestry may be said as unique way of management. The importance of forest and attachment with it is also reflected in the cultural life in the way of worshiping the deity lying under the tree like 'Sal/kurum or even in the foothill amidst jungle. The sanctity of the place is maintained by forbidding to cut the trees of the area. It bears the evidence of conserving and preserving the forest which is embedded in their cultural life. Even, they have own traditional committee to have a watch on the sustainable use and make themselves aware about the renewbility of the forest.

Next to forest, land is a vital natural resource to the Malpahariyas, since it provides stable and other subsidiary food to them. Land especially of hill slope and foot hill is a major source for resource utilization in the area of Pahariya concentration of Rajmahal hills. Likewise, more than 60% of land of the Malpahariya village at Amirjola lies on foothill and hill slope which is also the major natural resource. The basic principle in operating traditional wisdom for the purpose of land management is the traditional knowledge about nature and land which actually helps them to identify different types of land including farming land i.e. 'Bari' land (shifting cultivated land), 'Bitho' land (foothill land) and 'kheti' land (wet land). The basic idea about slope (dhasna), stone (chatan), foothill Godi), direction of wind, colour of soil and basic properties of it specially the degree of dryness of soil has led them to identify farm land which is principally of two types i.e. 'Bari' land, 'Bitho' land including 'Bitho aaol', 'Bithodoyem' and 'Ghar Ingna' falling under dry land, while 'kheti' including 'aaol', 'doyem' and 'sem' falls under wet land. In addition to it, they identify jungle as 'Bon' and water reservoir as 'jola'. Again, the basic features of farm land as perceived through traditional wisdom has led them to select way of cultivation such as 'kuruwa' (shifting cultivation) in 'bari' (slope land), 'Bitho chas' in 'Bitho' Land and 'dhan chas in kheti land. Similarly, the farming methods and techniques i.e. selection of crops and variety, crop season, sowing and harvesting method, implements used and preparation of land which vary with different suitabilities of land as understood by them. As for examples, the principles of putting seed in the hill in 'bari jami', broadcasting in 'bitho' jami and transplantation in 'kheti' are basically guided by the variation of slope in different land types. Similarly, dao (cutting implement) and 'dangua' (hole making implement) required for 'bari jami'; kodal (spade) used at Ghar Ingua (homestead land – part of 'bitho jami'); 'kodal' (spade), 'hal' (plough), mai (leveller) used at 'bitho jami'; hal (plough) and mai (leveller) required at kheti jami indicate the level of comprehensions through close set observations froming the basic perception. It is also striking to note that the idea behind cutting the trees at the height of 1.20m – 1.50m at 'bari jami' (shifting cultivation land) before starting 'kuruwa' cultivation is developed with this principle that does not affect soil erosion. In this process, the left out portion of tree would also help the creeper 'gangra' (bean plant) to get support for rise. The principle of avoiding to cut useful and valuable trees clearly indicate their understanding of the preservation of forest. Their traditional wisdom is also working deeply in selecting the nature of seeds as per nature and circumstances of the soil type. They know heavy and larger size seed can tolerate the resistance as put forward by slope. There is also variation in selection of heavy and darker type paddy seed in thick cover of soil and wet most place of 'kheti' and lighter type in thin cover of soil and less wet place of 'kheti'. The choice of 'gangra' (bean) in the first year 'bari' land fixes nitrogen in the soil which enhances the fertility of soil. The cultivation of maize and millet crops like 'bajra', 'joar' etc. is due to dryness of soil and fertility level. At organizational level, preparation of land including procedure of turning forest residues into organic manure, weeding and selection of time schedule for each stage of preparation is determined by the suitability of land. In cultural life, it is seen that they observe different types of rituals and customs in anticipation of good crop and in resisting the bad effects of the environment.. This belief pattern, whatever may be its scientific explanation is deep-rooted into their mind. Though the performance of different worships like 'Jara puja' (worship done in eve of 1st year shifting cultivation), 'makai puja' (worship held in the event of maize harvest), 'maghi puja' (worship held in Jan-Feb) to mark the harvest of crops, 'Bhudeo puja' (worship held in the name of earth). In respect of land holding, it may be said that per capita land holding for 'bitho' is much higher than that of 'kheti' or 'bari' land actually used for the year. The figure for 'bitho', 'kheti' and 'bari' is .56, .13 and .14 acre respectively. Again, at community level it is seen that Pahariya holds 81% 'bitho' land and the rest is held by the Santal. But this figure in case of 'kheti' land is 85% for 'Pahariya' and 15% for Santal. But 'Bari' land is owned only by the Pahariyas.

In respect of water management, it is seen that the scope of water management was limited initially, though its scope is presently extended to 'fishing, when the water reservoir has been extended by the Govt. in 1965. Again, the construction of earthen bundh along the contour technically known as contour bundh is a unique device for regulating water flow.

Therefore, it is clearly seen that the heritage of management of natural resources continues to operate through the following of deep-rooted traditional wisdom of the people concerned. But this wisdom has become weakened gradually in consequence of the impact of modernism especially with the introduction of modern management through science and technology, opening up of new avenues for livelihood, contact with outside through the development of communication net work and increasing education. However, it is suggested that there are some basic positive qualities in traditional wisdom in tribal societies which are to be utilized for the management of natural resources as and when necessary even in the era of modern management due to its eco-friendly role and easy understanding at the cognitive level of the tribal people concerned.

References

1. Chowdhury, P.C. Roy 1965 Bihar District Gazetters, Santal Parganas, The Superintendent Secretarial Press, Patna.
2. Ghosh, Saswaty 2000 'Abode of God' in the Impressions of the Sunday Statesman, 4th June, 2000.
3. Hunter, W.W. 1968 Annals of Rural Bengal, Smith Elder, London.
4. Kumar, A. 1986 Tribal Culture and Economy. The Malpahariyas of Santal Parganas. Inter-India Publication, London.
5. Mc. Pherson, Sir, H. 1909 Final Report on the Survey and Settlement Operations in the District of Santal Parganas, 1898-1907, Calcutta.
6. O Malley, L.S.S. 1938 District Gazetter Santhal Parganas. Bengal Secretariat Book Depot, Calcutta.
7. Prasad, N. 1961 Land and People of Tribal Bihar, Ranchi.
8. Prasad, S. 1974 where the three tribes meet – A study in tribal interaction. Indian International Publication, Allahabad.
9. Risley, H.H. 1891 Tribes and Castes of Bengal, Vol. I and II, Government of India Printing Offices, Calcutta.
10. Sarkar, S.S. 1934 The Maler and Malpahariyas of the Rajmahal Hills, Current Science, Vol. 1, No. 2.
11. Sarkar, S.S. 1935 'The Racial affinities of the inhabitants of Rajmahal Hills, The Transactions of Bose Research Institute Vol-XI, Calcutta.
12. Sagwal, S.S. 1999 Forest Management in India, Employment News, 29th May – 4th June, 1999.
13. Sharma, B.K. 1992 Habitat, Economy and Society to Tribal Core – A Case study of Damin-i-koh, Inter-India, Publications, New Delhi.
14. Singh, K.S. 1994 The Scheduled Tribes, National Series Volume III, Anthropological Survey of India. Oxford University Press, Calcutta.
15. Vidyarthi, L.P. 1964 Cultural Contours of Tribal Bihar, Punthi Pustak, Calcutta.

4

Management of Environment and Natural Resources: A Study on Traditional Wisdom of the Sauria Paharias of the Rajmahal Hills

Archana Datta and Sanchita Ghatak

Introduction

Emergence of worldwide consciousness of saving this earth from pollution and environmental degradation has encouraged to undertake the study of the Sauria Paharias of the Rajmahal Hills. This indigenous people of the region were born and brought up in the lap of the nature and have adopted a system of their own to maintain their environment through utilisation and preservation of natural resources. The region is located in the north eastern part of the erstwhile Santal Pargana district known as *Damin-i-Koh*. The Sauria Paharias are mainly found in Kathikund and Gopikandar blocks of Dumka Damin, Boarijore and Sundar Pahari blocks of Godda Damin, Littipara and Amrapara blocks of Pakur Damin and Borio, Barhait and Pathna blocks of Rajmahal Damin areas (Fig.1).

Sherwill (1851 : 544-45) referred that the Rajmahal Hills were inhabited by two distinct races - the Paharias living on summits of the forest claded hills and the Santals residing in the valley. O'Malley (1910: 71) stated that the Paharias were divided into two branches : (1) the Maler or the Sauria Paharias and (2) the Mal

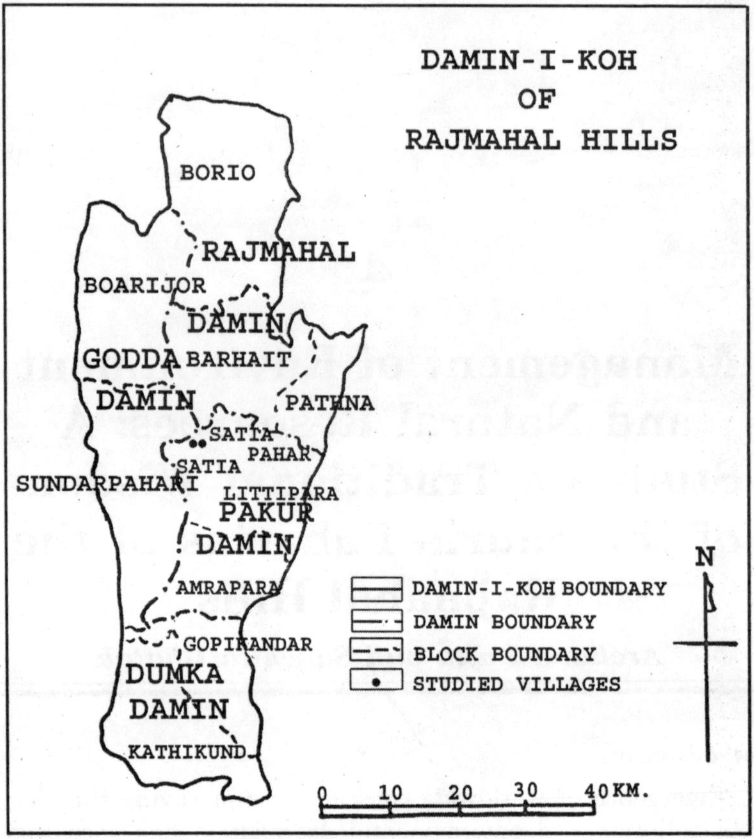

Fig. 1.

Paharias. Maler is the plural form of *male* meaning man in Malto language of the Saurias. Although, for the term of Sauria Paharias, it has been suggested that it was originated from the term Savala Pahar applied by the Hindus for the Rajmahal Hills.

The historical background of the Sauria Paharias of the Rajmahal Hills shows a conflict and confrontation with the Muhammadan kings, Zamindars and Britishers. Contact with the Santals for a long period as the close neighbouring community, as well as plain dwellers that they say *goler* has helped them to adopt some cultural traits of those people.

The studied region is marked by a series of flat topped plateaus and ridges dissected by a number of rivers. The Rajmahal Hills as the extension of Deccan Peninsula, have basaltic rocks, responsible and congenial for formation of rolling topography of the region. Soils vary according to the nature of parent rocks. Alluvium soils are found near the river beds. The region is dominated by monsoon climate. In this natural set up of the region Satia village of Littipara block of Pakur district was studied to acquire a clear knowledge about the traditional process of management of environment and natural resources by the Sauria Paharias who claim themselves as indigenous people of the area. They are still practising shifting cultivation.

Physical Environment of the Village

Physiographically, Satia is situated on a saddle between two hills. Average height of the village is a little over 152.4 meters. Maximum height of the village is 157.58 meters. The terrain character, in general, is undulating in nature, but a few patches of flat table lands are also observed in some areas, The height of the adjacent Satia Pahar, where the people of Satia practise shifting cultivation varies from 152.4 meters to more than 304.8 meters. The maximum height of this hilly tract is 396.24 meters.

As Satia village and Satia Pahar are situated on the Rajmahal range, both are characterised by basaltic rocks and laterite soil. It may be said that laterite has an intimate relation with the underlying basaltic rocks.

The village is dissected by a number of streams which are rainfed and remain almost dry during the summer and the winter seasons. The cross section (Fig. 2) depicts that slope is gentle in nature at Satia village (1° approximately) and steeper at

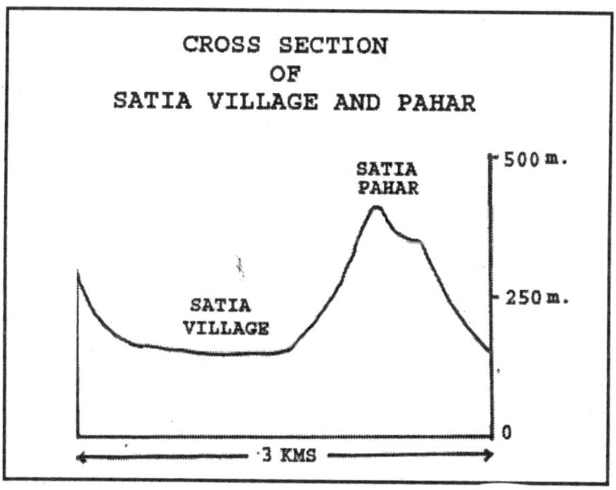

Fig. 2.

Satia Pahar (20° approx). Gentle slope of the village is used for settled plough cultivation whereas steep slope of Satia Pahar has no scope for ploughing. Shifting cultivation using only digging stick is practised there.

Kurni (summer), *eikdu* (rain) and *phania* (winter) are the three identified seasons of the Saurias of Satia. They apprehend the seasons marking the direction of wind. The climate is not an exception here from that of the Rajmahal hill region as a whole. It is marked by hot summer, moderate rainfall and cold winter.

Khajdu (soil) is being classified by them as (1) *kitro kaji* — gritty soil, (2) *keso khajdu* — red or laterite soil, (3) *margaro khajdu* — black soil, (4) *troke khajdu* — soil of red and black mixed found on the hill i.e. in Satia Pahar, and (5) *birinda khajdu* — white soil. Where there is no soil and parent rock has come out that portion is termed as *bija*.

Cultural Environment of the Village

The Sauria Paharias call themselves as Samaria Paharia. Satia, our studied village, is exclusively inhabited by the Saurias. Total population of the inhabited village in 1961 was 197 and it increased by 32 percent in 1999 (the year of study). The lowest percentage of population at the age group of 55+ category (Table - 1) reflects their short life span. Malnutrition, suffering from malaria and different other ailments are main causes for this.

Whereas, marital status shows the highest concentration in the age group of 35—54 followed by 15—34 and 55+ respectively. They want to get their daughters married at the age of 15—16 years and their sons at 20 to 25 years of age. But with the small holding size, low rate of production of crops as well as bride price system make them unable to marry their children in proper time. Only 10 percent of male and 11 percent of female got married at the age of 20 to 25 years.

Geographical distance for marriage of the Sauria Paharias has a great relevance with their management of land and forest resources. It is observed from the field survey that they generally like to arrange marital relations for their sons and daughters within a commandable distance to maintain a co-operation during clearing of forest as well as agricultural operation in their *khallu*, *bitta*, *bakri* and *keskette* lands. Specially, they need a huge number of labour force to complete their cultivation in *khallu* land. Besides that the Saurias, being a small community, want to make relationship within a commandable distance, so that, they

Table – 1 : Age Group and Marital status

Age Group	*Unmarried*			*Married*			*Widow*			*Population (Percentage to total population)*		
	Male	*Female*	*Total*	*Male*	*Female*	*Total*	*Male*	*Female*	*Total*	*Male*	*Female*	*Total*
0 – 4	25	23	48	-	-	-	-	-	-	25	23	48
Percentage	52.08	47.92	100.00	-	-	-	-	-	-	9.61	8.85	18.46
5 – 14	34	36	70	-	1	1	-	-	-	34	37	71
Percentage	47.89	50.70	98.59	-	1.41	1.41	-	-	-	13.08	14.23	27.31
15 -34	11	10	21	29	37	66	1	1	2	41	48	89
Percentage	12.36	11.24	23.60	32.59	41.57	74.16	1.12	1 12	2.24	15.77	18.46	34.23
35 – 54	1	-	1	21	14	35	1	9	10	23	23	46
Percentage	2.17	-	2.17	45.36	30.43	76.09	2.17	19.57	21.74	8.85	8.85	17.70
55 +	-	-	-	2	2	4	1	1	2	3	3	6
Percentage	-	-	-	33.33	33.33	66.66	16.67	16.67	33.34	1.15	1.15	2.30
Total	71	49	140	52	54	106	3	11	14	126	134	260
Percentage	27.31	26.54	53.85	20 00	20.77	40.77	1.15	4.23	5.38	48.46	51.54	100.00

Source : Field Survey.

Table – 2: Geographical Distances for Marriage (in Kilometres)

0 km.		0.1 - 5 kms.		5.1 – 10 kms.		10.1 kms. and above		Total Marital events
No. of marital events	Percentage to total events	No. of marital events	Percentage to total events	No. of marital events	Percentage to total events	No. of marital events	Percentage to total events	
32	51.61	12	19.36	14	22.58	4	6.45	62

Source: Field Survey.

can help each other at the time of needs and also can share the pleasure of different festive occasions and sorrow during their distress or unhappy affairs, through reciprocal exchange of rendering co-operation and good wishes. The frequent visits, in many times, lead to love affairs among the young boys and girls which may ultimately end in marriage. About 51.61 percent marriages have occurred within the village, They try their best to make negotiation of marriage within 10 kms. (Table 2). When biological distance is considered they generally practise endogamy at community level and avoid 3 to 4 generations in negotiation of marriage. Normally, marriage by negotiation is the customary rule of their society. But cases of elopement are not uncommon. Polygyny is allowed but at Satia only one such case has been identified. Gasi Malto, the Pradhan of Satia said that he had to marry more than once to maintain the agricultural operation and to manage the production and preservation of crops.

Role of Social Organisation in the Process of Management: Family is the primary social institution and plays a significant role in the management of social environment with the utilisation of natural resources. In general, a Sauria family consists of husband, wife and their unmarried children i.e., nuclear family. A son makes his own hut in his village immediately after his marriage. Albeit, a son lives in a separate hearth, he maintains a cordial relation with his parents and his brothers and shares the common *bakri*, *keskette*, *bitta* and *khallu* lands. About 58.49 percent families are nuclear in nature (Table3), 28.30 per cent families appear to be extended type. But uniqueness is observed in the structure of the extended families i.e. absorption of wife's widow mother, unmarried brothers and sisters in a family which is the legacy of the *addakundrupe* system. This is a unique customary law of the Saurias. This development of uniqueness in their family structure has a direct bearing in the management and utilisation of natural resources available in and around their habitat. A Sauria family is patrilineal and patrilocal in nature. Father's property is inherited by his sons. But in absence of a male issue daughter inherits father's property. In such case, the daughter along with her husband lives in her father's house, When a person lives with his wife in his father-in-law's house is known as *addakundrupe*.

Table 3: Family Structure

Family structure	*Nuclear*	*Extended*	*Broken*	*Incomplete*	*Total*
No. of families	31	15	3	4	53
Percentage of the total	58.49	28.30	5.66	7.55	100

Source: Field survey.

Family members of the Sauria Paharias contribute some efforts to manage their socio-cultural environment. When a male member goes to his agricultural field or to the forest it is the duty of his wife to look after their small children. As soon as he comes back home he uses to take care of their children allowing wife to take bath and other household work. Again, when his wife goes to the agricultural field for weeding or harvesting, he takes the responsibility of their children. When their children become grown up and able to take their food by themselves, they leave them alone and go to their own job. Boys and girls of above ten years of age also take part in the process of management in different ways. They take care of their younger brothers and sisters in the absence of their parents and they also take care of their domestic animals. Sometimes, they earn money by working as *bagal* or taking part in weeding and harvesting of crops. Thus, the Sauria families manage their social and cultural environment through reciprocal co-operation and understanding specially for sustenance.

Role of village authorities: Panchayat is the political unit of the Sauria villages. The *pradhan* and the *gudit* are the two important village authorities. Pradhan is the headman of the village and *gudit* plays the role of messenger. Besides these two they have a few more village officials, viz.; (1) *nado* - the priest, (2) *situ* - the marriage negotiator, (3) *kotwar* — subscription collector and (4) *demano* — communicator with *gossayans*.

The posts of *pradhan*, *gudit*, *nado*, *situ* and *kotwar* are hereditary and usually the eldest son succeeds father. But, if any one of them is thought to be incompetent, a new one is nominated from the village. The post of *demano* (shaman) depends on the nature of man who has achieved the skill of shamanism (skill of communication with *gossayans* or spirits). Apart from these, village authorities and all the adult male members take part in the village administration.

Role of education: Spreading of education also has an important role in the socio-cultural life of the Saurias. The table 4 depicts that literacy of the village has been limited in the age group of 5-14 and 15-34. It may be apprehended that the Saurias of this village have started formal education after eighties. About 30.33 percent of population are literate in the age group of 15-34.

Education of their children makes them conscious about cleanliness. They admit that at present they are taking bath at least twice a week. But previously, they used to take bath once in a month or so. They are also aware of cleanliness of their clothes and washes clothes in the streamlets off and on. Earlier, they were reluctant to avail of medical facilities from hospital, but now, they avail of it.

Although, the Sauria Paharias are backward in achieving formal education, they have a vast knowledge of herbal medicines (their informal education) which has been acquired by them due to the long close association with nature. This knowledge of herbal medicines has been transmitted among them through generations and till date they are greatly dependent on that knowledge to get rid of various diseases such as, malaria, T.B., different skin diseases, caugh and cold, etc.

Role of occupation: Occupation is the manifestation of traditional wisdom of a community through the mode and cause of uses or application of available natural resources for sustenance. Hilly terrain, forest clad landscape, and paucity of water for agriculture motivated the Saurias to undertake the practice of *khalllu* cultivation in this area, although, at present they are encouraged to practise settled cultivation on the foot hills. Now, no household is solely dependent on *khallu*. About 96 percent households of the village are engaged in practicing both shifting and settled cultivation and about 2 percent are depending only on settled cultivation. It is revealed from the table - 5 that about 81.25 percent of the households are earning their livelihood from their own agricultural land and working as agricultural labourers. In the lean period of cultivation they are engaged to clear rocks and pebbles either from the *bitta* land owned by themselves or by others to make it suitable for cultivation. Sometimes, they earn money, but very occasionally, as labourer working in the construction of the roads.

About 10.42 percent of households are dependent on carpentry work in addition to their engagement in agricultural

Table – 4 : Age group wise literacy and level of education

Age group	*Literate*		*Illiterate*		*Primary*		*Secondary*		*Above Secondary*		*Student*	
1	*M*	*F*	*M*	*F*	*M*	*F*	*M*	*F*	*M*	*F*	*M*	*F*
	2	*3*	*4*	*5*	*6*	*7*	*8*	*9*	*10*	*11*	*12*	*13*
0 – 4	-	-	25	23	-	-	-	-	-	-	-	-
	-	-	100	100	-	-	-	-	-	-	-	-
5 – 14	13	7	21	30	10	7	3	-	-	-	12	6
	18.31	9.86	29.58	42.25	14.09	9.86	4.22	-	-	-	16.90	8.45
15 – 34	23	4	18	44	8	3	15	1	-	-	5	1
	25.84	4.49	20.23	49.44	8.99	3.37	16.85	1.12	-	-	5.62	1.12
35 – 54	-	-	23	23	-	-	-	-	-	-	-	-
	-	-	50	50	-	-	-	-	-	-	-	-
55 +	-	-	3	3	-	-	-	-	-	-	-	-
	-	-	50	50	-	-	-	-	-	-	-	-
Total	36	11	90	123	18	10	18	1	-	-	17	7
	13.85	4.23	34.61	47.31	6.92	3.85	6.92	0.39	-	-	6.54	2.69

Source: Field Survey.

N.B: Lower figures under columns 2, 3, 4, 5 indicate percentage to the total population and 6-13 indicate percentage to the total literates whereas upper figures indicate number of population.

land as well as agricultural labourers. About 6.25 percent households have their own agricultural land, in addition, two are engaged in service at Paharia Seva Samity and one i.e. the *pradhan* is engaged in collection of taxes. Only one person is totally dependent on service at Paharia Seva Samity. Agricultural land provides food to the Saurias for not more than six months, so, they have to depend on forest produces in various ways: *mahua* flowers followed by *simri* (sea-cotton), *tetli* (tamarind), *tatge* (mango) and *kochra* (*mahua* seed), respectively are regular money yielding trees of the village. Besides these they sell fire wood in the local markets and each household earn at least Rs.40/ for a bundle of wood in a week.

Except those assured income from the forest produces of their *khallu* land they also earn some money from *kote* (Aegal Mermelos), *chakjo* (custard apple), *ilkru* (plum) and different other fruits of the forest selling in the market. A few of them sell bamboo also. *Kher*, another forest produce fetches some money for the Saurias.

Table 5: Dependency of families on different occupations

Total number of families	*Number of families dependent on*			
	A+AL	*A+O*	*A+AL+O*	*O*
48	39	3	5	1
Percentage of the total	81.25	6.25	10.42	2.08

Note: A = Agriculture, AL = Agricultural labourer, O = Other occupation

Management through market: Markets or *hatias* to the Sauria Paharias are the places of communication and interaction. They communicate all of their news i.e. their date of *bhoj* festival or *aher* (hunting expedition),etc.through *hatias*. Most of the negotiations of marriage are performed in *hatias*. Young boys and girls often choose their partners from within the gathering of the weekly and bi-weekly markets. Trends of solidarity also are noticed in their movement in groups to the market along with their commodities.

The market is a place of interaction with other communities also. The Santals and the *dikus* (plain dwellers) purchase fire wood, *masdu* (bamboos), *khosre* (beans) and other agricultural and forest produces from the Saurias. On the other hand, the Saurias buy paddy and rice from the Santals and edible oil, spices, salt, sweets, parched and puffed rice, kerosene oil, etc. from the *dikus*.

The market as a place of contact with different cultures plays a significant role in the material culture of the community. Now, the Saurias have learnt to lit the lamp of kerosene oil, more after they use umbrella, iron cooking pans, enamel plates and bowls, etc. which they purchase from the market. Interaction with other communities has introduced wearing of saris among the female members of the Saurias instead of their traditional dress of *jangha* (the lower garment) and *anga* and *dubba* (the upper garments). Male members, at present, sometimes use shirt and pant or dhoti instead of wearing loin cloth.

Management of Natural Resources

The process of management of environment of an area depends mainly on the management of natural resources and this process of management is the reflection of wisdom of local people. Land, forest and water are the three primary natural resources for the survival of the tribal people of the Rajmahal Hills. So, to understand the traditional wisdom of the Sauria Paharias for management of environment and natural resources, one should know the process of management of land, forest and water resources adopted by them for their existence.

Management of land

Management of land means the devices and techniques adopted by the people to get maximum benefit from the land with minimum investment and loss maintaining through balanced eco system. Here, the process of land management denotes the agricultural management which has been reflected in: (1) management of land under *khallu/ khaldu* (shifting cultivation), (2) management of land under settled cultivation.

1. Management of land under *khallu/ khaldu*: The traditional wisdom of the Sauria Paharias of Satia has been reflected in the process of management of *khallu / khaldu* land located at *doni* and *troke* of Satia Pahar, the uninhabited hill adjacent to Satia village. Here shifting cultivation has been practised through individual holding.

Table 6 : Management of land at Satia Pahar

Total Area	*Khallu*	*Bitta*	*Forest*	*Total forest land (khallu + forest)*
120.98	41.24	12.10	67. 10	108.88
100	34.09	10.00	55.91	90.00

Source: Land record and field investigation.

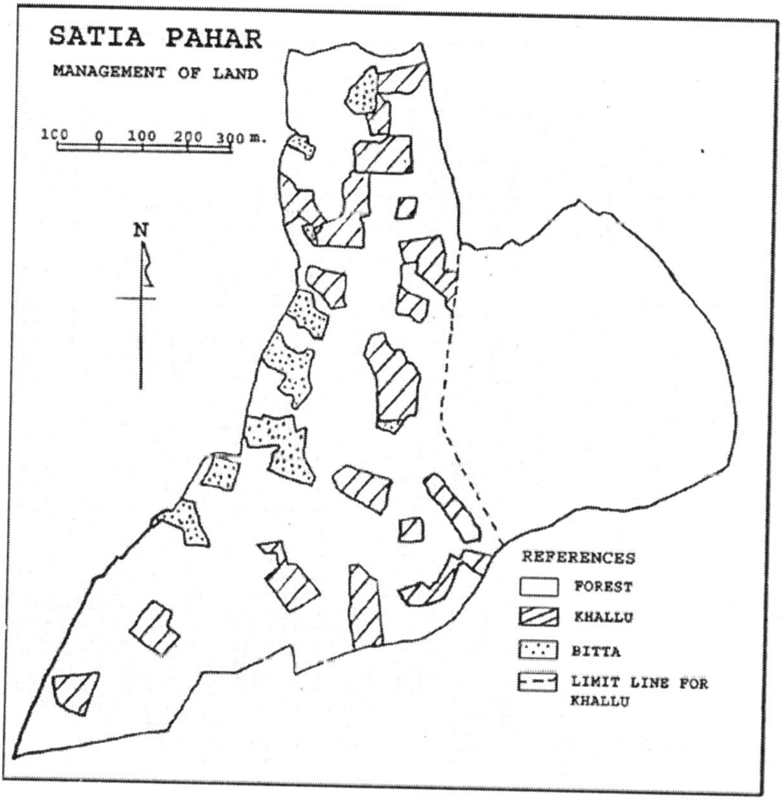

Fig. 3.

Total geographical area of Satia Pahar is 120.98 hectares of which about 90 percent of land are under forest and 10 percent land belongs to settled cultivation (table 6 and fig. 3). Shifting cultivation practised by the Sauria Paharias has occupied 41.24 hectares of forest land. Albeit, they often encroached the lands of Government protected forest adjacent to their *jamabandi* land (land in ownership record). Average holding per family in *khallu* for the current year (year of field work i.e. 1998—99) is 0.55 hectares (including Govt. land) and about 1.52 hectares per family are kept fallow for regeneration of the forest cover.

The *khallu* land located within the forest area is divided into two types: (1) *doni* — more or less flat land situated either between two ridges or cols. To clarify the structure of *doni* they mention that it is similar type of the land occupied by the Santals. Inspite of having smooth terrain condition they cannot use these lands for plough cultivation because these lands do not have any water source, they have to cross hilly tract to reach these lands; more over, these are located away from their settlement sites, (2) *troke* – the slope of the hill. Generally, land having slope of above 5° with no scope for ploughing are being mostly used for *khal1u*.The slope of *khallu* lands varies from 5° to 15°.

The *simi* (boundary) of the *khallu* land of a particular family is marked by boulders and different trees like *mahua* (bassia latifolia), *simri* (sea-cotton), *tatge* (mango), *chakjo* (custard apple), *tetli* (tamarind), etc. those have commercial and subsistence value. It may be said that this process of maintenance of boundary helps the Saurias to maintain their livelihood in one hand simultaneously it also prevent soil erosion to some extent in that sloppy areas, on the other hand. One plot of the forest is cultivated for two years then it is kept fallow for 3 to 4 years for regeneration. Cultivation in the *khallu* land is marked by a series of process.

(i) Management of *khallu* land in the first year: Busy agricultural operation for the Sauria Paharia families in the *khallu* land is marked by the clearing of under growth of selected forest tracts. Before selection of forest land for cultivation they first mark the trees, those will not be cut down, either by tieing ropes of straw around those trees or by different marking of symbols. The female folk clear the undergrowth with the help of *kudtatrudu* (sickle). Then the earth is dug with *jogi* (digging stick) made of branches of *karam* trees available in their forest and the holes are made 0.05 metre to 0.08 metre deep and 0.20 metre to 0.23 metre apart with regular interval for proper growth of the plants. Two to three seeds of *khosre* (bean) of large size are put into those holes to get at least one plant from each hole. Holes are covered with soil to protect seeds from monkeys, those are abundant in that area. Sowing is done both by males and females. After sowing seeds of *khosre* they (male folk) start cutting of big trees leaving the trunk on the ground upto 0.30 metre to 0.90 metre in height. Branches of big trees and twigs are also cut and arranged by them to be used as raised platforms that support the creepers of *khosre* to climb properly. This system also protects the crops from wild boars and monkeys and check soil erosion. It is noteworthy that they never cut the fruit bearing trees such as *tatge* (mango), *kathare* (jackfruit), *chakjo* (custard apple), *tetli* (tamarind), etc. and also trees having commercial importance such as *kendu* (leaves of which are used to make *bidi*), *simri* (sea-cotton), *makke* (shorea robusta) and trees having medicinal value such as, *aora* (amloki - emblic myrobalam), *pusre* (kusum – Schlechera oleosa), etc. The process of *kamkude* (weeding) takes place at least twice from germination of seeds to harvesting for better growth of plants. Watching of fields is the other important agricultural stage to protect the plants from wild animals and pilferers. They make a temporary hut on a high platform in the field; it is known as *khallu kuriya*. They also make *change* (a high platform) to watch the field. It is reported that the process of this first year cultivation itself creates barrier to pilferers and animals to reach the plants. So, they do not give much importance in watching *khosre* on the *troke* as on the *doni* land which has comparatively easy accessibility.

This system of cultivation in the first year is locally known as *jara* and to the Saurias it is known as *khosre dari*. It is found from the field survey that average holding during the first year of cultivation is about 0.52 hectares per family. Since, the productions of *khosre* in their *khosre dari* is comparatively high than that of other crops (about 252 kg/hectare) produced in *khallu* field and as this crop has high demand and price the Saurias try to clear at least some portion of the forest for cultivation of *khosre*.

(ii) Management of *khallu* land in the second year: After harvesting of *khosre* from the field of the first year, they sell the forest logs and woods; these were cut after sowing the *khosre*, in the local *hatia* (market). Some woods and twigs are also used as fuel and the fields are left as fallow for about three months i.e. up to April to regain fertility of soil. During this period leaves and dried creepers are allowed to be rotten to add organic manure in the soil. Moreover, in April - May they collect dried leaves and twigs which are heaped at different places away from the fruit bearing and other valuable trees and conveniently put fire to it. This system as one of the processes of resource management helps in various ways - (1) the grounds are made clear without any additional expenditure for labour, (2) this firing helps to ripe *mahua* fruits quickly due to the heat, (3) this method also helps them to collect *mahua* fruits and flowers from the clean ground. With the onset of the first shower some grasses and plants grow again; these are uprooted and left to rot. The ashes, rotten leaves and plants are spread all over the field. After this process the field becomes ready for cultivation. The agricultural system of the second year is called by the Santals and plain dwellers as *kurua* and by the Saurias as *khallu kude*. With the break of monsoon, in the month of *ashar* (June-July) seeds of *gangi* (maize), *arhar/ rahar* (pulse), *masi* (pulse), *bajra* (millet) and *khosre* (beans) are mixed in a basket with a ratio of 10: 10: 1/4: 1: 1/4 respectively for 0.13

hectares of land. Measurement of seeds is done with the help of a *pie* (measuring containers, 1 *pie* = 400 grams). They sow large size *gangi* seeds in the *khallu kude* as it is to survive at an adverse condition. Mixed seeds are dibbled, by the *jogi* into the same hole. As maize and *arhar* occupy their major diet they give more seeds of those two crops to get more yields. Mixed cropping has been practised to get many crops at a time. Some times they produce also *tur* (a kind of pulse) in the mixed cropping. However, sometimes they sow seeds of *arhar* in a separate hole. Sometimes they sow seeds of *kudrum* along the boundary of their *khallu* land. Weeding is done as and when required and it is mostly done by the members of the family.

Crops of the *khallu kude* require more protection than the first year crop from wild boar, hen, rat, monkey, parrot and pilferers when crops begin to ripe, because, access to the fields becomes easier in this phase than the field of the first year due to clearing of the jungle. They construct *khallu kuriya* or *change* again to watch the field. The Saurias stay there with spears, bows and arrows from September till the harvesting of crops. They also make sound by bitting tin or by shouting to drive the wild animals or pilferers away.

The process of harvesting of crops also shows the traditional wisdom of these tribal people. Gangi and *khosre* are plucked while harvesting of other crops is done with *tatrudu* (a kind of sickle). They harvest their crops very judiciously one after another. Gangi is harvested first in the month of September - October followed by *masi, bajra* and lastly, *arhar*,respectively. They collect maize by hand and leave the stalks for creeping of *khosre* plants. Khosre and *masi* become matured simultaneously, fruits of *masi* are harvested before *khosre* because the pods of *masi* are spilt out earlier than that of *khosre* and the *arhars* are harvested last because the absence of other plants during this period facilitates the growth of this plant. It is learnt that *khosre* are cultivated in *khallu kude* only for domestic consumption. They pluck it as and when required. It may be mentioned that only 7 families of Satia referred that they have done *khallu kude* in 1998—99 in 3.37 hectares of land.

It is noteworthy that the *khallu* cultivation practised by the Sauria Paharias of Pakur district is unique and different from the *khallu* cultivation practised elsewhere in the Rajmahal Hills. Unlike other places burning is done after harvesting of first crop(khosre) and a leguminous crop is sown only in Pakur district as first year crop. The field of the first and second year cultivations is termed in other areas as *khallu* (fresh plot) and *pachcha khallu* (old plot) respectively. There they practise mixed cropping both the years. Although it is observed from the previous work (Datta: 1991, 104—111) that the soil is comparatively infertile in Pakur district than that of other areas.

Management of land under settled cultivation

To know the management of agricultural land under settled cultivation by the Sauria Paharias one should be acquainted with the process of agricultural operation undertaken in different types of land, such as (i) *bitta* land, (ii) *bakri* land and (iii) *keskette* land.

(i) Management of *bitta* land:- Management of *bitta* land is the second stage of evolutionary process of agricultural operation in the area. This land lies on the foot hills between *khallu* and *bakri* lands and has been used as initial stage of settled cultivation. Despite the undulating nature of terrain character its gentle slope allows ploughing. The Sauria Paharias have converted their *khallu* land of this nature into bitta land to have an assured crop every year. They used to remove boulders and pebbles from this land and start ploughing. But mixed cropping system as in *khallu* and broadcasting system as in *bakri* land shows its transitional character. At present, the *bitta* lands near the streamlets or nalas where soil receives some amount of moisture and after repeated cultivation the depth of the soil increases to a great extent, are converted into paddy land. Following are the systems of mixture of different seeds for *bitta* land:-

1. *bajra + arhar + masi + gangi*
2. *bajra + arhar + masi+ kurthi*
3. *bajra + arhar + khosre*
4. *bajra + arhar + masi*
5. *khosre + kurthi*
6. *bajra + arhar*
7. *bajra*
8. *kasu* (paddy)

It is noteworthy that *bajra* is the dominating crop of *bitta* land followed by *arhar* and *masi*. Although they practise broadcasting method in *bitta* lands, exception is found for cultivation of *khosre* which is being dibbled with *jogi* as done in *khallu* land. Sometimes maize is produced along the boundary of *bitta* lands.

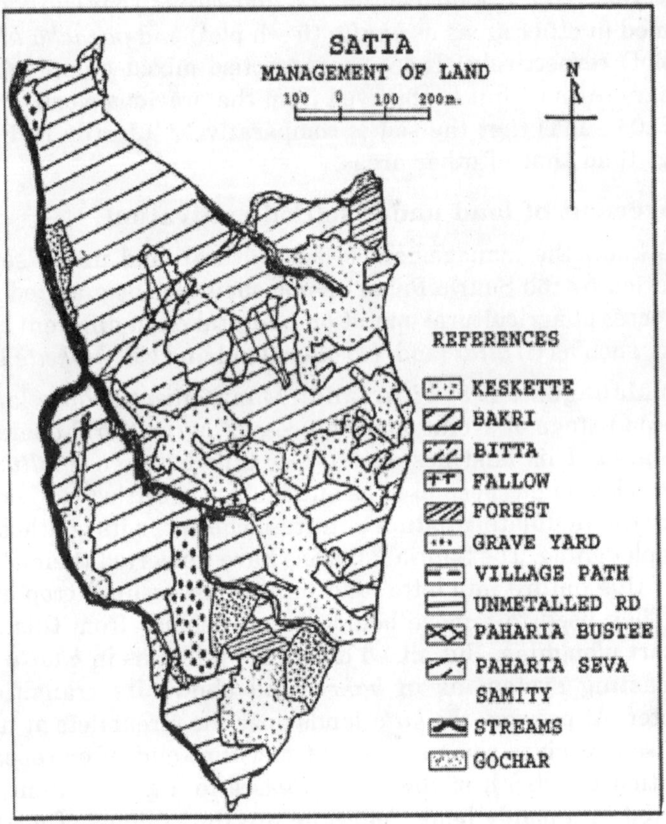

Fig. 4.

(ii) Manaqement of *bakri / bargi / bari* land: This land is located mostly near the homestead (fig.4) and soil is mixed with pebbles. The land is not fertile enough and water retention capacity is poor. This type of land may be placed between *bitta* and paddy land. Bakri land is termed by the Santals as *bargi,* by the non-tribal as *bari* and by the Sauria Paharias as *bakri.* It is unterraced highlands.

Gangi is the principal crop of *bakri* land, following crop sequences are found in *bakri* land of the study areas:

1. *gangi -sarso* (mustard)
2. *gangi - kurthi* (a kind of pulse)
3. *gangi - arhar* (pigeon pea).

Dominance of *sarso* or *kurthi* as second crop in the *bakr*i land is the common feature in the Sauria Paharia villages. The Sauria

Paharias, who have cows / bullocks, store cow dung in a fixed place for one year and mix this organic manure with the soil of *bakri* land before ploughing to increase the fertility.

Sometimes they also produce *adrosak* (leafy vegetables), cucumbar, etc. in their *bakri* land. Boundaries of their *bakri* lands are demarcated by different fruit bearing trees like *mankumde* (papaya), *chakjo* (custard apple), *kheldi* (banana), *ilkru* (plum),etc. Sanjari (drumstick) is a very common tree found either along the boundary of *bakri* lands situated near their homesteads or in the land adjacent to their homesteads.

It is observed from their *jamabandi* record that about 73.20 percent land of total cultivated area and 56.89 percent of total geographical area of Satia village is under *bakri* or *bari* land (Table - 7). Average holding size of *bakri* land is about 0.57 hectares. Sometimes they take land on *bharna* (lease) to repay the loan of *bhagats* (money lenders). As maize is one of the staple foods of the Sauria Paharias, they try their best to cultivate all of their land that is in their possession to produce maize. But about 15 percent of *bakri* land is kept fallow either due to non availability of plough or want of money after harvesting of maize.

(iii) Management of *keskette* or paddy land

The Sauria Paharias have acquired some traditional wisdom of the Santals for plough cultivation in their *keskette* land (paddy land). More or less leveled lands, in the foot hill region or near the streams, streamlets or nala bed, are used as *keskette*. A rudimentary terracing is found in the paddy lands situated at different levels (terracing is not uniform). Rain water or water of stream or streamlets is retained on terraces with the help of contour binding. They release excess water, when the field becomes sufficiently saturated, to the adjacent field lying at a lower level. The Sauria Paharias of Satia village have broadly classified their paddy land into two: (1) land for *mota kasu* (coarse paddy) and (2) land for *danga kasu* (highland paddy).

Lands located at the lower level congenial for wet cultivation are used for cultivation of *mota kasu*. The soil of this land is very fertile. The Sauria Paharias call it as *margaro khajdu*, colour of this soil is grey. It can retain water for a longer period of time due to high clay contain. Here coarse varieties of paddy are grown through the process of transplantation.

Lands for *danga kasu* have no irrigation facilities. Cultivation in this land is totally dependent on rain water and that also cannot be stored for a longer period. The soil of this land is termed by the Saurias as *birinda khajdu*. The colour of this soil is white. Finer varieties of paddy are grown in this land, through broadcasting of seeds. Weeding is done as and when required. Male, female, boys and girls of 10-12 years take part in harvesting operation.

Watching of agricultural crops in the field is an important aspect in agricultural operation. They have to keep watch through–out the day and night from ripening of paddy to harvesting in order to save the crops from wild animals. They prepare *kumba* (guard house) in the paddy field and stay there to keep watch on their crops and follow their indigenous method as mentioned earlier to protect their crops.

It is observed from the *jamabandi* record that about 24.96 percent of total agricultural land at Satia village is under paddy. Average holding size is 0.38 hectars per family. Four households out of 39 stated that they could not cultivate their land either due to lack of financial means or want of seed or non-availability of bullocks/cows.

The Sauria Paharias had an aversion to paddy cultivation due to slushy nature of soil of the paddy land. So, they used to give their paddy land on *batai* (share cropping) to the Santals, the neighbouring tribe, till seventies of the twentieth century. However, they did not have plough and they did not use plough for *bakri* land till that time. Now, they are trying to cultivate their paddy land themselves. The Santals are occassionally called for to extend their expertisation in sowing their paddy seeds or take part in transplantation as *berni* (labour). Table 6 and 7 depicts how the Sauria Paharias are managing their land resource in Satia village and Satia Pahar.

Management through rearing of livestock

Bullocks, cows, pigs and fowls are important livestock resources of the Sauria Paharias. Its importance to them is both economic and social. They use bullocks, cows and sometimes buffaloes for agricuirural operations. Pigs and fowls have ritual significance and all of these livestock as a whole have commercial as well as subsistence value to them. But for this study importance will be given on the cattle rearing process which is related to the management of land and forest to some extent as well as management of their economy also.

Analysis of the household schedules of Satia shows that about 61 percent households possess cattle of which 71 percent have

Table 7: Land Management at Satia Village

Total area	Keskette	Bakri	Bitta	Total agricultural land	Fallow	Forest	Pasture	Grave yard	Paharia bustee	Paharia Seva Samity	Road and village path	Streams	Barren land
78.09	15.15	44.43	0.46	60.04	0.94	3.20	3.20	2.82	2.77	2.29	0.25	1.92	0.66
100	19.40	56.89	0.59	76.88	1.20	4.10	4.10	3.61	3.55	2.93	0.32	2.46	0.85

Source: Land record and field observation.

cows followed by 20 percent possessing bullocks. Only Pradhan of the village possesses 3 buffaloes. Preponderance of cows is due to the liking of the Saurias to use cow in ploughing. Because, it will not only take part in ploughing operation in addition will multiply the cattle population also to enrich their economy. So, cows are not only the working force, but also a good commercial value to the Saurias. About 52.17 percent families of Satia possess plough and plough cattle ratio is 1:2.5.

About 4.10 percent of the total area of Satia are used as permanent *owacharipo* (grazing land). The person who is engaged to graze the cattle, is known to them as *bagal.* Early in the morning the boys and girls of 10 to 12 years of age usually go with the herds of cattle either to the grazing ground or to the left out *khallu* or *bitta* land. It is a very common picture of the village. Generally, one *bagal* takes the cattle of 4 to 5 families for grazing. Payment of a bagel is made @ Rs. 300 to 400 per year per family. In addition the bagal gets day meal from every family. Thus the foods usually suffice the meal of all members of his family. Generally, boys are involved in this work. Girls, generally, take cattle of their own for grazing. Moreover, the *bagal* gets yearly clothing from the owners of cattle. Thus cattle herding becomes a means of economic support to the distressed families of the community.

On the other hand, they graze their cattle in *khallu* and *bitta* land, immediately after harvesting till the onset of rain. This process of grazing helps to increase the fertility of the soil with the droppings of the cattle. Similarly, they graze the cattle in their *bakri* land also just after harvesting of maize. The green plants are consumed by the cattle. Thus they clear their land with the help of the cattle and add manure in the soil. In this way the Saurias manage to increase the fertility of their arable lands as well as manage the fodder for their livestock simultaneously. It is noteworthy that the Sauria Paharias usually do not drink milk. They believe that if they take milk of the cow, the calve will be deprived of its sustenance. Thus, through this rearing process and domestication of livestock the Saurias maintain a balance between their cultural life and utilisation of natural resources available in and around their habitat for subsistence.

Management through land tenure system

Roy Chowdhury (1963, 471-90) said that according to Santal Parganas Settlement Regulation III of 1872 all the Paharias of this district got occupancy right on their land. They were also allowed to practise shifting cultivation on their *raiyatee* land.

Generally, sons inherit fathers property in their society. But, if a man does not have any male issue and has only daughter, his son-in-law will live in his house as *adda kundrupe* (when a son-in-law lives in father-in-law's house). If there are two or more daughter then property will be equally shared by them. This customary law is prevalent only to take care of land and forest resources along with the wife's mother, unmarried sister and unmarried brother.

The Sauria Paharias also follow *batai* (share cropping) system in land management, in which they get half share of production incurring half of the agricultural expenditures. This system was very much prevalent among them when they did not acquire expertisation for paddy cultivation. They often used to give their paddy land on *batai* to the Santals who had an expertisation on paddy cultivation. The Saurias have a system of giving their lands on lease to others or taking of land from others on lease in lieu of some money for one, two or three years. They have to lease out their land either for want of money, seeds or for nonavailability of labour or sometimes for lack of plough for settled cultivation.

Management of Forest

As the culture of the Sauria Paharias originated, developed and flourished in the lap of the nature, they depend largely on forest resources for their survival. Forest resources provide them food and shelter. So, it is very much essential to know the effort of this community in management of forest resources and how far their traditional wisdom plays in the management process. Literal meaning of the forest management is economic utilization, conservation and propagation of forest resources.

Utilization of forest resources: In general forest is termed by the Saurias as *dadde.* Forests may be classified according to their utilization:

(1) *khawardu* — forest not being used for cultivation,

(2) *khallu* — forest land used for slash and burn cultivation.

They depend on forest resources in many ways:

(1) Forest resources provide them food, drink and shelter (Vidyarthi, 1963: 16) and help them to earn money for their survival.

(2) Forest resources supply them various medicinal plants to get cured of different diseases.

(3) Forests provide them suitable games for hunting.

(4) Forest resources supply them raw materials for cottage industries.

1. Use of forest resources for food drink and shelter and to earn money: The Sauria Paharias practise shifting cultivation in the forest clad hilly tract for their sustenance. But their agricultural land at *khallu*, *bakri* and *keskette* provide them food for six months only. On the contrary, surrounding forests of their habitat provides them various types of edibles throughout the year.

Mahua or *madgi* is an important forest resource to the Saurias of the Rajmahal hills. Mahua flowers are generally collected by women in the month of March-April and are consumed in various ways. However, the main use of *mahua* flowers is to prepare liquor. It plays a significant role in their religious life. They offer it to the spirits on the occasion of their different ritual performances.

Mahua fruit is known as *kochra.* The outer portion of this *kochra* is taken as fruit and oil is extracted from seeds. Mahua oil is used as body oil and cooking media. Sometimes, this oil is used to lit the lamp also. Mahua flowers and fruits are saleable items in the local markets.

Apart from *mahua* they also largely collect *tatge* (mango), *kanthare* (jackfruit), *kend* (a kind of fruit), *tentli* (tamarind), etc. in the summer season for their own consumption as well as to sell those items in the local market. In the rainy season, *chakjo* becomes almost a staple diet of the Saurias.

Major fruit of winter season is *ilkru* (palm). A very common picture of Littipara *hat* in winter season is that their male and female members come in the market with some *ilkru* to sell and they purchase some necessary commodities with the money received thereby.

In the month of March-April they sell *kendu* / *tela* leaves to the *dikus* (as middleman) @ Re. 1/- per 100 leaves.

Besides these individual gathering which is done by all the family members when they also go to the forest jointly (the village as a whole) for collection of fruits, roots and vegetables. This gathering is performed twice in winter and thrice in summer season.

In addition to food and drink the forest provides them *tela* leaf and *sal* leaf for making *chutti* (country made cigar). The Saurias like handmade *chutti* of *sal* leaf. They generally avoid smoking *chutti* made of *tela* leaf. They have a belief that *tela* leaf causes cough. The forest not only gives food to the Sauria people, their domestic animals are also fed by the fodders available from the forest.

Besides food and drinks, forest provides them materials to build their huts for shelter. About 41.67 percent huts of Satia have thatched roof. There is a luxuriant growth of *kher* (a kind of grass) in the forest and the Saurias use *kher* to thatch the roof of their hut. They prepare a frame of bamboos for the roof and that is thatched with *kher* and again it is tied with bamboo frame to get it protected from strong wind. After completion of harvesting of all crops, when they have no work to do, they collect *kher* from the forest. They rethatch their roof in every alternate year, so that rats cannot enter easily into the huts through the roof and cannot make harm of their *gangi*, which are hanging from their roofs. Roof thatched with *kher* keeps the room cool during the summer. Bamboos are also used to make doors and frames of the walls on all four sides. The bamboo walls are plastered with mud. The mud is white in colour and is collected from the hill known as *makoli*. Sal wood is used as central pole of the hut to enhance the strength as a whole. Besides *sal,* wood of *jirke, gamar, murga*, etc. are also used as poles and beams. They believe that these timbers are not prone to white ant. The Sauria Paharias use planks of *jirke* tree to construct wooden doors. They collect *rundu* sticks from the forest to make fence around their houses. Thus the Saurias depend on the forest for their shelter.

Apart from food, drink and shelter, the Sauria Paharias are largely dependent on forest produces to earn money and to meet necessities of life. Simri (sea cotton) is a good source of income of the Saurias of Satia. Troke *khajdu* is suitable for the growth of sea cotton in the Satia Pahar and many families earn some money for their survival from it.

The Sauria Paharias collect wood from the forest throughout the year and sell it to the market. It is seen that both males and females of the Sauria Paharias coming down from the hilly forest always have head load of logs. It is the duty of the male members to make the logs sizeable and tie these in bundles with *tiriali gatha* (rope of a kind of creepers) which is also available from the forest. These bundles are prepared to be taken to the next *hatia* for sale. Wood of *edic*, *jammu*, *sidi*, *kurchi*, etc. are used and sold as fuel wood.

2. Forest resources supply medicines: The forests of the Sauria Paharias are also very rich in various medicinal plants. Malaria, cough and cold, tuberculosis, diarrhea, etc. are the common diseases of the Sauria Paharias. Once, *kala-azar* (a type of fever) was also a very common disease. Generally, they apply their traditional medicines to be cured from these diseases and all of these medicines are prepared from different roots, tubers, barks or leaves of plants. Oil of *kujri* fruits are used with boiled egg to be cured from tuberculosis. Oil of *pusre* (kusum) is used to check blood vomiting. Dry barks of *doka* plant, mango and *lode* trees are used for curing diarrhoea. Globules made of pounded *tulsi* leaves, ginger, molasses and black pepper are taken to cure cough and cold. As they live in the area surrounded by forest they sprinkle water mixed with pounded roots of *sanjori* (drum stick) to prevent snakes to enter into their homestead. It may again be said that all these plants, roots and leaves, etc. are collected from their surrounding habitats.

3. Forests provide suitable games: The forest is also the abode of suitable games for the Saurias. Although hunting as an occupation is obsolete now-a-days, but the Sauria Paharias prefer to go to the jungle for hunting till now just as sports and past time. The young boys and middle aged persons of neighboring villages participate in this occasion. After fixation of date through a meeting a person with a twig of mango or *sal* branch announces the date in the *hatia*. The willing persons, even be Santals may also attend the expedition.

4. Forest resources supply raw materials for cottage industries : The forest provides them plants and trees from which they get raw materials for cottage industries. The Sauria collect *tiriali* for making ropes. Kudrum is also planted by them in the forest for making rope to make *bora* (gunny bag) for preservation of crops as well as to make cot. However, the Saurias have no skill to prepare *bora*. They sell the threads to the *dikku* and buy *bora* from them.

The Sauria Paharias have to depend largely on the forest product for preparation of their household materials and agricultural implements. The Mahulis collect bamboos from them and supply them ***kaithandu*** (winnowing fan) and *tokri* (basket) of different sizes. They use *ukhri* (mortar) and *manu* (pestle) for pounding their grains and those are made of some hard wood of the forest. Ukhri is generally made of the trunk of *kend* tree. Kando (wooden seat), frame of the cot, etc. are also prepared by the forest wood. Jogi and wooden part of different implements like plough, *tatrudu*, *kudtatrudu*, etc. are generally found in every house of the Saurias, prepared from forest wood.

Conservation of forest resources

Forest is the major controlling force to maintain biodiversity of a region. So, the whole world has given stress on the conservation of forest. The practice of conservation of forest resources among the Saurias are prevailing through generations. Manifestation of this has been reflected in the management process for cultivation in *khallu* land to retain the valuable trees. They do not cut any fruit bearing trees such as *mahua,* mango, custard apple, *bel*, etc. and money yielding trees like sea cotton, *sal,* etc. as well as medicinal plants like *kusum*, *mimi*(nim), etc.

Conservation of forest also has been reflected in the form of sacred groves. In Satia village, they have a sacred grove within the forest area. It is known as *jahirathan.* It generally consists of *sal* -30, *mahua* -1, *asan* -12, *murga* - 3 and a few other trees also. They do not allow cutting of a single tree from that sacred grove. Even after conversion to Christianity, they maintain its sanctity and traditional values and ethics.

The Saurias are very much conscious about the fire catching capacity of different trees. They always keep clean the grounds under *mahua*, *tatge*, *kanthare*, *jammu*, etc. in their land under *khallu*. Because, these trees are very much fire prone. Whereas, they do not clear the undergrowth of *simri* as water retaining capacity in the trunk of this tree is high, it is less prone to fire.

Their conservation system is reflected in other way also. Before clearing the jungle for *khallu* they go to the forest and select the land for *khallu* cultivation where trees have attained 1.52 to 1.83 metres height and forests have accomplished with sufficient density and growth. Old knowledgeable persons mark the valuable trees not to cut down.

Propagation

The Sauria Paharias also plant valuable trees like tamarind, *mahua*, mango, etc. in and around their *khallu* land. In one way, those trees demarcate the boundary of their *khallu* land; on the other hand these also protect the soil erosion to some extent. But the idea of protection for soil erosion by planting trees is not very much clear to them. They have been doing this to maintain their tradition only. Most of the villagers of Satia have *mahua*, mango, tamarind and sea-cotton trees around their *khallu* land. The following table (table – 8) shows an approximate estimate of ownership of some important trees in their *khallu* land.

Table 8: Ownership of some important trees

Name of trees	*No. of families*	*No. of trees*
Mahua	42	272
Mango	23	151
Sea cotton	19	350
Tamarind	14	60

It is observed from the field survey that most of the families of Satia has at least one grove of bamboo which is mainly used for the construction of their houses. Mahua and sea-cotton are used as major money fetching trees of the Saurias. Thus, it may be said that through the propagation of different trees the Saurias are trying to maintain an ecological balance in the forest cover.

Management of Water

Water plays a vital role in the land management process as a source of irrigation.

Jore (river / stream / streamlets) and *jarna* (springs) are the main natural water resources. As the Sauria Paharias are to collect their drinking water from a distant place they never waste a drop of water. They always in the habit of pour into the container the remaining water of the glass after taking it. Jore and *jarna* are their traditional source of drinking water. Previously, the water of the Kalchapre, Maskere, Kandejore and Saharjore were sources of drinking water of the Saurias of Satia. Now, two natural springs have been converted into wells and Saurias collect drinking water from those wells. However, about six years back, three tubewells were sunk by the Littipara block office for the benefit of the people. But, all of those tube wells are out of order at present. They also collect drinking water from the tube wells of the Paharia Seva Samity.

One thing is interesting that they never contaminate the water of these wells and streams used for drinking purposes. They teach their children also not to contaminate these water sources.

Now, the Sauria Paharias of Satia have learnt to use the water of rivers, streams or streamlets for irrigation through contour binding. But, this is not the indigenous art of the Saurias. It has been borrowed from the Santals.

Management through rituals, beliefs, customs and taboos:

Rituals, beliefs, customs and taboos have also some important role in the process of management of environment and natural resources of the Sauria Paharias. Living in the hilly terrains surrounded by forest they always have to fight against adverse circumstances which have created a feeling of uncertainty and insecurity. This feeling is responsible for the belief on supernatural powers or spirits of benevolent nature known as *gossaiyans* and of malevolent nature known as *marcambe*. Vidyarthi (1963:140) mentioned that the frequent occurrance of diseases and death in the hilly and forested habitats have made the Maler dependent upon supernatural and spirit world. Their abode is in the forested hills *(kuri gossaiyan),* within their village (*charka gossaiyan*), in their sacred grove (*chalnadu*), in the central pillar of their hut (*adda gossaiyan*) and in their hearth (*atto gossaiyan*).

They believe that if they do not propitiate them properly they have to face diseases, accidents, death, crop failure and various other hazards. They do ritual performances before their agricultural operation in their *khallu* land and before harvesting of crops. All the rituals are observed at village level as well as at family level and sacrifice is offered according to the instruction of *demano*. They believe that *demano*, has the shamanistic influence. So, what he will instruct that is oracle. During their festival they propitiate their ancestors at family level as well as at village level. This festival has also other role in their social management. It acts as the place of negotiation or selection of mates by the youngsters.

The Saurias of Satia have been converted to Christianity about 5 years back. They have left all those rituals after the Christianisation. But they cannot totally avoid their own traditional beliefs which have been reflected in their preservation of sacred groves through which they are indirectly maintaining the balance of bio-diversity in the natural environment. It is also reflected in the offerings of each harvested crops to their heavenly God at Church prior to consume and prayer made in the church during ailments. They still follow the customary law of *bewatorna* (in which a member from each family participates in harvesting operation of *khosre* of Pradhan) and taboos of menstrual woman to enter into the *khallu* land as it is to them a sacred place. After the assessment of the total situation it may be said that these rituals, festivals and customs have some social value. They are maintaining their solidarity and community feelings through there village level rituals, festivals and customs.

Thus, it is observed that the Saurias are controlling their environment and natural resources by applying their endegenous force i.e. their traditional wisdom. But role of some exogenous forces are also observed in this management processes. They are the Santals, the *bhagats*, the *dikus*, government and non-governmental organisations.

The Santals being the expert paddy cultivators have occupied the fertile paddy lands of the Saurias. On the contrary, the Saurias have accepted many of their methods of cultivation. With the introduction of paddy in their agricultural scenario they have included rice as one of the staple food in their diet list. Impact of the Santals is also found in their dress.

Bhagats in their society play a vital role in management process. They think that the *bhagats* are the only saviors in their distress by giving them loan easily in order to meet up their needs. But these *bhagats* are one of the causes of their poverty. They cannot even preserve their seeds for future cultivation for the retaliation of loan, because, the bhagats, virtually, snatch their produces at low price in the name of retaliation.

Besides *bhagats*, other people known to them as *dikus* are also exploiting them by collecting grains or forest wood at low price. Thus they have been exploited in every step of their life by those plain dwellers and it is very difficult for them to get rid of poverty. In this context, it may be said that the Sauria Paharias are using their forest and land resources only to meet up their immediate needs. But, these plain dwellers of the civilized world are trying to commercialise their forest resources and produces of their land alluring these poor people. As a result green coverage of the forest is thinning out leaving this forest people in uncertainty. So, it may be inferred that it is not the hunger of this tribal people but the greed of the civilized people is fully responsible for this degradation of environment. Inspite of their wisdom the hunger of the civilised world has thrown them in a precarious condition to earn their livelihood.

Role of Government and N.G.O. also may be referred here which have some impact on their management process. Government Programme of 'Indira Awas' was initiated by making 20 houses at Satia village from which they have learnt to live in the houses constituted by mudwall and tiled roof, about 16.66 percent houses have been constructed with this plan by their own effort. Government has many plan and programmes for the upliftment of the tribal society. But, all of its efforts become frustrated due to negligence and indifferent attitudes of the Government officials. Spreading of education, which has been initiated at Government level, has induced among them sense of cleanliness such as habit of bathing and washing of their clothes.

NGO, like Paharia Seva Samity is encouraging them to educate their children. They also encourage the Sauria Paharias by taking their expert opinion about herbal medicines.

The study depicts that two forces are in action in the management of environment and natural resources by the Sauria Paharias of the Rajmahal Hills. One is the endogenous force and other is the exogenous force.

Endogenous force is their traditional wisdom. In management of social environment it has been manifested and reflected in their marriage rule, marriage distance, imposition of customary law, process of interaction through market and maintenance of solidarity and community feeling through rituals, customs and other aspects. Their traditional wisdom also has been reflected in their process of cultivation in *khallu*, *bitta* and *bakri* land, in their sacred groves, preservation of valuable trees, selection of forest for cultivation, process of demarcation of boundary and their vast knowledge in herbal medicines. The exogenous forces are the Santals, bhagats, dikus, Government and non-government organizations those have brought some changes in their cultural landscape.

Lastly, it is revealed from the study that the traditional wisdom which is the endogenous force of a tribal society supported by exogenous forces plays an important role in main- taining some ecological balance through the process of preservation, conservation, manipulation and proper utilisation of the natural resources available in and around the habitat of the tribal people. In fact the traditional wisdom of the tribal world is undoubtedly very much useful to the environmentalists, sociologists as well as the anthropologists to save the world from the burning problems of environmental crisis.

References

1. Datta, Archana, 1991: Shifting Cultivation in Santal Parganas of Bihar, published in *Shifting Cultivation in India* edited by Dr. Saradindu Bose, Anthropological Survey of India, Calcutta, pp. 104-111.
2. O'Malley, L.S.S., 1910: *Santal Parganas Bengal District Gazetteers*, B.R. Publishing Corporation, Delhi.
3. Roy Choudhury, P.C., 1965: *Bihar District Gazetteers Santal Parganas*, Secretariat Press, Bihar, Patna.
4. Sherwill, Captain Walter Stanhope, 1951: Notes upon a tour through the Rajmahal Hills, *Journal of Asiatic Society of Bengal*, Vol. xx.
5. Vidyarthi, L.P., 1963: The Maler – A Study in Nature – Man - Spirit Complex of a Hill Tribe in Bihar, Book Land Pvt. Ltd., Calcutta.

5

A Study of Traditional Wisdom among the Bison Horn Maria of Bastar

Amitabha Sarkar and *Piyush Choudhury*

INTRODUCTION

The fertIlity in our country which is tropical, in looked into the forest canopy itself rather than stored in the soil as in the temperate zones. Once the forest is cleared the blazing sun and torrential rains rapidly leach and bake the land into a barren desert or scrub zone. In short, we are rapidly changing our local niche i.e. by deforesting the eye lash green belt into a sterile one (Singh, 1989).

In India different tribal people live in different eco-setting and for sustenance the immediate natural resources are utilised by them with their traditional knowledge and techniques. Since physical environment is the key factor for utilizing such resources, it is obvious that their social environment also cherished under such environment. The ecological setting is reflected in the technology, world view and the belief system of the tribes as a whole. Their economic pursuits are usually linked with the ecology, environment and the technology which allow them to adjust themselves with the situations in different interactional situations. These interactional activities have crystallised to some extent in the form of cultural traits. As these communities possess different level of cultural development, the nature of their response to their immediate niche might be different.

Forest constituting an important component of land environment is a renewable natural resource and contribute substantially to economic development. Therefore, proper management of forest ecosystem is an essential pre-requisite for sustainable development of human civilization. Thus, management of forests and Other natural resources become a new dimension to understand the great cultural heritage of our country in which about 7% population are tribal people and majority of their cultural life is imbibed and cherished under forest natural environment. It reveals from record that rate of literacy among tribals are very poor. But they possess the knowledge of their great cultural heritage through oral tradition whicn is being transmitted over generation. Since most of the tribal population of our country are living in and around forest environment and exploit it resources in search of livelihood, therefore, it is obvious that they also possess the indigenous knowledge of their niche which is otherwise known as traditional wisdom through which they not only exploit the natural resources but also conserve and preserve their bio-diversity which is again insearch of their subsistence. These two things are closely interlinked with their socio-cultural fabric of relation. The present discourse will also try to highlight about the same.

The present study is carried out among the Dandami Maria or Bison Horn Maria. The area occupied by the Bison Horn Maria lies in Bastar district of M.P. (now Chhattisgarh). It extends from the River Indravati to almost 18°N and is bounded longitudinally by 81°E and 82°E. Most of their abode is approachable by Jeep. At the moment distrièt Bastar is divided into Kankar, Danteweda and Bastar. The chief concentraction of Bison Horn Maria are Dantewada basin of Bastar district (Undivided).

Methods and Selection of Village

In order to understand the management of environment by Bison Horn Maria we have selected three locale basing on natural resources and its exploitation viz. (a) Practise of slash and burn cultivátion along with plough cultivation (b) settled cultivation and (c) wet cultivastion under the impact of mining area. Our main interest is to collect data from each eco-zone of at least 20 household censuses along with qualitative data. The duration of field work is about 54 days and data are collected with the help of an interpreter.

Record reveals that Bison-Horn Maria are mainly settled cultivators but due to pressure on land some of them have migrated to Marh area where there is abundance of forest land and whole area is unserveyed. Contextual observation reveals that Bison Horn Maria are very rough, clever and opportunist. Traditionally, the abode of Bison Horn Maria is South of Indravati river. A few among them crossed the Indravati river and pushed them towards north which is Marh area and settled there after taking formal permission of Abuj-Maria village headman and in this zone they practice slash and burn cultivation along with their neighbour. Koduli is one of such village where they practise *penda* (slash and burn cultivation. It is situated in Abujhmarh. In this village a few Abujhmaria families also live. Bison-Horn Maria are numerically dominant group in the village. There are altogether 31 families and we have covered all those in collecting household census.

In the settled cultivation based eco-zone we have selected Burumpal village under Tokapal block of Jagdalpur and about 39 km. away from District Head Quarter. The village cultivable lands are situated in undulated terrain. There are about 240 families. It is an uniethnic village distributed in seven hamlets. We collected 20 household census from this village. The unique observation is there no Mahua tree in the village. They usually purchase the same from weekly market and the fertile lands are situated in low terrain near stream while lands on upper terrain are barren and full of rocky surface.

Lastly, in the mining area eco-zone, we selected Padapur village which is very close to NMDC mining area. Bacheli (Dep. 5). is 3 km. away while Kirandul (Dep. 14) is about 10 km. away from the village. This is also uniethnic Bison Horn Maria village having 3 hamlets and there are tentatively 50 families of which we have collected 22 household census. being quantative data. Therefore, altogether we have covered 73 household of Bison Horn Maria for the present study.

Regarding data collection the investigators not only depended on household census but they collected requisite data through structured schedule, observation, case studies, and took group interview on a specific topic. Along with this technique of data collection the investigators also were depended on their legends, proverbs, songs which were tape recorded and lastly with the help of their performing arts especially dance, the investigators were able to collect their wisdom in relation to their forest environment.

Objective

The main objective in this particular study is to understand management of environment vis-a-vis their traditional wisdom in three different eco-zones and to examine the reflection of changing perspectives in a synchronic dimension.

Regional Background

Till date Bastar is one of the most forested district (i.e. undivided Bastar District) in Madhya Pradesh (now Chhattisgarh) with a forest cover estimated about 55.4 percent. The Bastar forests are of the tropical moist deciduous variety with Sal shading into teak. "Both Sal and teak have several associates (including *bija*, *saja*, *haldu*, *dhaora mahua*, *char tendu* which together constitute nearly 85%) including bamboo which today forms 20% of the forest cover". (Sundar, 1997). As per M.P. Environmental Status Report, Bhopal, 1991 per capita Forest Area in hectares available at Bastar is 9.5.

Both ecologically and culturally Bastar is part of the Dandakaranya forest. It is reported that in the Dandakaranya region there are about 72 identified dailects and several languages. Telegu influences is found in the Southern area like Konta, Marathi is mixed with Gondi in the western part while Halbi is the lingua-franca of Bastar since 17th century when Halbas of Bade Dongar (under Kondagaon teshil) recruited as Paik and soldiers of Bastar king.

According to 1991 census, the ST population at Bastar is 67%. There are small pockets of the following tribes namely, Munda, Gadaba, Saora etc towards the eastern part of Bastar but they are not the major tribal groups of Bastar. The important caste groups of Bastar are Mahara, Panka, Ganda, Kallar, Sundi, Raut, Dakad, Kumhars, Teli, Kewat, Panara, Marar, and Ghasia/Gadwa etc. It is important to mention that Maria (both Hill and plain), Muria, Dorla etc. tribal people of Bastar identify themselves as *Koitor*. The main tribal groups of Bastar are Abujh Maria, Bison-Horn Maria, Muria, Dorla, Dhurwa, Bhatra and Halba. They have their own habitation zone in the district (sketch map showing distribution of each tribal groups in the Bastar). Apart from this a sizeable immigrant are also found in Bastar. In this forest clad region-Dandakaranya, various historical eventualities have reached and these tribal people came in contact with those antequated consequences since time immemorial.

Historical Background

Various prehistoric remains excavated from Bastar prove the fact that from the prehistoric times there was human culture in Bastar. On the banks of the rivers reminicent of human culture of prehistoric times are found. Report of Bastar development plan by the State planning board opines that, "about 350 A.D. Vyaghra Dev of Nal dynasty is said to have conquered northern parts of Dandakaranya and founded his dynasty" and thus the Nal dynasty began. After Nal vans, Bastar passed through a dark era approximately for five hundred years. During this period the Chalukyas and the Ganga Kings of Orissa, some other Kings of Trikuta, Vakatakas ruled over Bastar. After that historically famous Chhindak Nagvanshi kings became the ruler of Bastar.

They are supposed to have started their reign from the middle of eleventh century. It is supported by the inscriptions, and ruined temples at Bhairamgarh, Barsur, Dantewada, and Kuruspal that in the eleventh century, a Telugu line of Nagvanshi kings reigned at Barsur in Dantewada tehsil and at Kurushpal near the Chitrakote falls of Indrawati river at Jagdalpur tehsil then known as Chakrakot (Grigson, 1991). Some 200 years ago or less there were several Zamindaris at Bastar of whom Bhopalpatnam, Sukma, Kutru, Kotapalli-Pamer still continuing through time. In Kutru again there were three or four sub-zamindars under the Zamindar. It can be told that before the kings migrated from Warangal, a nominal suzerainty of Warangal was there. Bastar was really ruled by the local chiefs or heads of the old tribal council. With the end of Nagvanshi dynasty Bastar passed through a trasitional period. It was ruled by the Chalukyas. There were several raids between 844 and 1150 by the Chalukya and Hoysala princes (*ibid*, 1991).

The first member of Kakatiya dynasty entered in Bastar and established his kingdom there was Raja Annam Deo. He was the younger brother of Raja Rudra Pratap. Actually Pratap Rudra was a member of Chalukya Vansh but adopted by Rudmma of Kakatiya dynasty and as soon as he was adopted he became one of the members sof the Kakatiya Vansh and then he became the King. Grigson has mentioned that Annam Deo established his kingdom in Mudhota and Raipur in 1424. Raja Annam Deo ruled for 45 years and after his death the thorne was succeeded by Hamir Deo followed by Bhairam Deo. After Bhairam Deo Raja Purushattam Deo became the king of Bastar. He shifted his kingdom in Bastar. He visited Lord Jagannatha at Puri of Orissa on foot. Seeing his devotion Lord Jagannatha became very pleased with him and as per the order of the deity he was offered a Chariot, He was the first king of Bastar started the festival of Goncha at Bastar. After him the fifth Kakatiya king was Jaisingh. Then Narayan Singh Dev ruled and succeeded by Raja Pratap Raj Deo. Raja Pratap Deo was succeeded by Jagdish Deo. Next serially it was ruled by king was Vir Narayan Deo, Bir Singh Deo, Digpal Deo, Rajpal Sing Deo, Raja Dalpat Deo. Raja Dalpat Deo shifted his capital to Jagdalpur. After him Daviya Deo became the king. He was succeeded by his son Mahipal Deo. Raja Bhupal Deo succeeded him and nextly he was succeeded by Raja Bhairam Deo. During his reign in 1854 direct political relations with the British Government of India was started. He was succeeded by his son Rudra Pratap Deo. Rudra Pratap Deo was succeeded by his daughter Prafulla Kumani Devi in 1921. During her reign the hereditary title Raja became Maharaja in 1932. After her death his son Maharaja Pravir Chandra Bhanj Deo became the ruler. He was the last Kakatiya King at Bastar before independence. During the Kakatiya dynasty the present day Bastar was divided into two feudatory states named bastar and Kanker. Among these two the Bastar state had five tehsils namely Narayanpur, Kondagaon, Jagdalpur, Bijapur and Konta and four zamindanis namely Kutru, Bhopalpatnam, Pamed and Sukma for the necessity of the administration. The Kanker state had only two tehsils.

The Kakatiya Kings mainly dealt with the administration of Bastar. They had an assistant called Dewan. In the tehsil level there were the Teheshildars and Managers.

In 1948 these two feudatory states that is Bastar and Kanker are brought under the state of Madhya Pradesh.

IMMEDIATE ENVIRONMENT AND TERRESTRIAL SET UP

The greater part of Bastar District is a plateau, about 600 m. high, leaving a narrow lowland margin on the north and south. The plateau continues eastwards to Jeypore in Orissa State. The Indrawati river bisects the district into almost two equal halfs

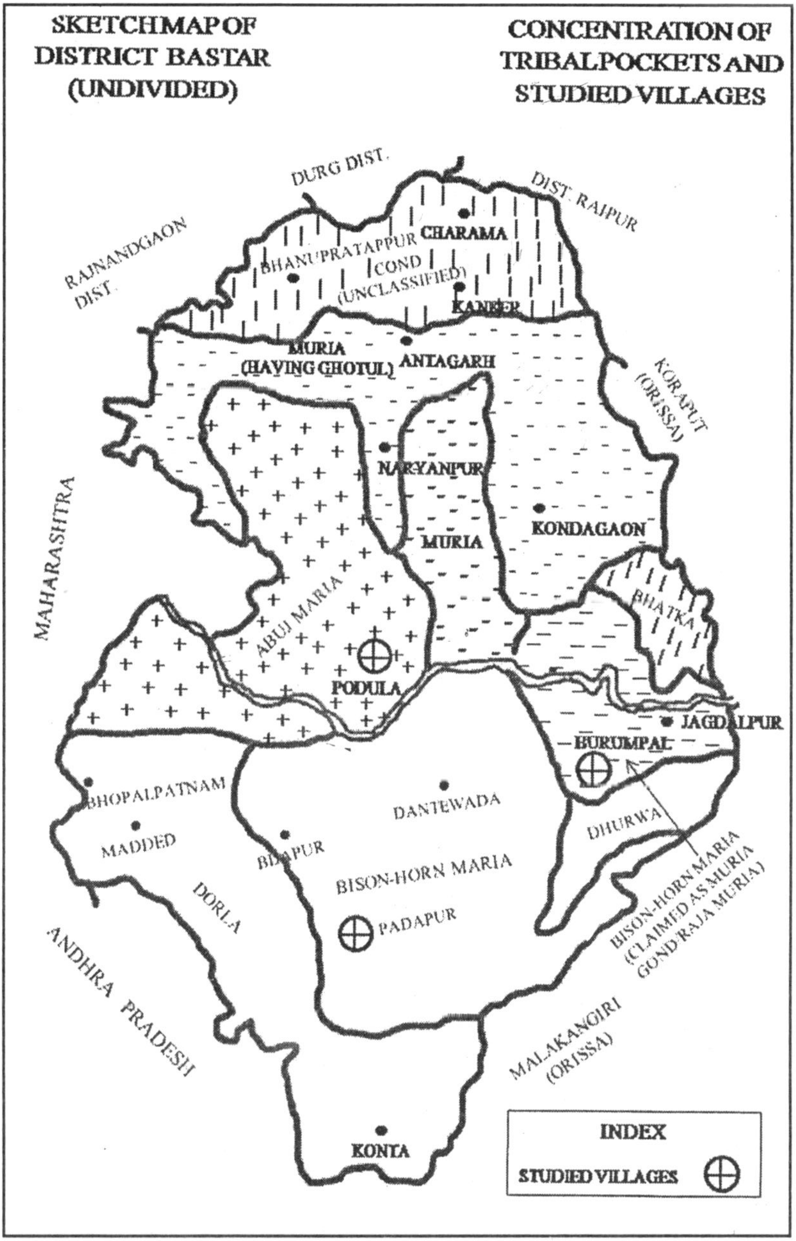
SKETCHMAP OF
DISTRICT BASTAR
(UNDIVIDED)
CONCENTRATION OF
TRIBALPOCKETS AND
STUDIED VILLAGES
DURG DIST.
DIST. RAIPUR
RAJNANDGAON
DIST.
CHARAMA
BHANUPRATAPPUR
COND
(UNCLASSIFIED)
KANKER
MURIA
(HAVING GHOTUL)
ANTAGARH
KORAPUT
(ORISSA)
NARYANPUR
MAHARASHTRA
KONDAGAON
MURIA
ABUJ MARIA
BHATKA
PODULA
JAGDALPUR
BURUMPAL
BHOPALPATNAM
DANTEWADA
MADDED
DHURWA
BIJAPUR
BISON-HORN MARIA
DORLA
PADAPUR
BISON-HORN MARIA
(CLAIMED AS MURIA
GOND/RAJA MURIA)
ANDHRA PRADESH
MALAKANGIRI
(ORISSA)
KONTA
INDEX
STUDIED VILLAGES

and the Sabri river which flows along the South-eastern boundary, bring this district in the Godavari basin.

Physiographically the district can be divided into the six divisions, viz.,

1. Northern lowland - The Kotri-Mahanadi plain stretches from the northern boundary of the district for about 25 Km. covering most of the parts of Kankar, and Bhanupratappur tehsils and the northern part of Narayanpur Teshil
2. Keshkal Scrapment - South of northern lowland the land rises steeply for abàut 150 m to 300 m along the Paralkote. Pratappur - Koelibeda - Antagarh - Kanker line.
3. Abulhmar Hills - The land surface along the Paralkote-Keshkal-Kutru is maintained at a height of 600 to 750 m throughout the central part of the district except that in western part it is so dissected as to possess a local relief of 150 to 300 m. giving it a hill form, knows as Abujhmarh hills, in the Southern part of Narayanpur teshil and the northern margin of the Bijapur tehsil.
4. North eastern Plateau - The North eastern plateau lies east of the Abujhmarh hills and extends upto the eastern boundary of the district. It is the Bastar highland.
5. Southern Plateau - A slightly lower plateau region of about 300 to 600 m. elevation extends to the Southwest of the North-eastern plateau, covering Dantewada teshil and the northern parts of Bijapur and Konta teshils. The Southern plateau starting from the Tangri Dongri hills on the east continues to the Indrawati River on the west and to the north.

   The Bailadilla hills, a double ridged range running north-south along the western boundary of the Dantewada teshil and attaining about 1100 m. elevation are the expression of the folded and highly elevated Dharwar formations.
6. Southern lowland - The Sukma lowland with a surface height of 150 to 300 m. continues as a wide strip of roughly 25 km. Along the district boundary to Konta and thereafter crossing the moderately high Golapalli hills, there is lowland stretching northwards to Bhopalpatnam. The Godavari - Sabri lowland extends from the Southern boundary of the district to the base of the Southern plateau. The descent from the Jagdalpur plateau to it, marked by the Darbha

Ghati is very steep.

Lithology

The mass of earth's crust in the District is formed of various old rocks belonging to the pre-cambrian and cambrian era and this can be classified as

(a) The Dharwar,

(b) The Archean granites and Gneisses

(c) The older trap

(d) The Cuddapaha

(e) The Vindhyans

It is reported that in Bastar District Dharwar rocks found in (a) Bailadilla hills on the Western Boundary of the Dantewade teshil. The Bailadilla series belonging to the upper Dharwar age, correspond with the iron ore series of Singhbhum of Bihar. They comprise haematite - quartzite, iron-ores, haematite - chlorite and haematite garnierite rocks, ferruginous conglomerates and white quartzite. (b) The Raoghat hills on the northern margin of the Abujhmarh hills, between Antagarh and Naryanpur in the Narayanpur teshil and (c) Chain of hills running from the midst of Pratappur and Koelibeda in Narayanpur teshil, northwards to Bhanupratappur teshil. And about three-fourth of the area'of the district is covered by Archean granites and gneisses. Studied village under Tokapal block is under this category of rock formation.

Soil

Laterites and lateritic soils cover a large area of Bastar district. In Abujhmar tract where the trap rocks occur the slopes have thin, light soils rather than the deep black cotton soils, whereas fresh alluvial soils are found in the beds of rivers and streams. The texture of the soil varies from Sandy to fine textured clayey soils. The fine quality of Sal is found in the valleys of Secondary lateritic deposit. The lateritic soils are the result of high humidity and tropical conditions. Hydrogen ion concentration (pH) of the soil is less than seven and therefore the soils are acidic.

Climate

Bastar district can be divided into three regions based on climatic condition viz. (i) Humid, (ii) Moist-Subhumid and (iii) Dry-Subhumid. The climate ingeneral is of monsoon type.

(a) **Temparature** - The climate of northern parts of the district is comparatively warmer than the central region of Jagdalpur. Temparature during the months of April to September remains higher from December to February are cooler.

(b) **Rainfall** - The monsoon sets in the month of June and continues upto September-October. Occurrence of rainfall during the monsoon season is due to the South-West monsoon winds The incidence of rainfall is different in the various parts of the district due to physiographic conditions. The Matalghat - Abujhmar - Baladilla-Golapali hills running north-south, through the middle of the district. Average rainfall varies between 1000 mm and 1500 mm in different region.

(c) **Humidity** - Relative humidity remains higher during rainy season followed by winters. Summers are marked with minimum relative humidity.

Eco-Climate

The eco-climate of the district is estimated on the basis of monthly rainfall data and mean monthly temperature. The district Bastar can be classified eco-climatically in three regions viz.

(i) Humid - The Southern plateau - West of Bailadilla and Tikanpalli Hills, mostly constituted of Bijapur Teshil. Usur hills lies South-West of the region.

(ii) Moist-Sub Humid - Abujhmar hills, north-western parts of Kotri-Mahanadi plain, eastern parts of Southern Plateau covering Dantewada plains, right upto Sukma and Southern parts of N.E. Plateau covering Indrawati plains of Jagdalpur region constitute this zone. Most of the area under Bhanupratappur, Naryanpur, Dantewada and Jagdalpur teshil comes under it.

(iii) Dry-Sub Humid - Eastern parts of Kotri - Mahanadi plain constituted of Kanker teshil, northern parts of N.E. plateau covering Kondagaon teshil and very small region South of Golapalli hills situated in Konta teshil forming this zone.

The Drainage

The drainage condition of the district is very well owing to its physiographic conditions. Most of the rivers are perennial. The chief rivers are Indrawati, Sabri, and Godavari. The drainage system of Bastar divides it into two unequal parts viz. (a) the

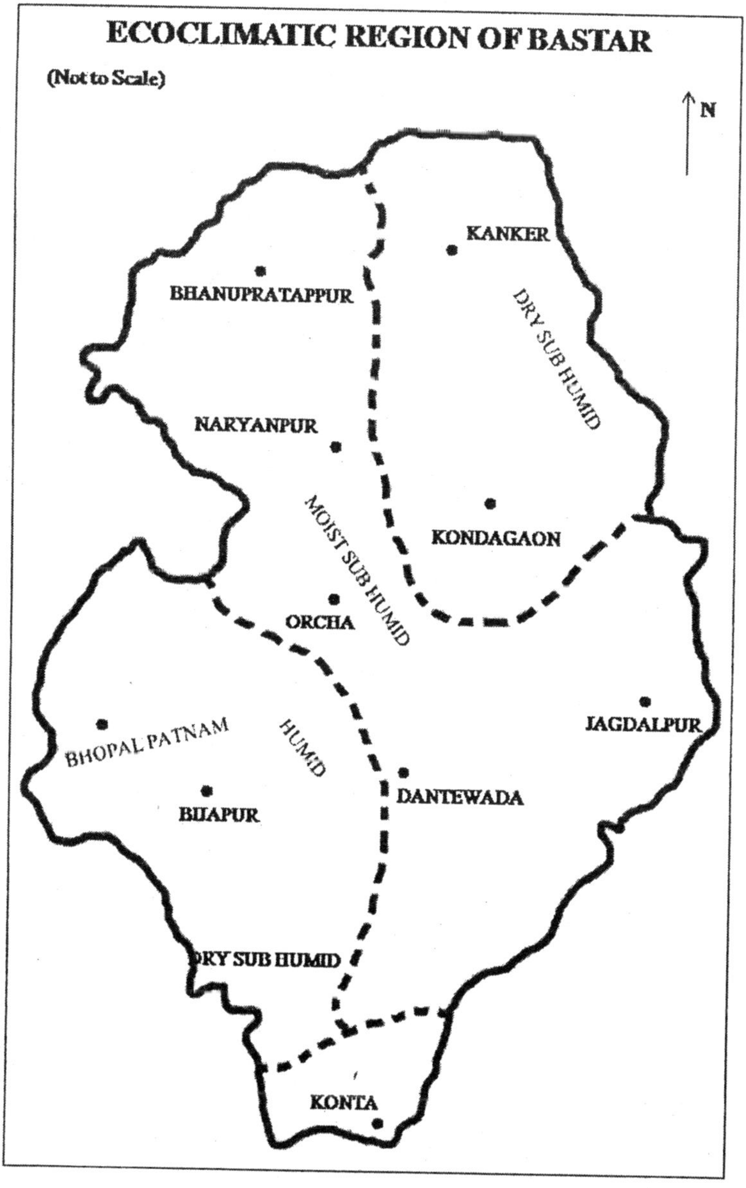

Source: Meteriologicval Office, Jagdalpur, Bastar, MP.

Godavari basin and (b) the Mahandi basin. Telinghati hills form the main watershed between them.

Flora

Tropical dry deciduous to moist deciduous types of forest found in this region. An interesting overlap of the Southern and northern forms of the tropical dry deciduous forest characterised by teak and Sal, respectively, occurs in Bastar division. The natural regeneration is fair but slow except under shade. The characteristic associates are *dhawra* (Anogeissus latifolia), Saja (Terminalia alata), bija (Pterocarpus marsupium), Karam (Mitragyna parviflora), bamboo (Dendrocalamus strictus), gardena, (Boswellia serrata), tendu (Diospyros melanoxylon), char (Buchnania lanzean), Kulu (Sterculia), amtar (Bauhinia). Among shrubs Woodfordia, Indigofera and Carissa Spinarum are abundant. Heteropopan contortus and Sabai (Eulalipsis binata) are the characteristic grasses. Terminalta arjuna (Arjun) and Morus albal (Mulberry) plantations are also found.

Fauna

Bastar region is rich in fauna especially wild animals like Tiger, Panther, Sloth bear, Gaur (Indian Bison), Swamp deer, Spotted deer (Sambhar and Chital), Nil-gai (Blue bull), Barking deer, Mouse deer and Wild Boar are common. Wild buffalo (Bubulus bubalis) is often found in two or three pockets of Bhairamgarh-Hingun-Jegur... Mingachal-Matewara tract, west of Kutru and Talperu-Chintavagu basin adjoining the Andhra. Indrawati National Park is declared as Protection of wild life Sancturies which is situated in the South of Abujhmar hills and on the bank of Indrawati river and under Bijapur tehsil, where special care is taken to wild Buffalo being endangered species and tiger. Apart from this, various kinds of birds are also found but their number is very few in comparison to the vast tract of forest due to hunting propensity prevails among the tribal people who roam in the forest either with *gulel* or *tir-dhanush*.

Terrestrial Set up

Keeping in mind the objective of project the investigators have selected three locale considering its available local resources which are being exploited by the Bison-Horn Maria. Practically speaking they are settled cultivators and as such they are highly aware of the technology of wet cultivation.

(a) Penda or Slash and Burn Cultivator-Bison-Horn Maria at Koduli

The village Koduli is a forest village situated in Orcha block of Naryanpur teshil of Bastar district. There is one fair weather Jeepable road.On its north hills and forest, Chotetondabeda village in the east, Japgunda and Duseli in the South while Bada Tondabeda in the west and orcha at North-west. The village is having one Primary Ashram School, devoid of electricity. In this village a few Abujh Maria families also live; infact Sarpanch is from Abujh Maria and with his due permission Bison Horn Maria community who migrated from Lohandiguda area of Jagdalpur are settled here and practise penda cultivation. During the period of investigation it is found that Bison-Horn Maria in this village are the dominant group. There are altogether 31 families while 5 families are Abujh Maria. Only due to the prassence of Abujh Maria the village has Ghotul and interestingly it is found that Bison-Horn Maria are also coming and attending all function at Ghotul, though Ghotul system is absent among them. For drinking water they till depend on rivulet- Marin, perennial source of water and tubewell. There is one Anganbari in the village. The instructar of Anganbari has also arranged night school in the village for adults. The surrounding of the village is full of forest and wild life. Many among this tribe are often engaged in this deep forest for installing trap through which their hunting expedition is going on.

It is noted that the co-relation between the house type of these people and the forest based environment is conspicuous here. The village is dispersed type . The huts of the Bison Horn Maria in the village are scattered and each hut is having with bari land. Their *penda* lands are situated outside the village. The village possesses *tallur* (sacred groves) where female are tabooed to enter. The trees at *tallur* are treated as sacred and these are tabooed to cut or destroy. In each and every tallur there is at least one sacred tree-Aden, which is very popular and- hence it is never destroyed by them. They attend weekly market at Orcha on wednesday where they sale and exchange their minor forest products and engage themselves with alcohol (Sulphi or Mahua) and gambling by arranging cock fighting.

The houses of these people are having some compartments viz, *wija-lon* (place for seed grain cereals and dried fruit like Mahua-a kind of storing place, situated in the rear), the *narma – lon* – it is in the middle and used as bedroom, it is made first and front room, and having a verandah or *oser* is added with slightly lower height with a slope, so that one have to enter in the room in a stooping posture. The material used in making the houses are bamboo, split bamboo, sal log, and thatched with either Sadka or Sabai grass or leaves of dwarf palms/*chind* grass or khaddar (Phoenix sylvestris and Phoenix farinifera). These are available in plenty in the forest. The walls are made of mud or bamboo splits. The doors are usually pieces of bamboo wicker-work sliding between pairs of vertical posts but sometimes the sections of wicker work are hinged on to a door post by knotted pieces of split bamboo. The typical sketch of their house is given below

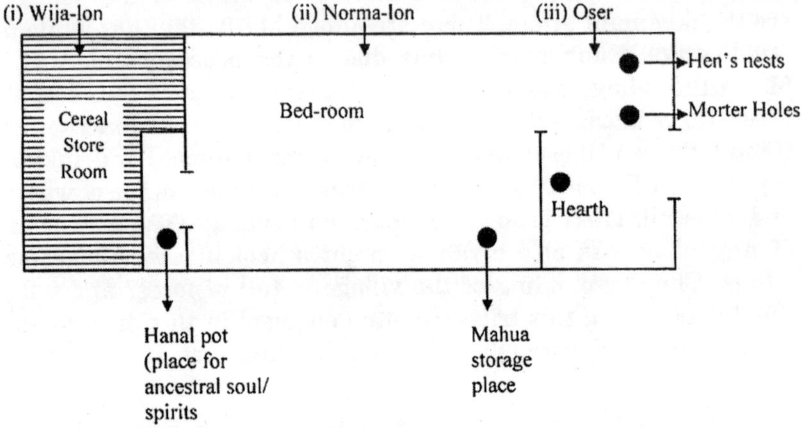

(b) Burumpal - Bison Horn Maria practise Wet Cultivation in Plain area

It has already been mentioned earlier that village concerned is situated 39 Km. away from Jagdalpur town under Tokapal block. As per record the total area of the village is 1129.24 hectres of which forest area is 69.92 hectres, cultivable waste land including *gauchar* and groves is 324.88 hectres and area available for cultivation is 19.45 hectres. It is reported that the studied village is under Chitapur Pargana.

The approach road of the village is through *metta* (chatan) type of land and slightly at the lower region the village is formed. The houses are clustered in various *paras* viz, *Sandhi para*, *Koton para*, *Lohar para*, *Sarpanch para*, *Pujari para*, *Patel para* and *Nanga para*. The village is completely uni ethnic and is exclusively inhabited by the Bison-Horn Maria. In each para there is one place of *pen-rahwar* or devigudi (a place of their deity) were there are small clusters of trees signifying the sacred place of their deities. A sacred value is always attached with this site and the trees here are tabooed to cut/destroy. There are about 240 households. The village cultivable lands are in undulated terrain. There is one Ashram School upto Vth standard, having an angan bari. A few houses here are also found to have electricity and gobar gas plant. They fetch their drinking water from the tubewell. A few co-coanut trees are also found. The idea of cocoanut plantation, electric facility and gobar gas plant installation were brought by Prof. B.D. Sharma who himself also lives in the village occasionally and there is one house for him at Pujari para. The place for *deogudi* (village deity) is in the east, the place for *moth* or *urskal* (memorial pillar) is in west. The village cultivable lands are situated in various undulating terrains. The cultivable lands near the low terrain having a natural irrigation facility due to pressence of prennial source of *nala.* Some among them also use this water for drinking purpose. The lands close this water source are *munda jamin* and produce both kharif as well as rabi crop. It is also reported that clan wise area have been demarcated for cremation and for child they bury the dead. The most striking observation is that there is big and old trees in the village and not a single Mahua tree is found. They borrow the mahua from market since *eiru* (liquor made of mahua) is favorite drink among them. In addition to *eiru* the other drink is *gorgha* (Sulphi), it is available in nature from Sulphi tree.

The houses of this village are of red soil or *lal tori* and thatched with either *khapra* (made of local clay) or rock slab (Potorlikal chatang) which are available from neighbouring area like Raikot, Dornapal villages. Along with these they use Sal balli, bamboo, bamboo splits. The bamboos are usually procured from their homestead land and the Sal logs are collected from the neighbouring forest area.

In the Pujari para and Lohar para the homestead lands are almost barren due to the influenced of stratified rock slabs. Regarding the internal arrangement of hut it is more or less same as observed in Koduli - a forest village.

(c) Padapur - A Village in NMDC Mining Area

The Bailadila project of NMDC ia located in Dantewada Teshil of Bastar. Bailadila derives the name from shape of the Hills. Literally, the word 'Bailadila' means the hump of an Ox.

It is a range of fourteen iron ore Hills. This hill range is situated in Dantewada teshil and 75% population here are tribals. Nearly 71% of the total geographical area of teshil is avilable for cultivation. The Bailadila project was assigned to NMDC in pursuance of an agreement between Government of India and Japan in March, 1960, for the supply of 4 million tonnes of iron ore to commence from 1966, for a period of 15 years initially. The Bailadila project had significant impact on the economy of hinterland tribal villages to the project area. The villages in and around the project area are the abode of Bison-Horn Maria tribal people. Their traditional subsitence economy seen to be influenced by their socio-cultural life. Their world view, income level as well as expenditure level become higher incomparison to their traditional villages which are away from the project area. Their needs are changing and materialistic attitude is observed. Under this circumstances Padapur village is studied by us with an expectation that their traditional wisdom in relation with their subsistence pattern may be affected due to the impact of industrialisation in this remote forest clad tribal pocket of Bastar.

The village Padapur is a mining area village. It is about 130 Km away from Jagdalpur town under Dantawada teshil towards south-west (Presently Dantewada is a separate district). The impact of mining industrial environment is marked. It is 3 km away from Bachaeli and 10 Km off from Kirandul iron ore mining plant of NMDC of Bastar. The record reveals that the total area of village is 252.56 hectares of which forest area is 15.56 hectares, cultivable waste land including *gauchar* and groves is 55.85 hectares and area not available for cultivation is 13.81 hectares. As per 1981 census there were 42 households with a total population 252. During field investigation it is reported that there are 50 households with three paras viz. Badepara or Patel Para, Sarpanch and Thota para. It is also an uni-ethnic Bison Horn Maria village.

The village is electrified, having an anganbari centre and having 51 students of which 30 are male child and 21 are female child and a school upto 7th standard. In one house (ex-Sarpanch) we observed T.V. facility. In the village some are engaged in plant (of NMDC) being unskilled worker. A few villagers are engaged in *Ghuti-Khadan* (of tin); they collect tin ore from Ghunti Khadan and sale these to State Mining camp office, infront of the School, at the rate of Rs. 80 per kg. Since the village is at the proximity of modern urban environment it is observed their dress and attire has changed, many among them having wrist watch, Transister, casseette tape recorder. Their way of life has greatly been influenced in this sort of contactive environment. Moreover, their subsistence economy has changed to full blown commercial economy. They are inclined towards more cash earning, one of the respondent was tea-garden worker at North-east, but now he is in tho village and is working in the Mining office. This we mentioned only in the background of their changing perspective of world view due to exposure of outside their natal place. Most striking observation is that there is enoromous number of Mahua trees, tamarind trees and a considerable number of Sulphi trees. They have high addiction to liquor and *eiru* is prepared in the village especially just before market day at Bachali on Tuesday where they sale it and earn some cash. The distillers are only one or two in the village.

There is one *utul* or *thanagudi* at Thotapara. It is a resting place for outsiders. Most interestingly it is found that in the record the whole village having only 18 *pattas* in different family heads of the village. In each *patta* there is vast stretch of land which is again given to their *akomama/saga* and *dadabhai* kins. In this way village land is distributed among their *dadabhai* and *akomama* groups. As per oral tradition the first settlers in the village was Elami and who bought their akomama i.e. Kunjami. Then Elami *bas* (clan) bought his *dadabhai* Marvi and Emla groups and in this way land was distributed. But in Govt. record there is no change in *patta's*. The Padapur village Panchyat consists of following neighbouring villages viz., Bade Bacheli, Bengpal, Benur, and Padapur. The Sarpanch of this panchyat is a woman of Bison-Horn Maria lives in the village while upa-sarpanch is also from this village, a Bison-Horn Maria candidate. Of the total five panch members all are living in this village, Kotwar lives in Pina Bacheli. It has been observed that impact of urbanization and politicisation in the village is marked. The *tallin* (sacred grove) is situated in the west under big shady trees. In fact this small patch of forest being sacred in their value system which is preserved with great care.

The houses in the village are thatched with khapra. They use bamboo splits also and walls are of laterite soil. But few (incidentally they are NMDC worker and earn cash in considerable amount) procure stone powder from Bhansi-quarry crushing plant of NMDC, use it in their houses after mixing it with cement and prepared bricks out of it. These bricks are used it in their walls while roof is thatched with khapra (prepared from local clay and burnt it). During Khapra preparation they ask the help from *dadabhai* group and in lieu of their service they are served with food and drink. In this way they exchange labour when needed.

Now in the following lines we shall try to depict the demographic aspects of the studied sample' from three eco-zone.

It reveals from Table 1 of three studied villages in three different eco-setting that sex-ratio Koduli, Burumpal and Padapur villages are 102.6, 103.8, 81.36 per 100 females respectively. 1981 census reveals that sex-ratio of the district was 1003 females per 1000 males.

Table 1: Age group wise Distribution of Three Studied Villages Eco-zone Village

Age Group	*Koduli*		*Burumpal*		*Padapur*	
	Male	*Female*	*Male*	*Female*	*Male*	*Female*
0-5	14	12	1	7	5	8
6-10	13	13	8/	8	7	12
11-15	8	5	9	3	8	6
16-20	8	8	6	4	1	2
21-25	4	5	6	6	2	6
26-30	5	5	5	5	7	7
31-35	7	7	5	6	6	5
36-40	10	7	2	5	6	3
41-45	-	-	3	1	2	-
46-50	3	5	4	6	1	2
51-55	1	2	3	2	-	2
56-60	3	4	3	-	2	1
61+	4	5	-	-	1	4
Total	**80**	**78**	**55**	**53**	**48**	**59**

Table 2 (a): Age-group wise Level of Literacy in Three Studied Villages of Bison-Horn Maria

(a) Village: Koduli

Age-group	*Illiterate*		*Upto Secondary level including Anganbari*		*Above Secondary to Higher Secondary*		*College level / Technical*	
	M	*F*	*M*	*F*	*M*	*F*	*M*	*F*
0-5	12	8	2	4	-	-		-
6-10	2	3	11	10	-	-	-	-
11-15	5	2	3	2	-	-	-	-
16-20	7	8	-	-	-	-	-	-
21-25	4	5	-	-	-	-	-	-
26-30	5	5	-	-	-	-	-	-
31-35	7	7	-	-	-	-	-	-
36-40	10	7	-	-	-	-	-	-
41-45	-	-	-	-	-	-	-	-
46-50	3	5	-	-	-	-	-	-
51-55	1	2	-	-	-	-	-	-
56-60	3	4	-	-	-	-	-	-
61+	4	5	-	-	-	-	-	-
Total	**63**	**61**	**17**	**17**	**-**	**-**	**-**	**-**
	(39.88)	**(38.6)**	**(10.76)**	**(10.76)**				

Table 2 (b): Age-group wise Level of Literacy in Three Studied Villages of Bison-Horn Maria

(a) Village: Burumpal

Age-group	*Illiterate*		*Upto Secondary level including Anganbari*		*Above Secondary to Higher Secondary*		*College level / Technical*	
	M	*F*	*M*	*F*	*M*	*F*	*M*	*F*
0-5	1	6	-	1	-	-	-	-
6-10	4	4	4	4	-	-	-	-
11-15	1	0	8	3	-	-	-	-
16-20	1	2	5	2	-	-	-	-
21-25	4	5	2	1	-	-	-	-
26-30	2	5	3	0	-	-	-	-
31-35	4	6	1	0	-	-	-	-
36-40	1	5	-	-	-	-	1	0
41-45	2	1	1	-	-	-	-	-
46-50	3	6	1	-	-	-	-	-
51-55	3	2	-	-	-	-	-	-
56-60	2	0	1	-	-	-	-	-
61+	-	2	-	-	-	-	-	-
Total	**28**	**42**	**26**	**17**	**-**	**-**	**1**	**-**
	(25.92)	**(38.89)**	**(24.07)**	**(10.19)**			**(0.93)**	

Table-2 (c): Age-group wise Level of Literacy in Three Studied Villages of Bison-Horn Maria

(a) Village: Padapur

Age-group	*Illiterate*		*Upto Secondary level including Anganbari*		*Above Secondary to Higher Secondary*		*College level / Technical*	
	M	F	M	F	M	F	M	F
0-5	2	7	3	1	-	-	-	-
6-10	3	4	4	8	-	-	-	-
11-15	4	3	4	3	-	-	-	-
16-20	1	3	-	-	-	-	-	-
21-25	1	6	1	-	-	-	-	-
26-30	7	7	-	-	-	-	-	-
31-35	6	5	-	-	-	-	-	-
36-40	6	3	-	-	-	-	-	-
41-45	2	0	-	-	-	-	-	-
46-50	0	2	1	-	-	-	-	-
51-55	0	2	-	-	-	-	-	-
56-60	2	1	-	-	-	-	-	-
61+	1	4	-	-	-	-	-	-
Total	**35**	**47**	**13**	**12**	-	-	-	-
	(32.71)	**(43.93)**	**(12.15)**	**(11.21)**				

The contextual data reveals from Table 2(a), (b) and (c) that of the total population in Koduli village their rate of literacy is 21.52 percent while illiterate are 78.48 percent. In Burumpal village it reveals from Table 2(b) that of the total household under census, there are altogether 64.81 percent are illiterate and only 35.11 percent are literate. While in Padapur village the literacy rate is 23.36 percent only. Data also reveals that their level of literacy in most of the cases is limited to secondary level which also includes Angan Bari facility in the village. As a whole the literacy level in the district is poor. According to 1981 census 14.13 percent are only literate.

Family

Table 3: Structure of Family in Three Studied Villages of Bison-Horn Maria

Family Type	*Villages*		
	Koduli	*Burumpal*	*Padapur*
1. Nuclear with or without dependent	19 (45%)	9 (77.27%)	17 (61.29%)
2. Horizontally Extended	2 (6.45%)	2 (10%)	2 (9.095)
3. Vertically Extended	3 (9.67%)	5 (25%)	1 (4.55%)
4. Incomplete with or without or without dependent	4 (12.9%)	4 (20%)	2 (9.09%)
5. Broken	3 (9.67%)	0	0

Table 4: Size of Family in Three Studied Villages of Bison-Horn Maria

No. of individual in family		*No. of family*		
		Koduli	*Burumpal*	*Padapur*
Small size	One	0	0	-
	Two	4	2	1
	Three	5	3	4
	Four	1	3	3
Medium size	Five	7	5	9
	Six	8	1	3
	Seven	2	2	1
	Eight	2	1	-
Large size	Nine	2	2	-
	Ten	-	-	-
	Eleven	-	-	1
	Twelve	-	1	-
Total		**31**	**20**	**22**
Average family size		**5.09**	**5.4**	**4.81**

It reveals from above tables that prevalence of nuclear family in Koduli, Burumpal and Padapur are 61.29%, 45%, and 77.27%

Table-5: Age-group wise Marital Status in Three Studied Villages of Bison-Horn Maria

Age	*Village*	*Unm-arried*		*Married*		*Widow / Widower*		*Divorce / Separated*	
		M	*F*	*M*	*F*	*M*	*F*	*M*	*F*
0-5	Koduli	14	12						
	Burumpal	1	7						
	Padapur	5	8						
6-10	Koduli	13	13						
	Burumpal	8	8						
	Padapur	7	12						
11-15	Koduli	8	5						
	Burumpal	9	3						
	Padapur	8	6						
16-20	Koduli	5	5	3	3				
	Burumpal	5	2	1	1				
	Padapur	1	1	-	2				
21-25	Koduli	2	1	2	4				
	Burumpal	3	1	3	5				
	Padapur	1	0	1	6				
26-30	Koduli	-	-	5	5				
	Burumpal	-	-	4	5	1			
	Padapur	-	-	7	1				
31-35	Koduli	-	-	7	7				
	Burumpal	-	-	5	6				
	Padapur	1	0	5	5				
36-40	Koduli	-	-	2	5				
	Burumpal	-	-	6	3				
	Padapur	-	-	-	-				

(contd...)

Age	Village	Unm-arried		Married		Widow / Widower		Divorce / Separated	
		M	F	M	F	M	F	M	F
41-45	Koduli	-	-	3	1				
	Burumpal	-	-	2	0				
	Padapur	-	-	3	5				
46-50	Koduli	-	-	3	5				
	Burumpal	-	-	4	5	-	1		
	Padapur	-	-	1	1	-	1		
51-55	Koduli	-	-	1	1	-	-		
	Burumpal	-	-	-	3	-	2		
	Padapur	-	-	-	1	-	1		
56-60	Koduli	-	-	3	0	-	-		
	Burumpal		-	-	2	1	-	-	
	Padapur	-	-	3	0	-	-		
61+	Koduli	-	-	4	4	-	1		
	Burumpal	-	-	-	-	-	-		
	Padapur		-	1	0	-	4		
Total	Koduli	42	36	36	2	6			
	Burumpal	26	21	28	31	1	1		
	Padapur	23	27	25	26	-	6		

respectively. It is evident from the data that in forest environment based village like Koduli where resources are plenty but to exploit such resources technology and labour or man power are essential, moreover in this adverse geographical terrain the Bison-Horn Maria are migrant therefore due to such social and environmental constraint they are more intended to maintain nuclear family, while in Burumpal village which is located in plain area there nuclear family is 45% while extended family is 35%. In Padapur village where industrial impact is noticed in their way of life there are about 77% nuclear family and average family size also vary in three different eco-zone like in Koduli it is 5.09 while it is higher in Burumpal - 5.4, but very less at mining situation in Padapur village - 4.81. In both the villages of Burumpal and Padapur the are settled cultivator and they have more security in their economic life in comparison to penda cultivators of Koduli village. Data also reveal that the influence of terrestrial set up is highly markei in their way of life.

Marital Status

It has been observed from studied group that they practice polygamous system which is more prevalent in Burumpal and Padapur villages where Bison-Horn Maria have secured economic life due to the practise of settled cultivation. Usually their marriages performed within age group 20-22. The bulk of their work force are within the age- group from 16-59 and most of them are married. Not a single case is recorded as divorce or separated which is also prevalent among them as per their customary rule. The contextual data, that is through Household Survey Schedule it appears that marriage distance in Koduli is varied from 3 to 35 km. (due to non availability of *akomama* the village endogamy is not possible). Infact the Bison-Horn Maria in this Koduli village are immigrant from Lohandiguda area or Geedam area which are south of Indrawati river and this place is their traditional abode. Due to shortage of cultivable land which is one of the chief factor for sustenance the Bison Horn Maria are pulled towards Abujh Maria habitat where abundance of land and forest are easily available. In case of Burumpal and Padapur villages where communication facility is available, the marriage distance in both the villages are maximum 60 km. From the studied respondent it can be said that topographical constraint is not a factor of Bison-Horn Maria due to their existence for survival, tenacity and perseverance towards the envoronmental control by means of adaptation. They possess a good technology in comparison with their neighbour - Abujh Maria at Koduli, who are *penda* cultivators.

Bison-Horn Maria

Marias of Bastar may be categorised into two viz., Hill Maria or Abujh Maria and Bison-Horn Maria or Dandami Maria. The former name originates from the habitat which are the high hills of Abujh Maria region and later on account of horned head gear during dancing. The names were given by Grigson.

The Bison Horn Maria of the open plain tracts have given up their shyness owing to outside exposure and communication facilities in their habitat. They are advanced and sophisticated in their way of life in comparison to Hill-Maria. The cultural differentiation is also found due to wide dispersal over a large part of the district. They are just taking wet cultivation though *penda* cultivation is still observed in some packets of the district. Their technology in agricultural activities are developed in comparison to Hill Maria. Infact, Bison-Horn Maria living with non-tribal or in areas with easy communication facilities to accept settled cultivation. There are pargana headman - Majhi, in the areas of Bison Horn Maria habitat, who possess wide influence and authority. In the traditional set up they had to deal with villages of many different clans and for larger number of village In fact in Bastar every tribe has a system of village panchyat and a higher authority for the clan or community depending upon the areas to be controlled.

NATURAL RESOURCES : MANAGEMENT AND UTILIZATION

Now, let us clarify the meaning and significance of natural resources. Since the tribal group like Bison- Horn Maria are nourished in the lap of forest environment and simultaneously they are wet cultivators in the plain area, while *penda* (slash and burn) cultivators are seen in the area where forest is abundant and in other eco-zone they have come in contact with mining industry. In the mentioned three eco-zone of Bison-Horn Maria settlement their primary natural resources are forest, land, water and solar energy. It is therefore essential if we primarily depict a picture of their gainful economic involvement/activities for maintaining their livelihood in three different studied area.

Table 6: Involvement in Economic Pursuits at Koduli (Below 5 yrs are not in the Table)

Sl. No.	*Nature of Economic Activities*	*Male*	*Female*	*Total*
1	Penda Cultivation (M) and Hunting(S)/ Wage labour (S)	44 (27.84%)	-	44 (27.84%)
2	Household work and collection (M) and Penda cultivation (S)/Wage labour (S)	-	42 (26.58%)	42 (26.58%)
3	Cattle Herding	4 (2.53%)	4 (2.53%)	8 (5.06%)
4	Student (M) and Cattle herding (S)	1 (0.63%)	1 (0.63%)	2 (1.26%)
5	Household Work (M) and collection (S)	-	5 (3.16%)	5 (3.16%)

(contd...)

(contd...)

Sl. No.	*Nature of Economic Activities*	*Male*	*Female*	*Total*
6	Penda Cultivation (M) and Cattle herder (S)	1 (0.63%)	-	1 (0.63%)
7	Agricultural labour/Wage labour only	1 (0.63%)	-	1 (0.63%)
8	Angan Bari Worker	-	2 (1.26%)	2 (1.26%)
9	Student	14 (8.86%)	11 (6.96%)	25 (15.82%)
10	No Work	4 (2.53%)	5 (3.16%)	9 (5.69%)

M=Main; S= Subsidiary

Table 7: Involvement in Economic Pursuits at Burumpal (Below 5 yrs are not in the Table)

Sl No.	*Nature of Economic Activities*	*Male*	*Female*	*Total*
1	Cultivation/quarry mine work or both (M) and Wage labour (S)	11 (10.18%)	-	11 (1.018%)
2	Cultivation only	14 (12.96%)	-	14 (12.96%)
3	Household work (M) and cultivation and Wage labour (S)	-	33 (30.55%)	33 (30.55%)
4	Household work only	-	2 (1.84%)	2 (1.84%)
5	Service only	4 (3.70%)	-	4 (3.70%)
6	Cultivation (M) and Wage labour (S)	4 (3.70%)	-	4 (3.70%)
7	Cultivation along with involvement in village Panchyat	1 (0.92%)	-	1 (0.92%)
8	Household work (M) and cultivation and Cattle herding (S)	-	1 (0.92%)	1 (0.92%)
9	Politics	1 (0.92%)	-	1 (0.92%)
10	Student	16 (14.81%)	12 (11.11%)	28 (25.92%)
11	No work	4 (3.70%)	1 (0.92%)	5 (4.62%)

M=Main; S=Subsidiary

Table 8: Involvement in Economic Pursuits at Padapur (Below 5 yrs not in the Table)

Sl. No.	*Nature of Economic Activities*	*Male*	*Female*	*Total*
1.	Cultivation (M) and Goti (tin ore) collection and Construction labour (S)	18 (16.82%)	-	18 (16.82%)
2.	Cultivation or cattle herding or both time to time (Mainly by children)	6 (5.6%)	-	6 (5.6%)
3.	Household work (M) and cultivation and wage Labour or Goti Collection (S)	-	29 (27.10%)	29 (27.10%)
4.	Mining worker (M), Cultivation during season (S)	6 (5.6%)	-	6 (5.6%)
5.	Household work only	-	6 (5.6%)	6 (5.6%)
6.	Cultivation (M) and involvement in village Panchyal	2 (1.87%)	-	2 (1.87%)
7.	Cattle herding as well as well as household work	-	1 (0.93%)	1 (0.93%)
8.	Construction wage labour	2 (1.87%)	-	2 (1.87%)
9.	Labour in Tin ore Mine (M) and Wage labour (S)	1 (0.93%)	-	1 (0.93%)
10.	Student	11 (10.28%)	11 (10.28%)	22 (20.56%)
11.	No work	-	4 (3.74%)	4 (3.74%)

M = Main; S = Subsidiary

It reveals from above three tables of involvement in economic pursuits in the three different eco-zone that Bison-Horn Maria of Koduli village who are primarily *Penda* (Slash-burn) cultivators, where forest resource is abundance. It is observed that 27.84% male are practising *penda* cultivation as main while hunting and or wage labour is subsidiary to them. On the contrary household work and collection of edible roots, fruits, vegetables, tubers and leafs etc. as main and cultivation/wage labour as subsidiary type is practised by 26.58% women. Cattle herding only is done by 5.00% population. In Burumpal where Bison-Horn Maria are settled cultivators in plain area shows that altogether 64 (59.25%) are directly involved in settled cultivation along with other gainful economic activities too. In this eco-zone quarry wage labour is also noticed and they are about 10.18% while 3.70% are service holder. In Padapur - mining impact village, it is found that various gainful economic pursuits are noticed of which most lucrative is *goti* (tin Ore) collection as well as service in mining. They still think land is bread earner for them and cash earned from gainful economic activities are spent on their land. Cultivation is practised along with various economic activities in the village by 61(57%), wages earned from *goti* collection are 44.85% and there 6(5.6%) are service in mine who are also during season involved in other gainful pursuits especially in agricultural activities.

Data clearly reveal that as per eco-zone of Bison-Horn Maria settlement area their occupational opportunities are also developed and changing and they exploit such situation in search of their livelihood.

Forest Management

The practical application of the scientific, technical and economic principles, to forestry is referred to as forest management. The modern man sees forestry as an Industry and hence forest management is akin to the management of any industry. Present day forest management is based on two important aspects viz, multiple use and sustained yield (Negi, 1994). In short, forest management mean utilisation as well as preservation/conservation of forest through such practices which have direct bearing on the sustainable living.

"If you come to help me, you can go home; but if you see my struggle as a part of your survival then perhaps we can work together". Thgere is a relevant saying in this regard which has been quoted by an Australian Aborigine (quoted from Srivastav and Khanna, 1995).

Man has so far acted as both an inhabitant and manipulator of the his local environment. He tries to overcome all the hurdles by his effort either by appeasing or by force or through mutual adjustment etc. Unfettered use of technology has given him mangnificant economic growth on the one side and at the same time brought him on the brink of disaster'. Forest resources are one of the major natural resources in which about 35.7% tribal people of India are living and maintain their livelihood. At a glance one can see the major activities of forest in our country from time immemorial.

Year	*Activities*
2000 BC - 300 BC	Medication, Hunting, Religious Studies.
300 BC – 650 BC	Hunting, Clearing of land for grazing, Domesticating wild animals.
650 AD – 1700 AD	Hunting, Shifting cultivation, Invasions and settlements, Revenue collection, Encroachment for agriculture.
1700 AD – 1850 AD	Timber production for ship building, Revenue collection, Hunting, Land for Agriculture, Shifting Cultivation, Human settlement.
1850 AD – 1947 AD	Deforestation of valuable timber for railway line and enormous supply of timber, bamboos, and grasses to I & II World Wars.
1947 AD – 1980 AD	Agricultural activities, irrigation, river valley project, industry and development of township, road and transmission of high voltage power line etc.

Source: Srivastav, A.K. and Pradeep Khanna "Restructuring forest eco-system", Social Change Vol. 25, No. 1, 1995, pp. 64-68.

India is the abode of tribal people and about 35.7% are living in dense forest (Singh, 1994). These tribal people also exploit the forest resources for their own survival, The Bison-Horn Maria of Bastar whose life and culture are chcrished under the lap of forest environment. Now in the following lines we shall try to highlight the interaction and inter-relation of Bison-Horn Maria with their immediate niche. The major thrust is given on their utilisation aspect in one hand and preservation or conservation on the other hand.

It has been observed that except at Koduli village, the forest of the region is owned by government. In Koduli village forest is owned by these community as a whole. It has already been mentioned that Koduli village of Abujh Marh region is unsurveyed hence no tax, and allow to practise *penda* cultivation.

Utilisation of Forest Resource

The Bison-Horn Maria have been traditionally living in forested areas and are dependent on the forest for their sources of livelihood. The ecological setting of their abode makes a deep impact on their life which gets adequately reflected in their economy as well as in their belief system. All the raw materials for hut coastruction are collected from the forest especially in Koduli village.

Especially the Bison-Horn Maria of Koduli have forest based economy and they satisfy most of their requirements by exploiting their immediate niche. i.e. forest. The forests not only supplies a patch of land to construct a hut but also provide them with wooden log, bamboos and thatching grass like *Sadka* and *chind* or *Ind kata* grasses.

They also collect various food items from forest which constitutes major economic activities among Bison-Horn Maria especially among their woman it is one of the chief economic pursuits. They exploit the forest and its produce to the maximum extent to meet their bare necessities. In the season of mahua, imli, kosa (Cocoon) and tendu they devote all their time in such collection from forest. It has been observed that these people have a very wide range of indigenous knowledge of edible roots, tubers, herbs, leaves, fruits, wild animals and medicinal plants etc that have been developed in them through a long course of experience. Due to close association with the forest environment they have secured an intimate knowledge on some bitter or sour taste food materials and non-edible *velra/puta* or mushroom etc. They process these food materials to make those edible one by washing those in running water or through boiling; they wash these repeatedly and when these would be ready for edible purposes. Collection plays a major gainful economic pursuit among them and it is chiefly done by their women folk who are assisted by their children. It has been observed in each morning that women are moving towards forest with a *tokna* (basket made of bamboo) and a digging stick (*pushal*) or (*korki*). According to their elderly members women are most competent in the activities of collection. They possess a basic knowledge about the availability of tuber. By observing upper surface of earth and vegetation they understand whether particular tuber is available there or not. It has also been observed that after getting the desired tuber or root in a place, they donot uproot the whole tuber or root on the contrary they keep some portion inside the earth inview of furure rejuvenation. Before going into the forest in the very early morning they go to near about jungle for fresh up and after defication they use either leaves or pebbles. Collection work continues till mid-day or when sun is on the top of their head or during summer when mahua flower falling from tree is stopped. Throughout the year they collect various edible and non-edible forest product for their sustenance. A list of such is illustrated below to understand seasonal variation of collection. It is also observed that the collected edible products are of highly nutritious having sufficient calorie value. They recognise three seasons *garmi* (summer), *barish* (monsoon), and *jara* (winter). The cognizance of their environment is as follows. When mahua flower blooms they think garmi (summer) is approaching, when Sal seed falls and mango becomes ripen they think barish or monsoon is approaching while when Kosra and paddy becomes matured for harvest and when chind juice becomes more tasty and sweet they think sardi or winter is approaching.

In the material possession forest also plays a significant role. It has already been discussed earlier that the materials required for construction of a hut is usually procured from local niche. Since they consider Saja or Aden (Termina tomentosa) tree as a sacred, so they try to apply some twig of Saja in the house construction. Their household goods of daily use and the materials associated with their economic life, and various types of weapons and implements are mostly made of wood, bamboo, grass and leaves etc. all are procured from the forest. The handle of an axe is made of wood, mushal (or wooden husker), gudari (hoe) etc. are prepardd from local wood available from forest. In case of hunting implements, arrows are made of bamboo splits while agricultural implements, and digging stick are made of wood which they acquire from forest. The cot is made of *bija* or *dhaman* tree while netting is done by the Siyari creeper (rope/ thread is prepared from Siyari creeper bark). Bamboo is another important item in their life since they prepare various shapes and sizes of *tokna* or baskets for keeping and also carrying cereals or any items purchased from bazar they use this for carrying. It is also taken to the deep forest during collection.

The table 9 clearly depicts a picture of seasonal variation of collection materials from forest which also has a major role in their sustenance pattern.

Table 9 : Seasonal collection from Forest Resources

Season	*Edible*	*Non Edible*
Garmi (Summer) (February-May)	*Mati or Tubers:* Kodo, Kaska, Gone, Kotosh, Kai, Kaiman, Keku, Lekh, Rasa, Nangal, Tule, Gunga, Rash, Nager etc. *Sag or Green Vegetable:* Velvetun, Kodeli, etc. *Phool or Flower* Velvetun, Tund, Mahua (Eiru) *Phal or Fruit:* Kohka/Velva, Mango, Char, Phanos (Jackfruit), Ind, Yurguna, Tendu, Imli Harra, Baira, Tummer etc. *Bija or Seed:* Tora, Sal; Juice or (Gohgha); Gorga (Sulphi) and Chind (Palm)	*Seed:* *Sal.* *Twig:* Sal, Harra, Neem Mango twig. *Leaves:* Siyari or Elephant Creeper, Tendu, Tummer, Sabai grass, Chhind, Epur (Phool Jharu) {incase of Bison-Horn Maria of Abujh Marh region} Bamboo Kosa (Silk Cocoon)
Barish (Monsoon) (June September)	Mati/Tuber Kash, Pad, Kaiman, Tule, Kotosh, Bada (a kind of Tuber grown under the foliage of sal leaves in forest; it is Highly nutrient). *Sad:* Kahak, Mugur, Erbor, Koliari etc. Basta-Young bamboo shot or Bans karil. Various kind of Kuhku or Putu or Mushroom.	Bamboo, fuel wood.
Sardi (Winder) (October-January)	Tuber: Pidu, Pad Gali; Fruit : Harra or Karka, Bayra or Jahka; Juice: Sulphi and chind (Tad) in case of Bison-Horn Maria of Sukma region.	Sal leaves for doni (bowl) preparation. Sabai grass, and bamboo for basketry.

The rain coat and rain hat are prepared out of various leaves act as a shield and thus protect from rain. Their personal tobacco pouch or *gota* is made of timas wood and lime container or *chuna goruli* is made of bamboo. Now-a-days in the mining area villages it is replaced by small tube having lime which is available in the local market. For sweeping in their courtyard they use Epur (Phool jharu) which they procure from forest or they use broomstiàk of the bamboo splits. They also possess various kinds of musical drums. This drum is also made of dried up trunk of Sago palm tree and for producing various rhythm of sound they use hide of cow on one side and another side with hide of goat or deer. The beating stick is made of wood. All the aforementioned items for their daily use in various socio-cultural functions are having impact of their forest environment. In all cases they procure the raw materials from local niche. Since they live in uncertain environment they keep a peacock and fowl feather in their respective houses as they believe that these items possesses some magical power to drive out malevolent spirits.

The another major area of sustenance from forest to the Bison Horn Maria is hunting. The Bison Horn Maria are expert in hunting and they also possess an indigenous knowledge to catch various hunts. Now-a-days due to non-availability of hunts it is not considered as an economic pursuit. Hunting is collectively done in certain occasions and there are festivals to grace such occasions. But they always carry bow and arrow when they go to forest. If par chance they get a bird, kotri, wild boar, fowl etc. they try to kill these and make a grand feast. According to their comprehension summer season is considered ideal for hunting

They catch rat which grow in the field. This is very delicious item to them. They first identity the holes in the paddy field. After that they dig a little portion of the hole and keep some Kosra grain fixes in the rat trap which is finally installed in the hole.The rats are very fond of Kosra grain, and as soon as they try to eat Kosra, they are trapped.

The hares are trapped in the night. During day time these take rest under the hole of some big trees specially chhind tree. It is the duty of a hunter to identify the place of movement first and install there *moler funda* which is also known as *jali funda* among Bison Horn Maria of Padapur and Bade Bacheli villagers. They dig hole very close to the trap and urinate in it. The hares get attracted with the smell of salt and are trapped.

Once it is observed that Dandami Maria or Bison Horn Maria were running behind wild boar at early morning with several bows and arrows and making various sorts of hurla sounds from mouth and drum. The animal was encircle with group of hunters and atlast became tired and caught.

They catch various birds by using their traditional wisdom based on extracting oil from valva green seed mixes with resin extracted from *Eva marandu* tree, prepare a paste which is annointed on some foliage leaves and branches of *dasing* tree. Then they keep this on a fruit bearing tree, when bird comes to eat those fruit, they are caught. The said birds are unable to fly due to sticky resins were hugged with their wing.

The womens are not allowed in any hunting expedition. Hunting is regarded as an auspicious event as it is mainly connected with certain rituals.

Lastly it can be said that they possess some cultural bindings by which local ecological balance is maintained. Such as they are tabooed to kill any animals or cut any tree/ plant which are their totemic object. It is found that most of their clans are totemic in nature.

Indigenous Health Care Practice

Forest plays a major role for providing medicinal herbs to their dwellers from time immemorial.

Disease is very common phenomenon in every society and to cope with such adverse condition they have to depend on medicine for which local environment plays a key role. It is known to all of us that before the advent of modern medicine/ therapy the people all over had developed culture specific beliefs and practices regarding their health care issue and diseases. The term ethno-medicine connotes "those belief and practices relating to health and disease which are products of indigenous cultural development and not explicitly derived from the conceptual framework of modern medicine" (Hughes, 1968), Indigenous health care practise in our country may be termed as ethno-medicine.

It has been observed that the experts who prèscribe and given a particular herbal plant for treatment, possess a deep rooted knowledge of their immediate niche. But before prescribing it he performs some ritual performances to identify the cause of diseases and the malevolent spirits, if any. Historical record reveals that the classical work the Atharva veda, ancient Indian Scholars like Charak, Sushrutha, Bagvatta and several others have produced remarkable descriptions of Indian medicinal plants. Rigveda which is considered to be the oldest available record dating back to 2000 - 1000 BC recognised the importance of several medicinal plants. It is obvious that the people who live in forest environment are primarily dependent on their immediate resource for their ailment and in India majority tribal people are living in forest based environment, who also use the herbal plants of their niche for curing the ailment.

The present treatise is confined among the Bison- Horn Maria of Bastar who exploit their natural resources for their ailment. Now in the following lines we will present the use of herbs and plants of their niche for their ailment.

Table 10: Use of Indigenous Knowledge for Ailment

Sl No.	*Use of Local Herbs/Plants/Seed*	*Disease/Treatment*
1.	Sarpagandha (Rauvolfia serpentine)	Roots of plants is used in blood pressure, hysteria, snake bite and mental derangement.
2.	Charota Seeds	Oil is used for Skin disease
3.	Kali musli (Curculiza orchiocdes)	Tuber is used as Health Tonic.
4.	Sadabahr (Vincarosea, Family-Apocynaccae)	Flower is used for diabetic and Cancer.
5.	Sarpunka (Indigofera angulosa)	Roots, Fruits, Seeds and Flower are used during acidic pain, wormicide and piles.
6.	Banjira (Carum nigrum)	Seeds are used for rheumatic pain.
7.	Jamun Seed (Syzygium cumini)	After crushing it is consumod for antidiabetic action.
8.	Harra fruit (Terminalia chebula)	Digestive and clear of Stomach
9.	Behra fruit (Terminalia bellirica)	do
10.	Aonla fruit (Emblica officinalis)	do

(contd...)

Sl No.	*Use of Local Herbs / Plants / Seed*	*Disease / Treatment*
11.	Kala Haldi (Curcuma caesia)	It's paste is used for Leprosy treatment.
12.	Chiraita (Swertia Chirata)	Plant is soaked in water and water is consumed. It is used for blood- purifier, anti diabetic and anti- malarial.
13.	Shivalingi Seeds	It removes barrenness.
14.	Arjun bark (T. Arjuna)	It is soaked in water and water is taken for heart problem.
15.	Kakai bark	It is also soaked in water and water is taken by the females as tonic after delivery.
16.	Jangli Kela (Musa sepintum)	Seed of fruit is used and used in Small Pox.
17.	Jangli Payar (Urginea indica)	Its tuber is used during diarrohoea and epilepsy.
18.	Bhui Aonla (Phyllanthis nurarii)	Whole plant extract is used during Jaundice and anaemic.
19.	Hadjod (Vitis quadrangularis)	Tip of leaf is used for bone fracture, rheumatism, acidic and worm.
20.	Kala dhatoora	For asthma leaves are smoken.
21.	Tad/Sulphi	Use during dental pain.
22.	Bajradanti root	Dental disease and for Stomach-ache problem.
23.	Nirmali Grass (Strychnos potatorum)	The plant is grounded and put in water immediately it is observed that water becomes crystal clear and drinkable.
24.	Velva Seed (Semicarpus anacardium)	After burning the seed oil is extracted and it is put drop by drop in the affected parts of headache.
25.	Kusum seed and bark (Schleichera trijuga)	Extracted oil is used in skin disease, rheumatic pain, itches etc.
26.	Babachi (Psoratea corylifolia)	Seeds are used in leucoderma leprosy, fistule, diarrohoea, and promoting urination.

(contd...)

Sl No.	*Use of Local Herbs / Plants / Seed*	*Disease / Treatment*
27.	Amaltas (Cassia fistula)	Fruit and flower are used for dengue fever, piles, gastric and constipation
28.	Dhaura (Anogeissus latifolia)	Bark and entire-plant are used for astringent antidote to snake, scorpion bite.
29.	Kurchi (Horlarrhena antidysentrica)	Bark and seeds are used in amoebic dysentery.
30	Erand seeds (Castor) (Ricinus communis)	Extracted oil is used for snake bite and pulp used oil is useful for purgative.

It has bveen understood through close investigation that the use of *tora tel* (from mahua seed) makes the hair black and grayness is low, and use of such oil in body restrict the feeling of cold in winter season; it is also antidot against dandwarf.

It reveals that exploration of this sort of natural treasure is very valuable as it has developed among the Bison-Horn Maria tribe over generations through prolonged association with their local environment. Infact, they have acquired the knowledge and learnt the ways and means for the sake of their survival in such adverse environment where the light of modern medical facility is poor.

Now it can be summarised that :

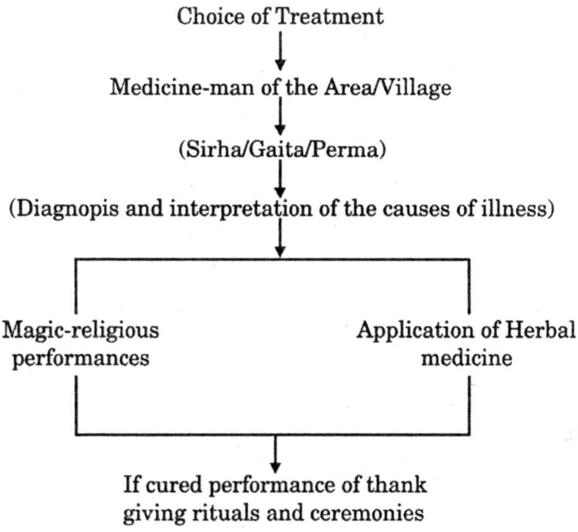

Conservation of Forest

According to Singh (1994) 402 tribes live in hilly terrain while 226 live in dense forest. It is obvious that forest resources play a great role on their sustenance pattern and due to this reason they also try to protect their physical environment through their traditional knowledge. Their way of life is closely imbibed with physical environ which form an inseparable component ofthe eco system and maintained unmediated relationship to the natural resources. Since they utilizes the natural resources for their livelihood they are well aware of their surrounding niche for over generation and also expect that the resource base would sustain their future generations as well. Before going into depth we would like to describe the term "conservaation" and "preservatioon". The difference between the two terms lies mainly in functional aspect, i.e. conservation of forest is mainly done by indigenous people themselves for their own sustenance through their age old traditional knowledge and oral tradition while where forest is protected for comtnercialisation it is known as preservation.

It has been observed that traditional practices of preserving sacred grove as per the tribal value system is a vast patch of container of various biological diversity. Paranjpye (1989) also expresses, "sacred groves refer to a patch of forest, or a patch of large forest which is undisturbed by the local inhabitants for all practical purposes". Buchman (1992) says sacred grove contains a large number of species and is considered to be a true ecological jewel. This territory harbours an immense wealth of biological and genetic diversity and provide safety for more endangered animal and plant species and probably constitute only representation of forest in its virgin condition". Gadgil and Vartak (1976) also expresses their thanks to such traditional practices which are operating in various tribal pockets of our country. The present observation is restricted on the Bison-Horn Maria tribe of Bastar, their practices of conservation based on traditional knowledge and culture of both material and spiritual operations are taken iflto consideration.

Among the Bison Horn Maria the sacred groves or *tallin* are patches of forest or a part of large forest usually untouched by local lo inhabitants. It is dedicated to their mother goddess-*deogudi* who is supposed to protect and preside over the grove and intruders who violate their customary law, that is, prohibition of cutting tree and violation of maintenance of this *tallin*. These primitive virgin of forests among Bison-Horn Maria also preserves wild varieties of diverse flora. Usually the *tallin* or sacred groves are situated in each and every villages and at the periphery of the village boundary. Most of the communal worship, annual worship, *pen* (clan deity) ritual and all celestial rituals are performed in their *tallin*. These virgin forest patches contribute significantly in the maintenance of 'biological diversity' and ecological balance of their environment. Record reveals that the sacred groves of ancient times have become the Biosphere Reserves of today and are found in several parts of India (Sinha, 1995). It is also reported that in Madhya Pradesh, having largest tribal population, alone has 42 such Biosphere Reserves (Sinha, 1995).

Apart from sacred grove there are various cultural bindings of prohibition in cutting and burning some specific trees in their *penda* land. They are tabooed to eat certain edible fruits, flowers, leafy vegetables like mango, mahua and Koliyari bhaji etc. prior to the performance of rituals. It reveals that their religious value system restrict them from destruction of these edible items before their maturity as well as further germination of these is highly effective in this restriction pattern.

It is worthy to mention that in each *tallin* of Bison-Horn Maria village there are several trees which are considered as sacred. Saja or aden, Jagdumar, Dhaura (Anogcissus latifolia) and Bargat (or Baniyan) are thopught to have sacred values) are have thoughtto sacred values. During field investigation it has been observed at *tallin* that there are Saja, elephant creeper, harra, ao bans (bamboo) and mango, bija and Jagdumar trees and the people are only allowed to collect dried up twigs and fallen leaves but are tabooed to cut any of those. Their ritual bindings imposed restrictions which are directly meaningful for their conservation aspect.

The Saja tree (Terminalia tomentosa) and its leaves are very important in the life and culture of Bison-Horn Maria. The religious value oriented sentiment is attached with Saja. When a Siraha (priest) becomes possessed by a deity, he keeps Saja or aden leaves in his hand. The deity responds on the Sirha which is marked by shaking of body.

They usually keep a dried up aden log/twig in their house which is becoming a social norm inveiw of protection from evil eye or malevolent spirit. Apart from this aden tree is also beneficial for them inview of their economic aspect; cocoon or kosa insect lay their egg on the aden leaves since aden leaves are delicious for the silk worms. They collect matured kosa and sell these at weekly market. The silk threads are extracted from the kosa. Therefore Aden tree is related with their religious and economic life and due to such restriction it is possible for cocoon to complete their life cycle. The dhaura tree has also economic importance like aden because Silk coooons are also prefer this tree to lay their eggs. They never urinate or spit under aden, dhaura, char, jagdumar trees since these are sacred to them.

They never cut trees like mango, tamarind, aonla, bayra, harra, mahua and char since these are fruit bearing trees on which their livelihood is imbibed and some trees are having medicinal value as well as economic importance. They also never cut trees at bij *patar* of the village where they perform *bij putni* and ama khani rituals. In this way conservation of their environment through their traditional wisdom is performed.

After plucking tamarind from the tree they usually pruning the twigs for good yield in the next year and it is found very successful.

In their surrounding environment bargat (baniyan) tree holds top position for it's ritual importance. It gives shade to all, many of their deity resides here, its fallen leaves and foliages on the penda field act as manure either by decomposing or after burn it's ashes becomes manure for *penda* field which act as fixation of nitrogen in the land which uttimately help in increasing of crop yield. The bark of baniyan is used in many ritual performances for purification by sprinkling water on the purification ceremony. Similarly the resin is extracted from Sal tree trunk and it is used as incense in their ritual activities. Velva tree (Semicarpus anacardium) and Dhaura tree has also medicinal value to them and due to such they donot cut this tree. There are some trees which are regarded as their asset and possession of these trees ascribe social status and these trees are Mahua, Tamarind, Sulphi, Tand, etc. Juice of Sulphi and Tand are intoxicating and in their ritual this juice is used as offering. The old and dried up Sulphi tree trunk is used as their musical drum, the pith of the said trunk is edible one by making powedered and prepare bread out of it. There fore, it is observed that conservation of their environment is maintained by their age-old traditional knowledge inview of their sustenance in such forest-clad environment.

It is reported that whenever they prepare *penda* field by clearing forests, by cutting trees, these are never uprooted but the tree are cut leaving at least 2 feet to 3 feet height of the tree from the base. This is not only for checking soil erosion but also helps to rejuvenate the remaining parts of trees in subsequent years. It has been observed that after one shower new leaves come out from the chiseled trunk but in most cases such tree trunks are burnt and damaged due to fire at the *penda* land. Incase of extraction of tuber from forest for their livelihood it is also reported that they never uproot the whole root system and tuber but allow to remain some portions of these under the earth inview of further rejuvenate in the subsequent year which will be in the interest of their survival. So their rich indigenous knowledge also helps to conserve their immediate niche in view of their sustenance. It is also found that they never hunt their clan totem which is tabooed and in this way also ecological balance is maintained.

In the preservation practices social forestry is done at mining area of Bacheli and also at Tokapal block where mainly eucalyptus, arjun, Sal and Cashewnut trees are planted which help to improve the biosphere of the area as well as when these trees except cashewnut become matured it is cut into pieces of log for commercial use.

Therefore, from the above discussion it can be said that forest management of Bison-Horn Maria are highly dependent on their traditional knowledge which they acquire over generatton.

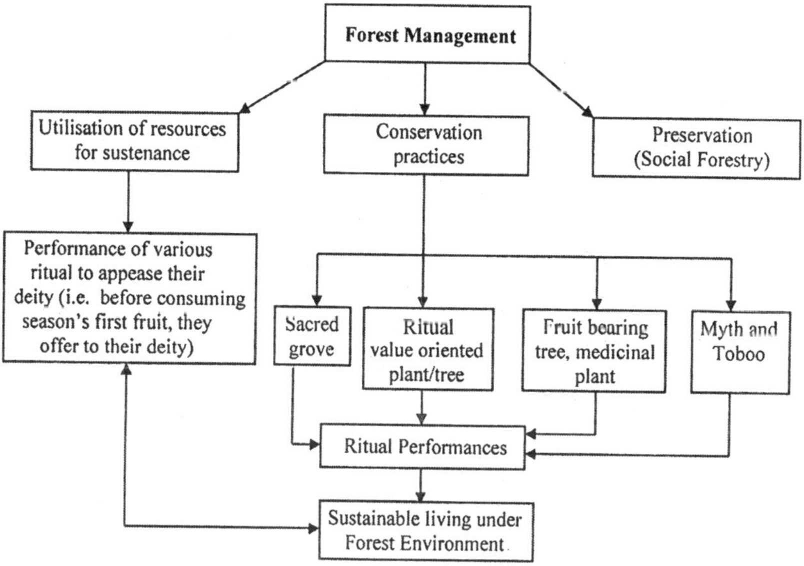

Land Management

The chief economic pursuit on which their livelihood depend is cultivation. It is estimated that producing yield is sufficient in most of the Bison-Horn Maria families at Marh area due to land holding capacity while in the wet cultivation area in plain land they have also produce sufficient and some of their yield is marketed in the weekly bazar. But in mining area though they practise wet cultivation but due to local niche i.e. mining and land quality, their production is not sufficient.

Since the subsistence base among the Bison-Horn Maria is agriculture, it becomes a family enterprise among them - those who share the hearth, share in the work and the harvest. It has been observed from three studied villages that family size among Bison Horn Maria are as follows:

Table 11: Family Size of Studied Villages

Koduli	Small (1-4 member)	10(32.25%)
	Medium (5-6 member)	15(48.39%)
	Large (7 member & above)	6 (19.36%)
Burumpal	(Small (1-4 member)	8(40%)
	Medium (5-6 member)	6(30%)
	Large (7 member & above)	6 (30%)
Padapur	Small (1-4 member)	8(36.36%)
	Medium (5-6 member)	12(54.55%)
	Large (7 member & above)	2 (9.09%)

It has been observed that in the *penda* cultivation area small (32.25%) and medium (48.39%) size family dominates while in plain area, wet cultivation zone medium (30%) to large (30%) family dominates. There is a proverb that in settled/ wet cultivation more hands mean more works which is essentially required in agriculture. While in Padapur, which is having an impact of urban environment due to mining industry which is reflected through the data on family size and i.e. Small family 36.36%, Medium size family 54.55% and Large size is only 9.09%.

Cultivatéd land is categorically identified by the Bison-Horn Maria themselves (i.e. emic view) in several ways relevant to its production of cereals/crops. Probably the most important distinction is between land which is on the hills/ hill slopes, table land and in the plains.

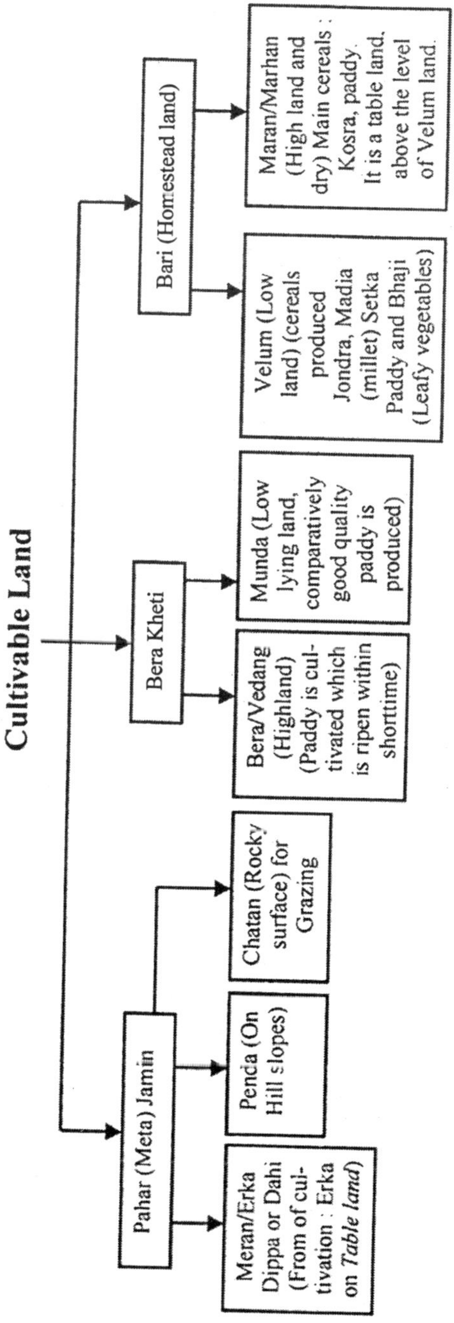
Cultivable Land
Pahar (Meta) Jamin
Bera Kheti
Bari (Homestead land)
Meran/Erka Dippa or Dahi (From of cultivation : Erka on *Table land*)
Penda (On Hill slopes)
Chatan (Rocky surface) for Grazing
Bera/Vedang (Highland) (Paddy is cultivated which is ripen within shorttime)
Munda (Low lying land, comparatively good quality paddy is produced)
Velum (Low land) (cereals produced Jondra, Madia (millet) Setka Paddy and Bhaji (Leafy vegetables)
Maran/Marhan (High land and dry) Main cereals : Kosra, paddy. It is a table land. above the level of Velum land.

It has been observed from three studied villages that Bison-Horn Maria or Dandami Maria possesses various types of land according to their local niche for their sustenance. Here in the following lines a comparative picture is illustrated to understand environmental impact or impact of local niche on their sustenance pattern.

Table 12: Total Available Cultivable Land under Possession in three Different eco-setting of Bison Horn Maria

Land Typed	*Possession of Land in Acres Villages*		
	Koduli *31 households*	*Burumpal* *20 households*	*Padapur* *22 households*
A. Penda, Erka/ Dippa, Marham (Marhan land only)	163 Acres (40.8%)	127 Acres (37.12%) (Marhan land only)	40 Acres (30.02%) (Marhan land only)
B. Bari	93.5 Acres (23.3%)	81.5 Acres (23.72%)	23.5 Acres (22.92%)
C. Bera	143.5 Acres 35.9%	134.5 Acres 39.16%	39 Acres 38.04%
Total	400 Acres	343.5 Acres	102.5 Acres

It reveals from above table - 12 that in Koduli where slash and burn and shifting cultivation dominates there only about 41% land is under shifting cultivation and Kosra is cultivated in this lands, while about 36% land is under paddy cultivation in Bera land and only about 23% land is available for Jondra (Maize), and Sarsoo (Mustard) and vegetable cultivation in *Bari* or Homestead land. In Burumpal Kosra is cultivated in Marhan land and only 37.12% land is available for this while for paddy cultivation in Bera land 39.16% lands are available and for Zondra cultivation in Bari land 23.72 lands are available to them. The village Padapur which is situated under mining environment and land quality is not good, soil is reddish in colour (mixed with iron), hill slopes land are rocky surface and in some pockets of such land tin ore is found; collection of tin ore is one of the economic pursuit among some villagers. Here, villagers cultivate Kosra in Marhan type of land which is 39.02%, and for paddy cultivation 38.04% lands (Bera land) are available while homestead Bari land is available only 22.92% where chiefly Zondra (matze) is cultivated.

Table 13: Nature of Land in Possession by Households in Three Different Eco-setting Bison-Horn Maria

Villages : A. Koduli, B. Burumpal, C. Padapur

Types of land	*Upto 1 Acre*			*Upto 3 Acre*			*Upto 5 Acre*			*Upto 8Acre*			*Upto 10 Acre and above*		
	A	B	C	A	B	C	A	B	C	A	B	C	A	B	C
1. Pahar : (Penda, Erka/Dippa, Marhan)	4	4	10	5	6	3	11	4	1	7	2	3	4	2	0
2. Bari	9	6	13	10	6	3	9	4	2	1	2	0	1	1	0
3. Bera	2	2	8	9	5	6	10	5	1	8	1	0	2	7	2

The Table 13 reveals that altogether in three villages 73 households are studied; of which 66(90.41%) families possesses various quantity of Penda, Dippa and Marhan type of land where chief cereals cultivated are Kosra, Kodu, Kulthi, Tilli, Chikma, rahar (Pulses). In the *marhan* land of Burumpal and Padapur some variety of paddy also cultivated viz., *Luchai*, *Garakuta* and *Barangi* etc. In Bari land mainly Zondra (maize) and Sarsoo (mustard) are cultivated and in altogether 67 families (91.78%) in various sizes possesses this type of land and paddy is cultivated in Bera land where mainly water storing capacity remain and for which contour bunding is formed or hedge is formed in between the land; of the total altogether 68(93.15%) families possesses this type of land in various sizes which are shown in Table 13.

Table 14 : Possession of Total Cultivable land by Households in three Different Eco-setting

Possession of total cultivable land	Villages		
	Koduli (A)	*Burumpal (B)*	*Padapur (C)*
No Land	0	0	5
Upto 3 Acres	0	2	5
Upto 5 Acres	3	1	6
Upto 8 Acres	5	2	1
Upto 10 Acres	3	5	3
Upto 20 Acres	14	8	2
Upto 30 Acres	6	1	0
More than 30 Acres	0	1	0
Total Households	31	20	22

Both table 13 and 14 reveal that 400 Acres of cultivable land are possessed by 31 households families of Dandami Maria at Koduli village on which 158 persons are dependent for their livelihood, while in Burumpal and in Padapur 343.5 acres and 102.5 acres of cultivable lands are available by 20 and 22 families respectively. In Burumpal 20 families having 108 persons while in Padapur 22 families having 106 souls. Therefore, it can be assumed from the contextual data that Land - Man Ratio in Koduli is 2.53 acres of land is available, while in Burumpal it is 3.18 acres and in Padapur it is 0.96 acres only.

Bison-Horn Maria practised Penda (slash and burn) cultivation at Marh area such as at Koduli village. Before going into detail perhaps it is wise to describe the land types; on the basis of such categorisation of land they practise cultivation of various cereals or crops as per land types. In the selection of nature of lands for raising various crops they directly depend on their traditional knowledge.

The high land on the hills is known as *Pahar* or *Meta Jamin.* When such cultivable land is situated at table land on hill top it is called as Maran/ Marhan. This type of land is smaller in size in comparison to penda land on hill slopes and usually in the marh area they practise two types of cultivation, viz Erka and Dippa or Dahi. The next variety of land on hill slope is *penda* and third form of land is *chatan* or rocky surface and it is essentially used as grazing field of their livestock.

The other quality of land is *bera*, which is comparatively flat and low land and suitable for paddy cultivation. The soil in this land is sticky and having capacity for water storage and they also prepare contour bunding between the land for water storage. Bera land is again divided into two categories according to its production capacity. The high land *bera* is known as *vedang* where paddy is also cultivated but it is ripen within short time. It is a coarse variety while low lying bera land is known as *munda* where good as well as finer quality of paddy is produced and in this land regular ploughing is essential. Usually *munda* land are situated very close to nallah or rivulet in the village where automatically water is stored due to the low lying nature.

The other cultivable land which occupies a major share in their economic life is homestead land or *bari* land; again this type of land is classified into two according to its position. It has been observed in the studied villages that their huts are situated in such a position which is attached with some cultivable land. In this type of land which is low lying known as *velum*, cereals produced are Jondra (maize), Madia (millet) Setka (a kind of paddy), bhaji (leafy vegetables) and sometimes Sarsoo (mustard) etc. Incidentally this land is highly fertile because their livestock live and roam in this land and the excrement found here and there in the land act as a fertilizer. The *bari* land which is situated in high level, it is obviously dry, and known as *marhan*; in this land they cultivate a kind of paddy known as *atwanji* which requires less water. It is a high yielding variety. The seeds are sown sometimes in April which are matured before Dusehra. Apart from *atwanji* paddy, they also cultivate Kosra of various types. Infact, this is also a table land and situated above the level of *velum* homestead land.

Table 15: Nature of crop and land type

Sl. No.	*Land type*	*Chief Cereals / Crop produced*
(i)	Maran/Marhan	Kosra, Oil seed like tili, Koreh, Paddy, Arba, Kulthi, Urad, Chikma
(ii)	Bari	Jondra, Rahar, Tomato, Kulthi, Chikma, Sarsoo, Tilli, Guard, Pumpkin, Barbaati, Sim (Jata)
(iii)	Bera	Paddy, Wheat

Type of Cultivation : (a) Penda

The Dandami Maria/ Bison-Horn Maria of Marh region practise penda cultivation. Infact, this is shifting cultivation which still exists throughout the world with certain variations due to ecological variation. It is the duty of the head of the family to decide as to which of the forest tract is to be cut in a particular year. Usually it happens that senior and experienced agnatic kin member of the family watches the growth of vegetation in forest tracts with a motive to select the suitable areas for *penda* cultivation. Penda includes several stages of operation. The first stage is the selection of the site and this is done usually a year in advance. The patch of land is selected on the basis of vegetation whether it is dense or not. According to their version *penda* is most suitable and preferred due to large quantity of yields.

From February to March in the specified patch of selected site are cleared by felling of trees and shrubs. Then these wooden logs are spread in the place for their drying. Lighting of such heaps of logs are done before the performance of Holi in the new moon of the month Phagur/ Fagun. The *penda* lands are set on fire, the ashes are diffused and then the land is ready for sowing. According to their traditional norm one is not allowed to lite fire in the forest prior to the performance of Holi. It is tabooed among them. Probable reason behind it is that during this time they have just completed harvest of Os kosra, these are lying in the forest land and liting of fire in jungle may cause destruction of their crop. It is also reported that before felling of trees, shrubs for *penda* land they usually perform a ritual to appease the Bhum deity - *Tallin*; this is practised when first time new *penda* land is prepared for cultivation.

The Bison-Horn Maria of Koduli village, who are immigrant in this zone, also follow the norms of Abujh Maria regarding selection of *penda* plots by their family members through mutual discussion; As per their bare economic necessity the area of *penda* plot is alloted to each family members.

Generally after the conduction of successive cultivation for at least four years the cultivators shift to another plot for *penda* cultivation. The demarcation between two person's *penda* land is done by raising row of some shrubs or plantation of til oil seed or making some tree trunks as the identity of demarcation line. They are to receive three yield of Kosra from a *penda* plot. During the month *mur* (April-May) after one or two showers the seeds of Kohla/ Kosra are sown broadcast. This is known to them as Chhota Kohla/ Kosra or *ghatka*. They are busy in their bera land for paddy cultivation during the months of *Na* (May-June) and *Hai* (June-July), Harvesting of Kosra is completed within Eranj (August-September) when they also harvest mountain rice in the same plot which is also matured along with Kohla. There are various types of small Kosra viz., *ghatka*, *chikma*, kodon, *mandia* etc.

The other type of Kosra, which is otherwise known as big kosra sown in *Hai* (June-July), consists of Kutki, Kang etc., harvested during *Pandi* (November-December). Along with this they also cultivate in the same plot by broadcasting the seed of various pulses like arhar, urad and jata (Sim-Dolichos lablab).

During Eranj (August-September) *Os Kosra* is sown in the penda plot of Chhota Kosra. Along with this they cultivate Kulthl and mung pulses and it is harvested during *Pusi* (December-January).

(b) Erka Cultivation

In this type of cultivation first the trees are felled in the forest then these are brought to a flat table land and spread out the logs and twigs and allow them to dry there after which these are burnt, usually before shower. The ashes act as fertilizer which totally mixes with soil. Then the seeds are broadcast. Erka cultivation is usually done in flat *marhan* land where they even produce rice.

(c) Dippa or Dahi Cultivation

This type of cultivation is very much akin to *erka* cultivation. It is also done in flat land but the said piece of plot can be cultivated only for two years. In the first year they cut smaller trees, shrub, under growth etc. of the particular plot. But in the second year they cut big trees and then only burnt. It is told that during first year the capacity for fertility of the land is high and therefore they cut only small trees for clearing the plot and then only burnt. But in the next year after harvesting of cereals the land fertility becomes reduced and therefore they cut big trees, dried up and burnt. The ashes act as a fertilizer of the plot.

(d) Plough cultivation

Plough cultivation is mainly done for raising the paddy. Bera land is mainly reserved for paddy cultivation. In the month of May-June they prepare the land by tiling the soil. After first shower in the month of June they again till the soil and then only sowing operation starts. Comparatively Bison Horn Maria are good cultivators and they are well aware of the technology of plough cultivation.

The Bison Horn Maria of Burumpal village who are well aware of this cultivation, also practise Rabi crop cultivation. As soon as they harvest Jondra (Maize), again ploughing for Rabi crop like sarsoo and tilli, since in this area there is irrigation facility by a stream. In the *marhan* land they cultivate urad, *arhar* (perhmi), chikma, kosra, kulthi and tilli etc., in *bari* land they cultivate also kulthi, Jondra (maize), sarsoo (rabi crop), and tilli (rabi crop). While in *bera* land they chiefly practise paddy cultivation; the low lying *bera* land attached with perenial water source - stream, also produce rabi paddy and wheat.

In Burumpal there are seven hamlets which are attached with the cultivable lands and bird's eye view of such lands are in undulated position. Therefore, contour bunding in between two plots are prevalent for water storage. The same picture of land is seen in Padapur village.

Land Holding

Land holding system in the marh area is very much typical. The Bison-Horn Maria in Marh area are immigrant, They got the land from the headman of Abujh Maria. Again plots of land are distributed among their family as per their bare economic need. Once a piece of plot is abandoned after Erka or Dippa cultivation then any one among them may occupy the plot for further cultivation. In this sort of transfer ot land holding there is no legal record.

While in Burumpal where all are settled cultivators have their own *patta* (land record) of land and for which they pay tax.

In case of Padapur village the whole village lands are under the possession of eighteen Dandami Maria families and hence there are only 18 pattas. They are settled cultivators. Again in due course they bought their *dadabhai* (brother's clan) and *akomama* (wife's clan) kins in the village and distributed the lands among them and for which there is no Government paper till date since 1900 or more. So it is revealed that they have a social control for sustenance on their land management pattern for cultivation and this is running without disturbance for years together.

Conservation of Land

Traditional system of conservation of land is still seen among the studied group. It has been observed in Koduli village where Bison-Horn Maria are *Penda* (Slash and burn) cultivators that during cutting of trees and shrubs for the preparation of *penda* land, care is given to leave such trees which are useful in their subsistence pattern namely, fruit bearing trees, like mahua, imli, aonla, mango, tendu char and religious value oriented tree like 'dumar, pipal, aden or saja, bargat (baniyan). They also take care to preserve the trees like bamboo grove, tendu and dharua since these trees/plants are economically helpful in their livelihood pattern. For basketry bamboo is essential, while tendu leaves are collected and sold in the market or forest department and lastly, Kosa (Cocoon) is also collected from forest and sold in the bazar. Incidentally Kosa is grown and nourished in *dharua* tree for which it has special importance to them and hence it is also protected. They even donot cut Sulphi tree due to its importance not only in their daily life but also it has importance in their economic and religious life.

During field investigation it is found that in cutting the grown up trees, lower portion of the trees about 24" to 30" are left in the field from the root. These trunks of cutting trees serves also in conservation practices like (i) to check soil erosion; (ii) after one or two shower it has capacity to rejuvenate twigs from the tip of slaughted tree trunk.

In Burumpal and Padapur villages where wet/settled cultivation is practised there we find that their live stock are confined in their *bari* land during night and the cowdung stored there in various corner of the plot act as an organic fertilizer which inturn increases their crop yield. Here their lands are having contour bunding. In Burumpal village the contour bunding of their cultivable lands are arranged like stairs. Therefore, they make a hole in such contour bunding which helps them to pass on excess rain water to its lower level land and in this way each and every piece of land is getting sufficient water to produce paddy. This traditional technological knowledge they have adapted for their sustenance in such topographical area of their land. This system is otherwise known as gravitational irrigation (i.e. rain fed).

It has already been discussed earlier that Bison- Horn Maria (Dandami. Maria) of Burumpal village are now very much interested for social forestry since their village is almost devoid of trees. Depth interview reveals us that before 1950's there were various trees in the village and even wild life was also prevalent but now-a-days due to the ignorance of their old people the village site now-a-days is looking completely barren. As a result of the present day activities of the panchayat in the conduction of social forestry the people concerned are trying their land and increase of water level capacity beneath the land and develop local environmental niche.

Role of Market

Market study is the cross-sectional study of a given group. It is a place of exchange of ideas, commodities etc. According to Hodges (1988) "the market is one of the most ubiquitous of human institution, and it is hardly necessary to insist upon its power to transform the lives of those who produce and consume the goods in which it deals".

Bastar is the abode of tribal people and the most parts of the district are ill communicated. Therefore, tribal people of the villages are solely dependent on local weekly market day for exchange and purchase of their daily needs. It has been observed that tribal people from the far of villages come on foot to visit such market places. They come in groups, so that when they spent their night in deep forest by liting fire, they are comfortable and save. In this country market, thousands of tribals "peasants' (Wolf, 1966) are busy for hours together with noisy activity; usually this Hat (weekly market) starts from 8 to 9 A.M. and continues upto 4.30/5 P.M. The people come for gossip, merry making/ courtship, playing bait, exchange of their goods, enjoy their time by drinking of Sulphi juice or Landa and exchange of ideas through induction of new technology in their subsistence sector especially in agricultural sector by using high yielding seed, and use of chemical fertilizer and insecticides etc. Above all, they come for business - to sell or exchange the tiny surpluses of their produce in lieu of their daily necessities.

Weekly market is the only spot where this tribal people are able to dispose their surpluse produce and Minor Forest Produce (MFP). It has already been stated earlier. Here in the following lines a list of such items are presented with it's price which they sell to the LAMP, or Co-operative or Forest Dept. Counter.

Table 16: Forest Produce and Market Price

1.	Aonla	Rs. 15/- to Rs. 1/-8 per kg.
2.	Sal seed	Rs. 4/- per kg.
3.	Hill grass or Epur (Phool Jharu)	Per bundle Rs. 4/- or Rs. 7/- per kg.
4.	Harra	Rs. 5/- per kg.
5.	Duli (by broading) fruit of Embelia tsjeriam Cottam)	Used as medicinal purpose, Rs. 130/- per kg.
6.	Karkatiabija (seeds of Ipomoea purpurea)	Medicinal purpose, Rs. 10/- to Rs. 30/- per kg.
7.	Kosa	i) Full size Rs. 0.80
		ii) Medium (where Cocoo himself Rs. 0.45 came out of such cover)
		iii) Where it is broken into Rs. 0.25 piece.
8.	a) Imli Athi (with seed)	Rs. 6.25 per kg.
	b) Imli Phool (without seed)	Rs. 13/- per kg.
	c) Imli Bija (seed)	Rs. 5/- per kg,
9.	Mahua Phool	Rs. 10/- per kg.
10.	Dhoop	Rs. 12/- per paila (One paila 1700 gm)
11.	Lasa (Gum)	Rs. 10/- per paila
12.	One Tumba Honey	Rs. 5/- in the market.

Apart from these they also exchange/ sell their cultivable produce during economic need and Bison-Horn Maria of Padapur and Burumpal villages are in the habit of selling their surplus cultivable produce regularly in the weekly market. Some of such cultivable produce which they sell in the market are:

Table 17: Cultivable Produce and Market Prince

1.	Paddy	Rs. 16/- per paila
2.	Kosra	Rs. 20/- per paila
3.	Mustard (Sarsoo)	Rs. 22/- per paila
4.	Jondra (Makai)	Rs. 25/- per paila
5.	Urad dal	Rs. 20/- per paila
6.	Arhar dal	Rs. 25/- per paila
7.	Jata (Sim)	Rs. 2/- per paila
8.	Papaya	Rs. 5/- for 6 to 8 pieces
9.	Gourd	Rs. 2/- per piece
10.	Lady's finger	Rs. 2/- per doni (consist of 8 to 10 pcs)

Therefore it reveals that market in the tribal habitat of Bastar plays a major role in exchanging or selling their agricultural products as well as MFP for their sustenance chiefly through land and forest. The distribution, exchange and sell of goods in such weekly bazar at the abode of tribal habitat penetrates in remote corner which affect their pattern of livelihood and they even brought into the main stream of population through the process of political network where such market plays an important role.

Management in other sphere of Natural resources

Apart from land and forest management there are also other spheres where management is necessary like water, solar energy and wind.

In the three villages under study it is observed that there is one lift irrigation system at Padapur - a mining village, through which a Bison-Horn Maria family try to produce rabi crop, incidentally it is the village sarpanch house, but her effort is not successful due to bad quality of water (i.e. water discharge from NMDC after washing iron-ore is not suitable for cultivation). While the Bison-Horn Maria of Burumpal village have a permanent perennial source of water, which they utilize in their cultivation. They even produce rabi paddy and other rabi ereals with the help of such water.

The use of Solar energy for sustenance is widely practised by Bison-Horn Maria of Bastar. The harvested crop and cereals are dried through solar rays. The grains of Jondra, mohua flower etc. are dried in sun ray and stored by them in their granary. During monsoon they are to face some scarcity in food material, due to such, they have a habit; to dry up the pieces of mutton of cow or pigs, which they spread on the roof of their huts for dry up and store these in their room. During necessity they use these by placing these in the hot water for sometime, then cook it and consume it. They are of opinion that above all without sun ray no life can be flourished.

Lastly, inview of wind management among Bison- Horn Maria it is observed that winnowing of harvested crop is fully dependent on flow and direction of wind at the threshing ground. More so, by examining and feeling the direction of wind certain aged persons canassess the change of environment i.e. from summer to monsoon, monsoon to winter and even guess the out burst of thunder shower.

Culture and Management of Natural Resource

The life and culture of Bison-Horn Maria of Bastar are governed under the influence of local environment. It has been keenly observed that socio-religious life is closely imbibed with environment inview of their livelihood. The relationship between a man with his immediate environment is like a meshed fabric due to various supernatural beliefs for their survival. Since their existence is very much linked with forest and land, they try to appease them in various ways.

Bison-Horn Maria - a sub-division of Gond are divided into number of septs. A group of septs are called *bhaiband* or *dadabhai* to each other, that is, in the relation of brothers or cousins being the sons of brothers. Marriage within same *bhaiband* is probthited-while the other group of septs known as *akomama / mamabhai* or *saga* and *mamabhai* means a maternal uncle's son and *akomama* signifies having the same maternal grandfather. Marriage between a person of *dadabhai* group with a girl of *mamabhai* group is allowed. Geneologital data and kinship data reveals that they practise cross-cousin marriage and it is preferred most, Broadly the tribe is divided into two broad exogamous halves again each of such exogamous halves have some classes (i.e. phratry) and each class has a number of septs or clans in it. Each sept possesses a clan or *pen* deity of their own who' are again having dadabhai and Saga/*akomama* relations in their clestial world. The clan or deity among them in Bastar district form a great family in which they are all related to one another and these tribals are well aware of their (i.e. *pen*) genealogies. Often, a clan god visits his/her relations in other village since one may be the wife or another a child or nephew or sister and so on. Their clans are totemic in nature, like Sodi. (tiger), Marvi (goat), Oyami (tortoise) etc. They are tabooed to kill these and in this way fauna of their niche are protected.

Traditional belief associates the clan god with territory in which the members of clan reside. A special priest called *perma* or wadde lives near its shrine; it is his duty to guard the clan god and to preside over its worship at all clan / *pen* festival.

The solidarity and unity among members of a clan ensure through the performance of annual clan god festival. It is, above all, the faith in its power to detect sorcerers, witches and breaches of taboo.

When a man suffers from frequent setback in his life like casualty to his live stock, his relatives falling ill or his crops failing etc. then he may requisition the services of his clan god.

The earth goddess - *bhum* or *tallin* is believed to be the ultimate source of all life, the mother who feeds and sustain her children. The village priest-*bhum gaita* may commune with her or solicit her help. On the onset, she divided the land into areas, one for each clan and fixed its boundaries. To every clan priest she revealed the territory alloted to his clan. The sacred information is being handed down through succeeding generation to descending one. Many festivals are designed to ensure the benevolence of the earth goddess. Tallin is the abode of their *bhumdevi*. They are not allowed to pollute the place. They consider they are the children of *bhum*. Tallin is vast stretches of land in the corner of village, which is considered as sacred grove. Each and every tree standing at *tallin* are considered as sacred, especially aden/Saja tree; the *deogudi* or place of their *bhum* deity - earth goddess is situated under aden tree. They do not cut any tree or its twigs at *tallin*. So more trees are grown in this place through easy germination. In this way through age old value system they practise conservation of their niche.

The religious activities of Bison Horn Maria are closely connected with their sustenance pattern in such ecological background. Each and every of their cultivated cereals, or fruits/flowers which they collect from forest are first offered to their deity and *bhum* deity and then only they are allowed to eat these. They always try to appease their supernatural power by offering the first cereals, fruits and thereby get blessings. Infact they observe various festivals connected mainly with agriculture and ancestors of clan god. These festivals are observed to seek benevolence and to ward - off evil spirits and are timed with the beginning of each agricultural operation.

Following are some importent and major *pandum* or festivals of Bison Horn Maria which are deeply connected with their subsistence pattern.

(a) Jare Pandum

It is performed in Magh or early February for cutting of timber for erka cultivation in hill slopes. *Weta Parad Pandum* or ceremonial communal hunting expedition is also performed during this time-Until *Kare Pandum* has taken place it is taboo or mela among them to cut any timber for *erka* cultivation. After this *Pandum* they are allowed to harvest forest grass crop.

Therefore, it is seen that the religious value system among them prevent them from doing injurious activities towards the nature which ultimately helps them in its conservation. Practically speaking harvested *Ghatka* is lying in the *penda* field during the period, so if firing is done in forest before *Kare pandum* it may be damaged. The ritual bindings restrict them from such activities.

(b) Bhimul Pandum

It is celebrated in the middle of February for good rains during the coming agricultural season. Through this *pandum* they try to appease the nature for their subsistence.

(c) Irpu Pandum or Mahua Pandum

Celebrated at the time of Mahua flowering first fruit ceremony. It is held sometimes in March. It is performed just after *Bhimul Pandum*.

(d) Marka Pandum or Ama Khani

Celebrated in little later part of March at the time of mango fruiting. The village priest or *perma* of the village fixes a day which is always in bright half of the month, in consultation with the *peda* or headman and village elders about a week beforehand.

When *peda* sees that young fruit has formed on trees he arranges for *Sari bori* or village subscription (often these are collected from passerby of main road) and perform the *Pandum*. In each *pandum* the men observe sexual continence on the night before the ceremony. It is also observed that mahua tree plays more important role than mango tree since mahua has a tremendous importance in their economic as well as religious life.

(e) Wjja Pandum

Celebrated in March or April during preliminary agricultural operations in the field. It usually starts on Sunday, five or six days after *marka pandurn.* Village priest or *perma* performs ritual activity in the name of *bhum* or *tallin* and sacrifices in his name black cock, egg etc. With these they try to appease the earth goddess with a hope that after sowing of seed a good yield is expected. Along with this they also perform *Mati teohar* to appease *bhum*-earth goddess.

(f) Hareli Pandum

It is a ceremonial worship for good crop. In the morning of the auspicious day the village elders assemble at *perma's* house and then go to the hut of the log-god-Anga or to the mata's hut - *deogudi* or *matatagudi*. No sacrifice is done but he lights a fire in front of god or goddess, burns a Sal resin in the fire and bows before the deity and it is followed by all the elders assemble there. The religious value behind such *pandum* is that well branched plant like paddy, kutki seed sown in the field should produce more.

(g) Kurum Pandum or Kurmim Kortang

It is performed towards the end of August when the new millet crop is cooked and eaten for the first time. These early ripening millets are from *penda* field, especially Chikma (Panicum miliare) variety. It is also performed by *perma* infornt of village log- hut or village *bhum Jaga* or *Kadri bera* field (a piece of land in the field of religious headman - *perma* assigned for certain village religious activities and sacrifices) before *bhimul* post which is regarded as village mother for this *pandum.* The *pemna* sacrifices cock and pig and sprinkles their blood over the goddess. This is often known as Nawakhani or *Ikma Pandum.* Without the performance of it consuming of the seasonal vegetables which is grown during that time is tabooed.

(h) Korta Pandum / or Punang Kortang

It is the ceremony to mark the first eating of the new crop of rice. This *pandum* comes about a month after the *Kurum Pandum.* This *pandum* not only celebrates first eating of new rice but also of new cucumbers, pumpkins and gourds. This *pandum* is clearly individual family oriented unlike the *Kurum Pandum.*

(1) Jata - Pandum

It is a ceremony to celebrate eating of new crop of beans and pulses. This *pandum* performs sometimes near the full moon of Pus. It is performed communally at the village before *deogudi* or the hut of log-god where sacrifices are done and the departed souls are invoked.

In this way they are prohibited to take mango, mahua and any new crop of their field prior to offer these to their deities and ancestors. It is believed that breach of such taboo may bring catastrophes to the family as well as to the village. Through various ritual bindings and their value these fruits of the year and new crops etc. are restricted to eat before the performance of ritual which indicates germination of new fruit tree is ensured since by this time matured fruits may available. In this way conservation practices through ritual performances are prevailed among them.

It reveals from above discussion that the socio religious life of Bison-Horn Maria are very much dependent and influenced on their local niche from which they eke out their livelihood.

WORLD VIEW AND CONCLUSION

The World view of people i.e. the way the people see themselves in relation to the world around them might give us a clue to the nature of their techno-economic adaptation as well as perpetuation of their distinct socio-cultural identity and would help us in comprehending the meaningful world they live in (Adhikary, 1984). According to Redfield (1971) it is the real whole of the little community that awaits the insider's total vision and conception of everything. During the presentation of their world view the researchers have initially collected the data on the universe of the people studied–the interaction with such universe for their sustenance and above all the cognitive aspect or emic views are gathered which they have acquired after prolonged association with such niche.

Native concept of Environment and Natural Objects

When mahua and mango flower are blooming they think *garmi* or summer is approaching. When they are able to collect sal seed or *tora* and when mango becomes ripen they understand that *barish* or monsoon is coming. When paddy is matured in the field and when sweetness is increased in *chind* palm juice itis apprehended that *sardi* or winter is approaching. On seeing more brownish tender leaf in *mahua* trees and size is big in April they take the situation as a sign of better monsoon It is the result of their close and continuous association with the forest.

The concept of day time is realised by the movement of *parad* or sun and length of daram or shadow and during night they depend in Cackle's sound. The Bison-Horn Maria's conception of eclipse or *gharnash* is that when both *parad* or sun or *lenj* or moon is captured by others; they consider this time as inauspicious and they donot eat during this period and to overcome this phase of nature they used to start hue and cry and become restless and express the condition by making noisy sound from their utensils. It is reported that *lenj* is the wife of *parad* and *ukkas* or stars are their children. Thunder is *markamutta* and as soon as it is seen the rain will follow. Till date in the remote abode of Bison-Horn Maria their idea regarding T.V. and radio are - person's are inside the TV/Radio. *Bhimulbil* is rainbow, if it is found in *peitaram* or in the direction of east then rain will be active while if it is found in *purdaimaito* or in west then rain w'ill be stopped but if this *bhimulbil* is found in either side after rain, then there is no further hope of rain again. The Bison-Horn Maria reckon their universe, natural objects and time mostly interms of concrete, predictable immediate environmental phenomena and this knowledge they acquire from their ascending generation. Similar observation has also been made by Morey (1971) and Evans-Pritchard (1940) who termed it as 'ecological time', i.e., "reflections of their relations to environment".

Use of Traditional Knowledge in Daily Life

They are fond of hunting and fishing. Bison-Horn Maria observe *parad pandum* at the time of starting of the agricultural season when all able bodied men go for a day long hunt with their bows, arrows, axe and spears. They are also expert in trapping the animals; *tarnone* is one such hare trap. Poisoning of fish is also practised by them by herbs, namely, *Kehkar* creeper or bark of *Karta* tree or with various poisionous vegetable products, which are all available in their local niche and are well recognised. They also use nets and snares. 'Lava Jaal', is used to catch *lava* - a kind of small bird, after harvest of paddy. Gum coated bamboo sticks called 'Chick' are also used for the same purpose. Often, they poison the water pits with herbs for catching fish. They never cut Aden, Sarai, Dhaura, Seona, Bhat trees because these have got not only religious value to them but kosa or cocoons are developed and nourished in these trees. The people collect cocoon and sale these to bazar, so it has also economic importance to them.

Apart from this, many of their traditional knowledge which are applied in their sustenance pattern, are discussed in the foregoing pages under different heading. This will also reveal that they have acquired this knowledge for their survival in such environment where resources are gathered from their habitat.

Traditional Wisdom

According to the myth and legend of Bison-Horn Maria - rain in Magh and Aghan is specially lucky for a good year. Fagun rain is unlucky for agriculture and means a bad year. Rain after Vaisak fullmoon means good year. When a warm eats away teak, sal leaves which it called *baisakoda* it gets up a tree, eats away all the leaves and then gets down. On its getting down rain begins to fall. If this warm get down in the beginning of *Asadh* it signifies for good year, if they come down earlier then there will be delay in raining. If it glows near the surface rain is soon to come. Fish can be caught in the field water during *Bhado* (August - September), if it is possible to catch in *kuanr* or *aswin* (September-October) good rain and good crops are promising.

Folk Song/Folktale

It reveals from their folk song that they always have a belief in supernatural power or benevolent spirit who are always appeased with their producing crop. It is thought without their blessings it is not possible for them to produce crop. Their each and every *pandum* or festivals are related with their economic activities and followed by dancing, singing and consumption of liquor like *mahua*, or *sulphi* or *chhind* etc.

On the eve of *bhimul pandum*, in the middle of February their song address to rain deity is as follows, Here in the following lines in Hindi version of such song :

"Phool Khile, Phool Khile Bhim
Dhan Phool Khile, Am Pake Bhim
Kosra Phool Khile Bhim Khile,
Mung Phool. Khile Bhim Khile,
Kulthi Phool Khile Bhim Khile
Tili Phool Khile Bhim Khile
Mahua Phool Khile Bhim Khile,
Manjar Khile Bhim Khile
Imli Phool Khile Bhim Khile
Jamun Phool Khile Bhim Khiie
Phool Khile, Phool Khile".

From the above song it is also evident that they have got a close association with nature, they always pray before the almighty that without rain their survival will be impossible and flower of mango, tamarind, kosra, paddy, Mahua etc. will bloom only after rain and for which they pray before Bhimul - the rain deity.

Concept of Supernatural Power in Relation to Management

Among Bison-Horn Maria every natural phenomenon is animated and presided by some spirits. These supernatural spirits have an important role in their way of life. The earth goddess - *bhum* is worshipped at their tallin (sacred grove). In the beginning of the year they celebrate *mati teohar* where *bhum* deity is appeased fcr good yield. The *bhum* deity is a woman, who looks after almost all the natural resources and creatures on the earth. *Bhun gaita* is the priest of such village ritual. These deities who control natural phenomena are worshipped in time and offerings are made before them..

Conclusion

From the aforesaid discussion it is clear that Bison-Horn Maria of Bastar whose life and culture are nourished in the lap of forest environment, are having close knit organisation with each aspect of their sustenance pattern which may be visualised in the following way -

Relation of Bison - Horn Maria with Sustenance pattern in relation with Management of Natural Resources

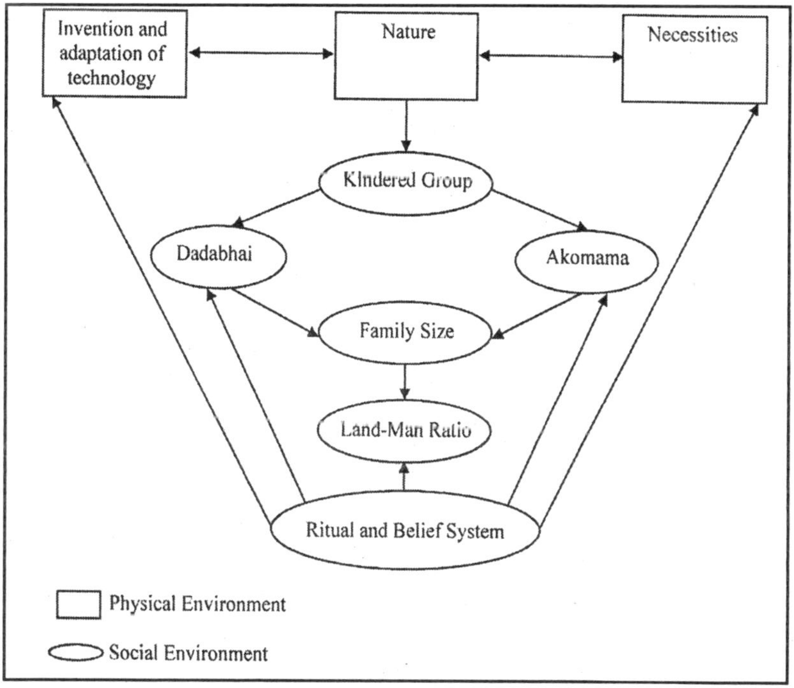

Now from the above discussion it can be concluded that environment limits the cultural development among Bison-Horn Maria or it is clear that culture development among Bison-Horn Maria is dependent on environmental opportunity in which natural resources play a key role. In other words if we consider Stewwrd (1955) view of 'culture core', it can be compared with Bison-Horn Maria of Bastar situation especially found in Burumpal and Padapur villages where Bison Horn Maria are wet cultivators and exploiting local resources which they practise not only with their traditional knowledge but also modern impact of communication is observed to work in them. In this habitat, technology is the key factor for their development and sustenance, since they are wet cultivators in this eco-zone,while in Koduli - a forest village eco-zone, where Bison-Horn Maria, are immigrant at the traditional habitat of Abujh Maria, practise *penda* cultivation after cleaning forest mercilessly and it is preferred most by them. It appears from close observation among Bison-Horn Maria that they are very much loose tempered, arogant and merciless in destroying forest, even they are reluctant in learning the utility and conservation of forest due to it's abundance in this eco-zone. In this eco-zone (i.e. Koduli Village of Marh area). White's (1959) observation on culture may be compared, that is, sum total of their cultural development is 'man-power (i.e. energy) implied by them in such environmental niche and harness of technological know how i.e. culture–technology x energy (Because they practise *penda* at Koduli and vast stretches of forest land is under their possession; a person's ability, energy and necessity are the main criteria for doing *penda* or increase *penda* plot for cultivation).

For the sake of survival they have been use their indigenous knowledge in exploiting as well as conserving their activities with traditional wisdom and over all in all those area of their survival where natural resources play a key role. There we witness a deep rooted shadow of supernatural belief systems. The core of the culture or value system of their society prevails in such beliefs. Therefore, shadow of belief system among Bison-Horn Maria or Dandami Maria also controls conservation of their bio- diversity with their indigenous traditional knowledge which is otherwise known to us as their traditional wisdom. In this context one environmentalist - view may be quoted on tribal wisdom, "the belief of Indian tribal peoples ..... that their culture was born and nourished in the forest, and their dependence for survival upon its continued existence has imbued in them a respectful attitude to nature, and given rise to the development of the most basic principles of forest management. Around the world the encyclopaedic knowledge of indigenous people on local plants and their application is an important basis for the development of medicines for the wider good of mankind" (Strong, 1992).

Thus the present study reveals that the management of environment and it's natural resources by the Bison-Horn Maria tribe of Bastar (M.P) is very much alike with Geertz (1963) approach - "Cultural Eco-systemicism" (interdependence of culture and physical factors is primary objective)- an approach of understanding culture and environrnent-with the help of sketches this may be focussed :

Bison-Horn Maria : Interaction of Culture and Environment

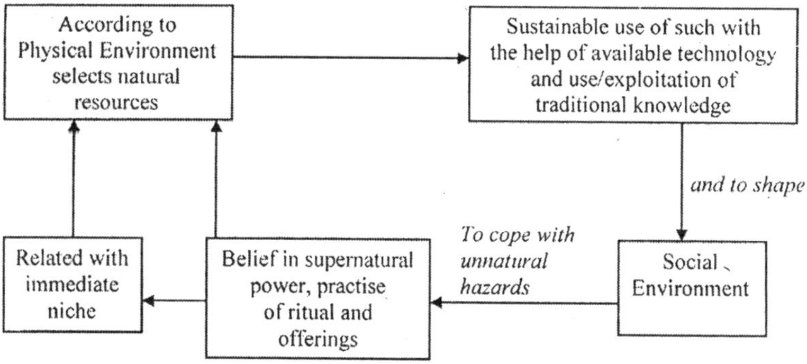

Thus, Bison-Horn Maria - a forest based tribe, nourished his culture under the influence of local envtronment and use it's local resources for survival with the help of their age old folk knowledge.

References

Adhikary, Ashim, K. 1984. *Society and World View of the Birhor,* Calcutta: Anthropological Survey of India, Memoir no. 60.

Bennett, John, W. 1976. *The Edological Transition: Cultural Anthropology and Human Adaptation*, New York: Pergamon Press Inc.

Buchman, U.K. 1992. *Mythen*, Geowissen: Hamburg.

Crookshank, H., 1963. *Geology of Southern Bastar and Jeypore from the Bailadila Range to the Eastern Ghats.* Memoirs of Geological Survey of India, Vol. 87.

Elwin, V. 1991. (Reprinted). *The Muria and their Ghotul,* Delhi : Oxford University Press and Vanya Prakshan.

Evans-Pritchard, E.E. 1940. The Nuer, Oxford : The Clavendon Press.

Gadgil, M. and V.D. Vartak, 1976. "The Sacred groves of Western Ghats in India", *Economic Botany*, Vol. 70, pp. 152-160.

Geertz, Clifford, 1963. *Agricultural Involution: The Process of Ecological Change in Indonesia*, Berkeley : University of California Press.

Gell, Simeran Man Singh, 1992. The Ghotul in Muria Society. Switzerland: Hardwood Academic Publishers.

Glasfurd, Capt. C.L.D. 1862. Report on the Dependency of Bastar.

Grigson, Sir Wilfrid, 1991. (Reprinted). The Maria Gonds of Bastar, Delhi: Vanya Prakshan and Oxford University Press.

Hodges, Richard, 1988, Primitive and Peasant Markets U.K.: Basil Blackwell Ltd.

Hughes Charles, 1968. "Ethnomedicine", in *International Encyclopaedia of Social Science,* Vol. IV, New York : The Macmillan Co. and Free Press.

Morey, Robert, V. 1971. Guahibo Time – reckoning" Anthropological Quarterly, Vol. 44, No. 1 pp. 22-36.

Negi, S.S. 1994. India's Forests. Forestry and Wild Life, New Delhi : Indus Publishing Co.

Pranjpye, 1989. "Deoral", in Deforestation and Drought (Ed.) N.D. Jayal, INTACH: New Delhi.

Rappaport, Roy A. 1967. Pigs for the Ancestors: Ritual in the Ecology of a New Guinea People, New Haven :Yale University Press.

Redfield Robert, 1971 . The Little Community and Peasant Society and Culture, Chicago: The University of Chicago Press.

Singh, K.S. 1994. People of India. Vol. VII, Identity, Ecology, Social Organisation, Economy, Linkages and Development Process. A Qualitative Profile, Delhi: Oxford University Press and Anthropological Survey of India.

Singh, Pramad, 1989. "A Collapsible Forest Ecology of India", in Problem of Waste Land and Forest Ecology in India (ed) Pramad Singh, New Delhi, Ashish Pub. House, pp. 227-245.

Sinha, Rajiv, K. 1995. "Contribution of Indian Tribals to Modern Civilization", in Tribals in India, ed A.K. Singh and M.K. Jabbi, New Delhi : Har-Anand Publication.

Sinha, Rajiv, K. 1992. "Eco-system Preservation Through Faith and Tradition in India Jr. of Human Ecology, Vol. II, No. 1 pp. 21-24.

Steward, J.H. 1955. The Theory of Culture Change, Urbana : University of Illinois Press.

Strong, F.M. 1992. "Only the Earth", Indian International Centre Quarterly. Vol. XIX, No. 1 & 2, pp. 49-52.

Sundar, Nandini, 1997. Subalterns and Soverigns : An Anthropological History of Bastar, 1854-1996, Delhi : Oxford University Press.

Tribhuwan, R.D. 1998. Medical World of the Tribals, New Delhi : Discovery Pub. House.

Vartak, V.D. and M. Gadgil. 1991. "Studies on Sacred Groves along the Western Ghats from Maharashtra and Goa : Role and Beliefs of Folklore", in Glimpses of Indian Ethnobotany, (ed.) S.K. Jain, New Delhi: IBH.

White, L.A., 1959. The Evolution of Culture, New York : McGraw Hill.

Wolf, Eric R., 1966. Peasants, New Jersey : Printice Hall, Inc.

Govt. Record:

1991 – Madhya Pradesh Environmental Status Report, Vol. XI, Bhopal.

1984 – Bastar Development Report, M.P. State Planning Board, Bhopal.

6

Study on Traditional Wisdom in Baiga Society

Samit Ghosal and *R.B. Thakre*

INTRODUCTION

The present study is an attempt to examine the Baiga, a primitive forest dwelling tribe of Madhya Pradesh, in the specific eco-cultural surroundings of their traditional environment. The enquiry shall centre around primarily to an understanding of their traditional wisdom and natural resources.

LOCATION AND AREA OF STUDY

The study under the project "Management of Environment and Natural Resources: A Study on Traditional Wisdom in Tribal Society" was conducted at Chara forest village (Location Code No. 582), situated in the Bajag Block of the Dindori district of Madhya Pradesh. The study area is known as 'Baiga Chawk" and it is located between 22°31′ and 22°35′ north latitude and 81°14′ and 81°23′ east longitude. Dindori is a new district formed by bifurcating the old Mandla district of Madhya Pradesh. The high and rugged table land of the district separates the cotton growing country of the south from the wheat growing extension of the Malwa plateau on the north. On the east and southeast it culminates into the gentle slopes of the lowland of Chhatisgarh.

Historical Background

The etymological meaning of the word Mandla leads to several conjectures. Some relate Mandla to the Sanskrit word 'mandal', meaning a circle, because the river Narmada almost girdles the district on three sides. According to others, mandla is a survival of the word 'mandala' or feudatory state (Mandla District Gazetteers, 1912). The early history of the area is obscure. The available historical accounts of the district suggest that the area was ruled by the Kalchuri or Chedi kings of the Jabalpur from 875 A.D. to 1180 A.D., till the rise of the Gond kings of Garha-Mandla, who ruled the country through the Gond chieftain's up to 1789 A.D. Since the 'Mutiny of 1857' the district was permanently administered by the British Rule (District Census Handbook, 1961).

Objective of the Study

The project seeks to understand how the tribal communities, living in relatively inaccessible and forested areas since time immemorial, are managing their natural resources, an integral part of their environment, e.g. land, water, forest, by using their traditional wisdom. The traditional knowledge pattern of the tribal people concerned is found to be integrated into their life-philosophy. They nurture the nature in their own age-old thinking orientation which is spontaneously fashioned in such a specific way which is pledged to perpetrate the ecological balance and biodiversity. Their cultural tie with local environment is unique. It is to be noted with great concern that the traditional wisdom of these tribal groups is fashioned with their basic philosophy centering round their conventional appeal for an amicable relationship with nature. This indigenous knowledge is needed to be respected. The study also tries to integrate the indigenous knowledge of the tribal people as would it be of considerable help if it is applied at the time framing the programme of development of the tribal people.

With this view in mind the Baiga, a primitive forest dwelling tribe of Madhya Pradesh, was studied to fulfill the required objective of the project. The Baiga was selected for the study because of their legendary knowledge of forest and forest produce, as the bulk of their economy even today is extracted from the forest resources. Attempt has been made to examine their traditional knowledge about utilization, preservation and conservation of natural resources that are still in vogue in their day to day life. Though mixed with superstitious belief the Baiga

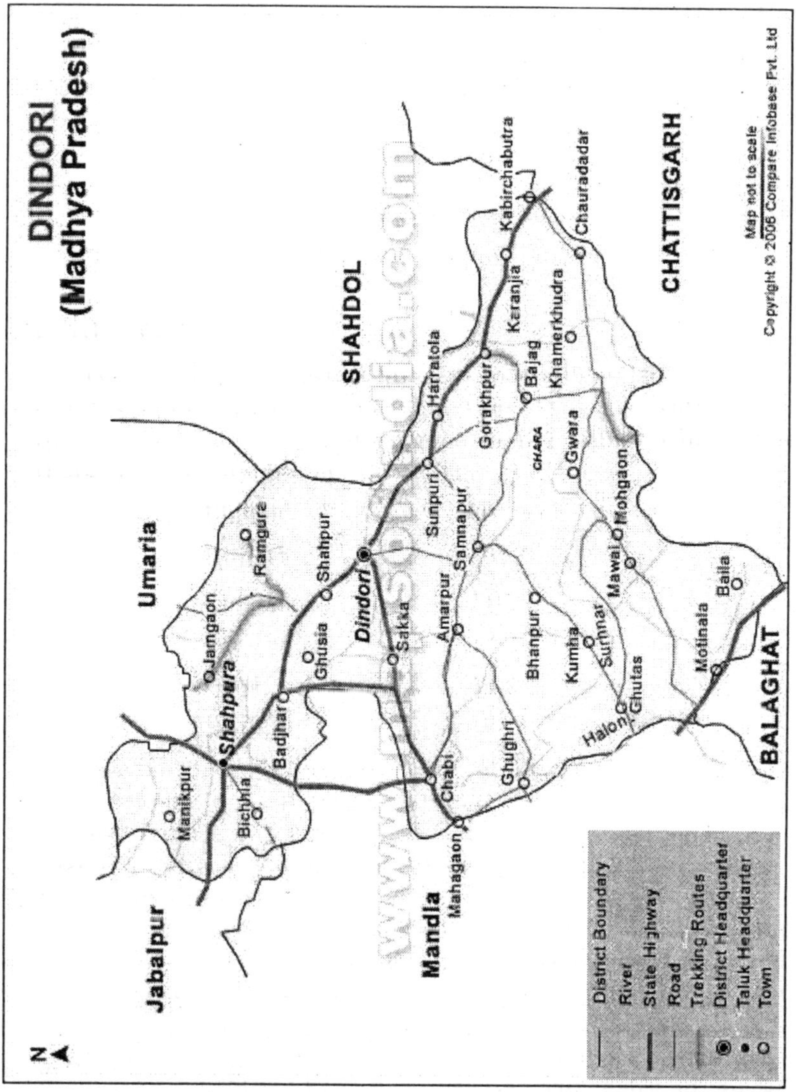

DINDORI
(Madhya Pradesh)
N
Jabalpur
Umaria
SHAHDOL
Mandla
CHATTISGARH
BALAGHAT
Dindori
Shahpura
Manikpur
Bichhia
Jamgaon
Ramgura
Badjhar
Ghusia
Shahpur
Sakka
Chabi
Mahagaon
Ghughri
Amarpur
Samnapur
Sunpuri
Harratola
Gorakhpur
Bajag
Karanjia
Kabirchabutra
Chauradadar
Khamerkhudra
Gwara
CHARA
Mohgaon
Mawai
Bhanpur
Kumha
Surhnar
Ghutas
Halon
Motinala
Baiha
District Boundary
River
State Highway
Road
Trekking Routes
District Headquarter
Taluk Headquarter
Town
Map not to scale
Copyright © 2006 Compare Infobase Pvt. Ltd

possess some degree of practical knowledge of animal behaviour, medicinal properties of plants, selection of specific crops suitable for particular field, crop rotation, forestry and craftsmanship. Baigas expertise as a medicine man *parexcellence* and their belief in supernatural power to control the menace of Tiger put them in a relatively superior position amongst the neighbouring tribes.

Selection of Study Area

Chara, a forest village situated deep inside the Reserve Forest in the 'Baiga Chawk", was selected as study area because it was observed that at Chara the Baiga were living in a close, intimate and harmonious relationship with nature, less disturbed by the outside world due to inhospitable terrain condition. The Baiga Chowk, a reservation, was created by the British administration in 1890 comprising of eight forest villages, namely, Tantar, Silpri, Kandapani, Dhurkuta, Lamota, Ajgar, Rajnisarai and Dhaba situated in the southern highland of Maikal range. This was done in order to rehabilitate the Baiga in a confined area, who chose to continue '*bewar*'. The timber in this area was of little value owing to the indiscriminate practice of '*bewar*' cultivation. Out side the chawk, all the Baiga were ordered either to abandon *bewar* or move into the reserve, where a tax @ Rupee one (Rs.1/-) per acre was assessed for *bewar* cultivation. Outside its limit *bewar* cultivation was strictly prohibited. The Baiga who had refused to abandon *bewar* or to move into the reservation, migrated to the neighbouring Pandaria Zamindari or Kuwardha Estate of Bilaspur.

The Baiga Development Authority was formed in 1978 and 52 villages were clustered in the Baiga Chawk area from Bajag, Samnapur and Karanjia blocks of Dindori district in 1980. On the eastern side of Baiga Chawk is Konta taluka of Bilaspur district, on the western side is Seoni district, on the north is Sirdhi district and on the south is Rajnandgaon district. Average height of the area varies from 2000 feet to 3000 feet altitude above sea level.

Methodology Used

Categorical methodological principles were adopted in the conduction of field work amongst the Baigas and village as a unit of study has been taken up for investigation. Standard ethnographic method applied according to the specific need. Efforts were made in collecting data through concrete case studies. As per very nature of the study attempts have conspicuously been made to spend more time on associated with observations as well as open end questionnaires and schedules and informal interviews, both directed and undirected. The approach of participant observation has been adopted but being outsider it was limited largely to informal social situation.

Land and People

A brief overview of the land and people of the area studied is to be helpful for proper understanding of the objective of the study. Nature of landscape, terrain and ethno-history of the people play an important role in the management of their surrounding environment and natural resources.

Geographical Setup

Dindori district is marked by the rugged Maikal hills, an eastward extension of Satpura range, which forms the watershed for the source of holy Narmada. The spurs and sub-ranges of the Maikal hills divide the country in the east of the district into a number of valleys and table land. The range of elevation of Maikal hills is from 2000 feet to 3000 feet.

Burner, the principal river of Baiga Chawk, flows west from Baiga Chawk and after being joined by the river Halon, empties its water into the Narmada at Deogaon.

The general rock structure of the district consists of granite, limestone and syanite. Lateritic murram is the commonest soil in the district but also in between there is decomposed trap known as black cotton soil. However, the most dominating soil of the area is described as 'skeleton soil' which consists of *Bherra* soil and *Sehra* soil. The *Bherra* soil is reddish in colour, full of gravels and not suitable for cultivation. *Sehra* soil is pale yellow in colour, mixed with clay and contains hymus, is ideal for cultivation.

The climate in the region is temperate in general. Even during the hottest days of summer, the temperature does not exceed 40°C. During the winter months, i.e. in December and January, the temperature goes down to 0°C. The canopy of thick forest keeps the temperature a little moist throughout the year. The average rainfall of the area is 1576 mm.

Natural Vegetation

Dindori district is rich in forest wealth. The *sal* (*shores robusta*) is the timber tree *par-excellence* of the district. Beside *sal*, *saj* (*terminalia tomentoss*), *bija* (*pterocarpus marsupium*), *tendu* (*diospyros melanoseylon*), *harra* (*terminalia chebula*), *dhawa* (*anogeissus latifolia*), *jamun* (*Eugenia jambolana*), *aonla* (*phyllanthus emblica*) and *achar* (*buchanania latifolia*) fruits, which yields *'Chiranji'*. The grassland of the district provides for an excellent grazing ground for the cattle. *Musail* (*iseilema wightie*) and *Kel* (*andropogon annulatus*) are the two main varieties of grasses which have a great value as fodder. Two types of bamboos are found in the area, *bana bans* or common bamboo (*dendrocalamus strictus*) and *Kattang* bans or thorny bamboo (*bambus rundinacea*). (The non timber forest produce will be discussed in subsequent chapters).

The Tribe: Baiga

According to 2001 Census the total population of Baiga is 3,32,936 in Madhya Pradesh. Of which 1,67,810 is male and 1,65,126 is female i.e. a sex ratio of 984 female per 1000 male. The population of Baiga in Mandla district is 59,370 (1991 Census).

One of the earliest account on the Baiga tribe written by Thomson (1867) says "they lived in the most inaccessible hills and remotest forest, were mere food gatherers and subsisted on forest products and hunting. Some of them raised wild grains in small trips on the hill sides".

The Baiga tribe is subdivided into a number of endogamous subgroups or sub-tribes, such as, Binjwar Baiga, Bharotia Baiga, Narotia Baiga, Raibhania, Kathbhania, Kundi, Gondwani, Kurku Baiga, Sawat Baiga, Budh-Bhania and Bhumia Baiga (Elwin, 1939). Each of the sub-tribe has further san subdivided into a number of exogamous *jat*. Besides this the baiga have also a number of non-tometic clans or septs, called *goti*, probably taken after the Gond, as some of the Gond clans are identical with that of the Baiga. The Baiga *gotis* play no role in marriage alliances.

Rusell and Hiralal (1916) regarded the Baiga as a branch of the primitive Bhuiya tribes of Chhotanagpur. Verrier Elwin (1939) also considered the Baiga as an offshoot of the great Bhuiya tribe of Chhotanagpur plateau who had migrated to this area via the plains of Chhatisgarh.

The Baiga of Baiga Chawk consider themselves 'Bhumia Baiga' – the Bhumia subdivision of the great Biaga tribe. The legend says, the God created Nanga Baiga and Nangi Baigin, the ancestor and ancestress of the Baiga tribe, from his naval. They were gifted with an axe and were asked to go to the jungle and maintain their livelihood by gathering forest produce and hunting animals. They are considered to be the oldest settlers of the region. The Baiga in this area live with other ethnic groups such as, Gond, Pradhan, Agaria, Ahir, Panka and Dhoba. They maintain a close relationship with the Gond whom they consider as elder brother and accepted their supremacy and higher social status. The Gond is *barki* and the Baiga is chotki. Culturally Dindori district and Baiga Chawk area is a part of Chhattisgarh which is mostly influenced by the Chhattisgarhi culture and language, Baigani, the language spoken by the Baiga is a corrupt form of Chhatisgarhi (Grierson; Linguistic Survey of India, Vol. VI, p. 235).

Material Life

Hutton (1944) defined material culture as "the study of those objects (other than human) and all those artifacts with which man surrounds himself in his attempt to ameliorate his position in his environment.

Material life is a fair index of the general level of knowledge and of the intellectual attainment of the people. Ecological factors play a great role in the various aspects of culture, especially in the case of material culture. Man utilizes his environment to the fullest extent possible with the technology at his disposal. He adapts himself to it and exercises his control over it. As a matter of fact material life of a man is the rendezvous of external environment and socio-cultural representation, manifestation of ecological relation.

Settlement Pattern

Generally Baiga villages are situated by the side of a river or stream. Most of the Baiga villages at Baiga Chawk are located at the top of the hills, always a stream flows below the hills as a source of water.

The Baiga build their houses either in the form of a large square or with houses lining the sides of a street. The village boundary is usually marked by a pile of stones. When the villages are built around a large square, three sides of the area are closed by houses and the fourth is open to the air but fenced with bamboo or cactus hedge. They fence their *bari* field with *Kharia, Katbalang* tree and *bakkal* (bark) of *mohlain* tree. The *sar* or cattle shed is also situated adjoining the houses. Outside the square, there is a garden land called *bari*. All the refuse of house and animal excreta are collected and allowed to decompose in a pit and utilized in the field. Being well manured it gives a good harvest of crops. Baiga houses, unlike the Gond, stand very close, usually five or six feet away from each other.

In a forest village, all the materials that are needed for a house – a few heavy wooden pillers, some poles, split bamboo, a few yards of bark, some thatching grass, mud, cow dung and white soil, are obtained from the forest free of cost. Walls of a Baiga house, rectangular in shape, is made of *chirree* straw and *birhol* (indigoferapulchella) branches. They are plastered with a mud made by mixing *lalmati* (red soil) and chaff of paddy, *Kodon* or *Kutki*. Two beams called *mayer*, placed horizontally on the mud walls across the breadth of rectangular house. Two vertical pillers, thunki – with a forked top, are rested on these *mayers* at the central position. The one horizontal beam *churia* is placed over the two inserted vertical pillers or *thunki*. Then a number of slanting *malga* around the house, runs down to the four walls to hold the slanting roof. Outside projection, on all four sides of the house is held by *patoti melga*, which runs on all sides of the projected roof. The roof of the house is thatched by *moya* grass (pennisectum alopecuros) or *rusa* grass (andropogon schaenanthus). They also use Khapra for roofing. *Shera* soil is mixed with the straw and husk of *Kodon*, *Kutki*, *Ramtilla* and the dough is put into a mould. At a makeshift kiln they first keep firewood, then cow dung and over it keep the stuff and put fire at the bottom, it burns for the whole night. After 2-3 days it gets cool and is ready to use. They use khapra because it lasts long but it is used by those who can afford it. The rest use grass as thatching material. The husk of cereals is used for cementation of the surface.

Sal is mainly used as an ideal timber for house construction. Beside hard and strong, sal wood can withstand the attack of insects. White *chuhi* soil is used for plastering of the walls; inside the house they use red soil or *lalmatti* for flooring, mixing it with hays of *kodon* at the ratio of 1:1.

Crafts

Basketry is very popular among the Baiga. They make it from the various types of bamboos – grown abundantly all over the area. They also make various traps to catch fish and birds. They prepare fish trap in which small fishes enter with the flow of water but cannot come out. Bow and arrow and all the agricultural implements are made by the Baiga, with the exception of iron parts which they buy from the Agaria. The Baiga are very expert in rope making from local grasses, especially from *mowa* and *sowa*. They made soil levellor (*bhakar*) with *sal* and plough with *dhanwa* wood. The Bhakar is used both for removing of the roots of earlier crops and leveling of soil. For eruption of roots they fit a iron share at the dorsal side and for using it as a levellor, they, detach the iron share, reverse it and use the ventral surface of the body for levelling.

The Baiga extract oil from *ramtilla* and mustard (*rai*) seeds with the help of a simple indigenous machine called *pelta*. The oil produced in the *pelta* is for their own domestic use only.

Storing

Food grains are stored in *koti* – a storage compartment made of mud. Food grains stored in the air tight container remains safe from insects at least for a year. They use two types of grinding implements, the heavy stone grinder is used for maize (*maka*) etc but a lighter earthen grinder is used for husking *Kodon*, *Kutki*. They have also several types and sizes of bamboo storing container such as, *jhel* (capacity – 10 kara, i.e. 50 kg), *dati* (capacity – 5 kara, i.e. 25 kg) and *jhapi* for keeping clothes. *Supa*, winnowing fan, is an important item in Baiga life.

Dress and Tattoo

The Bhumia Baiga living in and around the Baiga chawk are scantily dressed even today. Males put on a '*lingoti*' (loin cloth) in the waist and nothing above it. The women wear a short *sari*, ending much above the knees and put on a short blouse. Tattooing is very common among the Baiga women, especially after marriage when legs, thighs and breasts are also to be tattooed. Tattooing among the unmarried girls is limited to forehead and hands only. Tattooing (*gondna*) is done by a Badnin woman. The ink is prepared from snake skin and *ramtilla* oil. Badnin charges Rs.200/- for doing tattoo on entire body. For one leg Rs. 50, is charged for hands and breasts it is Rs.100/-, Baiga woman believes that if she is not tattooed before death, thc God will perform the tattooing on her body more painfully after her death and she will suffer more. Tattooing of the females is an identity of the Baiga tribe. In course of discussion, Dr. Seshan, the Block Medical Officer called it a natural acupuncture. According to him, in joints it helps in curing rheumatism and in the nymph glands around breast it helps in increased lactation and prevention of breast cancer. There is no single case of breast cancer reported among the Baiga women.

Food Habit

The staple diet of the Baiga is characteristically primordial in nature which is suitable to his life style for centuries around food gathering and hunting economy. *Pej* is a sort of thin gruel prepared by boiling the millet – *Kutki* (*panicum psilopodium*) in a large quantity of water, normally taken in the morning before going out for work. *Kodai* is a sort of porridge made of husked and cleaned *kodon* (*paspakum scrobiculatum*) forms a part of evening diet. These food items are however supplemented by leaves, roots, tubers, fruits and at times fish and pork. The Baiga are very fond of leafy vegetables, such as *charota vaji*, *Pakri vaji*, *Purpuin leaves*, *Chench leaves*, as well as roots and tubers like *dourchi kanda* and mushrooms. They use to catch field rat (*musa*) using rat traps and eat it after roasting in fire. The liver of bear is also eaten after frying it and adding salt. This is believed to have medicinal values and cures diseases of the testicles.

The Baiga wash their clothes with the ash made from the bark of *saja* (*termanalia tomantosa*) tree.

Cultural Set Up

The Village: Chara

Chara, a forest village in the Dindori district of Madhya Pradesh, is situated at an altitude of 2975 feet (892.5 meter) above sea level in the Maikal hills.

Chara is bounded on the north by Serajar village and Raijal River, on the south by Burner River, on the east by Tatar village and on the west by Silpiri village.

The Chara village is situated on a flat plateau, looking like a table top from a distance. Beside Burner, two small rivulets, Amadoba and Raijal run through the village boundary. One is neded to climb up from the river side to reach the top where settlement is situated on a flat piece of land, called *dadar*. The village has two hamlets, namely, Dadartolla and Nichetolla. *Dadar* means flat table land on the top of the hill. The original tribal settlement is in Dadartolla. Nichetolla is populated mainly by the non-tribal outsiders who live here on a temporary basis for different purposes. The study was conducted at Dadartolla and by Chara we will mean Dadartolla only. In Dadartolla there are 62 Baiga households, 14 Gond households and one Pradhan household. Our study is concentrated on the 62 Baiga households. In Nichetolla forest staff and some outsiders like shopkeepers and businessman live. There is a thin forest between Dadartolla and Nichetolla. A footpath runs through the forest from Dadartolla to Nichetolla which extends up to the river Burner. At Chara the main village road runs from east to west. Arterial roads connect it from north and south. Concentrations of the houses are on the southern side of the main road. At the slopes after some patches of agricultural fields, sal forest starts on all sides. The population of the Baiga in Chara is 341, of which 169 (49.56%) are males and 172 (50.44%) are females. The sex ratio (females per 1000 males) is 1017 (see Table 1 on population).

Table 1. Population *(Age-Group wise)*

Age Groups	*Male*	*Female*	*Total*
0 - 4	28	30	58
5 - 9	31	32	63
10 - 14	22	24	46
15 - 19	8	15	23
20 - 24	12	10	22
25 - 29	19	16	35
30 - 34	12	12	24
35 - 39	10	8	18
40 - 44	5	5	10
45 - 49	8	3	11
50 - 54	4	5	9
55 - 59	3	3	6
60 - 64	1	1	2
65 - 69	-	3	3
70	6	5	11
TOTAL	**169**	**172**	**341**
Percentage (%)	**49.56**	**50.44**	
Sex Ratio 1017			

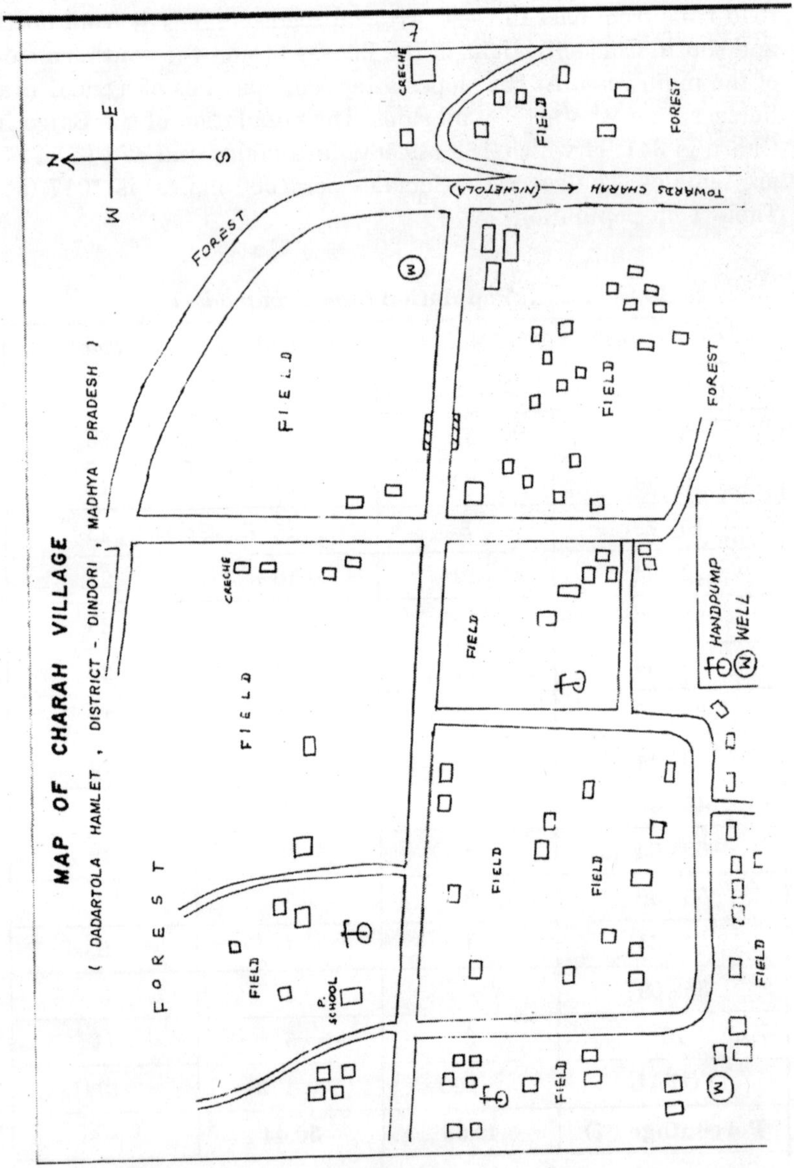
MAP OF CHARAH VILLAGE
(DADARTOLA HAMLET , DISTRICT - DINDORI , MADHYA PRADESH)
N
E
S
W
FOREST
FOREST
FOREST
FOREST
FIELD
FIELD
FIELD
FIELD
FIELD
FIELD
FIELD
FIELD
FIELD
CRECHE
CRECHE
P. SCHOOL
TOWARDS CHARAH (NICHETOLA)
HANDPUMP
WELL

Accessibility and Transport

Chara is located at a distance of about 70 km south – southeast directions from the district headquarter of Dindori. The distance of Chara from the block set up of Bajag is about 18 km. This entire stretch of 18 km. has a fair weather road which runs through the Reserve Forest. Being a member of forest tribe by nature the Baiga prefer to live in inaccessible areas like forest and hills, always far away from the urban centers. The main factor which governs the construction of roads and transport system in Baiga Chawk is for the interest of the convenience of the commercial exploitation of trees. Roads are being made to bring the timber out from the forest. Communication facilities of the tribal people living in the area are never thought of by the local administration. As a result all season roads are still lacking in Baiga Chawk. Inter village communication is maintained through the narrow forest footpath which is often infested with bears and other wild animals. In the absence of any regular public transport they have to depend on transport trucks, coming for timber transportation, as a means of communication. Electricity is available to the tribals at a subsidized rate.

Chara : A Forest Village

From administrative point of view forest villages are quite different from the revenue villages. They are situated in forest land and not in revenue land. Absolute ownership right is never given to the tribals living in a forest village. They cannot sale the land. They are just given some land on lease for cultivation. In return the villagers are expected to work as labourer in the forest department. The Baiga of Chara are mostly employed as labourer in the forest department. The welfare of these villages, in case of natural calamities or otherwise, vests on the Forest Department as its primary responsibility. The people living in forest villages and the villages (revenue) situated within a distance of 5 km. from the forest are allowed, as a special concession, to carry a bullock cart full of M.F.P. (Minor Forest Products). In Forest Villages (F.V.) roads are also built and maintained by the forest department. Minor irrigation and waterways are also looked after by the forest department. Likewise, land records are maintained by the Deputy Ranger of the forest department. The recommendation of the 1981 committee on Scheduled Castes and Tribes, to convert those 'forest villages' into 'revenue villages' is yet to be implemented in the area. In 1984 the Ministry of Agriculture (Government of India) advised State

Governments to give them 15-20 years 'long term heritable but inalienable rights which has been followed at the Baiga Chawk. The system was declared by Kerala High Court as ultra vires to the constitution. The 1978 state forest and Tribal welfare ministers' conference has also recommended conversion of forest villages to revenue villages (Roy Burman, 1999). However, the FRA, 2006 is likely to change all this in due time.

Total land of Chara village is 502.7 hectares and the total land for settlement as well as land under settled cultivation is 155 hectares. Total forest area of the village including public utility is 192.7 hectares.

SOCIAL DIVISION

The Baiga are found to be divided into numerous jatis, such as Deoria, Odoria, Bhusandia etc. The total number of such jatis are 26, as reported from Chara. The maximum number of persons belong to the Deoria *jati*, which is 68 (19.94%). Next comes Kuraki, in which there are 42 (12.35%) persons. Beside jatis, the Baiga also belong to some gotis, the number of *gotis* at Chara is only six. Majority of the people belong to either Marabe or Dhurbe *gotis*. The detail list of *jati* and *goti* names and the number of persons belonging to each *jati* and *goti* are given in tables 2 and 3.

Table 2. Baiga jatis

Sr. No.	*Name of the Jatis*	*Number of Persons*
01.	Deoria	68
02.	Kurakia	42
03.	Ghungaria	25
04.	Rathoria	25
05.	Karkutia	23
06.	Nandia	23
07.	Paria	22
08.	Mundakia	20
09.	Bagdaria	12
10.	Barangia	12

(contd...)

Sr. No.	*Name of the Jatis*	*Number of Persons*
11.	憑araria	11
12.	Lamotia	10
13.	Bhusandia	10
14.	Jhumaria	9
15.	Bundaria	6
16.	Kusaria	4
17.	Jhajotia	4
18.	Odaria	3
19.	Khoria	3
20.	Khoria	2
21.	Panchgania	2
22.	Machia	1
23.	Sutkaria	1
24.	Bhaina	1
25.	Samdaria	1
26.	Amdaria	1
	TOTAL	341

Table 3. Baiga Gotis

Sr. No.	*Name of the Gotis*	*Number of Persons*
01.	Dharbe	172
02.	Marabe	164
03.	Markan	2
04.	Parastha	1
05.	Darotia	1
06.	Parteji	1
	TOTAL	341

Marriage and Family

Marriage, as a social institution, particularly among traditional communities and is something more than just a regulated sex relation. Marriage is an institutional device for evolving family types through which the economic needs and sustainability of the individual are fulfilled. Eco-cultural adaptation of a traditional hunting and gathering tribe like the Baiga is reflected through the monogamous marriages and nuclear families. Anything bigger than nuclear family cannot be supported by their traditional hunting and food gathering economy. Edible gathering produce from the forest cannot sustain a large number of persons. Moreover, it is to be consumed within a day or two because scope of storing is also limited. In a traditional community like the Baiga, occurrences of types of marriage are adaptations to the demanding ecological, economic and cultural need of the people. However, most functions of marriage and family are overlapping and are so intricately related that it will be a futile exercise to try to delink them.

Marital Status

Out of 169 males 90 (53.25%) are unmarried, 76 (44.97%) are married and 3 (1.78%) persons are widower or divorcee. Out of 172 females, 94 (54.66%) are unmarried, 71 (41.28%) are married and 7 (4.06%) are widow or divorcees. The details of the marital status of the people concerned have been presented in Table 4.

Table 4: Marital Status

Sr. No.	*Status*	*Male*	*Female*	*Total*	*Percentage (N=341)*
01.	Unmarried	90	94	184	53.96
02.	Married	76	71	147	43.10
03.	Widow / Widower	3	7	10	02.94

Marriage Distance

From our data collected on marriage distance and place of marriage on 58 cases, it is revealed that the brides come to Chara from as many as 27 villages, of which 18 villages are situated within the district Dindori and 9 villages are situated in the adjoining district of Bilaspur. Out of the 58 marriage cases reported in the village household census, 46 (79.32%) marriages took place within the district and 12 (20.69%) marriages took place by bringing bride from Bilaspur district. From table 5A it is seen that the

Table 5A : Villages for marriage

Sr. No.	*Name of the Village*	*No. of Cases*	*Distance in Kilometer*
DINDORI DISTRICT			
01.	Silpiri	13	4
02.	Durkutta	4	10
03.	Lima	4	10
04.	Tarach	4	6
05.	Kandatolla	3	10
06.	Tatar	3	3
07.	Khamera	2	12
08.	Panpur	2	18
09.	Saraijhar	2	6
10.	Sarangpur	1	18
11.	Rangjara	1	12
12.	Sindurwar	1	12
13.	Hirakun	1	14
14.	Kandapani	1	5
15.	Kolaidoba	1	7
16.	Gara	1	14
17.	Talridora	1	5
18.	Chaklapani	1	6
BILASPUR DISTRICT			
19.	Pandripani	3	40
20.	Saraipani	2	28
21.	Ajwainbagh	1	35
22.	Dhuba	1	20
23.	Lodhra	1	25
24.	Chakmaktola	1	35
25.	Vaisadeoba	1	35
26.	Ghumra	1	50
27.	Sindurpani	1	25

Table 5b: Marriage range and distance

Distance from Chara (in kilometers)	*No. of Cases (N=58)*	*Percentage %*
Within 10 kilometers	30	51.73
10 to 20 kilometers	16	27.59
20 to 30 kilometers	5	08.62
Above 30 kilometers	7	12.06
TOTAL CASES	58	100.00

highest number of brides (22.4%) came to Chara from Silpiri village located at a distance of 4 kilometers, maximum number of marriage took place within a distance of 10 kilometers from Chara. From table No.5B on marriage distance it is seen that 30 brides came to Chara from villages situated within a distance of 10 kilometers. 16 brides came to Chara from villages situated between a distance of 10 and 20 kilometers and 5 brides came from villages situated at a distance between 20 and 30 kilometers. 7 brides came from villages located above 30 kilometers from Chara.

The fact that 51.73 percent of the marriages are settled within a distance of 10 kilometers is mostly regulated by eco-cultural factors. A distance of 10 kilometers in the rugged forested terrain of Baiga Chawk that has to be covered on foot for marriage is not an easy affair. Beside the nearby in-laws would also come handy at the time of crisis. Probably these are the reasons for the high priority of short distance marriage. It is also interesting to note that the marriage distances are being gradually increased. In recent past 7 (12.06%) marriages took place above a distance of 30 kilometers. This is due to availability of transport and opening up of the area.

Family Type and Structure

All the Baiga families studied at village Chara are monogamous. Polygamy is not practiced by the Baiga. Out of 62 Baiga families 42 (67.75%) are nuclear families, 19 (30.64%) are extended family and 1 (1.61%) family is incomplete. Detail of family type is shown in Table 6. The average family size 6.0.

The norm of nuclear family is preferred by the Baiga because it goes well with their tradition of hunting – food gathering economy. It is believed that the area of exploitation that is available to each family especially during lean months is capable only to support small sized family. The presence of extended families

Table 6 : Family Type

Sr. No.	*Types*	*Numbers (N=62)*	*Percentage %*
01.	Nuclear	42	67.75
02.	Extended	19	30.64
03.	Incomplete	1	1.61
	TOTAL	62	100.00
	Family Size: 6.0		

is only due to the reason that the agricultural land available to them is limited under the forest act, and the married sons stay with their parents because there is no scope for further ownership of agricultural land for them. The family amongst them is the basic unit for economic endeavour.

It is the family members who very often go to the forest for the collection of forest produces. They collect from forest fruits, roots and tubers, leafy vegetables for their daily consumption. Along with this they also gather economically important M.F.P. such as non-timber forest produces for selling in the local market. This specific situation has resulted in them the occurrence of small-sized nuclear families as an adaptation to suitably manage and exploit the environmental resources.

Family Welfare Programmes

The facility of family welfare or family planning is not available in the villages of Baiga Chawk or at Chara. Only a few women have opted voluntarily for sterilization operation. Operation is done only if someone comes forward and makes an affidavit before a Gazetted Officer that she or he is willing for the operation. The Baiga are not encouraged for sterilization as a matter of policy because their population growth is not much as a member of the 'primitive tribe'. However, use of medicinal herbs and prolonged lactation period help them to delay the monthly cycle (M.C.) among the females.

Literacy and its Role in the Management of Natural Rasources

Out of the 169 males among the Baiga of Chara, 124 (73.38%) persons are illiterate and 45 (26.62%) persons are literate. Among the females, out of the total of 172,171 (99.42%) persons

Table 7: Literacy

Sr. No.	Sex	Illiterate	Percentage	Literate					
				Primary (I – IV)	*Middle (V – VIII)*	*Secondary (IX – X)*	*High School & Above*	*TOTAL*	*%*
01.	Male	124	73.38	32	10	2	1	45	26.62
02.	Female	171	99.42	1	--	--	--	1	0.58
	TOTAL	295	86.52					46	13.48

are illiterate and only one female is literate. Detail is shown in table No.7 on literacy. The literacy rate among the Baiga is very low. At Chara the rate of literacy is only 13.48 percent, however it is above the state literacy rate of the Baiga which is only 3.62 percent (1981 Census). Owing to the low rate of literacy the impact of education is very negligible among the Baiga tribe of Chara. This lack of modern education has enabled the Baiga to continue with their traditional belief and practices, specially in the field of herbal medicines of which they have a vast repertoire of knowledge. This knowledge passes through generations.

The village Chara has one co-educational high school run by the tribal department. Teachers in this school are the employees of the tribal department, not of education department. The facility of this school is more enjoyed by the Gond than the Baiga.

Cattle Wealth

The number of livestock present in a village is the reflection of the economic status of its inhabitants. The following chart on the numbers of cattle and ploughs in the village Chara where there are 62 families of the Baiga.

Plough	-	60
Bullock	-	104
Cow	-	119
Pig	-	23
Goat	-	48
Buffalo	-	10

Considering family as a unit of production, ideally each family should have a 'pair of bullock' for use in the plough. The plough: bullock ratio should be 1:2. On examination it is seen that the ratio of the number of ploughs and bullocks does not tally with the common procedure. Out of 62 Baiga families two amongst these do not have plough. The rest 60 families through these have got ploughs but the number of bullocks is less than the requisite member. There are only 104 bullocks, indicating the shortage of 16 bullocks from the requisite ratio. So, there are eight families who do not have any bullock. They get the bullocks on loan or hire from others. The price of an adult bullock is Rs. 1500/- and that of an adult cow is Rs. 1100/-. The cost of an adult buffalo is Rs. 5000/-. The price of a small goat is

Rs.200/-. The mawasi bring the cattle from Chhattisgarh and sell these to the Baiga.

Occupation

The traditional occupation of the Baiga was shifting hill cultivation (*bewar*) and collection and gathering of forest produces – roots, tubers, fruits and vegetables along with the hunting of games. Their traditional economy, in the remote hills and forest, had continued for a pretty long time, till the time when British administration put a restriction on their practice of cutting *bewar*. Their economy has received a further jolt after independence when the Government nationalized the forest and their right to forest has become a mere concession. During summer they use to go to the forest in small groups for clandestine hunting. They hunt deer, sambar, wild bear etc. They catch rat with the help of rat trap and eat it after roasting it in the fire. Their food habit of eating rats keeps the rat population under control in an indigenous way, which otherwise would have damaged the food grains in a larger scale.

At present the Baiga of Baiga Chawk are heavily dependent on forest for their survival and subsistence i.e. because they practise agriculture to some extent in a limited scale due to non-availability of sufficient arable land. All lands in a forest village are legally owned by the Dept. of Forest. The occupants of a forest village are given a small patch of land for cultivation, as in the case of Chara it is only 2.5 hectare per family. Besides, the Dept. of Forest also provides employment to the Baiga of Chara in various capacities in the form of daily wage labour or as contractual labour of the forest department.

The Baiga when engaged by the Dept. of Forest for forest road construction, get @ Rs. 53.99 (Rupees fifty three and ninety nine paisa only) per day as labour payment. In Department of Forest both men and women get the same remuneration. But under contractor, men get Rs. 40/- per day whereas women get Rs. 30/- per day. For tree cutting they get Rs.70/- per cubic meter. For lopping of branches they get Rs. 50/- per cubic meter. For collection of firewood they get Rs. 32/- per *chatta*. *Chatta* is a bundle of dried firewood having 1 meter 10 centimeter in height, 1 meter 25 centimeter in length and 2 meter in breadth. They also earn some remuneration from the marking of trees in the forest @ Rs. 1.60 per marking. A person usually earns Rs. 20/- per day from markings of the trees.

They catch fish in the rivers for self consumption with the help of hooks, nets and traps. It is seen that even girls also go for fishing in the river. They make mud embankments to stop and encircle the flow of water in the shallow water. The fishes get trapped inside it and which are caught by them. They also use poison for catching fish. They mix *munga* (*moringa obifera*) or *Koiler* (*banhinia purpurea*) in the water. They also use the powdered bark of *chirecher* (*fluggea microcarpa*) or *guhalari* (*mainphal or randia dumetorum*) or the *bheri* (*caesaria tomentosa*) fruit. When put in the river water the fishes become stupefied and drowsy and are collected down stream.

Role of Market

Weekly markets, called *haat* and annual trade fair, popularly known as *marai*, are the main platform of economic transaction in the tribal area. The annual *marai* besides its economic role has a cultural aspect too. Lots of tribal dances, music, songs and various other cultural performances are observed at the *marai*. The *marai* of Dhurkutta village held in the month of March is an important event of the area. Boys and girls from far off places come to the *marai* and matches are also made in the *marai*.

Also there is a weekly market at Chara which sits on every Friday. Traders, mostly non-tribal outsiders, bring their goods and commodities on the pony's back. Pony is the most suitable mode of transportation in the hilly terrain of Baiga Chawk. Tribals also visit the hut for selling and purchasing of goods. Selling of forest produces and buying of essential commodities are mainly done by the womenfolk. Men come to the haat for enjoying and merrymaking. Drinking of alcoholic beverages, mainly by the men, are a part and parcel of the *haat* in Baiga Chawk.

Items which are available in the weekly market at Chara are listed as below –

1. Clothes
2. Shoes
3. Fishing nets
4. Iron implements
5. Vegetables
6. Forest produces
7. Cheap cosmetics for ladies
8. Toys
9. Food grains

The articles which are sold and purchased by the Baiga of Chara village.

Sr. No.	*Name*	*Nature of Transactions*
1.	Fuel Wood	Sold by the Baiga women @Rs.30/- per head load. (approximate weight 40 Kilograms)
2.	Mahua flower	Sold by the non-tribal traders @Rs.10/- per Kg.
3.	*Kanda* (a generic term for tubers)	Sold by the tribal women @Rs.8/-per Kg.
4.	Mustard seeds	Sold by the Baiga @Rs.15/- per Kilo.
5.	Ramtilla	Sold by the Baiga @Rs.12/- per Kilo.
6.	Safed Musli	Sold by the Baiga after washing in alam water @Rs.10/- per Kilo.
7.	Resin (*rar*)	Sold by Baiga @Rs.7/- per Kilo.
8.	Honey	Sold by the Baiga @Rs.50/- Per bottle of one litre.
9.	Mahul leaf	Sold by the Baiga @Rs.4/- per Kilo.
10.	Chindi grass	Sold by the Baiga @Rs.2/- per broom.
11.	Aaonla	Sold by the Baiga @Rs.10/- per Kilo.
12.	Gur (jaggery)	Sold by the non-tribal traders @Rs.8/- per Kilo.
13.	Mohua liquor	Purchased and sold both by non tribals and tribals @Rs.10/- per bottle.
14.	Iron spade	Sold by the Agaria @Rs.70/- per piece.
15.	Plough share	Purchased from Agaria @Rs.30/- per piece.
16.	Tangya (battle axe)	Purchased by the Baiga @Rs.100 per piece.
17.	Rice	Purchased by the Baiga from non-tribal traders @Rs.8/- per Kilo.
18.	Harra	Sold by the Baiga @Rs.2/- per Kilo.
19.	Sal seeds	Sold by the Baiga @Rs.2/- per Kilo.

Beside their economic importance these weekly markets have a social role to perform. It acts as a meeting place for boys and girls, marriage negotiations and courtship often take place in the weekly market which is the specific significance of it. Tribal medicine men and allopath quack doctors are found treating their patient in these weekly markets. A remarkable thing about these markets is that the goods and commodities of the traders are carried on small horses. These horses of the traders are always seen grazing in the nearby forest and pasture land at the vicinity of the village.

Jajmani System

The Baiga have jajmani or service relations with various communities. Agaria blacksmith in exchange of repairing work of his iron implements gets 5 *Kura* (25 kilograms) of *maka*, *kodon* and *kutki*. In exchange the Baiga only give food grain but not the oil seeds or any other cash crops. The Panka weave sari for the Baigin but now-a-days he demands cash payment instead of food grains.

Religious Belief, Practices and Festivals Related to the Management of Natural Resources

A great part of Baiga social life is associated with magic and religion. Sacrifice of pigs, goats and fowls play an important role in their magic and rituals. The Baiga are considered magicians and medicine men *par excellence*. They act as intermediary between various tribal groups and their respective Gods and Goddesses whether it is charming the fertility into the seeds or the propitiation of the deities for some gain or protecting a person from the witchcraft, the Baiga *gunias* are always remembered. Two Baiga *gunias* of Chara, Ghoran and Bhobla are quite often called for their magical prowess. They are able to drive away the wild animals from the village boundary. The Baiga are traditionally believed to have known the *mantras* and rituals to drive out the tiger. Beside stimulating the growth of crops, they can also protect them from hailstorm and wild boar or able to keep cows from straying. It is widely believed that the Baiga medicine-men know the herbs, a sure cure for snake bites. The inheritance of *guniaship* is carried from father to son. The *gunia* stands between mankind and all the malignant forces of nature and he drives them away by using his supernatural powers. A Baiga priest can also control the pest and insects from the *Kutki* field by performing puja with coconut and *mohua* liquor. When insects attack the *Kutki* crops they catch a few insects alive and burn them. They believe that the smell of the burnt insects drives away the insects out of the field. While doing so the priest invariably chant *mantras* and hymns for impression management. It is observed that the two *gunias* of Chara, Ghoran and Bhobla even when administering herbal medicines to their patient take the recourse of appeasing some or other deity through *pujas* and rituals.

They artfully mix ritual and religion in the treatment of diseases just to boost up the morale of the patient knowing their psychology.

Thakur deo is the strongest of all Gods. *Buradeo* and *Ajadadi* are the house deities. *Muamatli* is the deity who looks after the agricultural field and is required to be propitiated by sacrificing hen or cock. *Jet* is an agricultural ritual jointly performed by the villagers to worship *Thakur Deo*. *Maswasi* is the hunting god who is worshipped with coconut, fried rice and a red cock. Water deity is called *Paniharin*. *Nangbansi Bagaisur, who* lives at the outskirts of the village and it is the belief that due to him the Baiga can not be eaten or overpowered by the tiger. They also worship *dhartimata* or mother earth. *Maradeo, Banjari, Biranti, Chaonga pat* are the evil spirits. The Baiga consider Monday and Wednesday as auspicious but Saturday and Sunday are inauspicious to them. *Baisakh* and *Pus* (pous) are the best months for animal sacrifice and hunting. Because during the dry months moving around the forest is comparatively easy. The earth is placed on the head of *Burangaa*, it caused earth quake when he shifts it from one head to another. The Baiga believe that they take rebirth after death into his own family. They worship various trees such as *Aam* (mango), *Behi* (guava) as abode of the God but interestingly they only worship those trees which are planted by themselves. This is perhaps because of the fact that the Baiga plant only those trees which are useful to them and are not grown naturally within a approachable distance. They prudently ensure the survival, continuance and growth of these trees by worshipping these as sacred trees and even ensure the judicious use of the by-products like fruits, leaves and flowers etc. The Baiga of Baiga Chawk are quit Hinduised at present – they worship *Hanuman* before hunting and greet each other with the uttering of 'Ram-Ram' at the time of meeting. Among the gods and goddesses of Hindu pantheon they worship *Narayana*, *Siva* (Mahadeva), *Kali* etc.

Role of Village Authority: Traditional and Modern

The Baiga traditional panchayat is constituted by the *Mukaddam*, *Diwan*, *Samrath* and *Kotwal*. *Mukaddam* is the head of the village who looks after the village activities. *Diwan* assists *Mukaddam* in day-to-day activities. *Samrath* looks after the social activities, specially the visitors. *Kotwal* is the messenger who also keeps the records of birth and death and inform the

Forest Deputy Ranger if there is any crime committed for further necessary action.

Environmental awareness of the Baiga is recently observed when the educated Baiga jointly politicized the issue. In February 1999, a Baiga sammalayam (gathering) was held at Mohai when all the Baigas of 52 villages of the Baiga Chawk and also a few villages of Kowardha district participated. They took up the following issues for discussion and future course of action.

1. Regeneration of sal forest.
2. Village problems such as water scarcity etc.
3. Defending their right to the land and demanding compensation for the inhabitants of ten villages who are being displaced for the setting up of an aluminum factory.

Statutory Village Panchayat

The panchayat raj in Madhya Pradesh consists of a three tier system, at the lowest level is *gram* panchayat. Three neighbouring forest villages, namely, Chara, Silpiri and Tatar constitute one *gram* panchayat. The present *sarpanch* is a Gond. The area of these three villages is divided into 20 wards, each having a representing member. So, there are 20 representatives at the gram panchayat. As per rule there has to be one woman member, one *sarpanch* and 20 panchayat members are elected by direct vote.

The composition of the 20 seats and the representation of the Baiga are as follows –

Chara	- 8 members (2 Baiga, one is woman)
Tatar	- 7 members (2 Baiga)
Silpiri	- 5 members (2 Baiga, here also one woman member is Baiga)

These 20 members have elected one upa-sarpanch, who is a Baiga from Tatar.

Next tier is called *janapad*. Entire Bajag Block is one *Janapad*. There are 20 *Janapad* members at the ratio of one member for 3 panchayats who are elected by direct votes from villages. Bajag block has 44 *gram* panchayats which are represented by 20 *Janapad* members. The *Janapad* members elected one *Janapad adhyash* or president.

The 3rd and last tier is the Zilla Panchayat, called Zilla Sarkar i.e. local self government. There is one Zilla member for 20 gram panchayat. Jilla Parishad members are also elected by direct vote from the village level. Therefore, each person has to cast 4 votes, one for sarpanch, one for gram panchayat members, one for janapad members and one for Zilla Sarkar members.

Developmental Programmes

In forest villages, the panchayats are only allotted work of petty nature which are of small budget in comparison to the revenue villages. Developmental work given to the Chara panchayat under various schemes are, making of small stretch of road, patch repairing of roads, construction of well under Jawahar Rojgar Yojana (JRY). The panchayat has recently got the work of panchayat bhavan out of the grant sanctioned by Vth Finance Commission. They are also making a primary school building under Rajiv Gandhi Siksha Yojana. For plastering of a *jhira* (spring) at Tatar they received monetary grant of Rs.10,000 from the Baiga project (ITDP).

The *Sarpanch* alleged that all the major developmental work such as big road construction, deep wells, hand pumps, land development, minor irrigation and bridges are undertaken by the forest department itself and are not given to the panchayat. Even the money allotted by the Baiga Project under its various schemes are utilized by the forest department. Forest department is the supreme authority in the matter of developmental work in the forest villages of Baiga Chawk.

Non-Governmental Organisation (NGO)

In recent years the NGO have made their presence and have started work in the Baiga Chawk. They are engaged in different developmental activities at the village level. A N.G.O from Nagpur, known as '*sanstha*' in collaboration with Oxam International has adopted seven forest villages in Baiga Chawk, viz. Chara, Silpiri, Tatar, Dhurkutta, Kandapani, Jhilong and Saraijher.

They have initiated the following welfare programmes –

1. A *Balwadi* was set up at Chara where food and basic education has been provided to the tribal children.
2. For digging well and construction of road the villagers are to give their labour (*sramdan*) free and the organization (N.G.O.) provides them food and the cost of plastering of the wells and top surface, dressing of the roads with murram.

3. They established grain bank from which the tribals are supplied food grain on loan during lean season. The tribals refund the same quantity of grain back to the bank after the harvest of crops. This has helped the Baiga to come out of the evil clutches of money lender, *sahukar*, who use to exploit them. The N.G.O has raised the slogan that they are here to save *jamin* (land), *jan* (man) and *ban* (forest). The Baiga knew the importance of *jan*, *jamin* and *ban*. The N.G.O owns the confidence of the tribals through the implementation of parallel developmental schemes. Tribals are involved in the process by adopting PRA (Participatory Rural Appraisal) technique. They identify the problems and extend instant relief at the time of crisis, unlike the government, whose help could not reach them in time due to 'red tapism'. The villagers of Tatar have recently refused to participate in a programme of well digging taken up by panchayat because the N.G.O. has already built wells in the village.

Indebtedness

The Baiga avail loan both from Bank and private parties. There is a branch of PNB at Chara itself. The Bank (PNB) disburses loans to tribal under IRDP Programmes for development of land, purchase of sewing machine, bullocks and cows and conducting of petty business like grocery shops etc. The Bank disburse loan up to Rs.13,000/- and charges interest @ 15% per annum. The tribal subsidy is 50% of the loan amount with a ceiling of Rs.6,000/-. The Baiga, being a primitive tribe, get over and above this subsidy another 30% special additional subsidy which is allowed without any upper limit of ceiling. Thus the Baiga get 80% subsidy of the loan amount which is 30% more than the Gond. The Baiga has to repay only 20% of the loan amount.

The Baiga during lean season take loan in the form of food grain from *sahukar*. In exchange of one *bora* (100 kilograms) of *Kanki* (fractured rice) they have to repay after harvest one bag (100 kilograms) of *ramtilla* or *rai* (oil seeds), the market value of which is much higher. The market price of one quintal (100 kilograms) *Kanki* is Rs. 65/-, whereas the price of one quintal (100 kilograms) of mustard is Rs. 1,800/-. At the time of emergency to meet up the requirement of cash they use to sell food grains, mainly maize (makai) @ Rs. 20/- per Kuru (5 kilograms), which is also lower than the market rate. For taking cash they are to pay

25% interest per annum.

Their land though are held on occupancy basis can be used as security against loan from Bank only. This mortgaged land can be attached for debt towards Bank loan and can be auctioned only to the fellow tribesmen. Standing crops, cattle and movable property are their only security for getting loan from private agencies, so the rate of interest is very high.

Management of Land Resources

Due to the undulating nature of the terrain and topography there is considerable variation in respect of soil types from land to land in the Baiga Chawk area. Cultivable land is categorized by the Baiga in several ways according to its nature and productivity. Probably the most important distinction is between land which is irrigated and that is not. Nature of ownership of the land and its tenure system are the two other important features of land management.

Total area of land under the jurisdiction of Chara forest village is 502.7 hectares, of which 155.00 hectares each is under cultivation and settlement. The land under forest (including public utility) is 192.7 hectares. The detail of the utility pattern of the land in Chara is given in Table 8.

Table 8: Utilisation of Land

Sr. No.	*Nature of use*	*Area (in hec.)*	*Percentage*
01.	Under Settlement	155.00	31.07
02.	Under Cultivation	155.00	31.07
03.	Forest & Public Utility	192.7	37.86
	TOTAL	502.7	100.00

Ownership and Tenure

Chara, like all forest villages, came into existence to cater the needs of forestry operation, mainly supply of labour. Land were given to the occupants in lieu of their service as forest labour. Originally each of the 27 families was distributed 'patta' for 2.5 hectares of land. Rests of the 35 families are not allotted any patta for land, though each of them possesses 2.5 hectares of cultivable land. Therefore, out of the total 155.00 hectares of land under cultivation, 67.5 hectares of land owned by 27 families having patta and 87.5 hectares of land occupied by the remaining 35 families are not having patta or legal documents. Nonetheless, the measurements of the land held by them are taken and they are asked to apply for patta by the forest authority. No further lands are allotted to the Baiga even though the numbers of families have increased. This factor forced the adult sons, with their own families, to stay in joint family of his father since no further land would be available to them for cultivation. He has to share the land along with his brothers and father. Generally the patta is given on lease for 15 years in a renewable basis. It is given in the name of the head of the family and in the event of his death his wife or eldest son is registered as patta owner though it is actually shared by the family. They manage the land and control its production effectively by stopping the division of families and sharing the land amongst family members. The Baiga of Chara do not have the right to sell or mortgage the land, if they take loan from nationalized bank against the security of the land and fails to repay the debt, the land may be auctioned to a tribe only for the recovery of the loan amount.

A nominal fee of Rupee one is charged as tax from the patta holder by the forest department.

Land and Soil Types

The Baiga conceive and catagorised mainly two types of land, viz. *Bari* and *Kheti*. The Bari land are situated near the homestead, well manured, fenced and generally produce winter (ravi) crops having cash value such as *rai*, *ramtilla* and at times maize are grown here. The *Kheti* lands are situated far away places from the settlement, not manured, generally low lying for retention of rainwater. Crops like paddy, *kodo* and *kutki* are grown in this type of land. They use both the types of land for growing of winter and monsoon crops.

The Baiga identify various types of soils and grow specific crop in specific type of soil. *Kalimatti* (black soil) is called *sahra*. Slightly white soil is called *sira* and lateritic blackish murum is called *bharra soil*. Detail of the crops grown in particular soil are given below –

Crops	*Soil Types*
Paddy	Black soil, called *sahra*, found in *doba* or *jhila* land.
Kodo, Kutki and Ramtilla	Red soil, lateritic in texture.
Maize and Rai	*Bharra* soil in *Bari* land – using compost manure.

In *lalmati* and *bharra* soils, with the help of manure double cropping is done. In *bari* land maize and *rai* are grown and in paddy land gram and wheat are grown as mixed crop during winter.

Traditionally shifting hill cultivation or *bewar* happened to be their indigenous method of cultivation. But the Baiga have stopped this type of cultivation long ago. At present they are totally dependent on permanent cultivation, more aptly called agriculture, with a pair of bullock and plough.

Crop Pattern

Major crops which are grown by the Baiga of Chara village are given below in order of their importance, which are paddy, *kutki*, maize, *kodo*, *rai*, *ramtilla* and *jowar*.

The most important crop produced by the Baiga of Chara is paddy. Out of the total production of food grains of 36470 kilograms, the production of paddy is 10190 kg which is 27.97 percent of the total crop produced. The average production of paddy per household is 164.35 kilograms. The Baiga built bunds across the contour of the paddy fields which serve the dual purpose of retention of rain water for irrigation and to make the undulating terrain plain and even. The bunds also help in controlling soil erosion and maintaining soil fertility by preventing the wash of important soil nutrient. The Baiga built the *bundhia* with stones, dried up tree trunk, hays and mud.

The second most important crop of the Baiga agriculture is *Kutki*. The total production of *Kutki* in Chara is 8305 kilograms, which is 22.77 percent of the total crop production. The average production of *Kutki* per household is 133.95 kilograms.

The third important crop produced by the Baiga of Chara is maize or *maka*, which is 7690 kilograms. If accounts for 21.08 percent of the total production. The average production per household is 124.03 kilograms.

The fourth important crop is *Kodo* (millet). The total production of *Kodo* is 4459 kilograms. This is 12.20 percent of the total production of crop. The average production of *Kodo* per household is 71.77 kilograms.

The next two crops in order of importance are *Rai* (mustard) and *Ramtilla* or *jugni*, both are cash earning oil seeds. Chara grows 4150 kilograms of *Rai* which is 11.37 percent of the total production of crop and average production of *Rai* per household is 66.93 kilograms. The total production of *Ramtilla* in Chara is 1585 kilograms, which is 4.34 percent of the total crop production and the average production of *Ramtilla* per household is 25.56 kilograms.

Jowar produced in Chara is only 100 kilograms. It has recently been introduced which is negligible.

Detail of the production of crops in Chara village is given in Table 9 and in the histogram (bar chart).

Table 9 : Crop Pattern *(1997 – 1998)*

Sr. No.	*Crops*	*Production (in kg.)*	*Percentage to Total production*	*Average production Per household (kg)*
01.	Paddy	10190	27.97	164.35
02.	Kutki	8305	22.77	133.95
03.	Maize	7690	21.08	124.03
04.	Kodo	4450	12.20	71.77
05.	Rai	4150	11.37	66.93
06.	Ramtilla	1585	4.34	25.56
07.	Jowar	100	0.127	1.61
	TOTAL	36470	100.00	

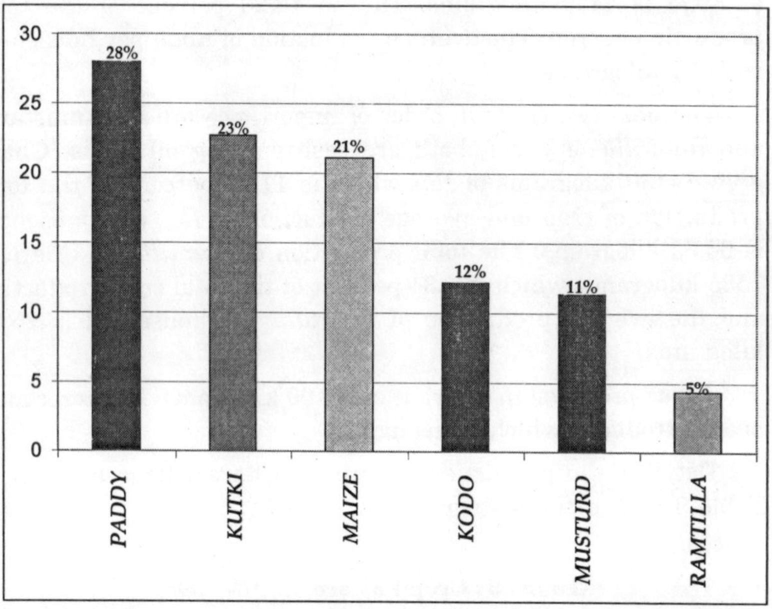

Graph showing crop pattern in Charah village district Dindori (Madhya Pradesh)

The traditional wisdom of the Baiga acquired through the practice of shifting cultivation over the years has motivated them to cultivate varieties of crops either simultaneously in different types of land or one after another in the same piece of land. By adopting this technique they get the advantage of different sowing, tending and harvesting time as associated with different crops, which also helps them to successful management and deployment of labour force at their disposal.

The Baiga follow rotation of crops to get more production and to maintain soil fertility. They show their traditional wisdom in rotating *Kodo*, *Kutki* and *Ramtilla* alternately in the same land. Maize and *Rai* also follow the rotation as double cropping without irrigation in the same land. Sometime they grow gram and wheat in the same land after paddy is harvested.

Basically it is observed that crop wise the Baiga have three types of land, as follows:-

Type	*Crop Cultivated*
I (*Bari*)	Maize and Mustard
II	Paddy, *Maka* and wheat
III	*Kodo, Kutki, Ramtilla*

The following illustration shows the crop layout of village Chara :

Land Type	*Crop Layout*
I	Maize and Mustard
II	Paddy, Gram and Wheat
III	*Kodo, Kutki* and *Ramtilla*

From the above example we know the extent of wisdom the Baiga traditionally possess and have applied in their agriculture through this unique concept of crop rotation and the optimum utilization of land they have at their disposal.

Method of Cultivation

The Baiga had to intensify their agriculture due to total stoppage of shifting cultivation. In *bewar* cultivation they have ample leisure time, which they sacrificed in the era of settled agriculture for increased working hours. The increasing demand of food supply due to increase in population have been negotiated by the Baiga through increasing labour input to intensify the agriculture, increasing their time in forest collection and supplementing the demand through cash earning in the form of forest labour.

The Baiga agricultural season start from the month of *Chait* (March-April). Roots and other remains of the earlier crops are taken out with the help of *bhakar*. These residues are then burnt to ash, which act as manure for the next crop. Except paddy, all other crops grown by the Baiga are sown by broadcasting method, paddy are sown by transplantation technique.

First they sow maize or *maka* in the month of Jet (May-June) by broadcasting method. They sow paddy by transplanting from seed beds in the month of *Ashar* (June-July). In the same month they also sow *Kodo* and *Kutki* in different fields. They sow *Kodo* and *Kutki* in the same land, keeping a gap of 15 days. Weeding is done from August onwards in respect of the crops mentioned above. In the month of *sawan* (July-August) they sow *ramtilla* in the same field where they already sowed *Kodo* and *Kutki*. As a matter of fact *Kodo*, *Kutki* and *Ramtilla* are sown in the same land one after another. In this way they get a gap in the harvesting time also. Harvesting of crops starts from the month of October. Maize is the first crop to be harvested in the end of *Kuwar* (September-October). Maize is harvested from middle of September to middle of October. After the harvesting of maize in October, mustard (*rai*) is sown on the same land. After maize other crops to be harvested are paddy, *kodo*, *kutki* and *ramtilla*. Paddy is harvested in the month of *Kartik* (October-November). *Kodo*, *Kutki* and *Ramtilla* are harvested in the months of *Agan* (November-December) and *Push* (December-January). The process of weeding of *rai* is done in the month of November and December. *Rai* (mustard) is harvested in the month of *Magh* (January-February). Domestic animals are fed on green fodder of crop residue. Again the preparation of land starts from the middle of February. This is the annual cycle of agriculture practiced by the Baiga.

The baiga cultivate two varieties of *Kutki*, the white one is called *nangdawan*, which is sown in *sawan*. The black variety is *sitahi* and it is sown in *Bhado*. Before cultivation of *Kutki* they perform a puja but it is not done with any other crops. The husking of paddy is done with the help of bullocks or buffaloes. They use the husk and straw of paddy, *Kodo* and *Kutki* as a fodder for animals and as a cementing material, mixed with soil, for the construction of house. For winnowing of mustard they use winnowing fan called *supa* and take the help of wind energy.

Family provides the main labour force in the Baiga agricultural operation as they have got small quantity of land. At times they depend on mutual exchange of labour from other families. They rarely engage hired labour in agricultural operation. Rate of hired labour is different for different crops. For Paddy, *Kodo* and *Kutki* it is 6 *baria* (2 kilograms) for both sexes. For *Ramtilla* they pay 4 *baria ramtilla* or Rs.20/- per day. For *Rai* it is 4 *baria rai* or Rs.20/- per day.

The Baiga agricultural calendar is shown in Table No. 10.

Table 10: Baiga Agricultural Calendar

Sr. No.	*Months*	*Activities*
1.	Chait *(March – April)*	Preparation of field, Harrowing and ploughing for the first time.
2.	Baisak *(April – May)*	Removal of roots of previous crops 2nd ploughing.
3.	Jet *(May – June)*	Sowing of maize by broadcasting.
4.	Ashar *(June – July)*	Sowing of paddy by transplantation after the arrival of monsoon. Sowing of Kodo and Kutki in different land by broadcasting.
5.	Sawan *(July – August)*	Sowing of Ramtilla (Jugni).
6.	Bhado *(August – September)*	Completion of sowing and growing of crops. Weeding process carried cut.
7.	Kuwar *(September–October)*	Harvesting of maize and sowing of mustard (rai).
8.	Kartik *(October –November)*	Harvesting of paddy.
9.	Agan *(November December)*	Harvesting of Kodo and Kutki.
10.	Push *(December –January)*	Harvesting of Ramtilla and weeding of Rai.
11.	Magh *(January – February)*	Harvesting of Rai.
12.	Phagun *(February – March)*	Remains fallow. Used as pasture for domestic animals. Grazing of cow, goat and buffaloes.

Their horticultural activities are very limited. In and around their homestead they grow guava, tamarind, banana, papaya and jackfruit. Some of those are also planted in the *bari* land. They also grow tobacco for self consumption.

Baiga agriculture shows us how they manage the land resources through the application of traditional wisdom in soil types, crop rotation and process of cultivation. It is also reported that, they discreetly cultivate poppy plants along with maize. Poppy being a dwarf variety grows under the cover and canopy of maize and can not be seen.

Management of Forest Resources

The ethnographic data (Elwin, 1939) on the Baiga show that they were formerly hunters and food gatherers/shifting cultivators, when the population was spare and resources were plenty, there was no special restriction on hunting space and forest patches for *bewer* cultivation. But, when population increased territorial limitation of economic activities came about. The village population living in a particular territory had to confine their exploitation within their territorial limits. A radius of approximately 20 kilometers is considered as the territorial limits of a Baiga village.

Forest has been and still is an integral part of the Baiga way of life. Only the dependency on forest resources has decreased over the years due to various exogenous factors, mainly government policies on forest starting with 1952 forest policy. These government policies on forest are specially relevant for a forest dwelling tribe like the Baiga.

National Forest Policy Of 1988

The new forest policy of 1988 takes into consideration the symbiotic relationship between the tribal people and forest.

The slient features of the new forest policy are :-

1. All the agencies responsible for forest management including the Forest Development Corporations should associate the tribal people closely in the process of – protection, regeneration and conservation of forests.
2. Meeting the basic requirements of the tribal people by providing them fuel wood, fodder, minor forest produce and timber.
3. Providing gainful employment to the people living in and around the forest.
4. The rights and concessions enjoyed by the tribal should be fully protected.

Types of Forest

There are mainly three types of forest in the area, viz. (1) Reserve Forest (2) Protected Forest and (3) National Park.

1. Reserve Forest – Where permission for collecting forest produces (MFP) mainly non-timber produces, is not supposed to be given as per rule, but as a concession the tribals living in the villages within it are allowed to collect fallen twigs and small dry branches (not the green ones) from the ground in head load.

2. Protected Forest – Where collection of MFP is permitted and selective residence is also allowed.

3. National Park – Where nothing is permitted, even residence and village settlements within the boundary of the National Park is not allowed.

In Dindori district the forest area is 2888.281 sq. kilometers, out of which 2853.54 sq. kilometers is Reserve Forest and 35.038 sq. kilometers is protected Forest. In Bajag block the area of forest is 224.114 sq. kilometers, out of which 215.802 sq. kilometers is Reserve Forest and 8.312 sq. kilometers is Protected Forest. Baiga Chawk comprising Bajag, Karanjia and Samnapur blocks, has 42.50 percent of the total forest area of Dindori district. In Bajag block there are seven forest villages the Names of which are given below showing their areas –

Sr. No.	*Names of Forest villages*	*Area (in hectares)*
1.	Khamera	862.7
2.	Tarach	788.7
3.	Silpiri	394.8
4.	Tatar	732.1
5.	Chara	502.7
6.	Khapripani	605.7
7.	Sitalpani	403.3

Nationalised Forest Resources

In general tribals are allowed to collect M.F.P. as a concession from the forest, as allowed by the Dept. of Forest.

But three major M.F.P. viz., *sal* seeds (*sal* seeds oil is now imported for use in medicines and perfumes), *Tendu* leaf (used in *Bidi* industry) and *Harra* (used for tanning of leather) are not permitted to sell in open market by the tribals directly. These forest produces are nationalized. They have to sell these items to the Dept. of Forest at a fixed price. *Tendu* leaves (*diospyros molanoxyla*) are stacked in a bundle of 50 leaves called *pura*. These bundles (*pura*) are sold for forty paisa. One thousand of such bundles are sold at the rate of Rs. 400/-. *Sal* seeds are sold at the rate of Rs. 2/- per kg. But at present collection of *sal* seeds have been stopped at Dindori for regeneration of *sal* forest. *Harra* fruits (*terminated chabula*) is priced Rs. 2/- per kg.

Nistar Right

This is some sort of concession given to the tribals. Under the Nistar the Baiga can collect fuel wood and other M.F.P. (non-timber forest produce) from the forest in head loads. They can also get timber from the forest depot for own need, e.g. House construction. There are different depots in the range where bamboo and timber are stored for selling. The *sarpanch* of the panchayat in the tribal area has to write a letter to this effect, that this person is a bonafide residence of such and such village and a member of this particular tribe. He will get the bamboo and timber from the forest department at half price for his personal use. The facility of Nistar is available to all the forest villages and the villages which are situated within a radius of 5 kilometers from the forest.

The forest produces, both non-timber and timber, are centrally auctioned by the forest department from Bhopal at a rate quoted by the highest bidder. The traders then come to the respective range depot, show the letters for rate/price etc and take delivery of the goods by paying the amount. The traders require permission from the forest department for taking the M.F.P. out of the forest area; even if it is purchased directly from the tribals at the weekly markets. Like this the forest department maintains records of the quantity of M.F.P that has been generated from the forest.

Forest Economy

By tradition the Baiga are forest dweller. Forest has shaped their habitat and economy. Even after the stoppage of bewar cultivation (shifting hill) in 1952, after the nationalization of forest, a bulk of their economy is still depending on forest. Fruits, leaves, roots and tubers which supplement and balance their cereal diet are obtained from forest. Fish, a delicacy in Baiga diet, are caught in small streams in the interior pockets of forest. Medicinal plants (mainly herbs), a must in Baiga life, are grown in the forest. Their only sweet dish, the honey, is also collected from the forest. Bamboos, timber, thatching grass, fibers for rope making and clays for his hut come from the forest. The fuel for his hearth in the form of firewood also comes from the forest. Forest also provides pasture for grazing of their cattle. Though hunting is not allowed as per rule, the Baiga still continue to do so clandestinely. When they see the foot step marks of wild boar they follow it stealthily and kill it.

They also hunt sambar, gotri (type of wild goat) etc. During summer the animals come near the water source where the Baiga waits for them. During menstruation period Baiga women do not go to the forest for collection of edible plants because it is believed that bears attracted by the smell of menstruating women and attack them. They besmear the arrow heads with a paste prepared from *mita* roots. They eat the animals killed by poisonous arrows by simply removing the wounds.

They purchase another arrow poison called *mahul* from market for Rs. 25/- per 10 grams which is a paste prepared from the root and they besmear it on the arrow heads with saliva.

Collection and selling of M.F.P strengthen their economy. Earlier when selling of *sal* seeds at the open market was allowed, a person used to earn Rs. 2,000/- per annum from it. They believe that paste of the bark of mango tree would cure '*janundice*'. This belief is responsible for the destruction of mango trees. They collect two types of edible mushrooms from the forest. One grows on the ground called *bhonra pihiri* or *sarai pihiri* and the other grows on tree called *khatta pihiri*. They sell the *khatta pihiri* to the traders for Rs. 6/- per kilogram but the *bhonro* or *sarai pihiri* is not sold.

Dependency of the Baiga on forest resources is manifold, which are catagorised as under –

1. Full time or part time wage labour employed by the Dept. of Forest
2. Craftsmen dependent on forest producc.
3. Part time hunter inhabiting the forest villages partly deriving livelihood.
4. Extractors of grass, bamboo, firewood, dried logs and twigs as head loads for personal use or local sale.
5. Gatherers of NTFP (Non Timber Forest Produces) such as mushrooms, fruits and tubers, medicinal plants for self consumption, barter or sale.

Minor/Non-timber Forest Produce

Minor forest produce (M.F.P) includes all kinds of forest produce except timber and firewood. The M.F.P plays a major role in Baiga economy. Baiga's knowledge of local flora and courage to go to the deep forest, have become quite useful in this regard.

M.F.P collected by the Baiga can be classified into three categories viz., non-edible, edible and marketable.

Non-Edible M.F.P

Non-edible M.F.P mainly provides materials for the hut and fencing of *bari* field adjoining the house. Bamboo and grass are the two main non-edible M.F.P. Grass is used for the thatching of roof. Bamboo is used for house construction, for making the handle and shaft of tools, making of basket as well as musical instruments. Bamboo forests are demarcated into several coups. At a time only one coup is open for extraction each year, while the remaining coups are left untouched. The working coups are allowed then to remain fallow for at least three consecutive years. The rotation in the extraction facilitates the regeneration of the clumps. Tender clumps below six inches are neither allowed to cut nor are the diggings of rhizomes permitted. Every year a small patch in the working coup is earmarked for *nistar* of the local villages, which includes (a) dry fuel wood (b) dry bamboos (c) grass (d) thorns (e) leaves and (f) bark or bakal. Baigas normally do not extract bamboos for commercial purpose. They use these to make basket, mat, cot etc for domestic use only. Since the Baiga do not extract bamboos for commercial purpose we find a healthy bamboo forest in the neighbourhood.

A study conducted by the Administrative staff College of Hyderabad in 1977-78 indicated that in a forest village households having less than five acres of land mainly depend on M.F.P. collection in Andhra Pradesh, Bihar, Madhya Pradesh and Orissa (Roy Burman, 1999).

Edible M.F.P

The most important edible M.F.P is *mahua* flower – as diet, as drink, as cooking medium and as source of light but due to excessive cold climate *mahua* tree is hot grown in Chara. For collection of *mahua* flower the Baiga go to Bilaspur district during the season (March-April) where *mahua* is grown profusely in the hotter climate. Mango, *Jamun*, *Gular*, *Ber*, *Bel*, *Mahul* etc are some of the important fruits available in Baiga Chawk.

The Baiga are very fond of leafy vegetables. Some of the popular leaves are *chinch*, *munga*, *chakoora*, *pipel*, *kajra*, *pakhri* etc. A large variety of roots and tubers are collected by the Baiga, which include *Kanhia Kanda*, *Kirchi Kanda*, *Kundru* etc.

Marketable M.F.P

Tendu leaves, *harra* fruits, *safed musli*, *rar* (resin) of *sal* tree and some medicinal plants are sold by the Baiga in the local weekly market. The *rar* which comes out naturally from the trunk of *sal* tree is sold by the Baiga for Rs. 5/- per kg. It is famous for its aromatic quality and used in the preparation of incense stick. *Sal* resin (*rar*) is boiled and oil is collected through distillation which is useful for skin diseases. *Safed musli* (*chlorophytum tuberosum*) or *Koinjar Kanda* was sold at the rate of Rs. 8/- per kilogram after it is washed in *alam* water. They sell *aonla* (*emblica officinates*) fruits for Rs. 10/- per kilogram. Honey is sold at the rate of Rs. 50/- per bottle. They sell *mahul* leaves (*banhinia vahisi*) for Rs. 3/- per kg. The Baiga women sell fire wood for Rs. 2.50/- per head load at Chara market.

Medicinal and Economically Useful Plants

For collection of edible, medicinal and economically useful plants the Baiga are to travel a lot in the forest. The Baiga perceive forest up to a radius of 10 kilometers from their village as their own territory. Beyond 10 kilometers they usually do not go. The Baiga have thorough knowledge of their territory. Natural resources are detected with the existence of plants in a particular location. Ground water can be detected in such sites where a normally armed plant grows without thorns. Bark of a tree indicates the amount of water present in the substratum layer. Whitish coloured bark indicates presence of good ground water but dark coloured bark pointsout scanty ground water. Termite hills are also considered clues to ground water.

Plants are considered as the principal source of all essentials in life, such as food, fodder, fiber, fuel and medicines. Many useful flowers, fruits and whole plants have been used as offerings in worship. These practices of the regular requirements of these plants for worshipping keep them available in the neighbourhood for recurrent use. Some plants such as *tulsi*, mango are worshipped and protected in the form of sacred plant. Among the Baiga it is more of sacred plants than the sacred grooves. This practice prevents these useful plants to pass into oblivion. There has always been some form of magical practices associated with the administering of these medicinal plants. The magical practices associated with the administering of these medicinal plants are mostly psychosomatic in nature.

A list of medicinal and economically useful plants used by the Baiga are given below –

(1) *Arjun (terminalia arjuna)* – Bark of the tree is used for heart ailments.

(2) *Van haldi (curcuma aromatica)* – Root of the shrub is used for skin diseases.

(3) *Haldi (curcuma longa)* – A paste of turmeric and oil is applied all over the body of the young women as a skin conditioner, antiseptic agent and germicide.

(4) *Mahua (madhuca latifolia)* – Flower of the tree is used as a beverage and food.

(5) *Munga (moringa olifera)* – Bark of the tree in paste form is used as poison for arrow heads.

(6) *Bach (acorus calamus)* – Root of the herb is used for vitality, blood purifier and cold.

(7) *Safed musli (chlorophytum tuberosum)* – Root of the herb is used for vigour.

(8) *Baichandi (dioscores hispida)* – Bulbs of the climber is used as food during illness.

(9) *Kali haldi (curcuma caesia)* – Root of the shrub is used for various diseases.

(10) *Sal (sorea robusta)* – Resin of the tree is used as astringent and in weak digestion.

(11) *Neem (Azardirachta indica)* – All the parts of the tree is used in the treatment of ulcers and skin diseases.

(12) *Ber (zizyphys maaritiana)* – Fruit of the tree is used for diarrhea and dysentery.

(13) *Kalmagh (andrographics paniculata)* – Roots and leaves of the herbs are used for liver diseases.

(14) *Aonla (emblica officinalis)* – Fruit of the tree is used for laxative and asthama.

(15) *Bon-ramtilla (vicoa auriculata)* – Leaves are made into paste and used for the treatment of skin diseases.

(16) *Ghunghuria (crotalaria alata)* –Root is made into paste and given for diarrhoea.

(17) *Jangli piyaj (urginea indica)* – Bulb of the herb is used for paralysis.

(18) *Kalihari* (*gloriosa superba*) – Plant itself is poisonous but root is considered as antidote in cobra poisoning.

(19) *Maibela* – a creeper. It is used to increase the breast milk in women after delivery.

(20) *Tajraj* – Root of the plant cures impotency in men.

(21) *Bhojra* – Root of the plant cures frigidity in women.

(22) *Bramhakash* – Tuber is mixed with gur and is given for stomach pain.

(23) *Tulsi* (*Ocimum sanctum*) – The worshippers of *Narayana* must worship *tulsi* which is believed as incarnation of goddess *Lakshmi*. This is a very useful plant – leaves of which have cusing effect on common cold, cough sore throat and ulsers.

(24) *Aparajita* (*clitoria ternates*) – Given for liver disorder.

(25) *Moa* grass (*pennisetum hohenackeri*) – Used for roof thatching.

(26) *Sabai* grass (*eulaliopsis binata*) – It is used for rope making.

(27) *Rusa* grass (*eymbopogon martini*) – It is used for rope making.

(28) *Chindi* grass (*photonix acautes*) – It is very useful plant. Required for broom making, thatching, fencing etc.

(29) *Semal Kanda* (*bombase malabaricum*) – It is a tuber.

(30) *Baichandi* (*diorcorea daemonia*) – It is a leafy vegetable.

(31) *Char/Chiranji* (*buchanaria lonjam*) – It is a very useful fruit.

(32) *Kania Kanda* (*dioscorea bilophylla*) –It is an edible tuber.

(33) *Kiolar bhaji* (*bauhinia purpuria*) – A leafy vegetablc.

(34) *Khachnar bhaji* (*banhinia variegate*) – A leafy vegetable.

(35) *Durba* grass (*eynodon dactylon*) – One of the most essential items used in rituals, worship and ceremonies, it is useful in the healing of old wound.

(36) *Dhatura* (*datura metal*) – It is used to worship Lord Siva. The flower of thc curative properties for various ailments.

(37) Banana (*musa paradisiacal*) – This plant is used by the Baiga as a holy symbol in marriage and other rituals.

Indigenous Forest Management

The Baiga being a primitive forest dwelling tribe know the forest best. They have known the traditional and indigenous way of managing the forest resources – herbs, shrubs and trees and the animals who are dependant either on plants or on other animals for survival. They are in the habit of living in complete harmony with nature until the equilibrium was disturbed by way of intrusion of the outside influences. The intruders, either government agencies or private parties, indiscriminately use their power, authority and shrewdness to exploit the forest depriving the tribals from their right to the forest resources. Useful fruit bearing trees are being replaced by timber yielding trees through commercialization of forest keeping corporate interest in mind at the cost of basic needs of forest dwellers.

The Baiga are not allowed to manage the forest in their traditional way, it is now governed by forest rules and managed by forest official – not any more by the tribals to whom it actually belongs. In the past, the use of forest products by the tribals was never at the cost of forest degeneration. Being too aware of the importance of forest in their lives, they developed norms and conventions, guarded by myths and folklore, which forbade destruction of scarce and vital trees, limited their utilization to certain seasons and otherwise promoted a culture that was protective for the trees and the animals.

Deforestation is increasing at a steady rate due to alien technique of tree felling. According to the Baiga the cutting of *sal* trees by using saw under the management of Dept. of Forest by forest department is the main cause for the degeneration of the forest. They prefer to cut the trees with axe, a few feet above the ground keeping the stumps intact for regeneration. They never extract the roots. It is said when trees are felled with axe the sprouts come out from the side after one or two monsoon since the trees are not fully dead. The same will not grow when the trees are felled by cutting with saw, as it has been increasingly done with the commercialization of forest, because the cross sectional cutting of the trunk by saw dried up the water content in the trunk and as a result xylem, phloem and other delicate plant tissues are destroyed making regeneration impossible. Before the nationalization of forest, the felling of trees were done by axe but after the take over by the forest department cutting is done entirely with saw. Presently the forest in Baiga Chawk area has become very much prone to insect attacks. An insect called *sal* borer (*hoplocerambyx spiniceonis*) has almost ruined the forest of the Baiga Chawk area. The epidemic disease of the *sal* tree is spread over a large area of forest tract. The insect, *sal* borer, makes hole in the trunk, the female insects lay eggs in the hole. As the young larva come out, they drink up the juice of the tree; it becomes pale and dry and dies a natural death within a short span of time. Forest department and local people are trying to control and eradicate this *sal* borer disease. It is believed by the Baiga that, in early times when they were allowed to put fire to the dried up leaves and under growth of the forest during summer (May-June) there was no incidence of *sal* borer attack. As this would effectively control the insects by killing them without any harm to the trees and the ashes, as manure, would help in the regeneration of grass for grazing. Beside the trees are also grown, as the insects are now dead they could be no longer put evil effect on the healthy trees. Moreover, the absence of dry leaves will not produce any noise from the foot steps while chasing the wild games for hunting.

Grazing (Chaoshira) of Animals

Grazing of cows, goats and buffaloes have become another reason for concern. Forest department has fixed some land for grazing, called *dudhiya jamin*, where grazing can be done for five consecutive years if managed judiciously. But unfortunately, excepting a few this plan is not followed by the Baiga at grass root level. One sq. kilometer of pasture land in the forest is supposed to support 100 units for grazing bovine. Cow above four years of age is considered one unit, buffalo (above four years of age) is two units, cow below four years of age is half unit and buffalo (below four years) is one unit.

Joint Forest Management (JFM)

On first June 1990, the Ministry of Environment and Forest sent out a Circular supporting the involvement of village communities and NGOs in the regeneration, management and protection of degraded forest.

To identify and solve the problems at grass root level JFM has been introduced in the forest villages of Madhya Pradesh. Chara, Tatar and Silpiri – the three forest villages which come under one panchayat, have one JFM. All the families are involved by making atleast two persons (both husband and wife) as members of the JFM committee. A governing body is set up of 10 to 11 members, which is as follows:

1. One teacher
2. Two persons from families below poverty line (BPL)
3. One panchayat member or *sarpanch*

4. One woman member
5. One beat guard or Deputy Ranger representing forest department.

First of all with the help of P.R.A. (Participatory Rural Appraisal) technique they identify some basic problems and needs of the village folk. JFM committee firstly ensures sustainability of the people by providing some help during the lean (e.g. food grain) season as per the need and requirement of the people. One such area identified is the deforestation due to grazing of animals. They select and marked some five to six patches in the forest. They oversee that in the first year only one or at the most two patches are used for grazing and collection of fire wood and *nistar* and not to disturb the remaining demarcated patches. In one year time the other 4/5 patches get regenerated and become ready for exploitation. Then in the second year they select one new patch for use for *nistar* and the cycle continues. This way by judicious use, grass and plants grow up in subsequent years and only a small area could support the grazing needs and provides *nistar* materials to the entire village. Thus, by proper management only one sq. km. of land could support 100 units of cattles.

Management of Other Resources

The Baiga's relationship with nature and environment is not the result of clash with and victory over nature but of a harmonious adaptation with natural surroundings.

Water Resource Management

Burner, Raljal and Amadoba are the three hilly streams flowing around the village Chara. Burner is the main river of the area, rests are its tributaries. The Baiga use their traditional wisdom in digging wells along the side of river Burner. This makes the wells perennial in nature as it draws the recharge of water through the constant seepage from the river, these rivers play a great role in the day-to-day activities of the Baiga. Besides taking bath and washing of clothes, they also prepare liquor from the *mohua* flower in the river bank. The Baiga have some indigenous methods of using and storing of river water. They block the flow of water in the river with the help of earthen *bund* and boulders. The trapped water creates a pool and is used for bathing, washing and at times for fishing also.

Wind And Solar Resources

Use of wind energy is only limited to the separation of husk from the grain. They extensively use solar energy for drying of food grains and vegetables. Mushrooms are dried in the sun for long hours and the dehydrated mushrooms are stored for future use.

Ideas About Nature and Natural Objects

The Baiga have definitely been lacking any positive or concrete ideas of astronomical perspectives. Their domain is limited to the earth and earthly phenomena.

They consider sun as male and moon as female. The rising of sun and moon conducted by the command of God. The day and night are caused by the magic of God. The eclipses, earthquake and thunder storms are due to the curse of God. The creation of all watery objects – oceans, seas, waves, tides, rivers, lakes, springs and flood are all due to rainfall and the rain itself is the incarnation of Lord Indra – the rain maker. The Baiga do not use the stars for divination. The moon has an influence on the menstrual cycle of women, but otherwise is mainly important as a source of light to dance by. They consider the earth a flat and round object – like a chapatti, not an oval one. Various marks on the moon are considered as tattoo marks. Moon is a woman and it was necessary for her to be tattooed. The Baiga are oblivious to the eclipses of sun and moon. An eclipse takes place in the sky and it has nothing to do with the earth for whom they are most concerned. The rainbow is thought as a water horse and is considered as an indication that rain is coming.

The Baiga, as a forest tribe, have a deep knowledge about plants and animals. Detail of which has already been discussed elsewhere in the report (Chapter on forest management). But it is worthwhile to mention about one wild animal which has great cultural significance among the Baiga – the tiger. The Baiga are widely believed as a manipulator of the movement of the tiger in the forest through their divine power. The Baiga themselves also believe that they have been blessed by the God that no tiger would harm them and a true Baiga should not afraid of tiger. A Baiga is always seen leading the hunting party of the forest tribes.

Summing Up

Being a forest tribe the ambience of the Baiga is unique and quite different from the tribes who are living outside. They live in forest villages which are administered differently from the revenue villages. Forest laws enacted from time to time play a vital role in shaping their economy and ecology. Forest department also provide them with employment.

National Forest Policies that are adopted since independence restricted their economic freedom to a great extent in the form of banning shifting hill cultivation and their privilege to the collection of forest resources has also been checked by the authority. They have been forced to shift towards settled agriculture. Nevertheless their dependences on forest still continue to exist. In Chara the maximum amount of land could be owned by a family is 2.5 hectares. In this meager land by judicious use of crop rotation and selecting particular land for specific crop as per soil types, they grow rice, maize, *kodu*, *kutki*, Mustard and *ramtilla*.

The Baiga select their mates mainly from nearby villages situated within a distance of three to five kilometers. Weekly markets beside their economic function play an important role in the negotiation of marriage. Marriage exogamy is maintained through the presence of numerous *jatis*.

The Baiga respond well to the changing scenario, as for as the environmental awareness issue is concerned, through their willful participation in joint forest management. The Baiga, at present, at the cross road of modernization along with their vast repertoire of indigenous knowledge of forest and medicinal plants and their knowledge could be used side by side with the present scientific technology for the regeneration of forest, e.g. trees should be cut with axe as per Baiga technique and not by saw as it is done now by the outside agencies. The felling of trees with axe helps in the regeneration and re-growth of forest, which is a reality as supported by the evidences based on time-long observations of the Baiga.

The Baiga, a primitive forest dwelling tribe, have come a long way outside forest economy and are looking forward to join the main stream of Indian society.

On the whole, it grievous and painful to note that the Bio-diversity convention adopted during the Earth Summit at Rio in 1992 has advocated that the knowledge and skill of the indigenous population about conservation and use of bio-diversity to be respected and documented, but it does not provide for conferring intellectual property right to such knowledge system on the plea that the same has no element of innovation in it but only carrying traditional knowledge.

References

1. Census of India, 1961, Madhya Pradesh District Census Handbook, Mandla District, Government of Madhya Pradesh.
2. District Gazetteer, Mandla District, 1912, Volume 'A' Discriptive account of Central Provinces, Times Press, Bombay.
3. Elwin Verrier, 1939, 'The Baiga' Reprint in 1986 Gian Publication, New Delhi.
4. Grierson Linguistic Survey of India, Vol. VI, p. 235.
5. Dr. Jagdish Swarup, A.K. Dwivedi, S.B. Rizvi, 'Ekikrut Gramin Vikas Yojanass Labhanwit Anuswhit Janjati Ke Hitgrahiyoka Mulyankan Adhyayan". District Mandla, Vikas Khand Dindori, Published by Adimjati Anusandhan Sansthan, Madhya Pradesh Bhopal, May, 1992.
6. Mohammed Amanullah, Dr. G.P. Patel, S. R. Patil and S.P. Bhat, March, 1990. 'Mandla Zilla Ki Baiga Janjati Me Paramparagat Chikitsa Paddhati'. Published by Adimjati Anusandhan Sanstha, Madhya Pradesh, Bhopal.
7. Nahagriya A.L., A.K. Dwivedi, V.K. Kesharvani. 'Baiga Vikas Adhikaran Dwara Kriyanvit Karyokramoka Mulyankan Adhyayan'. Published by Adimjati Anusandhan Sansthan, 35, Shyamla Hills, Bhopal – 2 (Madhya Pradesh).
8. Pandya, A.K., 1974. 'District Census Handbook Mandla District, Madhya Pradesh. Village and Town wise Primary Census Abstract Series X A and B.
9. Roy Burman B.K. 1999. 'Right of forest worker and their charter of demads' Journal of Indian Anthropological Society, No.34 (1), pp. 49-55.
10. Russel and Hiralal, 1996. Tribes and Castes of Central Provinces of India, Vol. II, Reprinted 1975. Cosmo Publication, New Delhi, pp. 77 92.
11. Thomson W.B., 1867. Report of the land revenue settlement of Seoni District, p. 39.
12. Dr. Vaishnav T.K., Mohammed Amanullah, S. R. Patil, Pravin Narad. August, 1991. 'Baiga Janjati Ka Jansankhi – Kiya Adhyayan'. Published by Adimjati Anusandhan Sanstha, Madhya Pradesh Bhopal.

7

A Study on Traditional Wisdom among the Munda and Oraon of Sundarban

Samira Dasgupta and *Amitabha Sarkar*

Introduction

The name Sundarban name may have been originated from 'Samudra-ban' or Samundar-ban' – the forest on the fringe of the sea. Sundarban is the largest delta of the river Ganga (Bhagirathi), is a unique bio-climatic zone in a tropical geographical niche of the coastal Bay of Bengal. The Southernmost part of W.B. which is a landmark of great ancient cultural heritage of mythological and historical events and confers with wonderful scenic beauty and natural resources of wide bio-diversity of mangrove forest is of immense curiosity among the scientist especially the anthropologists. Sundarban is also the largest natural mangrove resources in the world having about 102 low-lying islands of which 54 are reclaimed and in habitable condition while 48 are under reserved forests. The total area of Sundarban is 9630 sq. km. which is located between 21°32′ and 22°40′ north latitudes and between 88°05′ and 89° east latitudes bounded by Dampier – Hodges line.

Sometimes in 1830 Dampier and Hodges delimited the territory as a special forest and fixed the northern boundary of the forest. The major part of the area is being cultivated since 1830 when grants of the forest land started. About 1460 sq. miles of forest are out of 3089 sq. miles region south of Dampier Hodges line has been cleared and is being cultivated since 1830. There were primarily two objectives for reclamation of Sundarban – (a) to gain revenue from land and (b) to obtain a reserve rice against draught, the crops of Sundarban being very little dependent upon rainfall (Saha, 1999). In order to clear the vast tract of land for reclaimation the tribal people from Chotanagpur and other adjoining parts were brought and awarded settlement right by the then Jamindars and Jagirdars. After independence in few pockets of Sundarban were also reclaimed especially by the refugees from Bangladesh in the P.S. like Bansanti, Gosaba, Patharpratima, Hingalgang, Namkhana and Sagar etc. With the onset of roytwari settlement act in 1904, the influx of tribal population were started especially from Chotanagpur plateau, Santal Pargana and Mayurbhanj area of Orissa, who came in group with a hope of new economic opportunity by clearing forest, vast patches of forest land under the grant holders of *lotdars / latdars* and the people of the area were known as *latua / leto*.

Objective

The field work was carried out at Deltaic of mangrove forest of Sundarban in order to get an empirical data on management of natural resources as well as traditional wisdom (or deviation from such wisdom) of the tribal people who were once immigrated in this region from Chotanagpur, Orissa area and settled and eke out their subsistence from surrounding niche of Sundarban where brackish water plays a key role in their existence of survival.

Methodology

Sundarban in one of the biosphere reserve in our country and for its management the entire area is divided into: (a) 1700 sq. km. is declared as *core area* (including 1330 sq. km. National park); (b) forestry zone covers an area of 2564 sq. km; Here support activities for development of mangrove – eco-system will be allowed with stress on forestry and allied activities for the benefit of fringe area population; (c) the other area is known as Restoration Zone, which covers an area of 450 sq. km. mainly degraded forest areas, saline banks, mudflats and embankments etc. while (d) agriculture is practiced in 4916 sq. km. outside the forest area and declared as Manipulation Zone. All sorts of developmental activities with tidal resource management are performed in the area and we have carried out our filed work in this area.

The field work was carried out at Mathurapur II block in Dakshin Kankandighi of Kankandighi G.P. and Pachpukur village of Kumrapara G.P. among Munda and Oraon – these areas are far away from forest while Moghkhali, UttarMokamberia of Sonakhali (Basanti) and Ranipur, Rangabelia of Gosaba are fringe area to forest.

Physical Features : River

The Sundarban area is criss-crossed by the network of tidal rivers which play a chief role in communication system through water vessels. Rivers of this area are tidal and free tidal flushing of their spill areas has been stopped owing to premature reclamation; almost each and every part of Sundarban is washed or inundated for greater or longer peiod every day. In time the river swells up and again subsides. There are two tides and two ebbs in a day. The effect of tides and ebbs pay a significant role in the economic life of the people of Sundarban. All the rivers in Sundarban are connected with each other by some cross channels, forming a number of criss-cross canals, creeks, nalas or rivulets and also forming a network system in those areas by saline water. It is estimated that total area of river system of Sundarban is 1895. 88 km. There are number of rivers such as Hooghly, Muriganga, Bidya, Matla, Mani, Hatania, Raimangal, Hena, Piyali, Bidyadhari, Kalindi, HariaBhanga, Hogol, Kulti, Ichamati, Saptamukhi, Mridangebhanga etc. and all those rivers along with their tributaries have formed a number of islands at the mouth of Bay of Bengal.

Soil

Soil of the region may be broadly categorized as :

(i) Clayey or *antial* soil

(ii) Loamy or *doash/baliara* soil

(iii) Sandy loam

(iv) Sandy and

(v) Silty or *pali*

The salinity of soil varies with season and depending on the distance from sea. The PH of soil usually varies in between 6.5 and 8.9.

Climate

The network of creeks and rivers as well as closeness of the sea help the territory in controlling the extreme climatic condition. The cognizance of climate by the local people are as occasional

Nor'waster or *Kal Baisakhi* during March and April in the beginning of summer while winter is cognized through the performance of Diwali and availability of *patali gur*.

The average maximum temperature varies from 28°C to 30°C and raises upto 37°C in May – June while the average minimum temperature varies from 21° to 28°C and decreases upto 10° to 11°C in December – January. The average rainfall is 180 cm. The maximum rainfall occurs in September – October due to active monsoon. Wind velocity during cyclonic storms then reaches 120 km/hr; the natural mangrove forest on the coastline of Sundarban area often act as a natural barrier from any such natural calamity.

Flora

The flat swampy islands of Sundarban are covered with dense forest of mangrove vegetation. The well-known species in the area are *Kaora,* (Sonneratia apelata), *Sundari* (Heritiera fomes), *Hental* (Phoenex paludosa), *Garan* (Ceriop sroxburghianus), *Geoa* (Excoecaria agallocha), *Hargocha* (Acanthus ilicifolius), *Keya* (Pandanus fascicularis), *Golpata* (Nypa fruticans), *khalsi* (Acgiceras corniculatus), *garjan* (Rhizophora apiculata Blume), *Bhola* (Hibiscus tilliaceous) etc.

Fauna

Sundarban is rich in faunal diversity with Royal Bengal tiger at the top of the aqua-terrestrial food chain. In creek salt water crocodile is found; it is also the abode of imperil species like fishing cat, leopard cat, smooth coated otter (Lutra perpesillata), Gangetic dolphin etc. About 400 species of birds are available. This area is also known as goldmine of fishes and various sizes of crabs are also common. Catching of fish and crabs are one of the major economic pursuits among local people. The one of the most economic as well as commercial importance insect in this area fetch a good amount of money among local people (i.e. to *moule*) from collection of honey through honey Comb of rock bee (Apis dorsata).

Sundarban People

The scheduled castes and scheduled tribe population of Sundarban region play a vital role in the composition of population. This scheduled tribes of this area are mostly the descendants of those who were once brought over to this area, for clearing the forest and making the land cultivable, from their original homeland of Chotanagpur plateau of present day Jharkhand state and adjoining Orissa state (Das and et al. 1981).

There ae altogether 6 major scheduled tribe at Sundarban region who are numerically dominant tribal group in this region; They are Bhumij (88.8%), Munda (82.3%), Oraon (63.3%), Santal (65.7%), Kora (91.9%), and Mahali (89.5%) etc. (These data are based on 1971 census). It is also reported that Mundas are chiefly found in Gosaba, Sandeshkhali, Hasnabad and Canning while Orans are found in Mathurapur, Basanti, Sandeshkhali, Canning etc. police station of 24 Pargana district (Undivided).

History of Migration

The history of present habitation in Sundarban goes back to the early 18th century. The labourers were engaged for clearing jungles and for reclaiming lands criss-crossed by rivers and rivulets and often inter-connected by canals. The basic labour force was drawn mostly from Chotanagpur area (at present in Jharkhand state). With the gradual settlement of different ethnic groups into a close of the new habitations there emerged a new society with heterogeneous culture.Because of estuarine feature of this area the periphery of those habitations is protected by *bunds* or dykes which almost always run along the village boundary. These dykes are erected to keep out salt water of the tidal rivers and inter-connecting channels. Often the dykes are used as roads to the inhabitants of villages.

It reveals from both empirical and textual information that Oraons (often called as Uran/Dhangar) of this area migrated from Ranchi (undivided) district of Jharkhand. They trace their origin from Chotanagpur plateau but none can remember the exact place name of their origin. Historical information speaks that they immigrated at Chotanagpur where "they came in contact with Munda who had already settled there for a long time. The Oraons with a comparatively superior material condition and with better knowledge of agriculture spread their dominance over the land and gradually occupied the territory, though in certain pockets of relics of the Munda continued to persist". (Das and et al. 1981)

During British period when reclamation work of Sundarban was in progress, Munda, Oraon and others were brought by the Zamindar as cheap labourers from Ranchi area in connection with clearing of forest tracts and marshy lands and reclaimed. 'With this a huge amount of revenue was earned by the then government. A majority of tribal people of present day Sundaban are the descendant of those early setters. It is also reported that on reaching Sundarban these people changed their settlement from one place to other inview of their livelihood. The present young generation who are born and brought up in this situation are having a culture which is not at per with their traditional abode of Chotanagpur. They have lost their original/ traditional cultural behavior and present day Sundarban becomes the traditional homeland to them. It is also reported that their forefathers left their ancestral villages in Chotanagpur under adverse economic pressure. During present field investigation it is observed that some of them trace their clan name from their ancestral place name like *tamariya* and *silli* etc. though they don't know the meaning of such and don't possess any idea regarding Tamar and Silli area of present day Ranchi district of Jharkhand.

House Type

The houses in case of both the Oraons and the Mundas in general are large, spacious having one or two rooms with a large covered varandha. The house is generally constructed in a courtyard locally called as *uthan* or *angan*, sometimes at a corner or nearly in the middle of the courtyard. In the courtyard there is a threshing ground and there are places locally known as *gola* where they store paddy grain. The straw is staged in one or two places of the same courtyard. Their houses are mostly of four slopes. In the houses windows are rarely seen and if there is any it is a very small one. There are one or two doors. The houses are always constructed facing towards the courtyard. Each and every house has a cattle shed and a smaller place used as poultry. The house is provided with a kitchen garden attached with the hut. It is locally known as *bagan*.

In house making they are dependent on the locally available natural resources. The structure of a house is constructed by bamboo and then plastered with clay. The central pole of the house and also the room is the main support of a house and these are constructed by either bamboo or other materials like, some strong tree such as palm, geoa etc. The walls are plastered finally with the paste of cowdung, earth and water. The structure of the roof is constructed by bamboo and thatched with slightly wet straw. They use wet straw to set the straw properly. Each and every year they change the thatch during the month *Fagun* (February – March) with the of newly harvested straw which is harvested during the month *Pous* (December – January). During rainy season, straw gets spoilt so every year they change the straw. After thatching the straw it is tied with strong ropes as a protection. Otherwise the wind may destroy the thatching. In this way they use the natural resources for house making.

The roof of the house in a very slanting condition is constructed. It is the specific style that is suited to the environment. It obstructs the high wind to enter into inside the house proper. In this area all the houses are constructed in this style. In this area rain and storm is more or less a regular phenomenon, Which damages their huts, their crops etc. To protect their huts from such type of disturbances they construct the roof of their houses in such an excessive slanting condition.

In this way they apply the traditional knowledge of the locality for house building which is appropriate in that environmental condition using the natural resources available in that locality.

Village and the People

In order to get qualitative and quantitative empirical data of the Munda and Oraon tribes of Sundarban we have collected data from Pachpukur, village of Kumrapara Gram Panchyat, Dakshin Kankandighi village of Kankandighi G.P. The data were also collected from Moghkhali village of Basanti block and only qualitative empirical data were collected from Uttar Mokamberia village of Basanti block and Ranipur and Rangabelia villages of Gosaba block.

(a) Village-Panchpukur

It is a multi-ethnic village of Mathurapur II block of Kumrapara Gram Panchyat of South 24 Parganas. There are about 250 families in the village having following hamlets viz. Munda para, Oran para, Mahishya para, Paik para, Sardar para, Baidya (Napit) para, Naiya para, Tanti para and Haldar para. It is partially electrified. The village is bounded by Goalara village in north, Baidyapara in the east, Paikpara in south while Sutarbhag river is flowing from west. The village is having one primary school (which is very close to Munda and Oraon hamlet) and one junior high school.

In Panchpukur village there are 19 Munda families and 14 Oraon/Orang families. The Table 1 shows sex ratio of Munda in this village is 95 females per 100 males. The Table 2 is the literacy rate of Munda and it appears that 51.29% are illiterate. The Table-3 is the marital status of Munda and it shows 48.8% are unmarried and it is perhaps due to economic instability. The Table-4 is the occupational structure of Munda and it reveals that 27% are involved in cultivation as one of their economic pursuits and 42% are engaged in wage earning.

Altogether there are 14 Oraon families in Panchpukur village and Table-5 reflects sex ratio is 109 females out of 100 males. The Table-6 shows that there are about 49% are literate of which among present young generation age-group from 6 – 25 it is found that 70.58% are literate. The Table-7 shows 50.72% are unmarried among Oraon. The Oraon population at their marriageable age i.e. from 16 – 30 age-group it is found that 6 (8.7%) are unmarried among male of 16 – 20 age-group. It appears from Table-8 that cultivation as one of the major economic pursuits. Among the Oraon 14 (20.28%)are cultivators, and , wage labour 17 (24.63%). Among female Oraon household work as main economic pursuits with wage labour as subsidiary is 9 (13.04%). The collection work as subsidiary economic pursuits is practiced by only (5.79%) female; They usually collect crab, snail, and occasionally prawn seed from neighbouring rivulet.

Table 1: Village – Panchpukur
Age-group wise sex-ratio among the Munda

Age-group	Male	Female
0 – 5	6	-
6 – 10	5	9
11 – 15	7	4
16 – 20	4	4
21 – 25	2	1
26 – 30	5	4
31 – 35	1	3
36 – 40	1	1
41 – 45	3	5
46 – 50	2	2
51 – 55	1	1
56 – 60	2	2
61 and above	1	2
Total	**40**	**38**

Table-2: Village – Panchpukur

Age-group wise Literacy rate among the Munda

Age-group	*Illit-erate*		*Levels of Literacy*							
			Can sign only		*Primary level*		*Secon-dary / H.S. level*		*Higher Education*	
	M	*F*	*M*	*F*	*M*	*F*	*M*	*F*	*M*	*F*
0 – 5	5	-	-	-	1	-	-	-	-	-
6 – 10	3	2	-	-	2	7	-	-	-	-
11 – 15	2	2	-	-	1	1	4	1	-	-
16 – 20	-	2	-	-	2	-	2	2	-	-
21 – 25	-	1	-	-	1	-	1	-	-	-
26 – 30	3	4	-	-	-	-	2	-	-	-
31 – 35	-	2	-	-	-	-	2	-	-	-
36 – 40	-	1	-	-	-	-	1	-	-	-
41 – 45	2	4	-	-	1	1	-	-	-	-
46 – 50	2	4	-	-	1	-	1	-	-	-
51 – 55	-	1	-	-	-	-	1	-	-	-
56 – 60	-	2	1	-	1	-	-	-	-	-
61 and above	-	2	1	-	-	-	-	-	-	-
Total	**15**	**25**	**2**	**-**	**11**	**10**	**12**	**3**	**-**	**-**

Table 3: Village – Panchpukur
Age-group wise Marital status of the Munda

Age-group	*Unmarried*		*Married*		*Widow / widower*		*Separated / Divorced*	
	M	*F*	*M*	*F*	*M*	*F*	*M*	*F*
0 – 5	6	-	-	-	-	-	-	-
6 – 10	5	9	-	-	-	-	-	-
11 – 15	7	4	-	-	-	-	-	-
16 – 20	4	2	-	2	-	-	-	-
21 – 25	1	-	1	1	-	-	-	-
26 – 30	-	-	4	4	-	-	1	-
31 – 35	-	-	1	2	-	-	-	1
36 – 40	-	-	1	1	-	-	-	-
41 – 45	-	-	2	5	-	-	1	-
46 – 50	-	-	2	2	-	-	-	-
51 – 55	-	-	1	-	-	-	-	1
56 – 60	-	-	1	-	-	-	1	2
61 and above	-	-	1	-	-	-	-	2
Total	**23**	**15**	**14**	**17**	**-**	**-**	**3**	**6**

Table 4: Village – Panchpukur
Various Economic Pursuits among the Munda

Sl.No.	*Name of economic pursuits*	*Male*	*Female*
1	Cultivation (M) and wage labour (S)	10	-
2	Household work (M) and wage labour (S)	-	5
3	Student	2	10
4	Service (M) along with cultivation	6	-
5	Office bearer of gram panchyat (M) and cultivation (S)	1	-
6	Household work (M), Cultivation wage labour and collection (S)	-	14
7	Wage earning only	3	1
8	Cultivation only	4	-
9	Household work only	-	5
10	No. work	6	1
	Total	**32**	**36**

*M = Main * S = Subsidiary

The table-4 shows that 10 (12.12%) male are involved in cultivation as one of the main occupation while wage labour is subsidiary to them. There are 14 (17.94%) female involved in household work as main economic pursuits and cultivation, wage labour and collection as subsidiary to them. Altogether 21 (about 27%) male are practicing cultivation as one of their economic pursuits while male wage earner is 13 (16.66%) and female wage earner is 26(25.64%).

Table 5: Village – Panchpukur

Age-group wise sex-ratio among the Oraon

Age-group	*Male*	*Female*
0 – 5	3	9
6 – 10	4	7
11 – 15	4	2
16 – 20	6	2
21 – 25	1	1
26 – 30	2	4
31 – 35	3	4
36 – 40	4	3
41 – 45	3	-
46 – 50	1	-
51 – 55	1	1
56 – 60	1	1
61 and above	-	-
Total	**33**	**36**

Table 6: Village – Panchpukur
Age-group wise Literacy rate among the Oraon

Age-group	*Illiterate*		*Levels of Literacy*							
			Can sign only		*Primary level*		*Secondary / H.S. level*		*Higher Education*	
	M	*F*	*M*	*F*	*M*	*F*	*M*	*F*	*M*	*F*
0 – 5	3	9	-	-	-	-	-	-	-	-
6 – 10	-	1	-	-	4	6	-	-	-	-
11 – 15	-	1	-	-	-	-	4	1	-	-
16 – 20	-	1	-	-	3	-	3	1	-	-
21 – 25	-	-	-	-	-	1	1	-	-	-
26 – 30	-	3	-	-	1	-	1	1	-	-
31 – 35	1	3	-	-	-	1	2	-	-	-
36 – 40	1	3	-	-	1	-	2	-	-	-
41 – 45	2	-	-	-	1	-	-	-	-	-
46 – 50	1	-	-	-	-	-	-	-	-	-
51 – 55	1	1	-	-	-	-	-	-	-	-
56 – 60	1	3	-	-	-	-	-	-	-	-
61 and above	-	-	-	-	-	-	-	-	-	-
Total	**10**	**25**	**-**	**-**	**10**	**8**	**13**	**3**	**-**	**-**

Table 7: Village – Panchpukur
Age-group wise Marital status of the Oraon

Age-group	*Unmarried*		*Married*		*Widow / widower*		*Separated / Divorced*	
	M	*F*	*M*	*F*	*M*	*F*	*M*	*F*
0 – 5	3	9	-	-	-	-	-	-
6 – 10	4	7	-	-	-	-	-	-
11 – 15	4	2	-	-	-	-	-	-
16 – 20	6	-	-	2	-	-	-	-
21 – 25	-	-	1	1	-	-	-	-

(contd...)

Age-group	*Unm-arried*		*Married*		*Widow / widower*		*Separated / Divorced*	
	M	*F*	*M*	*F*	*M*	*F*	*M*	*F*
26 – 30	-	-	2	4	-	-	-	-
31 – 35	-	-	3	4	-	-	-	-
36 – 40	-	-	4	3	-	-	-	-
41 – 45	-	-	2	-	1	-	-	-
46 – 50	-	-	1	-	-	-	-	-
51 – 55	-	-	1	1	-	-	-	-
56 – 60	-	-	1	-	-	3	-	-
61 and above	-	-	-	-	-	-	-	-
Total	**17**	**18**	**15**	**15**	**1**	**3**	**-**	**-**

Table 8: Village – Panchpukur
Various Economic Pursuits among the Oraon

Sl. No.	*Name of economic pursuits*	*Male*	*Female*
1	Cultivation (M) and wage labour (S)	12	1
2	Household work (M) and wage labour (S)	-	4
3	Student	11	9
4	Household work (M), Cultivation wage labour and collection (S)	1	4
5	Wage earning only	4	1
6	Household work (M) and Cultivation (S)	-	3
7	Cultivation only	1	-
8	Household work only	-	5
9	No. work	4	8
	Total	**33**	**36**

*M = Main * S = Subsidiary

(b) Village – Dakshin Kankandighi

Dakshin Kankandghi village is under Kankandighi gram panchyat of Mathurapur-II block of South 24 Parganas. The nearest big business centre is Raidighi. In between Raidighi and Kankandighi there flows river Moni. Kankandighi is an island where a large part of cultivable land is cultivated by tribal people. It is a multi-ethnic village consists of Munda, Santal, Kora (Modi), Bhumij, Mahishya, PoundraKshtriya, Kaura Bagdi, Goala (Christian), Teli and Muslim. The Kankandighi (G.P.) island is having following villages viz. Uttar Kankandighi and Dakshin Kankandighi. The present investigation is carried out at Dakshin Kankandighi village at Munda para which is situated by the side of river Moni; On the east of this village is Jata Jogendrapur village. Moni river is on west, Nalgora is an north and on south is Nagendrapur fifth division. It is also reported that a number of archaeological findings were also recovered from excavation. The village is having Primary school and Junior High School but the High School is situated at the Jata Jagendrapur. There is no electric facility. The island roads are Kachcha but bricked for smooth moving of van rickshaw. The brackish water plays a major role in the economic life of the people. The source of drinking water is from well. The Munda are settled almost at the bank of river Moni. To escape from tidal effect there lies an embankment between Munda hamlet and Moni river. The investigation carried out in 31 Munda families of this village.

The Table-9 depicts age-group wise sex-ratio among the Munda of Dakshin Kankandighi village. It is found that sex-ratio is 96.7 female out of 100 males in the population. The table-10 shows that 53.73% are found in 11 – 15 age-group. The Table-11 depicts that the 56.98% are unmarried. It is found that in the marriageable age-group from 16 – 30 there are 26 (14.52%) males are engaged in cultivation while Meendhara as one of the economic pursuits is practiced by 69 (38.54%) male and 64 (35.75%) females. The said Table also reflects that 47 (26.25%) students are also engaged in Meendhara as gainful economic pursuits. Meendhara as one of the occupation among studied group at Sundarban is especially seasonal i.e. during monsoon it rises in the peak while it is down during winter. Most of the family members are involved in *meendhara* as one of the gainful economic pursuits at this village and fetch Rs. 400-500/- per month average.

Table 9: Village – Dakshin Kankandighi
Age-group wise sex-ratio among the Munda

Age-group	*Male*	*Female*
0 – 5	9	8
6 – 10	15	14
11 – 15	14	13
16 – 20	11	13
21 – 25	5	3
26 – 30	6	10
31 – 35	7	8
36 – 40	6	5
41 – 45	5	3
46 – 50	2	1
51 – 55	3	4
56 – 60	1	3
61 and above	7	3
Total	**91**	**88**

Table 10: Village – Dakshin Kankandighi
Age-group wise Literacy rate among the Munda

Age-group	*Illit-erate*		*Levels of Literacy*							
			Can sign only		*Primary level*		*Secondary / H.S. level*		*Higher Education*	
	M	*F*	*M*	*F*	*M*	*F*	*M*	*F*	*M*	*F*
0 – 5	9	8	-	-	-	-	-	-	-	-
6 – 10	4	6	-	-	11	8	-	-	-	-
11 – 15	2	4	-	-	12	9	-	-	-	-
16 – 20	4	9	1	1	2	3	4	-	-	-
21 – 25	2	3	-	-	3	-	-	-	-	-
26 – 30	-	8	1	-	3	1	2	1	-	-
31 – 35	3	6	1	1	3	1	-	-	-	-
36 – 40	2	4	1	-	2	-	1	1	-	-
41 – 45	1	3	1	-	3	-	-	-	-	-
46 – 50	1	1	-	-	1	-	-	-	-	-
51 – 55	1	4	1	-	1	-	-	-	-	-
56 – 60	-	3	-	-	1	-	-	-	-	-
61 and above	5	3	2	-	-	-	-	-	-	-
Total	**34**	**62**	**8**	**2**	**42**	**22**	**7**	**2**	-	-

Table-11: Village – Dakshin Kankandighi
Age-group wise Marital status of the Munda

Age-group	*Unma-rried*		*Married*		*Widow / widower*		*Separated / Divorced*	
	M	*F*	*M*	*F*	*M*	*F*	*M*	*F*
0 – 5	9	8	-	-	-	-	-	-
6 – 10	15	14	-	-	-	-	-	-
11 – 15	14	13	-	-	-	-	-	-
16 – 20	11	10	-	3	-	-	-	-
21 – 25	3	-	2	3	-	-	-	-
26 – 30	2	-	4	9	-	-	-	1
31 – 35	-	1	7	7	-	-	-	-
36 – 40	1	-	5	5	-	-	-	-
41 – 45	-	1	5	1	-	1	-	-
46 – 50	-	-	2	1	-	-	-	-
51 – 55	-	-	3	3	-	1	-	-
56 – 60	-	-	1	2	-	1	-	-
61 and above	-	-	6	2	1	1	-	-
Total	**55**	**47**	**35**	**36**	**1**	**4**	**-**	**1**

Table-12: Village – Kankandighi
Various Economic Pursuits among the Munda

Sl. No.	*Name of economic pursuits*	*Male*	*Female*
1	Cultivation (M) and wage labour with Meendhara (S)	33	-
2	Household work and cultivation (M), wage labour and Meendhara (S)	-	35
3	Wage labour (M) and collection of Meen (Prawn seed) [S]	4	7
4	Household work only	-	4
5	Cultivation only	4	-
6	Service only	2	-
7	Household work (M) and Meendhara (S)	-	5
8	Household work (M) and Cultivation (S)	-	3
9	Meendhara only	2	-
10	Cattle rearing	1	-
11	Student (M) with or without Meendhara (S)	30	17
12	No work	15	17
	Total	**91**	**88**

C. Village – Moghkhali

Village Moghkhali is situated in Sonakhali (Basanti) police station of South 24 Parganas. It is under Amratala (J.L. no. 130) Gram panchyat, Uttar Mokamberia Anchal and under Naryantola Post Office. On its north Tetultola village, Charankhali in South, Uttar Sonakhali in east and in west Amratala village and river Matla. It is a multi-ethnic village and Oraon is numerically dominant in the village. It is estimated that apart from Oraon Scheduled tribe (25 families) the other communities are Bairagi (5 families), Bhumij (12 families), Napit (3 families), Hindusthani (3 families), Muslim (2 families) etc. Village having thatched house. The thatched roof of the house is tied with storng string in order to protect from storm which is very frequent in this deltaic zone.

It appears from table-13 that sex-ratio of Moghkhali village among the Oraon is 100 that is 100 female out of 100 males in the population, while in Table-14 it reveals that about 51% are illiterate. It also appears from same Table that there are 39 (34.82%) literate person in the age-group of 6 – 30 which indicates present young generation are more inclined towards education. Table-15 reflects that about 43% are unmarried of which 18 (16.07%) are unmarried in 16 – 30 age-group. From table-16 it reflects that 24 (21.42%) males are involved in cultivation as one of the economic pursuits and 29 (25.89%) males are earning their bread through wage earning as one of the economic pursuits. While among women 27 (24.10%) are wages earner along with other occupational opportunity available to them.

Table-13: Village – Moghkhali
Age-group wise sex-ratio among the Oraon

Age-group	*Male*	*Female*
0 – 5	7	4
6 – 10	4	8
11 – 15	6	1
16 – 20	7	10
21 – 25	8	5
26 – 30	3	6
31 – 35	4	3
36 – 40	3	5
41 – 45	3	2
46 – 50	4	4
51 – 55	4	2
56 – 60	1	2
61 and above	2	4
Total	**56**	**56**

Table 14: Village – Moghkhali
Age-group wise Literacy rate among the Oraon

Age-group	*Illit-erate*		*Levels of Literacy*							
			Can sign only		*Primary level*		*Secondary / H.S. level*		*Higher Education*	
	M	*F*	*M*	*F*	*M*	*F*	*M*	*F*	*M*	*F*
0 – 5	7	4	-	-	-	-	-	-	-	-
6 – 10	1	-	-	-	2	7	1	1	-	-
11 – 15	-	1	-	-	-	-	6	-	-	-
16 – 20	3	4	-	-	1	2	3	4	-	-
21 – 25	2	3	1	-	2	-	3	2	-	-
26 – 30	-	3	1	-	-	1	2	2	-	-
31 – 35	1	2	-	-	-	-	3	1	-	-
36 – 40	1	4	-	-	1	1	1	-	-	-
41 – 45	-	2	-	-	-	-	3	-	-	-
46 – 50	1	4	1	-	-	-	2	-	-	-
51 – 55	4	2	-	-	-	-	-	-	-	-
56 – 60	1	2	-	-	-	-	-	-	-	-
61 and above	1	4	-	-	-	-	1	-	-	-
Total	**22**	**35**	**3**	**-**	**6**	**11**	**25**	**10**	**-**	**-**

Table-15: Village – Moghkhali
Age-group wise Marital status of the Oraon

Age-group	*Unmar-ried*		*Married*		*Widow / widower*		*Separated / Divorced*	
	M	*F*	*M*	*F*	*M*	*F*	*M*	*F*
0 – 5	7	4	-	-	-	-	-	-
6 – 10	4	8	-	-	-	-	-	-
11 – 15	6	1	-	-	-	-	-	-
16 – 20	7	6	-	4	-	-	-	-
21 – 25	4	-	4	5	-	-	-	-
26 – 30	1	-	2	4	-	1	-	1
31 – 35	-	-	4	2	-	1	-	-
36 – 40	-	-	3	5	-	-	-	-
41 – 45	-	-	3	2	-	-	-	-
46 – 50	-	-	4	3	-	1	-	-
51 – 55	-	-	4	1	-	1	-	-
56 – 60	-	-	1	1	-	1	-	-
61 and above	-	-	2	-	-	4	-	-
Total	**29**	**19**	**27**	**27**	**-**	**9**	**-**	**1**

Table 16: Village – Kankandighi
Various Economic Pursuits among the Munda

Sl. No.	*Name of economic pursuits*	*Male*	*Female*
1	Cultivation (M) and wage earning (S)	18	-
2	Household work (M), Cultivation and wage earning (S)	-	10
3	Household work (M) and collection (S)	-	9
4	Household work (M), wage earning (S)	-	11
5	Cultivation only	3	-
6	Service only	1	-
7	Wage earning only	11	6
8	Household work (M) and Cultivation (S)	-	5
9	Service (M), and Cultivation (S)	2	-
10	Household work (M), cultivation and Auganbari helper (S)	-	1
11	Student (M) and cultivation (S)	1	-
12	Student	11	10
13	No work	9	4
	Total	**56**	**56**

Management of Forest

To deal with the management of forest in the Sundarban area by the Oraon and the Munda – the two studied groups–it is astonishingly found that they have very less interaction with the forest. Though some of them live in the fringe area of the forest even then generally they avoid to go in the midst of the forest to fulfill their economic want. They have got other avenues through which they can earn their livelihood. According to them their forefathers used to go to the forest and were much dependent on it. At that time other economic resources were less and they were brought for cutting the forest so that they had lesser choice and opportunities. But now-a-days they have their natural resources such as land and water which give them several sources of earning and thus their opinion is that when there are ample other sources for livelihood, there is no basic necessity to go to the forest where every moment is full of insecurity and uncertainty.

Even then sometimes though very rarely, they go to the forest. Generally they go there in a group. Sometimes they go either for collection of honey, or fuel wood or sometimes for big wooden logs for house-making.

Sometimes (only a very few cases are there) they accompany the *mouleys* (the professional honey collectors)) in the forest. Honey collection is a seasonal operation which starts from the month of Chaitra (March – April) and continues atleast for three months. With the end of the season of neem flower it is the time when the of beehives are steeped in honey as all the flowering trees are full with bloom. The *mouleys* locate the beehives tracing the velocity of the northerly wind. Mouley is a group of people specialized for honey – collection. Whenever a group of honey collectors go to the jungle for honey collection, side-by-side they also collect the fuel wood. They collect *hental* leaves and honey. They collect *hental* leaves to use as broom, chappals and shoes, for honey collection and also for salt preparation. They collect honey from the beehives on the trees like Geoa, Bani, Keora etc. For collection of honey, the set fire to the mixture of the dried and fresh *hental* leaves and with the smoke of the burnt leaves the bees are driven away. After setting fire they hold it in favour of the wind. The smoke reaches to the honey – comb, irritates the bees and ultimately the bees leave the bee hive when they collect honey. The honey is either sold in the market or in some co-operative society. The price depends on the variety and quality of the honey.

Generally their necessity of fuel wood is fulfilled by the paddy straw and the branches of the trees locally available. For house making they arrange many a time to get wooden logs from their neighborhoods. If these are not available there they go to jungle to collect the wood. But in all the cases they never cut a tree from its base. They cut it leaving atleast 2′ height from the base. They cut it learning at least 2′ height from the base. They have a belief and also their practical experience says that in those cases the trees may not die and there are chances of their re-growth. In this way conservation of plants both in the forest and in their locality is done. There are certain trees such as Neem, Jagdumur, Bel, Gab, Bot, Asattha, Gaha/Geho, Tulsi etc. which are never felled by the people. According to them they are tabooed to fell those as all these plants have certain religious importance. Again they are not allowed to cut any tree and even a little shrub in their religions and sacred places which are known as than in this locality –

similar to the concept of *Sarna* in the Chotanagpur Plateau. All these religious beliefs and restrictions ultimately help in the conservation of forest.

Whenever they dig out any tuber from the earth, they do not take out the whole portion out of it. Always they leave some or a little portion of it under the earth. Gradually it grows again for future use. In this way conservation of tubers is done indirectly.

The tribal people here think that there are several items found both in forest and also in their habitat. Some of these constitute their food while others have medicinal value. As for example *Kukri* or mushroom and *hawnk* or young bamboo shoot are very delicious and costly items in their food materials. They do not consume all these varieties. The yellowish *kukri* grown on the decomposed straw is edible. When a young bamboo shoot grows, sometimes they cover it with an earthen pitcher locally known as *handi*. The bamboo shoot grows in circular fashion inside the *handi* which looks like a cabbage. They consume it. Though it is a delicious item even then they avoid to take it as it hampers in the growth of bamboo.

There are so many food items directly or indirectly come from the nature around them. In addition to these there are several plants which have some medicinal value and the people of the locality utilize these for their recovery.

Sl. No.	*Disease*	*Medicinal Herbs / Plants / roots / tubers etc.*	*How to use*
1	Cough and cold	Leaves of Manasa Plants, salt/honey	The juice of the leave is extracted and then mixed with salt or honey and taken.
2	Cuts	Leaves of marigold plant and sundried rice	The leaves are ground along with the sundried rice and then applied to the cut.
3	Cough and cold	Leaves of Tulsi plant and honey	The leaves are ground then mixed with honey and taken.
4	Boil	The roots of Ketki plant	The roots are ground and then applied to the area.

Sl. No.	*Disease*	*Medicinal Herbs / Plants / roots / tubers etc.*	*How to use*
5	Bone injury	Stem of the Harjora plant	The stem is ground and then applied to the place and bandaged.
	Sprain	The leaf of Nishindi leaf	The leave is crushed and applied to the place. It gives relief from pain.
6	Stomach upset, dysentery	Thankuni leaf, Mustard oil	The leaf is ground and mixed with mustard oil and taken with hot rice.
7	Headache	Telkucho leaf	The juice of the leaf is applied to the affected zone.
8	Stomach upset	Unripe banana	Preparation of the banana in boiled condition con summed.
9	Stomach trouble	Leaf of Dhutra leaf	It is crushed and applied on belly. It gives relief from any type of disease.
10	Sprain	Turmeric and mustard oil	Paste of turmeric added with mustard oil heated and applied to the affected zone.

Now-a-days they have started the plantation of coconut tree, date palm, palm and the bamboo trees in their locality and even in their homestead land. Previously their older generation had a belief that plantation of all these trees is not auspicious. It may cause unfortunate circumstances in their life. This belief gradually became faded. The usefulness of the plants and trees have been understood by these people from the neighbouring other communities. All of those have economic value. The fruits of these plants are very nutritious and are very tasty. These are the choiceable items to entertain their guests and invitees. Thus they have in due course given up those superstitious beliefs, they have adapted the knowledge of plantation of these trees from the local people.

Hunting in the forest is an obsolete phenomenon. But hunting is an amusement – it is liked by all of them and they hunt several birds, field rates, hares. These are generally available in their fields and surroundings. They have several traps to catch these.

According to them the field ratcs are very tasty during the summer season. During the winter season and till the beginning of the summer season, there are plenty of crops, vegetables and cereals in the field. So this creature gets plenty of food and become fat and tasty. They catch those for their own consumption; catching of field rats helps them in two ways. It adds a tasty dish in their food items and to save their crops, cereals and vegetables from destruction (as these are rigoroushy eaten by these creatures) they catch those with the help of rat trap.

In their field, during the harvesting season, Dhankhauri – a variety of bird come to eat the cultivated product. In order to resist this the cultivators catch these birds with a variety of trap, locally known as *atol*. During the harvesting season they prepare *atols*. An *atol* is constructed by a bunch of small thin bamboo sticks tied by the strings prepared out of palm leaves. For preparation of strings they have got some knowledge from the local people. According to them they extract the strings from the butt end of a leaf which is the joining end with the trunk of the palm tree. At first they take the portion and it is pounded. During the process of pounding fibers come out of the portion. The fibers are very strong. They keep these dipped into thc water for atleast one hour. Then the strings are isolated from one another and the bamboo sticks are tied with these strings to prepare an *atol*. It is told that during night they spread the *atol* in the field. Early in the morning the birds come to eat the harvested cereals, and crops. When they chase the birds, those run in a hurry try to run way and get trapped in those *atols*. In this way they catch the birds from the field.

From the above discussion on the forest management it is clearly noted that they have a very minimum interaction with forest. Very occasionally they go to the forest for collection of fuel wood, honey, wooden logs, some tubers and also the plants with medicinal value. As all these materials are available in the neighbouring ares of their habitat; the people do not like to visit the forest to collect these. Along with the utilization of these things they have got knowledge of conservation and preservation of these items which is not only helpful for the future utilization but also helpful to keep balance in the local bio-sphere.

Land Management

Similar to the Oraons and the Mundas of the Chotanagpur Plateau, the Oraons and the Mundas of the Sundarban area are primarily the cultivators. Cultivation is one of their most important occupations to maintain their livelihood. Along with cultivation, especially those who live very close to river, also earn their livelihood through *meendhara* or collection of prawn seed, or shrimp or finger ling which will be discussed later on.

In the Sundarban area the land which is termed as *ote* by the people is primarily of three types namely :

Classification of Cultivable Land

1	the Ora ote	the land attached with their huts (homestead land). It is generally used as kitchen garden
2	the Nicha/Nabal/Sali/Khala ote (Baria fasal or doo fasal jamin	low land with high productive value. In this type of land paddy of coarser variety is cultivated. This type of land is preferably used for Boro cultivation. Now-a-days after Boro cultivation, they also cultivate the paddy of Aman variety.
3	Danga/Ucha ote	this is high, less irrigated, rain-fed land, preferred for Aman cultivation. The paddy grows here is of finer variety but the quantity of the production is less than the paddy cultivated in the Khala ote. In this type of land Khesari (a kind of pulse) is also cultivated.

Type of land vis-à-vis Wisdom involved in Cereal Cultivation

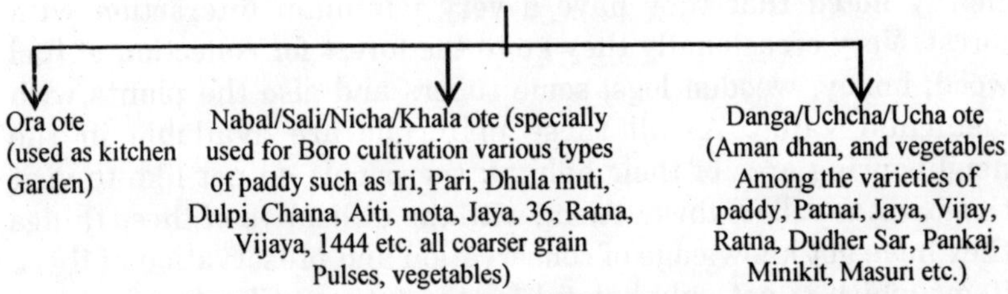

Now, in the following tables the land holding by the Mundas and the Oraons of the three studied villages are given.

Table – 17 (a): Land holding
Village – Panchpukur of Kumrapara G.P.
Community – Munda

Type of land	*Upto 10 kathas*	*11 kathas to 1 Bigha*	*Upto 3 Bigha*	*Upto 5 Bigha*	*Above 5 Bigha*	*Total Families*
Ora ote or Bastu	12	3	1	-	-	16
Nabal/Sali/ Nicha/Khala etc.	-	4	7	4	5	20
Uchcha/Danga ote	4	2	3	-	-	9
Total land	**16**	**9**	**11**	**4**	**5**	**45**

Table – 17 (b): Land holding
Village – Panchpukur of Kumrapara G.P.
Community – Oraon

Type of land	*Upto 10 kathas*	*11 kathas to 1 Bigha*	*Upto 3 Bigha*	*Upto 5 Bigha*	*Above 5 Bigha*	*Total Families*
Ora ote or Bastu	11	3	-	-	-	14
Nabal/Sali/ Nicha/Khala etc.	2	4	5	1	1	13
Uchcha/Danga ote	4	1	-	1	-	6
Total land	**17**	**8**	**5**	**2**	**1**	**33**

Table 17 (c): Land holding
Village – Kankandighi Community – Munda

Type of land	*No land*	*Upto 10 kathas*	*11 kathas to 1 Bigha*	*Upto 3 Bigha*	*Upto 5 Bigha*	*Above 5 Bigha*	*Total Fami lies*
Ora ote or Bastu	6	21	4	-	-	-	31
Nabal/Sali/ Nicha/Khal a etc.	-	5	13	5	-	-	23
Uchcha/Da nga ote	-	6	2	-	-	-	8
Total land	**6**	**32**	**19**	**5**	**-**	**-**	**62**

Table – 17 (d): Land holding
Village – Mogkhali
Community – Oraon

Type of land	*No land*	*Upto 10 kathas*	*11 kathas to 1 Bigha*	*Upto 3 Bigha*	*Upto 5 Bigha*	*Above 5 Bigha*	*Total Families*
Ora ote or Bastu	3	9	3	3	-	-	18
Nabal/Sali/ Nicha/Khala etc.	3	1	2	10	4	1	21
Uchcha/Danga ote	3	5	4	4	1	1	18
Total land	**9**	**15**	**9**	**17**	**5**	**2**	**57**

Table – 17 (e): Family wise land holding
A complied table of table 1 (a), (b), (c), (d)
(Total studied Munda family – 50, Oraon family – 38)

Type of land	*Villages and communities*				*Total Families*
	Munda of Panch-pukur	*Oraon of Panch-pukur*	*Munda of Kankan-dighi*	*Oraon of Kankan-dighi*	
Ora ote or Bastu	16	14	25	15	70
Nabal/Sali/ Nicha/Khala etc.	20	13	23	18	74
Uchcha/ Danga ote	9	6	8	15	38
Total land	**45**	**33**	**56**	**48**	**182**

It is found from the complied Table 17(a), (b), (c), (d) of land holding that in all the three villages the Munda and the Oraon communities under study possess *Nabal / Sali / Nicha / Khala ote* (low land). Now, among total 80 families it is found that 70 (87.5%) possess Ora ote or *Bastu* and 74 (92.5%) possess *Nabal / Sali / Nicha / Khala ote* and only 38 (47.0%) families possess *Uchcha* or *Dangaote*.

It is found that their *Ora ote* is also situated in or very close to the *Nabal / Sali / Nicha /Khala ote*. As they live in the Sundarban-the deltaic region, the land is mainly situated at the lower level and the *Ucha ote* is not so sufficient in the area and due to this reason their lands are mostly situated in close to the *Nabal ote*.

On the other hand, the Oraon and the Munda of Chotanagpur plateau live in the hilly region where the land is mainly of *Ucha* variety in the hilly terrain. They live in the *Uchajamin* area and their cultivable lands are situated in the *Ucha jamin.* Due to this reason the process of cultivation and the products are different from those of the Sundarban area.

It appears from the Occupational tables that the majority of the people have taken cultivation as one of their most important economic pursuits and practice settled plough cultivation.

Table 18: Cultivation with Other Occupations
Villages – Panchpukur, Kankandighi, and Mogkhali
Communities – Munda and Oraon

Sl. No.	*Name of the economic pursuits*	*Primary*			*Subsidiary*			*Total*
		Male	*Female*	*Total*	*Male*	*Female*	*Total*	
1	Cultivation (Primary), Wage labour (Subsidiary)	40	1	41	-	-	-	41
2	Service (Primary), Cultivation (Subsidiary)	-	-	-	12	-	12	12
3	Household work (Primary), Cultivation wage labour and collection (Subsidiary)	-	-	-	1	20	21	21
4	Household work (Primary), Cultivation (Subsidiary)	-	-	-	-	20	20	20
5	Cultivation (Primary)	12	-	12	-	-	-	12
6	Cultivation (Primary), wage labour with meendhara (Subsidiary)	33	-	33	-	-	-	33
7	Household work and cultivation (Primary), wage labour and meendhara (Subsidiary)	-	35	35	-	-	-	35
	Total	**85**	**36**	**121**	**13**	**40**	**53**	**174**

It is found earlier in the table of occupations (table 4, 8, 12, and 16) that there are 34 males and 30 females who have no occupational involvement to earn their livelihood. There are altogether 348 working persons. Among these 348 working persons 174 (46.03%) have taken cultivation as their one of the sources of earning and in case of 121 (32.01%) persons it is their primary occupation and in case of 53 (14.02%) persons it is the subsidiary occupation.

Therefore from the above table it is found that cultivation as an occupation is very important. As the land is fertile and suitable for paddy cultivation, they utilize it to produce the crops, cereals and vegetables.

After their settlement at the Sundarban area, to adjust with the ecological condition of the particular area, the presently studied groups have to share the traditional knowledge of the local people. It is told that the plough used in the Sundarban area for cultivation is different from the plough used in the Chotanagpur plateau. In the Chotanagpur plateau they use an iron shaft in the plough to till the hard rocky soil. In the Sundarban area, the soil is very easy for tilling so instead of an iron shaft a wooden shaft easily workable as well as upto satisfaction. Presently in the Sundarban area in some places they are using tractor instead of plough which indicates mechanization of agriculture.

It is told that before paddy cultivation they plough their land atleast for three times which are known as *karana* or *niyan chash, doyat or baria chash,* and *kada chash or apaiya* accordingly. The system is largely in vogue during the recent time also.

The first ploughing or *karana* or *niyan chash* is done in the month of *ashad* (June-July) after two or three showers. On the day of ploughing they plough the field for atleast three times. And in this process the mud is overturned. Along with the mud of upper layer, all the waste, leaves etc. accumulated in the field go downward. Again after three to four days they plough the same field and leave it for another three to four days. This is the *doyat* or *baria chash* that is second ploughing. The third ploughing or *apaiya* or *kada chash* is done with a *moi* (leveler) after three to four days of the second ploughing. It is done for leveling of the soil. It is told that when they plough, the mud of the upper layer along with leaves, cowdung, and all the waste products are overturned, those are pressed and get decomposed very quickly and in this process the fertility of the soil is increased. The other important point for ploughing is to loosen the soil which helps in water absorbtion and also for ventilation purpose. These all are the traditional knowledge associated with ploughing.

They generally prepare seed bed, locally known as *tolakhuti* separately at a corner of the field where they broadcast the seed. It is done earlier, probably in the month of Vaisakh (April – May). Transplantation or *ropni* is done later in the month of Ashad (June-July) just after ploughing. Weeding or *ghasnikat* is done in the month of Bhadra (August – September) by a comb like implement. The bunches of paddy plant are separated and lightened. Crop cutting starts in the month of Kartick (October – November). Paddy plants in the highland grow quicker than those of the low land. The paddy of low land is reaped in Aghran (November – December). When they observe that the paddy became golden coloured then it is the time for harvest. When it is observed that the paddy is going to be matured, they broadcast the seed of the Khesari pulses in the same field. At the time of the harvesting of paddy, the Khesari plants are already grown to a considerable height, so in most of the cases the upper portion of those Khesari plants also get cutting which is not at all a loss for them. On the contrary they intentionally do it. According to them from the cut portion several new branches grow.

At the top of each branch a handful of Khesari pulse grow. So, more branches give more quantity of pulses which is definitely a benefit to a cultivator and due to this reason they do khesari cultivation during this period. Here also they have borrowed the traditional knowledge of the local people. Kehsari is matured and reap during the month of Magh (Jan-Feb). Now, after its harvesting, once they plough the land and again broadcast the *chait kadai* or *mung* another variety of pulses. They say that till the time the soil has got its own potentialities and the soil is still wet and juicy, helpful for nourishment of the plant. Even then if there is one or two showers in the field, the field becomes more juicy which is a positive sign to get healthier plant with more product. After its harvest they leave the field atleast for three months when they cultivate nothing in the field. By this time the soil gets back its productivity and aging become suitable to produce crop.

When they cultivate *kadai* in the field, for the first year they have to spread a large quantity of seed but in the subsequent cultivations they need lesser quantity of seed in the same field. According to them once after production of *kadai* at its harvesting time, many *kadai* fall on the ground which is not destroyed but again give rise to new plants in the next season. When they see that the *kadai* plants get a mass of malted fibres at its fruit bearing end, they become sure that the plant become infected and no *kadai* will grow in those plants. All these are the traditional knowledge which they have acquired from the local people.

After harvesting of paddy they store it in granary or *gola*. Inner portion of the *gola* is anointed with cowdung paste to protect the harvest from the attack of insects.

The river water is never suitable for cultivation because of its tremendous salinity. If a land is accidentally influenced by saline water, they immediately stop the source of it and the land concerned is left till the rainy season. After one or two heavy showers the salt is washed out and after that it becomes suitable again for cultivation. This process is known as *dhoyani*.

According to them they do not like to use the canal water for cultivation as it is filthy. It is told by them that in such cases plants grow healthy as those get plenty of food from the filthy water but after sometimes these are attacked by various types of insects, some of which grow in the same filthy water. So if they use the canal water for cultivation, they take several measures to protect the plant from the attack of insects.

They have noticed that the insects get more attacked to the plants which are green and very fresh looking. So when the plants are grown up, they stop irrigation in those lands for at least fifteen days. By this time the field becomes dry and the green colour of those plants are faded to some extent so the insects would be less attracted. In this way they protect their plants.

As their lands in most of the cases are very low they feel difficulty to produce crop. So sometimes they do dredging in the canal, after which the mud is collected and then put on the *nabal* or the low land to make it raised considerably.

They produce both *aman* and *boro* types of paddy. During the rainy season *aman dhan* is cultivated. Boro dhan is Rabi crop, cultivated during the winter season. There are varieties of paddy grain, some of which ae already mentioned in the table of varieties of land. In the low land, paddy of coarser variety is grown where as in the high land the finer variety grows. They prefer the coarser variety. Generally they can produce six to seven maunds of paddy grain per *bigha* of land in the average. They use calcium, uria, phosphate, sulphate, D.A.P. and other chemical fetilizers and various types of insecticides are also applied in the field whenever necessary.

Their traditional knowledge indicates that foggy weather is not good for cultivation because of the fact that fog or mist hampers the growth of the cultivable products. It acts in the same way in case of the mango bloosom and also for the small mango. But if there is shower after the fog there will be no harm as it washes out the sticky fog.

The straw, known as *nara*, is staged to feed the cattle. It is also used as fucl.

To drain the excess water staged in a land, they keep a hole at a corner of the contour bund (locally known as *pokar/gheri/bheri*). The excess water passes to the land just beneath high land through the hole.

After cultivation they produce vegetables specially in their highland which is locally known as *bagan kara*. They produce various types of items such as *barbate* (beans), tomato, *uchchhe* (bitter gourd), *karala* (a larger variety of bitter gourd), *lanka* or *jhal* (chilly), *kumro* (pumpkin), *surja mukhi* (sun flower), *bhindi* (lady's finger), *lau* (gourd), *puisak* (a variety of leafy vegetable), *lal alu* (sweet potato) etc. Each of these has its own method of plantation requiring, varieties of soil, irrigation pattern, duration etc. The basic knowledge on all these affairs are borrowed from the people of locality. As for example *uchchhe, karala, lau* etc. are preferably grown in the high land. Similarly *begun* and *bhindi* and *lanka* are not only grown in the low land. These also grow in high land. *Lal alu* grows better in the *bheri* or contour bunding. All grows in sandy soil. In case of *lal alu* when it is matured, it cracks the soil and comes outside. When potato grows in the sticky soil, it cannot come outside and then it is grown under the soil. They have understood that *bhindi* (lady's finger) with lesser seed is of better quality and the cost of which is high. Bhindi with seven veins are of indigenous type. There are four varieties of *bhindi* and those are *sat sira,* (seven veins), *panch sira* (five veins), *tin sira* (three viens) and *secha bhindi* and among these *tin sira* type is costliest. They have got the ideas that the cuttings of the *alu* branch again give rise to new *alu* plant. Generally after harvesting of *alu* plant they sow the seeds of *kumro* and after that *chichinga* (a kind of green vegetable). Then in the same land they cultivate paddy.

In case of the cultivation of *barbate*, a creeper, they give it support by a stalk of jute plant, locally known as *pakati* for its upward growth. Previously they used to spread straw in the land and the creeper used to grow on it. Subsequently they observe that in such cases the colour of the plant and the fruit is not so attractive but when it is grown upward climbing on a stick instead of spreading on straw, its cotour is very charming. The reason behind it is not known but through their practical experiences they have got the knowledge. Similarly when they produce *uchche*, tomato etc. creepers, they instead of spreading straw give support for climbing. On the contrary they have noticed that *patal* (a kind of green vegetable) grows better if the plant is spread on straw as the juice of straw is very good for its growth. In such a case the product is healthy having a bright colour. It is noticed that the plant grows on floor, it gets rotten. If it climbs up, it becomes dry.

During cultivation they add the Potassium Permanganate with the soil to get healthy and storng root of the plant and the paddy grown in that land is of good quality.

Now-a-days there are hybrid varieties of these vegetables with which they are also acquinted. There are slight differences in some cases for the production of these varieties. They have acquired the knowledge from the local people to cultivate these and to have a successful production.

In the various ways as mentioned above they utilize their land as much as possible. The vegetables are mainly grown for cash earning. They sell these items in the markets at the Satjele, Beltoli, Chhotamollakhali, Canning, Kumir mari, Nyajjat, Gosaba, Dhamakhali etc. and even in Sealdah (Kolkata) market.

Beside utilization of land, at the Sundarban area, the Oraons and the Mundas of the same area have acquired the knowledge how to increase the fertility of the land. When they find that the quantity of the harvest is less, paddy stalk is being smaller in size, there is a quantity of paddy stalk without any grain (locally called as *chite dhan*) they get assured that the productivity is lessened. Then they generally abandoned the field for sometimes for its recovery from its in-fertility. But usually they change the variety of the paddy grain. In case of single crop land, the land is left uncultivated for atleast six to seven months within which period the land would regain the productivity. In this way they do conservation of land.

Therefore, it is observed that the Oraon and Munda of the Chotanagpur area, who were brought to the Sundarban area to clear the jungle, after settling in the new ecological zone gradually learned the traditional wisdom of the local people in connection with land management, which are very much suitable with the local ecological niche. By the application of these they have been able to adapt themselves with the different eco-cultural setting.

Water Management

Sundarban – the largest deltaic region of the world is constituted by of several small and large Islands which are surrounded by several rivers and rivulets such as Bidyadhari, Matla, Moni etc. which have ultimately flown down to the Bay of Bengal. So the people of the Sundarban area live in the landmass surrounded by water and automatically water has got a special importance in their life and culture.

The Oraon and the Munda – the people of the present study are the original inhabitants of the Chotanagpur plateau where the geographical condition is very different from that of the Sundarban area. The Chotanagpur plateau is a hill-clad area with hard rocky surface. The cultivable lands are less irrigated dry upland locally called as *tanr*. They primarily depend on the rain water for cultivation. They have scarcity of water. If there is any river, it is just a thin silver line running through the hill slpes and going downwards to the plains and ultimately across the border of their territory. In such a situation, to cope up with the local ecological niche they have taken some measures and ultimately which became their traditional wisdom. In case of water management their the traditional wisdom taught them nicely how to survive with lesser water and how to conduct the maximum utilization of that very limited water.

In Sundarban area, the geographical condition is completely different, the Oraon and the Munda after their migration from the Chotanagpur area have to share the traditional knowledge of the local people. Here they have to settle in plains in the deltaic region. Here instead of scarcity of water they got it in plenty. So the process of the management of water in that place is totally different. To cope with local ecological niche, they have to share the traditional wisdom of the local people.

Among the studied villages, village Panchpukur is situated very close to the river Moni and the village Kankandighi is situated just by the side of the same river. There is a river named Mridangabhanga which flows very close to the village Mogkhali. Bidyadhari and Matla – these two rivers flow near Gosaba,

Rangabelia etc. places. Except these rivers there are also ponds, canals, tube wells in those villages. The water of the tube-well is utilized by the people for cooking and drinking purposes. Pond water is used for cleaning, bathing, and also for fish cultivation. Except these there are some fisheries found in the nearby blocks such as Minakha, Bhangar etc. where they do fish cultivation in large scale. The Oraon and Munda are not found engaged in such fisheries.

It is seen that though they have plenty of water in their surroundings, even then they are to depend on the rain water for cultivation. The rain water absorbed in the soil is utilized in cultivation especially for gardening in their area. As they live very close to the sea, the water of the rivers is highly saline and this brackish water is totally unsuitable for cultivation. If the brackish water flows through a cultivable land, the land becomes less productive. In such cases a cultivator stops cultivation in that land and waits for next monsoon when the salt is washed out of the field and again drained towards the river. It is called *dhoani*. To protect the cultivable land from the brackish water, they prepare some barrier by the mud. Sometimes in such a cultivable land instead of cultivation they do prawn cultivation. After sometimes when the field becomes dry again, they wait till the *dhoani* in the monsoon and use it for agricultural purposes.

If the land is flooded by brackish water and becomes a ditch, they do prawn cultivation in that place. Gradually the place is filled up by the slit or deposition carried by the brackish water and the place becomes high. Then either they do agricultural work in that place after *dhoyani* as it is mentioned earlier or they dig out the mud of that area and use the mud in local brick kiln for preparation of brick. Again the place becomes low and filled up with brackish water and prawn cultivation is done. This is specially done in the Minakha block of the Sundaban area.

It is found that there is a vast land with mangrove growth by the sides of the rivers. Some of those are *Gargan*, *Geoa*, *Keora*, *Garan* etc. These all protect the river bed from erosion. The roots of these mangrove tighten the soft siltation locally called as *poli mati* and protect the bank of the river from erosion. In the Bay of Bengal tide and ebb happens twice daily. The rivers also experience tide and ebb twice daily. During the tide the water of the sea rises high and becomes very rough. Automatically it affects the rivers. Due to the effect of the tide the rough sea water proceeds on the upward direction and as a result the river water also becomes very rough and it even crosses the level of the river bed. When the tidal water which is very rough and powerful comes across the bank of the river, the mangrove growth protects the bank from erosion. The mangrove growth gets flooded or submersed twice daily due to the high tide in the river. During low tide which also occurs twice daily the water reseeds and flows down towards the sea. During the low tide the outward growth of the roots that is the areal roots of the mangrove vegetation which gets submerged during high tide, are seen. As these roots have continuous contact with the water, huge quantity of algae and water born small creatures are grown on these roots. All these are the nutritious food for the prawns, crabs and fishes of the sea which come towards the mangrove forest along with the tidal water.

During both full moon and new moon days, the intensity of tide and ebb is very high. The tides on these two days are called as *Kotal*. The *Kotal* of the full moon day is regarded as a *madi* or female *Kotal* and that of the new moon day is called as *madda* or male *Kotal*. The force or intensity of the male *Kotal* is more than a female *Kotal*. There is a myth behind it. It is told that the female *Kotal* wants to run away from the male *Kotal* and the male *Kotal* runs behind her to catch hold of her. The effects of the *Kotals* are continued till next three to five days. After that gradually it is minimized. The tide with lesser force is called as *marani* tide and *marani* ebb.

In the Sundarban area prawn cultivation is one of the most important occupations. It is very commonly seen that there are a huge number of people specially the small boys, girls and the women who are engaged in mindhara or catching of prawn seed or finger ling or shrimps from the rivers which ultimately grows to prawn.

Mindhara as an occupation is very popular to the people of the area. The studied groups of people also have taken it as an occupation. The following table shows how many persons have taken this as one of their occupations.

Table 19: Collection of Meen or Prawn Seed

Sl. No.	*Name of the economic pursuit*	*Male*	*Female*	*Total*
1	Household work (M), cultivation, wage labour, collection (S)	1	18	19
2	Cultivation (M), wage labour along with Meendhara (S)	33	-	33
3	Household work and cultivation (M), wage labour and Meendhara (S)	-	35	35
4	Wage labour (M), collection including Meendhara (S)	4	-	4
5	Student (M), Meendhara with or without (S)	30	17	47
6	Meendhara (M), Household work (S)	-	11	11
7	Meendhara (M)	2	-	2
8	Household work (M), collection (S)	-	9	9
	Total	**70**	**90**	**160**

It is found that among 374 working persons 160 (42.76%) persons are engaged in *meendhara*. Among these 160 persons there are 70 (18.71%) males and 90 (24.06%) are females who do *meendhara* as an occupation.

It is told by them that previously they used to go to the forest to collect fuel wood and honey but the terror of tiger resists them to go to the deep forest and instead that they have taken *meendhara* as an occupation. Along with the collection of finger ling, they also collect crabs and small fishes. Incidentally it is found that most villagers of the village Kankandighi which is situated at the bank of river Moni, Male, are engaged in meendhara and have taken it as one of their most important occupations. On the other hand the villagers of Mogkhali and Panchpukur villages though collect the fingerlings even then it has not got a very important position among their occupations. These two villages are situated at a considerable distance from the river and which is the reason that diberrs the people from shrimp collection. So it can be said that immediate geographical condition has an impact on their economic life.

In case of catching of fishes, crabs, snails etc. it is observed that generally the children along with one or two women go to the nearby river to catch small fishes, crabs etc. The small fishes and crabs come to the river side along with the tidal water. Generally they catch the fishes with Chhakni jal. The crabs come with the tidal water towards the bank of the river (locally called as khari) and these take their shelter in the holes of the river side. During the ebb when the water level comes down they dig out the crab by an iron stick. Sometimes they hang a small fish tied in a thread, attached with a stick or a branch of tree by the side of the river, very close to a hole when a crab gets attracted and come catch the fish, it is caught by the group of people aimed to catch it. There are various types of crabs such as *tele, chiti, nona,* etc. Among these *chiti* crabs grow profusely in summer. The *tele* variety is found during monsoon in the ponds and even in the saline water. The *nona* and *hero* crabs are available throughout the year in rivers.

Small boys and girls also collect snails from the Khari. Except the fingerlings, the other items that are collected from the rivers are for their own consumption. The collected items are share equally by all the persons of the group. If there is any elderly person in their group, he or she (generally she) gets a little more share.

As the presently studied groups of people are the original inhabitants of a plateau (as already pointed out), they had no idea or knowledge on the catching of crabs, snails and also on the meendhara. All these are acquired by them after their coming over here in the Sundarban area.

Generally they do fish cultivation in a very small scale only for their own consumption in their ponds. They generally do not sell those in the market. It is also observed that neither they accompany a fishing party for fishing expedition nor they are interested to get attached with any fishery. In case of fish cultivation, they prefer to cultivate fish in fresh water. According to them the fishes which grow in the filthy water as in a canal grow quicker and are healthier than the fishes grow in the fresh water as those get plenty of food in the filthy water. Even then they prefer to cultivate it in fresh water. It is comprehended by them that the fishes of canal water get rotten very quickly and it is not tasty like those grow in fresh water. The fresh water fishes are not only tastier and but also these do not get spoilt quickly. Its cost is also more than the canal water fishes. One can easily identify the difference between a canal water fish and a fresh water fish. The abdominal part of the fresh water fish is harder than that of the canal water. The fishes of the canal look slightly black in colour.

The is told that the fishes like to stay in a very calm and quite place. It is also observed that by nature fishes like to stay in water and also where the current of water is high they get more fish during tide. In the river they get fishes such as prawn, *gule*, *parse*, *bhetki*, *murli*, *pabda* etc. Among these *gule* fish stays in the holes beside the river.

They use lime to filter the water of the *bheri* or *gheri* (fishery). In the sweet water pond, when they observe that the water is spoilt, they keep banana leaves in such *bheri* and the secretion of those leaves purify the water. They add the *mahua Khaili* in the water. After a few day the *mahua Khaili* get completely spoilt and various types of small creatures are born in that water. Then they add lime and alam in that water for final filtration and the water is stirred. When the filteration process is completed then they start fish cultivation. Even there is need of the more filtration they add potassium permanganate. In the deposited spoilt *Khali* the small creatures born in that pond which are delicious food for the fishes Besides this they sometimes keep a bag full with mustard *Khaili* in the pond. There are several pores in the bag. The fishes take out their food from these pores. In Chotanagpur plateau fish cultivation is impossible. So they have no idea on this. The knowledge of fish and fish cultivation have naturally been acquired after coming over here by the Oraon and the Munda.

It is told that instead of fish cultivation they are very much interested in the activities of *min* or fingerling. They occupation is known as *Mindhara* and the people who do this are also called as *Mindhara*. This occupation is also not their traditional occupation but they have acquired it from the local people. The people of both the sexes go to the river to catch the fingerling. Meendhara is specially the work of the women folk and the children but in the villages of the river side it is done by the men folk also. During the duration of high tide they go to the river to catch the *meen* by the *meenjal* (a type of net) net with very fine weaving. During the time of ebb, they drag the net towards the bank of the river and the fingerling which come with the wave of the river are caught in the net. These are then separated from the net. It is told that when the force of the tide is high they stop *meendhara* for sometimes as during that time it is difficult to stand in the water with the net. Due to the force of water the net may be torn and due to this they stop the work of *meendhara* for sometimes. Again when the force is less, they start the work of *meendhara*. During ebb also they catch the *meen*. After ebb the work of *meendhara* is completed now, the *meen* are equally distributed in four plates. The *meen* are sold to the people who do cultivation of prawn. In some cases a middle man acts in the sale and purchase of the *meen*. A finger ling costs Rs. 0.50/- approximately but the cost varies according to the seasons. During the months Magh and Falgun it costs Rs. 1/- per piece of finger ling. During this time the fingerlings are not easily available so the costs is high. On the other hand during the months Bhadra, Aswin, Kartick, the cost of the fingerling is less as these are easily available and it costs even 0.03 paisa to 0.05 paisa per piece. In the other months it is 0.50 paisa to 0.90 paisa. The *phares* (middle man) collect the fingerlings visiting each and every door of the village. Sometimes the *meendharas* directly sell the *meens* in the local market to the fish cultivators and also to the fishery owners.

Generally three are three types of fingerlings namely *Chhati* or *Galda*, *Bagda* and *Mocha*. Galda may grow especially in sweet water but also can grow in slightly saline water. Bagda grows in saline water. It is told that for prawn cultivation they are very much dependent on the tide and ebb of the river.

They collect fingerlings with the help of *meen jal*. It is a big net. The holes of the net is very small and the net looks just like a mosquito net. After catching the fingerlings they separate each of those from the net and keep those in a jar filled with water. The water needs change after one or two hours and the water always must be vibrated. At times instead of selling these they themselves cultivate these in their own pond. It is done only for their own consumption.

It is very frequently noticed that there is a type of land which is called as *patit jamin*. It is nothing but a barren land. A fertile land may be transformed into *Patit jamin* if saline water from the river is flooded on it. Owing to the happening the *jamin* becomes unfertile and regarded as *patit*. Such a land is called as *bhasa badha* where they cultivate prawn and for prawn cultivation they collect the fingerlings of the Bagda variety of prawn and grow those in that land which is flooded by saline water.

It is told that a fingerling takes six to seven months to get full maturity. The *patit jamin* where they do prawn cultivation must be flooded with saline water again and again after two to three days' interval. Sometimes they intentionally open the lock gate of the river and allow the saline water to flow on that *patit jamin*. A continuous stirring is necessary in that water for which sometimes artificially they have to create wave. Cold water is another important item for prawn growing. In hot water prawn cannot survive. It is also observed that in that *bhasa badha* where the prawn is grown they spread a net over the place. It is kept for the protection of the shrimps. So that those cannot come out of the water. This net is known as *jopat jal*. It is made of bamboo.

In Chotanagpur plateau, the traditional abode the Oraon and the Munda, there is no scope for prawn cultivation as the geographical area is not suitable for growing prawn and even for fish cultivation. So the process of prawn cultivation is learnt by them at the Sundarban area from the local people. Though it is not their traditional wisdom even then gradually they have taken it as their own.

In the river boat is the only transport for them to visit the jungle and to go to the other villages across the river. Now-a-days launch or the mechanized boats are also introduced in their area and they enjoy the facility from it to visit the places.

Salt preparation – The informants have informed that previously their ancestors used to prepare salt from the saline water which is again learnt by them from the local people of the Sundarban area. Now-a-days they do not prepare salt. They purchase it from the local market. Even then some of them know to extract salt from the saline water of the Sundarban area through the indigenous process of the locality.

To prepare salt they first prepare a piece of land on the slopes of river bank. It is them dug-out to form a rectangular container and in the downwards slopes adjacent to previous container shaped area they prepare small rectangular hole where water can be accumulated. Then on the big rectangle shaped container they spread *hental* leaves which is again a mangrove vegetation and on the *hental* leaves they pour saline water which they fetch from adjacent river. After sometime the distilled water they use to collect from small hole and which they brought to their respective houses where they begin to boil the said distilled water which ultimately formed salt. But this is lengthy and hectic process; now in the market salt is easily available with cheaper rate. So it becomes obsolete.

Therefore, the above mentioned discussion gives an account on the water management of the Sundarban area by these two tribal people. These tribal people have acquired the knowledge of water management from the people of the locality suited for the place to cope up with the local ecological niche.

Rituals and Festivals in Connection with Management of Environment and Local Resources

The Oraon and the Munda of the Chotanagpur plateau have their own religious beliefs and practices adjusting with their local ecological niche. After migration to the Sundarban area – a completely different geographical area, they have to adapt with the local environment (both physical and cultural) for their survival. To cope up with that particular ecological niche, they began to share with the local culture, which gradually even penetrated into the core of their culture that is their own religious beliefs and practices. In this way modification has been affected in their religious life.

In the Chotanagpur plateau they have a belief that they have originated from Bhagwan or Dharmesh whom the Oraon call as Biri Belas and the Mundas call him as Haram and address as Gomke (means lord). He not only has created them but also created sun, moon, stars, sky, earth, air, forest, water sources – all the living and non-living objects of the universe. So during the time of prayer for good rain, good harvest, welfare of the cattle and mankind they worship him.

In the Chotanagpur plateau they have their own sacred place of worship – the *Sarna*. Sarna is a sacred grove with various types of trees, plants, herbs and bushes. Among these Sal (Shorea robusta) is the most important one. Sarna is the abode of their deities. They play, sit, and take rest in the place. So nobody is allowed to cut those even not permitted to break a twig of those trees. On the contrary they take care of those, so that the deities get comfort. In this way the trees of the sacred grove get protection and the preservation – a part of management is done.

In the Sundarban area the people informed that instead of *Sarna* they have village *than* and where they perform some the rituals in village *than*. They have also a sacred place behind their house where some of their traditional rituals (though modified a lot) are performed.

Amongst all of their rituals and festivals Sarhul is the most important festival. There are two types of Sarhul or baha namely Bada Sarhul or *marang baha* and the Chota Sarhul or *Uding Baha*. The Bada Sarhul is performed during the month Vaisakh (April – May). This Sarhul is performed at a corner of their homestead land. In the Chotanagpur plateau sal twigs, sal leaves are used in this ritual but in the Sundarban area as those are not available and instead of those they use banana leaves. Bada Sarhul is very important to them as after its performance they are allowed to take season's new mango and other items. This festival has got a specific significance in their economic life also. Before the performance of Sarhul they are not allowed to start ploughing. With the performance of Sarhul they seek permission and blessings from the deities and their ancestors to start ploughing and to have a good harvest. It is very interesting to note the time of performance of Sarhul coincides with the exact time of ploughing. A cultivator cannot till the soil as per his wishes but has to wait till Sarhul which helps him indirectly to do ploughing or to utilize the land (a part of management) in proper time.

Now-a-days both in the Chotanagpur plateau and in the Sundarban area importance of forest is becoming less, so the importance of Uding Baha or Chota Sarhul which is associated with forest is also lessened. In the Chotanagpur plateau it is still practiced and it is practiced in the *Sarna*. But in the Sundarban area they previously used to perform it in the forest and now they have stopped to perform it and on the other hand they perform the puja of *banadevi* or Banbibi– the local forest deity to have a safe life in Sundarban.

In addition to these rituals and festivals there are some festivities with their agricultural operations; that is a part of land utilization. As for example prior to sowing of seed perform *dhan-buni* ritual. Hariali or Batauli is performed before transplantation and *nayakhani* the eating of new rice is performed prior to the consumption of new rice. They are allowed to consume it after offering it to their deities and ancestors. They also perform a ceremony known as *bheloa-phari* through which they break all the evils and malevolent spirits. It is done in order to protect their crops and cereals from all types of destruction. With the performance of all these rituals they get strength in mind that their ancestors and deities give them support for proper utilization of land.

In the Sundarban area both of these groups have started to worship many of the Hindu deities. The Munda perform *goch purnima* prior to transplantation when they worship Lakshmi Devi – presiding deity of land and wealth. She is worshipped along with her husband Narayana. *Soso thapa* is another ritual through which they seek blessings from Narayana for a good harvest. Nawa bonga or *Nawa Khani* is the ritual through which they offer the newly harvested crops and cereals to the deities and ancestors specially Lakshmi and Narayana and after that they are allowed to consume it.

In the Sundarban area the Oraon and the Munda also worship other Hindu deities such as Sitala, Kali, Manasa, and other important local deities such as Banabibi or Banadevi, Sahjangali, Dakshin Roy, Kalu Roy, Narayani, Badar Saheb etc.

Banabibi or Banadevi is the presiding deity of the Sundarban area. She is worshipped by both the Hindus and the Muslims. Hindus call her as Banadevi and she is Banabibi to the Muslims. Many times the Hindus and the Muslims together perform the puja of the deity. The Oraons and the Mundas also participate in her rituals collectively with the villagers, performed in the village *than*. Previously her rituals used to be performed in the forest. Presently, as the frequency of forest going is lessened, they perform her ritual in the village itself. But whenever a party goes to the forest, they offer her sacrifices and seek her blessings for a safe venture. If any person goes to the forest, he or she definitely remembers her to get protection from tiger and all other ferocious animals and from all other evils of the forest. Sahjangali is her brother. Whenever she is worshipped, her brother also gets offerings.

Dakshin Roy – the presiding deity of the tigers is also propitiated to get protection from tiger. He is also remembered in sickness. He is believed as a reliever from it.

When fisher folk go to the river or deep sea, or when a boat man starts his boat they together remember, Badar Saheb – a Muslim saint, uttering his name thrice for a safe journey. The Hindus along with Badar Saheb also remember Ganga Mai to have a safe journey.

It is seen that the Oraon and the Munda very rarely accompany a fishing party or join in the party of honey collectors. Even then whenever there is any ritual performed in honour of Banabibi or Dakshin Roy or any other above mentioned territorial deities, they always participate in those rituals and festivals.

Therefore, it can be said from the above discussion that the Oraon and the Munda of the Sundarban are for the better management of environment and local resources have adapted the beliefs and ritual practices of the region for a peaceful and prosperous life.

World View

The Oraon and the Munda at the Sundarban area know that Sundarban – the place of their habitation is their own world. All their views, thoughts activities and everything are associated with that world where they live. They have nearly forgotten their own legends, stories and myths about their origin, the universe and have taken all of those of their present place of habitation. Which are assimilated in their life and culture gradually in a very long spell of time.

According to them, there are three seasons namely *garam* (summer), *varsa* (rainy season), and *thanda* (winter). They have informed that with the performance of Sarhul they feel that the summer season is approaching. Again with the blooming of flowers in the *Khalse*, mango, and neem trees they are sure that the days of scorching heat is very near. During summer season when they observe that the ants, especially the black ants are moving in rows towards a safe and comparatively high land from a low lying place with eggs in their mouth, they get the signal of the rainy season. There are some ants which start flying during this time. It is time when the sky is oriented with clouds, the environment is very hot and the wind start blowing from the southern direction, they think that the rainy season is approaching. Again, the frog's croak is the confirmation of the rains.

According to them if there is plenty of mango production, they get assured that in the same year the rainy season will help them to get sufficient water for cultivation and they will get bumper crop. If the production of tamarind becomes excessive they are afraid that there might be excessive rain and as a result there will be flood situation; it may happen similarly when the crabs crawl on the plants and snails are seen to climb on the trees it is definite that there will be flood.

When they observe that there is wind, blowing from the northern direction, the date palm trees are ready with juice, in the morning there is mist and there is a feeling of cold they say that the winter season has arrived. According to them during the winter season if the wind blows from the southern direction, they are sure that next in the morning there will definitely be a foggy situation. Intensity of fog is heavy in the months *pous* (December – January), *magh* (January – February) and *falgun* (February – March). Fog or mist hampers the buds in the mango trees. After sunrise the fog fallen on the buds is dried and become a sticky coating on the buds and ultimately the buds become dry and cannot bloom.

When it is observed that just with sunset the sky becomes red, it is indication rain. When there are two stars called as Jele and Jeleni found in the same line in the *nairit* (south – west) corner of the sky, it is sure to them that there will be rain in abundance, if they see any water vapour circle around the moon, they are sure to forecast a rain. The water vapour circle is known as *paras* or *chander sabha* or *ber* or *pani mandav*. If the circle is found to encircle the moon from a closer will be rain at distant place. If the circle encircles the moon from a larger distance then it will be rain in the neighbouring areas.

Lightening is believed as the fighting between Ram and Bijli Kanya but about her they know nothing.

To them *Ramdhanu* or *Ramer Gandi* or rainbow occurs generally in the sky, especially in the eastern side when there is chances of rain. Generally in such cases the rain is not heavy as *gandi* has protected the water from falling. After shower they say *gondi chan* is completed.

Another signal for rain they get from the *jhinjhi poka* (a little creature) which lives on the top of the tree. When these come down in a row then there will be rain.

Bhag jugnu (firefly) is generally seen in the summer season and also just after shower.

If a *tiktiki* or lizard sounds *tik tik* at the time of some discussion they say the words are going to be happen truly.

They have a belief that the earth goddess or Vashumata is holding the earth on her head when she gets tired, and changes her position, the earth is shaken and it is called *bhumikampa*.

About eclipse the people are of opinion that it occurs both in the cases of sun and moon. If it is solar eclipse then they say that the sun has taken loan from the moon and as could not meet the debt the moon arrested and swallowed it. After the payment of the debt the sun gets free. On the lunar eclipse the case is just reverse. During the duration of eclipse they do not cook and eat as they believe that the environment gets polluted during that time.

Generally they calculate time seeing the position of sun, moon, and stars and also their own shadows. When the shadow is found straight on the head and the sun comes on the top of the head, it is just 12 noon. During night they calculate time through the stars. The whirlwind is known as *ghurni pak*. It is nothing but hot wind in which there is evil spirit. If a child falls in it, he or she becomes sick. Those who commit suicide especially by hanging, they become ghost. Those roams in the wind.

They are very much afraid of ghost. They believe that person died through unnatural death, becomes ghost commonly known as *churin darha*. The women ghosts are called as *petni* live in the *seora* tree and the male ghosts are the *bhut* live in the *keora* tree. They roam wearing white dresses. Their feet are just over turned.

Omens

When a dog barks facing upward or a cat or dog weeps, these are all very bad omen. Sneezing during the start of any journey or crossing an ass or tortoise on the way is also not good. To see a jackal on the left side or a snake on the right side during the starting of journey is also not good. They never cross a broom as it is very inauspicious. If one sees any vacant pitcher or a crow hits anyone's head, result in inauspicious circumstances. White owl is a good omen and gray owl is not good.

Conclusion

The Oraon and the Munda of the Chotanagpur plateau have their own traditional wisdom for the management of their local resources to maintain their livelihood. When they have migrated to the Sundarban area, at the beginning they struggled in each and every sphere of their life to adjust with the local environment. It is felt that their own traditional wisdom is not suitable in the Sundarban area – a different geographical area. In due course their own traditional wisdom is modified to suit with the local environment. It is also observed that they have taken the traditional knowledge of the local people to adapt in that different geographical area. Gradually with the span of time those all are assimilated in their own life and culture and ultimately became the traditional wisdom of their own.

Literature Consulted

Das, A. K., Sankaranda Mukherji and M.K. Chowdhuri (edited). 1981. *A Focus on Sundarban.* Calcutta; Editions Indian.

Das, A.K. and M.K. Raha. 1963. *The Oraons of Sundarban.* Calcutta; Govt. of West Bengal.

Dey, N.K. and A.K. Bose. 1989. 'Forest Resources of Sundarban' in *Problems of Wasteland and Forest Ecology in India*, ed. Pramod Singh, New Delhi; Ashish Publishing House.

Mukhopadhyay, Sankarananda. 1976. *A Profile of Sundarban Tribes,* Calcutta; Firma KLM Pvt. Ltd.

Niyogi, T.K. 1996. *Tiger cult of the Sundarbans*, Calcutta; Anthropological Survey of India, Memoir no. 95.

Ponette, S.J. (edited). 1978. *The Munda World,* Hoffman Commemoration Volume, Ranchi; Catholic Press.

Saha, Bikashkanti. 1999, Mangrove Tigerland, Sundarban, Calcutta, Intelsoft.

Sarkar, R.M. 2001. "Work and understanding in Dasherchwak – A Fishing village in Mangrove Ecosystem", in *Man in India,* Vol. 81, No. 1 and 2 (pp. 23-48).

8

Management of Environment and Natural Resources–

Study on Traditional Wisdom among the Bhil of Jaisalmer, Rajasthan

Santanu Mitra

Man is part of nature and which is in the broadest sense, the entire world – all its processes and contents including man and culture. If man is excluded, nature is the physical environment which includes the non-human biological environment – everything in the world except man and culture (Watson and Watson : 1969:17).

Man's physical environment, that is, nature excluding man, consists of the total ecological community – its physical features and its living inhabitants – in which man lives and with which he interacts. The physical environment consists of the earth – its rocks, soil, surface waters and atmosphere; its weather and climate; its plant and animal life including man – and all the forces and process, including solar radiation, that integrate the elements of the earth into a worldwide thermodynamic system. In the world no animal is self-sufficient; if all plants on earth were to die, soon all animals would die as well. And for photosynthesis, plants depend also on soil, water and the atmosphere. The physical conditions necessary to the growth of plants result from the actions of certain forces on the matter of the earth actions initiated and sustained primarily by the force of gravitation. Man has altered his position in the earth's ecological community by gaining more and more control over the physical environment through his creation of culture. Among the products with which man directs, modifies, and controls the physical environment are fire, tools and social institutions that regulate conduct. All cultural accomplishments depend on the use of symbolic language, man's major cultural product. The products of man's activity are, therefore, part of both the cultural and the physical environment at the same time. In their physical manifestations, these cultural products are certainly part of the physical environment, subject to the laws of nature. It is their direct or indirect production according to man's intentions that makes them part of the cultural environment as well. Since man is a part of nature and since he acts upon and modifies the natural physical environment, he produces a natural result. But for the purposes of indicating that he proceeds with artifice, his results can be said artificial and the products he has made and the environment he has modified cultural (Watson and Watson : 18-21).

The existence of supernatural environment can easily be understood from the study of Professor L.P. Vidyarthi among the Maler. He opined, 'in moving to understand the "complex" of this hill community in a systematic manner, I could realise that I cannot begin everywhere; I must begin at some point. For me, at the level of observation, this starting point was the forest and the field, the village and the houses, the tools and implements, the work of the houses and the forests, the food and the dress and so on. These, evidently, provided the ecological base for the Maler culture, and in describing it, the other parts of its "complex whole", could gradually emerge. Keeping the focus on "Nature", thus, I could further see its interactions with the "Maler Man" and in the light of these data, I could realise the importance of the "Nature-man" approach in analysing a primitive culture (Evans-Pritchard, 1940; Redfield 1955; Thomas 1956). But, as I proceeded ahead from the level of observation to the level of cogitation, it became more and more clear to me that this Nature-Man relationship was not only confined to the ecological or subsistant level along. I noted an "Environment" of supernatural beliefs and rituals modifying and influencing the Nature-Man inter-relationship.

As I went deep with the analysis of the Maler forest economy, the cycle of *Khallu* cultivation, and the various dimensions of the man-to-man interactions, the functions, of the "spirits" (Grossaiyans) in regulating Nature-Man relationship and over all, moulding their culture, became clearer still. It appeared that by large the Maler represented a style of life in which maize, man, and the "god" have definite mutual roles to play. Focussing on Spirit (Gossaiyan etc. or "Gods") it was also recorded that with "sacred centres", "sacred performances", and "sacred specialists", it constituted a complex in itself and thus, I felt the necessity and confidence for introducing "Spirit" as another dimension to be considered with Nature-Man approach for the holistic portrayal of a primitive style of life. With these, I discovered the Nature-Man-Spirit approach which I found useful for the depiction of the Maler culture, (Vidyarthi : 1963 : 175-176).

Micklin (1973 : xiii) opined that human history is often calibrated in terms of a series of critical events that have marked drastic turning points in the evolution of society. At least three such "revolutions" are generally recognised: the tool-making, the agricultural and the scientific-industrial; and one might well add a fourth, the nuclear. While the social implications of these developments are obviously numerous and diverse, two consequences common to each stand out in the broad picture of the evolution of social organisation. First, man has become increasingly independent of the constraints of nature, and has developed successively greater capacities to manipulate and control his environment. Second, each of these revolutions has resulted in greatly expanded potential for supporting increasingly large popualations.

According to Micklin (1973: 3-4), the human ecologists try to observe the relationships among human organisms and their environments and their unit of study is the population, not isolated individuals. These aggregates may range from highly localised to widely dispersed groups. Relationships among members of populations as well as between distinct populations are socially organised suggesting temporarily persistent though highly modifiable patterns of social interaction. Indeed, it is through social organisation that populations are able to co-ordinate diverse skills and activities and thus satisfy the requisites of prolonged survival. Important aspect of ecological organisation is reflected in regularities and variations in spatial and temporal patterns of relationships. Ecological relationships are best represented in terms of sets of activities, e.g. working, travelling, exploiting etc. On the individual level these might well be viewed as "social roles", but on the collective level they are more adequately designated as "social processes". Ecological analysis should and can contribute to our populations are static phenomena and as one or both undergo alternation, relationships between them are also transformed. Underlying these shifts in ecological organisation is what is perhaps the most significant attribute of social organisation : its capacity for changing as well as adapting to external conditions.

He further opined that there is a growing awareness that man's environment is being manipulated and utilised irresponsibly. Natural resources are being depleted, air and water are becoming increasingly unfit for human consumption, human settlements are deteriorating in organisation as well as physical structure. At the same time, people are being born much more rapidly than they are dying, they are living longer and human communities are becoming increasingly congested. Consequently the human population is a point of imbalance with its environment. In short, the basic element of the human condition, the man-nature relationship, once again appears to be in a precarious state (Micklin, 1973: iii).

Therefore, the question of proper management of environment and natural resources arises. Consideration of the tribal communities in our country for the present study is due to their dependence and close attachment with their environment and their expertisation in proper management of the natural resources. The knowledge or wisdom beyond such expertisation is inherited through generations and it becomes a tradition which sometimes remains ethnic specific but in most of the times it becomes the part of a larger social tradition crossing the boundary with the contact and continuous interaction with other communities in the same ecological niche.

The present study is undertaken in the desert ecology to understand how people cope up themselves with the aridity in their natural setting. According to Ron Cooke, Andrew Warren and Andrew Goudie (1992:2) most deserts are areas of aridity which are defined in terms of some measure of water shortage. Further, "such measures, *indices of aridity,* are commonly based on relationships between water gained from precipitation and water lost by evaporation or transpiration ...... The aridity index is P/ETP (where P is the annual precipitation and ETP is the mean annual potential evapotranspiration, based on Penman formula). Aridity increases as the value of the ratio declines, and four zones of aridity are delimited :

(a) sub-humid zone : (0.50<P/ETP<0.75)

(b) semi-arid zone : (0.20<P/ETP<0.50)

(c) arid zone : (0.03<P/ETP<0.20)

(d) hyper-arid zone : (P/ETP<0.03)

Bharara (1999:6) describes that out of the total land area of 32,82,016 sq. km. in India, 3,87,300 sq. km. (11.80 percent) and 9,70,530 sq. km. (29.57 percent) fall under arid and semi-arid zone respectively which are distributed in the states of Jammu and Kashmir, Uttar Pradesh, Madhya Pradesh, Rajasthan, Gujarat, Punjab, Haryana, Maharashtra, Karnataka, Andhra Pradesh and Tamilnadu. Chouhan (1995:1-3) opines that the arid and semi-arid regions include that part of Rajasthan which lies west of the Aravalli range. This comprises the districts of Barmer, Jaisalmer, Bikaner, Churu, Ganganagar, Nagaur, Pali, Sikar, Jodhpur, Jalor and Jhunjhunu and these areas are situated between $24^{0}30'$ east longitude. He further opines (1995: 2-3) that hyper arid zone or true desert is situated in extreme west of Jaisalmer having an area of 9320 sq. km. (4.47 percent of the total area of 2,08,487 sq. km. of the western Rajasthan) which corresponds to real desert climates with very low and irregular rain with almost no perennial vegetation and where interannual variability of rainfall can reach 100 percent. Arid zone comprises an area of 1,32,420 sq. km. (63.52 percent) which is distributed in the districts of Jaisalmer, Barmer, Bikaner, Ganganagar and part of Churu, Nagaur and Jodhpur districts. Vegetation of this zone is scattered and includes according to the region, bushes and small woody, succulent, thorny or leafless shrubs. Very light pastoral use is characterised by annual rainfall of 80-100 mm and 100-300 mm; inter-annual rainfall variability is 50 to 100 per cent.

It's a well-known fact that deserts in the world are of two types hot and cold. Hot deserts have high temperatures for most part of the year and the winds are dry often blowing at gale speed. Due to high temperatures during summers the air rises up creating a low pressure area and to fill up the loss of this vertical movement of air, the air from surrounding areas pushes in often at great speed which may vary from 50 to 120 km/hour causing most serious effects of wind erosion. Important hot deserts of the world are Sahara (Africa), Kalahari (Africa), Arabia (Asia), Great Thar (Asia), Australia (Australia), Eurpoean (Europe), Colorado-Mexican (North America) and Peruvian (South America). The hot deserts may be of three types – (a) *Hammada* – these are rocky deserts with a desolate surface of bedrock having scattered patches of loose sand and rubbles, (b) *Reg* – they are stony deserts with a mantle of gravels, pebbles and rubbles as found ion Libya, Algerian

Sahara and Egypt, and (c) *Erg* – these hot deserts have a thick mantle of loose sand often occurring in the form of huge heaps called sanddunes. The larger particles of sands are blown away by high speed winds and so erosion, transportation and deposition are most common land form features of these areas. The Indian Thar desert for the most part is an erg but in small patches 'reg' and 'hammada' types are also found such as near Jaisalmer. On the other hand cold deserts have low to very low temperatures but lack of humidity in the air causes arid conditions. Antarctica is the biggest cold desert of the world (area 13,338.5 sq. km) where extreme cold conditions exist. Vast areas of Siberian Russia called 'Tundras' and a greater part of northern Canada, Alaska and the Arctic islands remain under the cover of permanent snow and ice and are thus cold deserts because they are totally devoid of vegetation. The other cold deserts of the world are Sinkiang, Gobi, Takla Makan (China), Tibet, Laddakh (India), northern parts of Norway, Sweden, Finland, Iceland and Greenland (Mathur : 1994 : vii-x).

Mathur opines, due to population stress in the hot deserts, there is a global problem of environmental protection today. To sustain the growing population extensive agriculture even on marginal lands is being done which causes loss of soil fertility and heavy soil erosion. Complementary to it is the problem of over-usage of surface water and subterranean water, beyond the limits of its annual replenishments which are now being exploited for irrigation, domestic use and drinking purposes. Denudation of natural vegetation chiefly for the purposes of firewood, animal grazing and the land-usage for agriculture has dwindled the natural environment to its greatest magnitude. ..... felling of trees, cutting of shrubs and even the grasses for burning is today leading to degradation of natural environment and the extension of the process of 'desertification'. In the process of desertification, the changes in climatic regimes may not be obvious over a short span of time but the climatic changes and weather phenomena may exhibit vacillating effects which may ultimately lead to desertic conditions in a larger period and thus causing extension of deserts. (Mathur, 1994: x-xii)."

Gurjar (1992) observed that radical changes in the environment and ecology of Thar desert are possible through irrigation because widespread canal irrigation in the area (Indira Gandhi Canal Command Area) has brought radical and beneficial changes in the harsh geographical environment and adverse desertic conditions have almost disappeared. The changes that irrigation begins in desert environment are of the two kinds – physical and social; physical changes include gradual changes in the micro climate, changes in the soils, stabilisation of sand dunes, afforestation and increase of cultivable land. Social changes include increase of population, literacy status, economic status and development of various amenities. These physical and social changes transform the desert conditions into an ideal environment which is very suitable for human habitation and development. Further he observed that irrigation brings some negative impacts also in form of water logging, salinity and alkanity and number of social evils, which needed to be tackled and controlled so that they do not hinder in any was the future development of the area.

So from the above discussion it may be concluded that, first, deserts are areas of aridity which is determined by aridity index P/ETP. Where value of P/ETP is less than 0.03 is called hyper-arid zone or true desert, where it is in between 0.03 and 0.20 is called arid zone. In Rajasthan extreme western part of Jaisalmer is hyper-arid zone while rest part of this district falls under arid zone. Jaisalmer is emphasised here as the present study is undertaken in the district of Jaisalmer. Rajasthan desert is the extension of great Thar desert. Second, in this desert climate inter-annual variability of rainfall can reach 50 to 100 percent with very low and irregular rain and scanty vegetation. Third, Jaisalmer desert though basically is an erg desert but it shows also the characteristics of hammada and reg. Fourth, due to several reasons population here is increased day by day and over-exploitation. Fifth, desertification can be checked by afforestation and implementation of canal irrigation in the area. From the study of Gurjar (1992) it is revealed that Indira Gandhi Canal has brought radical changes in the environment and ecology and also in the life of the people though it has some negative impacts as well.

The tribal communities are kith and kin with the physical environment around them who have developed their own system of managing the environment. Rizvi (1989) observed that there is a system of preserving a young sapling by planting it inside a hollowed tree trunk among the Hill Korwas of Chhattisgarh. He (1993) further observed among the Balti in Jammu and Kashmir that they have adopted some measures to utilise the water available to them properly. He observed that as there is acute water shortage each lineage of Hardas village gets its share of water after 9 days from the canals or aqueducts (*kuhls*). The maintenance of *kuhl* is the collective responsibility.

So it can be assumed hypothetically that the tribal communities residing in desert area must have adopted certain measures for proper maintenance of the natural resources available in their environment. Desert is a condition of aridity and lack of resources which if are used improperly can lead towards further desertification. Therefore, the present study has been undertaken in the desert ecology. Geo-morphologically Jaisalmer desert shows all typical characteristics of a hot desert. Further establishment of new avenues has brought certain changes in the ecology of Jaisalmer both in its natural environment and in the social environment of the people living here. Therefore the district of Jaisalmer has chosen for the present study. As the Bhil is the only tribal group residing here, the study has been undertaken among them. Further, numerically the Bhils are the second largest tribal group in Rajasthan after the Mina and second largest in India after the Gond. According to 1981 Census the Bhil population in India was 7,367,964 while in Rajasthan 1,840,966.

Objectives

Management of environment and natural resources means how people manipulate the resources available to them and what sort of relationships they form in doing such. Keeping this in mind the following objectives are set for the present study:

(i) To observe the natural resources and other resources available to the Bhils in this area.

(ii) To observe how they manipulate and maintain the natural resources and the economic activities associated with the resources available; and

(iii) To observe what sort of relationship they form with the resources and the people in their environment.

Methods

To fulfill the above-mentioned objectives all anthropological tools are applied for data collection like observation, interview, group discussion, key-informant technique etc. Statistical methods are also applied whenever required, for example during analysis census data. Photography is done as an aid to observation.

Selection of site

The fieldwork has been carried out among the Bhils in two

villages Bharamsar and Roopsi in Jaisalmer district. Bharamsar is at a distance of 15 km from Jaisalmer city located beside Bikaner Road. It is 09 km to the north-east of Roopsi village. Roopsi is at a distance of 18 km to the south-west of Jaisalmer. Both the villages are connected through metalled road with the city of Jaisalmer. The reasons behind choosing these two villages for the present study are as follows :

(i) Preliminary information collected from Jaisalmer suggest that a good number of Bhils reside in these two villages. Further the history of the Bhils in Roopsi goes back at least to 150-200 years.

(i) Informatiopn regarding geology suggest that both the villages exhibit all characteristics of hot desert, that is erg, hammada and reg.

(iii) Though both the villages are situated within 20 kms of Jaisalmer which is a small town. An urban complex or a city nearby is Jodhpur which is far away from these villages. Further these two villages are at a distance of 65-80 kms from newly evolved industrial complex of Ramgarh, Tanot where discovery of natural gas has given an impetus to the people to concentrate there. These two villages are far away from Indira Gandhi Canal Command Area also.

Time period

Fieldwork was undertaken within the period from 19th July 2000 to 25th August 2000. Ten months time is taken for required analysis and writing of the report.

Chapterisation

Apart from this introductory chapter the report is divided into five sections. Section one describes the Bhil in their village setting. Though the Bhils do not live in isolation in these villages but emphasis is given to them only being the unit of study. Whenever it is observed that they are showing a common practice in the locality is mentioned in the respective sections. The second section is dealt with the economic resources available to the Bhils in the desert ecology while the third section describes associated economic activities. The fourth section describes economic relationship formed with the nature and environment both living and non-living creatures and relationship with man belonging to their own community as well as of other communities. It describes also the relationship of the Bhils with the local bodies, government agencies and officials etc. The fifth and final section summarizes the findings.

Section I

The Bhils in the Village Setting

The landscape in the villages of Bharamsar and Roopsi is undulated with desert terrain. In both the villages sandy soil is prevalent soil which is a type mixed with gravels. Roopsi is shadowed in the west by small hillocks with a downward slope towards the east. Sand dunes, small in size, are observed to the north-east stretched for atleast a mile. In the hillock area soil type is hard stony.

Climatic condition is extreme in nature with severe hot during the summer and cold in winter. Rainfall is trace. Dust storms are frequent during summer, though nights are pleasant. On the other hand winter days are pleasant while temperature falls even as low as 3-1°C during winter mid-nights. Summer is the longest season running from March to middle of July, Rainy season starts from middle of July and lasts upto middle of October; Winter starts from middle of October and lasts upto February. Though the rainy season lasts for three months – rain occurs occasionally.

Flora

Vegetation is scanty and sparsely distributed. Grasses, shrubs, thorny bushes and very few varieties of trees dot the landscape. Among the grasses six types are available in this area, viz. *seban* or, *siwan, ganthil, muroth, bhuroth, naredon* and *morion*. Among other flora the local varieties are *mithajhal* or *barapilu, kharijhal* or *chhotapilu, bon* or *ker, babul, kumbhat, lowa, ak* or *akra, bordhi* or *behr, ruida, khajri, thor, safeda, neem, tulsi, saris, kakonda* etc. Most of these plants are deciduous and thorny in nature[1].

Fauna

According to the peoples' perception in this area, animals can be divided into several categories, for example, *paltoo janwar* (domesticated animals), *pakshi* (birds), *sarp* (snakes and reptiles), *kire* (insects) and *jangle janwar* (forest animals which are not reared). They domesticate animals like *behl* (ox), *gai* (cow), *baqri* (goats), *bhehr* (sheep), *unt* or *dago* (camel), *kutta* (dog) and *billi* (cat). A few of them rear a bird, *titr* (grey partridge). They identify other birds in the locality like *kabutar* (pigeon), *kowa* (house crow), *ghugu* (dove), *gaguraja, maur* (peafowl), *battebari, gatta, gorana, gironj, sounri, hauli, hada, dolar, chiri, lili, pencha* (owl), *sugan chiri, putrio* (a bird which sleeps keeping legs upward on the branches), *batera, gadria, bugla, kachori* etc.

They named several insects like *chitia* (ant), *madhu-makshi* (honey bee), *kira* (medium insect), *chhote kiri* (small insect), *bare kiri* (large insect), *makora* (spider), *makkhi* (fly), *machhehhar* (mosquitos), *gunga, udai (lokri* or timber eating insect), *ger* (white colour insect available under the earth surface).

Various reptiles and snakes are : identified in the name of *sanda, go, pukorgoera, channango, sera, bichhchhu* (scorpion), *gelar* etc. and *lundi* (black and white colour, deadly poisonous), *goraba* (yellow in colour, keep themselves hidden in the sand, 6 ft. in length, deadly poisonous), *pina* (sind krait) etc. respectively.

The *janglee janwar* are known by *hiron* (deer), *khorgos* (hare), *gidhor* (fox), *jarokh* (hyena), *janglee sour* (wild boar), *rojra* etc.[2]

Water Resources

Priviously there was plenty of water in both the villages and main water resource was the stream. At present stream is dried up completely and now major water sources are *talab* (pond) and tubewell from where everybody in the village is allowed to collect potable water. These are government properties. There is also other water resource like the *beri* or *bauri* (wells) made both by individual effort and government effort. However, the other Bhils also can use the water of wells made by individual efforts. The Bhil also prepare *tanka* or water reservoir like people of other communities in the village, in their individual houses and no other person except his family and kin members are allowed to take water from that.

The Bhils have the notion of salt water (*khare-pani*) which is not available in these two villages but they reported that it is available in the villages near Sam about 25-30 km from Roopsi. Rain water which they call *pular pani* is sweet in taste and it is accumulated in the local tanks and pools and is one of the major sources of potable water in the villages.

Road Condition

Apart from the main *pakha* roads in both the villages all other lanes and sublanes are entirely *kachcha*.

Electricity

Electricity is available in both the villages. However except in a few Bhil houses including its *Sarpanch* and her opponent in Roopsi village other Bhil do not enjoy the electric facility in both the villages.

Drainage and Sanitation

A *gadda* or large hole is dug in every village hut to store drained water for feeding cattle and other domestic animals. Excess water is absorbed by the dry soil in the courtyard.

For toilet the Bhils and other villagers have to go outside either at the back of sand dunes or behind shrubs or on the hill top. The males and the females use separate toilet places.

They take bathe beside reservoirs their houses taking water from those but they never use water of such village tubewell, well or pond which are used only as potable water.

The Bhil in the Villages

Population

The Bhil settlement in Bharamsar is located in the western half of the village while in Roopsi it is located in the south-western half. The Bhil population in Bharamsar is 83 in total residing in 17 household. Of these 14 household are located in the village Bharamsar itself and the rest 3 at its *dhani* (hamlet) situated in Baisakhi at a distance of 2.5 km to the north. Likewise the Bhil population in Roopsi is 290 in total, residing in 51 households of which 48 are situated in the village and 3 in its *dhani*, 1.5 km to the south of the village. Sex ratio in Bharamsar is 804 female per 1000 while that in Roopsi is 859 per 1000. Both are below the sex ratio of the state of Rajasthan which is 910 female per 1000 male[3]. The married girls are not counted in the census as after marriage they become member of other families where they got married. The Table 1 given overleaf shows the age and sex wise distribution of the Bhil population in the two villages. The percentage shown in this table is calculated in terms of the total Bhil population of the respective villages.

Family types according to size

Among the 17 household of Bharamsar and 51 of Roopsi, majority of the families are of medium size (with 5-8 members). Table 2 shows the distribution of the households according to family size.

Bhil Population : Marital Status

In both the villages number of unmarried persons are higher than married ones. No cases of divorce or separation found in any of the villages. The distribution of the Bhil population according to the marital status is shown in the Table 3. Percentage is calculated in terms of the total population of the respective villages.

Clan

The Bhil are divided into twelve exogamous *gotra* (clan) which are as follows : Kaliana, Chudi, Sindhania, Liria, Malkat, Jakhtia, Lautia, Ghantar, Dubka, Sundia, Dedonta and Kaluda. Roopsi shows an interesting feature that all male Bhils of this village belong to Kaliana. It was reported that when the Bhil settlement started here around 150 – 200 years back, two Bhil brothers belonging to Kaliana group came here to reside with their families. The present Bhils are the successors of them. On the other hand majority of Bhil men of Bharamsar belong either to Malkat or Sindhania clans. The Bhil of these two villages reported that by the blessings of goodess Kali, the Kaliana Bhils originated from 'Sivjike Mal ke Kokanse' (from knees of the Lord Siva). The Sindhania Bhils got name after their original abode of Sindh. However, the people were not aware about the genesis of other clans.

Marriage Distance

Village is treated as an exogamous unit regarding marriage and all marriages took place so far among the Bhils were inter-village marriage. Case in Bharamsar where a Bhil lady of that village married a Bhil man of village Kita at a distance of 55 km from Bharamsar. However at present that man came with that Bhil lady, his wife, to reside at Bharamsar for last two years, constructing his own hut and maintaining own hearth being separated from his wife's father's family. Table 4 shows the marriage distance maintained by the Bhils of Bharamsar and Roopsi. The cases of marriage in Bharamsar and Roopsi are 18 and 66 respectively in total.

Marriage Types

The main marriage type is *beon* (marriage by negotiation). Marriage is prohibited in the same clan, in mother's previous clan (clan before marriage) and father's mother's previous clan. Marriage is preferred with distant relations of *nanihal* (mother's parental house). A few preferences are shown in Table 5 overleaf.

Widow remarriage is permissible but it holds a lower status. It is called *dusragharana.* Saturday is treated inauspicious for *beon* while, the event of *dusragharana* takes place only on Saturday. This can take place between a widow and a widower or a widow and a bachelor. In the second case the boy may go to marry with *bharat* (marriage procession). Marriage by capture is permissible but rarely takes place. It is accepted within the community after payment of some punishment cost fixed at that time by the head of the community. At present there is no such case in both the villages.

Family Types

Nuclear family formed of both the spouses and their unmarried children is the prevalent family type in both the villages followed by vertically extended family formed of ego, his family of procreation and any of the member of his family of orientation (his both parents/widower father/widow mother). Other family types are nascent – formed of only with the ego and his spouse; and broken – formed of widow mother or widower father and her/his unmarried children. Table 6 shows the distribution of Bhil households according to family type.

Language and Education

The Bhil speak in Marwari language and use Devnagari script for writing. They also speak in Hindi with outsiders. A few of them can speak English also. There are one primary school and one middle school (upto class VIII) at Bharamsar and two primary schools (upto IV) and one secondary school (upto class X) at Roopsi village. However, the literacy rate among the Bhils is poor. Percentage of non-literate Bhils is higher in both the villages than that of the literates. Females are educated maximum upto the primary level. In Bharamsar a few males have education upto the maximum of secondary level while that in Roopsi upto graduate level.

Table 1 : Age and Sex wise distribution of the Bhils in the villages of Bharamsar and Roopsi in Jaisalmer District, Rajasthan

	Bharamsar						*Roopsi*					
Age group	*Male*	*%*	*Female*	*%*	*Total*	*%*	*Male*	*%*	*Female*	*%*	*Total*	*%*
0 – 4	05	6.02	08	9.64	13	15.66	22	7.59	25	8.62	47	16.21
5 – 9	10	12.05	06	7.23	16	19.28	35	12.07	34	11.72	69	23.79
10 – 14	10	12.05	04	4.82	14	16.87	25	8.62	09	3.10	34	11.72
15 – 19	03	3.61	02	2.41	05	6.02	14	4.83	10	3.45	24	8.28
20 – 24	03	3.61	01	1.20	04	4.82	14	4.83	06	2.07	20	6.90
25 – 29	02	2.41	05	6.02	07	8.43	09	3.10	15	5.17	24	8.28
30 – 34	06	7.23	04	4.82	10	12.05	13	4.48	08	2.76	21	7.24
35 – 39	02	2.41	02	2.41	04	4.82	07	2.41	08	2.76	15	5.17
40 – 44	02	2.41	-	-	02	2.41	11	3.79	06	2.07	17	5.86
45 – 49	-	-	-	-	-	-	01	0 34	01	0.34	02	0.69
50 – 54	-	-	-	-	-	-	02	0.69	04	1.38	06	2.07
55 – 59	-	-	-	-	-	-	02	0.69	05	1.72	07	2.41
60 – 64	-	-	03	3.61	03	3.61	-	-	01	0.34	01	0.34
65 and above	03	3.61	02	2.41	05	6.025	01	0.34	02	0.69	03	1.03
Total	**46**	**55.42**	**37**	**44.58**	**83**	**100**	**156**	**53.79**	**134**	**46.21**	**290**	**100**

Table 2 : The distribution of households according to Family Size among the Bhils in the villages of Bharamsar and Roopsi in the Jaisalmer District of Rajasthan

Name of village	*Bharamsar*		*Roopsi*	
Family types according to size	*No. of Family*	*%*	*No. of family*	*%*
Small (0 – 4 members)	06	35.29	14	27.45
Medium (5 – 8 members)	11	64.71	33	64.71
Large (9+ members)	-	-	04	7.84
Total	**17**	**100.00**	**51**	**100.00**

Table 3: The distribution of the Bhil population according to Marital Status in the villages of Bharamsar and Roopsi of Jaisalmer District, Rajasthan

	Bharamsar						*Roopsi*					
Marital status	*Male*	*%*	*Female*	*%*	*Total*	*%*	*Male*	*%*	*Female*	*%*	*Total*	*%*
Unmarried	30	36.14	19	22.89	49	59.04	100	34.48	69	23.79	169	58.28
Married	16	19.28	16	19.28	32	38.55	55	18.97	55	18.97	110	37.93
Widow	-	-	02	2.41	02	2.41	-	-	10	3.45	10	3.45
Widower	-	-	-	-	-	-	01	0.34	-	-	01	0.34
Total	**46**	**55.42**	**37**	**44.58**	**83**	**100**	**156**	**53.79**	**134**	**46.21**	**290**	**100**

Table 4 :Marriage Distance maintained by the Bhils of the Bharamsar and Roopsi in Jaisalmer District of Rajasthan

Marriage Distance (km)	*Bharamsar*		*Roopsi*	
	No. of cases	*%*	*No. of cases*	*%*
0 – 25	06	33.33	16	24.24
25 – 50	04	22.22	25	37.88
51 – 75	06	33.33	19	28.79
76 – 100	-	-	06	09.09
100 above	02	11.11	-	-
Total	**18**	**99.99**	**66**	**100.00**

Table 5 : Marriage Preferences among the Bhils as reported in Bharamsar and Roopsi villages of Jaisalmer District of Rajasthan

Marriage Preferences :	
Ego Fa Br So	= E Mo Br Da
E Fa Br So	= E Mo Fa Da/E Mo Fa Da Da
E	= EZ Hus Z
E	= EZ Hus Fa Br Da
E	= EZ Hus Fa Fa Da
E	= EZ Hus Z Da/EZ Hus Br Da

E = Ego; Fa=Father; Br=Brother; So=Son; Mo=Mother; Da=Daughter; Z=Sister; Hus=Husband.

Table6: The distribution of households according to family types among the Bhils of the villages of Bharamsar and Roopsi in Jaisalmer District of Rajasthan

Name of village	*Bharamsar*		*Roopsi*	
Family types	*No. of Family*	*%*	*No. of family*	*%*
Nascent	-	-	03	5.88
Nuclear	15	88.24	31	60.78
Vertically extended	01	5.88	16	31.37
Broken	01	5.88	01	1.96
Total	**17**	**100.00**	**51**	**100.00**

The age-group of 0 – 5 is not considered for literacy rate calculation as done by the Directorate of Census Operations. One category is made as only literate which means a person who can read and sign but cannot write properly. Among the Bhil population of 83 in total in Bharamsar 38 males and 27 females (65 in total) who belong to above 5 age-group are considered for literacy calculation. Simultaneously among the Bhil population of 290 in total in Roopsi, 124 males and 101 females (226 in total) belonging to above 5 age group are considered. Table 7 shows the literacy pattern among the Bhils of the two vilalges. From the table it would be found that the literacy rate in Bharamsar is 24.62 percent while that in Roopsi is 42.04 percent. The literacy rates for the males in Bharamsar and Roopsi are 34.21 percent and 57.60 percent respectively while those for the females are 11.11 percent and 22.77 percent respectively. Whereas according to 1991 census the literacy rate was 39 percent in Rajasthan compared to 52 percent in the country. The literacy rates are 55 percent for males and 20 percent for females in Rajasthan compared to 64 percent and 34 percent for males and females respectively, for India[4].

Occupation

Regarding occupation the Bhils of Bharamsar reported that traditionally they were labourers in different works and also in the agricultural field of upper caste people, mainly of the Rajputs. Presently most of them are engaged in several kind of labour works like stone cutting in road construction, in agriculture etc. A few of them traditionally were pastoralists while pastoralism has become a secondary source of income for a couple of houses.

On the other hand all Bhil families (51 in total) in Roopsi reported that traditionally they were cultivators. At present most of them are engaged in labour works like the Bhils of Bharamsar. A fragment of them are engaged in pastoralism and other occupations other than sevice and cultivation. Cultivation has become the major source of secondary and tertiary income for them. Table 8 will show the occupational pattern among Bhils in the two villages.

Table 7 : The Literacy pattern among the Bhils of Bharamsar and Roopsi villages of Jaisalmer District in Rajasthan

Educational status	*Bharamsar*						*Roopsi*					
	Male	*%*	*Female*	*%*	*Total*	*%*	*Male*	*%*	*Famale*	*%*	*Total*	*%*
Non-literate	25	65.79	24	88.89	49	75.38	53	39.55	78	71.56	131	59.96
Only literate	-	-	-	-	-	-	01	0.80	01	0.99	02	0.88
Primary (upto class IV)	11	21.05	05	11.11	11	16.92	52	34.40	30	21.78	65	28.76
Secondary (upto class X)	05	13.16	-	-	05	7.69	21	16.80	-	-	21	9.29
Upto Class XII)	-	-	-	-	-	-	03	2.40	-	-	03	1.33
Graduate	-	-	-	-	-	-	04	3.20	-	-	04	1.77
Total	**41**	**100**	**29**	**100**	**65**	**100**	**134**	**100**	**109**	**100**	**226**	**100**

Table 8 : Occupational Pattern among the Bhils in the villages of Bharamsar and Roopsi of Jaisalmer District, Rajasthan

Name of village	*Bharamsar*		*Roopsi*	
Occupational Pattern	*No. of cases*	*%*	*No. of cases*	*%*
Traditional	17	100.00	51	100.00
Labour	13	76.47	-	-
Pastoralism	03	17.65	-	-
Cultivation	-	-	51	100.00
Data not available	01	5.88	-	-
Present Primary	17	99.99	51	100.00
Labour	11	64.71	30	58.82
Cultivation	02	11.76	03	5.88
Service	02	11.76	04	7.84
Pastoralism	-	-	07	13.73
Others	02	11.76	07	13.73
Present Secondary	17	99.99	51	100.00
Cultivation	05	29.41	20	39.22
Labour	02	11.76	16	31.37
Pastoralism	02	11.76	01	1.96
Others	-	-	05	9.80
Having no secondary occupation	08	47.06	09	17.65
Present Tertiary	17	100.00	51	100.00
Cultivation	01	5.88	11	21.57
Labour	-	-	08	15.69
Pastoralism	-	-	01	1.96
Having no tertiary occupation	16	94.12	31	60.78

Food Habit

The Bhils of both the villages partake same kind of food. Previously they took flour made of *joar (Hordenivulgare)* and *Bajra (Pennisetumtyphoides)*. They also prepared flour by pestling the seeds of a kind of thorny shrub called *ghurat*. They ate then *barapilu*, sweet in taste, the fruit of *mithajhal; sangria-fruit* of *Khajri; Ker* – the fruit of *bon*. They also hunted *sanda,* a reptile; *gatta; battebari; titr* – among the birds and *hiron* and *khorgosh* among the animals to eat their flesh.

At present due to the ban of hunting animals as done by the government they have to leave the habit of hunting and compelled them be habituated in vegetarian diet. Very rarely they hunt any animal or bird to enjoy its flesh very secretly. Presently their staple food is flour of *bajra* and *genhu* (wheat : *Triticum vulgare*). Among the pulses they take *chana (Cana indica), moong (Vigna chinensis), urad* and lentil. All these they cultivate, but quantity is so insufficient that they have to purchase these from the local market. A few among them still have to depend upon *joar* for flour due to very poor economic condition. However, the Bhils in these villages purchase meat of goat for consuming from the city market rarely. Among the vegetables they use onion, brinjals, tomato, *bhindi, khakri, khorbuja* etc.

Among the fruits they consume directly *barapilu* and after some treatment *ker* and *sangria*. After plucking the green raw fruit of *ker* it is put into hot water for 12 hours. Then it is boiled in hot water. As a result it becomes sweet and edible. The *sangria* fruit is also boiled after plucking and dried. After boiling it becomes sweet and edible. In dry condition it can be restored for a long period. It is used to prepare curry when no other vegetables are available. They also use *karing*as vegetable which is actually *toomba* and cultivated in the field with *goar*. It is sweeter than *tarbuj* (water-mellon).

They consume some special item for almost daily use like *palli, dalia* etc. *Palli* is used as vegetables. The apex or outer skin of *chana* (gram) is dried and those dried leaves are used as vegables. The wheat corns are threshed in small pieces, water is added to it in required quantity, boiled and thus *dalia* is prepared. *Khatta / khatto* (sour) is another regular preparation from curd. After extracting butter the remaining portion of the curd is utilised both way – first, its liquid portion *chhanch* is taken as a drink to cool the body in hot wave of summer which is also called *khatto / khatta* and second its thick remains – *ghee*. Curry is prepared of *khatto* also. They drink milk of cow and goat regularly.

They also prepare some festive foods during any festival, ceremony or when guests come in their houses. A few of these items are described below :

(a) *Fofli* – At first wheat corns are pestle and then mixed with sufficient quantity of molasses. Thereafter, it becomes a thick paste, *roti* is prepared of it in round shape. Then these are cut into long pieces using a *sisa* (glass) and dried under sunlight. Thereafter, it is fried in oil and served.

(b) *Chaul*– Rice is fried in oil using salt.

(c) *Lopsi* – At first *dalia* is prepared. Then it is baked using *ghee* and thus *lopsi* is prepared.

(d) *Genju ki halooa* – At first ghee is boiled to some extent upon a tumbler, then flour in required quantity is put into that. This is made worm and then required quantity of sugar and water are added. Thus *halooa* is prepared.

(e) *Sebian* – They have one kind of machine in their houses called *ghori*. Flour is pestle in this machine for some time. Then it is kept as usual for some time and when slanted, thin long pieces of flour comes out. It is kept in hand, twisted within two palms and lift upon *charpai* (cot made of rope) to dry under sunlight. Before consumption it is boiled in water for some times and then water is driven out. It is kept on *parat* (large plate) and *ghee* and sugar is added to it in required quantity. Thus *sebian* is prepared.

They take meal twice daily besides a heavy breakfast with a few roti, curry and *chhanch* before proceeding to work and, another light one only with a cup of tea in the afternoon after their return. Meals consist of 3-4 roti made of flour, vegetables or dal and *khatto* or *chhanch* for adult. Children take 1-2 *roti* as per their capacity.

A few of them take liquor regularly. Sometimes they buy it from the market but generally they brew it in their houses. Bark of the *bawal* (*pangra*) tree is used for this purpose. They reported the brewing procedure with a rough estimation of the ingredients. First 10 kg of molasses and 2 kg *sode* (the pieces of bark) are put into an earthen pot and 14 kg water is added to it. They use *narangi*, a monsoon fruit, which they buy from market in huge quantity, as fermenting reagent. 1-2 kg of *narangi* is required to ferment the above mentioned mixture. For proper fermentation the pot is kept under earth surface for 6-8 days during summer and 10-12 days during winter. Sometimes they use *paisa* (copper coins) as fermenting reagent by which it is prepared within 3 days. Next it is brought outside. A container having capacity of keeping 15 kg of such mixture (dalda tin) is taken and the entire mixture is placed within it. Required quantity of water is added to it and then boiled for sometimes. After it becomes cool, is filtered and poured into 11-12 bottles each having the capacity of one litre. Thus 11-12 litres of liquor is prepared.

House Types

Three types of houses are found among the Bhils of Bharamsar and Roopsi villages. First, the *Jhupura* or cottage type mainly observed in the Bhil *dhanis* (hamlets) situated beside *khet* (small agricultural lands) to protect crops and also for temporary dwelling.

Next is the *kacca* or clay hut used for permanent dwelling within the village and the third type is the *pakka* hut also used for permanent dwelling within the village. Apart from these another type of house is observed among them which is a mixed type, made of any two types of houses mentioned above. Atleast two rooms are required to form a mixed type house where the rooms are of two different types either *jhupura* and *kacca* or *jhupura* and *pakka* or *kacca* and *pakka*. Number of rooms vary from one to four in each type of houses.

The following materials are required for the construction of a *jhupura*. Small stones, *gobar* (cowdung), *chiknimitti* (from soil available in agricultural field), water and *lakrian* (dry wood of locally available trees and shrubs) are required for wall construction. Specially the dry wood of *jhal* is used for making the frame of roof and thatching is done by *chog-khip* is thorny dry wood of local bushes. Knitting of materials done by home-made rope of goat wool. Sometimes the upper portion of the roof is covered by plastic sheet bought from market to protect the roof materials from heavy wind blow in the area. It is with conical top and circular ground plan.

Kacca houses have either conical or triangular roof with rectangular ground plan. Materials required for preparing *kacca* houses are small stones, cowdung, *chiknimitti,* water, *lakrian, khip* etc. *Baru* variety of stone having iron as its prime ingredient is used here.

The *pakka* houses have obviously rectangular top and ground plan. *Kansia* (yellow stone) and *baru* are used for its wall construction and construction of roof along with cement, water and *bajri* (sandy soil). The doors (*darwaja*) are made of both wooden and iron frame with wooden pair of leaves. Windows are made by iron frame and wooden leaves while *jhorokhe* (ventelators) are made of *lakrian* (wood).

Unara (summer) and *Siara* (winter) are good seasons for construction of houses. This because during summer they avail long day time and much working hours while during winter they can do hard labor work easily in comparatively low temperature.

However, *barsala* (rainy season) is treated as dull season for house construction. This is because their work may spoil by rain water and also its treated as inauspicious due to the starting of inauspicious *chaturmas (Shravan, Bhado, Aswin, Katik)* from the rainy season.

Table 9 shows the distribution of the house types and number of living rooms among the Bhils in these two villages.

Household Material

Among the household materials there are different types of utensils which they use for cooking, eating, drinking water, storage materials; then the materials for other activities including recreation. The utensils they used previously were made of *kasa*/brass while majority of them are now using steel utensils. Clay pitchers and wooden materials are also used for these purposes. Majority of the utensils are bought from market of Jaisalmer while wooden materials and clay materials are available in the village which are prepared by craftsmen in the village belonging to other castes[5].

Among the recreation items transistor is found almost in every houses while television and tape-recorder are found in a few houses. Majority of them use twigs of neem, *jhal* or *babool* for brushing teeth though at present a few of them are using modern tooth pastes and tooth brushes. A few of them are using modern towels, though majority of them use cotton clothes of daily use as napkin. Previously they used *pagarsi* (Rajasthani shoes) made of camel leather which the old persons still use, while the young generation people at present are using *chappals* (slippers), cambice and leather shoes, sandals etc.

Dress materials and Ornaments

They have to purchase the dress materials from the market of Jaisalmer. Neither, they produce it themselves nor there is any tailor individual or community within the villages from whom they can purchase. The adult males use *dhoti* or *kurta* for lower half, *kamij* or shirt for upper half and saffa (turban for head. Except the old males who use white turbans, the other aged males use colourful turbans, mainly red in colour. The married females use *odon* (scarf) on the head; *ghagra* for the lower half; *kanchli* (bodies) to cover breast, *kurti* to cover *kanchli, jamphar* to cover the entire upper half of the body. Married ladies use *ghunghat* (veil) in front of the elderly members of the family, community

Table 9 : Distribution of Housetypes and number of living rooms among the Bhils in the villages of Bharamsar and Roopsi of Jaisalmer District in Rajasthan

Village : Bharamsar	*Number of living rooms*									
House Types	*1*	*%*	*2*	*%*	*3*	*%*	*4*	*%*	*Total*	*%*
Jhupura	01	5.88	-	-	-	-	-	-	01	5.88
Kacca	04	23.53	01	2.88	-	-	-	-	05	29.41
Pakka	03	17.65	02	11.76	01	5.88	01	5.88	07	41.18
Mixed (Pakka+Kacca)	-	-	01	5.88	01	5.88	-	-	02	11.76
Mixed (Pakka+Jhupura)	-	-	-	-	-	-	-	-	-	-
Mixed (Kacca+Jhupura)	-	-	01	5.88	-	-	01	5.88	02	11.76
Total	**08**	**47.06**	**05**	**29.41**	**02**	**11.76**	**02**	**11.76**	**17**	**99.99**
Village : Roopsi										
Jhupura	07	13.73	02	3.92	01	1.96	-	-	10	19.61
Kacca	02	3.92	02	3.92	01	1.96	-	-	05	9.80
Pakka	04	7.84	09	17.65	07	13.73	02	3.92	22	43.14
Mixed (Pakka+Kacca)	-	-	05	9.80	01	1.96	01	1.96	07	13.73
Mixed (Pakka+Jhupura)	-	-	04	7.84	-	-	01	1.96	05	9.80
Mixed (Kacca+Jhupura)	-	-	01	1.96	01	1.96	-	-	02	3.92
Total	**13**	**25.49**	**23**	**45.10**	**11**	**21.57**	**04**	**7.84**	**51**	**100.00**

and of other communities. The girls use *odon* upon head, *chaddi* upon waist and *ghagri* covering upper half of the body and also the lower half upto knee height. The boys use *dhoti, kurta,* and *pajama* (patloon). However at present the adult males, boys and girls are also using modern garments like trouser, skirt, t-shirt, jeans, suit etc. and the ladies saree and blouse.

Males use *gohhru* (ear-rings) of different size, mainly small round tops while the females use different kinds of ornaments like rings, necklace, *gajra* (ornaments used upon wrist), *katria* (for married ladies only) of different size, from elbow to armpit on both hands which are white or off-white in colour; *boria* (tiara), *bichhuri* (anklet), *pagphul* (in the fingers of foot) and ear-rings. Ornaments are also bought from markets and these are made of plastic, iron, silver or gold.

Section II

Economic Resources

The economic resources utilised by the Bhils in this area are obviously different types of land available in this area like household and agricultural land, hillock, grazing and forest land, water-bodies etc.; then the labour force available from them in the form of main work force (age group between 15 to 65) and auxiliary labour force (age groups below 15 and above 65); and the movable and immovable property like cattle, personal belongings, savings, kitchen garden and horticulture product, land etc. which they can use as capital for economic production. They also capitalise the environmental forces like solar and wind energy applying traditional wisdom.

Land

Total land area in Bharamsar including Baisakhi is 8,905 hectare while that in Roopsi is 5491.36 hectare. Un-irrigated land including fallow land in Bharamsar and Roopsi are 620 and 863.62 hectares respectively. The cultivable waste land area including gauchar and groves in Bharamsar is 6583.65 hectare while that in Roopsi is 2954.31 hectare. The area not available for cultivation in Bharamsar is 1701.35 hectare and that in Roopsi is 1673.43 hectare[6].

Land types

The Bhils of these villages classify land in the following manner:

On the other hand *anubjao jamin* are such land which are not available for cultivation. This again can be classified in three types :

(a) Akhor land or *sukha jamin* : Completely dry land used for grazing animals and building houses.

(b) Khatedari jamin : This is the land where houses are constructed. Generally they prefer highland for construction of houses. Therefore the hilly land (*magre ki jamin*) is widely used making it plain for this purpose. They also build house upon the plains on the ground.

(c) Pali bheudi : This is permanent pasture and grazing land. Only wild grasses are observed here and they cannot cultivate as this is completely sterile for cultivation.

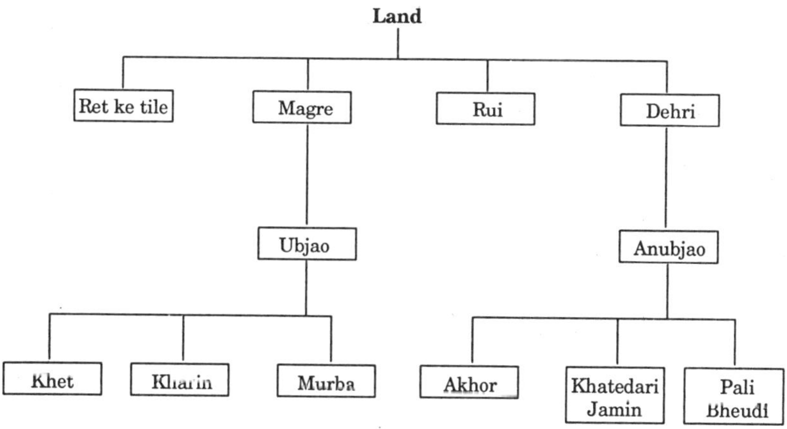

Among these land types the *khatedari* and *akhor* land on one hand and the *khet, kharin* and *murba* on the other come under individual ownership. Again according to ownership, land for cultivation may be classified as follows :

(a) *apna chas jamin* (own agricultural land)

(b) *sajedari chas jamin* (shared land for agriculture)

(c) *sarkar se mila jamin* (Land for agriculture either given on lease or donated by the govt.)

Table 10 shows the land holding pattern among the Bhils of the two villages.

Table 10 : Nature of landholding observed among the Bhils of the villages of Bharamsar and Roopsi in Jaisalmer District, Rajasthan

Nature of land holding	*Amount of land (hectare)*	*Bharamsar*		*Roopsi**	
		No. of household	*%*	*No. of household*	*%*
Own Land	0.01-5	09	52.94	29	54.72
	6-10	01	5.88	01	1.89
	10+	-	-	01	1.89
Share Land	0.01-5	01	5.88	-	-
	5+	-	-	-	-
Lease Land/Donated land	0.01-5	01	5.88	-	-
	5+	-	-	-	-
Landless	0	06	35.29	16	30.19
Total		**17**	**99.99**	**53**	**100.01**

*In Roopsi household number is 51 in total. However two households occupy both

Table 11 shows per capita land holding observed among the Bhils in these two villages.

Table 11 : Distribution of per Capita land holding observed among the Bhils in the villages of Bharamsar and Roopsi in Jaisalmer District, Rajasthan

Nature of land holding	*Amount of land (hectare)*	*Bharamsar*		*Roopsi**	
		No. of household	*%*	*No. of household*	*%*
Own	0.01-0.50	05	29.41	21	39.62
	0.51-1.00	04	23	07	13.21
	1.01-1.50	-	-	02	3.77
	1.51-2.00	01	0.53	01	1.89
	2.01+	-	5.88	-	-
Share**	0.01-0.50	-	-	06	11.32
	0.51+	-	-	-	-
Lease/Donated land	0.01-0.50	01	5.88	-	-
	0.51+	-	-	-	-
Landless	0	06	35.29	16	30.19
Total		**17**	**99.99**	**53**	**100.01**

*Total household number is 51 in Roopsi. Two household occupy both own and share land, hence the no. of household increases to 53.

** For percapita calculation of share land, the total land cultivated is divided by 3 as sharecropper receives 1/3rd share. Then that amount is divided by total no. of members in the share-cropper's family.

The following table shows distribution of cultivable land type pattern observed among the Bhils on these villages.

Table 12 : Distribution of cultivable land types observed among the Bhils in the villages of Bharamsar and Roopsi of Jaisalmer District in Rajasthan

Sl. No.	*Nature of land owned*	*Bharamsar*		*Roopsi*	
		No. of household	*%*	*No. of household*	*%*
1.	Murba+Khet	03	17.65	02	3.92
2.	Khet+Kharin	-	-	02	3.92
3.	Khet+Akhor	01	5.88	-	-
4.	Khet only	05	29.41	19	37.25
5.	Khain only	-	-	10	19.61
6.	Murba only	01	5.88	02	3.92
7.	Akhor only	01	5.88	-	-
8.	Landless	06	35.29	16	31.37
	Total	**17**	**99.99**	**51**	**99.99**

Soil Types

Again they have their own notion of the soil types available in this locality which they use for different purposes. For example:

(i) *retili mitti* (sandy soil) : used for shining utensils.

(ii) *chikni mitti* : black in colour, used for cultivation of gram and wheat, also used for wall construction in *jhupura* and *kacca* hut, mainly available in *Kharin* land.

(iii) *nehi kali nehi retili* : The soil which is neither sandy nor chikni mitti mainly available in *khet*, used for cultivation of goar, bajra etc.

(iv) *patthure mitti* (stoney soil) : It is not used.

(v) *moram mitti* : reddish in colour used for road construction. This is full of gravels and also called *murod*.

Resources - Stone cutting

Presently many of them are engaged in the profession of stone-cutting. As a result they know very well from where they would get the stones. Roopsi is surrounded by hills and hillocks on its west which is the main resource of stones in this village while stones are available from hillocks outside the periphery of the village in Bharamsar. According to the nature, they classify stones in the following manner :

(i) *Lal patthar* or *baru* (Red stone) : Heavy in nature having iron as its major ingredient used for house construction.

(ii) *Pila patthar* or *kansia* (Yellow stone) : It is again of two types, viz :

(a) *Karak* (hard) : used for house construction.

(b) *Naram* (soft) : used for making images, ports, bowls etc.

(iii) *Sakhe* or *sabna* : Large stones for constructing ceiling in *pakka* houses.

(iv) *Safed Pathar* (White stone) : Hard in nature used for making railway slipper available in villages farway from this area.

They can cut upto 50 feet of *baru* in one hour while in the same time they can cut either upto 100 feet of *Kansia* or 100 feet of *Sabna*. For cutting of *baru* they receive rupees 50/- per hour while for *Kansia* Rs. 100/- per hour and for *sabna* or for *safed patthar* Rs. 300/- per hour.

Forest Resources

Though forest resources are very scanty in this region and forest area is sparsely distributed at a distance of 2-10 kms from the villages in all direction, its importance among the Bhil, once hunting and collecting community, still persists to a great extent. The trees available in the forest are already mentioned in the 'flora' part of the first section. Though forest is unreserved in nature and is owned by the Forest Department of the Government, the Bhils have no restriction to collect forest products except hunting of wild animals available in the forest. They need not to pay any tax to enjoy their right over the forest products, however due to government rule they try to avoid hunting of wild animals in the forest. Even if they hunt they do it secretly. People of other communities including the villagers from other villages also visit these forests enjoying equal right over forest products. The Bhils in these two villages collect litter, timber, fodder, fruits, mushroom, honey etc. from the forest. Forest is also used for grazing of cattle because grass is available in plenty there. Forest is observed with great care as this is the abode of their deities.

Apart from these they plant several trees in their household premises, seeing their forefathers, which are useful in daily life in various ways like either supplying fuel in urgency or providing edible fruits or having medicinal value. 82.35 percent Bhil houses in Bharamsar have any kind of plant species like *jhal, khajuri* and *behr* in their household premises while 43.14 percent Bhil houses in Roopsi have plant species like neem, *babool, jhal, khajuri, behr, saris, safeda, akra* etc. in their household premises.

Labour Force

Another major economic resource of the Bhils is their labour force. Main labour force or work force is obviously the Bhil males and females belonging to the age group of 15 to 65. The age group below 15 are mainly school going children and they act as auxiliary work force helping their adult fellow men of the family in both household and outdoor work like fetching water, forest products etc. People belonging to above 65 age group are certainly old and feeble, however, they also serve their family as auxiliary labour force. Thus in Bharamsar main workforce is composed of 18 males and 17 females, 35 persons in total (42.17 percent of the total Bhil population of 83 in the village). Auxiliary labour force of below 15 age group in this village is composed of 25 males and 18 females, 43 persons in total (51.81 percent). Likewise in Roopsi the main force is composed of 73 males and 64 females, 137 persons in total (47.24 percent of the total Bhil population of 290 in the village). Auxiliary labour force of below 15 age group in this village is composed of 82 males and 68 females, 150 persons in total (51.72) percent) and that of above 65 age group is composed of 1 male and 2 females, only 3 persons in total (1.03 percent). Exchange of labour is also taking place whenever required.

Other Economic Resources

The other economic resources are the movable and immovable property like cattle, personal belonging, savings, kitchen garden and horticultural products, land etc. One Bhil in his distress can sell his land to another Bhil or one Meghwal in the buyer's name but not to any other person belonging to any other caste. On the other hand they can purchase land from higher castes but the deed has to be shown as deed of gift. As they are 'inferior' to the caste people they cannot sale land to a caste people showing it as a token of gift.

The kitchen garden and horticultural products are consumed in the respective houses first, then it is shared with the kin members and finally if there is a surplus among, that is either

Table 13 : The pattern of owning of Livestock in the village Roopsi of Jaisalmer District Rajasthan and the pattern of owning of Livestock per household and per captia

Name of village	*Total No. of House-hold*	*Total Popu-lation*	*Total No. of Livestock*				*Livestock per Household*				*Livestock per Capita*			
			Goat	*Sheep*	*Cow*	*Camel*	*Goat*	*Sheep*	*Cow*	*Camel*	*Goat*	*Sheep*	*Cow*	*Camel*
Roopsi	51	290	493	75	27	14	09.67	01.47	0.53	0.27	01.7	0.26	0.09	0.05

sold in the market or exchanged for other products with other Bhil neighbours in the village.

Personal belongings are sold whenever required but never exchanged. Savings is utilised in requirement for own family and for the kin members also.

Livestock

Cattle is an important resource which can be sold to others to get money in need. It is also the source of milk and milk products, fuel etc. They rear the animals like cow, goat, camel, sheep. Ox and camel is utilised for local transport of heavy materials by carts. Camel cart is also used for water transportation. Wool is sheared from goat, sheep and camel which is used to prepare rope for domestic purposes and also sold in market. Data on livestock rearing is not available from Bharamsar but it is available from Roopsi. Table 13 shows the livestock owned by the Bhils of Roopsi village and the pattern of owning of livestock per household and per capita.

Apart from all these they 'capitalise' natural forces like solar and wind energy according to their wisdom which will be discussed later.

Section III

ECONOMIC ATIVITIES

The Bhil traditionally worked as labourers in the Rajput houses and land, which they called *Mantak Majduri*. In exchange of their labour they received small amount of vegetables twice a day. For supplementing their meager income they had to collect food from forest by hunting and collecting.

After independence they were given small amount of land where they started settled cultivation. However, most of them were still engaged in labour work (*Mehenat Majduri*) by which they started earning cash money. With the flood of cash money their economic standard improved slightly. Some of them were also engaged in pastoralism and animal hunbandry. Later on they shifted to the profession of stone cutting and other hard labour work like road construction to get better wages and to improve them economically. Their perception about locally available stones and its application, helped them immensily in stone related professions. Agriculture remains subsidiary source of income for them as it is very much dependent upon rain water, as in the desert situation the rainfall is scanty, agriculture activities and other related works instead of still they are very much dependent upon forest products and mainly the auxiliary work force is engaged in this work. Only, as hunting is banned due to government rule they generally avoid hunting animals. Their expertise in forest bound activities would be explored later on.

Agriculture

Though agriculture is mostly the mode of secondary occupation (29.41 percent in Bharamsar and 39.22 percent in Roopsi) and to a little bit the mode of tertiary occupation (5.88 percent in Bharamsar and 21.57 percent in Roopsi), but it is discussed here first for two reasons – (a) by agriculture a vast amount of land is utilised for economic purposes and (b) traditional wisdom is very much associated with agricultural practices.

Land Types and Productivity

Agriculture is performed on two types of land, viz. *khet* and *kharin*. Double cropping can be done in *kharin* while single cropping is possible on *khet.* Table 14 shows the crop season observed by the Bhills in this area.

Wheat, gram and mustard can be cropped separately or

Table 14 : Crop Season observed by the Bhils in the villages of Bharamsar and Roopsi in Jaisalmer District of Rajasthan

Name of crop	*Sowing Season*	*Harvesting Season*
Bajra	Ashad-Shravan (July)	Katik (Oct-Nov)
Goar	-do-	-do-
Khakri	-do-	-do-
Khorbuja	-do-	-do-
Til	-do-	-do-
Moong (Pulse)	-do-	-do-
Joar	-do-	-do-
Wheat	Katik-Meghar (Oct-Dec)	After four months
Gram	-do-	-do-
Mustard	-do-	-do-
Jamba (mustard like)	-do-	-do-

simultaneously. It holds good for *bajra* (a millet crop), *goar* (a fodder crop), *khakri* (cucumber like), *joar* (millet), *khorbuja* (musk-melon), *til* (sesame) and *moong* (a kind of pulse) to cultivate simultaneously. It depends upon the desire of the cultivator. Table 15 describes the nature of yield per kg/ hectare in the previous year in Bharamsar and Roopsi.

Table 16 shows yielding of crops per capita among the Bhils of these villages. As a few of them are share croppers and receive 1/3rd share of the crop produced, the following method is applied to calculate per capita yielding of them:

(i) Noting of total yielding and total land area.
(ii) 1/3rd share received: hence total yield is divided by 3.
(iii) Share portion is yielded from 1/3rd portion of land, hence total land area is divided by 3.
(iv) Yield in kg/hectare is calculated by (ii) divided by (iii)
(v) For per capita yield in kg/ hectare (iv) is divided by total member of the share cropper's family.

Manure and Fertilizer

They use only cowdung as manure which according to their belief is the best manure giving a bumper crop. Chemical fertilizer (*khad*) like urea or potash are believed to spoil natural fertility of the soil. They never utilise any pesticides and any sparaying is yet to be adopted though they know that crop is affected by some insects. Shrubs like *jhal* or *babool* are not allowed to grow near their fields as they are to affect the crops adversely.

Seed

The seeds are preserved from earlier crop to utilise for the next sowing. They also purchase seeds from market or collect from Panchayat. They have their own perception of seed quality, for example, for wheat two types of seed are used – a red variety and another white variety. They widely use the red variety because less amount of water is required for its cultivation. On the other hand if there is a moderately good rainfall they sow the white variety of wheat which absorbs more water. The yield of white variety is very high and healthy.

Crop rotation

Crops are rotated as per the crop season shown earlier in three ways; first in the single- cropped land one crop is produced in one year followed by another one in the next year, second a summer crop is followed by a winter crop and third, a few crops are cultivated simultaneously of which some are much water consuming and some are less, thus neutralising the water requirement. To them it is the best method because they can utilise the scanty amount of water available for agriculture to produce 3 to 4 types of crop at a time in the small plots of agricultural land they possess.

Agricultural Implements

Traditionally for ploughing and sowing they use plough driven by *bhel* (ox). Only a few of them utilise mechanised tractors. Majority

Table 15: Nature of crop yielded last year (1999-2000) and yielding of crops in kg/hectare observed among the Bhils in the villages of Bharamsar and Roopsi in Jaisalmer District, Rajasthan

Yield kg/ hectare	*Name of crops*									
	Goar		*Bajra*		*Wheat*		*Horsegram*		*Mustard*	
	Bh.	*Ro.*	*Bh.*	*Ro.*	*Bh.*	*Ro.*	*Bh.*	*Ro.*	*Bh.*	*Ro.*
0 – 50	-	04	05	01	-	01	-	-	-	-
51 – 100	-	02	04	-	-	03	-	-	-	-
101 – 150	06	02	-	-	-	-	-	-	-	01
151 – 200	02	02	-	-	-	03	-	-	-	02
201 – 250	01	01	-	-	-	01	-	-	-	-
251 – 300	-	-	-	-	-	05	-	01	-	01
301 – 350	-	-	-	-	-	01	-	-	-	-
351 – 400	-	-	-	01	-	03	-	01	-	-
401+	-	03	-	-	-	08	-	02	-	-
Total household	**09**	**14**	**09**	**02**	**-**	**25**	**-**	**04**	**-**	**04**

Bh. – Bharamsar; Ro. – Roopsi;

Table 16 : Per capita yield of crops observed last year (1999-2000) among the Bhils of Bharamsar and Roopsi villages of Jaisalmer District, Rajasthan

Per Capita yield of crops kg/ hectare	*Name of crops*									
	Goar		*Bajra*		*Wheat*		*Horsegram*		*Mustard*	
	Bh.	*Ro.*	*Bh.*	*Ro.*	*Bh.*	*Ro.*	*Bh.*	*Ro.*	*Bh.*	*Ro.*
0 – 20	-	05	08	01	-	05	-	-	-	-
21 – 40	06	05	01	01	-	04	-	-	-	04
41 – 60	03	02	-	-	-	08	-	02	-	-
61 – 80	-	-	-	-	-	04	-	-	-	-
81 – 100	-	01	-	-	-	02	-	-	-	-
100+	-	01	-	-	-	02	-	02	-	-
Total household	**09**	**14**	**09**	**02**	**-**	**25**	**-**	**04**	**-**	**04**

Bh. – Bharamsar; Ro. – Roopsi.

of them cultivate with help of wooden harrow, yoke and wooden plough. For leveling the land they use *kulhari* (axe). A wooden hollow cylinder (*nai*) is attached to the back portion of plough by which they sow seeds. *Kasi* and *paora* are two kinds of spade which are used to clean the land. *Datri* (sickle) is used to cut grains. *Sajra,* a type of sieve, is used for threshing while a few of them are utilising modern thresher at present. The grains are stored in *bhori* (sacks), *kothi* (container made of mud) and *dol* (iron made). 76.47 percent of Bhil houses in Bharamsar and 60.78 percent in Roopsi have their own agricultural implements. They have to borrow modern thresher and tractor from other caste people.

Agricultural Operations

Clearing of land : At first weeds and stalks of previous crops are cleared using *kulhari, kasi and paora.*

Manuring*: B*efore the onset of agricultural operations the cattles are left in the agricultural field for grazing. The dung and urine left by the cattles get mixed with the soil in due course.

Sowing: Before sowing seeds they plough the land once for cultivation of *goar, bajra* etc. and twice in a gap of fifteen days for horsegram and wheat. Then the land is left for another fifteen days. After that another plough is given for sowing seeds. It has already been mentioned that there is a hollow cylinder (*nai*) attached to the *hal* (plough) by which they sow seeds in rows.

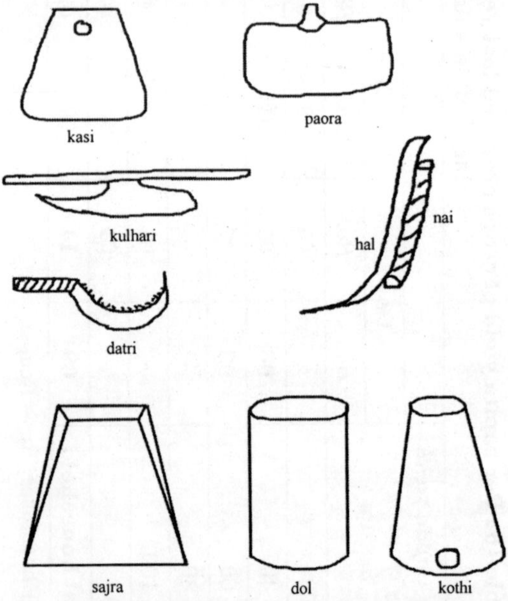

Fig. 1 : Sketches of Agricultural implements used by the Bhils. (not to scale) (SM-2001)

Irrigation

Irrigation is dependent upon rain water, which by the downward flow from hill /hillock tops, gather in the agriculture land. The demarcation boundary (*dhore*) between two lands are kept high to store water in a particular land thus acting as a binding measure of water. However, beneath that boundary a drain is kept having both openings closed in normal condition. When sufficient water is gathered in one land, the excess is drained through the channel opening its both mouths. Thus the next land gets its water share for irrigation.

Protective Measure

They use fencing by dry twings of thorny shrubs or by iron wire bought from market to protect crops from cattles. The landowner acts as watchman in the field to protect crops from birds, cattles etc. He sometimes takes help of his family members, kin members, neighbor or sometimes employ on hire labour for this purpose. If cattles are found grazing the standing crops, the landowner holds them captive in a *bara* (enclosure for cattles). The owner of the cattle has to release his cattles from the *bara* by paying the damages to the land owner in case the cattle has damaged the crop and also gives an undertaking that in future his cattle will not enter into the field with standing crop.

Harvesting Method

Apart from providing protection of the crops, the farmers do not require to do anything before ripening of crops. However, when they cultivate *goar and bajra,* there is chances of growing other weeds in the field, which may damage crops. If they find such, they simply cut it from the root by *kasi*. As three ploughs are given for sowing horse – gram and wheat, there is no chance for any weed to grow.

In case of *bajra,* the part where grains occur is called *sora*. First they cut the grains by *datri* from *sora*. Then they separately cut the grasses which are used as fodder for the cattle. For *goar,* horse – gram and wheat, the plant is cut from the upper surface of the land, leaving the stalk and root underneath; by help of *datri*.

Threshing and Winnowing: Use of Wind Energy

At first, a place beside the agricultural field is cleared and prepared for threshing. This place is called *khala or khalihan.*

It is smeared with soaked cowdung (*gobar*). Then the crops are kept upon that to make a heap (*dheli*). In past, ox or camel were driven upon that *dheli,* which they called *gaona*, to separate the grass and grains. They utilise camel still now to a great extent, though a few of them are using modern thresher nowadays for this purpose.

After separation of grains, these are put into *sajra* for winnowing and kept before the wind blow, that is, the face of *sajra* is kept on that direction from which wind is coming. The heavy wind blow separates the minute *kachra* (waste particles) and the skin from the grains. As a result out- skinned grains remains within the *sajra* and skins and other waste particles are blown away.

Preparation of Box, Basket for Storage and Preparation of Granaries

It has already been mentioned that three types of containers, viz, *kothi, dol and bhorni* are used for storing grains. They are preparing *kothi* for generations using camel dung and *chikni mitti.* Dried camel dung is smeared by *chikni mitti* to prepare *kothi. Dol* is made of iron and bought from market, hence not widely used. *Bhori* or sacks are generally cement bags collected from neighbours or are jute made sacks.

After winnowing the grains are put into these containers. Previously they used bullock carts to carry this material to their houses. At present they use *unt gada* (camel cart). Some of them also hire tractor or truck for this purpose. Then these are put into one of the living rooms within the house. No other granaries are made for this purpose.

Manual Labour

Previously every work related to agriculture was performed manually. Dependence on manual labour still exists among them to a large extent. Majority of them are still using bullock driven plough for ploughing and sowing; they clean land and cut crops manually; thresh applying bullock or camel; winnow manually using *sajra;* put grains manually into *bhori, kothi or dhol* and bring the containers home using camel cart. Only a few of them nowadays, are ploughing and sowing seeds using mechanised tractor, threshing crops using modern thresher and bringing crops home either on tractor driven troly or on truck.

Extent of Dependence and Adequacy of Agriculture

Agriculture is very much dependent upon rain water. Previously, when heavy rainfall occurred, they managed to store one to two year crop by a single cultivation. Otherwise they had to depend upon labour works. Nowadays the situation is almost same. With the increase of population, land is distributed among the children and they are producing a lesser amount of crop in small lands they own. The landless Bhils solely depend upon labour work while the land owners, according to them, can manage to fulfil part of their requirement of livelihood by agriculture and for the rest they also have to depend upon labour work and other activities.

Organisation of Agricultural Activities: Division and Exchange of Labour

Mostly all sort of agricultural works are performed by the male members belonging to main work force category. The children generally go to school or act as shepherd. The female members belonging to main work force look after the household work and bring meal of their family men engaged in agricultural work during noon. Sometimes they help also for one to two hours in agricultural works. If there is more than one adult female in any household, they, except one, who looks after the domestic chore, all others go to the agricultural field to help their male counter parts. However, during harvesting, females play the major role in cutting crops and winnowing grains.

Three kind of labour exchangeship is observed among the Bhils in this area. First, mutual labour exchange is observed among kin members and close neighbours where labour is reciprocated by labour and no food or monitory transaction take place. Second type is observed among the Bhils belonging to two different villages or among the Bhils and Meghwals of the same village where labour is reciprocated by labour and mid-day meal and no monitory transaction take place. The Bhil and the Meghwal feel themselves close to each other being placed at the bottom in caste hierarchy. The third type of labour exchange is that when the Bhil employ a hired labour, a person belonging to any other caste or sect other than the Bhil or the Meghwal. In this type of labour is reciprocated by cash money and mid-day meal. A male labour is paid Rs. 80/= per day while a female Rs. 50/= per day for their labour.

Land Conservation

Since long past they are applying certain methods to protect land from erosion and to maintain its fertility. First, within two lands they keep high demarcation boundary (*dhore*) to prevent dispersion of soil particles from one land to other during wind blow. To protect the soil, they plant trees upon the *dhore*. Further *dhore* acts as water binder of a particular land. Previously *dhore* was prepared by themselves. Nowadays they receive money and labour provided by the government. Barren land is utilised for grazing of cattles. They sometimes prepare sandy soil for cultivation of *bajra* by cutting weeds and herbs.

Pattern of Change in Land Ownership

Since 1947 a change has taken place regarding right of the ownership. Previously a few landlords were owner of all lands. After independence through land sealing the government has become the owner of a vast amount of land which is again distributed to the Bhils and other deprived communities. Thus, nowadays a Bhil farmer has his rights upon the land he owns and cultivates.

Beliefs, Taboos and Religious Activities Associated with Agriculture

The Bhils in this area have certain kind of beliefs associated with agriculture. For example, if they observe *titr* or *suganchiri* on their right side before proceeding for any agricultural activity, treat it as auspicious while observation of such in the left is believed to be inauspicious. Next if they observe a vessel full of water before proceeding to land preparation for agriculture, believe that good rainfall and good cultivation will take place; while an empty vessel on such occasion is treated as indicator of bad rainfall and bad cultivation. For sowing seed and cutting grains Saturday is believed to be auspicious being the date of *Grahadevta Shani* (the Saturn-the King of planets). Therefore before proceeding for such operations they offer food to *Shanidevta* and partake that as his grace. A few of them sacrifice he – goats also and prepare food beside the agricultural land.

They can predict the occurrence of rainfall performing a ritual. Four earthen pot full of water are kept at four sides. The pot of which side breaks early is treated as the side where good rainfall will occur.

They do not perform or start any agricultural activity on Tuesday. It is believed that on Tuesday, *Dhartimata* or the Mother Earth takes a bathe leaving her clothes. *Dhartimata* is the land where they cultivate. Thus if they go for agricultural operation on that day, they will be cursed by *Dhartimata*, because she will think that her children-the Bhils are insulting her seeing their Mother in bare body.

There is no other taboo associated with any other days. Monday is the day of Lord Shiva, Wednesday of Ganeshji, Thursday the day of *guru Behaspat* (Jupiter) and Friday is the day of *Santoshimata.* Hence all these days are treated auspicious for daily life, however, there is no such belief regarding agriculture associated with these days. Though Saturday is treated auspicious for agriculture and also for preparation for butter, in general it is treated as an inauspicious day to go outside.

They perform three rituals in the month of *Vaisakh (*April-May) associated with agricultural activities. First, the *Amabos* (the last day of the dark fortnight), next is the *dooj* (the second day of the bright fortnight succeeding *Amabos*) and finally *akhateej* (the next day of *dooj).* On the day of *Amabos*, they proceed towards the nearest forest early in the morning and search for *titr or suganchiri.* After observance of such, they believe, whatever they will think will be fulfilled. If they think good rainfall and good harvest will occur, it will occur; and if they think, less rainfall and poor harvest will occur; that will happen. After that they return home. In the village 20-25 plates of the grains of *bajra* are collected from 20-25 families and these are kept in four large plates in the four directions. A boy is called for to touch any plate and nothing else is said to him. It is believed that if he touches the plates of North or East, good rainfall and good harvest will occur and if he touches the plates of South or West less rainfall and poor harvest will occur. Then the male members prepare *dalia* of that *bajra* outside the room which they call *khij* and take it collectively. No female member is allowed to come outside at that time. It is believed to be inauspicious if a lady comes outside at that moment removing her *ghunghat* (scarf upon the head). On the day of *dooj* and *akhateej* they take molasses, coconut, *fofli* prepared from wheat collectively. They believe performing of such rites will bring good harvest.

Water Conservation and Water Management

In a desert ecology the conservation of water resource and proper management is very important. Water is utilised for drinking purposes for the human being and the cattle, for other household activities and for irrigation.

Agriculture in this area solely depends upon rainfall. They prepare *dhore* (contour) between two lands to utilise rain water properly and for preserving it. They open the both ends of a channel lying behind the *dhore* to drain out the water from one land to the other. If two lands are situated in a manner, that *dhore* cannot be constructed in between, then a flat piece of wood is kept there in between the lands by which the excess water of one land can be drained to the other. If any stream emerges there from the hill top by heavy rainfall, that water is also restored either preparing a *dhore* at the bottom or a tank (*talab*). One such *talab* is located in Roopsi surrounded by hillocks in its three sides having the other side open, through which man and cattle can reach there. The taste of this water is so sweet that it is still used as one of main sources of water for both human being and cattle. Neither they perform any other domestic work there nor they go for nature's call upon the hill slopes to avoid spoiling of such water. For domestic work, they use water of *pani tanka* (water reservoirs) made in individual houses which are filled by fetching water from tube well or by water brought there using camel tankers. Large tubewells are made by the government in Vaisakhi and Ramkunda from where potable water is supplied to Bharamsar and Roopsi respectively and also in other villages through *pakka* pipelines.

Previously they prepared *pakhals* (leather sac) of cattle leathers in which water of 4-5 large *matka* (clay pitcher) can be poured. Two *pakhals* full of water were kept in both sides of a camel to keep proper balance and thus camel was used to carry water from one place to the other. This was the only measure of water supply. But at present supply is mainly done by *pakka* pipelines. For this purpose large reservoirs are made in certain villages at a particular distance from the tubewell. Water transport by camel or tractor driven tankers are widely observed.

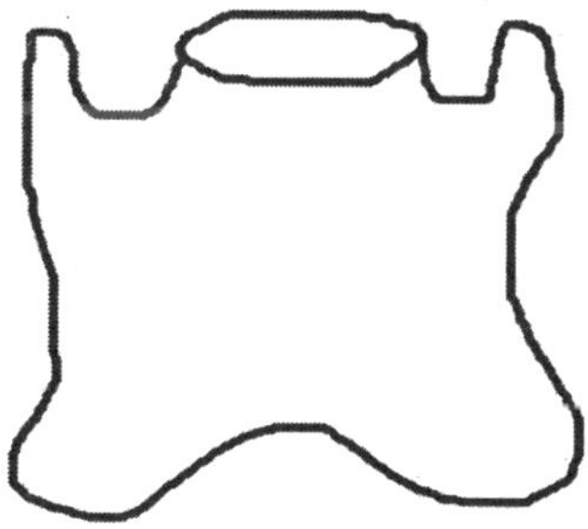

Pakhal

During dry season *berry* (well) are dug. If it is found that water of that well is *khara* (saline), then in a distant place, another well is dug and water of that is tasted. If that is found sweet in taste, then used for all sort of domestic activities.

The modern tubewell facility is available in Roopsi and Bharamsar till 1980s and now there is no shortage of water so far even during the summer. However, after rainfall, stream flooded water is still now bound preparing *dhore.*

Beforc cighties, before the establishment of modern tubewells and getting the supply water facilities, they faced problem of acute water shortage during summer. Once used wells became dried. They then used their expertise to search for underground water. They always kept observation upon those places where rain water accumulates to a great extent during heavy rainfall. They then dug well in those areas and easily got thc under surface water. Further perhaps observing their caste fellow men they believed that God Indra has mastery over rain and by appeasing Him they could get His blessings in form of occurrence of heavy rainfall. To appease Indra they collect a handful of wheat grain from every house and prepare of it *gugri* adding molasses, which is fed to the children. It was believed that Indra would be pleased by such practice and good rainfall would occur.

Economic Activity : Stone Cutting

It has already been mentioned that presently one of the prime sources of income of the Bhil community is stone cutting and associated labour work. Hills and hillocks in the surrounding area of the villages are the main sources of stones. It has also been mentioned that they have their perceptions of different kind of stones, their sources and utility and they receive different amount of money for cutting same quantity of different stones. Large hammer, axes, crowbar, pick axe etc. are used to cut the stone. First, a large stone is cut which is given a finer shape using small hammer before loading. They receive money for loading and unloading of stones in the cart driven by bullock and camel or in the tractor-troly or truck. Previously they received rupees six only for loading and unloading of 25 sq. feet stones in camel cart or 20 sq. feet stones in bullock cart. At present they receive rupees one hundred to two hundred only for loading and unloading of stones in tractor-troly and truck respectively.

Economic Activity Associated with Pastoralism and Animal Husbandry

It is reported that once upon a time pastoralism was one of major sources of income of the Bhils and still now a Bhil can earn a good amount in this profession.

However, only a few of them are engaged in this work because the number of cattle in the village are not sufficient for maintaining livelihood for each and every Bhil and the amount of income increases with the number of animals in the herd increases. These persons look after their own cattle, as well as the cattle of other Bhils and even of the cattle of the Meghwal or the Rajput or any other community in the village. They receive rupees twenty to twenty five per month for one cow or bullock while rupees fifteen per month for one sheep or goat. Thus if one goes with 50 goats, 50 sheeps and 20 bullocks or cows, then he can earn (50x15+50x15=20x25)=(750+750+500)=2000 rupees per month. Actually they go with more animals in one herd and earn more accordingly.

The shepherds go to jungle or hill top or permanent grazing land where plenty of grasses are available. They also go to *khet* and *kharin* when people do not cultivable.

It has already been mentioned that mostly they rear goats, sheeps, cows and camels. The caring of such animals in individual houses is done by the members of the respective family. A cow herder only looks after the animals in the day time when he goes out with the cattle for their grazing till he comes back home with the cattle.

They feed *seban* and *muroth* grasses (available in *khet, kharin*) to ox and cow and *ganthil grass* available in forest) to sheeps and goats. Leaves of *bordhi* or *behr* and *khajuri* are eaten by goats. *Morion* grass, available in lands submerged under water, are fed to every cattle. Camels take also different kind of grasses. Apart from that they also take thorny bushes locally available. These cattle are fed also grasses like *naredon, bhuroth* etc. in the jungle and hillocks. In individual houses they are fed *dala* of *goar* (the threshed mater of *goar* seed), water, grass portion of horse-gram, *goarti* (grass portion of *goar*), *sukhol* (grass portion of wheat) etc.

When the cattle get ill, they are fed ayurvedic medicines, either bought from Jaisalmer market or home made. For any skin disease or wound they apply *meda lakri* (small twigs bought from market) mixing with ghee, *surma* (which is applied in human eyes) and *mustis khand* (one type of molasses); externally upon that wound. For other illness they make an iron rod red burn and press it upon the body of the cattle by which it becomes well. This is called *dam*. During illness the cattle are fed coconut milk and skin of the camel.

Every individual can identify his cattle without giving any mark upon the body of the animal. They have their own perception and identifying capability which they cannot express in words. However, all the cattle of a particular village have an identifying mark upon its body. This distinguishes animals of one village with other village. An iron rod having a particular kind of shape in its one end, is made red burn and applied to every cattle at the time it is owned by any villager.

Milk Pouring

Camel milk is not utilised by the Bhils and hence camel milk is not poured. Milk of cow, she-goat and sheep are utilised for daily use. These animals are fed *goarti*, *goargom* (grains of goar). *Gul* (molasses), green grasses etc. to increase the milk quantity. Milk is available within the period of first delivery and next carriage of child.

Milk is poured in bucket or steal vessels. At first its calves are fed milk for a few minutes, then pouring is started. The back legs are tied with rope. Then the *anchal* (nipples) are cleared with water. After that they start pouring the milk.

Milk Products

After pouring of milk it is boiled. Some portion is consumed adding sugar and the rest is cooled. 4 to 5 drops of *chhanch* (curd extract) previously prepared, is added to it and kept in a cool place. On the next morning it becomes curd. Curd is also either directly consumed or curry is prepared from it. Some portion is kept for these purposes. Rest portion is added with previously prepared curd and placed in an earthen pot (*matura*) for preparation of butter and *chhanch*. For preparation of these they use *jharna-dadi*. *Jharna* is a wooden piece of instrument. A belt made of cow-leather is used to move it. It is called *patta*. The *matura* is placed in a manner that it remains unmoved. *Jharna* is placed inside the curd mixture and is moved by *patta*. One end of *patta* is kept in left hand and the other end is hold by right hand. When the right end is moved inward, the left one is moved outward at the same time and vice versa. This is done very fast for hours as a result thick butter is churned. Butter (*makkhan*) is separated by a spoon. Then water is added to the mixture and again the same movement is done. A thick layer precipitates downward having the liquid upward. The liquid is the *chhanch* or *khatto* which is collected first keeping the *matura* in a slanting position. The thick portion is used for domestic purposes as *ghee*.

Storing of dung

Generally cowdung is collected and utilised for several purposes. The female members of every household collect cowdung for domestic purpose. First they dump cowdung collected at different places in the courtyard and separate it in two halves according to requirement. From one half small round balls are prepared and dried under sunlight. These are used as fuel. *Chikni mitti* is mixed with the other half of cowdung and water is added to that in required quantity. After mixing water, a large dump is prepared by hand and for proper mixing it is chopped by legs. This mixture is utilised for smearing floors, courtyard, walls. It is also used on top of ceiling of *kacca* houses and *jhupura* to prevent dropping of rainwater inside the room and also to provide more cooling effect to the room.

Wool Shearing

In the summer goat, sheep and camels are given a bathe before sheering of wool. After giving a bathe the body hair of these animals are cut by *katera* (a large iron scissor). Then the hairs are dumped in the toom or in the courtyard and it is beaten with wood sticks to drive out the garbages inside. Then some portion of it is kept upon a flat stone and moved clockwise to prepare *undhaga* (round balls of wool). Sometimes a large wooden stick is taken and a portion of wool is tied in one end. The stick is moved and round ball is prepared. They prepare rope of this wool for domestic use like bringing bunches of wood sticks from jungle, lifting water by a bucket from the reservoir, to tie cattle during milking a cow or goat etc. For preparing the rope, two small twigs are taken and two persons stand each with one of these twigs atleast at a distance of hight two adult people and both twigs are moved in oppsite direction. Thus *duri* (rope) is prepared.

However, they cann't prepare carpet themselves out of this wool. They sell wool in the handlooms for this purpose at the rate of rupees thirty per kilogram. They receive carpet from the handloom at the rate of rupees sixty per kilogram which they not only use in their house but also sell in the market at higher rates. They also sell the wool balls directly in the market at the rate of rupees thirty five to forty per kilogram.

Role of men, women and children associated with animal husbandry

1. The work of cow-herding is done by the males both adult and child.
2. Generally adult females milk animals.
3. Milk products are prepared by the females.
4. Selling of milk products are done by the males.
5. Fetching of grasses for feeding cattle are done by both males and females.
6. Wool preparation and rope preparation are done by the males.

Thus there is a unique distribution of labour associated with pastoralism and animal hushandry.

Forest Management

It has already been mentioned that forest resources are scanty and the users are a large number who still depend upon forest for various things. Therefore, they always remain careful to maintain its proper utilisation. For example, they never cut the whole tree except the dried ones, rather collect the dry twigs of branches of the trees. Whenever a dried tree is cut off, another is replanted either by them or by the government staff as substitute to avoid deforestation in the locality. They do so because they know that 'galad istemalse kuch bhi nehi milega aur sab ret hi ret ho jayega, that is,' improper use will cause have creating lack of resources as well as expanding the desert in the area.

They collect a lot of items from the jungle. For example, they collect dry cowdung from the jungle as litter for fuel propose which is left by the cattle brought there for grazing and available in plenty. Further as fuel wood they collect dry twigs and branches of *khajuri, babool, jhal, lowa, bon, kumbhat, kakonda, ruida* and *akra.*

They also collect dry branches to use as timbers. For example, the door frame is made of the branches of *babool*. The branches of *khajuri* and *kumbhat* are used to make the plough and yoke.

The collect fodders from the jungle. *Ganthil* and *seban* are two types of grasses grow in plenty in the jungle which ae collected to feed the cattle in the houses. These are cut using *datri*, made of bunches, tagged by home-made rope, put upon the head and brought home.

They also collect a few fruits from the trees like *pilu* from *jhal, sangria* from *khajuri, ker* from *bon* and *bordhi* or *behr* from *bordhi* tree. They have their own grading system for fruits also. For example, two types of *pilu* are available here – one is sweet and the other bitter. Before plucking fruits they taste one piece from a tree and if it is found, sweet then only pluck fruits from that tree. Fruits collected from the trees are generally consumed by the members of the family and sometimes shared with the kin members also. In very rare case they sell the excess amount in the market. Previously they sold fuel wood in huge quantity in the market which at present they hardly do.

They also collect *khumbi* (mushroom) and honey from the forest but honey is rarely available. *Khumbi* is available from the onset of rainy season till the end of it but it is also collected occasionally.

All the forest products except timber and honey are collected by the female members. Only honey and timbers are collected by the male members.

Another important economic activity associated with forest is hunting which was once one of the major sources of maintaining livelihood. At present they hardly go for that being compelled due to the government banning over hunting of wild animals. However, still now they are very much fond of hunting and rarely they go for a hunt expedition, often hiding from others and return after hunting any wild boar, *hiron* (deer) or any bird like *battebari* or *titr,* the flesh of which they enjoy very much.

Hunting is collective effort of male members belonging to age group of above 12-14 who went for hunting and whatever they hunted were equally shared between every members after giving a good portion to the headman of the village and leader of that expedition and also to the person who hunted that particular animal. But as nowadays, being a secretive practice they form a very small group of persons either the members of a particular family or the member of the kin groups. However, they still distribute equal shares to the participants whatever they hunt.

Previsously they used *kulhari* and a large hard wooden stick (*danda*) as their hunting implements. At present they use double-barrel guns which were once given to them by the Rajput landlords for looking after their lands. They also use some traps which will be described later on.

They go for any hunting expedition in the dark nights and often on *Ambod* (the last day of the dark fortnight) to avail natural light. It is because they believe the animals would be aware of their existence in the moonlight. Further, they make it sure that on that night there must be heavy wind blowing from their opposite direction by which they would get the smell of animals but the animals would not get the smell of the hunters. Heavy wind blow also would hide the noise of their footsteps inside the jungle.

They also go with a few *Kotora* (utensils), large stone flakes and torch. For example, if they see any deer then one of them will create sound playing the *kotoras* to attract that deer, another will focus light of the torch in the eyes of that as a result its "*ankhen dhoudhia jayega*" that is, it would remain unmoved. The third person would hit upon its head by the *danda* by which it would become senseless. Then that is brought home.

Sometimes they use a trap called *kurr. Kurr* is iron made spring like instrument which in normal case remains wide and when any animal comes inside it gets closed and the animal cann't go out. Generally a small hole is dug in the path where the deers move and the *kurr* is kept inside it, then it is covered with leaves and wood-sticks so that no one can understand that there is a trap awaiting. When deer passes upon it and by any means one of its legs goes inside the *kurr* it cannot move any further and thus easily gets caught by the hunters. However, only the children use this trap, not the adult males; because hunting by traping one animal is treated as a matter of losing social prestige.

They also hunt one reptile called *sanda*, a squirrel like animal which generally remains under the earth surface in an area having sandy soil with stones and boulders and a source of water like stream or pool nearby. At that places the Bhils dig the earth using stones to collect *sanda*. They not only eat its flesh but use oil extracted from it as a medicine in pains also.

Religious beliefs and practices associated with forest

Forest is the abode of *Kolraidevi*, *Bhurebaba* and *Khetparji* – the Supreme Being in Bhil mythology. A temple of *Khetparji* who is equated with Lord Ganesha is situated at a distance of 5 km from Roopsi to the north-east. *Khetparji* is believed to be the deity by whose blessing they would get every success in activity. In the month of *Bhado* (August – September) and in the month of *Magha* (January-February) on the auspicious date of *Sukla Panchami* (the 5th day of the bright fortnight) in each month, *Khetparji* is worshipped there. People from each and every community gather there to take part. The Brahmans and the Banias (trading community) offer sweets to the deity while people of other communities sacrifice a goat in name of their community and village. A fair also takes place and both males and females participate in worshipping on such occasions. As *Khetparji* blesses people to achieve every success, he is worshipped on those particular dates and also before any lifecycle or annual ritual taking place in the village.

The temple of *Kolraidevi* – the mother goddess and source of energy (*Shaktimata*) is situated at a distance of 10 km. to the south-east of Roopsi beside *Tejwa ki Dhani*. People of every community come here also and there are separate temples for each and every community. Tehlaram, the Bhil *bhonpa* in Roopsi worships on behalf of the Bhils belonging to different villages in the temple for the Bhils. In the month of *Bhadra* and *Magha*, on the auspicious dates of thirteenth and fourteenth in the bright fortnight of those months, the worshipping take place. They offer butter, *misri* (one kind of dry sweet), coconut, *roti-churi*, goat and *gugri* to the deity. It is believed that by worshipping Her, they will get Her blessing by which good rain and good harvest will occur every season and everybody will remain well and prosperous.

It is also believed that *Bhurebaba* resides at that place where *Shaktimata* resides. He is the symbol of Lord Siva and worshipped by the Bhils only. His temple is located beside the temple of *Kolraidevi* within a *goopha* (cave). His worshipped takes place on the second days of the bright fortnight in the months of *Bhadra* and *Magha* and also during *Navaratri* in the month of *Ashuj* (September – October). He is worshipping during Navaratri as it is believed that during that period He had driven out the *Rakshasas* (evil forces) from the mountain and jungle to make the living of the Bhils peaceful there. On the other hand He is worshipped during the months of *Bhadra* and *Magha* as it is believed that He must be worshipped as "Father Shakti" prior to the worshipping of in "Mother Sakti" *Kolrai Devi* on these months. He is worshipped as the protector from all evil forces and it is believed that the Bhils can overcome every hazards by appeasing Him. He is offered coconut, *misri* and *batasa*. A goat is also offered in named of the Bhils.

They always try to maintain to save the purity of the forest. Though the temples of these deities are located at particular jungles but all jungles symbolically are treated as their abode. They believe that by maintaining the purity of the forest, they will enjoy the forest products for long days. Thus forest is kept in high esteem and looked after carefully so that nobody harms its sanctity. If they observe that any damage has taken place they throw cow-urine; which is believed to be as pure as the Ganga water, everywhere; sing devotional songs; offer fruits, sweets and a goat to the deities and partake such as their blessings as part of the purificatory rites.

Conservation of Forest

Not only to protect the sanctity of the forest, it is looked after carefully also as the Bhils receive a lot of things of their daily use from the forest still now. Previously they enjoyed each and every right in the forest land including hunting. However, though they do not have the ownership right over forest but they enjoy every right to collect forest products except hunting. Nowadays as forest belongs to the government, the government staff (Department of Forest) are looking after the trees and animals. They are always planting trees there to avoid deforestation and protect forest land.

The Bhils, as they are utilising forest products, also act as "volunteer guards" of the forest. They avoid lopping of trees without requirement and collect forest products in required quantity. The headman of every community and the Patwari of the village also look after that the forest products are collected properly. Forest is, thus, protected by the Bhils as a part of their life.

Solar Management

The Bhils are in the practice of drying up grains in direct sunlight. Therefore grains are kept in such places for drying up where sunlight falls through at the day long. As soon as the grains dry up, the seeds can be separated from it easily. Solar rays are also used in drying wet vegetables, for the preparation of *fofli, sebian* etc.

They generally build their houses when sunrays exist through long the day and no rainfall occurs. Thus they prefer summer and winter for this purpose. Cement and plaster in pakka houses and clay and cowdung in kacca houses require enough sunrays for drying up.

Role of Market

Nowadays, they are using two markets for purchasing or selling different commodities by monitory transaction. One is the village market situated in respective villages composed of a few general and stationary stores, from where they purchase flour, pulses, sugar, spices and other ration materials for their household use. It is found that as they produce only a few crops, they cannot subsist for the whole year. They are thus dependent on market for their subsistence to procure the crops. They also purchase soap, incense sticks, cosmatics etc. from the village market.

They also go to the city market of Jaisalmer at a distance of 18 km from the village Roopsi and 15 km from Bharamsar. They purchase there ornaments, dress material,, tea, *kumbhi* (mushroom), meat, wheat, horsegram, goar, vegetables, oils for cooking and kerosene etc. They sell sometimes wood-sticks, wool or any surplus forest fruits in the city market.

Sometimes *pashumela* (market for animal purchasing) take place in Jaisalmer from where they purchase and sell *pashudhan* (cattle).

Market is also the place of meeting where the Bhil of one village can interact with the Bhils of other villages in different matters. When a few members come for a purchase from the city market they also enjoy a movie in the cinema hall besides the work of marketing. Thus market secondarily acts as a media of passing leisure time and enjoyment. So the market has an important role in controlling the economic and social life of the Bhils in various ways.

Section IV

Economic Relationship

Man as a social animal always interacts with the surrounding environment. Thus, he establishes relationship ties with other men belonging to his family, kin, community, village and the broad environment formed of other villages. On the other hand he always is seen in interactional process with the physical or natural environment where he lives and acquires every resources to maintain his livelihood. Thus a man-nature relationship is specifically distinguished here. The human culture is shaped according to its environment both physical and social. The tribal culture as the economic organisation is related to the social organisation as well as ritualistic beliefs, hence it has to be seen holistically through the relationship formed by nature-man-spirit complex.

In a particular ecological set up the management of natural resources by a tribal community is determined by its wisdom coupled with its cultural norm and value system. This can be understood in terms of man-nature relationship, man-super nature relationship, man-plant relationship. The entire economic relationship by different economic activities exploiting different economic resources is the sum total of all these things.

Man-Nature Relationship

Man exploits nature according to his various requirements and nature appears to him in its various forms. For a Bhil the resources acquired from land, water, forest and hills are the gifts of nature. Therefore, it is observed that certain kind of nature are existing, certain beliefs and practices are taking place associated with agricultural activities where man exploits land or in a broader sense mother earth and again with forest. A mother-child relationship is always existing there which is described by the belief of not digging the earth on Tuesday when mother earth becomes bare-bodied to take a bathe. As they are cared by nature, they also take care of proper utilisation and maintenance of land, water, forest – all natural resources surrounding them.

Certain beliefs and practices are also existing associated with other natural objects and phenomena taking place in their environment which are described below.

Beliefs associated with the sun

According to them *subha* (dawn) is the period when the sun

appears in the east in the sky. From that period the sun starts his journey from east to west – the day time exists. When the sun becomes tired after reaching the west it starts sleeping – the twilight first and then the night begins. Thus they believe, like the sun, day time indicates the period of their activities and night is for sleeping. Therefore, they awake early in the morning, work throughout the day, return in the evening from work to take rest, take supper and go to bed at night. Again they awake with the awakening of the sun next day. Further they believe also that the time of sunrise – beginning of the day is the time of God. If the sun does not arise all animals and birds will die because they can't go to get their food. Setting of the sun on the other hand, is time of the end of the day, end time of the daily activities, time of taking rest as the sun set declares the starting of night. The sun is treated by them as a god who starts his journey in the morning to meet his mother every day during evening. As a result day and night occurs.

The solar rays are believed to be the grace of God. It was, be at a time used for fire making also. Previously they kept the dry wood of *akra* or *bordhi* upside and a white stone (*gachhia*) down and by friction of this, fire was produced. Then they applied glass to lit fire. Dry cowdung was kept at a place and solar rays passing through a glass upon the dry cowdung created fire. However, at present fire is produced using fuel and matches.

Moon

They have their beliefs associated with the states of moon which is a common belief of all the communities. They acquire this idea within the locality as well as by exchanging thoughts with other communities. According to this belief the moon had 27 wives of whom he loved one and drove away others. The fathers of other 26 wives cursed the moon that he would become short for ever. Then the moon agreed to accept his wives again but one day would be for accepting one wife. Thereafter the fathers said that whenever one wife would go to his palce his size would increase and whenever she would leave that place his size would decrease. On the day of *poonam* (fullmoon) all the 27 wives reside at the moon's house and his full size is observed. On *amabos*. all the wives leave his house and he never appears on that day. Moon is also treated as god. According to his appearance that is his size, they calculate *tithia* (auspicious dates). For example, during *ashad* (June-July) *dooj* (the second day of the bright fortnight) is an auspicious date treated as the day of Loard Siva. On that night seeing the structure of the moon the farmers assume whether good rainfall would occur or not. If it shapes like a plough, then it is assumed that good rain would occur. Again if its structure appears as 'U' in English alphabet, is the indication of poor rainfall. Thus this is directly associated with their economy.

Stars and Constellations

They believe that a man after death becomes star in the sky. When an honest man dies he becomes a shining star. Belief regarding *akashganga* (constellations) is associated with the Bhil life cycle rituals. During marriage a bachelor boy and girl drink a kind of syrup made of salt water which indicates the end of their bachelor life and starting of conjugal life procreating a legitimate family. It is believed that if a boy or girl dies before marriage then he/she is indebted of that salt; that is, before procreating a family they died and their this-worldly life ended incompletely. *Akashganga* is the *marg* (route) of those souls departed before fulfilling a compelte life. Their journey never ends. They throw salt in their part and *Kalindernag* (snake) drives them from the behind from one place to other through the route. *Kalindernag* thus symbolically represents here the pain of the death before fulfilling the complete life of a human being.

Planets

Beliefs associated with planets are again a common belief. Planets (*nabograha*) are controlling power of human fate and if one of these becomes angry, the human being falls in danger. The Saturn (*Shani*) is the most dangerous among all planets.

Comets

Comets are called *chotiwala taro* or *puchhwalo taro* (stars having tails). It is believed that due to the anger of any goddess, these stars appear. Then they prepare a star made of cowdung keeping it upon a stone slab. *Mehendi* (dye) and *chaul* (rice) are added to it and then a part is eaten by everybody. They believe that the goddess would become happy on the performance of this activity and no harm would be effected.

Beliefs associated with meteorites are related to black magic. When a magician comes in the village and shows his magic and on the same night if they observe any shooting star falling on the earth they believe, the star is broken by the magic of the magician and therefore it fell down on the earth.

Energy

They believe that energy exists in the sun, in the earth and in the human being, in the natural objects like stones, in the water. They observe when two palms are rubbed massively those become hot or when two stones are rubbed massively fire arises. These are the indications of energy. God creates this energy for the benevolence of all living creatures.

Space and Time

Space is above the sky having no limit and the abode of gods and goddesses, the sun, the moon, the planets, the stars and the constellations. Time is calculated showing the shadow of the trees during day time. Life grows with the advancement of time – a baby becomes adult then old. If a baby is observed with large ears is believed to be long living.

Gravitation

They narrated gravitational forces as everything comes downward towards the earth surface because *dhartimata* (the mother earth) loves everything and attracts everything towards her lap.

Season

They have conception of three seasons one succeeding another and treat it as a natural phenomenon. It is believed that this succession of seasons take place for their benefit as the grace of God Almighty. First season is the *Unaru* or *Unara* (summer) comprising four months – *Fagun* (February–March), *Chet* (March-April), *Vaisakh* (April – May) and *Jeth* (May – June). Then comes *Barsaru* or *Barsala* (rainy season) comprising another four months – *Ashad* (June – July), *Shavan* (July – August), *Bhado* (August – September) and *Ashuj* (September – October). It is followed by *Siaru* or *Siara* (Winter) comprising the rest four months *Katik* (October – November), *Meghar* (November – December), *Pous* (December – January) and *Magha* (Jaunary – February). From their observation they found that during the rainy season *badal* (clouds) appear from which rain showers and in the winter *kohra* (fogs) occur.

Eclipse

In long past the Bhil had no idea about eclipse. But when interaction started with other communities they hold a common idea about the reason behind happening of eclipses. In their language they call it *nonde*. According to their belief there was once a hill inside the sea.

The *Shankar Bhagwan* (Lord Siva) separates the poison from *Amrit* (the divine liquor). Poison was given to the *Rakshasas* (evil power) and *amrit* to gods. One rakshas partakas part of it sitting hiddenly beside the gods. The sun and the moon identified him and told Lord Vishnu about him. Vishnu killed him but as he had taken a part of *amrit* he did not die but became two *rakshasas* Rahu and Ketu. When they tried to eat the sun and moon, *nonde* occurs. The Bhils identify Sankar Bhagan as their Supreme Being *Bhurebada*. Previously the Bhils did not perform anything during eclipse but nowadays under the influence of the Brahmans and the Banias they at present observe fasting during this time.

Earthquake

They have related the earthquake with the perception about virtue and vice. Virtue is to maintain the life-style according to the cultural norms of their community and breach of such is vice. A vice made by one man damages the whole community and the village. They believe that when vice increases tremendously the mother earth cann't bear the strain and starts moving (*hilte hai*) and as a result earthquake takes place.

They have given two more popular narrations regarding earthquake. One, there is water at the bottom underneath the earth surface. There is the *sarpa nag* (a snake) upon the water holding an ox upon its hood. The ox holds *dhartimata* (mother earth) upon one of its horn. When the ox shifts the earth from one horn to the oher then the earthquake happens due to that movement. According to the second narration, there is one large bird which lay the egg from the sky. The baby bird comes out from the egg and start flying in the sky. The shell comes down upon the earth surface. As a result of which earthquake happens. Whatever may be the reason, the people believe that if earthquake happens heavy rainfall will occur. Thus it is also related with their economy.

Thunderstorm

Beliefs associated with thunderstorm is also a common characteristic feature of the villagers. According to their understanding, after the birth of Lord Krishna his father kept him in a house of Nandalala and brought his newly-born daughter. With their arrival in the prison of King Kongsho, the people who were sleeping, woke up and informed Kongsho about the baby. Kongsho appeared there and threw the baby in the sky. That daughter disappeared creating the thunderstorm. Kongsho becomes a metal of daily use today the *Kansa* (bell metal). At present whenever that daughter becomes angry she expresses her anger upon Kongsho and at that time thunderstorm takes place. At that time utensils made of bell-metal are not kept outside to save those from the anger of that daughter. That is done not to save a man of vice but to save their daily utensils, damage of which will cause economic loss to them.

They have given a second narration of thunderstorm also. *Ghor* (lightening) occurs when two clouds touch each other in joy and their laugh is expressed as thunder. Thus nature is expressing her happiness due to the arrival of rainy season and that she expresses by lightning and thunder. After a heavy shower *indradhanush* (rainbow) is appeared in the sky. According to their belief it is the facial expression of happiness of the nature being relieved by the shower after a hot summer.

Flood and Draught

Beliefs associated with flood and draught are related to some conception of auspiciousness – inauspiciousness. In normal condition rains during the rainy season makes every landscape green. After the end of the rainy season, due to lack of water, the greenery starts to dry up. They calculate the emergence and occurrence of draught and flood by seeing some inauspicious signs like a barren woman coming in front of male members without *ghunghat* or a newly widow coming in front of other male members wearing black *urni* (scarf). The first sign is the cause of draught taking a barren lady as the symbol of drought. Second sign is the cause of flood with the implication that when a recently widowed lady comes outside before another man means after killing her husband with the flood of her sex she is approaching to kill another man.

Again it is believed that when a man sitting upon a *tilla* observes a *behl* (ox) infront, treates it as a sign for good rainfall.

Rain and Frost

They believe that rains are a normal factor during rainy season by which people, plant, animal – everyone is benefitted. Frost, formulation is rare here in winter. Winter is oneway treated as a season of loss specially when it becomes so cool that frost is formed and it damages crops. Birds and animals die in extreme cold. Sometimes during winter rain takes place. The drops are formed of half water-half ice.

Wind

From their observation they have formed certain beliefs associated with wind blow. They observe that wind blows south to north during summer, north to south during winter and from every direction during rainy season which causes several natural phenomena. Heavy wind blow takes place during summer and light but cold wave occurs during winter. They perceive the hot wave (*loo*) occurs during summer because after becoming hot the sand and soil particles become light and fly from one area to other with the blow of the wind. To save themselves from *loo* they keep water and onion with them, which they drink and eat regularly. Sometimes *dhool bhori hava* or *andhi* (dust storm) blows during summer which is also caused by extreme heating of the sand and soil particles. It also creates problems to the shepherds. When *andhi* occurs they generally sit under a tree covering their faces to keep themselves safe from *andhi*. *Chakraborti Hawa* (whirl wind) takes place during rainy season. When the sky is shadowed by thick cloud no wind blows, soil becomes so hot that suddenly one wind blow is observed to move in a rotating movement from the earth surface toward upward. They relate the occurrence of *chakraborti hawa* to the movement of ghosts and evil spirits. At that time they pray to god to save them from the evil spirits. That is to say when they cannot get the proper explanation in their mind behind any natural phenomena, they simply relate it with the world of spirit or some supernatural objects. During rainy season storm or heavy wind blows frequently. The surrounding becomes smoky. Sometimes it becomes *bhutiara* (another kind of whirlwind) also. It rotates and suddenly becomes a heavy storm (*toofan*) and spreads everywhere creating a lot of damage. As they called it *bhutiara* or relate it with the ghost or spirit world, they pray to god to save them on such occasions.

Sound

They believe sound is created by friction of two hard things like two stones. When they talk sound is created by friction of palet and tongue. Friction between one hard and one soft things creates a low sound. They have given an example. If a metal body drops upon a stone creates a larger sound than when it drops upon sand.

Echo

They believe that during rainy season when wind blow is interrupted by hillocks (*mogre*) echoes occur there if anybody shouts loudly. However, auspicity inauspicity concepts are not associated with the origin of echoes.

Form

They perceive three kinds of forms–*gol* (round), *tinkhun* (triangle) and *chowkhun* (square). *Gol* and *chowkhun* forms are useful while *tinkhun* forms are not. A stone flake triangular in shape is of no work. Thus a man who does not come in the benefit of society, is commonly called as *tinkhuni admi*.

Colour

In their conception there are six type of colours viz. *seri* (white), *hari* (green), *geru* (red), *pila* (yellow), *bhura* (brown) and *kaile* (black). They conceptualise these six colours observing their surroundings.

Shadow

According to their perception shadow occurs due to the movement of the sun from one direction to another. There must be any object before the light source on the opposite of which shadow occurs. Shadow helps to calculate the time also during day and even now the olderly persons are observed to say exact time not seeing a watch, just looking a shadow.

Reflection

When the sunrays come upon a water surface it reflects which has been keenly observed by these people. They believe that if a baby observes such reflection he will fall ill and may suffer from loose motion. Then the baby requires treatment and the *bhonpa* (medicine man) drives away his disease by his supernatural power. However the young children or the adult are not affected by observing that reflection.

Water

They believe water is a supreme gift of the mother nature. According to their concept, being hot, the *bhutiara* (whirl wind) pulls the water of *samundar* (sea) in the sky. During rainy season that water moves in the sky as cloud and drops upon the earth surface as rain which reaches inside the earth surface. They dig it and make wells and thus get water from there. According to their concept *Samundar* (sea) is as large as the sky and full of water. This is the source of rain water. They said that *Samundar* is situated beside Karachi (Pakistan). When wind blows upon the sea, *lahar* (waves) are generated. Though they have no such idea about tides, they believe that in less depth no *bor* (current) occur. However, if a place of more depth is situated beside a place of less depth, the sea current occurs. Whirlpools, according to them, occur in the deep sea when water moves forming circles with the heavy wind blow. They call it *bhounrio* of water.

According to their perception a stream or river originates from the hills or hillocks. It comes full of water when there is heavy shower in the hills. However, lakes, according to them, is constructed by any person and it is not a creation of nature. They have given one example of lake Amarsagar situated at a distance of 15 kms from Roopsi and 18 kms from Bharamsar which was created by Raja Amar Singha of Jaisalmer. Floods happen when streams are overflowed with rain water however the belief associated with flood has already been described.

Among the hydrographic phenomena they describe *osh* (dew) which occurs during winter. They observe that it showers from the sky in the morning but the phenomenon is never seen in bare eyes. It is observed upon the grasses as dew and they also understand its existence when they see their garments become wet in it.

Water in both the villages are sweet in taste. However, it has been mentioned earlier that they have the concepts about salt water which according to them, is available in Sam and other villages nearby – situated at a distance of 25-35 kms from Roopsi. They observe huge foam occurs in salt water when people use soap. Further beside the sources white patches of salt are observed by them and from there people extract salt in that locality.

Registan (Desert)

The striking feature of this area is *ret* (sand) or *registan* (desert) which is caused by lack of water and rainfall in the area. *Ret* is used in their daily work like cleaning of utensils. Being the resident of *registan* where water is less, other resources are less, they become habituated to utilise the resources properly. Thus *registan* has a great role to shape their socio-economic life.

Magre (hillock/hill)

The Bhils conceptualise *magre* (hillock/hill) as land full of stones and small *kankar* (gravels) stand up above the earth surface. Land between two hills is called *jamin* which is almost plain and where water can be bound constructing *dhore.* Wheat and horsegram can be cultivated here. Caves are situated upon the hills and is the abode of one of their Supre Being *Bhurebaba.*

Up and Down

As there are hill areas people have the concept of *niche* (downward) and *chari* (upward). They perceive that water (rain water) flows always downward. If they throw something even towards upward direction that comes downward. However a man has the capability to go up or down stream by walking. According to their belief, it is the grace of god by which they are enjoying such power.

They perceive that everything in their surrounding is *'kudrat ke kamal'* or gift of the mother nature. Therefore, there is *hariyali* (greenery) in the *Kharins* within the *registan; patthar* (stones) in the hillock for their livelihood and whatever forest is available there with full of resources for them. Thus they feel happy with whatever is available to them from the nature.

They conceive it as the blessing of God Almighty. As they are nurtured by the nature, they also take proper care to protect the natural resources; thus a mother–child relationship exists between nature and the Bhils.

Man-Supernature (God) Relationship

Apart from the natural objects and 'super-natural' spirits mentioned so far, the Bhils have interactions with other 'supernatural' beings like gods and goddesses appeasing of which give them the surety of better livelihood – thus providing them prosperity and wealth. As a result, this kind of relationship comes under the discussion of economic relationship. It has already been mentioned that they worship *Khetparji*, *Kolraidevi* and *Bhurebaba*. Besides they also worship *Kalkadevi* (goddess Kali), *Pabuji* and *Samad*.

Kalkadevi is worshipped by all Bhils of the locality though worshipping of Her is organised by the Bhils of Roopsi village. All Bhils of Roopsi belong to the clan Kaliana, which according to them is derived from their origin of *Kalkadevi*. As she is their clan deity they organise the worshipping of Her. She is worshipped on the auspicious dates of 4th, 13th or 14th in the bright fortnight in the months of *Bhadra* and *Magha*. Tehlaram, the Bhil *bhonpa* in

Roopsi officiates the ceremony. She is offered butter, *misri,* coconut, *roti-churi*, *gugri* and a he-goat. All Bhils irrespective of age and sex participate in it and they make a common fund providing subscription for the expenditure of the worshipping. It is believed by them that she will protect them from every hazard.

Pabuji is worshipped by all Bhils irrespective of age and sex in the month of *Bhadra* on the auspicious nineth day of the bright fortnight. All of them provide subscription for its worshipping. He is offered coconut, molasses and *ghee*. He is worshipped as he protects their cattle from all problems. Thus it is directly related to their economic benefit.

Samad is not a deity. He was a *Bhagat* who took *jiut Samadhi* (He took burial while he was alive). All Bhils and people of other communities in this area worship him on auspicious 2nd day in the months of Bhadra and Magha.

Man-Plant and Man-Animal Relationship

Plant and animals are living creatures in the nature. Those may provide benefit to them or harm them. Thus the Bhil has distinct relationship with the plants and animals in the locality. Plants provide them fruit, fuel, timber on one hand and on the other some of the plants or plant parts or their derivatives have medicinal value. For example, neem is seen to be planted in the courtyard in majority of the Bhil houses. It is looked after with great care. All the Bhils know its medicinal value. A few of its leaves are pasted and the extracted juice is given to a person affected with fever every hour by which he is cured quickly. This juice is also applied locally upon the wounds and injuries. Leaves of neem are heated and applied to skin infections. Neem twigs are used to clean teeth. Ker, pilu, sangria are fruits they collect locally from trees available in the locality, one, herb called *Chandel* is also collected. Its juice is given to the adult pneumonia patients. For cough and cold they apply a mixture, locally called *kara,* made of cloves, black pepper, *shoont* and nutmeg at night. They cultivate *taramira,* a mustard like crop and extract its oil which is applied for burn case mixing with turmeric. On the other hand they treat *thor* and *akra* as poisonous and only dry wood of these pants are used as fuel.

They divide animals mainly in two categories – domesticated animals and wild animals. Among the domesticated animals there are the cattle and apart from those they domesticate dog and cat. All domesticated animals have economic values. Cattle are not only used for providing milk and milk products, wool but also as means of agriculture and transport (ox and camel). Further he-goat is used for sacrifice to the deities to appease them and get their blessings for economic prosperity. Dog protects their property and crop while cat kills mice in the house and agricultural field. Cow urine is used as a sacred object and treated as sacred like the Ganga water. It is used during worshipping or before threshing of corns to make a land sacred for use. Cowdung has multipurpose use as fuel, fertilizer and material for smearing floor, courtyard and also the walls and roof of *jhupura* and *kacca* hut.

On the other hand they divide the wild animals in two categories like harmful and non-harmful. Among the harmful animals, there are the birds like peacock which damages the crop. But it is beneficial also as it kills poisonous snakes. All the snakes in the locality are deadly poisonous thus causes human death and as a result labour force decreases. Therefore, they kill the snakes wherever found. They are aware of four types of *bicchu* (scorpion) – *kala* (black), *pila* (yellow), *urneoala* (flying) and *kambnia* —all of these are dealy poisonous and avoided with fear. *Kambnia* is so dangerous that touch of it will cause death. The insects found in the locality are also treated harmful and some of these are poisonous also. Previously they hunted a few birds like *battebari, gatta, titr* etc. And a few animals like *hiron* and *khorgosh* which nowadays they cann't do due to government banning over hunting. They avoid man-eating animals like *jarokh* (hyena).

Since long past they are treating observation of some birds like *titr*, *suganchiri* as auspicious before going for agricultural operations. Some birds and animals have medicinal values also. They believe as the *battebari* bird digests stones, eating its flesh they will be cured of diseases like kidney or stomach stones or urinary tract infections. *Bijii* – another animal, though at present found rarely, is also beneficial to them like *sanda,* a reptile. *Bijji* is as large as cat and hare. After killing it and *sanda*, oil is extracted from the fat portions of these animals. This oil is rubbed locally for any pain as this is a very good pain killer. Nowadays, killing of *bijii* is not easy because it moves fast and sometimes attacks a man from behind and bites the lower vein of leg from back. As a result the man loses his potentiality to walk and sometimes death occurs.

Man-Man Relationship

Man-man relationship is discussed here under three subheadings

– first, intra-community level, then inter-community level and finally interaction with other agencies.

(A) Intra-community Level

It has been discussed here in two forms – first relationship with the heads and second relationship between the commoners.

(I) Relationship with the Heads

The headman of the Bhil community is called *Jam*. In past days he was paid a great respect and he had the main decision making role. His decisions were final regarding any matter and everybody had to abide by his instructions. But at present as the Bhils find him making favour to somebody that is irrational, his status is decreased in the society. For example, in Roopsi, there is no single *jam* rather a group of elderly persons (*panch*), are taking decisions simultaneously and uniformly. In Roopsi case, it is found that the Bhils are divided in two large political groups – BJP and Congress (I). But whenever any dispute occurs the Bhil leaders of each party sit together to solve the matter. Further in any other dispute they proceed to court for solution.

Most of the people worship their household deities themselves and no priest is engaged for that. The community deities either are worshipped by *bhonpa* or by other elderly members of the community. Only during marriage the Meghwal *garg* (a priestly class) are appointed to officiate the matter whom they treat as *gurus*.

Bhonpa acts as *guru,* medicine-man and as the mediator between people and the God/spirit world. He is still now kept in high esteem. He drives away diseases by his spiritual power. The Bhils reported that whenever anybody gets ill either he chooses plant therapy or goes to the hospital for medical treatment on one hand and on the other still now they approach to *bhonpa* simultaneously to get his blessing to get relief from the disease.

(II) Commoner's Relationship

Coomoners' relationship is of brotherlyhood. Everybody treats his fellow Bhilman as his brother and helps him in his requirements. It is also found that the mutual exchange of labour are taking place during agricultural operations. When any worship takes place everybody provides equal subscription and labour for the purpose. Everybody participates and provides manual labour when birth of a baby takes place or any marriage or death occurs.

In the family level every member performs his and her duties according to the distribution of work without any hesitation.

(B) Inter-Community Relationship

The Rajput-Bhil interaction is this area started since long past when they served the Rajput landlords as their labourers and watchmen in agricultural fields. They were humiliated and received half-day meal from the Rajput whom they revered in fear and maintained a hatred for them. They were cheated by the *Banias* (merchant class) also and the banias were kept at a distance. After independence the situation has been better to some extent due to the introduction of formal education and distribution of lands to them by the government. With the greater political interest, interactions started also with these communities. The high castes are now somehow in closer relationship with the Bhils than the previous days.

Formerly the relation with the Meghwal, another low caste community was not amiable but now in the changed perspective it is warm. They are invited in the ceremonies and festivities organised by the Bhils. The Meghwal *garg* officiates in the marriage and naming of the newborn of the Bhils. This close relation is also found in labour exchange system which is described earlier.

In modern situation every community is divided into two political parties BJP and Congress (I). As a Bhil lady is the *Sarpanch* (head of panchayat) in Roosi, she and her Bhil supporters belonging to Cong (I) are receiving support from the followers of this party belonging to other communities. This lady is elected defeating another Bhil lady belonging to BJP and she also finds her supporters from every community. Thus modern politics on one hand divides the communities in two halves and also on the other hand it brings all the communities in close connection with the Bhils. In other ways it helps in developing their economic condition. As they belong to labour class they work and earn in any panchayat operation and receive full support from the high caste communities in doing such.

(C) Interaction with Other Agencies : Relationship with the Govt. and Govt. Officials

In general the Bhil observe that they are benefitted a lot from the government. Government provides them land, education for children, better medical facilities, potable water by making deep tubewells in the village, pakka house in the Indira Awas Yajana scheme, job opportunity in government labour works etc. However, they are a bit disappointed with the government for its banning over hunting wild animals and birds which they are very much fond of; though they believe excess killing of animals and birds is a social curse. They say they will be happy if government provides them a partial relaxation in hunting during occasions.

However, they are very much disappointed with the behavior and treatment they receive from the local government officials. They cann't meet the patwaris neither in his office nor in the village. Government has a monthly scheme to pay elderly persons an amount of rupees two hundred and fifty. Government has another scheme to provide their children books and exercise books free of cost which they do not receive. Even the officials encroach the government amount distributed for their treatment facility and they do not get the benefit of it. Cheating by government and bank officials also take place when they take any loan. They say that even if they pay back, that amount is not deposited to their accounts and digested by the particular official. As a result amount of loan never decreases. The Bhils hate these cheater officials very much.

The relationship with the local village panchayat is better. Commonly there is no direct role of the panchayat in the natural resource management and it is observed by the elderly members of every community, but panchayat interrupts in any local level dispute within the village and provides a friendly solution acceptable by all. However, if anybody does not have the *patta* or ownership of a *khatedari* land but uses it, the *sarpanch* can drive him out or give him the required *patta*. Nobody can challenge his decision in this regard. Panchayat decides the matter who will receive economic benefit from the government. In the Roopsi case as the Bhils are now in power, they can misuse it. But as they are divided and they have inter-actions with other communities there is no indulgence in this regard and they are happy with their panchayat. Both in Bharamsar and Roopsi the economic organisation of the Bhils is composed of community level organisation at the bottom and village level organisation at the top.

Section V

Summary and Conclusion

The resources available to the Bhil in the desert ecology and how they utilise their resources, how they interact with the nature and the people in their surrounding have been discussed in the preceding sections. It has been described how they are coping up with the changing situation applying their traditional wisdom. Culture is dynamic and therefore it accumulates new elements and once that becomes institutionalised, becomes part of that culture. Therefore, what is modern today will become tradition tomorrow. In this chapter the findings would be summarised and how the traditional wisdom helps them in managing their environment and natural resources may be reviewed here.

From the first section it is clear that the literacy rate among the Bhils is very poor. In this area very often they show cultural practices which are more regional than ethnic specific. It is because they do not live in absolute isolation and their contact with people of other communities exist here since long past mainly for economic reasons.

The Bhils of Bharamsar reported that traditionally they were labourers while Roopsi Bhils said they were cultivators. However, the Roopsi Bhils actually meant that they cultivated the lands of Rajput landlords as agricultural labourer (*mantak majduri*). Thus they got expertise in different sorts of labour work since long past. Only after the independence of India in 1947, they were given small amounts of land for settled cultivation where they started cultivation depending solely upon rainwater for irrigation.

In desert situation land is the prime economic resource. Jaisalmer desert shows all typical characterisitics of a hot desert on the one hand, like sand dumes made of loose soils; stony rocks with full of gravels, pebbles and rubbles and land with a desolate surface of bedrock; on the other. There is also green patches with full of grasses, bushes and thorny shrubs. Therefore, people living here for long periods have notions of different kinds of lands and their utility. Thus there are *khet* and *kharin* lands for agriculture; *pali bheudi* which is used as permanent pasture and grazing land, *rui* (forest), *magre* (stony rocks) and *ret ke tile* (sand dunes) as major land types in this locality.

A few among the Bhils reported that they own *murba* or fertile land beside the Indira Gandhi Canal but as quality of those lands are poor and that area is far away from these villages, they hardly go to cultivate there. Thus they cultivate only in *khet* and *kharin*. Table 12 shows that in Bharamsar 64.71 percent people have any kind of agricultural land and 35.29 percent are landless while in Roopsi 68.62 percent people own some kind of land 31.37 percent are landless.

Table 8 shows that only 11.76 percent Bhils in Bharamsar and 5.88 percent Bhils in Roopsi have agriculture as their primary mode of income. As stones are available in this area in plenty, and demand for stone materials in the modern world is vast, majority of the Bhils are engaged in stone-cutting and related labour works (64.71 percent in Bharamsar and 58.82 percent in Roopsi). Thus, it has become the prime income source. On the other hand as permanent pastures and gazing land is available here, a few persons have adopted pastoralism as their prime source of income (13.73 percent in Roopsi). As income in this profession increases with the increase in size of the herd, it is not possible for too many persons to accept this as their primary income source. The landless people are dependent upon stone related labour works and pastoralism while cultivation satisfies only as mode of secondary and tertiary income for the people having land (29.41 percent and 5.88 percent in Bharamsar and 39.22 percent and 21.57 percent respectively in Roopsi).

As agriculture is a work of hard toil they take every measures to have a good crop. Except using cowdung as manure they never use any chemical fertilizers which are believed to spoil natural fertility. They take care in seed selection also. Crop rotation also takes place and they prefer cultivation of a few crops at a time in the same land of which some crops are much water consuming and some are less, thus neutralising the water requirement. Traditional instruments and mechanisms are mostly used which is explored at length in the third section. *Dhore* (contour) are constructed within two lands to bind water and a few kind of trees are planted upon *dhore* to stop soil erosion. Crops are protected from cattles and birds carefully and the landowner protect crops from cattle and birds carefully and the landowner has every right to capture the cattle of others if are found to damange his crops and demand penalty from owner of the cattle. Threshing is done mainly in traditional way and wind energy is used for winnowing applying traditional wisdom. As modern education is penetrating among them, though in a slower speed than in other communities, a few of them are practicing mechanised ways of cultivation at present to some extent.

After adopting so many precautions they are not very much sure of producing a bumper crop which is reflected through their dependency upon supernatural beings for this purpose. Thus, before agricultural operation they perform a few rites to appease certain gods and goddesses, try to foresee the occurrence of rainfall by observing certain good signs which are mentioned before.

They have their notions about locally available soils and their utility. They know very well about the stones available in their surroundings. Stones are required in different modern activities like construction of buildings, road construction, construction of railway slipper etc. and hence demand for stones and stone related activities are increasing everyday. Yellow stone is an important feature in this area and it is utilised for building forts, palaces since long past. It is also utilised in construction of utensils, images etc. Any activity related to stone like cutting, loading and unloading requires hard labour and the Bhils are habituated in hard labour work since long past. Hence they easily have accepted this profession as their prime source of income. It is interesting to note that there is no belief in supernatural entities associated with stone cutting.

Lives-stocks in forms of cattle and other domesticated animals serve them as important resources. Cattles not only provide them milk, wood, fuel as dung; act as means of agriculture and transport but it also provides them money in need being sold to others in the market. Cats and dogs give them protection from mice, snakes and other animals. They prepare ropes in their houses made of wool of camels, sheeps and goats which are utilised in several domestic works and also sold in the market. The village animals are identified by special marks given upon the bodies of the animals, however, their traditional wisdom help them to identify their personal cattle without giving any mark of identification for such.

Though forest resources are scanty but those are managed with great care and utilised in plenty for different purposes. Forest is the source of litter, fuel, timber, fodder, fruits, honey, mushroom etc. The Bhils are basically jungle-dwelling community. Therefore, since long past they have the habit of hunting. Due to the government banning over hunting they have almost stopped this practice, however, rarely they go for a hunt secretly for enjoyment. Hunting was performed utilising traditional instruments and a hunt by trapping is treated as a loss of social prestige to them. A few animals were killed because of their medicinal values like *sanda, battebari* (bird), *bijii* etc. Forest is treated with a great esteem as there is the abode of their deities by appeasing whom they believe, they would overcome every hazard.

In all sort of activities the Bhil have a distinct division of labour work. Workforce is the forms of main workforce and auxiliary work force are important resource to them which help them in maintaining every activity in domestic sphere and outside, properly. Very rarely they require labour from other persons. Women share the workload with the men but in money-earning professions they are given a less amount of cash than their male counterparts. They have a distinct labour exchangeship also. When they exchange labour with the kins or the Bhils of the same village, labour is reciprocated by labour. When labour is exchanged with the Bhils belonging to other villages who are non-kins and with the Meghwals, labour is reciprocated by mid-day meal and labour. But while they hire labour from other caste people that is paid in cash. It shows the distinct relationship of the communities. The Meghwal is a scheduled caste community who are treated at par or just above them in the caste hierarchy and hence a warm relation is maintained with them which is reflected through the system of reciprocity.

Market plays an important role in present day Bhil life as a place of purchasing and selling commodities, cattle and as a place of meeting with the Bhils of other villages. It is also a place of passing leisure time by seeing movies etc.

In the desert ecology the conservation of water resources and its proper management is one of the prime requirements. Water is utilised for drinking purposes for the human being and the cattle, for domestic work and for irrigation. Irrigation solely depends upon rainwater in this area and therefore the Bhils construct *dhore* within two lands to bind that water. Rain water is also preserved constructing large *talab* (tank), well (*berry*) etc. Previously water was brought in *pakhals* (leather bags) by means of camel transport from remote places. Applying their wisdom they dug wells in such areas where they found rainwater accumulated during a heavy shower. Water is preserved in reservoirs in individual houses since long past. Nowadays after the implementation of modern tubewell in the villages the Bhils have overcome the problem of water shortage even during the summer. From the tubewell, water is brought in large scale by camel tankers or tankers driven by mechanised tractors in individual houses to preserve that in the reservoirs for all sort of domestic use. Potable water is brought by the female members from tubewells in buckets, pitchers and other steel vessels. They also take special care for proper use of that water.

The Bhils in the locality are very much dependent upon natural resources for their livelihood. Hence they treat themselves children of the mother nature and take proper care of the natural resources. Their beliefs in the virtue and vice, auspicity and inauspicity are associated with the natural phenomena and happenings in the natural environment take a great role in shaping their mental frame and culture. Therefore, they relate the period from dawn to dusk as the time of work with the movement of the sun, stars with the departed souls; constellations with the soles departed before completing lifecycle, time with the advancement of life and so on. Appearance of seasons are treated as the gift of mother nature, the supreme being, for different sort of activities. As agriculture solely depends upon rainwater, they try to foresee the occurrence of rain by certain kinds of signs of auspiciousness, inauspiciousness. Again certain kinds of phenomena or concepts narrated as part of a greater regional culture like earthquake, eclipse, planets, comets, thunderstorm, etc., meteorites are treated as black magical effect while the whirlwind which is a natural phenomenon during summer, is related to the ghost world. They conceptualise different colours and forms observing their natural setting. They believe that despite their serious effort they may not succeed unless get the favour of supernatural beings, gods and goddesses. As their technology is insufficient in agriculture they depend upon the gods and goddesses, on the other hand as stone related works are the demand of modern market economy, beliefs in supernatural forces are not associated with it. However, from their traditional wisdom they have developed certain measures to produce multiple crops by properly utilising the scanty water available to them.

They have knowledge about the medicinal values of certain plant and animal species. Due to non-availability of the animal species in plenty and government banning over hunting, use of animals for medicinal purpose is decreasing every day. As they believe life is the gift of god or nature, though they are adopting modern medicines, they go to the *bhonpa* simultaneously to get the favour of the gods.

They form certain kind of relationships with the people both in intra-and inter-community level. The elderly persons of the Bhil community (*panch*) and the *bhonpa* (medicine man and mediator with the supernatural world) are treated with great respect. The *panch* look after the proper utilisation of the natural resources available and also solve disputes arouse both in intra-community and intercommunity levels. All the Bhils in the village and of other villages maintain a relationship of fraternity and brotherhood while relationship with the Meghwals, the scheduled case group, is very warm. It is reflected through the labour exchange system and through the appointment of a Meghwal *garg* (priestly class) for officiating Bhil marriages. Though previously the Bhils revered the upper castes especially the Rajputs and Banias with a great hatred for them in mind, but at present modern politics bring these castes closer. However, though they have great respect for the government due to the launching of beneficial programme for them, but except the *Sarpanch* (headman of the panchayat) other government officials, bank officials are hated for their practice of cheating the simple Bhils still now.

So from the above discussion it is clear that the Bhils in this locality are very much eco-friendly in nature. As literacy rate is poor among them they remain more tradition-bound than any other community. The places where inter-annual variability of rainfall reaches from 50 to 100 percent and agriculture depends upon that rainwater for irrigation, it cannot become the source of primary income of the people. Therefore the people who practice agriculture to some extent take every care to be sure of success of their hard toil. This is reflected from not utilising chemical fertilizer according to their belief, cautiousness in seed selection, construction of contour to bind rainwater in one land and the system of draining it to the other, giving preference to multiple cropping at a time etc. On the other hand, to have bumper crop they appease the gods and goddesses and perform other rituals according to their belief. They take utmost care in utilising forest resources properly. Since long past they are habituated in all sort of labour works and they have proved themselves fittest in stone-related labour works. Their traditional wisdom helps them in this regard to a great extent. As this they perform in demand of modern market, an excessive amount of money which has improved their economic condition in one hand and on the other no beliefs in supernatural is seen to be associated with this profession. Their traditional wisdom helps them in searching new water sources while introduction of modern tubewell help the villagers to overcome the problem of water shortage to some extent. Applying their traditional wisdom they are looking after the natural resources with great care under the able guidance of *panch*. On the other hand, they are cordially accepting modern mechanisms to adapt themselves in the modern world. Modern politics has brought the upper castes closer to them which helped in other way to improve their economic condition. As they are habituated in labour works no body put objection when the Bhils are engaged in all labour works of the panchayat. In the new socio-economic and socio-political system the importance of *Jam* or Bhil headman has decreased due to his irrationality and importance of *panch* (collective heads) has increased a lot. When five heads gather to take any decision that becomes rational and acceptable to every person. As the supernatural world is of great importance to satisfy the traditional mode of economy the *bhonpa* (mediator with the supernatural world) is kept in high esteem. Their traditional system of labour exchangeship suggests the closeness and distance of the communities in this area. Thus in this area the tradition-bound Bhils are moving through a phase of transition towards the modernity and their traditional knowledge help them a lot to survive in this phase and in the proper utilisation of natural resources available them to the best they can perform. In this context certain measures may be taken for their economic betterment and also for proper utilisation of natural resources in the locality. For example.

(i) The practice of cultivation of multiple crops at a time in a particular land is wise because the crops in this pattern of cultivation people choose, are of different water consuming varieties thus neutralising the water requirement. This pattern of cultivation should be encouraged and introduced in those areas of aridity where cultivation is possible to some extent.

(ii) Panchayat should help in construction of the contours prepared for water binding.

(iii) Channels may be constructed from Indira Gandhi Canal in this area so that a flood of water can enhance irrigation and afforestation here which ultimately helps to stop soil erosion. This would increase cultivation in the area.

(iv) The females should be paid in equal amount with their male counterparts in any sort of labour work while they are providing equal labour.

(v) Government should assist through panchayat by providing monetary help and modern mechanism during cultivation.

(vi) Modern education should be spread among them without gender biasness and it should be provided to the poorer families free of cost upto that standard they want learning. This would help them in two ways: first, with the aid of Modern education they would avoid deceiving by other and, second, through modern education the scientific knowledge achieved by them would help them in all sort of works being supplementary to their traditional wisdom.

(vii) Government beneficial programmes should reach them properly and all officials should treat them as their fellow men. Panchayat should take care in this regard.

(viii) To encourage them further in stone related works they can be taught the techniques of grinding and polishing of stones so that to ensure the opening of new avenues in this profession.

Notes

1. See Appendix - I
2. See Appendix - I
3. See Bhasin & Bhasin, 1999:6.
4. See Bhasin & Bhasin, 1999:7.
5. See Appendix-II
6. Source : District Census Handbook – Jaisalmer : 1991 : 14-15.

Bibliography

Bates, Marston. 1972. 'Environment' in David L. Sills ed. *International Encyclopedia of the Social Sciences,* Vol.V (first published 1968) New York, The Macmillan Company Free Press; London, Collier Macmillan Publishers : 90-93. (reprint).

Bharara, L.P. 1999. *Man in the Desert : drought, desertification and indigenous knowledge for sustainable development*, Jodhpur, Scientific Publishers : 6.

Bhasin, M.K. and Veena Bhasin. 1999. *Rajasthan : ecology, culture and society,* Delhi, Kamla-Raj Enterprises : 6-7.

Chouhan, T.K. 1995. *Indian Desert : resources and perspective development,* Jaipur, Printwell : 1-3.

Cooke, Ron; Andrew Warren and Andrew Goudie. 1993. *Desert Geomorphology,* London, University College London (UCL) Press and New Delhi, Research Press : 2.

Gurjar, Ram Kumar. 1992. *Irrigation Impact on Desert Ecology,* Jaipur, Printwell : 138-148.

Mathur, H.S. 1994. *Arid Lands : people and resources,* Jaipur, RBSA Publishers : 7-12.

Micklin, Michael (ed.). 1973. *Population, Environement and Social Organisation; current issues in Human Ecology*, Hinsdale, Illinois, The Dryden Press : xiii, 3-4.

Samanta, D.K. 1998. "Bhil/Gametia" in K.S. Singh (Gend. Ed.) *People of*

India : Rajasthan, Vol. XXXVII, Part-I, Mumbai, Popular Prakashan Pvt. Ltd. (copyright-Anthropological Survey of India) : 150-154.

Rizvi, B.R. 1989. *Hill Korwas of Chhattisgarh : a study of tribal economy,* New Delhi, Gian Publishing House : 1-186.

Rizvi, B.R. 1993. *The Balti : a scheduled tribe of Jammu & Kashmir,* New Delhi, Gian Publishing House : 1-106.

Tomar, R.P. (ed.) 1994. Census of India : 1991, Series 21, Rajasthan, Part-XII A and B, District Census Handbook, District-Jaisalmer, Jaipur, Directorate of Census Operaztions, Govt. of Rajasthan; XIII, LILV, 6, 9, 14-15, 92.

Vidyarthi, L.P. 1963. *The Maler : a study in Nature Man-Spirit complex of a hill tribe,* Calcutta, Bookland Pvt. Ltd. : 175-176.

Watson, Richard A. and patty Jo Watson. 1969. *Man and Nature : an anthropological essay in Human Ecology;* New York, Chicago, San Francisco, Atlanta; Harcourt, Brace and World Inc : 17-21.

APPENDIX - 1

Flora

Local name	Scientific name
Seban or Siwan	*Lagiurrus sindicus*
Ganthil	*Eleugine compressa*
Muroth	*Panicum turgidum*
Bhuroth	*Cenchrus setigerus*
Naredon	*Cyperus longus*
Morion	*Chloris roxburtglina*
Mithaihal	*Salvadoora oleoides*
Kharijhal	*Salvadora persuca*
Bon or ker	*Capparis decidua*
Babul	*Acacia milotica*
Kumbhat	*Acacia senegal*
Lowa	*Haloxylon salic ornicum*
Ak or akra	*Calotropis procera*
Bordhi or Behr	*Ziziphus mauritiana*
Ruida	*Tecomela undulate*
Khajri	*Prosopis cineraria*
Thor	*Euphorbia spepcies*
Safeda	*Eucalyptus sp.*
Neem	*Azaduracta indica*
Tulsi	*Ocimum sanctum*
Saris	*Albezia sp.*
Kakonda	*Majtenus emaginatus*

Fauna

Local name	Scientific name
Titr	*Francolinus pondicerianas*
Kabutar	*Columba livia*

Kowa	*Corvus splendens*
Ghugu	*Streptopelia risoria*
Maur	*Pavo cristatus*
Sanda	*Urmaistic hardwiki*
Kalindernag	*Naia tripudians*
Pina	*Bungarus sindanus*
Khorgos	*Lepusnigricollis dayanus*
Gidhor	*Vulpes pusilla*
Jarokh	*Hyacnahyaena*
JangleeSuor	*Susscrofacristatus*

APPENDIX - 2

List of Utensils and Utility

Bagoli – Small flat bootomed utensil like tumbler for preparation of curry, tea etc. made of steel/brass.

Balon-chaklu – Wooden material for preparation of roti.

Parat– Large wooden or steel plate for preparing the the paste of *ata* before preparing roti.

Thali– Plate made of steel/brass/kasa for eating.

Batti– Bowl made of steel/brass/kasa for eating.

Lota– Made of glass or steel for drinking water.

Tipra– Kattle made of steel for boiling water or making tea.

Chhanni– Strainer to filter tea.

Cup– Made of glass or steel to drink tea.

Matura – Clay made material for preparing curd.

Jharua– Wooden material used for preparing butter and *chhanch.*

Patta – Cow-leather made belt attached to *Jharua.*

Makri – Wooden material for preparing butter and *chhanch.*

Tawa – Iron made pan for preparing roti.

Chamch – Spoon.

Degri – Large kittle for preparing tea in bulk amount.

Bucket – Iron/plastic/steel made for storing water.

Motki – Clay pitcher for storing potable water during summer.

Tambera – Iron pitcher to fetch water from outside.

Dhakkan – Clay lid of different pots.

Dholki – Iron made container to store flour.

Tiffin carrier – Steel made to carry tiffin/meal while going outside for work.

Jug – Steel made pot for bringing tea, water.

Chulhe – Clay oven.

Kerosene stove – Used in a few houses.

Charpai – Cot made of wood and rope.

Rele – Bed sheets.

Rajai – Cotton body cover used during sleeping in winter.

Takia – Pillow.

Chaste – Made of iron to store garments, *rajai, rele*etc.

Suitcase – To store garments in room and also for going outside for several days.

Glossary

Akashganga	:	Gonstellations
Akhor	:	Dry land
Amabos	:	The last day of the dark fortnight
Anchal	:	Nipples of female cattles
Andhi/dhoolbharihawa	:	Dust-storm
Anubjaojamin	:	Sterile land
Apnachasjamin	:	Own agricultural land
Badal	:	Cloud
Bajri	:	Sandy soil
Baqri	:	Goat
Bara	:	Enclosure for cattle
Bare-kiri	:	Insect of large size
Barsaru/barsala	:	Rainy season
Batera	:	A type of bird
Battebari	:	A type of bird used for medicinal purpose
Bauri/beri	:	Well
Behl	:	Ox
Beon	:	Marriage
Bharat	:	Marriage procession
Bhehr	:	Sheep
Bhonpa	:	Mediator with the supernatural world and medicine-man
Bhori	:	Sacks
Bhounrio	:	Whirlpool
Bhura	:	Brown
Bhutiara	:	One type of whirlwind
Bichhchhu	:	Scorpion
Bichhuri	:	Anklet
Billi	:	Cat
Bor	:	Current
Boria	:	Tiara
Bugla	:	A type of bird

Chakraborti : Whirlwind
Chanda : Moon
Channango : A type of reptile
Chappals : Slippers
Chari : Upward
Chhotekiri : Insect of small size
Chiknimitti : Black soil
Chiri : Sparrow
Chitia : Ant
Chotiwalo or puchhwala taro : Comet
Chowkhun : Acquire
Darwaja : Door
Datri : Sickle
Dehri : Plain land
Dhani : Hamlet
Dhartimata : Mother earth
Dheli : Heap of crops
Dhore : Contour
Dol : Iron-made container for storing crops
Dolar : A type of bird
Dori : Rope
Dusra-gharana : Widow remarriage
Gachhia : White stone previously used for fire making
Gadria : A type of bird
Gaguraja : A type of bird
Gai : Cow
Gaona : Threshing by camel or ox
Garg : Priest appointed for officiating Bhil marriage from the Meghwal
Community
Gatta : A type of bird
Gelar : A type of reptile
Ger : Insect, white in colour
Geru : Red
Ghor : Lightening
Ghunghat : Veil
Gironj : A type of bird
Go : A type of reptile
Goargom : Grains of guar
Gobar : Cow dung
Gohhru : Ear-rings
Gol : Round
Goopha : Cave
Goraba : A type of snake

Gorana	:	A type of bird
Gotra	:	Clan
Graha	:	Planet
Gul	:	Molasses
Gunga	:	A type of insect
Hada	:	A type of bird
Hal	:	Plough
Hari	:	Green
Hariyali	:	Greenery
Hauli	:	A type of bird
Hiren	:	Deer
Indradhanush	:	Rainbow
Jam	:	Headman of the Bhils in past days
Jangleejanwar	:	Forest animals
Jarokhe	:	Ventelators
Jhupura	:	Cottage type hut
Kaccamokan	:	Clay hut
Kochori	:	A type of bird
Kachra	:	Garbage
Kaile	:	Black
Kanchli	:	Bodies
Kankar	:	Gravels
Kansa	:	Bell metal
Kara	:	Medicine made of cloves, black pepper etc. used for cough and cold
Kasi	:	Spade
Khad	:	Chemical fertilizer
Kharepani	:	Salt-water
Kharin	:	Large agricultural land where double cropping is done
Khatedarijamin	:	Homestead land
Khet	:	Small agricultural land where single cropping is done
Khumbi	:	Mushroom
Kira	:	Insect of medium size
Kire	:	Insects
Kohra	:	Fog
Kothi	:	Clay made container for storing crops
Kulhari	:	Axe
Kurr	:	Trap used for hunting
Kutta	:	Dog
Lohar	:	Wave
Lokrian	:	Wood sticks
Lalpatthar/baru	:	Red stone having iron as prime ingredient

Lili	:	A type of bird
Lundi	:	A type of snake
Machhchhar	:	Mosquito
Madhumakhi	:	Honey-bee
Magre	:	Hillock/hill
Makkhi	:	Fly
Makora	:	Spider
Mantakmajduri	:	Traditional labour work where payment was made in kind
Matka	:	Clay pitcher
Mehenatmajduri	:	Labour where payment is made in cash
Burba	:	Canal water irrigated land
Murod	:	Soil full of gravels
Mustiskhand	:	One type of molasses
Nai	:	Hollow cylinder attached to plough for sowing seeds
Naihal	:	Mother's parental house
Niche	:	Downward
Nonde	:	Eclipse
Odon	:	Scarf
Osh	:	dew
Pagarsi	:	Rajasthani shoes
Pakhal	:	Leather sac used for water transport
Pakkamokan	:	House made of stones & cement
Pakshi	:	Bird
Palarpani	:	Rain water used for drinking, sweet in taste
Palibheudi	:	Permanent pasture and grazing land
Paltoojanwar	:	Domesticated animals
Panch	:	Council made of Bhil heads
Paora	:	Spade
Pashudhan	:	Cattle
Pashumela	:	Market for selling and purchasing cattle
Patta	:	Ownership right
Patthuremitti	:	Stony soil
Pencha	:	Owl
Pila	:	Yellow
Pilapatthar or kansia	:	Yellow stone
Poonam	:	Full moon
Pukorgoera	:	A type of reptile
Putrio	:	Bat
Registan	:	Desert

Ret	:	Sand
Ret ke tile	:	Sand dunes
Retilimitti	:	Sandy soil
Rajora	:	A type of forest animal
Rui	:	Forest
Safedpatthar	:	White stone used as railway slipper
Saffa	:	Turban
Sajedarichasjamin	:	Agricultural land used for share cropping
Sajra	:	Sieve used for winnowing
Sakhe/sabana	:	Purge stones used for ceiling construction in pakka houses
Samundar	:	Sea
Sarkar se milajamin	:	Land for agriculture either given or lease or donated by government
Sarp	:	Snakes
Sarpanch	:	Head of panchayat
Sera	:	A type of reptile
Seri	:	White
Siaru/siara	:	Winter
Sounri	:	A type of bird
Subha	:	Dawn
Suganchiri	:	A bird like sparrow treated as auspicious
Suraj	:	Sun
Talab	:	Pond
Tanka	:	Water reservoir
Taro	:	Star
Tinkhun	:	Triangle
Tithia	:	Auspicious dates
Toofan	:	Storm
Ubjao	:	Fertile
Udai	:	A type of insect
Unaru/unara	:	Summer
Undhaga	:	Round ball of wool
Unt/dago	:	Camel
Untgada	:	Camel-cart

Table 17: Age and Sex-wise Distribution of Population

Age Break-up	0-5		6-10		11-15		16-20		21-25		26-30		31-35		36-40		41-45		46-50		51-55		56-60		61+		Total		Total
Community	M	F	M	F	M	F	M	F	M	F	M	F	M	F	M	F	M	F	M	F	M	F	M	F	M	F			
Nai	4	-	2	3	1	2	3	3	4	1	1	1	-	1	1	1	1	3	1	-	1	-	-	-	-	1	19	15	34
Suthar	-	2	-	1	-	1	3	4	2	1	-	-	1	-	-	-	-	2	-	-	1	-	1	-	2	-	10	11	21
Lohar	1	1	-	1	1	-	1	-	-	-	-	-	-	1	1	-	-	-	-	1	1	-	-	-	-	-	5	4	9
Darji	1	-	1	1	1	-	-	2	1	-	-	-	-	-	-	-	-	1	-	-	1	-	-	-	-	-	5	4	9
Rajput	38	37	47	34	35	24	24	19	11	21	17	21	22	19	19	20	17	18	15	7	10	6	8	7	11	6	279	237	518
Bhil	14	10	6	11	6	4	9	6	-	7	8	3	2	3	7	5	3	2	3	1	1	1	2	1	1	-	62	54	116
Khatik	5	2	1	2	-	-	-	-	-	1	2	2	2	2	-	-	-	-	-	-	-	1	-	-	1	-	11	10	21
Regar	-	-	-	-	-	-	-	-	-	-	-	-	-	-	-	-	-	-	-	-	-	-	1	-	-	-	1	-	1
Salai/ Salvi	8	4	10	6	6	5	7	2	2	3	4	5	3	3	3	4	3	5	4	3	4	1	3	1	1	1	59	43	102
Bhambi	1	1	1	-	1	-	-	-	-	-	-	1	1	-	-	-	-	-	-	-	-	-	-	-	-	-	4	2	6
Kalbelia	7	2	6	5	2	-	2	3	1	2	3	2	1	-	-	1	1	-	1	2	-	1	1	-	-	-	25	18	43
Brahman	-	-	-	2	1	-	-	-	1	-	-	-	-	1	-	-	1	-	-	-	-	-	-	-	-	-	3	3	6
Nath	-	-	-	-	-	-	-	-	-	-	-	-	1	2	1	-	-	-	-	-	-	-	-	-	-	-	3	2	5
Bairagi	-	-	-	-	-	-	-	-	-	-	-	-	-	1	1	-	-	-	-	-	-	-	-	-	-	-	1	1	2

Table 18: Bhils in local hierarchy

Community	*No. of Household*	*Category*	*Remark*
Brahman	1	Priestly (Pujari Baba)	Water acceptable
Nath	1		
Bairagi	1		
Rajput	93	Farmer Ruler (Thakur)	
Suthar	2	Artisans (Kamin)	
Nai	6		
Darji	1		
Lohar	2		
Bhil	26	Adivasi	Water in branpot, not from earthenpot, no food
Khatik	5	Scheduled Castes (Achhyut)	
Regar	1		
Balai	24		
Dholi	1		
Bhambi	1		
Kalbelia	6		
Total	**171**		

Table 19: Community wise Distribution of Literates

Community	Literacy								Illiteracy				
	General Level		Higher Educaion		Literate		Total literate	%	Illiterate		Total Illiterate	%	Total
	M	F	M	F	M	F			M	F			
Brahman	1	2	2	1	3	3	6	100.00	-	-	-	-	6
Bairagi	1	-	-	-	1	-	1	50.00	-	1	1	50.00	2
Nath	-	-	-	-	-	-	-	00.00	3	2	5	100.00	5
Suthar	6	2	1	-	7	2	9	42.85	3	9	12	57.15	21
Nai	13	4	-	-	13	4	17	50.00	6	11	17	50.00	34
Darji	4	1	-	-	4	1	5	55.55	1	3	4	44.45	9
Lohar	3	1	-	-	3	1	4	44.45	2	3	5	55.55	9
Rajput	179	64	3	-	172	64	246	47.49	97	175	272	52.01	518
Bhil	15	5	-	-	15	5	20	17.24	47	49	96	82.76	116
Khatik	4	2	1	-	5	2	7	33.33	6	8	14	66.66	21
Regar	-	-	1	-	1	-	1	100.00	-	-	-	-	1
Balai	26	10	3	-	3	2	5	55.55	2	2	4	44.45	9
Dholi	3	2	-	-	2	1	3	50.00	2	1	3	50.00	6
Bhambi	2	1	-	-	2	1	3	50.00	2	1	3	50.00	6
Kalbelia	3	-	-	-	3	-	3	6.98	22	18	40	93.32	902
Total							**366**	**40.68**			**536**	**59.32**	**902**

Table 20: Community wise Control over of Resources

Community	*Land*	*Land Resource*		*Landless*		*Cattle Resource*			*Remark*
	....	*Peebal* ...	*Bida*	....	....	.....	*Goat*	*Bullock*	
Brahman	-	-	1	-	-	-	-	-	
Bairagi	1	7	-	-	2	2	4	-	
Nath	1	6	-	-	2	3	4	-	
Rajput	93	201.5	316	-	113	106	140	25	
Suthar	2	8	8	-	11	4	1	4	
Darji	1	2	-	-	1	1	2	-	
Nai	6	8	9	-	9	3	7	2	
Lohar	2	-	12	-	-	-	1	-	
Khatik	1	3	5	4	-	-	-	-	
Regar	-	-	1	-	-	-	-	-	
Balai/Salvi	24	26	32	-	22	8	50	6	
Dholi	1	2	-	-	2	-	1	-	
Bhambi	-	-	-	1	-	-	-	-	
Kalbelia	6	5	-	5	-	-	6	-	
Bhil	26	23.5	51.5	-	27	15	130	12	

Table 21: Community wise Distribution of Working force

Community		Farming	Ag Lab.	Daily Lab.	Lab. In Marble	Tailoring	Service	H.H.	Priestly	Trade	Driving	Barber	Carpentry	Sonithy	Mason	Cattle
Brahman	**M**	-	-	-	1	-	-	-	-	-	-	-	-	-	-	-
	F	-	-	-	-	-	1	1	-	-	-	-	-	-	-	-
Nath	**M**	1	-	2	-	-	-	-	-	-	-	-	-	-	-	-
	F	-	-	-	-	-	-	2	-	-	-	-	-	-	-	-
Bairagi	**M**	-	-	-	-	-	-	-	1	-	-	-	-	-	-	-
	F	-	-	-	-	-	-	1	-	-	-	-	-	-	-	-
Rajput	**M**	56	7	2	35	-	45	-	-	13	6	-	-	-	-	-
	F	-	-	-	-	-	-	145	-	-	-	-	-	-	-	-
Nai	**M**	2	-	-	3	-	5	-	-	1	-	1	-	-	-	-
	F	-	-	-	-	-	1	10	-	-	-	-	-	-	-	-
Suthar	**M**	2	-	-	-	-	2	-	-	-	-	-	6	-	-	-
	F	-	-	-	-	-	1	6	-	-	-	-	-	-	-	-
Lohar	**M**	-	-	-	-	-	-	-	-	-	-	-	-	3	-	-
	F	-	-	-	-	-	-	2	-	-	-	-	-	-	-	-
Darji	**M**	-	-	-	-	3	-	-	-	-	-	-	-	-	-	-
	F	-	-	-	-	-	-	3	-	-	-	-	-	-	-	-
Khatik	**M**	2	-	-	-	1	1	-	-	2	-	-	-	-	-	-
	F	-	-	1	-	-	-	4	-	-	-	-	-	-	-	-
Regar	**M**	-	-	-	-	-	1	-	-	-	-	-	-	-	-	-

(contd...)

Community		*Farming*	*Ag Lab.*	*Daily Lab.*	*Lab. In Marble*	*Tailoring*	*Service*	*H.H.*	*Priestly*	*Trade*	*Driving*	*Barber*	*Carpentry*	*Sonithy*	*Mason*	*Cattle*
Bunkar	**M**	4	2	-	9	-	-	-	-	-	-	-	-	-	8	1
	F	-	6	13	-	-	-	10	-	1	-	-	-	-	-	-
Bhambi	**M**	-	-	-	-	-	-	-	-	-	-	-	-	-	-	-
	F	-	-	-	-	-	-	1	-	-	-	-	-	-	-	-
Dholi	**M**	1	-	1	1	-	-	-	-	-	-	-	-	-	-	-
	F	-	1	-	1	-	-	-	-	-	-	-	-	-	-	-
Kalbelia	**M**	-	-	-	13	-	-	-	-	-	-	-	-	-	-	-
	F	-	1	4	3	-	-	4	-	-	-	-	-	-	-	-

9

Dynamics of Resource Management in Katchal Island

Umesh Kumar and *Samir Biswas*

Introduction

Islands have unique ecosystems because of their well-defined boundary and broad resource base both terrestrial and aquatic. The islanders have the advantage of utilising resources of the islands as well as that of the adjoining sea. Human survival in the islands depends not only on what type and quantity of natural resources are available there but also on the way these resources are used. Therefore, human adaptation to the island environment has peculiar form and processes. The Nicobarese of Katchal have adapted themselves to the island environment in a manner where social organisation and religion are outgrowth of the practical system for making a living, rather than their cause. Thus a close connection can be drawn between the ownership and management of resources and social organisation in the Nicobarese society.

The Andaman and Nicobar archipelago is like a chain of pearls in the Bay of Bengal. There are as many as 319 islands in the form of more or less an arch and have an area of about 8293 sq.km. spread over a length of 700 km. The islands are situated between 6° and 10° N latitudes and 92° and 94° E longitudes in the Bay of Bengal. The 10° channel with a uniform depth of 400 fathoms and an approximate width of 128 km separates the Andaman group of islands from the Nicobar. There are altogether 19 islands in the Nicobar archipelago out

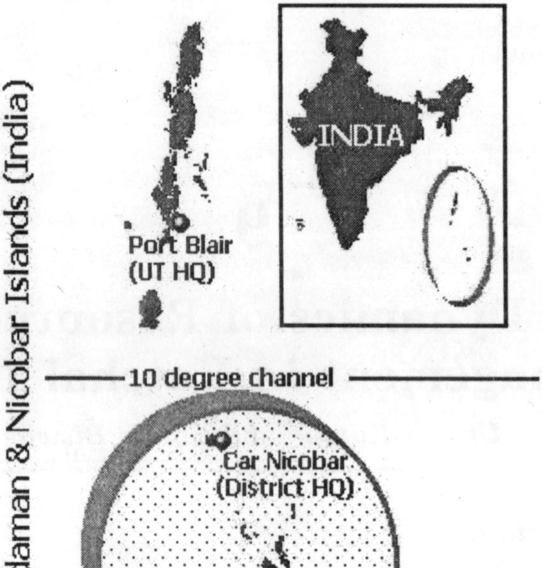

Katchal Island

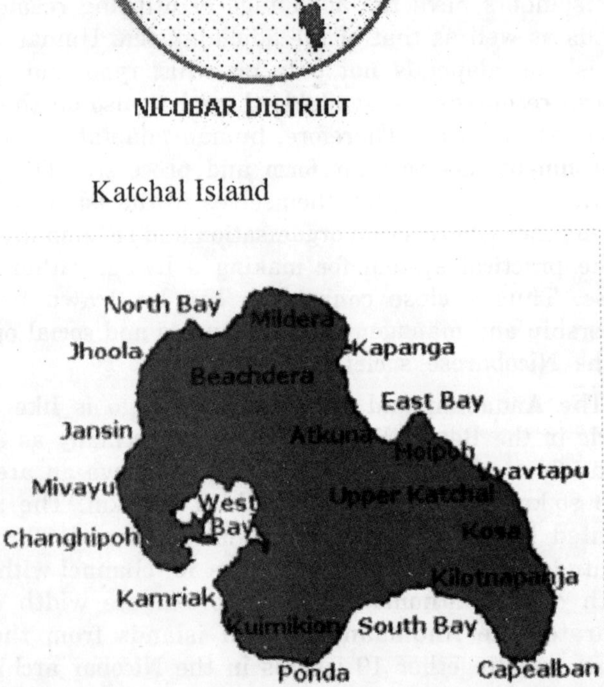

Fig. 1.

of which only 12 are inhabited. The inhabited islands can be divided into three groups viz. (1) northern group consisting of only Car Nicobar island (2) central group consisting of Chowra, Terresa, Bompuka, Camorta, Nancowry, Trinket and Katchal and (3) southern group consisting of Little Nicobar, Pulomilo, Kondul and Great Nicobar. Except in the Great Nicobar where the Shompen tribe of Mongoloid stock and a few ex-army personnel are living, in all the other islands the main population is Nicobarese.

Katchal, earlier known as Tihnyu, is the largest island of the central group of islands (Figure-1). It has been home to both indigenous and non-indigenous people. The Katchal Island is situated in the south-east side of Kamorta, Nancowry and Bompoka islands between 7°51′50″ and 8°01′56″ N latitudes and 93°17′41″ and 93°28′47″ E longitudes. It comes under Nancowry tehsil. It has an area of 174.4 sq km. It is situated about 1600 kms away from the mainland of India. It is 300 km south of Port Blair, capital of the Andaman and Nicobar Islands. The highest peak of Katchal is 835 ft. high. There are 35 villages in Katchal of which six are main villages (Table 1). People in Katchal speak Nicobari, Hindi, Tamil, Telugu, Bengali, Santhali (a tribal language from South Bihar) and English.

Table 1. Population of Different villages of Katchal and telephone facilities

No.	*Name of Village*	*Estimated Population as per preliminary data of census 2001*	*Telephone facilities*
1.	Jhoola	374	Available
2.	Jansin	211	Available
3.	Hitlat	103	NA
4.	Mayatapis/Maratapia	107	NA
5.	Chonghipoh	31	NA
6.	Sanaya	134	NA
7.	Alkaipoh/Alkripoh	93	NA
8.	Alhitoth/Alhiloth	81	NA
9.	Katahuwa	37	NA

No.	*Name of Village*	*Estimated Population as per preliminary data of census 2001*	*Telephone facilities*
10.	Kumikia	117	NA
11.	Kamriak	34	NA
12.	Hutnyak	84	NA
13.	Ongulongho	24	NA
14.	Chonsiyala	Nil	NA
15.	Hontona	71	NA
16.	Kulatapangla	52	NA
17.	Vyavtapu	173	NA
18.	Hoipoh	55	NA
19.	Mapayala	95	NA
20.	Chengtamilan	Nil	NA
21.	Atkuna / Alkun	57	NA
22.	Tani	23	NA
23.	Kalminikum / Kalmenkam	Nil	NA
24.	Hakonhala	58	NA
25.	Reakomlong	27	NA
26.	Sonomkuwa	18	NA
27.	Tavinkin/Tavakin	27	NA
28.	Hainatai(Hoinatai)	51	NA
29.	Altaful	209	NA
30.	Kavatinpeu /Karahonpoh	105	NA
31.	Alsama	60	NA
32.	Kapanga	866	Available
33.	Kupinga	100	NA
34.	Mildera	1844	Available
35.	W.B.Katchal(Hindra)	118	Available
	Total Population	**5386**	

Source: Census, 2001.

Among 35 villages, Mildera is the largest village and it is inhabited primarily by the non-Nicobarese. However of all villages, telephone facility is available in only five villages. Efforts were being made to connect al the settlements with telephone.

Facilities at Katchal Island

Health : Primary Health Centre – 1, Sub Centre – 3

Education: Primary School - 6

Middle - 2

Secondary - 2

Senior Secondary School - 1

Water Supply: There are no reported problems as regards water.

Power : Presently it is electrified but is proposed to augment the DG capacity at Katchal Islands by 3x128 KW DG Sets.

Roads : 23.66 KM Pucca road.

Cooperative Societies: 4 No's

Police Station : 1

Police Radio Station: 1

Present mode of main communication: By Shipping.

The present study was carried out before tsunami in the year 2000. Katchal was one of the worst effected islands of Andaman and Nicobar archipelago. Of 35 villages in Katchal Isalnd, thirty one villages were uni-ethnic and four were multi-ethnic. In the aftermath of tsunami which struck the Andaman and Nicobar Islands on 26th December 2004, settlement structures of these villages were badly affected. For time being there exist only four settlements. They were namely Slow Tegree (uni-ethnic), Oil Palm (uni-ethnic), Mildera (multi-ethnic) and Beach Dera (multi-ethnic). Also the sea water has advanced over a large area in the west Katchal. The total population of the island before tsunami was 5386 (Census, 2001), out of which 345 lives were lost and many were missing in the aftermath of tsunami. (Sinha Roy and Datta Chaudhuri, 2007).

Climate - The island has a semi-equatorial climate. Two monsoons pass over Katchal in a regular annual cycle. Taking these and the spells intervening them five seasonal phases can be distinguished, namely,

(a) the south-west monsoon, from June to September
(b) period of transition, in October.
(c) the northeast monsoon, from November to January.
(d) period of dull in February and March and
(e) the warm season of April and May.

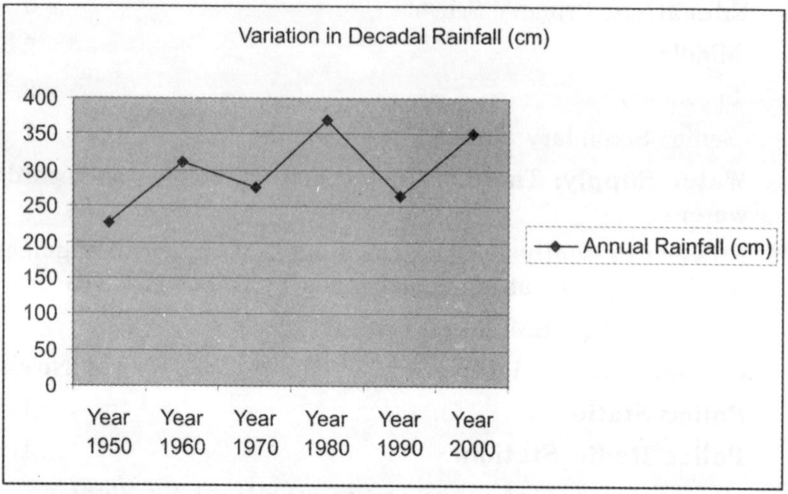

Fig. 2.

The southwest monsoon brings heavy and extensive rain that facilitates planting of food crops. The northeast monsoon is comparatively week but rain during this period helps in extending horticulture activities beyond wet days. Due to their location in the equatorial belt the islands have a warm and humid tropical climate. Temperatures range from 18°C to 34°C with a mean annual temperature of 26.4°C. The average relative humidity varies from 65 to 89 per cent (Roy *et al.*, 2003). The mean annual precipitation ranges between 3000 and 4000 mm (Fig. 2). The rainfall is influenced by the southwest and northeast monsoon winds. The southeast monsoon arrives in May, lasts until the end of September and is often accompanied by high winds. In November the northeast monsoon starts often accompanied by cyclones. The intensity of the rains decline from February onwards until the southeast monsoon starts again.

Flora and fauna - The tropical climate and fertile soil have favoured luxuriant growth of vegetation. The natural flora in the island consists of mangrove forest, pandanus, casurina, silk cotton, cane creeper, fish poison tree (*kinyaya*), neem, bamboo thickets etc. Besides, due to a long history of outside contacts many plants have been introduced in the Island. These are mainly coconut, areca, banana, jackfruit, mango papaya, pineapple, yam, tapioca, lemon etc. Generally the islanders get all the timbers they need from their own groves and forest. Where there is paucity of such resources, the requirement is met through inter-island trade. The avian and faunal life of Nicobar group of islands is not exotic. Among them are wild pigeons, python, green snakes, imperial pigeons, pigs, dogs, oxes, cats, rats, poultry birds, turtles, land crabs, sea cucumber, variety of fish etc

People - The Nicobarese is the generic name for indigenous people of Nicobar Islands. The term seems to be derived from the name of these islands which the Nicobarese as *takasstto*. The island community inhabiting different islands of nicobar identify themselves by different terms such as Tarik (native of Car-Nicobar), Som-poi (native of Chowra), Som—Tehiong (people of Teressa), Som-Payuh (inhabitant of Katchal), Som-Onhet (native of Nancowry), and Som-Long (inhabitant of Great Nicobar). Racially there are no differences among them. Mathur writing about the physical characteristics of the Nicobarese says that the people have in general Mongoloid features (1967: 42). E.H. Man (1889: 367) has emphasised the racial affinity between the Nicobaries and the Indo–Chinese. Grierson writing about the Nicobarese language says that Nicobarese also belong to Khmer branch Austro-Asiatic sub family that seems to form a connecting link between the Munda languages and Mon (reprint 1967:32-33). Each island constitutes a social system and the interaction amongst its population is direct and face-to-face. Everyone knows every other. Here interaction means cooperation (Hillery, 1968:34). In the island cooperation between and amongst families is not on the basis of individual settlements but on an entire island basis. Familial cooperation between and amongst families of the island during the life cycle as well as in economic activity is the *sin qua non* of the Nicobarese community of Katchal.

It is not exactly known when and from where the islands were first populated. Syamchaudhuri believes that the first immigrants were Mon-Khmer people starting from the Malay-Burma cost. He dates the arrival of humans on the archipelago in a time before the Christian era but not before 1000 B.C. (Syamchaudhuri 1977). But after some time of isolation an intermingling of the natives with the people of Burma, China and Malaysia, who visited these islands for trade, took place (Justin 1990). The legends of the Nicobarese themselves tell various different stories about how the first people arrived on the islands. This also makes it difficult to draw definite conclusions about their origin. Due to their location on vital sea routes through the Indian Ocean the Nicobar Islands have been used as resting point and secure harbor by ships of many nations. Before the beginning of the European colonisation of Asia the islands were already visited by Indian, Arabian and Chinese ships. At this time the Nicobarese traded food items in exchange for iron and clothes. Later the trade with coconuts, an occupation to which the Nicobarese stick to until today, became an important factor. After being a Danish and for a short time an Austrian colony, the Nicobars became part of the British colonies in 1867. The British were the first colonial nation, which could successfully install an administration over the islands. This event was significant for the Nicobarese society, as they were now forced to adapt to a foreign administration. Singh (2003:245) describes this period as follows:

"The foundation for future development in the Nicobars was already provided by the British during their seventy-eight years of control. In this period, the English achieved much success in setting up a regular system of administration over the Nicobars, which the Danes prior to them had repeatedly failed to establish. By the time India took over the Islands in 1947, a basic network of administering the islands had been set up. The authority of the administration came to be acknowledged by the Nicobarese as well. By now, the Nicobarese were somehow acquainted with the idea of being governed by a state and having to abide their written laws. Apparently, the Nicobarese had found it impossible to resist a power superior to their own, and had gradually come to integrate an external system of civic-state within their own traditional one."

The British period ended 1947 when the islands were taken over by independent India. The islands remained under the direct control of the central government in Delhi. The Nicobarese were listed as a "Schedule Tribe" in 1950. Two years later John Richardson, from Car Nicobar and bishop in Burma, was nominated to represent the tribes of the islands in the Indian parliament. This made Car Nicobar become the axis of the Nicobar archipelago, whereas Port Blair remained the administrative headquarters of the Andaman-Nicobar Archipelago.

In order to integrate the Nicobar islands into the development process, the administrative structure on Car Nicobar was further developed. Senior officers from several welfare and administrative departments were also positioned at Car Nicobar. However, besides carrying out development and welfare programmes, the local administration was not allowed to interfere in tribal affairs unless serious law and order issues arose. The Nicobarese continued to own their land legally, and to manage their own day-to-day affairs through their tribal system of leadership and elders that was recognised in lieu of the "Village *Panchayats*" (village local self governance elected bodies) on the Indian mainland.

In July 1956 the Andaman and Nicobar Protection of Aboriginal Tribes Regulation was enforced with the aim to protect the interests of the aboriginal population. Several parts of the Andaman and nearly the whole Nicobar group of Islands were declared restricted area. Entry into these areas was highly regulated and required a special pass, which could be issued by the deputy Commissioner, or his nominated representatives. A direct consequence of this development was that the old trading relations with the Burmese and Malays who came for coconuts, swiflet nests, sea cucumber and shells was disrupted. In 1992 the concept of "Tribal Council" was introduced on the Nicobar Islands. A tribal council was formed on every important island. Smaller islands were merged together with their neighboring islands. Members of the tribal council are the elected village captains and has a chairperson to head it. The tribal council is recognised by the Indian government as the only official institution. The administration must consult the tribal council before any projects are implemented and be responsive to requests from the council.

Occupation - The region appears quite attractive and blended with nature and surrounded by plant species of daily use. The basic occupation of the Nicobarese is horticulture and chiefly consists of raising plantation of coconut, areca nut, yam and other vegetables and fruits, making copra and fishing. By virtue of the fact that Nicobarese settlements are mostly concentrated near the coast as fishing, commonly practiced. The main stay of their economy is coconut followed by piggery.

The dominant layer is formed by coconut (*Cocos nucifera)* followed by areacnut (*Areca catechu*) and banana (*Musa paradisiaca*). Coconut is valued socially and economically as a keystone resource species of the tribal community. For ages, the tribe practices coconut oil extraction in an autochthonic manner, which is also their main source of economy. Coconut oil is extracted using indigenous methods and it is used for both self-consumption and trade. Areca nut also has prominent importance as edible nut, and is used as a masticator (Dagar, 1999). Apart from that among the Nicobarese aloo (*Tacca leontopetaloides*), papita (*Carica papaya*) and *Citrus* species (other than herbaceous life forms) dominated the second layer. Ornamental plants like *Croton* were planted around the hut to enhance its beauty. It can possibly be quoted that the coconut plantation and other plant species in vicinity of *Nicobari* settlements have both subsistence and commercial functions. Kloss (1903) has also enlisted articles like rice, sugar, iron, matches, red cotton, old clothes, oils, silver that were in great demand among the *Nicobarese* and that they exchanged these for coconuts, ambergris, areca nuts, bananas and other forest foods from Burmese and Arab traders. They also practice the canoe making (using *Callophylum inophyllum*, *Sterculia alata*) in order to facilitate transport to different places. The narcotic property of *Barringtonia speciosa* is made use for fish poisoning. The relationship the tribe shares with the environment is symbiotic. Besides these, when necessary they also make articles of handicraft such as mats and baskets.

Today the main economic activity of most of the Nicobarese is trade of coconuts particularly copra, the dried coconut-flesh. The copra is marketed to local co-operatives or to private traders in exchange for money or rice, sugar, clothes and other necessities. The form of the trade ranges from barter-exchange to typical cash-economy based trade. Food sources are: fish, coconut-oil, roots and vegetables grown in gardens, livestock (fowl goats and cows), rice and non-timber-forest-products (NTFP). Traditionally the locally available pandanus (*Pandanus sp.*) was the main stable food until it was replaced by rice. In the last five years the Nicobar group of islands were integrated more deeply in the regional/global economy. As a result, the fluctuations of the copra market had an immediate impact on the Nicobarese. Singh (2003) argues that the Nicobarese have been and still are involved in unequal trade relations. Considering Katchal as example and using the concept of Haustein (1989) he states that the islanders pay 43 Rupees per kilo import and receive Rs.18 for each kilo of export (i.e. copra). Of late due to spread of education, many Katchal islanders are in service and holding jobs in both public and private sectors.

Resource Management and Socio-Political System and Religion

The literal meaning of resources management is the use of resources in a manner through which one meets his needs without disturbing the recuperative rate of resources. The islanders of Katchal are successfully doing it. In the Nicobarese society of Katchal, the resource management is achieved through the island's social structure, economic organisation, political system and religion.

Social Structure

Nicobarese society of Katchal is a well-organised entity. Every inhabitant of the island has a strong attachment with the village of birth. Each islander who traces their descent from a common ancestor belongs to a descent group which is known as *ramage* in northern group and *kamunchiase* in central group. The *kamunchiase (ramage)* is a six level generation group related through consanguinity. The *kamunchiase* is exogamous in nature. After the marriage, either husband goes to live with her wife or wife joins her husband's *kamunchiase*. Through negotiation it is decided who will join whose family after marriage because leaving one's *kamunchiase* and joining another *kamunchiase* on account of marriage is considered to be depletion in the number of working hands. Both *kamunchiase* wants an increase in the number of working hands. As a logical corollary to it, when the husband joins the *kamunchiase* of his wife, his position is comparatively inferior to her wife and vice versa. The *kamunchiase* consists of a number of agnatic kin groups called *tu-het* in northern group and *nitakaru* in central group of islands. In other words, the *kamunchiase* usually consists of more than one household. A lesser group has a separate *nitakaru (tu-het)* but the land, plantation and gardens are generally not separated.

The resources of the island are controlled and supervised by the *kamunchiase*. In the social structure of the Nicobarese of Katchal Island, the individual can not accumulate and usurp any property or produce of garden. The distribution and allocation of resources like land, gardening activities etc. are done by the head of the *kamunchiase*. The size of gardening plots makes relocation easy and convenient. A big piece of land is divided into a number of sub plots and each sub-plot is used by a family. He also supervises day-to-day reciprocities of food, constitute canoe making teams etc. between *nitakarus*. In an island situation and from the view point of economy, it is always very prudent that that management of resources and related activities are not left to the individual. This way the economic interest of weakest and less intelligent is protected. Thus the socio-economic functions of the *kamunchiase* ensure the survival of *nitakaru* in particular and the entire island society in general.

At *kamunchiase* level, there is possession of common plantations and gardens. The *kamunchiase* works as an integrated economic unit for the production of food crops, copra, and grow piggery and poultry. The chief economic value of the land lies in its use, that is, the potential capacities of the *kamunchiase* to use the land for different economic purposes. The wealth of the *kamunchiase* does not depend on the area of the land it owns. Rather it is the productive capacity of its members that can increase the production. In absence of any individual title of ownership, its economic foundation is not perturbed. More importantly, the material resources are drawn out sufficiently when the *kamunchiase* works as an integrated whole under the leadership of the head of a *kamunchiase*.

The bonds between one *kamunchiase* and another are affected through mutual economic aids. For example, if a *kamunchiase* requires to cultivate a particular variety of plant for which there is no extra land, the head of that *kamunchiase* approaches the head of another *kamunchiase* of his village or a friendly one of another village to get a share in the garden for the plant which is to be cultivated. If the extra land is available, the request is complied with. At the time of gardening, the people of donating *kamunchiase* go to help that *kamunchiase*, which has received land for cultivation, in the garden preparation. But such usufructuary relationship in the use of land is declining with increasing population. The introduction of money has brought about a subtle change in the value of common ownership. Cash economy now getting ground, labour of the *kamunchiase* spent in output of copra is readily changed into money.

Form the study it appears that social organisation of the Nicobarese in Katchal Island is an outgrowth of the practical systems for making a living, rather than their cause. Thus a close connection can be drawn between the ownership and management of resources and social organisation in the Nicobarese society.

Village Council

The village council in the island is an outgrowth of an earlier informal political system that existed a few decades back. Earlier each island of the Nicobar used to have one chief. But the old system was replaced by the village council in the early quarter of twentieth century by British Government. Therefore the present setup is attributed to British administration.

Every village in the tribal area is having a village council headed by 1st captain and who is assisted by 2nd and 3rd captain. The Captains are elected democratically by secret ballot normally for tenure of 4 years. Every island/group of islands is having Tribal Council, which is constituted by the 1stCaptains of Village Council falling in their jurisdiction. These 1st Captains select Chief Captain and Vice Chief Captain of the Tribal Council. At present in Nicobar district, there are seven Tribal councils namely Car Nicobar, Katchal, Nancowry, Kamorta, Teressa, Chowra and Pilobhabi.

Village Council plays an important role in day-to-day life. They are the link between the Local Administration and the tribal people of the island. Now-a-day, most of the developmental schemes are being implemented through them only.

There is a functional difference between the village council and social organisation. Every *kamunchiase* in the village organizes and maintains social and economic activities as separate entities. But the affair that concerns the entire village and those between one *kamunchiase* and other are controlled and issue thereto decided by the village council. The village council acts as legislative, adjudicative and executive body in the Island. The main aim of the village council is to provide an orderly life and help the people in getting their basic needs satisfied. One of the ways through which the village council achieves its objective of resource management is through the economic and judicious use of resources. The council exercises regulation over the entire landmass of the island, but with regard to the use of the land, it is the head of the *kamunchiase* who regulates the allocation and use of the land. However, even here, if the council wants it can interfere and impose its decision. The council controls the spread of the settlement. For the school, dispensary, Govt's offices and quarters, the council earmarks the area after much consideration. For raising the ceremonial hut the formal approval of the council is needed. Similarly before burying or cremating a non-tribal person, the permission of the council is necessary for it is the council, which decides where the dead should be cremated or buried. Regarding the use of the forest the permission of the council is needed for as it approves which part of the forest should be exploited.

Any violation of norms in utilisation of land and forest is considered as an economic offence. Any economic offence is considered as an offence against the community. Under such situation the council gives the punishment which may range from simple economic penalty to excommunication.

Spirits and Shamanism

Prior to the occupation of these islands by the British, the people of the Nicobar group of islands were totally animistic. At the beginning of twentieth century Christianity entered into the Car Nicobar. Due to the effort of Rev. Gabriel and his fellow faithful, the Christianity made its presence felt in the Katchal in fifties. Today, in Katchal about 90% of islanders are Christian and rest of 10% are still following their traditional religion. The impact of Christianity on traditional religion is not so much as to shatter its system of adaptation but it has certainly effected the position of the *Menluena* and their popularity is on wane. However, people of both faiths have adjusted themselves with each other. The Christians of Island implicitly regard Christ as one amongst the benevolent spirits. In facts, it happens with first generation of converts because they have only normal understanding of Christianity and partial affiliation towards it. All the life cycle ceremonies amongst the Christians are performed according to the two traditions. Firstly, it is performed according to the Christian tradition then by the native tradition. An analysis of both the traditions helps us to understand as how both have mixed together without disturbing the traditional symbiosis of man nature and spirits.

For the Nicobarese, the religion is an adaptive mechanism to nature. The Nicobarese has their own cultural construct of nature in which they belong to a scheme of hierarchy to which both spirits and dead relatives who have become spirits belong. Propitiation of the spirits before the initiation of any economic activity is necessary and it, in turn, has caused the development of symbiotic relationship with nature whose outer manifestation is spirit-worship. Writing about the religion of Nicobarese, Richard Temple says, "Fear of spirits and ghosts is guide to all ceremonies and the life of the people is very much related with ceremonies and feasts of all kinds (1903)".

(a) Concepts of spirits and their forms: The Nicobarese believe that spirits regulates the entire universe. The Islanders conceive three categories of spirits. They are (1) malevolent spirits (2) benevolent spirits powerful (3) the ancestral spirits which are benevolent or malevolent depending on the nature of the dead when they were alive. The malevolent spirits are more powerful than benevolent spirits. These three categories of spirits are known as *Iwi*, *Sia and Ma-la-ha* respectively in the central group of islands

The *Iwi* are considered as very powerful and the islanders attribute to them different powers like control over climatic condition and the environment. The non-physical forms of the *Iwi* take the shape of forces of nature like a gush of wind, cyclone, monstrous waves in sea etc.

The pivot on which the old religion revolves is *shaman.* They are called *Menluena* in the central group of islands. They are the bridge between the supernatural and the mundane. The people still believe that *Menluena* control the forces of nature. More importantly, people believe that they not only control the spirits but also act through them. They are specialists in ethno-medicines also and in fact are witch doctors too. In the Islander's cultural construct of nature, man is embedded in nature and spirits possess nature. Interaction between man and nature take place through *Menluena* who helps propitiate spirits.

(b) Beliefs and management of resources and environment: At the beginning of every economic activity like gardening fishing, while making fishing and large outrigger canoes, while starting on a voyage to other island, the *Iwi* are appeased necessarily with sacrifices of pigs and chickens. People believe that if they do not appease the *Iwi,* anything unwanted and unexpected may happen to them. Further, there are some taboos connected with economic activities, which have to be strictly observed, otherwise the wrath of the *Iwi* may strike the offender in any form. For example a women during the menstrual period, and people after a death in their families are supposed to be under pollution and they are tabooed to enter their gardens, touch their fishing canoes, and equipments. To ward off the pollution and to bring them to the normal state of harmony with the cosmos, they require sacrifices of pigs and chickens to the *Iwi* spirits.

Since the Nicobarese conception of nature is intricately related with spirits, their every economic activity begins with the propitiation of spirits and it is marked by a particular ceremony. The occurrence of the feasts is determined by including three variables, one creating a cycle from 1 to 360 (one year) one from 1 to 720 (two years) and one from 1 to 3600 days (ten years). Thus four different kinds of festivals exist; small ones, occurring about three times a year, bigger ones every two years, even bigger ones every five years, and really large ones every ten years. The number of pigs demanded on such occasions is correlated to the size of the human population. The numbers of pigs slaughtered depends on the type of feast, on the human population and on the amount of available pigs. The pigs are ranked according to their weight and the heaviest are generally slaughtered first. When the demand for pigs is higher than the available numbers of pigs then only the male pigs are slaughtered. The following are important festival/ ceremonies:

Months	*Economic acitivities*	*Ceremony*
February-March-April	During these three months garden is cleared, leaves and twigs are burnt; new garden is prepared for new plants that are to be planted	*Kuikapa*- This festival is related with clearing of garden
May-June-July	During these months, coconuts *(Uyav)*, sweet potato, (*Kubang and Kani)* areca nut *(Hiyah*), banana *(Sia)* etc. are planted. Thereafter crab catching is begins.	*Vani-ayom*- This ceremony is related with the fencing of garden and plantation. *Kanacha*- It is held every year in the last week of plantation. *Isa-Yuang-Unviha*: This festival is also related with the crab catching and celebrated in the month of May. If viewed climatically, it is the time when the crabs are found in abundance. Secondly it the time when the monsoon sets over the island. The crab catching ends with *Idfat* festival.

Months	*Economic acitivities*	*Ceremony*
		Panuha-Minlan: This festival is related with catching of crab. It is celebrated in the month of June. *Panuha* is the name of the festival and *Minlan* is the name of the red crab.
August-September-October	It is the season of making racing canoes *(Reui)* and fishing spear (*Mi-am*). Some plantation is also done during this period.	*Idfat-* it is generally held in month of October. It means plantation is over and their washing themselves is over. If *Idfat* is not hold they would soon would grow old and die. Two or three *Idfat* are held every year. The last *Idfat* is held between October and November and the pig is sacrificed on the last Idfat in goal ghar *(Nyihopol)*. After *Idfat* no plantation is done. *Hahumsicaich* – It is related with canoe making.
November-December-January	Fishing activities in open sea begins. It continues up to march. It is also the season of making outrigger canoes.	*Kanaochilu or Anucha*-This ceremony is related with fish catching .The date for it is fixed on last *Idfat.* During this festival which is held on moon lit night people venture into sea in their outrigger canoe and fishing is done by spear with the help of mashal (torch). This festival continues for about 10 days. Sail is not hoist on canoe. It tells the onset of northwardly wind and is indicative of good weather condition also. *Yanata-kanyaum*-It is also an important festival. On this day young men do fishing with the help of hook, line and net. They also use the fruits of *tivila, yoanhoa and kinyav* trees to poison the fish.

The Human and the Natural Environment System

The social-ecological system can be disjointed into a "human system" and a "natural environment system". The activities of the humans in the "natural-environment systems" are hunting and gathering. Livestock, agriculture plantations etc. belong to the human-system. The building blocks of the "natural-environment systems" are the ecosystems. The Human system can be seen as a special case ecosystem, with humans as key-species. The human system contains the biophysical elements of the human society (humans themselves, stocks of society e.g.: buildings, livestock). These elements have to be maintained through the use of locally extracted or imported resources. This links the human system to the "natural-environment systems". The "natural environment systems" interact with the colonised (e.g. agricultural) elements of the human-system and provide essential ecosystem services. The requirements (needs) of the humans to maintain themselves and the rest of their system are composed of the basic-needs (food, shelter) and other culturally influenced needs.

The Human System

Humans are organised on different scales. They are part of a core-family, a household, a number of associated households etc. The form of social organisation is influenced by the worldview/perception and by constraints imposed by the natural-environment system. These forms of organisation are not static. They change over time. The decision if such changes are incorporated into a model depends on the anticipated speed with which these changes will occur and the possibility of forecasting them. The economic decisions on Katchal Island are taken at the level of the *Kamuchiase*. The humans interact with the other systems when they try to fulfill their needs. The worldview/perception field influences what these needs will look like. When extracting resources out of the environment the humans also receive feedbacks. How these feedbacks are interpreted again largely depends on the worldview/perception of the people.

The Pig System

For the Nicobarese their pigs are the most important livestock both in terms of numbers respectively biomass and social status. They use them for ritual purpose or ceremonial food at feasts. The status of a family is strongly linked to their ability of providing sufficient number of pigs. Due to this people are willing to invest more energy into pig keeping then they can gain out of this activity. More importantly, against the backdrop of the fact that 16 pigs require about one square km of forest to sustain and roam as they get 70% of their diet in forest (Vitousek et al 1995), a pig population of approximately 1000 domestic has a considerable influence on that ecosystem, especially as island-ecosystems are seen to be even more easily effected by a single species.

The Influence of the Pig (Sus scorfa) on Katchal Island Systems

Pigs can have a considerable effect on the ecosystems they dwell. Digging and rooting activities of pigs in forest soil has the potential to increase decomposition of leaf litter and the rate at which nitrogen and other nutrients become available. Due to the special conditions on islands (disharmony of species, e.g. missing functional groups, low species richness, high degree of specialisation and endemism, short food webs, under saturated communities, lower competitive ability) these effects can be fortified. In the case of Katchal pigs play important roles in altering the environment on Katchal. The island ecosystem would not look like it does today without the influence of the pigs. The underlying assumption is that most time used for pig rearing is spent in controlling the equal distribution of the feed. Especially the smaller and weaker pigs (infants and females) should benefit from this, which is reflected in a decreasing mortality rate in one year- old piglets.

The time spends for pig rearing is influenced by the variable "pig importance factor". It determines the human to pig ratio which together with the total human population gives the received "minimum pig requirement" which is the benchmark for the "time invested in pigs" e.g. if the "minimum pig requirement is below a certain percentage of the real pig population, the time spend on pigs increases and the mortality rate of piglets decreases (Singh, 2003). The reproduction derived from information of local veterinary indicates that it is influenced by age, sex and body weight. Generally a sow gives give birth to 5 – 12 piglets every eight months beginning at the age of 8 months. However, the weight of sow is an important determining factor. The more the weight the more piglets will be born. The pigs on Katchal Island have two food sources, one is the coconuts fed to them by the humans the other is the food they find while scavenging in the forest.

Economic and Allied Activities

The literal meaning of the resource management is the use of resources in a manner through which one meets his needs without disturbing recuperative rate of the resources. The islanders of Katchal are successfully doing it. In the Nicobarese society of Katchal the resource management is achieved through the island's social structure, economic organisation, political system (Village council) and religion.

Horticulture

Of the total land available in Katchal, approximately 60% land is under horticulture, 30 percent under forest and 10% under settlement. As discussed earlier, two categories of land ownership are found in Katchal Island. They are the land on which Island Council has control and is covered by such things as the ceremonial hut, burial ground, school, dispensary etc., while the forest and gardening land owned by them are other category of lands and are owned and administered by the *Kamunchiase.* Of all economic activities, the horticulture particularly the coconut plantation is most important activity. Horticultural garden needs harrowing, weeding and application of manure at regular interval for good crop. However, the Nicobarese are never seen to follow the said process. It does not mean that they are indifferent about good production of coconut. In fact aforementioned task is carried-out by the pigs. Piggery is the second most important economic activities after plantation. Each Nicobarese household keeps a good number of pigs. While roaming in the garden, pigs turnover the soil in search of roots. The turning over of soil kills the weeds. Besides, the excreta of pigs serve as manure. It is how the three stage process of harrowing, weeding and manuring is accomplished.

Water related activity

Since the time immemorial the Nicobarese of Katchal have been inhabiting the island. It has helped them understand the moods of sea and its relation with seasons. Accordingly they have developed a seasonal calendar, which helps them in fishing and journey.

(A) Fishing - The islanders of Katchal practice fishing for food. Arrows, spears, hooks, and lines are the traditional fishing instruments of these tribes. The Malaysian and Burmese merchants had introduced nets before the arrival of English colonists. The tribes also hunt crabs and shells for food. During such trips they generally use different types of pedals and oars for propulsion besides sails. Their favourite occupational interest is octopus fishing. They generally carry spears, arrows, and the seeds of *kanyov* tree (as narcotic), coconuts, and lime for catching octopus. They go in the night time irrespective of the phase of the tide. They sprinkle the extract of *kanyov* seeds and sometimes seeds of *Baringtonica racemosa* in water which narcotize octopuses and fishes.

The fishing activities of the Nicobarese can be divided into two categories viz. daily activity and seasonal activity. The fishing activity, which is carried out daily, is generally performed near the coast while the other one is seasonal and begins with some ceremonies. The methods of fishing followed by the Islanders are the hook-and-line techniques, spear fishing and torchlight fishing. Groups as well as individuals do hook-and-line fishing.

Spear fishing is of two types. They are:

(1) Simple spear fishing: In this method fish is killed with a long spear in the shallow sea water.

(2) Dive-fishing: It is mainly done by a group in open sea. Every one carries a spear attached with a long and strong rubber string. Success depends on alertness and perfection. Torchlight fishing is also a group activity. It is carried out in open sea. The light attracts the fish. When they approach near the boat/canoe, they are killed with spear.

(B) Canoe Making - Like the Nicobarese of other islands, the islanders of Katchal also make outrigger canoe. This activity takes place between the months of February and April. It is the period when the open sea fishing comes to an end and people prepare themselves for the next season. For canoe making generally the trees of Borneo mahogany, white Bombay and wild jackfruit are used. The canoe making is associated with a festival known as *Hanumsicaich.* Similarly when the canoe is ready for sail the *Hanuich-Nyi- Rsuax* festival is performed in front of the owner's house.

Housing

The houses in the Island have unique design and are generally of high standard. It is remarkable that these people had learnt to make good houses right from the remote past.

Broadly speaking, the houses are of three types- (a) dome shaped round houses on silts (b) Rectangular houses with sloping wagon type roof on silt and (c) pacca houses.

The dome shaped round houses look like giant beehives and is oldest. In these houses, the roofs and the walls are continuous and one hemispherical top serves both the purposes. The entrance to the house is by means of an opening at one edge of the floor on which a ladder is kept to climb in and out of the house. The floor is made up of horizontally laid split bamboo or areca nut, owing to this it is easy to clean the floor. An analysis reveals that their houses particularly dome shaped houses are an index of climate, made up of locally available materials and an epitome of their social requirements and religions faith. They are able to withstand the force of a cyclone as it deflects the force of winds in all directions.

Besides the lofty dome shaped, there are rectangular wagon type of houses also. The rectangular houses are also built on silts with floor raised about 6 to 8 feet above the ground level. But they are not as grand as the circular houses.

Oceanographic Knowledge

The Katchal islanders have a comprehensive and detailed knowledge about the sea and creeks of the islands. They also depend on the sea for their livelihood. Their navigational practices are quite interesting and intricate. Mostly the tribes are settled on the seashore. Their traditional knowledge about sea is unique and the seafaring activity of tribes is different from that of the settlers. Their knowledge about winds, waves, tides, current, etc., have been discussed below.

Waves

The islanders of Katchal have acquired intricate knowledge about different kinds of waves. However, they seem to identify one particular type of wave, which is the principal wave of each set of waves locally known as *Nayange*. They recognise that the sea is turbulent during new moon and full moon days. They are very careful and do not go for voyaging when the sea is too rough. Their decision is highly appreciated for avoiding such voyages.

Currents

The Katchal islanders on the basis of their flowing directions recognize four different types of currents: (1) *Heam Kudi* - from north; (2) *Heam Kulam* - from south; (3) *Heam Kuli* - from east;

and (4) *Heam Kuvath* - from west. These currents are very powerful when any of these four types winds- *Chu, Kaba, Susam,* and *Lohaah* - are blowing. These currents are generally useful to the Nicobarese for catching fish. They determine direction and nature of the current by putting the *Hallis* (pedal) over the water for sometime. The Nicobarese state that the currents are far fewer from the ninth day of full moon up to the 14th day and after that the currents again gain momentum.

Tides

Tides are useful for fishing activity. Having an exhaustive knowledge about tides and their usefulness, the tribal seafarers and sailors apply this knowledge for fishing trips. They authentically say that the low and high tides are caused by moon only. In order to predict the occurrence of low and high tide, they use indigenously made lunar calendar. They have, however, no idea of the exact time of their incidence. During new moon and full moon days, they avoid fishing both in high and low tides. Generally low tides are preferred for fishing trip.

For coastal fishing, during low tides in the inter-tidal region, they dig small pits and fill them when the tides turn high. Water is logged in the pits. Along with the receding water, women, small boys and girls splash the water with small sticks. Sometime they sprinkle the extract of the seeds of *kanyov* tree on water, which has a narcotising effect on the fishes.

Winds

The Katchal islanders also, like the mainlanders and settlers, have recognised four different types of winds in four seasons on the basis of their blowing direction. These different winds are identified just by feeling only. Each wind is predominant in a particular season. These winds are: (1) West wind- *Chu*- January to March, (2) North wind- *Kaba*- April to June, (3) East wind- *Susam*- July to September, (4) South wind- *Lohaha*- October to December. These winds are observed regularly. Among these four winds, the East wind is considered to be good for navigation and fishing trip.

Measuring Depth

The practice of measuring of depth by the people of Katchal is quite unique. The first method they adopt is by observing the colour of water. They state that a close relationship exists between colour and water. According to them the blue colour of water is considered to be deep and shallowness is indicated by green and pale colour of it.

The second method depends upon the sound produced between the vessel/boat/canoe hull and sea surface. The depth at the spot is determined by hearing the sound from underneath the vessel produced due to friction of hull bottom with water. The friction sound produced at the interface of water and hull is different at different depths according to them.

The third one depends upon simply looking at the water because the water of Andaman and Nicobar islands is crystal clear. They just jump into the water and confirm the depth of water. They never use any measuring device for depth finding.

Cyclone Prediction

Many methods are used by the Nicobarese of Katchal for predicting the arrival of cyclone, bad weather, thunder and heavy rain. They use several clues of nature and behaviour of animals around them for cyclone prediction. They tell that indication of arrival of cyclone and rough weather is predicted by the agitation and behaviour of pigs, and by the rolling of marine snakes. If they have any doubt regarding the cyclone or bad weather, they closely observe the pigs at home. Many islanders state that if the dark clouds meet together in large masses with heavy lighting and thunder, it is a sure indication of cyclone.

Time, Duration and place of Navigation

They have standard pattern for fixing fishing times and go for fishing trips according to their food requirements, mood, phase of the moon, nature of tide, etc. They generally go for fishing in the low tide period. The duration of fishing seems to be similar among all islanders. The duration of their voyage or fishing time never exceeds 3 to 4 hours. The fishermen go up to 10-15 km from the shore.

Direction, Finding and Stellar Knowledge

The Nicobarese never exceed 10 km distance from the shore for fishing so that they do not impose any necessity to know the exact position and direction. They have definite words for four directions, which are *tangale* (north), *tangange* (south), *tanganae* (east), and *tangiche* (west). They find the direction with the help of natural objects like sun, moon, and stars in their navigational activity. Generally they use the following stars during night hours.

Onchiana (Centaurus): A constellation, which appears in south during February to April.

Thyan (Orion): A constellation appearing in the east. One star in it is very bright.

Mahayuvan (southern cross): Visible in the south from December to April.

Sama (Al de Baron): it is a bright red coloured star visible in the East from May to September.

Balangkaruvya (Venus): single planet in the East.

Musaha (Ursa Major): it is a constellation appearing in the North.

Gna gna hyyam (Pleiades): Visible in the East from September to February.

Seafaring in Different Seasons of the Year

All the seasons of the year are not good for seafaring activity. The Nicobarese have definite seasons for navigation according to their calendar. The seasons of *Mukyop* (December-January), *Ranecaba* (January- February) and *Tutch* (February-March) are generally good for navigation and fishing. In *Bach* (March-April), the wind force is greater and the sea becomes rough and this season is not suitable for navigation. After this comes the *Amu* (April-May). During this season seafaring and fishing are altogether forbidden and nobody go for fishing. With the end of *Amu*, the wind force becomes normal and fishing and seafaring begin again from the month of *Tukai* (September-October).

Reciprocity and Resource Management

In Katchal the social and economic system still depends on the traditional system of gift, exchange and reciprocity. The significance of gift giving in such societies goes with three essential aspects, viz., (i) obligation to give presents (ii) obligation receive them and (iii) the obligation to repay the gifts received (Rappaport, 1968). Mauss (1954) call this as 'total presentation'. The same system of gift giving is found in socio-economic system of Katchal. Here the thing, which is given, is not important but the act of giving, receiving and repaying is important. Following salons partially the type of reciprocities practiced by the Katchal islanders within the island could be categorised into (i) generalised reciprocity and (ii) balanced reciprocity.

It has been observed that generalised reciprocities occur quite often within *nitakaru*. In this sector the obligation to repay is not strictly adhered to. Here the exchange of food, material, equipment and services is very frequent. At the inter-*nitakaru* and inter-*Kamunchiase* level, the obligation to repay is more than in the previous sector. The ceremony of 'ancestor' worship comes under inter-*nitakaru* level while 'pig festival' comes under inter-*Kamunchiase* category. Here co-operation in terms of men, material and services are provided to the head of the *nitakaru* who is organising it. It is done so because it is beyond the capacity of the host families to feed the invities from their own resources. Thus an examination of reciprocities and exchanges in the island suggests that it is in fact a way of resource management.

Tsunami and its Impact

The earthquake on 26 December 2004 with its epicenter at Sumatra, Indonesia triggered a tsunami which had a major impact on the Andaman and Nicobar Islands. The massive tsunami swept through the Indian Ocean region to become arguably the largest natural disaster in living memory. People ran out in panic and those riding cycles and bikes were forced to stop due to strong wobbling effects. The sea rose to about 4.25 metres above the high tide line in Nicobar Islands. The sea water surged at neatly 700 kms per hour at Great Nicobar and flattened whatever came in its way. It flooded the villages, breached the shore protection walls, certain sections of the low level roads, impaired some bridges and harbour structures and inundated the vast stretches of the shore line. It broke homes and hearts.

Social and economic infrastructures in Nicobar group of islands were severely damaged. Damages to infrastructure include 68 schools, 40 anganwadi centres, most of the health sub-centres, 84 fair shops, 13 storage godowns and 24 jetties. The power supply system in all the islands were badly damaged (www.nicobar.nic.in). Road network in most of the affected islands was severely damaged. In some places, the roads were washed out while in other cracks developed.

As a result of the killer tsunami, the economies of the Nicobar group of islands were severely affected. The business community suffered losses by way of damages to stock, loss of revenue, and losses to property and infrastructure. About 3950 hectares of paddy and 6660 hectares of plantation crop area were affected by the

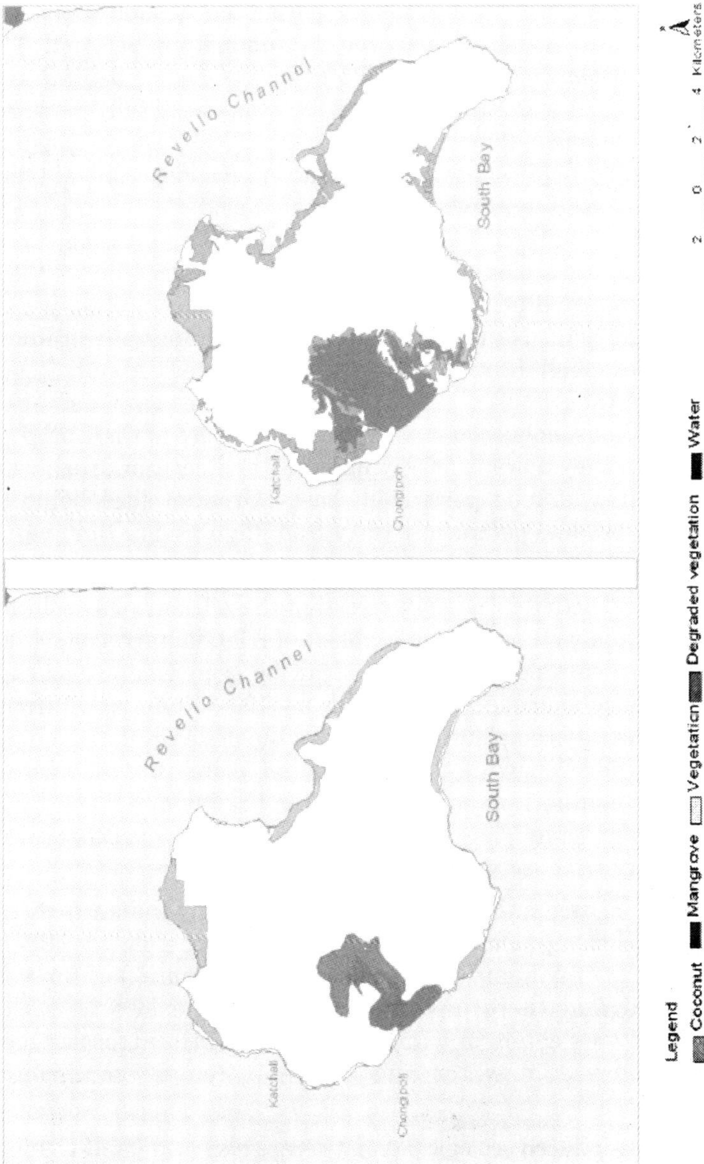

Fig. 3. Pre and Post.

ingress of sea water due to tsunami (www.nicobar.nic.in). More damaging than immediate loss was the increased salinity of soil. As per Central Soil Salinity Research Institute, Karnal major problems caused by tsunami water were : inundation causing anoxia, increase in soil salinity, enhanced dissolution of iron, manganese and aluminum. Large tract of land is permanently submerged and large areas are water logged due to subduction of land. The fishermen suffered enormously due to loss of boats, fishing nets and loss of live. It were estimated that 938 boats were fully damaged while 765 partially damaged in tsunami. Total loss of livestock estimated to be 157577 (www.nicobar.nic.in). Besides, central tribal co-operative societies, which were the backbone of the local economy, also suffered badly. The earthquake and the resulting tsunami had a severe impact on houses in the islands. The southern islands of the archipelago, mainly Chowra, Teressa, Bompooka, Katchal, Kamorta, Nancowrie and Trinket (Nancowrie group of islands), Campbell Bay were the worst affected. About 10,000 families lost their houses. A total of 16,603 houses were damaged. Majority of households could not return to the site of their original dwellings as they were in low lying areas and certain areas were inundated in water on permanent basis. Original sites being on coastal belt became potentially risky from high tide or high winds hazards.

Geological activity was so intense that these islands have shifted horizontally as well as vertically. Most of islands have gone down vertically by varying degrees. This can be seen visually as high tide line has advanced inland roughly by 100-150 meters. Intense geological activity completely broke down the underground drainage pattern. As per report of Central Ground Water Board, Eastern Region, the equilibrium boundary between saline and fresh water was broken at many place. This has increased the drinking water vulnerability of these islands.

Studies to assess the loss of flora and fauna by Indian Institute of Remote Sensing, Dehradun (Roy, 2003) by comparing IRS-1C LISS III data of January 4, 2005 with old information of the year 1999 reveal that there has been a considerable loss to coastal lands and a vast chunk of mangroves and the littoral forests have been submerged in water and at places coastal sands have developed.

Tsunami-induced ecological damages are also evident at Katchal. There are damages to the structure and function of all the coastal ecosystems such as coral reefs, mangroves, sea grasses, estuarine mudflats, etc. The biological structure of the ecosystem could be easily disrupted as various species at different trophic levels were differentially removed, and with the structure altered, ecosystem functions could also be altered. The satellite images clearly show the coastal landscape changes in Katchal. The inundated areas have severely affected the various ecosystems and the coastal organisms as discussed below.

Mangroves, whose tangled roots grow above the ground in coastal swamps, are a unique habitat for wildlife like migratory birds, monkeys, lizards and turtles. Mangroves contribute directly to rural livelihoods by providing forest products – timber, poles, fuel wood and thatch for houses – and indirectly by providing spawning grounds and nutrients for fish and shellfish. Mangroves, which lie in the inter-tidal region between sea and land, help protect and stabilize coastlines and enrich coastal water. They are more effective than concrete barriers in reducing erosion, trapping sediments and dissipating the energy of breaking waves. For example, villages in and around Bhitarkanika were spared much of the fury of the 1999 super cyclone due to the vast mangrove forest. Mangrove forests are themselves victims of the tsunami waves; young saplings in the island have been removed completely. Some of the larger trees have also been uprooted as the waters could easily enter these regions. Land-cover estimates of Katchal Island shows that the mangrove areas were affected to the extent of 339.03 ha (69%) in Katchal (Ramachandran *et al.*, 2005) (Figure-2). Such a major damage in mangrove area has severely affected the coastal productivity and destabilised coastal areas, which has accelerated shoreline erosion and increasingly affected the forest area due to salt-water intrusion into the forests. Since natural regeneration of mangroves will take considerable time (10 to 15 yrs), the impact on forest will be severe in these islands. Although corals occupy less than one quarter of 1% of the marine environment, coral reefs are home to more than a quarter of all known marine fish species. They provide food, livelihood and other essential services to hundreds of millions of coastal-dwellers, as critical fish habitat, popular destinations for ecotourism, or protection to coastal communities from storms and hurricanes. Coral formations act as buffers during storm surges and tidal waves. When giant tsunami waves smashed onto the shores, the massive backwash returned to sea carrying a deadly cargo that could destroy the vital coral reefs of the region. The coral in nearby shallow areas of Katchal have been destroyed, crushed and shrouded in debris. The tsunami surge, which has gone through mangroves, has ripped them completely, releasing silt, sediments, nutrients and pollutants. Coral reefs are mainly affected due to siltation, which occurs as a result of the tsunami. Siltation has led to choking and death of the live coral reefs. The effect of coastal pollution, added to raw sewage released by the disaster have further harmed coral habitats and threatened already depleted fish stocks. Extensive damage to coral reef is seen in Katchal Island. The extent of reef area affected is 49% at Katchal (Ramachandran *et al.*, 2005).

On the day of the tsunami and after, extensive silt-laden turbid waters were seen all over the reef area. Such turbid waters were mapped using satellite imageries by Indian Satellite Remote Sensing Organisation, Deharadun (Roy, 2003). The water receded after ten days, but silt and mud were found to be deposited on the reef area. Later, the mud settled on these reefs led to death of coral polyps. In future it may lead to permanent loss of coral reef in these islands. The physical structure has been damaged by the force of the wave itself. Physical removal of flora and fauna and increased sediment load have killed sediment-sensitive corals and sea grasses by smothering Considerable forest and plantation areas were flooded by the tsunami. The forest areas inundated by the tsunami are 1787 ha (18%) in Katchal. The flooded sea water remained in the area for days and when it evaporated, it increased the soil salinity. This has affected the entire forest ecosystem, especially the micro flora of the forest ecosystem that helps in remineralisation and fertilisation process of this ecosystem.

Sand bars and sand dunes act as a buffer against storms and tidal surges. Removal and deposition of sand dunes have been witnessed due to tsunamis. Sand dunes have helped reduce the impact of the tsunami and this has helped protect the nearby settlements from being destroyed. Changes in sediment transport pattern and loss of sea turtle nesting grounds due to removal of sand from the beaches have also been seen on the islands. The sandy areas have considerably increased in two of the four islands. The increase in the extent of sandy beaches after the tsunami was 1242.02 ha in Katchal (Ramachandran and et al. 2005). A change in the physical environment has affected the biodiversity of the region. Changes in the chemistry of the water are another factor that have affected biodiversity. For example, muddy coasts now have become sandy coasts and vice versa. Fish populations are greatly affected due to vibrations and shock. Immediately after the tsunami, mortality of shellfishes such as prawns and crabs was observed in the vicinity of mangrove areas due to leaching of acid sulphate salts and water quality deterioration (Dam Roy and Krishnan, 2005). There is concern that marine life in the island could take centuries to recover after being devastated by the tsunami.

During tsunami, it was experienced that coastal plantation particularly mangroves served as best defence against such disasters. Coastline protection drew special attention as the land mass had gone down vertically and new vulnerable areas were exposed to sea water. The mitigating effect of mangroves depends on their response to two physical processes of tsunami - (i) wave attack, and (ii) towing flow. Mangrove's response to wave attacks depends on its vegetation characteristics, whereas the response to towing flow relies on 'drag force' caused by the mangroves, resulting in prevention of coastal erosion. Thus the protective role of mangroves depends on: (i) vegetation characteristics such as, density, height, species composition, density of forest, diameter of mangrove roots and trunks, and elevation of habitats, as well as status of ecological degradation of the forests; and, (ii) tsunami wave characteristics such as, wave height, wave period, depth of water (Mazda *et al.*, 1997 a, b). The role of mangroves in reducing the sea-waves is scientifically proved. Harada *et al.* (2002) have conducted a hydraulic experiment to study the tsunami reduction effect of the coastal permeable structures using five different models - mangroves, coastal forest, wave dissipating block, breakwater rock, and houses. This work reveals that mangroves are effective as compared to concrete seawall structures for reduction of tsunami-hit house damages behind the forest. Mazda *et al.,* (1997a) have reported that six-year-old mangrove forests of 1.5 km width reduce the sea-waves by 20 times, from 1 metre high waves at the open sea to 0.05 metres at the coast. The reduction of wave amplitude and energy by tree vegetation has also been proved by measurements of wave forces and modeling of fluid dynamics (Massel *et al.,* 1999). Analytical model shows that trees in a 100m wide belt may reduce the maximum tsunami flow pressure by more than 90%, if the wave height is less than 4-5 m (Hiraishi and Harada, 2003). Forest Department has started coastal defence plantation. Cross section of such defence wall was decided to be made up of local endemic species to avoid ecological contamination due to import of external species. It is also important from the view point of restoration of biodiversity because regeneration of the habitat-specific seaweed populations depends on the restoration of mangrove plants (Mantri, 2005).

Resilience of people

Tsunami has itched a permanent scar in the memory of people of Nicobar group of islands. They will never forget the tsunami, but they have not allowed themselves to get cowed down. One is not entirely sure of reasons and factors behind this marked resilience. Generally bereavement has two components: forced and natural. The natural component results from the longing and love for the deceased person. It is a healthy psychological sublimation process`. The forced component, on the other hand, results from the perceived loss of socio-economic well being due to the departure of the earning member. There are certain factors in the Nicobar society which soothes out this forced component. These include:

1. The tribal community practice strong joint family system, locally called *Kamunchiase* (Ramage). It is more than a common homestead. People of the same *Kamunchiase* even living in separate houses consider themselves as a unified whole. The *Kamunchiase* headman takes care of the whole *Kamunchiase*. This provides an excellent social safety net, which is strongly seen in the language as the local language does not have any word for 'widow' or 'orphan'. Each individual belongs to community.
2. Gender relations are much healthier in the tribal society. Women do not face any structured discrimination in access to social and economic assets. This comforting feature has direct correlation with the well being of women and children. As a consequence even the death of an earning male member does not affect as much the socio-economic potential of the household as in case of a non-tribal community.
3. The tribal economy is mainly biomass based barter system. Most of the consumption needs are fulfilled by nature itself. It is this sense of consumption security which has helped reduce the psychological stress to some extent they were suffering due to perceived loss of economic potential of a household. Further, the main productive asset (the land) is held at joint family level under *Kamunchiase*. The individual

land records are not maintained. They are neither with the community nor the administration. Thus an asset position of a family does not have much co-relation with individual male members of the family. The resulting individual independent economic security soothes out forced component of withdrawal symptoms

4. Tribal community is demonetised to certain extent. As a result, unlike the non-tribal community, psychological distress due to legal constraints in compensation distribution is absent to some extent.
5. Being a close nit society they have stronger influence of religion. Thus, they are able to sublimate longing and distress via biblical medium in a more effective fashion.

To restore psychological health and to bring back normalcy among children, restoration of schools was considered to be of utmost importance. Church of North India CNI/ CASA took up task of creating permanent schools. Due to logistical constraints, it was a long duration task, meanwhile value added semi-permanent schools had been created. By the end of December 2005, many schools were made operational in Katchal. For quality up-gradation, local teachers were sent for multi-grade / multi-scale methodology training. Local youths were trained in under the skill building programmes by the Industry Department in association with CARE.

However, socially Katchal Island like other islands of the Nicobar has undergone a huge transformation and it might be the beginning of a whole new system in the villages, joint families have split and kitchens are no longer one for many families. Money has been looked at with power to buy things. The traditional houses of wood and leaves also known as "Ngyo-pul" or round huts are replaced with asbestos sheets and the cultural shift from a joint family to nuclear families is evident. The present semi wooden structures (houses) will remind us of the villages and traditional architecture that used to exist.

Conclusion

The island situation of Katchal has contributed to the development of organic relationship between man and nature. The most important element in the system of resource management is in Katchal Island is the social structure of Nicobarese in which the decent groups *(Kamunchiase)* exercise authority over land and forest and are responsible for distributing usufructury right to the individual families. Family, in turn, is responsible for making full utilisation of resources in cooperation with other such units. Religion in form of spirit worship is an adaptive mechanism to nature where the propitiation of spirits, prior to the use of resources, is considered necessary. It has led to the development of a symbiotic relationship with nature resulting into the sustainable use of resources.

However in the aftermath of tsunami, which had struck the Andaman and Nicobar archipelago on 26th December, 2004, the Nicobar group of islands was worst affected and Katchal was one of the worst hit islands. The magnitude of devastation in term of loss of life and destruction of property were immense. Unprecedented level of human loss had and would continue to have strong bearing on psychological well being of survivors. The colossal loss of lives has resulted into loss of expertise in different spheres of material culture and belief system. Now there is probably no *Menluena* alive in the entire island in the aftermath of tsunami. It will take a long time before this void is filled in. In this regard, the non-tribal population is more at edge as they do not have a strong traditional social security net like tribal society.

References

A & N Administration. 1966. *Statistical Hand Book, A and N Islands.* Port-Blair.

Bodley, John. 1976. *Anthropology and Contemporary Human Problems.* Cunnings, California, p. 99.

Bonnington, M. C. 1931. *Census of India, Andaman and Nicobar Islands,* Part II and Vol. II, Kolkata-1.

Dagar, J.C. and Singh, N.T. 1999. *Plant Resources of the Andaman & Nicobar Islands*. Bishen Singh Mahendra Pal Singh, 1: 987 (1999).

Dam Roy, S. and Krishnan, P. 2005. Mangrove stands of Andaman vis-à-vis tsunami. *Current Science*, 89 : 1800-1804.

Government of India. 1909. *Imperial Gazetteer of India, Provincial Series: Andaman and Nicobar Islands.* Kolkata.

Census of India. 1991. *Andaman and Nicobar Islands*. Govt. of India.

Census of India. 2001. *Andaman and Nicobar Islands: Provisional Tables*. Govt. of India.

Grierson, G. A. 1967. *Linguistic Survey of India.* Vol. I, Part 1, Kolkata, pp. 32-33.

Harada, K., Imamura, R. and Hiraishi, T. (1992). Experimental study on the effect in reducing tsunami by the coastal permeable structures. *Final Proc. Int. Offshore Polar Eng. Conf.* USA, pp. 652-658.

Harada, K., Imamura, F., Hiraishi, T. (2002). Experimental study on the effect in reducing Tsunami by the coastal permeable structures. *Final Proc. Int. Offshore Polar Eng. Conf.*, USA, pp. 652-658.

Hillary Jr. George A. 1968. *Communal Organisation: A Study of Local Societies.* Chicago, Univ. of Chicago Press, p. 34.

Hiraishi, T., Harada , K. (2003). Green belt Tsunami Prevention in South-Pacific Region. Available from : http://eqtap.edm.bosai.go.jp / useful_outputs/report/hiraishi /data / papers/greenbelt. pdf

Justin A. 1990. *The Nicobarese.* Calcutta. Anthropological Survey of India, the ASI Andaman and Nicobar Tribe Series.

Kathiresan, K. 2000. A review of studies on Pichavaram mangrove, southeast India. *Hydrobiologia*, 430 : 185-205.

Kathiresan, K. and Bingham, B.L. 2001. Biology of mangroves and mangrove ecosystems. *Advances in Marine Biology*, 40 : 81-251.

Kathiresan, K., Rajendran, N. 2005. Coastal mangrove forests mitigated tsunami. *Estuarine coastal and Shelf Science*, 65 : 601-606.

Kathiresan, K. and Rajendran, N. 2006. Reply to Comments of Kerr et al. on 'Coastal mangrove forests mitigated tsunami' (Estuar.Coast. Shelf Sci 65: 601-606. *Estuarine Coastal and Shelf Science*, 67 : 542.

Kloss, B. C. 1903. (reprint 1971). *Andaman and Nicobars* (reprint). Vivek, Delhi.

Kloss, B.C. 1903. *In the Andamans and Nicobars: The Narrative of a Cruise on the Schooner "Terrapin" with Notices of their Fauna, Ethnology, Etc.* John Murray, London.

Man, E.H.B. 1889. The Nicobar Islanders. *Journal of Anthropological Survey of India and Ireland*, Vol. XVIII, London, p. 367.

Mathur, K. K. 1967. *Nicobar Islands.* NBT, New Delhi, p. 42.

Mantri, V.A., 2005. Changes in local intertidal seaweed habitats in the Andaman and Nicobar Islands after 26 December 2004 tsunami. *Current Science*, 89 : 1071-72.

Massel, S.R. (1999). Tides and waves in mangrove forests: in fluid mechanics for marine ecologists. *Springer- Verlag*, pp. 418-425.

Mauses.1984. *The Gift.* Cohen and West Ltd., London.

Mazda, Y., Magi, M., Kogo, M. and Hong, P.N. (1997). Mangrove on coastal protection from waves in the Tong King Delta, Vietnam. *Mangroves and Salt Marshes*, 1: 127-135.

Mazda, Y., Wolanski, E., King, B., Sase, A. and Ohtsuka, D., 1997b. Drag force due to vegetation in mangrove swamps. *Mangroves and Salt Marshes*, 1(3) : 193-199.

Ramachandran, S., Anitha, S., Balamurugan, V., Dharanirajan, K., Ezhil Vendhan, K., Marie Irene Preeti Divien, Senthil Vel, A., Sjjahad Hussain, I. and Udayaraj, A. 2005. Ecological impact of tsunami on Nicobar Islands (Camorta, Katchal, Nancowry and Trinkat). *Current Science*, 89 : 195-200.

Rappaport, Roy, A. B. 1967. Ritual Regulation of Governmental Relation among New Guinea People. *Ethnology*, 6, pp. 17-31.

Rappaport, Roy, A. B. 1968. *Pigs for the Ancestors.* Yale University Press, New Haven.
Roy P.S. (Project Director) 2003. *Biodiversity Characterisation at Landscape Level in Andaman & Nicobar Islands Using Satellite Remote Sensing and Geographic Information System.* Indian Institute of Remote Sensing and Department of Environment and Forest, Dehradun.
Sahalin, M.D. 1968. *Tribesmen.* Prentice Hall, New Jersey.
Shyam, N.K. 1977. *Social structure of Car Nicobar Islanders.* Anthropological Survey of India, Kolkata.
Singh J.S. 2003. *In the Sea of Influence. A World System Perspective of the Nicobar Islands.* Lund. Lund University
Sinha Roy, K.M and Datta Chaudhury, S.S. 2007. "Tsunami 2004-A Disaster Unparallel: A Case Study of Katchal and Nancowry Island" in *Tsunami in South Asia,* Anthropological Survey of India, Kolkata.
Temple, R. C. 1903. *Census of India, Andaman and Nicobar Islands.* Vol. III, Part II, Kolkata.
Vitousek, P.M. and T.L. Benning. 1995. Ecosystem and Landscape Diversity: Islands as Model Systems. In: Vitousek, P.M., L.L Loope, H. Andersen, (eds.) *Islands: Biological Diversity and Ecosystem Function. – Ecological Studies ;* 115. New York. Springer.

10

Management of Environment and Natural Resources Study on Traditional Wisdom among the War Khasi of Meghalaya

R. R. Gowloog and *S. Mukherjee*

Introduction

Historical material on the Khasis, before the advent of the British, is scarce and scholars have had to deal with incomplete and inconsistent records. But it has been well established that the Khasi and Jaintia Hills formed one kingdom, which in course of time became divided to two separate kingdoms – the Khynriam and the Pnar(Jaintia). These kingdoms in turn, were divided into several political units (Bareh – 1967 – 13).

The Khasis are a Scheduled Tribe of Meghalaya and are divided into five groups known as (1) Khynriam, (2) Pnar, (3) Bhoi, (4) Lyngam and (5) War, occupying different parts of the state. The Khasis speak a Mon–Khmer language which belongs to the Austro Asiatic family. They follow the matrilineal descent system.

The Khasis belong to one of the earliest groups of people migrating to North–East India. They are the nearest cognates of the Austrics in view of anthropological and linguistic findings. That the ancient Khasis had settled in Assam before coming to this present abode is shown by the Austric names of ancient places in Assam. The remains of megaliths of Austric origin scattered over the hills and plains of North–East India also lead to the same conclusion (Bareh – 1967).

No separate historical account of the War Khasis is available. Thus the historical accounts relating to the Khasi people in general largely stand true for the West Khasi Hills also. There are historical indications to show that they had migrated from outside and had a fairly developed political organisation and detailed administration for the villages as well. They also had a highly developed technology of iron smelting and manufacturing iron tools which were exported to distant places on the south as well as north (Bareh – 1967, Dasgupta – 1984, Gurdon – 1907).

This present essay is based on the study conducted in Mawlam village under Pynursla Block, East Khasi Hills districts, Meghalaya. The study deals with tribal wisdom among the traditional War Khasi people who are spread throughout the Pynursla Block and surrounding areas. They are concentrated over the highly dissected plateau gradually sloping down towards south from the ridge and culminating abruptly in the Bangladesh plains.

Mawlam, a typical War village, was selected for detailed study mainly due to its location in a remote corner of the south western part of the Pynursla Block and still dominated by traditional religion called '*Niamtre*'. The village is approachable by a partially metalled road from Pynursla village, the block headquarters. One has to cover a distance of about 15 kilometres from the diversion point on the Shillong – Dawki Highway at 58 kilometres from Shillong, the state headquarters.

The village is mainly inhabited by the War Khasis. The few migrant labourers found there, however, cannot be considered as part of the village population and are not considered so by the villagers themselves. The total population of the local people, according to the records available with the Pynursla Block office, is 556 of which 254 are males and 282 are females. The total number of households according to the same source is 135. Such households are distributed over a number of clusters. sample

AREA IN FOCUS

The main objective of the present work is to study the traditional wisdom in relation to environmental resource use and conservation. Hence the enquiry was directed to document and understanding the indigenous knowledge of the people about their traditional sources of livelihood in West Khasi Hills district of Meghalaya; to understand the traditional forms of resource utilization, the traditional technology of preservation and conservation of natural resources, and to understand the changes, if any, in the above respects.

The study is based on a purposively selected village called Mawlam, located in interior part of Pynursla Block of East Khasi Hills Districts. The purpose of selecting this village was to find a village which was rich in traditional wisdom regarding environmental management. This was discussed with local knowledgeable officials and key informants at the Pynursla Block Office and finally the village under study was selected. The whole Pynursla C D Block is the traditional homeland of the War Khasis living in symbiotic relation with the environment for a few thousand years or so.

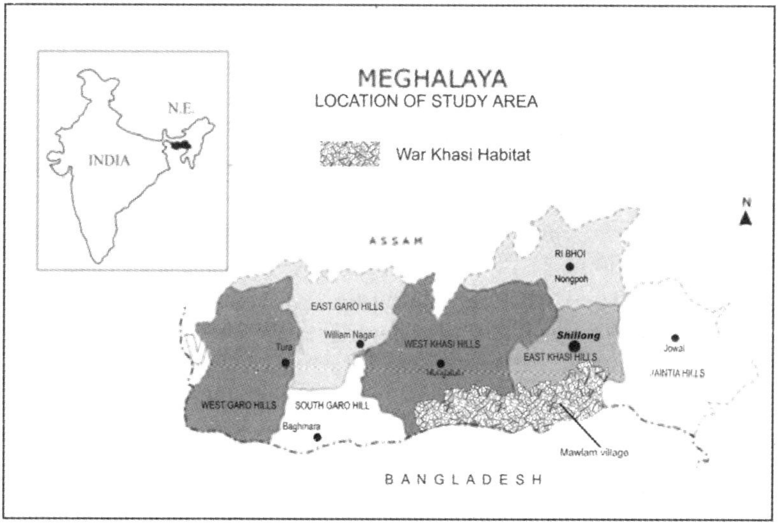

Fig. 1. Location of studied village in the Ri War or the War country, the traditional habitat of the War Khasi people.

The requisite data for the purpose were based on observation and interview. The interview was based on the schedule for village survey along with a detailed guideline provided by the office project coordinator. Schedules on household survey were used to take the information regarding demographic as well as resource possessions. Households were selected purposively again to get samples from various economic levels to get a complete picture of the different resources utilization patterns. In total 52 households were covered which included two Christian and one family of Bodo husband from Assam staying with his Khasi wife. All the interviews were conducted with the help of a qualified guide, a graduate, War boy, from Pynursla. Audio–visual tools like a tap recorder and a still camera were also used in the field. Finally, to gather a comprehensive account of various aspects like a role of market, irrigation and hunting technologies we visited several other places in the War area.

Regional background

Meghalaya was a part of Assam in the form of two districts, viz. the United Khasi and Jaintia Hills districts and the Garo Hills districts. They were autonomous districts of Assam under Paragraph 1 (1) of the Sixth Schedule to the Constitution of India. Meghalaya was born on the 24th December, 1969 following the 22nd Amendment of the Indian Constitution by passing the Assam Re–organisation (Meghalaya) Bill. On the 2nd April, 1970, the autonomous state of Meghalaya was inaugurated and the full fledged statehood was attained on 21st January, 1972, Meghalaya lies between 25° 47' and 26° 10' North latitude and 89° 45' and 92° 47' East longitude. It is bounded by Assam on the north–east, west and south by Bangladesh. Its area is 22,429 square kilometres.

According to Bareh, (1984) the Khasi Hills region is divided into three regions. 1) Bhoi region on the north which forms itself a compact plateau with associated flat lands and open valleys, its northern extremity gradually sloping towards the Brahmaputra valleys. Ri–Lum, an irregular plateau on higher elevation comprising of metamorphic rocks with some river basins are seen here and there. The highest table land extends from near about Mawphlang Upland on the west as far as the Raphlang Hills on the east and culminates at Swer and Lyngkyrdem on the south. The highest peak is Shillong or Laikor peak (6,449 feet) situated on the top of the capital city. The central plateau of the Jaintia Hills is formed mostly of small ranges of hills with extensive valleys amidst them. Towards the south of Ri–Lum lie the Mawsynram, Sohra and Syndai platforms renowned for the heaviest rainfall in the world. The last division is Ri–War forming a narrow belt full of oblong and sturdy ridges, abruptly terminating at the Surma Valley, forming a scene of mounted up precipices, occasionally coloured by deep gorges, carved up by magnificent rocks, intersperse by the elevated ravines and at particular points, the sparkling cascades can be clearly seen (Bareh, 1967).

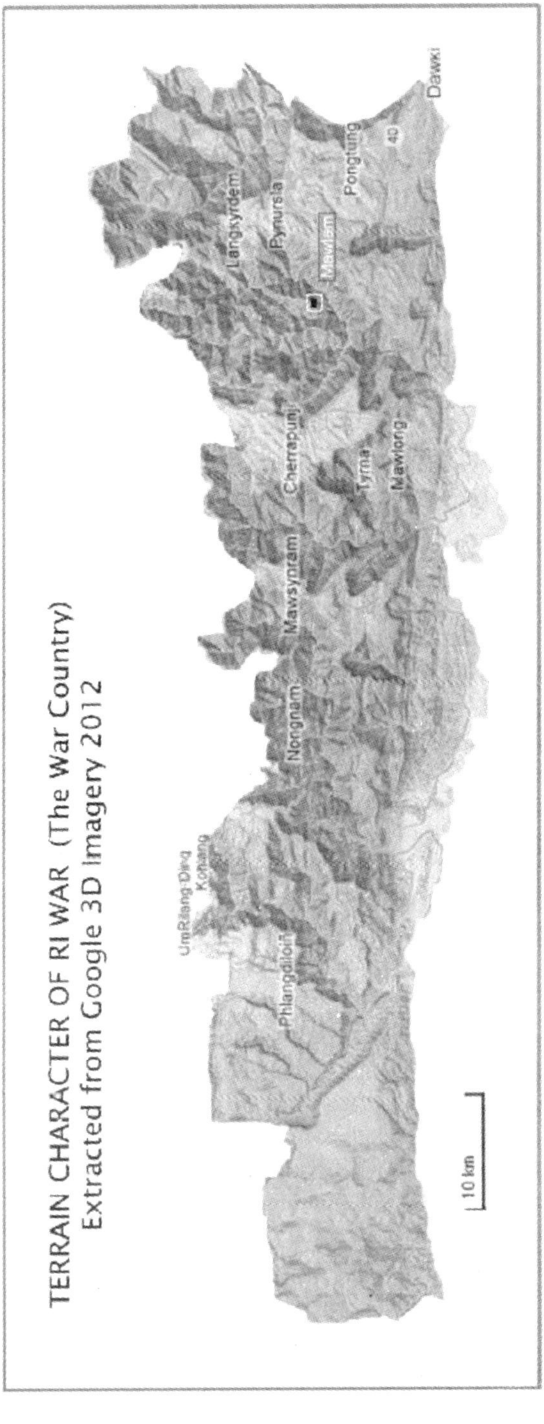

Fig. 2. The highly dissected War Country as visible in the satellite imagery

The climate of the region differs due to variation in altitude and terrain. Generally the high hills enjoy a salubrious climate through most part of the year. The region is directly influenced by the south–west monsoon. It is interesting to note that Cherrapunjee at the southern extremity of Ri–Lum received the highest rainfall and in 1961 the total amount of rainfall came up to about 900 inches but recently Mawsynram, lying west of Cherrapunjee, has received more rainfall than hitherto rainiest place.

The three main communities in Meghalaya are Khasi, Jaintia and Garo. The Khasis and the Jaintias inhabit the eastern and central portions of Meghalaya. They speak a Môn–Khmer language, where as the Garos inhabiting the western part of Meghalaya speaks a Tibeto–Burman language. All these three communities are distinct in terms of their matrilineal kinship system. More than sixty percent of its population are Christians, the remaining being distributed among "animists", Hindus, Muslims and Jains.

The origin of the name 'Khasi' is shrouded in mystery and no one has so far been able to come up with a satisfactory explanation of the term. It has been derived, according to some, from the Indo–Aryan word '*Khas*' signifying waste or scrub land. 'Khasi' or '*Khasia*' would thus mean, according to them, an inhabitant of scrub country (Meghalaya Districts Gazetteer, Khasi Hills Districts 1991: 1). To quote Bareh again "*The term Khasi has a particular significance. Kha means born of and Si refers to an ancient mother. It is relevant to add here that the various names of clans bear their mother's names. For instance Sawain clan owes its name to Sa, the ancestress; Ngap Kynta bears the name of Ngap, the ancient mother of that clan... This system of ascribing the names of clans after mother, is, as well, intimately related to a matrilineal system of the people themselves. Khasi therefore, indicated, an original derivation and a legacy bequeathed upon the descendants*" (1967).

The state is now divided into seven districts, each with an Autonomous Districts Council. These districts are (1) East Khasi Hills district; (2) Jaintia Hills districts; (3) West Khasi Hills district; (4) Ri–Bhoi districts; (5) East Garo Hills district; (6) West Garo Hills district and (7) South Garo Hills districts. The East Khasi Hills district is predominantly dominated by the Khynriam and War Khasis. The Jaintia Hills districts by the Jaintias or Pnars; the West Khasi Hills districts by Wars and Lyngngams; Ri–Bhoi by Bhois; and the three other districts by the Garos. The Districts Councils are not only autonomous in internal affairs but also act an intermediary body determining the relations between the people on one hand and the state and the Union Governments on the other (Bareh 1967).

Natural Resources

SOIL : There are three main types of soils in Meghalaya the red loam or hill soils, the laterite soil, and the old alluvium. The red loam or hill soils occupy almost the entire region except a limited tract in the foot hills and sub–mundane fringes and a pocket in the south western Mikir Hills adjoining the Jaintia Hills. These soils are generally loamy, varying sometimes between clay and sandy loam and are rich in organic matter and nitrogen. These are usually acidic and are good for the cultivation of fruits, potatoes and rice in hill slopes and terraces. The soil is, however, deficient in phosphate and potash.

The laterite soil of the plateau are confined to a small fringe extending from west to east in the northern border of the plateau with its important concentration in the south–western part of the Mikir Hills adjoining the Jaintia Hills. These soils are highly leached, poor in plant nutrients and acidic in reaction.

The old alluvium is found in the highland areas bordering the plains, all along the northern fringe of the region. These soils occupy very low percentage of the region and are usually very much acidic in nature. In texture they vary from sandy to clay loam with a varying degree of nitrogen from high to low content. They are deficient in available phosphate. These soils are used for the cultivation of rice, fruits, vegetables and tea (a limited average) in the Mikir Hills region adjoining the Nowgong and Sibsagar districts (Singh 1971).

The vegetation is rich. To quote Sir Joseph Hooker, "The flora of the Khasi Hills in number and variety of fine plants is the richest in India and probably in Asia" (1856: 490). Nature and climate have exercised a tremendous influence on the life and activities of the people. Impressed with the scenery of the Khasi Hills, the first English observer (1826) compared the country to the highlands of Scotland, whereas Sir Joseph Hooker in 1856 compared the pastures of Mairong to those of New Zealand. During the Second World War, the Khasi Hills was nickname 'the Scotland of the East' and Shillong (then headquarters of Assam) situated in the heart of the land was known as one of the lovely 'Queens of Hill Stations' in India. (Bareh, 1967: 9)

The region is very rich in mineral resources but so far only coal, limestone and sillimunite have, to some extent, been commercially exploited. Recent investigations have revealed the presence of clay, corundum, glass, sand, phosphate, iron, uranium etc. The important minerals of the region are:–

(1) Upper cretaceous and lower tertiary coal in Garo, Khasi and Mikir Hills;
(2) High grade numulitic limestone, in a belt extending from Garo Hills in the west through the Khasi, Jaintia, Mikir Hills in the east;
(3) Sillimanite and corundum deposits in Sonapahar area of the Khasi Hills;
(4) Clays including Kaolin or 'China–Clay' in the Garo (Tura area), Khasi (Mawphlang area), Jaintia and Mikir Hills, the Garo Hills alone having more than 35 million tons of kaolin and occurring in as many as ten places;
(5) Glass sands in the coal–fields of the Laitryngew and Cherrapunjee areas in the Khasi Hills;
(6) Banded iron–ore in the border areas of the Khasi Jaintia Hills and the Assam Valley;
(7) Copper, in the Umpyrtha and Ranighat areas in the Khasi and Jaintia Hills;
(8) Gold bearing rocks with a trace of 1.2 penny weight of gold per ton of rock, south–west of Mawphlang in the Khasi Hills; and
(9) Gypsum in the form of Sebémite crystals and disseminated in shale beds, near Mahendraganj in the Garo Hills and in some places in Mikir Hills.

Regarding regional distribution of the said potentially rich mineral wealth, Meghalaya plateau not only has the greatest concentration of minerals but also has accounted for a high regional income from mining in the Meghalaya. This section of Meghalaya produces more than 90% of the total sillimanite of India which is mined in and around the recently established mining centre of Sonapahar, about 3 kilometres north of Nongmaweit in the northern part of the Nongstoin state of the Khasi Hills, from 13 deposits in a belt, 20 kilometres long and 1.5 kilometres wide reserves of this natural refractory, world famous from the point of view of quantity and purity and for occurrence in the form of massive rocks from which blocks can be sawn for direct use in furnaces, have been estimated at about 0.5 million tonnes. Corundum, another valuable mineral, is found to occur in association with the sillimite deposits.

Coal has been exploited to a great extent in the Garo and the Jaintia Hills.

The exploitation of nummulitic limestone is also very significant in the region. Bulk of the limestone is being utilized in the cement factory at Cherrapunjee.

The wide variations in climatic conditions in elevation as well as in the character of the soil offer scope for the cultivation of a wide variety of agricultural crops and fruits trees, ranging from species adapted to tropical conditions to those that thrive in temperate climate. Major crops are rice, maize, millet etc. Productions of these are for self consumption only. The introduction of tapioca the Forest Department helped to stabilize the situation in time. According to the 1981 census report as many as 84 (eighty four) villages in the area raised tapioca. Many villages are large scale producers of potato. Potato was apparently introduced by David Scott into the Khasi Hills and immediately proved successful. The British Government started on an experimental farm at Upper Shillong in 1873 but discontinued the project after a short time because of the loss it sustained. The farm was, however, revived towards the close of the 19th century and the report for 1897 – 98 indicated that the potato experiment was very successful. It is also one of the major cash crops. It can be grown in rotation with rice, thus ensuring the maximum utilization of land as well as greater profit. Sweet potato and yam are grown for domestic consumption other important cash crops are areca nut, betel leaf, black pepper, bay leaves, ginger, broom stick etc.

Almost all kinds of vegetables suitable for varying climatic conditions are also cultivated, e.g. carrot, cucumber, turnip, varieties of beans and peas, cauliflower, cabbage, tomatoes, chillies, brinjal, okra, gourds etc. The soil and climate are also conductive for the growth of variety of fruits like orange, pineapples, lemons, bananas, guava, mango, jackfruits, litchi, pears, peaches, papaya, plums, etc.

Geographical aspects

The Southern portion of the Shillong Plateau under the East Khasi Hills District is dominantly inhabited by the War Khasi group stands as a distinct physiographic and cultural unit. In fact War Khasi villages are scattered all over this highly dissected plateau surface which, as per Dasgupta (1984) is bounded by Mahram state, Mawsynram state and Laitlyngkot on the south by Mymensing and Sylhet districts of Bangladesh and on the east by

Jaintia Hills with extreme point reaching Lubha River. Roughly within the co–ordinates of 25° 10″ to 25° 27″ north latitude and 91°10″ to 92°05″ east longitude the region spreads approximately 85 km. along the Bangladesh Border and 20 km. along north–south.

Physiography: The Khasi Hills as a whole may be roughly divided into three prominent physiographic zones from north to south. The Central ridge, the highest part of the Meghalaya Plateau is called Khasi Highland with average height of about 1000 m. includes Shillong Peak (1964 m.) stands mighty as the Central zone. On the north of it the plateau drops slowly stepwise upto the edge of the Brahmaputra plain of Assam. This moderately sloping rolling hills region is termed as Ri–Bhoi were altitude averages around 600 m. The third zone starts immediately the southern edge of the central Khasi upland roughly conforming to the 4000 feet (1000 m) contour line. This narrow elongated 'Ri–War' region is highly dissected by many small and big streams and rivers flowing south ward into the Bangladesh plains. The highest relative relief with deep gorges over the old erosional levels of the plateau are the most striking. Topographical features of the region is very heavy rainfall, mostly from the south west monsoon is the responsible factor for shaping the topography of this War region which includes Mawsynram and Cherrapunjee the worlds highest rainfall sites. The central ridge acts as the orographic barrier leaving the northern part as rain shadow area of the monsoon current.

The Meghalaya Plateau has a complex geological and geomorphological history being the part of the ancient Gondwana super continent separated by the Garo–Rajmahal gap on its western boundary. The plateau contains within its barren faceted marks of several peneplains or the old erosion surfaces, which ranges from Pre–Cambrian to Recent and Sub–Recent periods. This Pre–Cambrian Gondwana block experienced several emergence and submergence with erosion, sedimentation, diastrophism, intrusion, movement of land and sea and emission (Singh – 1971). The northern part of the War country, just south of the Shillong Hills, has a typical granitic topography with rounded hills and shallow valleys compared of the Myllium granite. Further south beyond Myllium there is a vast structure platform on which stands Cherrapunjee. This part is composed gently dipping sandstones of cretaceous age. This structural platform stands as an escarpment and its face has been attacked by flurried action due to extremely heavy rainfall and as a result of which a number of platforms, e.g.

Cherrapunjee, Lyngkyrdem and Mawsynram have been formed. From Cherrapunjee and Lyngkyrdem the terrain has a gentle slope southwards for about 7 – 10 km. and then falls rapidly to the Sylhet Plains (Singh, 1971).

The drainage pattern in the region represents a most spectacular feature of extraordinary straight river courses evidently along joints and faults. The magnificent gorges scooped out by the rivers in the southern Khasi Hills are the results of massive hardward erosion by the antecedent streams along joints of the sedimentary rocks over the blocks, experiencing relatively greater upliftment.

The War region is drained by several south flowing rivers and streams originates from southern flank of the Central Upland.

Along the eastern boundary of the War Um–Ngot River is one of the longest in the region. It originates near the Shillong Peak and has a straight flow southward with a westward bend in the middle and finally enters Bangladesh plains of Dawki taking the name Pigain Gang. It has a relatively large catchment area which includes the eastern part of the Shillong – Dawki Highway. This Highway runs along the narrow ridge between Laitlynkot and Pynursla forming the water divides with another important system on the west run by the river Umsohryngkew and its tributaries. In between these two drainage systems a small triangular segment of the lower plateau with its crest near Pynursla village, is drained by the river Umkrem. Further west the source flows just west of Shillong Peak. It has a narrow long course sandwiched between Cherrapunjee plateau on the east and Mawsynram and enters Bangladesh at Shella Bazar. The Umngi River drains the western flank of Mawsynram ridge. Finally the Kynchiang or Jadukata River, the longest river course of the War country forms roughly its western limit. However, all along the Bangladesh border there are some minor rivers or rather hilly streams like Ballat, Rengua, Mawkam, Armen, Erangaru etc. which along with all others rivers mentioned above are draining their waters into the Surma River in Bangladesh.

Climate: A huge difference in altitude, very high slopes of the valley walls, direct exposure to the strong tropical monsoon currents from Bay of Bengal are the important keys to understand the climatic characters of the War region. From more 80 m on the south to above 1000 m on the north is an immense altitudinal range within a maximum aerial distance of only 32 km (near Lyngkerdem village).

The meteorological significance of the War region is evident from the fact that two of the five major meteorological station of Meghalaya are located here, i.e. Cherrapunjee and Mawsynram, recording world's highest rainfall. These two stations are located only about 165 km apart and almost along 25°17"N Latitude. The normal annual rainfall recorded (Census – 1981) are 7.378.94 mm in Cherrapunjee and 10.093.53 m in Mawsynram most of which is received during the actual rainy season from May to September, though April and October are also fairly wet. The geographic feature of these two stations are unique in the sense that sheer cliffs of about 1000 m up to the edge of the table and faces directly south providing a huge barrier to the monsoon clouds. Thus, it is expected that even within this micro region we may get considerable variation of fall depending on the location and direction of valley walls. Likewise, air temperature varies with the altitude. The tablelands reaches above 900 m enjoy milder temperature compared to the deep valleys and low lying patches of plains along the Bangladesh border having hot–humid condition. The mean maximum temperatures for Cherrapunjee are 20.6°C and mean minimum is 14.3°C. But there are no such recordings in any low valley areas to understand the range of variation in normal monthly temperatures with 9.20°C in January the coolest month and the 16.91°C in the hottest month August. But as major part of the region is lower in altitude than the other stations, the general climatic conditions must be warmer with higher differences between winter and summer temperature. In fact in most part there is a short dry winter of moderate temperature between November and January followed by a dry pre–monsoon months of March–April characterised by very strong winds spreading wild fires over the grassy slopes. Then the long hottest and wettest season between May–October is prevalent along this southern plateau slopes.

Geology of War Country: The northern most part, which is in fact the southern flank of Central (Shillong) ridge is mostly Shillong group of quartzite lying unconformabely over the Archaran gneissic complex. Then the rocks are intruded by acidic silts and dykes around Myllium are hard Myllium granites. To the south of Lyngkerdem up to the Bangladesh border Cretaceous Tertiary Sediments occupies the thick and extensive beds, a continuity of the same series of Bangladesh Basin. The sediments are mainly sandstone and shale and most of the major coal and limestone deposits of the area.

Soil: The archaran and Pre–Cambrian rocks under the impact of heavy tropical rainfall have developed into Red Loam or Hill soils over most of the plateau with certain exception of Laterites and allumiums. These soils are generally loamy, varying sometimes between clayee and dandy loam and are rich in organic matter and nitrogen. These are usually acidic and suitable for orchards of fruits, potatoes etc. However, the soils are deficient in potash and phosphate (Singh, 1971).

On the southern part of East Khasi Hills District soils are of somewhat different types depending on the local geologic formation and climate. The Pynursla Block and the adjoining War country possess mainly two types of soils. Those are as per I.C.A.R. classification:

(1) Udalfs–Ochrepts–Orthents: – with high base status and of shallow black and brown colour, which have formed recently under humid climatic conditions. This type roughly occupies the portion north of Pynursla village over the high plateau slopes and tablelands when potato and orange grows well.

(2) Ustalfs–Ochrepts–Orthents: – the shallow black, brown and recent alluvial soils utilized well for oranges, betel nuts, betel leaves, all over the southern most part upto Bangladesh border (Census 1981).

Flora: Though the Meghalaya Plateau is well known for its unique bio–diversity having a wide range of endemic species the present day forest cover is far below the significant level from environmental point of view. Still the last traces of greens are found mostly in the form of sacred grove's and village or community forest which is preserved as part of the old tradition of these people.

In the Central and Eastern Meghalaya including Khasi and Jaintia Hills districts, the vegetation types can broadly be grouped into:

(a) The mixed tropical evergreen hardwood are found in the northern and southern parts upto an elevation of about 300 *m* where main species are Sal, Sam, Champa, Gamhari, Boli, etc. besides the thickets of bamboo, cane and wild banana trees in the slopes and narrow valleys;

(b) In the middle altitude belt between 300 – 700 m the rolling grasslands of the Central plateau trees and shrubs are bare with scattered pine trees;

(c) Mainly Pine trees are found along with Willow, Birch, Mokrisal, Oak, Mongolia, Beech and Rhododendrons etc over the highest part of the plateau around Shillong above 750 m.

One of the significant peculiarities in vegetation cover is observed in the southern faces of the Shillong Plateau including the War country. In spite of very heavy precipitation under tropical conditions we do not get a dense evergreen rainforest in the part. The entire area looks black and dreamy with hillocks and the landscape is characterised by occasional open grassland through which the underlying rocks project out. This is mainly due to two factors the steep slopes and the structural character of the horizontally laid limestone beds which helps quick draining of rain water leaving a very badly leached soil on surface (Singh – 1971). But over the lower slopes and the head ward region of the small and medium catchments one can find lush green blocks and strips compound of a very rich species of trees and under growth resembling rainforests. In brief the natural vegetation of Khasi Hills can broadly be divided into the Tropical (upto about 1000 m) and warm temperate type (on the higher region) (Simon – 1991).

The richness in floral diversity of the War country can well be projected from the comments made by Dr. Joseph Dalton Hooker in his Himalayan Journals (1850): *"It is extremely difficult to give within the limits of this narration any idea of the Khasi Hills flora which is, in extent and number of fern plants, the richest in India and probably in all Asia. We collected upwards of 2000 flowering plants within ten miles of the station of Churra (Cherra) besides 150 ferns, with a profusion of mosses, litchens and fungi"* and again *"In fact, strange as it may appear ... the temperate flora descends fully 1000* ft *lower in the latitude of Khassia (25 degree N) thus, and that of Sikkim (27 degree N) though the former is two degrees nearer to the Equator"*.

Further Hooker (1850) has given a first hand account of the vegetation on the southern slopes of the East Khasi Hills district. He observed many varieties of palm trees of those twenty kinds being indigenous including the cultivated betel nut with its graceful standard feathery crown adorned the verdant slopes. Trees like oaks, oranges, gamboges, diosphyros, figs, jacks, plantains, and screw pines and many more frequent here together with virus and peppers. The broader leafed wild betel nuts, and beautiful earyoter or wine–palms with huge leaves twelve feet long. There are usual prevalence of numerous parasites, epi–physical orchids, ferns, mosses and Lycopodiums – and host of bamboo species. (Dasgupta, 1983)

North Eastern India being declared as one of the eight 'Bio–Diversity Hot Spots of the world', faces a serious threat for steady depletion of its forest cover. In Meghalaya the situation is among the worst with only 42.34% of total geographical area under any type of forest cover which is second lowest only above Assam in North–Eastern states in terms of the rate of depletion of forest cover between 1993 and 1995. Meghalaya (39.78%) again came second only to Nagaland. The Forest Survey of India, Report (1995) further stated that the actual healthy dense forest cover, the environmentally useful land is only 20.96% of the total forest cover in Meghalaya, the lowest among all N.E. states. The remaining 79.04% of forest are the mixture of open and degraded types. The impact of the Supreme Court order towards the enforcement of Front Conservation Acts since 1996 has not yet been assured. But the sudden drying up of a major source of income generation through illegal sale of forest products may develop a paradox as the rural Meghalayans will not find any alternate occupation than their traditional Jhum Cultivation again. In fact, Jhum cultivation change forest on hill slope could not be stopped totally and some ...110 sq. km of forest waste converted to jhum fields during 1991 – 1993 and also to plantation agriculture (NEC, 1995). This jhuming or shifting cultivation is observed as the main factor responsible for depletion of natural resources. This is because due to increased population that the jhum cycle has become shorter from around 30 – 40 years to as low as 6 – 10 years or less at present (Simon, 1991). Hence usual term of regeneration of the forests on fallow jhum lands is not allowed and also as the forests and mostly owned by families jhuming cannot be prevented easily.

Cultural Set Up

Mawlam, the village under study, is mostly inhabited by the War Khasi people. People in the village believe the War Khasis to have migrated from the Cherra side. Those settled in the upper side are known as War *Phlang* (grass land) and those who settled down slope were known as War. Some also believe the term War to be an anglicised term from *Wah* meaning river. An interesting story is narrated by some elders as to why the name "Mawlam" meaning guiding stone. *'Maw'* meaning 'rock', *'Lam'* means 'one who leads the path'. Originally the village was far down the slope on the northern side. Once, a group of Synteng people from Jaintia Hills came to that village to capture some land. At the entry point one stone with a small stone resting on top blocked the way of the invaders. The villagers found the invaders trapped by that stone. The invaders begged pardon and promised never to come back again. So the villagers believe that they were saved by that stone. Since then they consider the stone as *Ublei* (God). Every year they worship the stone in the month of March. If anybody disturbs or touches the stone; a tiger with a man's head or a man without head will appear indicating God's wrath. They appease with some sacrifice and annual worship. The whole village was later shifted to the Upper part of the hill as they found a flat surface. But still they have much area in Podwar region.

Village Mawlam nestles on the southern slope of a hill and slowly descends to the Bangladesh plains. Viewed from the top, the village is hardly perceptible with the green foliage with which the southern slopes are clad. Thick jungle having large groves of betel nut and other fruit trees surround the main village. There is no paddy land in the village and the people do not cultivate the crop. Shifting cultivation is practised in the neighbouring jungles. Communication between houses are maintained with narrow footpaths or rough stone steps. Mawlam is one of the eleven Raids under Pynursla Block. The village comprises a number of hamlets or *Khels*. These *Khels* send their headman to represent them in the village council or *Dorbar Shnong*. The houses (mainly Katcha and semi Pucca) clusters together in various pockets. No area of the village is kept separate for any particular clan; all categories of people live together. There is one Government Lower Primary School for the whole village up to Class – IV, employing four (4) teachers. Recently they have built one community hall, which was yet to be inaugurated. Most interesting thing to be noted is the maintenance of traditional houses built with good quality of wood, type of bamboo, stone and thatched roofs. There were only two pucca buildings in the village viz. school and one shop, most houses were semi–pucca. The houses were constructed in such a fashion that they best suited this region and most materials used in construction were locally available. Triangular shaped plots of land are avoided because it brings bad luck and death occurs in that family ultimately leaving none. Boundary stones are always treated with respect. In case one happens to touch it or go over it, he/she will suffer rheumatic pains and victims are advised to tie a straw or creeper around the stone and thereby transfer the affliction to the stone. They prefer their houses facing eastward. A common playground lies in the centre of the village, which is typical of any large and important War village, which is meant for any kind of community gatherings like annual religious festivals and dances etc. The two main sources of water, natural springs, lies either side of the village inside the Law Adong Wah Shiep lies towards north east and Wah Tlang towards south–west of the village. Water scarcity prevails during winter months. To reach these two water sources needed quite steep descend. As told by the villagers during summer pits (*Shynkhah*) were dug at the front of the houses to store rain water for washing and other purposes.

All their fields of broomstick, orange, bay leaves and orchards lies away from the village and most of the family members leave their houses at dawn carrying their lunch packs (made locally from bark of betel nut trees) and return only after sunset.

Domesticated animals were mainly pigs, and fowls. They had no concept of consuming milk so no cows are reared. But spilling of milk on the fire is considered harmful to the animal from which the milk has been obtained and to ward off the injurious consequences salt is sprinkled on the fire immediately. Sometimes milk packets are brought for consumption from Shillong.

Regarding dress, majority of males have adopted the western type dress, i.e. coat, trousers and shirt. Their traditional dress was a small cloth round the waist and between the legs, one end of which hangs in front like a small apron (*Sleng*). A sleeveless coat (*Jymphang*) with a row of tassels across the chest which acts like button, elderly men wear turbans. A bag made of cloth or some back of a tree is slung across the shoulders for carrying their necessary things. Most women, particularly those of the rural areas are still conservative regarding their dress known as *Jainsem* (two pieces of cloth pinned over the shoulders). The undergarment of the women is a petticoat (*Kashimi*) and a blouse (*Ka Korkhakti*) is worn. Over these piece of cloth (*Jainkyrsa*) is used as an apron. A head shawl or *Tapmohkhlieh* knotted at the back of the neck. Over this a larger piece of thicker texture called the *Jainkup* is knotted in front. They are fond of ornaments of gold, silver, various coloured precious stones and beads.

The weapons of the Khasis are swords, spears, bows and arrows, mostly prepared by local smiths. They never use wood or bone handles for their swords, only iron and steel. The Khasi weapon par excellence is the bow (*ka Syntieh*). The bow is of bamboo, and is about 5 feet in height. The bow string is of split bamboo, the bamboos that are used are *Uspit*, *Uskhen* and *Usiej–lieh*.

The arrows (*Ki Khnon*) are of two kinds: (a) the bark headed (*Ki Pliang*), and (b) the plain headed (*Sop*). Both made of bamboo. The first is used for hunting, the latter for archery matches only.

Khasi society may be divided into three groups, the ruling class (*Syiem*), the priestly class (*Lyngdoh*) and the rest. In society, however, there is no separation of these groups and there is no bar to inter–marriage between one group and another. However, marriage within some clan is strictly a taboo. Even after marriage a man belongs to his own clan, though his earning goes towards the support of his wife and children and in case his wife is the youngest (*Ka Khadduh*) he lives in his wife's house.

Sickness is believed to be caused by acts of omission or commission against God or spirit. The reasons are sought by divination, by seeing the positions and shapes of egg shells or examining the entrails of the sacrificial cock, and appropriate remedies are resorted to.

When a person dies, his funeral and cremation are arranged on the third day, unless death is accidental. Normally, the dead are cremated, but in time of an epidemic particularly of the eruptive diseases like measles, chicken pox, and small pox, temporary burial is resorted to. After the epidemic has passed, the body is exhumed and then cremated according to the usual practice. Food is left for the use of the departed soul at the place of cremation. Fragments of bones are collected and taken by a female relative to the repository of the bones of the clan. She must walk steadily and look in front; not paying any attention to the possible distractions that unfriendly spirits may arise. When a stream has to be crossed, a string is run from bank to bank to serve as a bridge for the soul of the dead.

Demographic Profile

Demographically speaking the studied village represents a medium size Khasi village with 135 households of which 52 have been covered in detail as required for the study. Considering the clan of the head of the household, in this case that of the mother in a matrilineal society, 16 such clans are recorded among those sampled. However there were 22 clans found considering the clan of the husbands who reside at the in-law's house as per the Khasi traditions. Perhaps such a large number of clans may have emerged as a consequence of strict clan exogamy. Those clans are ranked as per total number of representative households and a comparative account is presented to examine the sex ratio, share of population and household size (Table 1).

Table 1: Clanwise population structure of sampled house holds, Mawlam 1999

Serial No.	Clan	No. of H.H.	Person	Male	Female	Female per '000 Male	Population share	Average H.H.Size
1	Khongbuteb	9	41	18	23	1278	15.4	4.6
2	Tyngsong	8	38	22	16	727	14.3	4.8
3	Khongsdier	7	36	15	21	1400	13.5	5.1
4	Khongkhlad	6	26	12	14	1167	9.8	4.3
5	Khongkrom	6	36	16	20	1250	13.5	6.0
6	Khongji	4	20	8	12	1500	7.5	5.0
7	Khongain	2	11	4	7	1750	4.1	5.5
8	Khonsbnan	2	6	3	3	1000	2.3	3.0
9	Nongsteng	1	8	5	3	600	3.0	8.0
10	Khongklan	1	6	2	4	2000	2.3	6.0
11	Mawpat	1	11	7	4	571	4.1	11.0
12	Khongshuin	1	4	3	1	333	1.5	4.0
13	Kaw-in	1	11	6	5	833	4.1	11.0
14	Rongjem	1	5	1	4	4000	1.9	5.0
15	Sabong	1	4	1	3	3000	1.5	4.0
16	Majaw	1	3	1	2	2000	1.1	3.0
	Total	52	266	124	142	1145	100.0	5.1

The emerging dominant clans here are Khongbuteb, Tyngsong, Khongsdier, Khongkrom and Khongkhlad sharing 66.5 per cent in together. This table shows that the size of the household in Mawlam size is 5.1. most interesting aspect of this village is the sex ratio per 1000 males, which ranges from a low of 333 for Khongshwin clan to an amazing high of 4000 for Rongjem clan with a average sex ratio being 1145. In fact four clans have more than 200 females per 100 males, one has 300 families per 100 males, and one of the clan has 400 females per 100 males. This strange picture depicted above relates to single household clans, and the total number of members in such households does not exceed 6 persons. Therefore, the peculiarity of the sex ratio appears to be a mere statistical coincidence. Nevertheless, it will be interesting to big deep into the phenomena especially in a matrilineal society where tradition of resident husband is still in vogue.

Age-sex Structure

Though the sample size is not sufficient for a viable demographic analysis the relationship between the age group and sex among the studied households is discussed in brief (Table 2). It is evident that population share falls abruptly above the age of

Table 2: Age-sex structure of sampled households, Mawlam village 1999

Age group	*Male*	*Female*	*Total*	*Sex Ratio '000 male*
0-4	18	24	42	1333
5-9	17	15	32	882
10-14	13	22	35	1692
15-19	12	13	25	1083
20-24	14	13	27	929
25-29	10	12	22	1200
30-34	9	9	18	1000
35-39	12	10	22	833
40-44	6	5	11	833
45-49	5	2	7	400
50-54	1	4	5	4000
55-59	2	4	6	2000
60-64	2	1	3	500
65-69	1	2	3	2000
70+	2	6	8	3000
All	124	142	266	1145

39 indicating a lower longevity. In fact there are only 15% male and 27% female population survived in 40+ age group among and respectively. On the other hand around 50% population in both sexes are in 0-14 age group indicating a higher birth rate.

Therefore, it may be deducted that though there is a healthy rate of survival of the infants and children but the loss of population at middle age poses questions to be answered by future researchers.

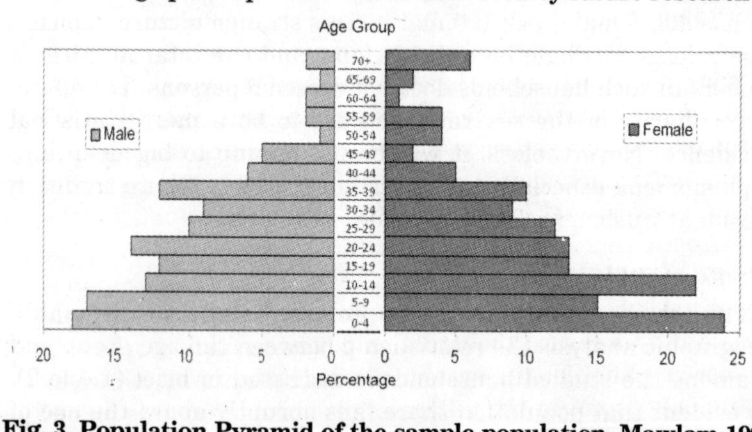

Fig. 3. Population Pyramid of the sample population, Mawlam 1999.

The population pyramid (Fig. 3) also conforms to the above analysis and represents a typical conical form. Another remarkable feature that sex ratio is remains high in favour of female since both in all age groups except in a few, which, in other words, possibly represents the culture of female preference in the Khasi society.

Marital Status

Table 3: Marital status and marriage distance of sampled population by age-sex, Maulam 1999

Age Group	*Married*		*Unmarried*		*Separated/Divorc*		*Marraige Distance*			
	Male	*Female*	*Male*	*Female*	*Male*	*Female*	*Male*		*Female*	
							Birt Place	*Dist. (Km)*	*Birt Place*	*Dist. (Km)*
15-19	1	3	11	10	0	0	Nongjiri	20		
20-24	6	9	8	4	0	0			Mawkhap	40
25-29	8	9	2	3	0	2	Mawbeh(2),Kokrajhar	25, 170+	NA	NA
30-34	5	8	4	1	0	0	NA	NA	Wah Umlun	5
35-39	9	10	3	0	1	0	Mawpat, Lyngdem	150,23	NA	NA
40-44	6	5	0	0	0	2	Lyngdem, Pyrnai(2)	23,6	Umniuh	8
45-49	5	2	0	0	1	0	NA	NA	NA	NA
50-54	1	4	0	0	0	1	NA	NA	NA	NA
55-59	2	4	0	0	0	0	Weilai (WKH)	150+	NA	NA
60+	5	9	0	0	0	1	Pyrnai, Mawbeh	6,25	NA	NA
All Age	48	63	28	18	2	6	12			

This table 3 shows that more than 50% unmarried persons have already either attained the age of marriage or crossed that age. Among such unmarried persons the males constitute more than half of the unmarried females. The percentage of divorced persons is incidentally rather low (1.8%), out of which three-fourth is represented by females. The reason for a low percentage of unmarried persons and high percentage of divorcees among the females is not clear. It would not be difficult to explain this if the inheritance of property was only among the female line. But since the War Khasis give more or less equal emphasis to both male and female in this regard the situation demands further research for an answer. Whether the system of visiting husband, which is very commonly found in the village is responsible for this or not is not certain.

Education

This table-4 shows that the total percentage of literacy is only 31.7. However, the percentage of females, despite being a matrilineal village, is far lower (26.3%) compared to the percentage of male literate (37.7%). It is also interesting to observe that 20 households in the village have no literate members at all. There are two other interesting educational features of this village:-

(1) there's no educated person, male or female above the age of 45 years and above the age of 40 years in the case of females. This shows that the spread of education in this village is about 40 years old.]

(2) the difference in the number of educated persons between primary and middle and levels shows that only one-fourth of the primary educated persons have continued their education up to the middle level, in other words drop out rate presents is an alarming figure by and standard.

Table 4: Educational status of sampled population by age-sex, Mawlam 1999

	Pre-Primary		*Primary*		*Middle*		*Secondary*		*Matric*	
Age Group	*Male*	*Female*	*Male*	*Female*	*Male*	*Female*	*Male*	*Female*	*Male*	*Female*
5-9	2	5	1	1	0	0	0	0	0	0
10-14	1	3	8	7	0	0	0	0	0	0
15-19	0	0	5	3	3	2	2	0	0	0
20-24	0	0	3	1	2	1	0	0	0	0
25-29	0	0	3	2	0	1	0	0	0	0
30-34	0	1	1	3	0	0	0	0	0	0
35-39	1	0	5	0	0	0	0	0	1	1
40-44	0	0	2	0	0	0	0	0	0	0
45-49	0	0	0	0	0	0	0	0	0	0
50-54	0	0	0	0	0	0	0	0	0	0
Total	4	9	28	17	5	4	2	0	1	1

Role of Social Organisation

The purpose of this section is to describe how the society has allocated roles/duties responsibilities to various social groups and institutions in the society with particular reference to use or exploit the natural resources. This may be discussed in this section with special reference of management of Podwar or Ryngko.

Podwar means the high slope land found around the river gorges and Ryngko is the land which is plains and dry. Podwar lands are ecologically fragile lands and use of any mechanical instruments is impossible Ryngko lands are basically used for the cultivation of broomsticks which at one time was the major source of income for the villagers.

Crops grown in the Podwar regions are mostly potatoes, yams, maize, millet and a few varieties of pulses. Fruits are widely cultivated like orange, jackfruit, pineapple, banana and varieties of lemon. Vegetables like pumpkin, gourds, beans, squash and a few locally available leafy vegetables are grown black pepper, chillies, ginger, turmeric, garlic are also cultivated. Betel nut and betel leaf are also grown widely both for consumption and commercial purpose.

The War Khasi families are small in size and nuclear family is the dominant type of family composition. The authority in the management of the family rests on the wife; but the role and position of a husband in the family are not insignificant inspite of the matrilineal and matrilocal set up. All the adult capable members of the family, both male and female work in the fields, cook and serve meals, wash clothes, fetch water and do the marketing. Generally the womenfolk carry the garden products to the market and sell them there and purchase there the domestic necessities. The daughter's friends help in each others family chores especially domestic help. Most of the heavy work is done by the men folk like construction repairing of roads/houses, carrying fuel from jungles, breaking stones, clearing of jungles and the outdoor work.

The wife manages all family affairs consultation with the husband and he represents her in the village councils and other extra domestic affairs. During the marriage of the children father's approval is necessary. Hence the position of father in a War family is much better among the Khasis. Except the youngest one, other daughters establish separate families with their husbands and expected to be economically independent. Sons, after marriage, leave parental house, and they also have equal right from the parental property, a unique feature of the War Khasis. The youngest daughter, with whom the parents live, looks after the main house and takes care of her old parents with the help of her husband. One very peculiar feature amongst them is that of the visiting husband. Husband stays with his parents and helps there only at night he comes to stay with his wife and family.

The present section is based on the data collected from 52 households, inhabiting two *Khels* or hamlets of Mawlam. The War Khasis are divided into a number of exogamous clans (*Kuror Jait*). We would identify total 22 clans within Mawlam. Among the War

Khasis, there is no trace of totemic clan (Dasgupta – 1984).

The clan or *Jait*, and not the individual, is the unit of the Khasi society in which the eldest maternal uncle or *U Khi* is the head. Clan organization and function among the War Khasis are not as elaborate as among the Khasi proper. Among the Khasi people the clan members are bound together by the religious tie of ancestor worship in common and a common clan sepulchre (Gurdon, 1914: 65). Among them a very large proportion of land is also the property of the clan which is known as *Rikur* and the youngest daughter or *Ka Khadduh* in the line of the clan, whose house is known as *Kaiing Khadduh* or last house, holds the obligation of performing the religious ceremonies of the clan (Gurdon, 1914).

Role of Village Authorities

Traditionally the Khasis were divided into numerous native states (*Syiemships*) that were administered by a king known as *Syiem* who had an executive council (*Dorbar*) consisting of *Myntries*. The *Myntries* in the *Dorbar* possesses judicial powers and in the past was the highest court of appeal inside the *Syiemship*. At the village level in the village *Dorbar* which looks into the administration of the village. The *Dorbar* is headed by the *Rangbah Shnong* of village council who is assisted by the leading members of the village. He convenes a full village *Dorbar* attended by all adults of the village when important issues are to be considered and upon which decision has to be taken. At the *Raid* level, administration is conducted by the *Dorbar Raid* headed by a person known by different titles as *Lyngdoh Raid* or *Syiem Raid* or *Bason Raid* who is assisted by representatives of certain clans lowest administrative unit for maintaining order and settling disputes is the *Raid Dorbar* consisting of 2 (two) or more villages represented in the *Dorbar* by a headman (*Rongbah Shnong*) and all adult men in the *Raid* and presided by *Sardar*. Besides judicial functions, the village resources, land and the collection of tribute for the *Syiem*, called *Pynsuk*. These collections are used for the state religious ceremonies for the *Syiem* who is also the religious head of the state. After Independence, the Sixth Schedule of the Indian Constitution created the District Council (1952) which is empowered to make laws concerning *Syiemships*. It has introduced certain changes regarding administration of justice and has classified the *Syiems* court as Additional Subordinate District Council Court. At present, there is a clash of authority between the *Syiemship* and the District Council a modern institution. It is difficult to say the future of the *Syiemship*. Considering the fact that the *Syiemship* reflects the political instincts of the fore–fathers of the Khasi people and continues to be a mark of their tribal identity its significance remains.

Education

On the educational status of the people of this village it may at first be pointed out that there is no non–formal education whatsoever. The villagers were totally illiterate until about 1960's when the first school in the village is reported to have been established. A few fortunate villagers went out of the village for educational purposes. Even now if any villager wants to study beyond the primary level he has to go out of the village because the only school in the village is a Lower Primary School, managed by four teachers.

The educational status of the villagers clearly reflects the above circumstances. For instance Table 4, shows that 81.7% of the educated persons in the village are primary or pre–primary educated 12.7% are middle level educated and only 5.6% of them are educated above middle level. It may also be noticed there is not a single literate person above matric level.

Age group wise it is seen that there is no literate person above the age of 45. In fact more than 50% of the literates are concentrated between 10 and 19 years. Above this age group the percentage of literates is not very significant. From the above it is indicated that educational spread in the village is quite recent and there is a high level of drop cuts at 20+ age.

With regard to male/female distribution the above table shows that the ratio is in favour of the female only at pre–primary level. In all other levels above pre –primary level the males have a clear dominance over the females except at middle level where the females seems to compete with the males.

Occupational changes

As regards traditional occupation all the 52 respondents reported that their parents and grandparents were engaged in agriculture, which earlier was of shifting type. Being located where it is there is very little occupational change even today. The present study table 5 shows that almost 90% of the respondents are still dependent on agriculture. But the dependence on Jhum Cultivation has declined much since horticulture was taken up during early British period and such plantation agriculture was intensified during

Table- 5: Occupational profile of sampled population by age-sex, Mawlam 1999

Age Group	*Cultivator*		*Agri-Labour*		*Daily wage*		*Business*		*Teaching*		*House Wife*	*Other*	
	Male	*Female*	*Male*	*Female*	*Male*	*Female*	*Male*	*Female*	*Male*	*Female*		*Male*	*Female*
15-19	5	4	0	4	0	0	0	0	0	0	0	0	0
20-24	9	9	2	3	0	0	0	0	0	0	1	0	0
25-29	7	8	3	5	0	0	0	0	0	0	0	0	0
30-34	4	6	5	1	0	0	0	1	0	0	0	0	0
35-39	5	6	3	4	1	0	0	0	1	1	0	1*	0
40-44	4	3	3	2	0	0	0	0	0	0	0	1**	1***
45-49	5	1	0	0	0	0	0	1	0	0	0	1#	0
50-54	1	3	0	1	0	0	0	0	0	0	0	0	0
55-59	1	2	0	2	0	0	0	1	0	0	0	1$	0
60+	5	0	0	0	0	0	0	0	0	0	9	1@	0
Total	46	42	16	22	1	0	0	3	1	1	10	5	1

*Carpentry+Masonry; **Sawing; ***Basketry; # Bee keeping; $ Blacksmithy;
@ Priesthood and traditional medicine man

the later part of the colonial regime. Only the popularity of broomstick plantation can be mentioned as a remarkable change in land use. The new occupations like business and teaching jobs do not even constitute together a total of 5%. What is however noticeable in the village is a fairly large category of agricultural labourers. This could be an indication of growing population with only about 5% of the respondents having secondary and above level education. With such a state of education in the village no significant occupational change can be visualized in the near future because education is one of the most important factors responsible for occupational change. Another important change in their economic world is in terms of free trade with Bangladesh which has a major setback after the partition of Bengal. This has made a big impact on many aspects of their peasant economy particularly the marketing of betel leaves.

Accessibility and Transport Network

The village Mawlam is located at a distance of 72 kilometres from Shillong. The village is approachable by a partially metalled road from Pynursla village, the Block Headquarters. To reach the village one has to cover a distance of about 15 kilometres from the diversion point on the Shillong. Dawki Highway lies at a distance of 58 kilometres from Shillong, the State Headquarter.

Modes of transport are mainly M.T.C. buses which started from (Nongjri) to Shillong via Pynursla local buses are more frequent during hot days. A few private vehicles are also occasionally seen plying on this road.

Role of market

A market, other than being the main centre of business transactions, needs to be viewed as an important traditional social institution; particularly in the tribal territories providing the base for both inter and intra community socio educational symbiosis. Among the Khasis of Meghalaya, a very long tradition of village markets is continuing till today with a well integrated and well distributed network throughout the region. The significance of Khasi markets in the Khasi society can easily be understood from the writing of P.T. Gurdon (1975) in his pioneering work The Khasis. He observed "The Khasi week has the peculiarity that it almost universally consists of eight days. The reason of the eight–day week is because the markets are usually held every eighth day. The names of the days of the week are not those of planets, but the places where the principal markets are held, or used to be held, in the Khasi and Jaintia Hills." The names of the week days and corresponding market places of the Khasi Hills were -

(1) Lynkah (Barapani or Khawang)

(2) Nongkrem

(3) Um–long (Mawlong the hat at Laban)

(4) Ranghep (Ku–bah at Cherri) (Mawtawar in Mylliem) (Umsaw in Nongkhlaw)

(5) Shillong (Laitlyngkot)

(6) Pomtih or Pomtiah (Mawkhar, small market)

(7) Umnih

(8) Yeo–duh (Mawkhar, large market)

It is obvious that the War area was traditionally rich producers of horticultural and mineral resources, thus experiencing higher trade and business activities in the whole Khasi land. It is evident from the fact that markets have always been held every fourth day at Nongjai, Mawbong, Tyliawp and Shella, all located along the border with present Bangladesh through which most of the export and import were made. The chief products were oranges, betel nut, betel leaf and bay leaf. Before partition the orange trade was mainly controlled by the Muslims of Sylhet, who used to visit many small and large village markets e.g. Theria, Bholaganj, Byrong, Phali, Mawdon, Rengua and Balat. Oranges used to be exported to Sylhet by the rivers. Chattak, in Bangladesh, just south of Shella, was the main centre from where oranges were consigned to different parts of Bangladesh and to Calcutta. But after partition, the War Khasi people were almost overnight reduced from prosperity to near poverty due to the banning of border trades resulting in the closure of most of the markets. Another factor that attributed to the fall in the prosperity of the War economy was abrupt decline in orange production caused by a widespread attack of blight (Simon, 1991) which recurs regularly in the orchards during the last two decades or so.

In cause of the present study altogether five such village markets were found in existence in the whole of Pynursla Block. Those are as follows:

S.No.	*Name of the village/market*	*Day of next two markets*	*Organised and managed by*
1.	Laitlynkot	12.2.99, 24.2.99 (every 8th day)	Khasi Hills District Council
2.	Pynursla	14.2.99, 18.2.99 (every 4th day)	Khynriem Syiemship
3.	Lyngkhat	15.2.99, 19.2.99 (every 4th day)	Khynriem Syiemship
4.	Hat Thymmai	13.2.99, 17.2.99 (every 4th day)	Khynriem Syiemship
5.	Hat Nongjri	12.2.99, 16.2.99 (every 4th day)	Ilaka Nongjri

Only the Laitlynkot market day falls every eighth day in accordance with the usual day for Shillong market (at present Bara Bazaar) because it is located at the northern tip of the Pynursla Block and does not fall under actual War country. All other markets are held every fourth day so that everyday there is a market in the region and thus the traditional eighth day cycle is maintained by doubling the occurrence. The village Hat Nongjri, Hat Thymmai and Lyngkhat are all located on the Bangladesh border from west to east respectively. All these village markets are connected by motorable roads, though mostly unmetalled. Nongjri gets two buses on bazaar days coming from Shillong and Pynursla Hat Lyngkhat and Hat – Thymmai. Buses ply from Pynursla and Pongtung on this route every bazaar day. Morcover trucks and other small and medium carriage vehicles also ply during the peak seasons. The traditional bazaar buses are unique in Meghalaya the rear half of which is meant only for commodities while the front half has a few seats.

The National Highway 40, the first highway laid in Meghalaya is responsible for the trade significance of the rural markets at Dawki of Jaintia Hills District on the border of Bangladesh close to Tamabil. The place is well connected by regular bus services and other public vehicles from Shillong via Pynursla and Jowai the district town of Jaintia Hills. In fact there are two markets running simultaneously on every fourth day. The old Dawki bazaar or Low Dawki has lost its importance mainly due to partition and a huge fire that completely gutted down the market place around a decade back. The piece of land on the south east bank of the river Um Nyat was provided by the rich Rynksai clan of Dawki for the purpose. At present the land holds one Hindu temple and a big betel nut garden, where some orange, betel nut and betel leaf are transacted on the bazaar days. But as informed by the present village secretary of Dawki, Mr. Mitford Ryngksai, the owner of the land, the old Low Dawki market was one of the two main outlets through which most of the famous War oranges, betel nuts and betel leaves were sold to big merchants of Sylhet. In those days's betel leaf was of great demand in Bangladesh and was exchanged through "Barter system" against rice, fish (fresh and dry). Even inferior quality betel leaves (smaller variety) used to find good markets and partition played havoc to the particular business of this highly perishable commodity. It is said that the present market of betel leaf here is only one tenth compared to earlier period. Even orange had a good open competitive market where growers used to get reasonably fair prices but at present the market is totally controlled and monopolised by a handful of orange exporters who fix up the rates at their benefits only. Moreover the local crafts from various bamboos and canes and the traditional Khasi iron tools and implements are of good demand in the market.

With the steady decline of the old Dawki market another plot of land was provided some 200 metres east of the old market by the Lamin clan of the Lamin village of Jaintia Hills. This new market is known as Bakur market and at present holds the main bulk of transaction leaving only orange which goes to Dawki market. The Bakur market is jointly managed by the village (Raid) authority and the District Council while the Meghalaya marketing board, a newly formed body, has provided infrastructural assistance by construction permanent sheds, stalls and storage etc. Permanent stalls and stores are allotted as per the recommendation of the Bakur Bazar society strictly only to the tribals. The roadside and pavement vendors are allowed on daily basis. In case of permanent stalls *Boidung* or one time salami is collected in addition to Rs. 15 as *Khajna* for the bazaar days only. The temporary vendors on the pavements pay Rs. 10/- or Rs. 5/- depending on the type and quantity of commodities brought that day. A petty yam seller pays only Rs. 5/- while a basket seller has to pay Rs. 10/- and so on as the place is well connected by roads many vendors seen attending from as far as Shillong and Jowai amongst the nearby villages.

Though not a single non–tribal was seen as seller in the market but the Khasis and Jaintias from Bangladesh villages have open access to the border and sell various articles as pavement vendors. Only the children and aged women folks of Bangladeshi citizen are allowed to come to the market and work as household maids or porters and earn a day's wage.

The Bakur market is placed over a small dome shaped hillock, left of the N.H. 40, behind the permanent Dawki Bazar area. There are five entry points from different directions corresponding five main sections e.g. the betel nut section, betel leaf section, baskets and steel implements section, garments and stationary section and fish and meat section. The main vegetable section, dry fish, tea stalls, etc. are more or less located around the central zone. During our visit betel nut and leaf were observed as the main item of transaction and these two commodities occupied almost 25% of total sale. Broomsticks along with betel nuts/leaf and charcoal were sold to the middle man buyers who ultimately export those to far away markets in Bangladesh and Assam etc. The service renderers like barbers, tea and meal stalls owners, herbal medicine man, studio photographers, tailors, even large departmental stores and grocery, pan and cigarette sellers, book sellers, etc. are mostly having regular, permanent shops and stalls also have to pay the *Khajna* for the bazaar days. There were a good number of vendors, the tribals from Bangladesh selling mostly second hand garments and warm clothes.

None of the aged local informants could mention any special social meetings or interactions during the bazaar days in earlier years. But in many ways the authors have depicted the local peoples activities revolve around the market to a large extent.

The most significant impact of the border trade on environment was reported by the elderly local people as related to the closure of huge betel/leaf market in Bangladesh due to partition. Earlier the forests were preserved carefully to cultivate betel leaf which suits well in an unaltered forest ecosystem. But as the demand of these some dwindled after 1947 the villagers started transferring those virgin forests in to jhum fields and then into broomstick plantation. The comprehensive assessment of this fact has never been attempted.

In this border market the relic or the residual of the large scale socio–cultural and economic interactions between the tribal groups and the non–tribal people of different ethno–linguistic groups of the earlier year could still be observed in Dawki. Both the Meghalayans and Bangladeshis try to converse in each other's language as and when required. The Khasi sellers interact with Bengali buyers in broken Sylheti dialect while most of the Bengali labourers use Khasi while conversing with their Khasi masters and traders.

Further, this particular market acts as the base of a dynamic functional interaction linking the traditional tribal economy with the larger economic system. The results of demonstrative effects are found among rural tribal communities most prominently in the form of adaptations and changes in dietary habits, dressing patterns, etc.

The roadway communication and transport system of the region becomes very much alive during the bazaar days. All the regular buses change their schedule times and reach early as the bazaar starts around 8 a.m. and leaves late in the afternoon when it is over. Many special buses including typical bazaar buses, small and medium four wheelers, trucks, etc. found occupying the one and a half kilometre long stretch of the N.H. 40 near the market. Most of the vehicles ply between various far flung villages of Pynursla Block which, it seemed, is the main hinterland.

Various other activities like a political meeting for the fourth coming M.P.C. election was held at the Bungalow near the market, a two day traditional dance festival with a small fair was organized by the local school. The famous boat racing festival of this year has been scheduled on next two consecutive bazaar days when a dance competition and fete are held in the market. The organizers of the competition get a good return of money from various sources of gambling and lotteries during the great gathering due to the bazaar and the boat festival on the same day.

Finally, for various officials and authorities of Dawki, the bazaar days become very busy days too. All the wage labourers come to receive their payments from P.W.D. contractors at the P.W.D. office. The schedule for next phase of work is also settled there. The officials of the village authorities meet and discuss many important matters regarding any problem or dispute ranging from allotment of jhum fields to selection of beneficiaries of different government schemes.

The Dawki Primary Health Centre, located at the main market, becomes truly busy with all the doctors and health workers present to serve the heavy rush of patients. The private pharmacy arranges a private practitioner too.

There are five export agency offices near Tamabil, border post about 1 km away, along with District Council Agents, Border Security and Passport office, Land Custom office, Land Clearing

Agents etc. play their respective roles in handling matters related to the export of oranges, betel leaf, betel nut, coal, limestone etc. to Bangladesh. But during our visit the border movement was restricted due to sudden spurt of security problems which made the business quite dull as reported by many of the villagers visiting the market.

Pynursla Bazaar

For the Mawlam villagers the nearest market place is Pynursla, the block headquarters. The place is well connected by roads with Shillong and Dawki, being located on the N.H. 40 at around 50 km from the state capital. As one of the important transport junction this large village has gained certain urban characteristics. Buses and other public vehicles ply from several directions connecting far away places like Nongjri, Laitlynkot, Lyngkerdem, Nongsken, Mawpram etc. mostly during market days. Villagers from all directions come to attend this market mainly by buses and other four wheeler vehicles. The sellers and buyers can broadly be divided into the following categories:

(1) Producer seller: They sell their own produce like agricultural surplus, minor forest produces and local crafts etc. forming the wide base of such rural markets. Products like yams, oranges, lemons, betel leaf and betel nuts, bananas, bay –leaf, fowls and birds and their products, pigs, goats, broomstick, canes, baskets etc.

(2) Middleman sellers: They are either from villages or urban areas who collect mostly the cash crops, village crafts etc. from the villagers at the villages and sell the goods to bigger businessmen or the middleman buyers in the villages or nearby urban markets.

(3) Non–farm good sellers: They are from urban areas who sell, besides food items like rice, cooked meat, tea and snacks, clothes, plastic wares, aluminium and brass wares, dry fish and iron tools which are commonly used in the villages.

Pynursla has permanent rows of shops on both sides of the N.H. 40. The village after having been given the status of Block Headquarters in October, 1960, a number of important government offices such as B.D.O., Post and Telegraph, Banks, P.H.C., S.D.O., P.W.D. (South Div.), P.O., Police Headquarters, etc were established in and around. One Secondary English Medium Boarding School, first one in the whole War area, founded by one Italian father –

Nicolas Chology is also located at the village hill top. Moreover, one Government Primary School is also in operation at present.

Though there is hardly any mention of the Pynursla periodic rural market in any of the literature available, the present study reveals this as one of the oldest traditional market still managed by the *Khynrim Syiemship* on a community land. Similar to all other such markets in the War country the market is held every fourth day. Bazaar *Khajna* for certain items like betel leaf and betel nut are collected in kind, i.e. for 40 taps, 1 tap is given as *Khajna*. For other items like vegetables, fishes, *pusari*, clothes, fruit shops (temporary and permanent) only Rs. 3/– is taken as *Khajna* on market days only.

One interesting thing to be noted is that all the roadside lands belonging to the *Raid* has now been leased out to Khasi students union, who also collect similar *Khajna* as stated above from different categories of shops, vendors and hawkers. Especially on market days, K.S.U. members would manage the heavy traffic and charge parking fee of Rs. 3/– for small vehicles and Rs. 5 for heavy vehicles, maintenance and cleaning is done by their members only.

The market area is cleaned every fourth day by the employees of the *Syiem* and are paid on monthly basis.

Religion, beliefs and practices

It has already been indicated that this village is the bastion of traditional religion called *Niamtre.* Besides the two Christian households, which have been mentioned earlier, all other households practise their traditional religion. This religion may in other words be equated with what is usually described as 'Animism'.

Among the War Khasis, worship is known as *Ainguh* (*Ai* – give, *Nguh* – worship). They worship numerous gods and goddesses. These gods and goddesses are supposed to exercise good or evil influence over human beings, according to whether they are propitiated with sacrifice or not. Thus, illness for example, is thought to be caused by one or more of the spirits on account of some act of omission, and health can only be restored by the due propitiation of the offended spirits. In order to ascertain which is the offended spirit; a system of divination by means of cowries, breaking eggs, or examining the entrails of animals and birds, was instituted.

They worship the creator *Ka Blei Nongthaw*. *Ka–Blaing* is the guardian spirit of the family. *Ka–Jymngiew* is the goddess of luck and is worshipped if any dire catastrophe befalls on the family.

Ryngkew bason is worshipped before any hunting expedition and again after they return from the same.

Ka–Jangrieng is worshipped before fishing.

The community or village worship is performed when some dire catastrophe befalls on the village. Four main gods are worshipped: (1) *Mawkhan* (2) *Maweh* (3) *Mawknoe* (4) *Shinteng*. This year (March – 1999) also they were supposed to perform this ritual due to very less production. Besides the usual religious paraphernalia (betel nut, leaf, certain plants, rice, eggs, liquor, one cock and goat, preferably black in colour are must for the sacrifice). Last they performed this ritual was inside the *Law Adong* in a particular place always. No presence of outsiders is allowed at that time and at that place. Christians and women are also not allowed to participate. The village elders and knowledgeable persons are allowed to take part along with the village *Lyndoh*. The total time for the ritual takes about 2 hours.

Lyngdohs (priests) are chosen from among six clans only (1) *Khongngain* (2) *Khongbutib* (3) *Khongsdier* (4) khongkrom (5) *Tongsong* (6) *Khongji*.

Every clan has got their own god called Lei–Phen, who protects the clan and is believed to reside in every home.

They never symbolize their gods by means of images, their worship being offered to the spirit only. The propitiation of these spirits is carried out either by priests (*Lyngdohs*) or by old men. Ancestor worship is an important duty of every Khasi individual. They believe that the spirits of the dead, whose funeral ceremonies have been duly performed, goes to the house or garden of god, where betel nut groves are there, hence the expression for the departed – *Uba bam Kwai Haiing Ublei* (he who is eating betel nut in god's house). Idea of supreme happiness to the Khasi is being able to eat betel nut uninterruptedly.

The memorial stone to commemorate the dead were huge flat stones known as Mawkrah to preserve the mortal remains of their dead, clanwise.

Their crematorium (*Jingthangbrew*) was placed inside the jungle. There were three in Mawlam.

Management of land

In the War country (Ri War) most of the land is with moderate to very high slopes, interspersed with restricted flat topped ridges and narrow valley floors. These highly dissected, high relief, high slope landforms are believed to be synonymous to the term Podwar, literally, Podwar might have been derived from Pudwah meaning steep valley walls on either side of the river (*Wah*). The almost flat or undulating ridge tops here most of the village settlements are located are called *Ryngko* which is almost equivalent to *Ka–Rilum* or *Ka–Riphland* of the highland Khasi area (Gurdon – 1975) or the high grasslands. But the wet paddy lands on the valley plains (*Hali* or *Pynthor*) are less common here excepting along the Bangladesh border. In the village Mawlam, which is situated on the northern border of Ri War, the village land other than the homestead area is divided into Podwar and Ryngko with pre–dominance of the former category.

The traditional War people of the village define the Podwar as sloppy land of vast extent usually on either sides of a big river. It is observed that slopes approximately above 20° and continuing for a considerable area is termed Podwar. On either side of the ridge (Ryngko), on which the village is located, Podwar lands start with declination ranging from 20° up to 50° or even more till it ends in the valley floor, some 2000 to 3000 ft below. Due to heavy rainfall these slopes are mostly under thick green cover either with the natural vegetation or orchard groves of various fruits and nuts. In the deeps of those narrow valleys the air remains warmer then the upper part which helps the growth of various trees and crops.

The Ryngko lands on the other hand are restricted along the swinging ridge tops varying in width from half a kilometre to as little as 150 m. In fact, the main motorable road from Pynursla upto the village and beyond runs through the Ryngko. This type of land is rocky and greasy in nature where trees and crops are hardly seen growing healthy. The wider parts and the occasional flat pockets of Ryngko are also called *Maidan* by the villagers. Now–a–days this category of land is used only for broomstick plantation other than its use as homestead land.

LAND MORTGAGE

We came across one interesting phenomenon regarding mortgage of orchard plots in the village. Mrs. Faith Khongshuin, 45 years was reported having three sohkwit plots mortgaged to her by three households in the village. She has paid Rs. 8,500/- in cash last year for those three plots through verbal contract only. Such mortgage contract is called *Babuh Bynda*, which gives the person the total right to harvest the fruits along with the responsibility of maintaining those orchards. The assessment of the value of harvest and the accounting is solely done by the lady mentioned above under mutual trust. The agreement will continue till the amount is balanced by sale of the fruits. Hence this agreement will be inherited by her family even after her death if necessary. In general the youngest daughter will inherit the same though all the children will share the benefit. She finds a good market for those fruits in Bangladesh through Nongjri market. So far we have not come across any such record of mortgage system in the available literature in War Khasis. It is further interesting to note that the same lady having a younger second husband (after death of the first) staying with her. She has also given shelter to a widowed relative (Mrs. Longba Tynsong) along with her two sons. They help her in the fields as well as in running the grocery shop. She has given them a separate room to live–in.

MEASUREMENT AND DEMARCATION OF LAND

In the study area no villager or village authority uses any kind of unit of measuring land, whether individual or community. But the practice of demarcating individual plots has become more common with the transformation towards settled cultivation. A large stone or *Mawpud* (corner stone) usually placed in one corner of the plot, adjacent to another plot. They perform certain prayers and sacrifice a cock on the stone before placing it on the field. This traditional practice was actually meant for protecting their crops by appeasing the relevant god. This is still followed by the villagers practising their traditional religion particularly for their jhum fields. But at present it seems that the stone plays a most important role as demarcation point between plots of different owners. Now they place some smaller stones along the boundary of the plots for clear demarcation. It is interesting further to note that even Christian Khasi villagers believe that if anybody steps or goes over the *Mawpud* he or she will be punished by god and suffers rheumatic pains on the joints and the only way to cure is to tie a straw over the *Mawpud* to transfer the pain as believed. Thus this old belief still continues to help avoiding probably property disputes till date.

LAND TENURE SYSTEM

In all over Khasi Hills, land tenure system is governed by a member of Khasi customary laws (Simon – 1991). Broadly, we come across two common types of land ownership:

(i) Ri Kynti i.e. owned by a particular clan or a family.

(ii) Ri Raid i.e. which belongs to a particular village or a group of villages. Hence *Ri Raid* is meant for community use under the supervision of *Sirdar*, the head of the *Raid* organisation.

The customs regarding inheritance of land or property among the general Khasi custom of female inheritance in the way that War children (both male and female) get definite share. As started by Khongphai (1974) only women keep the bones of ancestors in their family land (*Ri–Shieng*) adjacent to their own houses, but a man cannot. If a woman dies without daughters, her bones and those of her sons are kept by her female *Kur* (near relatives). The *Ri–Shieng*) land is given to the youngest female (*Ka Khadduh*) because she maintains the religion and keeps the bones. The property mostly consisting of groves (*ki-bui*) remains in the name of *Ka Khadduh* which she cannot sell or lease out. The management of this lies with the *Kurs*. The brothers and sisters of *Ka–Khadduh* can plant trees in the grove and get the share of the product, when there is any empty or unmanaged land in the *Ri–Shieng*. After the death of the brothers of *Ka–Khadduh*, their children cease to have the right to cultivate the land, but can take the fruits from the groves planted by their fathers. But in case of the children of the sisters of *Ka–Khadduh* they too have rights to plant trees even after the death of their mother. A woman having no children can give her *Ri–Shieng* to her youngest sisters. Now–a–days in the village, the *Ri–Shieng* land is left in the joint possession and engagement of all the daughters and not the youngest alone.

JHUM CULTIVATION

Jhuming or *Thang Shyrti* a very old mode of agriculture, involving slashing and burning of forests on slopes, is still in practice in the War area but due to its long history of plantation agriculture producing several horticultural crops the practice of jhuming remained comparatively less in this region then in the other parts of Meghalaya. As per 1981 census, the Pynursla Block as a whole had only 8.6% of total households in jhuming compared to 10.8% in the East Khasi Hills District (Tayang, 1983). Further in the Block 48% of all the villages had jhum fields involving about 60% of the total population during early 70's as per a more detailed study conducted by this office (Roy Choudhuri – 1991). The same study shows that there was 1755 hectares of land under jhum (2.07% area of the block) and 0.03% hectares jhum land per capita.

In the village Mawlam there was 13.5% of households practising jhum cultivation involving only 16% of the total population during 1981 (Tayang – 1983), compared to 8.6% Jhumia households in the Pynursla Block as a whole.

During the present study 26 out of total 52 households studied have been practising jhum cultivation in the Mawlam village. In total, 58 jhum plots of various sizes were reported under cultivation by those households, i.e. on an average 2.2 plots per household. This figure does not include all the jhum plots actually in possession of the households which should include the plots kept fallow during the year. Out of 26 households 10 had only one plot and eight had two plots each while the maximum five numbers of plots were possessed by three households only (Tayeng, 1983).

In this region villagers practise jhum cultivation mostly on the community land or *Ri Raid* controlled and managed by the *Raid* or the village organisation. *Raid* is formed by combining two or more adjacent villages. The *Raid* Mawlam also includes Ryngkew and is the smallest *Raid* out of 11 such *Raids* in the block. The land of *Ri Raid* is freely available to the villagers of that *Raid*. Any farmer can choose any part of the *Raid* land not cultivated by any other with former information to the *Sirdar* of the *Raid* before clearing the forest. There are no restrictions on the size and number of plots one family can possess but the cleared plots should be utilized regularly. Hence any cultivator in general clears jhum plots within the limits of his or their capability to cultivate the same depending upon:

(1) Availability of manpower within the household,

(2) Extent of family sustenance.

The Jhumia household will continue to possess the plot till he leaves the same as fallow which they decide by observing the yield and quality of crops grown in the plot. One can cultivate the same plot for as minimum as one year to a maximum of four at a stretch. Similarly the fallow period also varies from eight years to 15 years again depending upon the type of crop one wants to grow.

While clearing a new plot of land in the *Ri Raid* forest one has to be careful of not hampering the adjacent plots owned by other usually they leave a reasonable portion of land untouched in-between two such plots as the provision for further extension by either of those parties. The *Raid* organisation can impose fine if any Jhumia fails to sow seeds in the cleared plots and such failure for three consecutive years will automatically nullify the rights of possession of the holder and the same plot can be taken up by others.

During clearing of the forests all the vegetations are slashed off accepting the base of the large tree trunks just to avoid extra labour required to dig it out and for regeneration of the same. The cut trees and branches are kept on the same plot to be dried up under the winter sun (January – February). The *Raid* organisation does not allow the Jhumia to take away any such cut branches till a heavy shower of rain occurs which in fact occurs within a month or so. At first the large logs, if any, are taken away and utilized for house building and repairing and mostly as firewood. The branches with medium girth are kept mostly for making charcoal while the dried leaves and other smaller branches including some bamboos are left on the ground to be burnt afterwards (March – April). It is reported that the firewood, collected from jhum fields are meant mostly for their own use but they sell charcoal directly to the local markets. The details of charcoal making process will be given later on.

STAGES IN JHUM CULTIVATION AND IMPLEMENTS USED

To cut and clear the forest one iron axe or *U–Sdie* for cutting large trees and a dao or *Ka–Wait Lyndong* for cutting wood, bamboo etc., another smaller dao *Ka–Went Lung* for clearing bushes. In the village Mawlam Jhumias start clearing the forest in the month of November – December after completion of harvesting their orchards. Then the dried leaves and branches are burnt after around 6 – 8 weeks. The ashes or *U–dpar* are spread over the land as manure and the Jhumia wait for the rains to come. After two or three showers they sow seeds in the small holes made by the long digging sticks or *Lyngkha* which has become almost synonymous to the jhum cultivation itself. The holes are made with roughly 1 ft gaps in–between, but without maintaining any pattern. In each hole they put a mixed quantity of seeds which they carry in a small cloth bag hanging from his neck and then cover the hole with soil by foot. In case of tuber plants they cut segments of the matured tuber like arum or tapioca and plant one by one by digging holes. No more care is taken after sowing for the next two three months. Weeding is done twice in May and end of August depending upon the growth of unwanted vegetation. They still do not apply any manure.

In the village they usually combine maize with millet as staple cereals along with arum and tapioca as staple tubers, and also ginger, turmeric and rai (mustard seeds) are sometimes grown as popular cash crops here. Since a variety of crops are grown in the same plot the harvesting is done in different periods depending on the maturity of those crops. For harvesting they use a small dao or *Ka–Wait* and the *Lynkha*.

Men folk undertake the clearing of forest and burning the dried vegetation often in a group comprising relatives and co–villagers of the owner of the plot. The weeding, harvesting and carrying the crop to their houses are mostly done by the women folk of the farmer's household. Unlike harvesting the fruits and broomstick, hired labourers are not engaged for harvesting jhum fields.

The present generation Jhumias are found less involved and less informative about jhum cultivation because they have better alternative land use over the more laborious traditional one with less returns.

Cropping pattern in jhum

In Meghalaya and particularly in Khasi Hills cropping pattern varies a lot from place to place and year to year (Roy Choudhuri, 1991). But it was interesting to observe in Mawlam and surrounding areas that the traditional cropping pattern has been and still in the changing phase, though the higher hills of Pynursla block as a whole had no tradition of growing paddy in jhum fields the staple crops like arum, tapioca, maize and millet in combination with ginger and turmeric as cash crops have been largely altered. In fact almost all the households studied reported that after the first crop, e.g. arum, sweet potatoes, tapioca, etc. they switch over either to broomstick, bay–leaf or even to horticulture. They find it more profitable to grow those cash crops than continuing with traditional ones.

Depending on the quality of soils and the capacity of the Jhumia family the second and third year's land use is chosen. The crops which require minimum maintenance and gives reasonable return like broomstick and bay–leaf are taken up by the poorer and smaller households having limited capacity for horticulture and other plantation crops. Others plant orange, lemon, banana, pineapple, papaya etc. after one or two years of jhuming.

The probable reasons behind such trends in the War villages may be many folds;

(1) Primarily the success rate of permanent plantation crops in horticulture and broomstick is more compared to the low return from jhum crops.

(2) The Government policy discouraging and even prohibiting the jhum cultivation in the state as a whole.

(3) Growth of population leading to lower man land ratio and shorter jhum styles have compelled villagers to extract more from the same plot of land even in the absence of developed agricultural technology.

(4) By transferring jhum plots in the community land (*Ri Raid*) to permanent plantations private possessions of land.

On the whole the brighter side of such transformation can be felt in decreasing or stopping the degradation of the valuable top soil of hill slopes by keeping those under one or the other type of permanent plantation.

Plantation agriculture

As already mentioned Podwar lands are extensively and intensively used mainly for horticulture. The high slopes with thinner soil cover do not permit any physical alteration and as such these villagers do not have any tradition or constructing terraces. The degree and direction of slope and the availability of water are the important aspects villagers consider to plant different varieties of trees. The highest part of the slope just below the Ryngko with less moisture in the soil and colder atmosphere are planted with broomstick is continued upto the first break of slope downward. In fact this higher zone of Podwar was earlier used mostly for jhum cultivation, which had been transformed to broomstick fields since this cash crop started finding market around 20 – 22 years ago.

As the settlement of the village is situated at around 3,500 ft the orange orchards are found 500 – 600 ft below the top end extends well upto an altitude of 1500 ft or so. Hence, the narrow strip of slope upto the river bank on either side is meant mostly for areca nut and betel leaf which are inter–cultured. Black pepper is also grown in combination with areca nuts. Moreover, along the perennial streams and springs on the lower and middle Podwar, various fruit trees are grown like mango, jackfruit and papaya and climbers like betel leaf and pepper grow very healthy over the trunks of these trees as the traditional mode of inter–culture. According to the villagers perception south facing slopes are best suited for almost all these trees to grow depending upon the amount of sunlight available. The north facing ones can only be utilised for arum, tapioca and other local varieties of tuber plants due to exposure to dry and chilly wind blowing down from high plateau on the north.

The War area has a very long tradition of horticulture, which provided the early prosperity of its economy in contrast to the much poorer level of the other Khasi groups. Extensive plantation of orange, lemon and areca nut was encouraged by the proximity to the huge market through Bangladesh. Though the estimated area and production of plantation crops are supplied by the Pynursla Block office the exact areas under horticulture crops are not available at the village level.

In Mawlam village horticulture was observed as the main agricultural activity covering maximum portion of the village economy. From the household survey it is calculated that 33 out of 52 households (63.5%) possessed one or the other mentioned horticulture plantation in Podwar (Table 6).

Considering this year's production of plantation crops like orange, lemon, betel nut, bay–leaf, broomstick and also a number of jhum plots cleared by each household the total resource possession is worked out employing a simple scoring technique. Taking proportionate score points on each item of land use and production in both Podwar and Ryngko the total resource scores have been calculated household wise to get a uniform quantitative picture. Thus among all the studied households the average size of resource score is found to be 9.81 points with a range from as low as 0.2 to as high as 61.9. This indicates that there is considerable disparity in resource distribution among those households, with the co–efficient of variability 125%. Examining the distribution of those households among six resource score ranges the disparity is again revealed as 48% households have scored less than 5 points. Out of remaining 52% households 40% scored between 5 – 20 points while there were only 12% households having more than 20 points scores.

Orange: The importance of this citrus fruit in the War region in particular has been mentioned and discussed in several works.

Gurdon (1975) wrote: "The cultivation of orange in the southern portion of the district ranks equally in importance with that of the potato in the northern .... The orange of the Khasi Hills has always been famous for its excellence, and Sir George Birdwood ...referred to the orange and lemon of Garhwal, Sikkim and Khasia

Table 6: Average annual agricultural production score by category of land clanwise, Mawlam village1999

Serial No.	*Clan of Head of HH*	*Podwar land*				*Ringki land*	*Total Score pointa*	*No. of H.H.*	*Average Score*
		Orange+ Lemon	*Areca Nuts*	*Bay Leaf*	*Jhum*	*Broom Stick*			
1	Tyngsong	57.40	36.80	14.40	14.00	14.20	136.80	8	17.10
2	Khongkrom	34.30	1.30	10.60	8.00	16.80	71.00	6	11.83
3	Khongsdier	39.40	2.70	2.40	4.00	15.80	64.30	7	9.19
4	Mawpat	12.80	39.00	3.00	1.00	6.00	61.80	1	61.80
5	Khongbuteb	22.40	1.40	11.80	12.00	12.20	59.80	9	6.64
6	Khongain	3.80	2.20	8.00	5.00	4.80	23.80	2	11.90
7	Khongji	10.40	0.00	3.40	1.00	6.60	21.40	4	5.35
8	Khongsuin	4.10	5.30	4.00	3.00	4.00	20.40	1	20.40
9	Khongkhlad	2.60	1.30	1.60	6.00	1.80	13.30	6	2.22
10	Nongsteing	5.10	1.80	1.60	2.00	1.60	12.10	1	12.10
11	Khonsbnan	1.00	0.30	1.20	0.00	6.00	8.50	2	4.25
12	Rongjem	5.10	1.30	0.00	0.00	0.00	6.40	1	6.40
13	Sabong	0.00	0.00	0.00	2.00	3.20	5.20	1	5.20
14	Kaw-in	0.00	0.00	0.00	0.00	3.00	3.00	1	3.00
15	Khongklan	0.00	0.00	0.00	0.00	0.80	0.80	1	0.80
16	Majaw	0.00	0.00	0.00	0.00	0.20	0.20	1	0.20
	Total	198.40	93.40	62.00	58.00	97.00	508.80	52	9.78

R=–0.11.

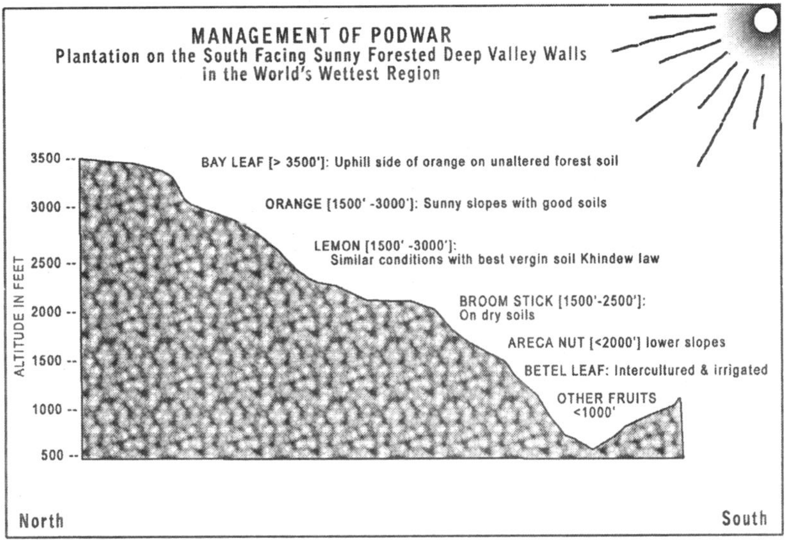

Fig. 4. A schematic profile of Podwar slope with altitudinal zonation for different plantation crops.

as having been carried by Arab traders into Syria, whence the Crusaders helped to gradually propagate them throughout southern Europe". Whereas the potato was imported the orange would appear to be indigenous in these hills. Further, Dr. Tanaka, a Japanese expert attributed the origin of the orange to the Khasi Hills itself (Simon, 1991). It is also mentioned that though orange is still being grown, in terms of quality and quantity it has become a mere shadow of its past glory, bringing about a swift decline in the economic prosperity of the War people. The main reasons behind the decline were damage caused by pests due to bad management of the orchards and closure of the direct international market through Bangladesh after the partition.

In the War Khasi region the orange or Soh Niamtra species grown traditionally is Khasi Mandarin which is believed to be the only species in India propagated directly through seeds. The plant needs warmer slopes and good rainfall and can be grown well roughly upto 3000 ft. above sea level, though the best quality fruits are harvested between 1500 ft. and 3000 ft. zone. These people understand that the quality of the fruit, i.e. the fructose content is higher with the longer time taken to mature. Hence, in higher altitude with slightly less temperature, e.g. middle part of the War country fruits are best in quality though lesser in quantity than the lower altitude. Mentioned was also made by the villagers about the Wakhen orange claiming it as the world's sweetest variety grown in and around the village of the same name. This village is located further north near Lyngkerdem in the Rumkheng river gorge at an altitude of about 2,500 ft.

The seeds are collected selectively from the most matured oranges including those which are over matured and damaged during transporting. The seeds are first dried completely in the sun, then, during December-February first nursery is prepared in the homestead land and is called *Share–Shyieng–Soh*. The ground is thoroughly hoed and soil pulverized completely. Then the nursery is fenced up with stones to prevent the movements of pigs and fowls. The seeds are sown in haphazard rows and a thin layer of soil is spread to cover the seeds. These nurseries are watered regularly to keep the top layer of soil moist and also being covered by leaves particularly on sunny days ensuring the retention of moisture.

As the seedlings (*Dieng–Soh–Niamtra*) in some War villages of lower altitude orange nurseries are raised commercially. The saplings of 3 – 4 years old (*Kwin*) are sold at the rate of Rs. 8/- to Rs. 10/- per plant. The War people believe that the saplings grown in Um–Syjem village are best though the village does not have any orange orchard. Even in Mawlam village when they are 3 – 4 inches tall they are transplanted in the second nursery or *Share–Dieng–Soh*, on a warmer slope in the lower Podwar. For the second nursery, villagers select a slope having rocky red hill soil of low depth. The seedlings are kept there for 4/5 years after planting at 2 ft. spacing. The reason for selecting the particular soil called *Daw–Maw* is that the roots would not penetrate deep into the soil and it will be easier and safer to transplant those tender plants with harder stems on the actual orchard.

The final sites for the orchard Bri–Soh–Niamtra are chosen by the villagers in their Podwar land avoiding the shady corners and exposure to strong winds. The mature saplings are planted with at least 6 – 9 ft. space in–between upon the angle of slope. The orchards are not cleared totally of all plants and trees naturally present. A few shady trees are kept during the growth of the orange plant. Those shady trees are gradually lopped off with the growth of the orange trees. Such trees act as wind barriers as well. The Khasi mandarin takes around 5 – 8 years from germination to flowering. At about 20 years of age the plant becomes fully mature and bears maximum fruits. The quality and quantity of production falls with its ageing if not maintained properly.

The flowering starts within one month of harvesting, i.e. in the month of March, the *Pyrem* (spring) in this region. Orange takes a longer period to start becoming red or orange in colour during October (which they call *Risaw* or month when the landscape (orchards) becomes red in colour). This month the villagers clear the undergrowth in the orchards for the second time after the first pruning and cutting of dead branches done in the post harvesting period. They spread those dead branches on the ground to add green manure to the soil. They do not use any other manure nor do they dig the soil to expose the roots which is a common care taken in other regions. The clearing of the tree trunk from mosses and other parasitic plants is also done along with the clearing of undergrowth. But these labours of intensive works are not done completely in each and every orchard in the village. This is one of the reasons the orange orchards in War country are affected by various pests and insects. It is recorded by Gurdon (1975) that a full grown tree yields as many as one thousand fruits in a year. But due to heavy damages done by different pests and also due to the old age of a large numbers of orange trees the production at present and particularly in this year was very meagre. As per the estimate given by the villagers this year they got a very low yield ranging approximately from 50 – 120 fruits per tree. In the village an old farmer narrated about the pests of the orange plants. They call it *Ksain*, a caterpillar like pest, which first appears on leaves and feeds on it, after being grown up it bores hole in the stems and fruits as well. They have even observed the life cycle of the *Ksain* as similar to that of butterfly. In fact, they do not know any proper effective measure to control such pests. At present they only plug the hole with a stick or *Shar* so as to check its movement. They have also observed that the attacks of such pests are more every year. In addition this year there were many unseasoned heavy showers with hailstones which have also damaged the crops heavily.

The orange is harvested starting from the orchards on the lower slopes in the month of December or *Nohprah*. They carry a medium size basket and climb on the tree to pluck the fruits carefully by hand. The fruits on the tips of the extended branches are also plucked carefully by their hands only. Till today villagers at large do not accept any exotic orange species or adapt to new farming techniques though they are very much concerned about the fall in production.

The village farmers as well as the middle men measure the fruits in traditional way and not by weight. For orange and lemon the smallest unit of counting is *Hali* (4 pieces). 16 *Hali* equals 1 *Bhar*, 16 *Bhars* equals 1 *Lenti* or 1024 numbers. Oranges are transported from the village to market packed in a conical bamboo basket called *Ka Khara* made in the village itself. This year due to very low production the villagers earned a good price of around Rs. 1000/- per *Lenti*.

Lemon: The lemon species grown here are locally known as *Soh Kwit* in War dialect and seems to be an indigenous one too. It requires some kind of environment like orange but latter grows in a particular soil called *Khyndew Iaw* meaning old undisturbed soils of the forest. Villagers plant *Soh Kwit* even at a higher altitude than orange. It fetches much lower price than orange. This fruit has a high demand in Bangladesh and is mostly exported there. The rate of production was almost similar to orange this year. But the harvesting is completed 2 – 3 months before orange.

Bay leaf: Bay Leaf or *Tezpat* (Cinnamonum zeylanicum) is another extensively grown indigenous crop in the East Khasi Hills. It is called *La–Tuson* in War dialect and *Sla Tyrpad* in Khasi proper. It is an aromatic plant having a wide market in India and Bangladesh. The saplings are collected from the forest and transplanted to the chosen plot of land in Podwar. The villagers prefer to plant bay–leaf on the uphill side of orange in a good unaltered forest soil. The collection of leaves starts after the plants are about 5 years old. Every year villagers harvest bay leaves in February – March as soon as the orange is completely harvested. The leaves are dried in the sun for a few days in the village and transported to market packed in gunny bags. In other parts of the Khasi Hills harvesting season starts in November. The plant hardly needs any care, once it is grown up except only a periodical cleaning of weeds and other unwanted vegetation. It fetches Rs. 450/- to Rs. 500/- per quintal.

Cinnamon: The local variety of cinnamon plants (Cinammomum temala) locally called *Tynsia* is recently being popularised as another cash crop in the village. The method of cultivation is almost similar to that of bay–leaf but it is propagated through cuttings and planted in Ryngko lands of the village at present. Both leaves and its bark are harvested and sold which is inferior in quality to the one cultivated in South India and famous for its aromatic use. Only after 14 – 15 years of growth the plant is ready to be harvested, though leaves are collected for use much earlier. They cut the matured branches along with leaves leaving only one or two feet of the main trunk to allow further growth. The bark of the branches are peeled off and dried in the sun for 2–3 weeks while the leaves dry quicker. They sell *Shimuth* (1 bundle) at Rs. 10/- per kg of dried bundle and Rs. 1/- per bundle of leaves. At present Cinnamon grown in the village goes mostly to Bangladesh through Nongjri bazaar. It seemed that this crop is a recent inclusion here and they neither knew the actual price in the outside market nor they are sure about the quality of the produce. Villagers reported that since last 20 years or so they are planting this spice though only around 14–15 houses are having the plantation at present.

Areca nut: Areca nut is the second major cash crop traditionally cultivated in the War country. This is perhaps the most widely consumed non–food item in the whole of Northeast India and is propagated over a vast range of eco–zones from riverine plains to low hills of the plateau and the foot hills of the Himalaya as well. As informed by the State Agriculture Department the areca nut species grown here is an indigenous one which shows variable growth and production depending upon the altitude, soil type and slope. The Kwai in Khasi and Kwei War country can be cultivated successfully even up to an altitude of 2000 ft on various soils but require good rainfall and warmer climate. In the village the areca nut plantations occupy the lowest part of the Podwar. But a few yards away from the river bed to avail water logging.

It is propagated through seeds in a common traditional way. The seeds are selected carefully from the mature trees. Experienced farmers select the seeds, identifying the mature ones observing the shape of a single nut, a nut with protruded tail part. Such nuts are produced only by the trees which are 25 – 30 years old. This is called *Sleij* when the *Pdeng* (tail part) is protruded. Usually all the saplings of areca nut are grown in nurseries in the low altitude villages bordering Bangladesh in a rich clayey soil. Many of the northern War villages mentioned that they best preferred saplings produced in Umkren village nurseries located close to the border some 6 – 7 km west of Dawki. The selected nuts are at first loaded in a bamboo basket and wrapped in gunny bags and rags etc on ground under shade and regularly watered till those are germinated. It takes around 3 – 4 weeks and usually done in the month of January – February then those are planted in the nursery called *Kwei–Share* and are watered regularly assuring no water logging. These saplings, when it reaches 2 – 3 ft height, are sold to the farmers from all over War areas as the hilly villages are not found suitable for *Kwei–Share*.

In the actual garden plot the saplings are planted about 4 – 6 ft apart so that no plant touches another when matured. The inter–plant distance is kept less over high slopes and higher altitude where they grow less tall. The garden plantation site is called *Tui Kwei* or *Barah Kwei*. The best soil for areca nut is clay loam type and results better on east facing slopes. On an average the fruiting starts from eighth year. One tree bears nuts even upto 60 – 70 years if proper care is taken. To avoid insects and pests the garden should be cleared off undergrowth and also the tree trunk needs to be cleaned from mosses and fungi, dried and old leaves are also pruned regularly.

Harvesting starts from December and continues upto March. In the Mawlam village harvesting is done very late in March for late maturity due to high altitude. It is reported that at the beginning between 8 – 11 years one areca nut plant bears 3 bunches annually called *Ka* containing 80 – 100 nuts in each. But with the maturity the production goes upto 5 *Ka* of 150 nuts each. Due to tall height of the trees the villagers employ unique technique for harvesting the nuts to reach the heights of around 40 – 60 ft any ladder cannot be placed on the slim trunk; neither would it withstand the weight of an adult person to reach the top. So the villagers have adopted a technique combining two usual methods within the limits of safety. They make a light ladder with a long one vertical pole of bamboo (18 – 20 ft) and fix up tangential bamboo pieces (1.5 ft. These tangential bamboo pieces are fixed equally extended on either side of the pole to be used as steps. The person, usually young males, hold another thin and long piece of bamboo fitted on the top with a sharp iron sickle and climb the ladder leaning on the tree keeping his balance as meticulously as an expert acrobat. Reaching around middle of the tree he holds the tree trunk with left hand and leg while the right leg holds the ladder and right hand operates the second bamboo pole to cut the branches from the tree. Another person who holds the lower end of the ladder at the beginning now plays the part of a catcher on ground. The catcher takes care of the branches falling free from such a height using an empty gunny bag, which he swings swiftly synchronising accurately to hold the branch safely in the sack. As it was observed the whole operation takes around just 2 – 3 minutes per tree.

The branches are gathered in one or two places in the garden to be sorted out and be classified into four grades, the biggest and most mature nuts called *Paduh* are kept for two purposes

(i) Making *Wisecup* by processing in water (*U'wei um*) for local consusmption and

(ii) For selling to various *'pan–masala'* manufacturing industries.

The second quality called *Kwei Soh* is to be sold for direct consumption (*U'wei khaw*). The third and fourth grades are called *Pdeng* and *Bia* are the smallest and defective ones. These are mainly sold in the markets in the plain areas outside Northeast region where dry *'supari'* is consumed. They count the nuts in a traditional way as follows.

10 Nos	= 1 Kati
10 Kati	= 1 Pai
40 Kati or 4 Pai	= 1 Kani
16 Kani	= 1 Lenti or 6400 nuts

After grading, the nuts are packed in bamboo baskets called *Khara* (large one) and *Khoh* (small one) and transported to the market.

Processing of areca nut: The traditional system of processing nuts in water for making and lightly fermented and stronger one different in War areas compared to that of making *Garuah Tamul* in Assam. The best qualities of nuts are put into huge, roughly made bamboo baskets called *Khara* (5 to 5½ ft high and 3 to 3½ ft diameter) and immersed in water pools called *Kwei Pukhri*. Such *Pukhris* are made near or along a natural stream. The continuous flow of water is allowed through the pool with only one inlet and one outlet point; to avoid strong smell to develop. Every day a person forces himself into each *Khara* full of nuts to assure that the nuts are immersed properly. After processing such a way for around 3 – 4 months the *Wisecup* or the *U'wei um* can be kept for 6 months without further decline in quality and it fetches around thrice of the normal *Kwei*.

Disease since last two decades or so a new and so far unknown disease has been found infesting areca nut trees mainly in the lower hills of the War area that is the largest producing belt. A kind of wilting starts usually from the tip of the mature leaves which become dry and dark in colour. Within a few weeks the whole tree upto the root gets affected and dies. The affected part smells rotten. So far no remedy is found other than detecting it early and cutting the affected leaves.

Betel leaf or tympaw: This is another important traditional agricultural product in Khasi Hills equally popular like areca nut. But betel leaf is not grown well on northern part of the War area. This delicate creeper plant needs a very restricted and specific environment to thrive. This tropical plant loves cool and shady places with enough moisture in soil and atmosphere. The plant is propagated through cuttings and planted close to shady trees on which the creeper will grow. At the base of the newly planted cutting they put some leaf mould to retain moisture and to help developing roots faster. They usually plant new cuttings during peak rainy season (July – August). The cuttings are made from full grown, healthy plants. About three–four pieces of the main stem of one plant are taken from a height of 8 ft upward so that the master plant survives.

On earlier days when forest was ample in the region they preferred undisturbed old forest areas for betel leaf cultivation. Big trees like *Dieng Bati, Dieng–Sohphang, Diengli, Dieng–Kya, Dieng–Taric* etc. were preferred as support trees on which the creeper got twined. After planting a new cutting they used to prune all the lower branches of the support tree to allow sunlight as the creeper grows faster initially in a warm–lighted and airy condition. The west facing slopes are preferred for betel leaf. They make leaf mould out of the cut branches and put those around the base of the tree. Now–a–days due to depletion of forest the betel leaf plants are mostly grown in the betel nut gardens. Before planting they clear the part of the forest. Once it starts growing steadily and new shoots come out it requires complete shade and regular watering. As winter season approaches the farmers prepare a unique network of dual irrigation in their betel leaf plantations (to be discussed later on).

Harvesting of betel leaf starts after four years of plantation, leaves are harvested regularly at an interval of two to three months in the lower or southern region. In the village Mawlam it is harvested only twice a year, once in July – August giving highest yield and the second time in March–April. In general at lower altitudes the best quality leaves are plucked during winter (December – February) when all the leaves excepting the very young ones are collected. This harvest is called *Kheit Lynghlaw*. The next harvest *Noh Tram* is done in April – May – June when they pluck selectively and screen out the diseased leaves. So the production remains low in quality and quantity. Again during rain another selective harvest they do which is called *Kheit Siediap* but do not prune the plant. They maintain very high level of hygiene during harvesting which is not always followed religiously by the present day farmers. Earlier any person was allowed inside these plantation areas only after taking bath and wearing a clean loin cloth or "*Gamcha*". They still believe that betel leaf plants are very sensitive to various bacteria and viruses foreign to the forest eco-system it is growing in, hence management of this plant demands higher attention of the farmers and the success depends upon the traditional wisdom in him.

The leaves are carefully sorted by size and maturity. The bigger and greener leaves are washed carefully in clean and fresh water before making bundles in a typical traditional way.

16 Jora (pairs)	= 1 Shong (32)
3 Shongs	= 1 Bhiah
4 Bhiah	= 1 Tap
20 Tap	= 1 Kwi
40 Tap or 2 Kwi	= 1 Khah (one basket full)

N.B. One Khah of best quality leaf is formed by only 5 Tap instead of 40 Taps.

Diseases and Pests: Similar to the disease in the areca nut trees, a new and unknown disease is affecting the production of betel leaf since the last 10 – 12 years. The villagers call it *Tram* when they find some leaves are getting black spots as if the portion is burnt. They believe this is an air-borne disease which spreads very fast by wind. At present they do not know any remedy for this disease and simply keep strict watch and cut the affected part immediately. After cutting those leaves, they are collected in a particular basket called kharatram and then thrown in a river or dumped in an isolated place. The Kharatram is washed and cleaned after every use and kept separately for this purpose only.

An important point was raised by an experienced farmer in Dawki, the border market, that after the partition with Bengal they have lost a huge market for betel leaf. This crop being very much sensitive to heat and dryness is very difficult to transport to distant markets in Assam without proper transport facility. Hence the loss of market has forced many farmers to switch over to jhum cultivation and timber trade by cutting of the healthy old forest which provided the necessary eco-system for betel leaf plant.

Broomstick: The long sticks of flowers of the Thysalolaema maxima species of Poicea family have extensively altered the face of the Meghalaya plateau by revolutionizing the rural economy at least the last two decades. This indigenously available grass can be grown even up to an altitude of 4000 ft but maximum concentration was observed roughly between 1500 and 2500 ft. It can thrive on a wide range of soil and slope. Usually the dry and rocky slopes with very thin soil cover and the jhum fallow lands are the natural habitat of this grass. So the plantation of it in commercial scale is a unique phenomenon in the history of agriculture in Meghalaya. Farmers simply transplant the naturally available plant by selecting the new shoots. But they usually prefer old and new jhum fallows as well as any vacant space in and around the homestead. Though the exact date is not known as to when the commercialization started most of the villagers said that it must be around 20 years before. Several probable causes were highlighted regarding the popularity of this plant. Firstly, as the yield in the jhum fields declined due to shortened jhum cycle and parallelly the Government campaign to give up jhuming, acted as the triggering effect. It seems logical because broomstick became popular at a very fast pace, mainly, in the lower and middle hill ranges of East Khasi Hills Districts where there was hardly any forest left, due to intensive jhum activities. So people had no option to substitute jhuming, unlike the West Khasi Hills where timber trade became the alternate while in the Jaintia Hills they had enough coal reserves to exploit.

On the other hand the less fertile or degraded and barren rocky plateau could not produce any other crop profitable enough to earn their livelihood.

The lucrative vast market all over India must have played encouraging role too. It is observed that slopes all along the highways connecting Shillong and Guwahati and the interior villages connected by motorable subsidiary roads have adopted this crop early and in greater extent.

The broomstick is called *Lynnai* in War district and requires least care to grow. After harvesting the sticks during January – March, they perform weeding and cleaning the fields and leave for the rain to come. Only once in two-three years they burn the grasses after harvesting believing that it will help the grass to grow better at par with their traditional perception and very old practice as in the case of jhum cultivation. Harvesting requires hard labour continuously for several months to avoid getting scratched on their legs, while harvesting by the sharp edges of the leaves. They use a kind of cover upto the knee with a cotton garter called *Jingropjat*. The harvested sticks are brought near the village settlement and spread over any dry ground mostly along the road side to dry it under the sun. Some households make bamboo stacks to hang or spread those sticks in their courtyards. It takes 2 – 3 weeks or more to dry depending on the sunny days. The dried up sticks are then thrashed on stone slabs thoroughly to separate the seeds from the sticks. After that these are made into bundles.

A small bundle (handful) is called *Shi Khim* while a big bundle (backload) is *Shi Kit* consisting of 9 *Shi Khim*. One backload of brown stick weighs around 35 kg, when it is brought from the field after harvesting. The same quantity weighs 25 kg (approx.) after drying backload (row) from the field to the owner's house as labourer gets @ Rs. 80 per kg or Rs. 28/- per *Kit* as the charges of harvesting and considering 2 – 3½ hours walk. An adult male can carry about 18-20 *Khims* a day (9 a.m. – 5 p.m.) and woman can carry 15-16 *Khims* a day. The *Khim* quantity depends on the person making it, so also the *Kit*. There is no standard weight for these measures. A very strong man can carry upto 70 kg backload. Normal person can carry 50 kg and a woman upto 35 kg.

There has been a huge fall in the sale prices of broomstick within the last 10 years, villagers reported that they started selling this crop as high as Rs. 1000 per quintal, which has come down to mere Rs. 100 this year. This is mainly due to the huge production of this crop and owing to a very large portion of land brought under this crop. The trade of broomstick was in their tradition as it is an indigenous species which people used to gather as a minor forest produce.

One old man in the village told that there is an old Khasi proverb saying – "*Broom is a good slave but a bad master*". At present these villagers have started realizing the truth behind the proverb. They now find it almost impossible to clear the broomstick plots to grow some other crop through jhum and plantation. In fact this grass can only be cleared by carefully uprooting the whole plant and drying under the sun, the secondary growth has to be cleared regularly. The mellowed officers of State Agriculture Office at Pynursla informed that this grass has a 15 – 20 years life cycle. At present the villagers are at a loss and do not find any alternative to it as the price has dropped considerably. Thus, the land less or marginal farmers in the village are getting lower and lower labour charges for harvesting proportionate to the price level. Hence, the same crop which once boosted the rural economy has turned to be a liability to them. Moreover, it is yet to be ascertained as to what could be the state of soil fertility after the plant is removed from the land. Experienced farmers in the village have noticed that whatever the quality of the soil the broomstick plots can be used for planting other crops only after minimum three years. During this first 3 to 5 years they used to continue weeding and uprooting of whatever secondary growth of the grass occurs. But to uproot the grass is a labour intensive job. They prefer to grow pineapple, arum, chillies, etc. But in Ryngko lands they still prefer broomstick as the most profitable crop with least labour required.

Basket making: The War people, like most of the tribal communities of northeast India, are well known for their experience in making a wide range of baskets. The most commonly used raw materials are bamboo and cane which are available naturally in the forests.

The Mawlam villagers make all the baskets for uses like packing and transporting their produces, fishing, food gathering and various domestic purposes. The baskets for packaging the fruits; in particular are required in large quantities and are done by some of the household commercially as a small scale household industry in their own houses. For making one '*Ka Khara*', the 'medium size basket to pack orange, a nine feet long piece of bamboo' – *Thyr* is required which is collected from the *Ri-Raid* land in the Podwar. Though both man and women participate in basketry works the latter are considered more expert. Experienced women can make upto 50 such baskets with split bamboo in a single day. The baskets are made in large numbers well in advance of harvesting orange and lemon. Due to very less production of fruits this year we found about 800 such baskets are left unsold only in one house. Moreover, they received only half the usual price i.e. @ Rs. 0.50 per basket this year.

Other kinds of baskets were seen in use in the village include *Ka Khoh* the conical and most common one, *Ka Polo* for storing fruits and vegetables, *Ka Kriah* a smaller with a square bottom used for keeping various kitchen articles including food items, *Ka Kuh* to collect fish during fishing, *Ka Prah* – a typical basket for winnowing the husks and dust from cereals and grains.

This traditional drip irrigation system practised by the War people is a unique example of their wisdom. Using only the locally available resource i.e. bamboo, a well developed dendritic network of bamboo channels are laid wisely utilizing the slope of the land. One natural stream or spring is selected at a higher level than the field. The water source is then canalised through a narrow outlet using stones and mud. Then they place a pipe made of a whole bamboo sometimes joining a series of such bamboo pipes depending on the distance to be covered. This main pipe is called *Kdung*. Then the subsidiary or the second order pipes (*Lar*) made of half split bamboo (*Shken*) are fitted with the main pipe in selected points. The third order (*Khliah*), fourth (*Pyntee*) and the fifth (*Pynjan*) other bamboo channels are connected stepwise to reach the water right up to the base of each and every betel plant. To control the flow of water they place a small piece of wood 2″ long tangentially fixed to a 3″–4″ long thin slice of bamboo through which water is diverted to the next order canal. Thus, at the end water falls at the root of the plant drop by drop whole day and night. The small piece of wood and bamboo part is called *Shyngliar*– which is only used at the junction between the last canal and the earlier one. At present, in most cases, polythene (flexible) pipes have replaced the first 2–3 stages of bamboo pipes but the *Pyntler* and *Pynjam* the last two channels are still in use if we compare the modern drip irrigation equipment and the cost involved in installation and maintenance it costs many times cheaper and equally effective indigenous eco–friendly technology requiring no power and exotic materials.

Management of forest

The Khasis have a long symbiotic relation between them and their natural surroundings. Till recent past these tribal group was highly dependent on its immediate natural resources for sustenance. Forests were the mother of all required resources to these people for several thousand years. Only after the development of road transport network from 1870's and the consequent impact of the huge markets of the northern and southern plains did the forest start depleting from the hills for commercial uses. On the other hand the continuously growing burden of population has made the once viable jhum land use system responsible for permanent degradation of forests and hill slopes by reducing the jhum cycle from 30–40 years to mere 6–10 years or less (Simon, 1991).

Types and ownership of forest

The United Khasi-Jaintia Hills Autonomous District (Management and Control of Forests) Acts 1961 passed in pursuance of paragraph 11 of the Sixth Schedule of Indian Constitution was extended to all forest land of the region except 722.30 sq. km (i.e. only 8% of the total forest) which is directly under the State Forest Department (Tiwari et.al., 1998). Therefore, almost all the forests (92%) are under the private control through the rules framed by the Executive Committee of District Council. These forests in Khasi Hills are basically divided into two depending upon their ownership (i) the village on community forests controlled by *Raid* and (ii) those of individual or clan holdings *Ri Kynti*. Since time immemorial all the forests were controlled and demarked through Khasi customary laws governed by the traditional *Syiems* of different Durbars. The forests were presented for specific needs and were utilized carefully.

Law Nian *Law Adong*	Forest protected by village Durbar.
Law Long Um	Forest with water source for winters.
Law Shnong	Village forest.
Law Kue	Clan (family) forests.

Several Acts, norms and religious sanctions were framed to conserve these forests were there before. The implementation of Forests Acts, signifies the depths and extent of the indigenous knowledge of environment of these tribal people.

In the village Mawlam a well preserved *Law Lyndoh* was observed other than the huge patch of *Iaw Adong*. But only a few households (6 out of 52 studied) have reported possessing purely private forests inherited from ancestors of their clans *Law Kue*. In all cases the area of these forests were not estimated either by the villagers or by the state administration as in the case of any land as such.

(I) Law Lyndoh: is a sacred grove of highest order kept under the stringent customary rules of total protection and control by the priest or *Lyndoh* selected by the village authority. This forest is the abode of the supreme guardian god. 'U Ryngkew U Basa' who from time immemorial guards the villages and the people from any harm. At present a small patch of about 50 *sq.* metres of undisturbed primary forest is housing the 'Mawlam' the 'Guiding Stone' of the village. It is a 2 ½ ft high, 2′x1′ stone block with another small piece of stone on top of it. The stone is worshipped every year in the month of March by the Lyndoh or priest who is deputed from the recognised clan council of the raid comprised of six clans, viz. Khongain, Khongitib, Khongsdier, Khongklan, Tynsong and Khongji. The ritual is performed after the burning of jhum field called Knai Khatrat on the 15th or 16th day of March as fixed by the Durbar. Prayers are chanted before the goat and cocks are sacrificed. Every tenth year they hold a special prayer where a cow is sacrificed. The villagers (other than the Christian families) believe that if anybody disturbs the stone by touching or hitting or verbal teasing the stone god will appear with the body of tiger and head of a man. In such incidence they have to perform ritual and sacrifice on animal by law of the Lyndohs even a dry leaf cannot be collected from the *Law Lyndoh*. Only the elderly men are allowed to take part in the ritual or the families who strictly follow the traditional religion. (Niamtre), neither any children nor any person of other religion is allowed. We were allowed to visit the forest after much pursuance. We observed a very old and huge rubber tree (*Jri*) by the 'Mawlam' rock. The tree is held in high reverence by the villagers and is seen as the Gateway of the village. In fact the typically laid root system of the tree is used as the god made stairs before construction of the road.

The *Law Lyndoh* forest still possesses a good species diversity including various medicinal herbal plants. The most valuable trees found in the forest as reported by the villagers are *dieng tusei, dieng shyrngan, dieng sohsyrlet, dieng sohsarat, dieng shoat, dieng jri, dieng lakhor, dieng pyrchit, dieng sohphi, dieng sohum, dieng bti, dieng sohniar, tuson, ka brah* etc. along with many varieties of bamboo (*Thyr*). The *'Kambiraj'* or the village medicine man collects many of these herbal plants from the *Iaw Lyndoh* when these are needed but only through proper channel i.e. permission and guidance of the *Lyndoh*.

(2) *Law Adong*: These are protected forests in the village meant for specific community needs and managed by the *Raid* organization as the local body of the *Syiem*, in this case *Khynriem Syiemship*. In the village most of the *Law Adongs* are present in and around the heads of the mini catchments areas, from where large and small streams originate (*Law Thang Um*). All the four natural water points supplying water to the villagers are all located inside the *Law Adongs*, which surround the village on three sides. Moreover the three crematoria for non-Christian Khasi villagers are also located inside these forests. Only with the permission of the *Sirdar* or the *Bah Shnong* of the Mawlam *Raid* villagers can utilize the forest produce for building materials, firewood and cremation. Compared to *Law Lyndoh* the forests of *Law Adong* are more disturbed and exploited.

(3) ***Raid***: organization also manages other categories of forest land under Ri Raid, which are non-protected forests. Villagers are free to these for jhum cultivation or plantation of any crop both annual and perennial. During the last few decades both area under jhum and jhum fields are decreasing with increasing land under plantation crops.

(4) The fourth category of forests includes those under family and clan possession under the Ri Kynti area. Such forests are kept for household level or clan level requirements like house building, jhum cultivation and firewood. In the village Mawlam land under such type of forest is very much restricted even today. Only 6 of the 52 household surveyed belonging to 3 clans (Khonghrom, Khonghitib, Nongsteih) reported having such forest through of negligible amount.

Utilization of forest resource

The forests of Meghalaya being very rich in flora and fauna with high species diversity have long been supporting the people with many of their needs. Broadly the War Khasi people utilize the forest resource to fulfil their basic needs through:

(i) Hunting and collection of food articles.

(ii) Firewood and charcoal.

(iii) House building materials.

(iv) Materials for making domestic crafts.

(v) Medicinal plants.

(i) Traditionally these jhumia populations have been practising hunting and food gathering to supplement their food shortage during the lean periods. Today hunting of games is practised more as a recreation than as a regular means of livelihood. As reported by the elderly villagers and documented by various earlier researchers; game hunting was a group activity in all the villagers of the region. In earlier days winter and spring (November – March) was the usual lean period for the Jhumia population. During these hunting of games like wild boar, deer, jungle cat, rabbits, mongoose, large rats and squirrel were hunted in the forests. Khasi villagers consume many varieties of birds starting from large eagles to small sparrows. Fish is also a favourite, available in rivers, streams and pools. Dry fish are mostly bought from Bangladesh.

A rich variety of tools and techniques were used during hunting which included bows and arrows, spears, daos or choppers, knives along with fishing nets and hooks supported quite a few simple and effective trapping systems. Dogs with specific traits known as *'Sew-beh'* were usually employed in a group hunting and game chaser (Caje and Syiemlieh 1998).

As a part of the traditional forest conservation customs the hunting activity was also guided by a set of rules and regulations. Firstly an individual or a group of hunters should give a general notice to the *'Rongbah Shnong* and village elders before venturing into the forests, usually the community forest, or *Law Adong* under the *Raid*. They usually avoid composing a hunting team of odd numbers (3,7,9,13 etc.) believed as unlucky, secondly, one or two village elderly people used to guide the hunting team in restricting them against killing any animal which is pregnant or nursing stage. Restrictions are also observed in choosing the right season and number of animals hunted, which usually does not exceed three per season for a group of hunters. These norms were common to almost all villagers with some variation depending upon the village *Dorbar's* decision.

Fishing is also a favourite to all the Khasis in general. An individual's family or a group of individuals go for fishing in the streams and rivers in their village surroundings. Unlike hunting fishing has no such restriction other than that odd numbers of participants which is usually avoided.

But certain traditional beliefs on natural phenomenon like rain, thunder, lightning etc. occurring during the start of the journey to forest would either delay or postpone their going. Hunting is always an all male affair, while for fishing both sexes may participate.

In the village Mawlam hunting and fishing are quite common still today. During harvesting season (October – March) they also go for hunting both in agricultural fields and *Law Adong* forests. They use guns (*Suloi*) for hunting monkey, fox, bear, deer, boars, wild fowls etc. Usually at least two males go together for such ventures. Sometimes hunting and harvesting of crops like *Tejpat* and broomsticks are done together. The guns are usually bought from nearby markets including cities like Guwahati and Shillong. But mostly shot guns with one/two barrels are crudely made by some local artisans and used due to its easy availability and low price (Rs. 1500 - Rs. 2500). These days use of trained dogs is no more common in hunting, guns have replaced bow and arrows and other weapons.

During our field study most of the Mawlam villagers were found experts in making various traps using nothing but natural raw materials available in the forests. For catching or killing different birds, squirrels, wild rats, rabbits, they lay different kinds of traps (*Pap*). A few of these traps are described below:-

(1) Riam Pap: The most common and effective trap meant for small animals like wild rat, mongoose, squirrel and rabbit. It is mostly laid in winter inside the broom stick fields or in the forests. They select a place which appears to be the shelter or path of such animals. They find a flat slab of stone of at least 1½ ft x 1 foot in size, which is called *Mawpap* or the trap stone. Then a piece of strong branch of tree of 1 foot length is collected, dieng Kynthei or female stick. Another piece of stick *Dieng Shynong* or male stick of 6-8" length is fixed tangentially in such a way that it holds the weight of the rock on the ground. To fix these two together a flexible piece of slit bamboo of 10-12' length is attached with one end pressed on the ground. The same piece is then laid round the *Dieng Kynthei*. Finally another piece of long bamboo stick of about 1.5 to 2 ft length, which is lighter and thinner is fixed as trigger passing between the twisted *Riwai* to reach well inside the raised stone (as in the sketch). The bait usually a small piece of carrot or bread is fixed tightly at one end of the long stick – *Dieng Bamkhana* reaching inside the rock. The tap laid in this way is left as such. Everyday a person will come and examine the tap trap and he may change the bait if necessary. Smaller animals are trapped or killed below the rock as it falls on them.

(2) Riam Khung: *Riam Khung* is the bird trap laid above ground using smaller trees and carefully keeping the natural lay out of the forest intact. This trapping system is engineered by employing the strength of the branches. At first a small tree is cut at around 3' – 4' height above ground in the forest preferably close to crop fields or streams. The cut away stem is made like a long wedge (*Dieng Kynring*) and fixed on the cut end of the stem standing on ground (*Dieng Jingbam*). Then a tender branch 2 ½″ is tied with the horizontal *Dieng Kynring* in the form of an inverted 'U' shape called *'Pyrdung'*. The next step is to pull down another young tree and find it by a strong string (at present a nylon string) with the horizontal pale (*Dieng Kynrieng*) – keeping the string in full tension. This second tree when fixed in tension acts as the main force of the trap. The string is then pulled down further and delicately locked with the help of one small wedge like stick (*Pyrson*) and another thin stick 1 ½ *ft* long) called *Kalar*, parallel to the horizontal which acts as the trigger. A loop is made with the loose part of the string and laid over the one end of the *Kalar* is the place for birds to sit and eat the bait. As soon as any bird put its weight loop the trap will go off and the bird will be tied by the legs in the string. In this region the common birds caught are *pyrsaw*, *sympohnei*, *slang*, per *kdait*, *mrit*, *purnei*, *pdit* etc.

(3) Pnah: *Pnah* is another kind of simple trap for birds. The *Thriang* the resin of the wild rubber tree *Dieng Jri* is collected first. A piece of tender bamboo (1′ to 1½′) is slit into thin sticks leaving some 3″– 4″ of the piece intact which acts as the handle. The resin is smeared over the slit part of the bamboo which holds the resin. Then the whole thing is placed on some tree close to water points or streams where birds used to perch after bathing. In fields or forests with no bait the gum is strong enough to hold the bird. A bamboo casing is also used to cover the gum while carrying it. This gum is also applied over a long bamboo pole (3" – 4") and tied horizontally over two vertical poles fixed on the ground with some baits kept close to this. The birds come and sit on it and get stuck. Even large birds like eagles are caught in this way. Attraction bait prepared from a fruit *Sohlang* was found sold in the village markets in the shape of a cricket ball they say it is effective bait for catching birds and fish.

Another common way of killing birds is with *Tehjiri* or catapult. Almost any young boy upto the age of 18 – 20 years and some elderly persons too carry a catapult while casually strolling around the homestead. Most of them are sharp shooters and kill one bird almost every hour. A few are really experts in whistling and imitating various sounds of birds with perfection. They stand quietly under a large tree or near a bush in the forest and whistle and the birds respond by coming closer towards him and then he targets the birds.

Fishing: The summer and rainy seasons (April September) are good for fishing in the streams, rivers and pools around the village. Khasis in general enjoy fishing and still find time to do so, unlike rare occasions for hunting. The Mawlam villagers have little access to large rivers and ponds due to its location on top of the range with average height of about 15007 ft from the main river – *Wah Umroh*. Hence they mainly fish in few natural water pools and streams using smaller hand nets (*Ka Bnij*) and cast nets (*Ka Billea*) and fishing rods (*Rong Wiang*) fitted with *Khwai* or the hook. They usually make their own nets (*Jer*) with thread prepared from barks of trees.

Normally they catch fishes like *Khasaw*, *Kharew*, *Khamongue* etc from rivers and streams *Snalynai*, *Doh Thli* and *Shee* are smaller fishes caught by small pieces of cloth or *'Gamchcha'* and hand nets. To keep such smaller fishes they carry small baskets (*Ruh*) tied around their waists.

Various superstitious, beliefs and fears restrict the villagers from over exploitation and disturbing natural habitats of the fishes. The medicine-man or *Kambiraj* narrated that they believe a *'Puri'* or female spirit of the river lives in the War Khas and (the river of fishes) if any body throws stones or disturbs the water too much, the *'Puri* gets angry. She then causes a storm with heavy rains resulting in certain epidemic diseases etc. or she makes particular males (single) go insane. Rituals are performed therefore before fishing to the *'Puri'*. Further in and around the permanent water sources in the *'Iaw Adong'* fishing by any kind of net is totally prohibited so as to maintain the natural flow of water.

COLLECTION OF FRUITS AND VEGETABLES

In almost all the seasons various roots, vegetables (mushrooms/ tits) and fruits form a portion of their diet. Fruits like banana, fig. jackfruits, etc. are widely available in the forests. They plant them in their homesteads too. The tender shoots of fig (*Lapong*), the tender core of banana trunk (*Pashor*) and flower (*Ka Siar*), jackfruits and their seeds are favourite vegetables to the people. Bamboo shoots are also collected for consumption similar to other parts is also consumed like *Jahjee*, *Shorblang* and *Jamgrdoh*. During monsoon at least 10 – 12 varieties of mushrooms (*Tit*) are collected, the most common ones are *Tit Tung* and *Tit Lakhek*. Squash plants, once planted grow without further care for which they get large quantity of vegetable, fruits, plant itself and its root.

BEE KEEPING AND HONEY COLLECTION

The War Khasi people has a long tradition of bee keeping and honey collection, using their own knowledge and techniques (Dasgupta, 1984) till today bee keeping is practiced almost in all villages through honey collection from the forests has become a low key affair due to the shrinking of forest cover. In the village we found only a few households not rearing bees.

The collection of wild honey is done during February – March and completed before the starts of the rains. There are two varieties of honey bees found in the forests:

(i) Uimai – the bigger one producing better quality and larger quantity of honey but more dangerous to handle and

(ii) Ungap – the common smaller variety is considered less pugnacious and chosen for keeping in a box. The collectors apply smoke to the hives by burning cotton rags to drive away the bees. But they avoid collection from *Uimai* hives during day time.

The box for keeping bees is made by scooping out a piece of 2" – 5" long log with 10" – 12" diameter to make cylinder sort of container (*Ka Ksing Ngap*). Two circular plates of wood are used as lids (*U Jong Sit*) for both ends of the cylinder making a small entry and exit slit passage on one end. Usually during the autumn season (*Symrai*) September – October they locate *U Ngap* hive in the forest. After collecting the queen bee (*Ka Sympa*) they carefully tie one of its wings and put it inside *Ka Ksing* tied with a stick then both ends are closed and slowly the other bees enter inside following the queen. Then the *Ka Ksing* is brought back to their house and kept usually on the raised platform of their huts selecting a corner with least disturbance or it is tied up in some branch of a tree in the courtyard.

The first collection of honey is done after around one year and subsequently they get honey 2 – 3 times a year, depending on the season and flora. One hive produces one to two bottles (700 ml bottles) per harvest. The rate per bottle is Rs. 150/- to Rs. 200/- per bottle. Maximum honey is available from the extraction made during spring and winter season. The honey is consumed as high energy substance and also for medicinal purpose especially for cold and cough. During winter months children are fed with honey, women during pregnancy and post delivery period are also given honey. The *Kambiraj* traditional medicine man also used honey as base for some of his medicines.

COLLECTION OF FIREWOOD AND CHARCOAL MAKING

In the village Mawlam people are totally dependent on firewood for cooking and heating their rooms during winter months. It was found that all the required firewood is collected from the forests under the *Raid* Mawlam jurisdiction. By the law of the *Raid* dry and dead branches of wood can be collected from all kinds of forests barring the sacred groves or *Law Lyndoh*. But nobody is allowed to collect leaf litters as those are meant for maintaining nutrients for the forests.

Most of the required quantity of firewood is collected and stored during the dry winter months after the jhum fields are cleared and plenty of dry woods are available in the forests. Collection of firewood from the fields and forests is mainly the job of adult male villagers but adult women and children also extend help for gathering smaller and lighter woods while coming back from fields and from around the residential areas.

Charcoal is another important commodity the villagers produce utilizing the selected portion of firewood they collect. After separating the good quality dried up wood as firewood from the newly cleared jhum fields they usually select the poorer quality wood for making charcoal or *Rnga*. One experienced adult male person from the family of that jhum field takes the responsibility of charcoal making as they think it as a specialized job and it takes a few days to complete the job. First a pit is dug on the slope of the cleared field itself. Due to hardness of the soil and rocky slopes only three sides of a square spot is cut to make a flat ground. The sides of this pit depend upon the quantity of wood one will use. Then the already gathered logs are cut into equal pieces (1.5" – 2" long) stacked carefully on that pit in a very compact manner so that there will be restricted amount of air passage. All the four exposed sides of the stack (*Thliew Rnga*) are covered with the dug up mud/soil to seal all the ventilation points except a few required ones on top. Then fire is lit from below through a few gaps left for this purpose. It is important to keep the fire steady at a regulated speed. The man in charge should keep strict vigil on the hearth so that there is no flame which may completely burn down the wood to ashes. The fire is controlled simply by blocking and opening the air passages on different points of the stack. One or two persons have to assist the man for at least 3 to 5 days depending on the stack.

Most of the charcoal produced is sold in the market to meet the needs in towns and cities even outside Meghalaya. This year they sold at Rs. 120/- to Rs. 130/- per bag of 40 kg of charcoal, which they consider was good return. The prices have risen with the Supreme Court judgement against felling and transport of timber and other forest products. The producer keeps only 2 to 4 bags of charcoal for using at home during winter months.

HOUSE BUILDING MATERIALS

In Mawlam village most of the houses or *Kaing* are of typically a traditional pattern built utilizing the locally available materials. Out of 52 households studied there were 23 houses having tin roof over the traditional katcha structure. Only one house is made of 80% R.C.C. and 20% wood. The traditional War Khasi houses are constructed on raised platforms whether on slope or flat ground. In the village even the recent houses are built using oblong shaped, single block of stones. Walls and floors are made of wooden planks. Wooden or bamboo poles are used to construct the sloped roof frame. Roofing materials are either straw or a variety of wild palm. Materials are usually locally available. Households having no private forest appeal to the village *Durbar* or *Raid* committee to supply the required timber and bamboo. In general they are allowed to collect the materials from the *Iaw Adong* and other community forest. But in case for large amounts a nominal amount is to be paid.

The most preferred woods for particular parts of the buildings are: -

(1) *Dieng Tusei*: Strong and heavy wood for main frame structure.

(2) *Dieng Bti* (jackfruit): For making planks.

(3) *Dieng Phoniew*: For walls and floors.

(4) *Dieng Rai*: For making most of the furniture with smooth finishing.

(5) *Thyr* (bamboos): of different varieties: Used for flooring, roofing and frames.

Belief still persists among the War people that any tree or bamboo felled and collected during particular seasons on new moon days the wood will remain good or less termite/insects will spoil them. Moreover, tree below the girth of less than 5 – 7 feet are prohibited to be used. Though these days, these beliefs are gradually dying out among the new generation.

BASKETRY

Baskets are made by the villagers themselves and certain households are engaged in making such baskets as a household industry. For making one such basket a 9 ft long bamboo (*Thyr*) collected from the community forests are utilized. Though both male and female make these baskets, females are more expert. Experienced women can make up to 50 baskets a day compared to men. Rate per basket is 0.50 paisa each. One household in the village, who made a large number of such baskets well before the harvesting of the fruits found a low demand and still around 800 pieces were seen, stacked unsold in his house. Due to low production this year the demand was less.

PLANTS FOR MEDICINAL AND SPECIAL USE

The *Kambiraj* or traditional medicine man Tilliw Khongbnan (M/60) is one of the eldest and most experienced in the village. He is regularly called by the villagers to treat any kind of persistent illness or disorder of body and mind. But from the way of treatment narrated by him it seems that they practice more of rituals and prayers and administer only a few herbs and natural medicines. But it is interesting to note that the person had no background of traditional medicine in his family. He said that he had discovered the first medicine by observing rats eating an herb and they hardly fall sick even after eating waste food etc. Once in his 20's he was suffering repeatedly with diarrhoea. He tried that herb fleshy creeper called *Laikad* and got cured. He now keeps the creeper dried and makes powder which is then mixed with a little bit of powdered molar tooth of an elephant (*Bniat hati*). This mixture advised to take 2-3 times a day for any indications of food poisoning, diarrhoea and acute stomach problems, *Soh Pryda* (a wide variety of guava plant) had many uses. The pastes of its leaves are applied over forehead to cure headache. The powder of the dried leaves is mixed with water to drink during any problem of indigestion or acidity. He has observed that the fruits and leaves of this plant are eaten by deer in the forests.

In most cases reported, the *Kambiraj* first performs ritual to detect the cause of illness by traditional method of breaking on egg on a wooden board called *Liang Shat Khan*. If the disease still persists even after performing the ritual the herbal medicine is used.

Diseases like measles (*Niang Blei*), cough and cold among children (*Niang Tmar*) are believed to be caused by god's wish either as blessings or teachings. So far in such cases the *Kambiraj* performed various rituals to appease the relevant god or spirit. They also use *Soh Kwit* juice over the whole body during measles.

Snakes, mainly pythons, are killed both for food and medicine. The python's fat is believed to be effective for curing joint/rheumatic pains. The affected person drinks a portion of fat mixed with water or rubs the fat over the affected area.

A kind of large, dark, round disk like seed of a tree is consumed as especially nutritious food. The hard outer shell is burnt to take out the kernel or actual seed. The nut-like seeds are then boiled in water and cut into pieces. Then wrapped in a clean cloth and kept immersed in a flowing stream for about 24 hours now it becomes ready to eat. They also grind the kernel and mix it with water to make smooth paste which is applied over the body as a skin nourishing and cleansing cream.

All the above mentioned medicinal herbs and many such others are available in the forests mostly in *Law Lyndoh* and *Law Adong*. But as informed by the village elders herbal medicine is a comparatively recent introduction (15-20 years) in the village and the knowledge has been disseminated by the *Kambiraj*. At present one health worker visits the village twice a week from Pynursla P.H.C. to provide the modern health care facility to the villagers.

TACKLING THE FOREST FIRE

Forest fire is a common event in the Khasi Hills particularly in late winters when villagers burn their jhum fields. Moreover, the villagers in War Khasi region still believe that if they burn the dry undergrowth during February – March, the soil on the slopes gets extra nutrition and get purified and vegetation grows anew. So burning slopes, whether bare or forested are a common site till today instead of prohibiting orders from the *Dorbar* and the state government as well hence, most cases of forest fire are man made only.

In the event of any such forest fire, spreading inside the village, all the villagers present in the nearby houses rush to the spot under the instruction of the Raid Committee or *Dorbar*. They carry buckets and mugs and fetch water to douse the fire. Depending on the size of fire they even spend days warding off the fire. In case of huge fires in a good forest villagers clear a strip of forest along the line of fire so as to check the further progress of the same beyond that vacant space. This cleared strip of about 6-10 ft wide, without any dry vegetation to catch fire, acts as the fire barrier. This traditional mode of tackling forest fire is very much followed by the Meghalaya forest department and state government machinery here at present.

If the fire is spread from the adjacent village or Raid, compensation is demanded from the responsible party. If a person of the same village is found guilty he or she will be fined in cash equivalent or kind by the Raid, and also he has to bear the cost of holding prayers to one of these village guardian gods. When nobody confesses or knows about the responsible person, the priests will declare that the almighty may punish the guilty person, who will ultimately fall ill or even die.

WATER MANAGEMENT

Due to its location in the world's wettest region and very high slopes of the terrain over most parts, the War country is posing a unique situation in terms of water resource and its management. During May to September the village gets rain water in abundance most of which gets drained away very fast through streams and rivers in the form of surface run off. In the process the narrow flat ridge top, where the village settlement is located, surrounded by high slopes and less vegetation cover fails to retain enough water. The red loamy soils add to the cause due to low water holding capacity. Hence only two points around the village settlement serve as natural perennial source of water for domestic uses. Those sources are located in the main-catchments on either side of the main road covered under *Law Adong* forests. There is no well system in the village. Only during the rainy season two or three more natural springs provides them clear water.

The main perennial source of water is located along a footpath only about 300 *m* down slope from the nearest homestead. There are three points on the same line at around 3-4 *m* of gap. The first spring just below the thick forests is made into a square tank using stones and cement and used only for drinking water or *Tynghoh-Um-Dih*. A wooden board is kept to cover the small tank to protect from gathering any dirt. The excess of this continuous flow of water gets drained away through a small outlet leaving a sizeable amount of water of 1.5" deep inside the tank. The same overflow of water is again gathered in a rocky natural pool, a little lower below the tank. This point is utilized for washing clothes and utensils and is called *Tynghoh-Um-Sait*. Further down, the same flow is again diverted through a larger square tank made by arranging stones. This tank – *Pukhri Kwei* is about 5 ft deep and has one inlet and one outlet each on opposite direction. This tank is used for soaking *'Kwei'* (betel nuts) towards fermenting it.

Some fifty metres down slope the same spring surfaces again to become a small slow flowing stream but this surface water is not used for washing purpose during dry season due to the amount of dirt in the form of dead leaf litters. The forest slopes around this small stream is only used as open air latrine of the villagers.

A deserted hut was observed on the other side of the path which was earlier used as country liquor distillation centre.

The second perennial source on the other side of the road is not equally managed and maintained by the *Raid* Committee. The water seemed to be not of equally good quality and volume. The collection point is located just 200 metres below the source region of a stream inside the *Law Adong* forest. But the flow of water is on the surface for a greater part and demarcation between the points of drinking water and water for other uses is less distinct. There is no concrete structure for the reservoir a small pool where water is collected from.

From these two sources villagers regularly collect and use water for their domestic consumption. For the purpose of drinking and cooking they have to carry the water from a distance of more than 500 metres depending upon the location of the particular house. This job of carrying water in large and small containers is literally an uphill task performed mostly by the women and children who stay home during day time. A conical bamboo basket is used for carrying the water containers, which they hang on their back with load taken on the head by a split bamboo sling. The little boys and girls also follow elders with smaller containers. Traditionally they used to carry water in bamboo containers known as *Ktang Um* or larger bamboo species with large diameter is used attaching a small sling to hold. Around 6-8 such small *Ktang Um* are placed inside the *Khoh* (bamboo) and hung on the back with the help of a sling or *Star* around the head. To avoid getting wet from the spilled up water they place a protective cover called *Trap*. A semi circular shield made of bamboo (*Skhen*) frame over which large dried leaves (*Lamet) is woven.*

During the rainy season villagers collect water dripping off from roofs of their houses as supplementary source of both drinking and other purposes. They collect rain water in the traditional way by digging hole on their courtyard number and size of which depend on the quantity of water required by that family. Such holes are dug in the place when there is a hard rocky impermeable layer below the surface. Small holes or small pools of water also called *Tynghoh* signify the long tradition of managing the water resources. It also indicates perpetual crisis of water in this village, particularly during dry season, paradoxical to the abundance of rainfall received.

On the other hand the high hill slopes having good vegetation cover either in the form of forests or plantation and the nature of soil holds the valuable rain water before it flows down to the valley. The villagers understand that the amount of water (or moisture) in the soils increases down slope and also around the prominent stream channels along the slopes. Their perception in this regard is well reflected in selecting the crop as per the character of this soil and the slope. In usual sequence the broomstick grass is grown on the highest and driest parts, followed by bay leaf, citrus, other fruit trees, bananas and lastly the betel nut plantations. The wettest and best soils (with higher water holding capacity) are utilized mainly for betel leaf, betel nut, papaya, black pepper, etc.

Water collected from the spring for drinking purpose is usually taken as pure potable water and consumed directly excepting a few enlightened families who purify it by boiling. When water become scarce and dirty they sieve it through a piece of clean cloth. In general all the Khasi families were found very particular about domestic hygiene like washing, cleaning the kitchen articles as well as their own hands and feet mainly after entering their houses from outside. It is a feast of one's eyes to see to glittering silvery utensils arranged systematically in their kitchens.

Both in summer and in winter they take bath twice or thrice a week in the spring or streams. Only very old persons and children are bathed at home with warm water at the backyard platform called *Rynsen*. In some new houses they have built separate washing room attached to the kitchen or *Ka Jing Bo-um* with cemented floor where they store water and also wash and clean things. Even this room is used as bathing room.

Almost all houses maintain kitchen gardens or *Kper* in the backyard. The kitchen and washroom outlets are directed to the kitchen gardens to re-utilize the water. The chickens feed on the left over food articles and water too. Otherwise there is no concept of drainage excepting in two of the houses we visited. A soak pit is made behind the kitchen while this water is soaked in the soil under the backyard platform *Rynsan* in most cases.

CONSERVATION

Throughout the War area were found isolated small patches of vegetation covering the micro-catchments areas particularly around the sources of first order streams. These patches of green were either *Law Adong* the protected forests or *'Law Lyndoh'* the sacred forests. This particular feature emphasizes the traditional concept and knowledge of conservation of two most important and interrelated resources the water and the forests among the War Khasi people at large.

In the village the Raid committee maintains the perennial water sources at the community level. Certain rules and practices are still in vogue among these villagers. Firstly, no tree is allowed to be felled particularly around the water points in '*Law Lyngdoh*'. Secondly, the community participates in cleaning and maintaining those sources once or twice every year. Thirdly, the *Lyndoh* or priest performs prayers at such sources every year to appease the Rain god responsible for providing water. Lastly, in times of draught or even temporary water crisis, the community members go to the water point in a big group. Through the day and night they clean the point by digging out the mud accumulated there and clear the path of flow. They search and dig points in and around the source area to find and create new sources. To maintain a good flow of water from the source they plant *Soh Um* tree which they believe produces water. Some of the elderly villagers pointed out that where there were a few plants of *Soh Um* in the forest there must be a water source nearby. Thus observing this plant they could locate probable water source.

SUMMARY AND CONCLUSION

As stated in the first chapter of the present report it is based on a preliminary study in a village called Mawlam, located in the East Khasi Hills district of Meghalaya. The stipulated sample size was 50 only, though we have made an effort to cover aspects of the village beyond what was specifically asked for. However, the findings of the present study should be taken as tentative.

The location of the village in a remote area with no infrastructural facilities until recently has influenced many of the characteristics of the society there. It is found that even the first primary school came up only about 30 years back. As a consequence of such a background, educational development in the village has been very insipient. About 90% of the villagers still depend on agricultural and economic diversification has been insignificant. With the closing of border with Bangladesh trade across the border, which was once an important activity; as almost come to an end. There are some external changes such as in their dress, household gadgets, etc. these are of recent origin and only the richer families have been able to exhibit such changes. People are generally very poor and men, women and children have to jointly eke out their living out of very difficult circumstances.

The present study shows that the dependence of the people of the village on the market is significant. What they grow and how much they grow, and when they grow; are largely decided by the market conditions. The vulnerability of the people was most evident when broomstick cultivation had to be discontinued as a result of drastic fall in price. While in one hand it was difficult for the villagers to switch over to some other form of cultivation there was hardly any government effort to bail them out of such a situation.

It is also observed that the villagers still have a very close association with the forest. They go to the forest for a variety of reasons such as collection of food, games and medicinal plants. Their reliance on the forest increases during the lean seasons. Perhaps, partly due to this reason, they have a rich knowledge of the forest resources. Being located in the wettest region of the world, and yet suffering from lack of portable water they have devised over the generation a system of water management which may be worthy of being emulated by hill villages elsewhere as well. Their total dependence on land has also made them experts in optimum utilization of various kinds of land for various crops. The nature of land ownership, which is one of the most complicated in the entire hill region, also reflects, to some extent their dependence on land. For instance a large part of the village land is under clan or community ownership, which makes the same plot of land much more viable than it would be under individual or private ownership.

Their association with the supernatural world is not yet disturbed significantly by the receding forest cover in the vicinity. They can still name innumerable gods and goddesses related to land, river, rocks, trees, ponds, sickness, disease, natural calamities etc. Even social control is partly taken care of by their strong belief in such god and goddess. Otherwise they have a strong tradition of village polity which is still continued. However, the authority of such traditional leaders, including the medicine man, is gradually fading as new values based on education and wealth, are beginning to challenge the traditional order.

In sum, this village exemplifies not only the predicament of shifting from a multi-crop based shifting cultivation to a single or dual based economy but also the predicament of the people who cannot make their voices heard on the corridors of power. This village exemplifies further uncertainties and vagaries of nature against which they have nothing to support them except their own traditional wisdom about their environment. Finally the present study depicts the community struggle for survival in a less bountiful nature and increase in population.

Bibliography

Allen, B.C. 1905/1980: Gazetteer of the Khasi and Jaintia Hills: Garo Hills Lushai Hills. Pioneer Press, Allahabad.

Aier, A & S Changkija, "Perspectives of indigenous knowledge for sustainable development of the Hill areas of North-Eastern Hill areas". Paper presented at the workshop on Anthropology and Allied disciplines in North – East India sponsored jointly by A.S.I. and N.E.H.U. and held in the Department of Anthropology, N.E.H.U. Shillong – March 1999.

Bareh, H. 1984: The History and Culture of the Khasi People. Guwahati Spectrum Publications, 1971 Khasi Fables and Folk-Tales, Firma, K.L. Mukhopadhyay Publication, Calcutta.

Borthakur, M. 1989: "Periodic markets in tribal areas (a case study in Meghalaya)". M. Phil. Dissertation, N.E.H.U., Shillong.

Cajee, L & H.J. Syiemlieh "Concept of environment protection and conservation among the Khasis". Paper presented at the seminar on Physical and Cultural Ecology of N.E. India, N.E.H.U., Shillong – September 1998.

Dasgupta, P.K. 1984: Life and Cultures of Matrilineal tribe of Meghalaya. Inter India Publications. Delhi.

Gurdon, P.R.T. 1907: The Khasis Cosmo Publications. Delhi.

Khongphai, A.S. 1974: Nater on Khasi Law. Ri Khasi Press, Shillong.

Mirani, R. 1979: "Khasi Symbolism". M. Phil Dissertation, N.E.H.U., Shillong.

Missa, P.K. & A. Rangad, 1997-98: "Sacred Grove and the Khasi society". Report submitted to R.C.N.A.E.B., Shillong.

Pakyntein, E.H., 1965: Census of India 1961: Assam United Khasi and Jaintia Hills. Published by Government of Assam, Guwahati.

Roy, Burman, J.J. 1994: "Sacred Groves: Symbol of self assertion" Economic News and Views, November 16th – 30th.

Sen, G. 1992 (Ed.): Indigenous visions: Peoples of India, attitudes to the environment. Sage Publications and India International Centre, New Delhi.

Simon, I.M. 1991: Meghalaya District Gazetteers: Khasi Hills District. Published Directorate of Arts and Culture, Shillong.

1966: Khasi and Jaintia Tales and Beliefs. Published by Department of Tribal Culture and Folklore Research, Gauhati University.

Singh, R.L. (Ed.) 1971: India: A Regional Geography National Geographical Society of India, Varanasi.

Roy, Choudhury, 1991: Shifting Cultivation.

Index

T

Abujhmaria in group hunting expedition.

Bison horn Maria--Mother and Child

Fisherman in his Boat for fishing at Sundarban

Bhil with Camel

Bison Horn Maria-- engaged in household chores at Bijapur

Bison-horn-Maria in dancing posture

Abujhmaria in group hunting expedition.

Nicobarese-- collection of non-vegetarian food item

Nicobarese- ways of inter sland transportation

Villagers engaged in Meendhara at the creeks of Sundarban